REEXAMINING CUSTOMARY INTERNATIONAL LAW

Reexamining Customary International Law takes on the complex issues and controversies surrounding the history, theory, and practice of customary international law as it reexamines customary law's increasingly important role in world affairs. It incorporates the expertise of distinguished authors to probe many difficult issues that remain unresolved concerning the doctrine of customary law. At the same time, this book engages in a profound exploration of the practical role of customary international law in a variety of important fields, including humanitarian law, human rights law, and air and space law.

Brian D. Lepard is the Harold W. Conroy Distinguished Professor of Law at the University of Nebraska College of Law. He has written numerous books and articles on international law, comparative law, human rights, and tax law, including *Customary International Law: A New Theory with Practical Applications*, published by Cambridge University Press in 2010. He is Chair of the Committee on Formation of Rules of Customary International Law of the American Branch of the International Law Association. He is also Academic Director of the Law College's LL.M. in Global Legal Practice Program for non-US lawyers and international students.

ASIL Studies in International Legal Theory

The purpose of the ASIL Studies in International Legal Theory series is to clarify and improve the theoretical foundations of international law. Too often the progressive development and implementation of international law has foundered on confusion about first principles. This series raises the level of public and scholarly discussion about the structure and purposes of the world legal order and how best to achieve global justice through law.

This series grows out of the International Legal Theory project of the American Society of International Law. The ASIL Studies in International Legal Theory series deepens this conversation by publishing scholarly monographs and edited volumes of essays considering subjects in international legal theory.

Volumes in the Series

International Criminal Law and Philosophy edited by Larry May and Zachary Hoskins
Customary International Law: A New Theory with Practical Applications by Brian D. Lepard
The New Global Law by Rafael Domingo
The Role of Ethics in International Law edited by Donald Earl Childress III
Global Justice and International Economic Law: Opportunities and Prospects edited by Chios Carmody, Frank J. Garcia, and John Linarelli
Parochialism, Cosmopolitanism, and the Foundations of International Law edited by Mortimer Sellers
Morality, Jus Post Bellum, and International Law edited by Larry May and Andrew T. Forcehimes
The Future of International Law: Global Governance by Joel P. Trachtman
Normative Pluralism and International Law: Exploring Global Governance by Jan Klabbers and Touko Piiparinen
Jus Post Bellum and Transitional Justice by Larry May and Elizabeth Edenberg
Negotiating State and Non-State Law: The Challenge of Global and Local Legal Pluralism edited by Michael A. Helfand
The Theory of Self-Determination edited by Fernando R. Tesón
Human Rights in Emergencies edited by Evan J. Criddle
Reexamining Customary International Law edited by Brian D. Lepard

Reexamining Customary International Law

Edited by
BRIAN D. LEPARD
University of Nebraska

CAMBRIDGE
UNIVERSITY PRESS

CAMBRIDGE
UNIVERSITY PRESS

One Liberty Plaza, New York NY 10006

Cambridge University Press is part of the University of Cambridge.

It furthers the University's mission by disseminating knowledge in the pursuit of education, learning, and research at the highest international levels of excellence.

www.cambridge.org
Information on this title: www.cambridge.org/9781107146914

First published 2017

A catalogue record for this publication is available from the British Library.

Library of Congress Cataloging-in-Publication Data
Names: Lepard, Brian D., editor.
Title: Reexamining customary international law / edited by Brian D. Lepard.
Description: Cambridge [UK]; New York: Cambridge University Press, 2016.
Includes bibliographical references and index.
Identifiers: LCCN 2016028356 | ISBN 9781107146914 (hardback)
Subjects: LCSH: Customary law, International.
Classification: LCC KZ1277. R44 2016 | DDC 340.5–dc23
LC record available at https://lccn.loc.gov/2016028356sw

ISBN 978-1-107-14691-4 Hardback

To my family

Contents

Notes on the Contributors

Noora Arajärvi is Fellow with the Berlin Research Group "The International Rule of Law – Rise or Decline?" She has served as an Associate Rule of Law Officer at the Executive Office of the Secretary-General of the United Nations. Before joining the UN, she worked as a lecturer at the University of Central Lancashire (UCLan), Cyprus; The University of the West Indies in Trinidad and Tobago; and Tilburg University in the Netherlands. She has also served at the Office of the Prosecutor of the International Criminal Court. In 2011, she received her Ph.D. from the European University Institute, where she also coordinated the Working Group on International Criminal Law. She earned an LL.M. degree at the University of Helsinki and an LL.B. degree at the University of Sheffield. Dr. Arajärvi has published numerous articles on international law and is the author of *The Changing Nature of Customary International Law: Methods of Interpreting the Concept of Custom in International Criminal Tribunals* (2014).

Els Debuf is currently on secondment from the International Committee of the Red Cross (ICRC) as Senior Advisor on Humanitarian Affairs to the International Peace Institute and the Independent Commission on Multilateralism in New York. Before assuming these positions, from May 2007 until September 2015 she was a legal adviser in the Legal Division of the ICRC, where, among other responsibilities, she served as head of the ICRC's project on customary international humanitarian law and the editor of the ICRC's online "CIHL Database" from 2011 to October 2014. She regularly makes presentations at conferences and has published a book and several articles on international law, international humanitarian law, and international human rights law.

Jean-Marie Henckaerts is a legal adviser in the Legal Division of the ICRC, where he has served since 1996. He was head of the ICRC's project on customary international humanitarian law from 2000 to 2010, and was one of the two authors of the ICRC's 2005 study on the subject. Since 2011 he has headed the ICRC's project to update the Commentaries on the Geneva Conventions of 1949 and their Additional Protocols of 1977. He has published seven books and numerous articles on international law, international humanitarian law, and human rights law.

J. Patrick Kelly is Professor of Law Emeritus at Widener University School of Law. Before his retirement, he was Vice-Dean and Professor of International Law. Professor Kelly received his J.D. degree from Harvard Law School and a B.A. from the University of Delaware. He founded and has directed the Nairobi International Law Institute since 1988 and founded the Sydney International Law Institute. His academic writings are primarily in international legal theory, international trade, and government regulation. His articles have appeared in many international law journals, including those of the Yale, Virginia, Duke, Cornell, Northwestern, and Michigan law schools. He has written a number of widely cited articles and book chapters on customary international law, including "The Twilight of Customary International Law," 40 *Virginia Journal of International Law* 449 (2000).

Thomas Kleinlein is Privatdozent at the Institute for Public Law of Goethe University in Frankfurt am Main and associate member of the Cluster of Excellence "Normative Orders." In 2014 and 2015 he was a visiting researcher at the Yale Law School and the University of Michigan Law School. In the winter semester 2016–17 he is a visiting professor at the Humboldt University of Berlin. He has published extensively on the theory of public international law. His books include *Konstitutionalisierung im Völkerrecht: Konstruktion und Elemente einer idealistischen Völkerrechtslehre* (*Constitutionalization in International Law*) (2012), and *Völkerrecht im innerstaatlichen Bereich* (*Public International Law in Domestic Legal Systems*) (2010) (coedited by Christina Binder, Claudia Fuchs, Matthias Goldmann, and Konrad Lachmayer).

Brian D. Lepard is the Harold W. Conroy Distinguished Professor of Law at the University of Nebraska College of Law. He has written numerous books and articles on international law, comparative law, human rights, and tax law, including *Customary International Law: A New Theory with Practical Applications*, published by Cambridge University Press in 2010. He is Chair of the Committee on Formation of Rules of Customary International Law of the American Branch of the International Law Association. He is also Academic Director of the Law College's LL.M. in Global Legal Practice Program for non-U.S. lawyers and international students.

Sofia Michaelides-Mateou is an expert on air law and is currently an Associate Professor of Aviation in the College of Engineering at the Abu Dhabi University. Her research is multidisciplinary, combining law and aviation. Her books on air law include *Flying in the Face of Criminalization: The Safety Implications for Prosecuting Aviation Professionals for Accidents* (2010) and *Air Law: A Practical Perspective*, published by Ant. N. Sakkoulas in Greece. She has presented many papers at international aviation conferences and has published articles on subjects such as unmanned aircraft systems, aviation security, safety, unruly passengers, the liability of aviation professionals, the protection of aviation safety data, and just culture. Dr. Michaelides-Mateou is also an aviation legal consultant who has participated in a number of aviation litigation cases and is an active member of the Eurocontrol Just Culture Task Force.

Niels Petersen is Professor of Public Law, International Law, and European Union Law at the University of Münster and Research Associate of the Max Planck Institute for Research on Collective Goods. His main areas of research are international law, comparative constitutional law, and constitutional theory. He holds a Ph.D. in law from the University of Frankfurt and an M.A. in quantitative methods in the social sciences from Columbia University. He was a Research Fellow at the Max Planck Institute for Comparative Public Law and Public International Law in Heidelberg from 2004 to 2006 and at the Max Planck Institute for Research on Collective Goods in Bonn from 2007 to 2014. Furthermore, he was Emile Noel Fellow at the New York University School of Law during the 2012–2013 academic year. Dr. Petersen has published many articles and book chapters on customary international law.

Anna Williams Shavers is the Cline Williams Professor of Citizenship Law at the University of Nebraska College of Law. Her primary scholarly interest is in the area of immigration and its intersection with gender issues. She serves as a member of the Nebraska Human Trafficking Task Force established by the governor of Nebraska. Recent articles she has published reflecting her interests are "Human Trafficking, the Rule of Law, and Corporate Social Responsibility," 9 *South Carolina Journal of International Law and Business* 39 (2012) and "Crossing the Border Through Immigration, Importation, Illicit and Other Means and the Implications for Human and Civil Rights," 27 *Journal of Civil Rights and Economic Development* 501 (2014).

Fernando R. Tesón is the Tobias Simon Eminent Scholar at the Florida State University College of Law. He has written many books and articles, including on customary international law. His books include *A Philosophy of International Law* (1998); *Humanitarian Intervention: An Inquiry into Law and Morality* (3rd edn. fully revised and updated, 2005); *Rational Choice and Democratic Deliberation* (Cambridge University Press, 2006) (with Guido Pincione); and *Justice at a Distance* (Cambridge University Press, 2015) (with Loren Lomasky). Before entering academia, Professor Tesón was a career diplomat for the Argentina Foreign Ministry in Buenos Aires for four years.

Frans G. von der Dunk holds the Harvey and Susan Perlman Alumni/Othmer Chair of Space Law at the University of Nebraska College of Law and teaches in its LL.M. Program on Space, Cyber, and Telecommunications Law. He is also Director of Black Holes BV, a consultancy in space law and policy based in Leiden, the Netherlands. He has written more than 130 articles and published papers on the subject of space law. He has also served as an adviser to the Dutch government, several foreign governments, the European Commission, the European Space Agency, the United Nations, and the Organization for Economic Co-operation and Development, as well as a number of private companies.

Michael Wood is a member of the International Law Commission and serves as its Special Rapporteur on the topic "Identification of customary international law." He is a Senior Fellow of the Lauterpacht Centre for International Law, University of Cambridge, and a barrister at 20 Essex Street, London, where he practices in the field of public international law, including before international courts and tribunals. He was Legal Adviser to the United Kingdom's Foreign and Commonwealth Office between 1999 and 2006, having joined as an Assistant Legal Adviser in 1970. He worked for three years at the Permanent Mission of the United Kingdom to the United Nations in New York, and has represented the United Kingdom in cases before the International Court of Justice.

Foreword

Michael Wood

Customary international law remains the bedrock of international law. Its merits and demerits as compared with that other great source of the law, treaties, have often been discussed. It used to be thought in some quarters that customary law would cease to be important as treaties multiplied. But that was never a realistic view. Even when whole areas of international law are codified in widely accepted international conventions, customary international law continues to play a vital role, as can be seen from the recent case law of international and national courts and tribunals. A good example is the law of the sea. As of August 2016, there are 168 parties to the 1982 United Nations Convention on the Law of the Sea, yet much scope remains for the customary international law of the sea. This is so not only in relation to those states (including important coastal states) and international organizations that remain outside the Convention, but also in order to complete the law in areas not covered by the Convention and to interpret and apply the Convention in areas that are in principle covered by it. Customary law is also relevant where the law is to be applied to events that took place prior to the entry into force of the Convention for the parties concerned. And it may continue to exist, and be applicable, separately from a treaty, even where the two have the same content and even among parties to the treaty.[1]

That customary international law may benefit from examination (or reexamination, as the title of this book suggests) is uncontested. The nature of customary law has led international lawyers over the decades to discuss the

[1] See *Military and Paramilitary Activities in and against Nicaragua (Nicaragua v. United States of America)*, Merits, Judgment of 27 June 1986, 1986 ICJ Rep. 14, 93-96, paras. 174–79; *Application of the Convention on the Prevention and Punishment of the Crime of Genocide (Croatia v. Serbia)*, ICJ Judgment of 3 February 2015, para. 88.

"complexities – indeed mysteries" of its operation,[2] a classical subject that is still debated in academic circles, even if not so much in practice.

Particularly interesting aspects, which Professor Lepard highlights in his introduction to the book, include the history of customary international law; the relationship between customary international law and politics, as well as ethics; why customary international law is law; what counts as relevant state practice; and how acceptance as law (*opinio juris*) is to be proved. These all raise a large number of questions, many by now relatively straightforward, some more difficult. They are also, for the most part, currently being addressed by the UN International Law Commission under the topic "Identification of customary international law."[3] The aim of that topic is "to offer practical guidance to those, in whatever capacity, called upon to identify rules of customary international law, in particular those who are not necessarily specialists in the general field of public international law."[4]

The debates in the International Law Commission (and in the Sixth Committee of the UN General Assembly) on the topic have evidenced a strong attachment to the "two-element" approach to the formation and identification of rules of customary international law. There is a general acceptance among members of the Commission – and among states – that customary international law requires, in the words of Article 38(1)(b) of the Statute of the International Court of Justice ("ICJ"), "a general practice accepted as law," that is, both a sufficiently widespread and consistent practice and *opinio juris* accompanying it. That is the starting position for the Commission's effort to clarify what these elements encompass and how they may be evidenced.

The present volume contains a range of essays that seek to describe the workings of customary international law from various perspectives and in various fields. It is striking that, however original and however innovative these essays are, for the most part the authors, too, adopt the two-element

2 Hersch Lauterpacht, *The Development of International Law by the International Court* (Cambridge: Stevens and Sons Ltd., 1958, reprinted by Cambridge University Press, 1996), 390.

3 At its sixty-eighth session (2016), the Commission adopted, on first reading, a set of sixteen draft conclusions (with commentaries) on the identification of customary international law. See the International Law Commission's 2016 report to the UN General Assembly, "Report of the International Law Commission," Sixty-Eighth Session (2 May–10 June and 4 July–12 August 2016), UN Doc. A/71/10 (2016), chapter V. See also the Special Rapporteur's first, second, third, and fourth reports (UN Doc. A/CN.4/663 (2013), UN Doc. A/CN.4/672 (2014), UN Doc. A/CN.4/682 (2015), and UN Doc. A/CN.4/695 and Add.1 (2016)).

4 Michael Wood, Special Rapporteur, "Second Report on Identification of Customary International Law," UN Doc. A/CN.4/672 (2014), para. 12.

approach, at least as their basis. This is particularly noteworthy given moves in some legal scholarship (including within this book) toward different approaches to the formation and identification of customary international law, in particular those seeking to rely predominantly on one or the other element.

For those authors who adhere to the two-element approach, as for the Commission, reexamining customary international law provides an opportunity to highlight the virtues (and address the challenges) of the approach widely seen as encapsulated in the Statute of the International Court and clearly endorsed in practice, and in doing so to contribute to the predictability and legitimacy of this important source of law. Restating the standard position may indeed be valuable in itself: as the Jordanian member of the Commission said, "The Commission should . . . clarify the process according to which customary international law was formed, its constituent elements and the kind of evidence required to establish its existence, all of which would serve to promote legal certainty."[5]

A key question to bear in mind when reading this book is whether the approach toward identifying rules of customary international law varies according to subject matter, or whether the same approach applies across the board, even if the available evidence, and its weight, may vary from field to field (or, perhaps more accurately, from rule to rule). Overall the chapters of this book tend to support a common approach (even if exact details may differ). The debates in Geneva and New York also assumed a common approach across the whole of international law. As Judge Greenwood has remarked, "International law is not a series of fragmented specialist and self-contained bodies of law, each of which functions in isolation from the others; it is a single, unified system of law."[6]

Another fundamental question for anyone currently confronting the so-called "mysteries" of customary international law is where to look for enlightenment on the appropriate methodology for identifying its rules. Do we find guidance in writings, in the practice and pronouncements of states and other subjects of international law, or in decisions of international and domestic courts? The answer, of course, is "all of the above." At the same time, it may be thought that the most authoritative instruction is to be found in the pronouncements of the ICJ, which "relies on customary international law constantly and

5 Provisional summary record of the 3183rd meeting of the Commission, 19 July 2013, UN Doc. A/CN.4/SR.3183 (2013), 6 (Hmoud).

6 *Ahmadou Sadio Diallo (Republic of Guinea v. Democratic Republic of the Congo)*, Compensation Owed by the Democratic Republic of the Congo to the Republic of Guinea, Judgment of 19 June 2012, 2012 ICJ Rep. 324, 394, para. 8 (Declaration of Judge Greenwood).

as a matter of course."[7] Such pronouncements have been and remain a central element in the current work of the International Law Commission, whose draft conclusions on the topic "Identification of customary international law" may now hopefully provide clear and accessible guidance as well.

There is agreement that the final outcome of the Commission's work should be a set of "conclusions" with commentaries, and that – given the inherent flexibility of the customary process – they should not be overly prescriptive. All this may sound far removed from the elaborate theories propounded in some of the writings on the subject. But that is not to say that such writings, and academic debate more widely, are unhelpful. Far from it, as the present fascinating volume illustrates. As a colleague and I have recently written with respect to customary international law, "academic disputes are bound to continue. That is not to be regretted; those engaged in the practice of law may benefit much from theoretical debate – and vice versa."[8] It is certainly to be expected that the current work of the International Law Commission will do so.

7 Lauterpacht, *The Development of International Law by the International Court*, 392.

8 Omri Sender and Michael Wood, "The Emergence of Customary International Law: Between Theory and Practice," in *Research Handbook on the Theory and Practice of International Lawmaking*, edited by Catherine Brölmann and Yannick Radi 133 (Cheltenham, UK and Northampton, MA: Edward Elgar, 2016), 159.

Acknowledgments

This book has been, from the beginning, a collaborative enterprise, which means I owe a great debt of gratitude to many others. It first took shape as the outgrowth of a conference on "Reexamining Customary International Law" organized by the International Legal Theory Interest Group of the American Society of International Law ("ASIL") and held at ASIL Headquarters in Washington, DC, in November 2010. Many of the contributors presented earlier versions of their work there and benefited from the stimulating discussion that ensued. I am grateful to the ASIL for sponsoring this gathering and to my colleagues in the International Legal Theory Interest Group, especially Mortimer Sellers. However, I also sought out additional experts who were not able to participate in that conference, and their contributions grace these pages as well. Some of them participated in a conference on "The Role of *Opinio Juris* in Customary International Law" held at the University of Geneva in Geneva, Switzerland, in July 2013 and sponsored by the Duke-Geneva Institute in Transnational Law. The American Society of International Law co-sponsored this program. In short, I am indebted to all these organizations and the contributing authors for helping this book come to fruition.

I am particularly pleased that Sir Michael Wood, Special Rapporteur of the International Law Commission on the topic "Identification of customary international law," lent his support to the project and kindly agreed to contribute the Foreword. His insights, and the Commission's work in general, figure prominently in the book.

I appreciate, too, the support of the former Dean of the University of Nebraska College of Law, Susan Poser, as well as the current Interim Dean, Richard Moberly. They have enthusiastically endorsed this project and kindly provided funding for my travel and research through offering Ross McCollum grants. Equally important, they have prioritized the study of international law within the curriculum of the College of Law. For example, I am privileged to co-teach a course on International Perspectives in the U.S. Legal System for all first-year Nebraska Law students, in which I have been able to share some of the concepts in the book with my students and benefit from their own perspectives on customary international law. I am grateful to them, as I have learned as much from them as they have from me. I especially appreciate the research and editorial assistance of Ciara Coleman, Kiersten Haugen, and Ken Smith, all former students of mine.

It has been a particular pleasure to collaborate with my colleagues Anna Williams Shavers and Frans G. von der Dunk, both of whom contributed chapters to the book, as well as Jack Beard and Matthew Schaefer, who have offered many helpful comments on my own theory of customary international law. Likewise, the staff of the Marvin and Virginia Schmid Law Library at the University of Nebraska College of Law provided invaluable assistance with my research, and I am especially grateful to Kris Lauber for finding many of the sources cited in my contributions to the book.

This book has undergone many revisions and refinements, and throughout the process all of the authors demonstrated good cheer and a willingness to consider, and learn from, the views of one another. We have all benefited immensely from the cogent suggestions of the anonymous reviewers for Cambridge University Press, which markedly improved the manuscript. My editor, John Berger, has, as always, been unflagging in his commitment to the project.

Last but not least, I could not have completed such a long-term and time-intensive undertaking without the loving support of my family, and in particular my wife Jenina and sons Brandon and Justin. Jenina has provided me with unceasing encouragement. And even though Brandon and Justin are now "out of the house" and pursuing their own passions in life, they have been a constant and permanent inspiration to me. Their optimism about the future and the possibilities for building a more just and peaceful world, including through the impact of international law, is a reminder to me that the issues discussed in this volume are not merely academic, but vital to the realization of just such a vision and to benefiting the lives of people around the globe.

1

Introduction

Why Does Customary International Law Need Reexamining?

Brian D. Lepard

1.1 THE INCREASING RELEVANCE OF CUSTOMARY INTERNATIONAL LAW

Customary international law has long been one of the cornerstones of the international legal order, alongside treaties. The international legal historian Arthur Nussbaum declared that customary international law "has always held a position equal or superior to treaties" "in the theory of the law of nations."[1] Hans Kelsen famously argued that customary international law provides in fact the "basic norm" of the international legal order; it is the foundation on which all international legal rules are built.[2] Thus, for example, the rules governing treaties themselves originated in customary international law, and numerous decisions of the International Court of Justice ("ICJ") have identified particular rules relating to the conclusion and entry into force of treaties, their interpretation, and their termination as rules of customary international law.[3]

The great international law theorists invoked customary international law. For example, Hugo Grotius (1583–1645), in his influential treatise, *On the Law*

1 Arthur Nussbaum, *A Concise History of the Law of Nations* (New York: The Macmillan Co., rev. ed. 1954), 201.

2 See Hans Kelsen, *General Theory of Law and State*, translated by Anders Wedberg (Cambridge, MA: Harvard University Press, 1945), 369. See also Nussbaum, *A Concise History of the Law of Nations*, 281 (affirming that "Kelsen attributes binding force above all to international custom," from which "the binding force of treaties is derived: *pacta sunt servanda* is in itself a customary rule").

3 See, e.g., *Land and Maritime Boundary Between Cameroon and Nigeria (Cameroon v. Nigeria: Equatorial Guinea intervening)*, Judgment of 10 October 2002, 2002 ICJ Rep. 303, 429–30, paras. 263–64 (on the customary law character of rules on the conclusion and entry into force of treaties); *Legal Consequences of the Construction of a Wall in the Occupied Palestinian Territory*, Advisory Opinion of 9 July 2004, 2004 ICJ Rep. 136, 174, para. 94 ("*Wall Advisory Opinion*") (on the customary law status of rules of treaty interpretation); *Gabčíkovo-Nagymaros Project (Hungary v. Slovakia)*, Judgment of 25 September 1997, 1997 ICJ Rep. 7, 38, para. 46 (on the customary law character of rules involving the termination of treaties).

of War and Peace ("*De Jure Belli Ac Pacis*"), first published in 1625, affirmed that customary law is the essence of the "law of nations," which supplements natural law. Grotius defined the "law of nations" as "the law which has received its obligatory force from the *will of all nations, or of many nations*."[4] He went on to state that the law of nations must be found from their customs. He wrote: "The proof for the law of nations is similar to that for unwritten municipal law; it is found in *unbroken custom* and the testimony of those who are skilled in it. The law of nations, in fact, as Dio Chrysostom well observes, 'is the creation of time and custom.' And for the study of it the illustrious writers of history are of the greatest value to us."[5]

The scholastic Francisco Suárez (1548–1617), in his great work *On Laws and God as Legislator*, similarly wrote that human communities

> need a law by which they are guided and rightly ordered in respect to communication and association. To a great extent this is done by natural reason but not so sufficiently and directly everywhere. Hence, certain special rules could be established by the customs of these nations [*gentes*]. For just as in one commonwealth [*civitas*] or province [*provincia*] custom establishes law, so among the human race as a whole rules of *jus gentium* could be established by usage [*moribus*]. This is true all the more because the rules pertaining to that law are few.[6]

One of the early positivists, Richard Zouche (1590–1661), professor of civil law at Oxford University, also characterized international law – *jus inter gentes* – as "a law which has been accepted by customs conforming to reason among most nations or which has been agreed upon by single nations."[7] He minimized the importance of natural law.[8] In keeping with this view, eventually the idea of natural law was weakened beginning with the rationalism of the eighteenth century and then abandoned during the tide of positivism that swept through the legal field during the nineteenth century.[9] Positivism maintained that states were bound only by treaties and customary international law because they had exercised their positive "will" in consenting to, or otherwise participating in the formation of, both forms of law.

4 Hugo Grotius, *De Jure Belli ac Pacis Libri Tres*, translated by Francis W. Kelsey (New York: Oceana; London: Wildy & Sons, 1964), book 1, chap. 1, ¶ 14, 44 (emphasis added).
5 Ibid. (emphasis added).
6 Francisco Suárez, *De legibus ac Deo legislatore* (1612), in *Selections from Three Works of Suárez*, translated by J.B. Scott (1944), vol. II., 19, § 9, quoted in Nussbaum, *A Concise History of the Law of Nations*, 87–88.
7 Quoted in Nussbaum, *A Concise History of the Law of Nations*, 167.
8 See ibid.
9 See, e.g., ibid., 135, 164–85.

Positivism still holds sway today. And because it endorses customary international law, customary law lives on in the twenty-first century, as vital as ever. Customary international law has been recognized in the Statute of the ICJ as one of the three primary sources of international law to be applied by the Court, alongside treaties and general principles of law.[10]

In keeping with this foundational status, many judicial decisions at both the international and national levels have identified and applied rules of customary international law. These rules have ranged across a vast legal terrain, addressing subjects as diverse as states' right to sovereignty, sovereign immunity and diplomatic relations among states, states' responsibility for international law violations, their rights to natural resources, the law of the sea, international environmental law, the law of international armed conflict, international criminal law, and human rights.

For example, the ICJ and its predecessor, the Permanent Court of International Justice ("PCIJ"), have held that states have a fundamental right to sovereignty under customary international law; indeed, state sovereignty has long been acknowledged as a foundational customary principle of the current global legal order.[11] In keeping with this principle, the ICJ has ruled that states have sovereignty over their natural resources.[12] Moreover, the Court has recognized the customary law right of states to immunity from lawsuits by other states.[13] It has, furthermore, identified many rules involving diplomatic privileges and immunities[14] and diplomatic protection[15] as customary law. At the same time, it has recognized the customary law status of norms relating to the responsibility of states for their wrongful acts.[16]

10 See Statute of the International Court of Justice ("ICJ Statute"), art. 38(1).

11 See, e.g., *Case of the S.S. "Lotus" (France v. Turkey)*, Judgment of 7 September 1927, PCIJ Series A, No. 10, 18 (stating that the "rules of law binding upon States … emanate from their own free will"). See also James Crawford, *Brownlie's Principles of Public International Law* (Oxford: Oxford University Press, 8th ed. 2012), 5.

12 See, e.g., *Armed Activities on the Territory of the Congo (Democratic Republic of the Congo v. Uganda)*, Judgment of 19 December 2005, 2005 ICJ Rep. 168, 251–52, para. 244 ("2005 *Armed Activities Case (Congo v. Uganda)*").

13 *Jurisdictional Immunities of the State (Germany v. Italy: Greece intervening)*, Judgment of 3 February 2012, 2012 ICJ Rep. 99, 123, para. 56.

14 See, e.g., *United States Diplomatic and Consular Staff in Tehran (United States of America v. Iran)*, Judgment of 24 May 1980, 1980 ICJ Rep. 3, 30–31, para. 62; *Arrest Warrant of 11 April 2000 (Democratic Republic of the Congo v. Belgium)*, Judgment of 14 February 2002, 2002 ICJ Rep. 3, 20–22, paras. 51–55 (affirming that the provisions of the Vienna Convention on Diplomatic Relations and the Vienna Convention on Consular Relations regarding diplomatic immunity reflect customary international law).

15 See, e.g., *Ahmadou Sadio Diallo (Republic of Guinea v. Democratic Republic of the Congo)*, Preliminary Objections, Judgment of 24 May 2007, 2007 ICJ Rep. 582, 599, para. 39.

16 See, e.g., *Difference Relating to Immunity from Legal Process of a Special Rapporteur of the Commission on Human Rights*, Advisory Opinion of 29 April 1999, 1999 ICJ Rep. 62, 87, para. 62;

The law of the sea originated as customary law, and international tribunals have issued many decisions identifying particular rules of the law of the sea as customary in nature. These include the freedom of all states to navigate on the high seas as well as a right of ships flying the flag of one state to pass innocently through the territorial waters of another.[17] They also include rules on delimiting maritime boundaries and fishery zones, and rules establishing rights to use the waters and the seabed adjoining the coast of a state.[18] Courts are more frequently recognizing norms of environmental law as customary rules.[19]

The ICJ has identified many norms of the law of armed conflict as having customary law status, including the rule that one state may not use armed force in the territory of another except in self-defense or as authorized by the United Nations Security Council,[20] and the rule that a state may not lawfully acquire territory by war.[21] The ICJ has affirmed a broader customary rule that one state

2005 *Armed Activities Case (Congo v. Uganda)*, 242, paras. 213–14; *Application of the Convention on the Prevention and Punishment of the Crime of Genocide (Bosnia and Herzegovina v. Serbia and Montenegro)*, Judgment of 26 February 2007, 2007 ICJ Rep. 43, 202, para. 385, 207–08, para. 398, 216–17, paras. 419–20 ("2007 *Genocide Convention Case*").

17 See, e.g., *Military and Paramilitary Activities in and against Nicaragua (Nicaragua v. United States of America)*, Jurisdiction and Admissibility, Judgment of 26 November 1984, 1984 ICJ Rep. 392, 424, para. 73 (asserting that the principle of "freedom of navigation" continues "to be binding as part of customary international law"); *Maritime Delimitation and Territorial Questions Between Qatar and Bahrain (Qatar v. Bahrain)*, Merits, Judgment of 16 March 2001, 2001 ICJ Rep. 40, 110, para. 223 (customary international law accords to ships "the right of innocent passage") ("*Maritime Delimitation Case (Qatar v. Bahrain)*").

18 See, e.g., *Continental Shelf Case (Tunisia v. Libyan Arab Jamahiriya)*, Judgment of 24 February 1982, 1982 ICJ Rep. 18, 74, para. 100 ("the notion of historic rights or waters and that of the continental shelf are governed by distinct legal régimes in customary international law"); *Continental Shelf Case (Libyan Arab Jamahiriya v. Malta)*, Judgment of 3 June 1985, 1985 ICJ Rep. 13, 33, para. 34 (holding that the exclusive economic zone "is shown by the practice of States to have become a part of customary law"); *Maritime Delimitation in the Area Between Greenland and Jan Mayen (Denmark v. Norway)*, Judgment of 14 June 1993, 1993 ICJ Rep. 38, 58, para. 46; *Maritime Delimitation Case (Qatar v. Bahrain)*, 2001 ICJ Rep. 40, 91, para. 167, 93, para. 174, 97, paras. 183, 185, 100, para. 201; *Territorial and Maritime Dispute Between Nicaragua and Honduras in the Caribbean Sea (Nicaragua v. Honduras)*, Judgment of 8 October 2007, 2007 ICJ Rep. 659, 696, para. 113, 703, para. 141, 739–40, para. 265 (quoting from earlier cases discussing customary rules of maritime boundary delimitation).

19 See, e.g., *Legality of the Threat or Use of Nuclear Weapons*, Advisory Opinion of 8 July 1996, 1996 ICJ Rep. 226, 241–42, para. 29 ("*Nuclear Weapons Advisory Opinion*") (affirming that "the existence of the general obligation of States to ensure that activities within their jurisdiction and control respect the environment of other States or of areas beyond national control is now part of the corpus of international law relating to the environment").

20 See, e.g., *Military and Paramilitary Activities in and against Nicaragua (Nicaragua v. United States of America)*, Merits, Judgment of 27 June 1986, 1986 ICJ Rep. 14, 98–101, paras. 187–90 ("*Nicaragua Case*"); *Wall Advisory Opinion*, 171, para. 87.

21 See *Wall Advisory Opinion*, 166, para. 74, 171, para. 87, 182, para. 117.

may not intervene in the affairs of another[22] and may not lend aid to subversive activities whose purpose is to topple the government of another state.[23]

At the same time, the ICJ has identified as customary law the right of states to use armed force in self-defense against armed attacks by other states,[24] and rules mandating that any such defensive measures be both necessary and proportional to the scope of the attack.[25] Similarly, the ICJ has recognized particular norms developed to govern hostilities as customary norms, such as the law of occupation[26] and the law of neutrality.[27] The ICJ has also recognized as a customary norm the principle that states should settle their disputes peacefully and without recourse to war.[28]

Furthermore, the ICJ has determined that many rules of international humanitarian law aimed at reducing the loss of life or harm to noncombatants in both international and noninternational armed conflicts have attained the status of customary international law.[29] In this connection, the International Committee of the Red Cross ("ICRC") has undertaken a massive study of customary rules of international humanitarian law[30] – a study analyzed in

22 See, e.g., *Nicaragua Case*, 126, para. 246 ("the principle of non-intervention derives from customary international law").

23 See, e.g., ibid., 108, para. 206; 2005 *Armed Activities Case (Congo v. Uganda)*, 226–27, para. 162.

24 See *Nicaragua Case*, 94, para. 176 (holding that the "right of self-defence" is "of a customary nature" and asserting that Article 51 of the UN Charter, which refers to states' "inherent right" to self-defense, constitutes a recognition of this preexisting customary norm). See also *Oil Platforms Case (Islamic Republic of Iran v. United States of America)*, Judgment of 6 November 2003, 2003 ICJ Rep. 161, 186–87, para. 51 (reiterating the requirement of an "armed attack" to justify the exercise of self-defense under customary international law).

25 See, e.g., *Nicaragua Case*, 94, para. 176 (stating that the rule that a right of self-defense warrants only measures that "are proportional to the armed attack and necessary to respond to it" is "a rule well established in customary international law"); *Nuclear Weapons Advisory Opinion*, 245, para. 41 (affirming that the "submission of the exercise of the right of self-defence to the conditions of necessity and proportionality is a rule of customary international law"); *Oil Platforms Case*, 187, para. 51 (similar).

26 See, e.g., *Wall Advisory Opinion*, 167, para. 78.

27 See *Nuclear Weapons Advisory Opinion*, 256, para. 74, 260–61, paras. 88–89.

28 See *Nicaragua Case*, 145, para. 290 (affirming that the "principle that the parties to any dispute ... should seek a solution by peaceful means" has "the status of customary law").

29 See, e.g., ibid., 113–14, para. 218 (treating the rules in common Article 3 of the Geneva Conventions, as well as other "fundamental general principles of humanitarian law" appearing in the Geneva Conventions, as part of customary international law); *Nuclear Weapons Advisory Opinion*, 256–60, paras. 74–87; *Wall Advisory Opinion*, 172, para. 89 (the "Court considers that the provisions of the Hague Regulations [annexed to the Fourth Hague Convention of 1907] have become part of customary law"); 2005 *Armed Activities Case (Congo v. Uganda)*, 243–44, paras. 217–19 (similar).

30 See *Customary International Humanitarian Law*, edited by Jean-Marie Henckaerts and Louise Doswald-Beck, 2 vols., Vol. I: Rules, Vol. II: Practice (2 Parts) (Cambridge: Cambridge University Press and ICRC, 2005).

detail by two of the contributors to this volume. The ICJ, and many other courts, have upheld the customary law character of the prohibition of genocide, reflected in such treaties as the 1948 Convention on the Prevention and Punishment of the Crime of Genocide.[31]

Many courts have recognized that serious war crimes are prohibited by customary law and that customary law now permits and sometimes requires their prosecution by states. In this connection, the statutes of international criminal tribunals, including those of the International Criminal Tribunal for the former Yugoslavia ("ICTY"), the International Criminal Tribunal for Rwanda ("ICTR"), and the International Criminal Court ("ICC"), refer to customary international law in their definitions of the crimes over which the tribunals have jurisdiction.[32] And, as discussed by some of the contributors to this volume, decisions of these tribunals often refer to customary international law.[33]

Moreover, the ICJ and other tribunals are increasingly recognizing a wide range of human rights as protected by norms of customary law and not only human rights treaties. For example, the ICJ has suggested that "the basic rights of the human person, including protection from slavery and racial discrimination" have risen to the level of customary international law.[34]

Alongside the recognition by international tribunals and organizations of this sweeping array of norms as having attained the status of customary law, national legal systems are now giving greater prominence to customary international law. Many national judicial decisions are applying it and affirming that particular norms are customary in character and binding internally.

For example, a number of state constitutions specifically incorporate customary international law into the national legal system in some way. Thus, the Constitution of South Africa provides in Section 232 that "customary international law is law in the Republic unless it is inconsistent with the Constitution or an Act of Parliament."[35]

[31] See, e.g., *Armed Activities on the Territory of the Congo (New Application: 2012) (Democratic Republic of the Congo v. Rwanda)*, Jurisdiction and Admissibility, Judgment of 3 February 2006, 2006 ICJ Rep. 6, 31–32, para. 64; 2007 *Genocide Convention Case*, 110–11, para. 161; *Application of the Convention on the Prevention and Punishment of the Crime of Genocide (Croatia v. Serbia)*, ICJ Judgment of 3 February 2015, para. 87.

[32] See, e.g., Rome Statute of the International Criminal Court, 17 July 1998, 2187 UNTS 90, art. 8(2)(b).

[33] See, for example, the decisions discussed in Noora Arajärvi, "From the 'Demands of Humanity': The Formulation of *Opinio Juris* in Decisions of International Criminal Tribunals and the Need for a Renewed Emphasis on State Practice," in this volume.

[34] *Barcelona Traction, Light and Power Company, Limited (Belgium v. Spain)*, Second Phase, Judgment of 5 February 1970, 1970 ICJ Rep. 3, 32, para. 34 ("*Barcelona Traction Case*").

[35] Constitution of South Africa, sec. 232, available at http://www.gov.za/documents/constitution-republic-south-africa-1996-chapter-14-general-provisions#232. See also *Kaunda v. President of*

Even in the absence of an explicit constitutional provision, many national courts have ruled or implied that customary international law plays some role in their domestic legal systems. For example, the High Court of Australia has implied that customary international law may influence the development of the common law of Australia.[36] The Supreme Court of Canada has affirmed that "following the common law tradition, it appears that the doctrine of adoption operates in Canada such that prohibitive rules of customary international law should be incorporated into domestic law in the absence of conflicting legislation."[37] The Supreme Court of India has declared that "it is almost [an] accepted proposition of law that the rules of customary international law which are not contrary to the municipal law shall be deemed to be incorporated in the domestic law."[38] The Supreme Court of Israel has repeatedly affirmed that customary international law is part of Israeli law. Thus, it has stated that the provisions of Geneva Convention IV, which relates to the protection of civilians in armed conflict, that have entered customary international law "constitute a part of the law of the State of Israel" and asserted that Israeli armed forces must comply with them.[39] The former UK House of Lords has generally endorsed the proposition that customary international law is part of the law of England and Wales.[40]

U.S. courts have made similar pronouncements. In the famous 1900 case of *The Paquete Habana*, the U.S. Supreme Court affirmed that "[customary] international law is part of our law, and must be ascertained and administered by the courts of justice of appropriate jurisdiction, as often as questions of right depending upon it are duly presented for their determination."[41] And the United States has a federal statute, on the books since 1789 and known as the "Alien Tort Claims Act" ("ATCA"), that establishes original district court jurisdiction over "any civil action by an alien for a tort only, committed in violation of the law of nations or a treaty of the United States."[42] U.S. courts have interpreted the phrase "law of nations" as a synonym for "customary international law." Many cases have been decided under this statute involving claims

the Republic of South Africa, Case CCT 23/04 (4 August 2004), para. 23 (Constitutional Court of South Africa quoted this provision).

36 See, e.g., *Mabo v. Queensland (No. 2)*, [1992] HCA 23; (1992) 175 CLR 1 (3 June 1992), para. 42.

37 *R v. Hape*, [2007] 2 S.C.R. 292, 2007 SCC 26 (7 June 2007), para. 39. See also ibid., para. 53.

38 *People's Union for Civil Liberties (PUCL) v. The Union of India*, [1997] 1 SCC 301 (18 December 1996).

39 *Physicians for Human Rights v. Prime Minister of Israel*, HCJ 201/09, [2009] IsrLR 1 (19 January 2009), para. 15. See also *Public Committee Against Torture in Israel v. Government of Israel*, HCJ 769/02 (13 December 2006), para. 19 (similar).

40 See *R. v. Jones*, [2006] UKHL 16 (29 March 2006), paras. 11–23.

41 175 U.S. 677 (1900), 700.

42 28 U.S.C. § 1350.

by non-U.S. citizens that their rights protected by customary international have been violated. U.S. courts have delved into the question of whether particular norms have attained the status of customary international law and thus whether their violation is a "tort" committed in violation of customary international law.[43]

Various national courts have also held that domestic statutes should be interpreted, if possible, to be consistent with customary international law. For example, the High Court of Australia has asserted that Australian courts should favor an interpretation of a statute that is in keeping with international law, including customary international law.[44] The Israeli Supreme Court has similarly affirmed that "an Israeli act of legislation should be interpreted in a manner that is consistent, in so far as possible, with the norms of international law to which the State of Israel is committed."[45] The Supreme Court of New Zealand has declared that statutory rights and powers "are to be exercised, if the wording will permit, so as to be in accordance with international law, both customary and treaty based."[46] The Competition Appeal Court of South Africa has said that in light of sections 232 and 233 of the South Africa Constitution, courts are required to prefer any reasonable interpretation of legislation that is consistent with international law over any alternative interpretation that is inconsistent with international law.[47] And the U.S. Supreme Court has affirmed that "an act of Congress ought never to be construed to violate the law of nations if any other possible construction remains."[48]

1.2 THE TRADITIONAL DOCTRINE OF CUSTOMARY INTERNATIONAL LAW

This brief review of judicial decisions clearly demonstrates that customary international law is increasingly relevant in the global legal order. But just what

43 See, e.g., *Filartiga v. Pena-Irala*, 630 F.2d 876 (2nd Cir. 1980) (holding torture to be prohibited by customary international law); *Sosa v. Alvarez-Machain*, 542 U.S. 692 (2004) (establishing standards that a norm of customary international law must meet for a case to be actionable under the ATCA); *Kiobel v. Royal Dutch Petroleum Co.*, 569 U.S. ___, 133 S.Ct. 1659 (2013), 1669 (holding that the ATCA has no extraterritorial application, and thus that it should not grant jurisdiction for lawsuits for torts committed outside the U.S that did not "touch and concern" the territory of the U.S.).

44 *Behrooz v. Secretary of the Department of Immigration and Multicultural and Indigenous Affairs*, [2004] HCA 36 (6 August 2004), para. 127.

45 *A v. State of Israel* (11 June 2008), para. 9.

46 *Attorney-General v. Zaoui*, [2005] NZSC 38 (21 June 2005), para, 90.

47 *American Soda Ash Corp. v. Competition Commission of South Africa*, Competition Appeal Court of South Africa, Case No. 12/CAC/DEC01, [2003] ZACAC 6 (30 October 2003), para. 15.

48 *Murray v. The Schooner Charming Betsy*, 6 U.S. 64 (1804), 118.

is customary international law? The traditional doctrine seems to provide a straightforward definition: Customary international law results from the confluence of two elements: (1) a practice among states that is relatively consistent (and thus a "custom"), and (2) a belief by the states engaging in the practice that it is legally required or permitted. The first element is often referred to as the "consistent state practice" requirement, and the second element as the requirement of "*opinio juris sive necessitatis*," or more briefly, "*opinio juris*."

The ICJ has, in a number of decisions, identified these two requirements of consistent state practice and *opinio juris*. Thus, in the 1985 *Continental Shelf Case (Libyan Arab Jamahiriya v. Malta)*, the ICJ announced that the substance of customary international law must be "looked for primarily in the actual practice and *opinio juris* of States."[49] In the 1969 *North Sea Continental Shelf Cases*, the ICJ affirmed:

> Not only must the acts concerned [constituting state practice] amount to a *settled* practice, but they must also be such, or be carried out in such a way, as to be *evidence of a belief that this practice is rendered obligatory by the existence of a rule of law requiring it*. The need for such a belief, i.e., the existence of a subjective element, is implicit in the very notion of the *opinio juris sive necessitatis*. The States concerned must *therefore feel that they are conforming to what amounts to a legal obligation*.[50]

In its 2012 *Jurisdictional Immunities of the State* judgment, the ICJ reiterated that "the existence of a rule of customary international law requires that there be 'a settled practice' together with *opinio juris*."[51] These statements of the Court at least enjoy significant persuasive authority regarding the foundational elements of customary international law.[52]

Many scholars and practitioners of international law have confirmed the "two element" test for customary international law.[53] For example, Michael Wood,

49 *Continental Shelf Case (Libyan Arab Jamahiriya v. Malta)*, 29, para. 27.

50 *North Sea Continental Shelf Cases (Federal Republic of Germany v. Denmark; Federal Republic of Germany v. Netherlands)*, Judgment of 20 February 1969, 1969 ICJ Rep. 3, 44, para. 77 (emphasis added).

51 *Jurisdictional Immunities of the State (Germany v. Italy)*, 122, para. 55.

52 The 2016 draft conclusions of the ILC similarly suggest that pronouncements of the ICJ relating to customary international law deserve to be given significant weight. The draft conclusions indicate in particular that decisions of international courts and tribunals, and particularly of the ICJ, "concerning the existence and content of rules of customary international law are a subsidiary means for the determination of such rules." "Report of the International Law Commission," Sixty-Eighth Session (2 May–10 June and 4 July–12 August 2016), UN Doc. A/71/10 (2016), 76–79, Draft Conclusion 13, para. 1.

53 In addition to the authorities discussed in the text, see, e.g., Restatement (Third) of the Foreign Relations Law of the United States, § 102(2) ("Customary international law results from a

in his second report presented in 2014 to the International Law Commission ("ILC") as Special Rapporteur on the topic "Identification of customary international law," reaffirmed the merits of the two-element test.[54] The draft conclusions adopted in 2016 by the Commission furthermore endorse this two-element requirement. Draft Conclusion 2 states: "To determine the existence and content of a rule of customary international law, it is necessary to ascertain whether there is a general practice that is accepted as law (*opinio juris*)."[55] Draft Conclusion 3 goes on to affirm that both elements are necessary to prove and should not be amalgamated, affirming: "Each of the two constituent elements is to be separately ascertained. This requires an assessment of evidence for each element."[56] Yet it also recognizes a certain flexibility in the process of evaluating evidence of both elements, stating: "In assessing evidence for the purpose of ascertaining whether there is a general practice and whether that practice is accepted as law (*opinio juris*), regard must be had to the overall context, the nature of the rule, and the particular circumstances in which the evidence in question is to be found."[57]

Furthermore, customary law is generally accepted as binding all states, with or without their explicit consent. However, traditional doctrine maintains that those states that persistently object to an emerging customary norm, beginning with the time of its initial articulation, are not bound by it. This exception has become known as the "persistent objector" doctrine.[58] The 2016 draft conclusions of the ILC reaffirm this doctrine, declaring: "Where a State has objected to a rule of customary international law while that rule was in the process of formation, the rule is not opposable to the State concerned for so long as it maintains its objection."[59] The draft conclusions reiterate the

general and consistent practice of states followed by them from a sense of legal obligation"); Rosalyn Higgins, *The Development of International Law Through the Political Organs of the United Nations* (London: Oxford University Press, 1963), 1–2 ("The emergence of a customary rule of law occurs where there has grown up a clear and continuous habit of performing certain actions in the conviction that they are obligatory under international law.").

54 See Michael Wood, Special Rapporteur, "Second Report on Identification of Customary International Law," 65, Draft Conclusion 3; ibid., paras. 21–31.

55 "Report of the International Law Commission," Sixty-Eighth Session, Draft Conclusion 2.

56 Ibid., Draft Conclusion 3, para. 2.

57 Ibid., para. 1.

58 On the persistent objector doctrine, see, e.g., Brian D. Lepard, *Customary International Law: A New Theory with Practical Applications* (New York: Cambridge University Press, 2010), 229–42; Jonathon I. Charney, "The Persistent Objector Rule and the Development of Customary International Law," 56 *British Yearbook of International Law* 1 (1985); Restatement (Third), § 102, comment b ("A principle of customary law is not binding on a state that declares its dissent from the principle during its development."); ibid., comment d (elaborating on the persistent objector exception).

59 "Report of the International Law Commission," Sixty-Eighth Session, Draft Conclusion 15, para. 1.

traditional requirement that "the objection must be clearly expressed, made known to other States, and maintained persistently."[60]

It is also established doctrine that some norms of customary law are so important that they have been accepted by states as "peremptory norms," or norms of "*jus cogens*," which have a privileged status and cannot be violated by states under any circumstances, including through contrary treaties. Article 53 of the 1969 Vienna Convention on the Law of Treaties defines "a peremptory norm of general international law" as "a norm accepted and recognized by the international community of States as a whole as a norm from which no derogation is permitted *and which can be modified only by a subsequent norm of general international law having the same character*."[61] Any treaty that conflicts with a peremptory norm is considered entirely void.[62] Moreover, peremptory norms bind all states, even persistent objectors.[63] Some examples of peremptory norms that have been widely recognized include the prohibitions of genocide, crimes against humanity, slavery and the slave trade, racial discrimination, torture, piracy, and the use of nondefensive force by one state against another.[64]

The ICJ has recognized another privileged category of customary law norms: *erga omnes* norms. These are obligations owed by a state to all other states, and their violation gives any other state, and not just the victim state, the right to pursue legal remedies against the offending state under international law. The ICJ affirmed in the 1970 *Barcelona Traction Case* that these norms "are the concern of all States. In view of the importance of the rights involved, all States can be held to have a legal interest in their protection."[65] It gave as examples of *erga omnes* obligations those derived from "the outlawing of acts of aggression, and of genocide, as also from the principles and rules concerning the basic rights of the human person, including protection from slavery and racial discrimination."[66] Despite this laconic statement, there are no obvious guidelines for determining whether a norm is an *erga omnes* norm. Furthermore, the precise relationship between *jus cogens* norms and *erga omnes* norms has been debated.[67] Nevertheless, the existence of *erga omnes* norms has been widely accepted in traditional doctrine.

60 Ibid., para. 2.

61 Vienna Convention on the Law of Treaties, 1155 UNTS 331 (1969), art. 53 (emphasis added).

62 Ibid.

63 See Lepard, *Customary International Law*, 250–52.

64 See ibid., 7.

65 *Barcelona Traction Case*, 32, para. 33.

66 Ibid., para. 34.

67 See generally Lepard, *Customary International Law*, 40, 261–69.

The concept of customary international law also seems clear enough because it has a parallel in domestic legal systems. Common law legal systems have long applied customary law in particular kinds of cases. English jurist William Blackstone's *Commentaries on the Laws of England* summarized fairly sophisticated criteria for determining when a common law court could find and apply customary law.[68] In addition, civil law countries have had a long-standing tradition of recognizing customary law. Many civil codes permit a judge to refer to customary law as a subsidiary source of law if no written law governs an issue. For example, Article 1 of the Swiss Civil Code of 1907 allows for reference to customary law in the absence of a statutory provision,[69] and the Louisiana Civil Code affirms in Article 3 that "custom results from practice repeated for a long time and generally accepted as having acquired the force of law."[70]

The first codification of the concept of customary international law in a broad-ranging international treaty occurred in 1920 in the form of Article 38 of the Statute of the PCIJ, which is now word-for-word Article 38 of the Statute of the ICJ. The Advisory Committee of Jurists, which drafted the provision, laid down the rules that would be applied by the new international court, the PCIJ. The members of the Committee said in this provision that the PCIJ would apply "international conventions, whether general or particular, establishing rules expressly recognized by the contesting states" (referred to here as "treaties").[71] However, they added that the Court would also apply "international custom, as evidence of a general practice accepted as law."[72] Third, they indicated that the Court could apply "the general principles of law recognized by civilized nations."[73] In adopting the language of "international custom, as evidence of a general practice accepted as law," the drafters of the Statute were drawing on an already well-entrenched history of customary international law, but also of customary law recognized at the local and national levels.

68 For a discussion of his criteria and their application by modern courts, see David Callies, "How Custom Becomes Law in England," in *The Role of Customary Law in Sustainable Development*, edited by Peter Ørebech et al. 158 (Cambridge: Cambridge University Press, 2005).

69 Swiss Civil Code of 1907 (status as of 1 January 2016), art. 1, para. 2, available at www.admin.ch/ch/e/rs/2/210.en.pdf.

70 Louisiana Civil Code, art. 3, Acts 1987, No. 124, § 1, available at www.legis.la.gov/Legis/Law.aspx?d=110037.

71 ICJ Statute, art. 38, para. 1(a).

72 Ibid., para. 1(b).

73 Ibid., para. 1(c).

1.3 WHY DOES CUSTOMARY INTERNATIONAL LAW NEED REEXAMINING?

If customary international law is now invoked so often by international and national tribunals, and if its history, definition, and doctrinal elements seem to be widely accepted, why does it need reexamining?

To begin, the history of customary international law is not as simple as the preceding account suggests. It may trace its roots to national law systems, but its emergence on the international scene was gradual and its doctrinal formulation took some time. It continued to be laden with many ambiguities and problems of definition (on which I touch later in this chapter) – so much so that when the Advisory Committee of Jurists drafted Article 38(1)(b), the language the jurists chose was not a model of clarity and in fact betrayed many of these unresolved problems.

For example, the Statute refers to "international custom" as a source of law, rather than "international customary law" itself. Normally, the word "custom" refers to a practice rather than a legal norm, although sometimes it has been used as a shorthand expression for "customary law" – as might have been the intention of the drafters here. On the other hand, the Statute's language refers to such custom as "evidence" of a "general practice accepted as law." This could be read as a reference to "custom" as "practice." Moreover, it could indicate that such a practice is to be referred to as "evidence" of a "general practice accepted as law." The main contribution of the latter phrase is to introduce the notion of *opinio juris*, or general acceptance as law. This *could* imply (as I have argued), that the drafters primarily viewed state practice as *evidence* of *opinio juris*.[74] Indeed, even statements by early international law theorists, like Grotius quoted at the beginning of the chapter, leave open the understanding that, in Grotius's words, "unbroken custom" (i.e., practice) is best viewed as "proof" (i.e., evidence) of the law of nations (and therefore customary international law), rather than a requirement in its own right to establish customary international law.[75] This fundamental interpretive issue, then, demands reexamination.

Furthermore, there is a tendency, certainly among lawyers, to view customary international law doctrine as entrenched and "ahistorical." What I mean by the latter adjective is that lawyers typically ignore the history of the doctrine and work with the concept of customary law as an isolated legal category.

[74] On this point, see Lepard, *Customary International Law*, 128–29.

[75] See Grotius, *De Jure Belli ac Pacis Libri Tres*, book 1, chap. 1, ¶ 14, 44.

However, an understanding of the history of the customary law concept is essential if states are to use it most effectively today. Thus, this history needs reexamining. And it is possible that such a reexamination might uncover uncomfortable facts. For example, contributor J. Patrick Kelly argues that historically the whole doctrine of customary international law was part and parcel of a broad effort by the great powers to justify their domination and pursue their self-interests. As another example, as just noted, I have argued that a careful perusal of the debates on foundational documents like the Statute of the PCIJ opens up the possibility that state practice was viewed as evidence of *opinio juris* rather than a free-standing requirement of its own.[76] Of course, such views based on historical inquiries do not sit easily with the ahistorical model.

Again, thinking broadly about customary law, it is evident that the legal concept is supposed to be detached from politics. The legal inquiry assumes an air of political agnosticism: We treat all states as juridically equal sovereign states, and ask whether there is a sufficient quantum of state practice among them accompanied by a sense of legal obligation. It would appear that we are to ignore the identities of particular states, their relative power on the world scene, whether or not they have a democratic form of government, and similar political issues. However, is this possible? Can customary law so easily be detached from the realities of power politics? And as soon as we admit that customary law can help states achieve their own interests, we have to ask troubling questions about whether some states' interests should count more than those of others. Moreover, is it really possible for international judges to avoid political bias in ascertaining whether there is "consistent" state practice and *opinio juris* given the ambiguities lurking in these concepts? (I explore these ambiguities later in the chapter.) In brief, the relationship between customary international law and politics deserves reexamination.

Traditional customary international law doctrine also adopts the pretense of being ethically neutral; it purports not to care whether a rule formed through the marriage of consistent state practice and *opinio juris* is ethically desirable or not. For example, it was generally accepted, prior to the adoption of the UN Charter in 1945 with its announcement of the concept of universal human rights and fundamental freedoms, that states treated their own citizens as they wished (establishing a consistent state practice) and evidently with the view that they had the legal right to do so (establishing *opinio juris*). Accordingly, there was, according to traditional doctrine, a customary norm permitting

[76] See Lepard, *Customary International Law*, 129 (noting that the word "evidence" was intentionally added by the drafters to an earlier proposal by Baron Descamps of Belgium that omitted this word).

sovereign states to violate the human rights (as ethically defined) of their own citizens. By contrast, it is now generally accepted that the old rule has undergone profound transformation, and there are today widely agreed customary law norms protecting many human rights, including the right not to be tortured, among many others. One might say, then, that there is a new customary rule favoring state deference to human rights (although which rights and how much protection they deserve are hotly disputed issues).

The traditional doctrine on its face holds that neither the old rule nor the new one is to be preferred to the other; state practice and *opinio juris* have simply changed and so has the rule. It would leave open the possibility that should states revert to their prior practices and go back to a view that they may lawfully treat their own citizens as they wish (as some have argued may now be happening regarding state views on torture and "enhanced interrogations"), then the old rule would come back into force.

Many, if not most, international lawyers would find a way to dispute such a conclusion. They might marshal arguments about there not being a sufficiently widely accepted new practice, or a true change in *opinio juris* among the majority of states. For example, they might cite evidence that states still claim that they do not practice torture. But at bottom, if they were to be perfectly honest, they would admit that one reason they resist the conclusion is because the current human rights–based rule is simply more ethically defensible. It is an ethically better rule. And to admit this means that ethics should (and perhaps must) play some role in the recognition of customary international law. Furthermore, it could be argued that even if the positivist pretenses of the nineteenth century, with their emphasis on unbridled state sovereignty, chafe at such an introduction of ethics, today we should (and must) adopt a more "enlightened" view of customary international law that opens the door to some ethical reasoning without undermining its status as law.

This aspect of customary international law, too, deserves reexamining, and the relationship between ethics and customary law has become the subject of a growing literature. For example, I have developed an approach to customary law that requires that state beliefs about the desirability of an authoritative legal norm (and therefore *opinio juris*) ought to be assessed with reference to a "background" system of ethical principles that states themselves have endorsed, and in particular to what I have called "fundamental ethical principles." I define fundamental ethical principles as principles identified in international instruments, including the UN Charter and the Universal Declaration of Human Rights, that are in turn rationally related to a preeminent ethical principle of "unity in diversity." According to this principle, all states and individuals form part of global communities of states and human beings that ethically should be united at the same time that they can take pride in their fundamental autonomy and diversity of culture, ethnic origin, religion, and belief.[77] (I discuss this concept in more detail in Chapter 8.)

Other scholars have similarly incorporated ethical considerations in their proposed approaches to customary international law. For example, legal philosopher John Tasioulas has argued that "the ethical appeal of a candidate norm" should figure "among the criteria for determining whether it is a valid norm of [customary international law] in such a way that a customary norm may exist even in the absence of widespread state practice, or even overwhelming state consent, in its favour."[78]

The subject of the relationship between ethics and customary international law also bears on the question of which customary norms should qualify as peremptory or *jus cogens* norms. What exactly, is the reason for recognizing some customary norms as having this privileged status? Is the reason because of their ethically compelling character – such as in the case of the prohibitions of genocide or torture? Some scholars have argued that ethics should play such a role.[79] And David Bederman has described some *jus cogens* norms as a "form of natural law 'super-custom.'"[80] On the other hand, other scholars insist that *jus cogens* norms have a privileged status because states resoundingly believe they should, whether or not they promote particular ethical values.[81] In brief, the problem of how to identify *jus cogens* norms, and the role of ethics in this determination, deserve reexamination. Similar problems exist, as we saw from an earlier discussion, regarding the identification of *erga omnes* norms.

Another fundamental question has also never adequately been answered: Why is customary international law law? There is no particular reason to draw legal inferences from any given practice; after all, states, like people, engage in a wide variety of practices for many reasons. Some reasons are found in self-interest; others may involve a sense of moral obligation, or even mere courtesy (often referred to as "comity" in the traditional language of international law). More broadly, why should any regularity of behavior give

77 Ibid., 8.

78 John Tasioulas, "Customary International Law and the Quest for Global Justice," in *The Nature of Customary Law: Legal, Historical and Philosophical Perspectives*, edited by Amanda Perreau-Saussine and James Bernard Murphy 307 (Cambridge: Cambridge University Press, 2007), 310.

79 See, e.g., Lepard, *Customary International Law*, 243–60.

80 David J. Bederman, *Custom as a Source of Law* (New York: Cambridge University Press, 2010), 159.

81 See, e.g., Rosalyn Higgins, *Problems and Process: International Law and How We Use It* (Oxford: Clarendon Press, 1994), 21–22 (maintaining that *jus cogens* norms have a special character not because of their "higher normativity," but because the international "*community as a whole* regards these norms as of critical importance, such that particular states cannot 'contract out' of them") (emphasis in the original).

rise to a *legal* obligation, permission, or prohibition? Thus, some meta-theory is required to explain this transmutation of consistent behavior into legal rule.

One might respond that the answer to the dilemma is found in the concept of *opinio juris*: A regularity of behavior gives rise to a legal rule only when states engaging in the behavior believe that it does. But why should mere state beliefs that their practices are legally permitted or required create a legal rule? Is it because each individual state with such a belief, and engaging in a practice, is "consenting" to being bound by the rule, thereby exercising its sovereignty? If so, we need a fuller "consent" theory of international legal obligation to support recognition of customary law. Alternatively, is customary international law law because it reflects a "global legislative" model according to which we essentially count states' beliefs as "votes" in favor of or against a candidate for a legal rule – and once the rule is recognized, like any legislation, it binds all states?

The global legislative model would seem to fit much of the traditional doctrine of customary law (except for the persistent objector doctrine) quite well. It would explain the generally accepted doctrine that a particular state does not have to consent to a customary rule to be bound by it, and the related rule that new states are bound by customary rules already in existence (and to which they necessarily could not consent).

On the other hand, the implications of such a model would need to be explored more thoroughly. One potential weighty implication of such a legislative theory is that so long as a majority of states believe that a rule exists (or perhaps should exist), it ought to be recognized as law. There would seem to be no necessity for consistent state practice as such under this legislative view – unless a state's conforming practice were characterized as evidence of its views about whether the rule exists or should be recognized. Indeed, some theories of customary international law incorporate such a perspective.[82]

Either the consent theory or the legislative theory of obligation of customary international law forces us to confront larger questions about why any rules of international law should be recognized as binding otherwise sovereign states. Is it because some legal rules can facilitate realization of states' own self-interests by allowing them to cooperate or coordinate their actions? Is it because some legal rules are desirable to further particular moral values? Even if we accept the realization of states' interests as a valid goal, why is a legal rule necessary as opposed to informal mechanisms of coordination and cooperation? Many jurists and scholars have turned to game theory to

82 See, e.g., Lepard, *Customary International Law*, 122–39; Andrew T. Guzman, *How International Law Works: A Rational Choice Theory* (Oxford: Oxford University Press, 2008), 200.

delve into these challenging issues, and to explore such related questions as whether the persistent objector doctrine ought to still be recognized and what its boundaries ought to be.[83] In any event, what is clear is that we need a fuller explanation of *why* concordant state practice and beliefs should be treated as sufficient to create a customary norm.

The inquiry does not end here. We can ask other telling questions about why a conclusion of legal obligation should follow from the admixture of state practice and *opinio juris*. For example, what if states are mistaken that their behavior is legally permitted or mandated? (This gives rise to the so-called "paradox of *opinio juris*," which I discuss in more detail later in the chapter.) Why should a legal rule be recognized based on a simple mistake? And, as we have already asked, what if states' beliefs that a certain behavior is legally authorized – say, "enhanced interrogation" of terrorism suspects – run counter to fundamental ethical values, either their own or the values held by their people or the values articulated by world religions or secular philosophies? Should states' beliefs and behavior always lead to recognition of a legal rule in these circumstances, without further inquiry?

Furthermore, the apparent consensus on the "technical" definition of customary law and its elements is superficial. It frays as soon as we attempt to probe such questions as whether state practice is always required, or *opinio juris* is always required, or how to prove up the existence of a sufficient "quantum" of either.

Let us first consider the state practice requirement. Just what is "state" practice? States are not people; they are complex entities, with multiple institutions – among others, executive, legislative, and judicial branches, not to mention layers of government authority from the national level down to the local, and countless departments, bureaus, and offices within each of these branches and levels of government. So which practices of which of these manifold actors count as "state" practice? The traditional theory seems to insist that we reduce all practice to that of a mythical, unitary "state." These kinds of problems are being given increasing attention by scholars and jurists – without a clear consensus.[84]

83 See, e.g., Niels Petersen, "The Role of Consent and Uncertainty in the Formation of Customary International Law," in this volume. Another, related promising area of inquiry involves investigating why states may choose to adopt customary law norms instead of treaties or "soft law" instruments as a means of pursuing their interests. See, e.g., Laurence R. Helfer and Ingrid B. Wuerth, "An Instrument Choice Perspective on Customary International Law," 37 *Michigan Journal of International Law* (forthcoming 2016).

84 See, e.g., Ingrid Wuerth, "Customary International Law as Constitution" (paper delivered at a conference held on October 31, 2014 at Duke Law School on "Custom in Crisis: International Law in a Changing World" (on file with the author)). I have also addressed the appropriate weight to be given to the views of organs of executive, legislative, and judicial branches. See Lepard, *Customary International Law*, 171–80.

Furthermore, what is a "practice"? Every day every state-affiliated entity undertakes actions – but also refrains from undertaking countless other actions. Which is the relevant practice for purposes of determining customary international law? Can a "nonaction" or "abstention from action" count as practice? Again, there are no universally accepted answers, and scholars and jurists are divided on the question.[85] The 2016 draft conclusions of the ILC reflect this paucity of explicit rules on practice, while at least recognizing that nonaction can sometimes be treated as practice. They thus state: "Practice may take a wide range of forms. It includes both physical and verbal acts. It may, under certain circumstances, include inaction."[86]

In the same vein, it can be difficult to know what kinds of state actions or inactions are relevant and how they should be weighted. The traditional view is that we can look at everything a state organ does. This is reflected, again, in the Commission's 2016 draft conclusions, which affirm: "Forms of State practice include, but are not limited to: diplomatic acts and correspondence; conduct in connection with resolutions adopted by an international organization or at an intergovernmental conference; conduct in connection with treaties; executive conduct, including operational conduct 'on the ground'; legislative and administrative acts; and decisions of national courts."[87] The draft conclusions also assert the majority view that no one form of practice is automatically entitled to greater weight than another: "There is no predetermined hierarchy among the various forms of practice."[88] These principles conceal many difficult problems of theory and application. For example, in the case of putative customary norms involving the conduct of foreign relations, an area of activities the primary responsibility for which most state constitutions assign to the executive branch, is it appropriate to treat national court decisions as having the same weight as executive policy?

Even if we manage to identify which state entities can act on behalf of a state and which actions or nonactions count as practice, at the global level we must determine a means for "adding up" the practice of the many states that exist in the world political system. According to traditional doctrine, there must be some kind of "consistent" practice globally that includes diverse states. The 2016 draft conclusions of the Commission manifest this view,

85 For a review of conflicting perspectives, see Lepard, *Customary International Law*, 219.

86 "Report of the International Law Commission," Sixty-Eighth Session, Draft Conclusion 6, para. 1. On inaction as a form of practice, see Michael Wood, Special Rapporteur, "Third Report on Identification of Customary International Law," UN Doc. A/CN.4/682 (2015), paras. 19–26.

87 "Report of the International Law Commission," Sixty-Eighth Session, Draft Conclusion 6, para. 2.

88 Ibid., para. 3.

asserting: "The relevant practice must be general, meaning that it must be sufficiently widespread and representative, as well as consistent."[89]

Nevertheless, what does it mean for a practice to be "widespread," "representative," and "consistent"? Do all 196-odd states in the international system have to engage in a practice for it to give rise to a customary norm? Do at least a super-majority of all states have to do so? Or is a simple majority sufficient – say, 99 out of the 196? Can the practices of less than a majority be sufficient to support a customary rule? In this regard, can we or should we focus on the practices only of states that are "specially affected" by a putative norm – for example, only coastal states in the case of norms of the law of the sea?[90]

In the same vein, should we give special weight – or perhaps even exclusive weight – to the practices of certain states, like powerful one or democratic ones? As an empirical matter, and as argued by J. Patrick Kelly in this volume, many rules of customary international law have been recognized mainly on the basis of the practice of the great powers. Indeed, customary international law has been roundly criticized by some observers as "undemocratic" on this score.[91] In this connection, what significance should be accorded to protests by less powerful states against the practices of more powerful ones? When can such protests defeat a finding that there is a consistent state practice or a sufficiently universal *opinio juris*?

Some commentators have argued, in fact, that the practices of powerful states *should* be entitled to more weight in any assessment of consistent state practice. For example, the Restatement (Third) of the Foreign Relations Law of the United States declares that "failure of a significant number of *important* states to adopt a practice can prevent a principle from becoming general customary law though it might become 'particular customary law' for the participating states."[92] These views might be an apology for a kind of neo-imperialism, or they might be based on a view that any legal rule calling for a practice that is not engaged in by the most powerful states has no real chance of being enforced and therefore should not be recognized as a legal rule in the first place. In any event, they run counter to a long-standing principle (of customary law) that generally upholds the sovereign equality of states.

89 Ibid., Draft Conclusion 8, para. 1.

90 On the concept of "specially affected" states, see *North Sea Continental Shelf Cases*, 43, para. 74.

91 In this connection, David J. Bederman, although maintaining that customary law is "a popular mechanism for law-making," acknowledges the "concern that customary regimes were actually the product of institutional elites, and were often wielded at the expense of the masses." Bederman, *Custom as a Source of Law*, 176.

92 Restatement (Third), § 102, comment b (emphasis added).

Moreover, is it ethically appropriate to count the practices of all states equally? Should certain ethical factors lead to giving more "weight" to the practices of some states than those of others? One ethical factor already suggested is that of the degree to which a state is affected by a rule. It might seem unfair to allow states not impacted by a rule to participate in its creation through their practice.

A second potentially relevant factor is the internal governance structure of a state, and the extent to which its institutions (and therefore practices) are democratic and supported by the people. In short, should the practices of democratic states be given more weight than those of autocratic states? Some scholars have argued that the practices (and views) of democratic states ought to be given more "weight" in a global assessment of state practice (and *opinio juris*) out of deference to respect for human rights values.[93] However, this argument may raise its own problems, especially because it contradicts the concept of "sovereign equality" of states, now reflected in Article 2(1) of the UN Charter.[94]

Other problems revolve around identification of the "sources" of evidence of state practice. These problems are related to all of those I have just identified. For example, how do executive actions and orders count in relation to parliamentary laws? What is the role of administrative regulations as evidence of state practice? Can courts participate in the formation of customary law through the treatment of their decisions as "practice"? The ILC's 2016 draft conclusions simply affirm that all of these are sources of evidence. One conclusion thus asserts: "State practice consists of conduct of the State, whether in the exercise of its executive, legislative, judicial or other functions."[95] Does it matter whether any of these actions are "unilateral" as opposed to "bilateral" or "multilateral"? Can a state's voting record in the UN General Assembly count as "practice"? Opinion among jurists has been sharply divided on these points.

Again, the Commission's 2016 draft conclusions reflect the challenges of resolving all of these questions, instead calling for a holistic approach: "Account is to be taken of all available practice of a particular State, which is to be assessed as a whole."[96] On the other hand, the conclusions call for less weight to be given in a global assessment of consistent state practice to practices of a state that are not uniform: "Where the practice of a particular State varies,

93 See Lepard, *Customary International Law*, 154–57.

94 See UN Charter, art. 2, para. 1 (providing that "the Organization is based on the principle of the sovereign equality of all its Members").

95 "Report of the International Law Commission," Sixty-Eighth Session, Draft Conclusion 5.

96 Ibid., Draft Conclusion 7, para. 1.

the weight to be given to that practice may be reduced."[97] These general principles, of course, may prove very difficult to apply in particular cases.

Even if we can determine how to assess state practice, which states' practices count, and how to weight them, we must also determine how long the relevant states must have engaged in the practice. Traditionally, a practice must have endured a very long time – even "since time immemorial," or, in Blackstone's formulation, "so long … that the memory of man runneth not to the contrary."[98] Grotius, we have seen, referred to "unbroken custom."[99]

However, a modern view has emerged that no fixed period of long practice is necessary. Thus, in keeping with Michael Wood's proposals in his 2014 report to the International Law Commission, the Commission in 2016 adopted a conclusion that "provided that the practice is general, no particular duration is required."[100] In its judgment in the 1969 *North Sea Continental Shelf Cases*, the ICJ stated:

> Although the passage of *only a short period of time* is not necessarily, or of itself, a bar to the formation of a new rule of customary international law …, an indispensable requirement would be that within the period in question, *short though it might be*, State practice, including that of States whose interests are specially affected, should have been both extensive and virtually uniform in the sense of the provision invoked.[101]

The flexibility reflected in the Committee's draft conclusions, Michael Wood's report, and the *North Sea Continental Shelf Cases* may be appropriate. However, it leaves open large questions about just how to figure out if a practice has endured for a "sufficiently" long time to generate customary law.

Finally, must the consideration of practice be limited to that of states rather than international organizations or nongovernmental organizations? The traditional view holds that we must look exclusively, or at least primarily, to state behavior to ascertain customary law. This view is evident in the draft conclusions of the ILC issued in 2016, which assert: "The requirement, as a constituent element of customary international law, of a general practice means that it is *primarily* the practice of States that contributes to the

97 Ibid., para. 2.

98 William Blackstone, *Commentaries on the Laws of England*, 1st edition, 76–77, quoted in Callies, "How Custom Becomes Law in England," 166. On the requirement of immemoriality, see generally ibid., 166–70.

99 Grotius, *De Jure Belli ac Pacis Libri Tres*, book 1, chap. 1, ¶ 14, 44.

100 "Report of the International Law Commission," Sixty-Eighth Session, Draft Conclusion 8, para. 2. See also Michael Wood, Special Rapporteur, "Second Report on Identification of Customary International Law," 67, Draft Conclusion 9, para. 3.

101 *North Sea Continental Shelf Cases*, 43, para. 74 (emphasis added).

formation, or expression, of rules of customary international law."[102] At the same time, the draft conclusions acknowledge some general role for the practice of international organizations, providing: "In certain cases, the practice of international organizations also contributes to the formation, or expression, of rules of customary international law."[103] Nevertheless, this general role is unclear, although Michael Wood addresses some relevant considerations in his third report.[104] And the draft conclusions assert that with this one exception for international organizations, "conduct of other actors is not practice that contributes to the formation, or expression, of rules of customary international law, but may be relevant when assessing the practice" of states or international organizations.[105] Again, this accurate summary of the traditional view leaves unanswered many questions about the relevance of the practice of nongovernmental actors.

The *opinio juris* requirement, like the consistent state practice requirement, at first glance seems easy enough to state, and even intuitive: States must engage in a practice with a belief that they are legally obligated or permitted to do so. This traditional understanding is reflected in the ILC's 2016 draft conclusions, which affirm: "The requirement, as a constituent element of customary international law, that the general practice be accepted as law (*opinio juris*) means that the practice in question must be undertaken with a sense of legal right or obligation."[106]

Certainly one function of the requirement is to distinguish behavior motivated by perceived legal rules from behavior motivated purely by self-interest, by a sense of moral obligation, or by a desire on the part of a state to treat other states with consideration, or "comity."[107] This function of the *opinio juris* requirement is readily understandable and defensible. However, when we try to "unpack" the requirement and apply it in concrete cases, a myriad of problems assert themselves, just as in the case of the consistent state practice requirement, and often of a parallel nature.

Thus, first of all, states are not people, so how can they "believe" or "think" anything? The whole concept seems artificial (but then, so is the concept of a

102 "Report of the International Law Commission," Sixty-Eighth Session, Draft Conclusion 4, para. 1 (emphasis added).

103 Ibid., para. 2.

104 See Michael Wood, Special Rapporteur, "Third Report on Identification of Customary International Law," paras. 68–79.

105 "Report of the International Law Commission," Sixty-Eighth Session, Draft Conclusion 4, para. 3.

106 Ibid., Draft Conclusion 9, para. 1.

107 In this connection, the 2016 draft conclusions of the ILC state that "a general practice that is accepted as law (*opinio juris*) is to be distinguished from mere usage or habit." Ibid., para. 2.

"state"). In practice, how is a jurist to ascertain the "beliefs" of a state when it engages in a practice? Here again, we are confronted with the fact that states are complex entities with many branches, organs, offices, and bureaus, each of which may express, through a wide variety of media, various "views." So to which of these sub-entities do we look? And what evidence of views or beliefs are we looking for? Public proclamations by executive branch officials? Public or private diplomatic communications by executive branch officials of a state with their counterparts of other states? Purely private notes made by executive branch officials? Treaties signed by executive branch officials and approved by a parliament? Treaties signed by executive branch officials but not approved by a parliament? Public affirmations by a parliament? Laws adopted by a parliament? Administrative regulations adopted by a government agency? Opinions of courts reflected in judicial decisions they render? The draft conclusions of the ILC issued in 2016 endorse all of these as evidence of *opinio juris*,[108] but they, like traditional doctrine, do not provide an explanation of how to weigh and balance these diverse sources of views.

Furthermore, must *opinio juris* be confined to the views of governments, or should it also encompass the views of nongovernmental organizations or even individuals residing in a state? Can their beliefs count as part of the beliefs of that "state"? The traditional Westphalian model emphasizing the sovereignty of states of course holds that we can only look to government views, but many scholars, and even jurists, are challenging that perspective, including on the ground that newly accepted values of democracy and human rights demand such a broadened concept of *opinio juris*.[109]

[108] Thus, the draft conclusions state in general that "evidence of acceptance as law (*opinio juris*) may take a wide range of forms." Ibid., Draft Conclusion 10, para. 1. They go on to specify that "forms of evidence of acceptance as law (*opinio juris*) include, but are not limited to: public statements made on behalf of States; official publications; government legal opinions; diplomatic correspondence; decisions of national courts; treaty provisions; and conduct in connection with resolutions adopted by an international organization or at an intergovernmental conference." Ibid., para. 2. They also assert that "failure to react over time to a practice may serve as evidence of acceptance as law (*opinio juris*), provided that States were in a position to react and the circumstances called for some reaction." Ibid., para. 3. On the relevance of national court decisions, the draft conclusions state that "regard may be had, as appropriate, to decisions of national courts concerning the existence and content of rules of customary international law, as a subsidiary means for the determination of such rules." Ibid., Conclusion 13, para. 2.

[109] See, e.g., Jordan J. Paust, *International Law as Law of the United States* (Durham, NC: Carolina Academic Press, 2nd ed. 2003), 4 (arguing that "contrary to false myth perpetrated in the early twentieth century, the subjective element of customary international law (*i.e., opinio juris* or expectations that something is legally appropriate or required) is to be gathered from patterns of generally shared legal expectation among humankind, not merely among official State elites").

Another problem with the *opinio juris* requirement is that it overlooks the potentially complex motivations for state behavior. It asserts that a legal rule emerges because states engage in a practice *out of a sense of legal obligation*. But states may engage in a practice for a kaleidoscopic variety of reasons, including self-interest. So what if a state, for example, provides "prompt, adequate, and effective" compensation for expropriation of property of foreign investors primarily because it believes that is the best way to encourage future foreign investment? What if state officials also happen to believe that a "prompt, adequate, and effective" compensation rule under customary international law might exist, and are aware that their actions would be consistent with it, but they do not really know, and they would act the same way even if they did not believe such a rule constrained them? How are we to "count" this state's views in the "*opinio juris* equation"? Must they be "discarded" because the exclusive motivation for the practice in question was not a sense of legal obligation? Must they be excluded because not even the primary motivation was such a sense? The traditional theory of customary law simply ignores these very difficult questions.

In addition, as many scholars have underscored, the traditional formulation of the *opinio juris* test results in a chronological paradox, at least with respect to the emergence of new customary norms.[110] In particular, it requires that before the customary norm comes into existence, states must believe that they are already bound by the (nonexistent) norm. This implies that states must mistakenly believe that a norm already exists as a precondition for it coming into existence. A rational observer might reasonably ask: What kind of theory of law bases its system of recognition on openly acknowledged mistakes?

One might respond to this concern by observing that all legal norms that are not enacted by legislation on a certain date, but rather evolve organically – and we might refer here to the common law as an example, by analogy – come into being as part of a *process* of norm proposal and recognition. On this view, there really is no mistake on the part of states; their very belief in an existing obligation is part of the process of creating that obligation. Another response to this concern might be that while it is problematic in theory, in practice courts and other decision-makers have had no trouble ascertaining whether there is a sufficiently widespread belief by states that a norm is legally binding, and thus the whole problem of the paradox is harmless. Furthermore, the

[110] On this paradox, see Bederman, *Custom as a Source of Law*, 20, 149. See also Anthony A. D'Amato, *The Concept of Custom in International Law* (Ithaca, NY: Cornell University Press, 1971), 73–74.

paradox does not even exist with respect to the *opinio juris* supporting norms that have, indeed, already entered the corpus of customary law.[111]

These responses, however, do not do justice to deeper problems that are revealed by the paradox. The first is a problem already touched upon: Why, normatively, should a belief by at least some states that a norm *is* the law be a sufficient condition (alongside the existence of consistent state practice) for it being recognized as law? This problem parallels what philosophers call the "naturalistic fallacy" – the belief that just because something "naturally" is, it *ought to be*. For example, let us assume that most states genuinely believe that legally they are currently permitted to engage in torture under limited and specific circumstances. Assuming that they also practice torture under these circumstances, does the confluence of their belief and practice mean that a new customary norm authorizing torture under these circumstances must necessarily come into existence? In other words, there is an ethical problem lurking in the "is to ought" connection made bare by the paradox. This might in fact be the most troublesome aspect of the paradox – not that states are simply mistaken about the content of the law.

In my own work I have sought to address these problems associated with the paradox by refining our understanding of *opinio juris*. In particular, I have proposed that *opinio juris* should be understood as a belief by states generally that it is desirable now or in the near future to have an authoritative legal principle or rule prescribing, permitting, or prohibiting certain conduct, apart from treaty obligations.[112] This refined definition of course "solves" the problem of relying on a "mistake" by states because the question it asks is not whether they believe a norm already exists, but whether they believe it *ought* to exist. It also takes a step forward in solving the problem of the naturalistic fallacy by requiring a belief by states that a particular norm would, in fact, be desirable to implement – not simply that states happen to believe they are in fact already bound by the norm, whether it is desirable or not. This is supported by the legislative function of customary international law.

I have also argued that this understanding of *opinio juris* is better supported by judicial "practice" in actually identifying *opinio juris* than is the traditional formulation. At the same time, the theory still recognizes the central role of states in forming *opinio juris*.

Other scholars have promoted a similar view that the *opinio juris* requirement should best be understood as an expression of state beliefs about what norms should be recognized as customary law. For example, Curtis Bradley

[111] See, e.g., D'Amato, *The Concept of Custom in International Law*, 73–74.
[112] See Lepard, *Customary International Law*, 8.

has developed a theory of customary international law that would take into account what states prefer the law to be.[113] A number of the authors in this volume address my reconceptualization of *opinio juris* and my new theory of customary international law more generally – in some cases approving of it, and in others, critiquing it.

Another problem revealed by the chronological paradox is how to identify the point in time when a sufficient number of states recognize, mistakenly or not, the existence of a putative norm, so that it becomes at that time customary law. We will see a number of examples of this problem in the contributions in this volume.

Having explored some of the particular problems lurking in the state practice and *opinio juris* requirements, we might step back and ask some broader questions about the necessity of either. Is either element, or at least proof of it, really required? To challenge the entrenched two-element definition might seem heretical, but the fact is that in practice, many courts, including the ICJ, have given it short shrift. So although one can find a few statements of the requirements in oft-cited opinions of the ICJ, such as in the 1985 *Continental Shelf Case (Libyan Arab Jamahiriya v. Malta)* quoted earlier in the chapter, in many cases the test is not clearly set out, and the Court finds a customary law without explicitly establishing the existence of both consistent state practice and *opinio juris*.

To give two examples, first, in the 1986 *Nicaragua Case*, the ICJ concluded based on the text of UN resolutions and the UN Charter that certain norms on the use of force were part of customary law, even though it admitted that supporting practice fell short and that state behavior often contradicted the norms. In particular, the ICJ found that a state has no right under customary international law to participate in collective military action based on a right of collective self-defense in response to an opposing military activity falling short of an armed attack.[114] In reaching this conclusion, the ICJ relied primarily on Articles 2(4) and 51 of the UN Charter and two UN General Assembly resolutions: General Assembly Resolution 2625, "Declaration on Principles of International Law concerning Friendly Relations and Co-operation among States in accordance with the Charter of the United Nations," adopted in

[113] See Curtis A. Bradley, "Customary International Law Adjudication as Common Law Adjudication," in *Custom's Future: International Law in a Changing World*, edited by Curtis A. Bradley 34 (New York: Cambridge University Press, 2016), 49 (arguing in favor of a "common law" account of customary international law adjudication under which judges make choices that "are informed by judgments about *the perceived preferences of the regulated states*, the likely consequences of adopting a particular formulation of the relevant international rule, and moral and ethical considerations") (emphasis added).

[114] See *Nicaragua Case*, 99–103, paras. 188–93, 110–11, paras. 210–11.

1970;[115] and the Definition of Aggression contained in General Assembly Resolution 3314, adopted in 1974.[116]

The Court's opinion was heavily criticized by many scholars for essentially ignoring the consistent state practice requirement and elevating the status of the *opinio juris* test.[117] As we will see, a number of the contributors to this volume agree with these critiques.

Another example of a court focusing on *opinio juris* in preference to state practice is the 2000 case of *Prosecutor v. Kupreškić*, in which the trial chamber of the ICTY concluded that there existed in customary international law a prohibition of reprisals against civilians, even though state practice was lacking in support of this prohibition. The chamber candidly said that clear *opinio juris* should trump spotty evidence of state practice. It affirmed:

> In the light of the way States and courts have implemented [the Martens Clause, a common treaty provision that appeared for the first time in the preamble to the 1899 Hague Convention II with Respect to the Laws and Customs of War on Land], this Clause clearly shows that principles of international humanitarian law may emerge through a customary process under the pressure of the demands of humanity or the dictates of public conscience, *even where State practice is scant or inconsistent*. The other element, in the form of *opinio necessitatis*, crystallising as a result of the imperatives of humanity or public conscience, *may turn out to be the decisive element heralding the emergence of a general rule or principle of humanitarian law*.[118]

In some cases the ICJ has referred to a common practice and declared it to be consistent with a customary law norm without any serious inquiry into the existence of *opinio juris*. For example, in its decision in the 1959 *Interhandel Case*, it stated, simply, that "the rule that local remedies must be exhausted before international proceedings may be instituted is a well-established rule of customary international law; the rule has been generally observed in cases in which a State has adopted the cause of its national whose rights are claimed to have been disregarded in another State in violation of international law."[119] The Court apparently relied on a widespread practice of states but made no detailed inquiry into *opinio juris*. Many other judgments contain a similarly

[115] G.A. Res. 2625 (XXV) (1970).

[116] G.A. Res. 3314 (XXIX) (1974).

[117] See, e.g., Anthony A. D'Amato, "Trashing Customary International Law," 81 *American Journal of International Law* 101 (1987).

[118] *Prosecutor v. Kupreškić*, 14 January 2000, IT-95-16-T, para 527 (emphasis added), available at www.refworld.org/docid/40276c634.html.

[119] See, e.g., *Interhandel Case (Switzerland v. United States of America)*, Preliminary Objections, Judgment of 21 March 1959, 1959 ICJ Rep. 6, 27.

terse statement about the content of customary law, based apparently on state practice alone.

This judicial agnosticism about the traditional definition has led many scholars to probe more deeply into the reasons for the two requirements and formulate new theories of customary law, some of which are alleged to provide a better "fit" with the actual record of judicial decision making on customary law than the long-standing definition. For example, the International Law Association's Committee on the Formation of Customary (General) International Law, under the leadership of Maurice Mendelson, published a report in 2000 that challenged the need for proof of *opinio juris* as a condition of recognizing a customary norm. It affirmed that "it is not *usually* necessary to demonstrate the existence of the subjective element [*opinio juris*] before a customary rule can be said to have come into being."[120]

On the other hand, other scholars, including myself, have asked probing questions about the need for the consistent state practice requirement. Some argue that it can effectively be dispensed with altogether, and that a clear expression of *opinio juris* can negate the need for a record of state practice, resulting in "instant" customary law. Thus, Bin Cheng famously affirmed: "There is no reason why an *opinio juris communis* may not grow up in a very short period of time among all or simply some Members of the United Nations with the result that a new rule of international customary law comes into being among them."[121]

I have expressed the view that state practice is best viewed as evidence of *opinio juris*, and the importance of this evidence can vary according to the type of problem a norm is intended to solve. Other scholars have echoed the view that state practice should be considered evidence of *opinio juris*.[122] Of course, all of these "modern" theories may challenge in some way the traditional conception of customary law as originating in, and being grounded in, "custom," that is, some form of recurring state behavior.[123]

120 International Law Association, London Conference (2000), Committee on the Formation of Customary (General) International Law, "Final Report of the Committee: Statement of Principles Applicable to the Formation of General Customary International Law," sec. 1, Commentary, para. (b)(4) (emphasis in the original).

121 Bin Cheng, "United Nations Resolutions on Outer Space: 'Instant' International Customary Law?" in *International Law: Teaching and Practice*, edited by Bin Cheng 237 (London: Stevens & Sons, 1982), 252.

122 See ibid, 251; Guzman, *How International Law Works*, 200 (affirming that practice "is best considered as evidence of *opinio juris*").

123 On so-called "modern" theories of customary international law, see, for example, Anthea Elizabeth Roberts, "Traditional and Modern Approaches to Customary International Law: A Reconciliation," 95 *American Journal of International Law* 757 (2001).

Recognizing that, in practice, courts will not often find compelling evidence of both state practice and *opinio juris*, some scholars, the most well-known being Frederick L. Kirgis, have advocated a "sliding scale" approach.[124] Under this approach, strong evidence of *opinio juris* can compensate for weak evidence of state practice, and vice versa.

Moreover, other scholars have developed Kirgis' idea that sufficient *opinio juris* can offset a relative paucity of state practice. Thus, Michael Scharf has suggested that some rules of customary international law can be created quickly based on new *opinio juris*, and with less state practice. He refers to such a rapid development of a customary norm as a "Grotian Moment."[125] He affirms: "The Grotian Moment concept illuminates how and why customary international law can sometimes develop with surprising rapidity and limited state practice. The concept reflects the reality that in periods of fundamental change, whether by technological advances, the commission of new forms of crimes against humanity, or the development of new means of warfare or terrorism, rapidly developing customary international law may be necessary to keep up with the pace of developments."[126]

In short, lurking behind the entrenched two-element definition of customary international law are many questions about the legitimacy and practicality of insisting on proof of both elements to find that a customary norm exists. All of the above theories raise important questions about these elements and their role on both theoretical and pragmatic grounds. These theories also call for a reexamination of the traditional doctrine of customary international law.

Questions about the role of the consistent state practice and *opinio juris* requirements also raise the thorny issue of how existing customary law norms change or terminate. Under the traditional model, it would seem that once both elements establish a norm, there must be a change in *both* state practice *and opinio juris* to modify the norm or reject it. Accordingly, a change in the practice of one or only a few states prior to an accompanying change in collective *opinio juris* could be characterized as a "violation" of the established norm. (This is often referred to as the "first mover" problem: The first state engaging in a new practice must necessarily be considered a violator of the existing norm.[127]) Moreover, even if collective *opinio juris* changed, the first

[124] See Frederick L. Kirgis, Jr., "Custom on a Sliding Scale," 81 *American Journal of International Law* 146 (1987).

[125] See Michael P. Scharf, *Customary International Law in Times of Fundamental Change: Recognizing Grotian Moments* (New York: Cambridge University Press, 2013).

[126] Ibid., 8.

[127] See Bederman, *Custom as a Source of Law*, 149.

states to engage in a new practice consistent with the new *opinio juris* could be viewed as violators of the prior norm, at least until a sufficiently consistent new practice among states developed. Indeed, there could be no new customary rule until a large number of states behaved contrary to the old rule. Thus, the traditional model leads to the judicially undesirable result that an existing law can only be changed by its own widespread violation. This type of problem has given some support to theories that emphasize *opinio juris*, because, under these theories, a change in *opinio juris* alone could be sufficient to modify a preexisting norm, and thus initial state practice consistent with the revised norm would not have to be viewed as a violation of the old one.[128]

Another constellation of problems revolves around the relationship between customary international law and other "sources" of international law. We have seen that Article 38 of the Statute of the ICJ lists the three principal sources of international law that the ICJ is to apply in determining disputes: international conventions (treaties), customary law, and general principles of law. This apparently simple list might give rise to the impression that there are bright-line boundaries demarcating each of these sources. The reality, upon closer examination – and certainly based on the experience of international courts in applying customary law – is that the lines between them are much blurrier. This is another reason that the relationship of customary law to other sources needs to be reexamined.

On the one hand, there are clear differences between treaties and customary international law. In particular, treaties are agreements among states that must be signed and ratified by a state for them to be binding on that state. They establish obligations only on the basis of explicit consent. By contrast, customary law, in principle, binds all states, with or without their explicit consent, except in the case of persistent objectors. Moreover, its rules derive from the confluence of state practice and *opinio juris*, rather than from meticulously negotiated and fine-tuned written text.

On the other hand, there is a close two-way relationship between treaties and customary law that merits examination: Preexisting customary norms can later be codified by treaties, and preexisting treaty norms can later give rise to new customary norms.

Thus, first, it is well accepted that particular treaties are intended to codify preexisting customary international law norms. For example, the ICJ Statute itself codified certain aspects of preexisting customary law on sources of

128 See generally Brian D. Lepard, "Customary International Law as a Dynamic Process," in *Custom's Future: International Law in a Changing World*, edited by Curtis A. Bradley 62 (New York: Cambridge University Press, 2016), 72, 89.

international law in Article 38. Furthermore, as confirmed by the ICJ in its 2015 Judgment in the case of *Application of the Convention on the Prevention and Punishment of the Crime of Genocide (Croatia v. Serbia)*, the 1948 Genocide Convention "enshrines principles that also form part of customary international law."[129] Similarly, the 1969 Vienna Convention on the Law of Treaties was consciously intended to codify many long-standing customary norms concerning how treaties are made, interpreted, modified, and terminated. The drafters of the 1982 United Nations Convention on the Law of the Sea sought to codify many of the rules that had governed use of the seas in customary law for centuries. The 2016 draft conclusions of the ILC reaffirm this codification function of some treaties, noting that "a rule set forth in a treaty may reflect a rule of customary international law if it is established that the treaty rule: (a) codified a rule of customary international law existing at the time when the treaty was concluded."[130]

This codification process seems natural enough, but critical questions about its impact on customary law abound. For example, if a broad, multilateral treaty codifies a preexisting customary norm, does the treaty "authoritatively" define and interpret the preexisting customary norm? When, if ever, does a treaty codification "extinguish" the customary norm? Can a customary norm continue to exist alongside a similar treaty norm, with varying characteristics? If so, which states are bound by which norms? On their face, treaties bind only parties, but can a treaty codification come to supplant the customary norm it codifies and effectively bind all states as customary law itself? When and under what circumstances? Does it matter whether the treaty is intended to be one that is universally ratified?

Second, it is also recognized that norms that originate in treaties can, over some period of time, come to be so broadly accepted by states, including non-parties to the treaty, and so widely implemented by states in practice, that they are transmuted into new customary norms. This recognition is reflected in Article 38 of the Vienna Convention on the Law of Treaties, which states: "Nothing in articles 34 and 37 precludes a rule set forth in a treaty from becoming binding upon a third State as a customary rule of international law, recognized as such."[131] Again, the ICJ acknowledged the legitimacy of this process in the *North Sea Continental Shelf Cases*, where it stated that a treaty provision could be

[129] *Application of the Convention on the Prevention and Punishment of the Crime of Genocide (Croatia v. Serbia)*, ICJ Judgment of 3 February 2015, para. 87.

[130] "Report of the International Law Commission," Sixty-Eighth Session, Draft Conclusion 11, para. 1(a).

[131] Vienna Convention on the Law of Treaties, art. 38.

> a norm-creating provision which has constituted the foundation of, or has generated a rule which, while only conventional or contractual in its origin, has since passed into the general *corpus* of international law, and is now accepted as such by the *opinio juris*, so as to have become binding even for countries which have never, and do not, become parties to the [treaty]. There is no doubt that this process is a perfectly possible one and does from time to time occur: it constitutes indeed one of the recognized methods by which new rules of customary international law may be formed. At the same time this result is not lightly to be regarded as having been attained.[132]

This process of treaty generation of a customary rule can involve either a rule that has begun to emerge as customary law prior to the treaty, but whose solidification the treaty fostered, or an entirely new rule given birth to by the treaty. Both cases are recognized in the 2016 ILC draft conclusions. Thus, they state, first, that a treaty rule may reflect customary law if the treaty rule "has led to the crystallization of a rule of customary international law that had started to emerge prior to the conclusion of the treaty."[133] And they recognize, second, that a treaty may have "given rise to a general practice that is accepted as law (*opinio juris*), thus generating a new rule of customary international law."[134]

However, the precise operation of this process of customary norm crystallization or creation by a treaty is mysterious. What requirements must be satisfied for a treaty norm to become a customary norm? Is it sufficient that parties to the treaties observe the norm and believe it to be (or that it should be) customary law for it to become customary law? Or must we instead focus solely on the beliefs and practices of nonparties, and ask whether their opinions and practice support recognition of the treaty norm as customary law? Or should we examine the views and practices of all states, both parties and nonparties? Must a certain "critical mass" of this group of states, however defined, support the treaty norm for it to become customary law? These kinds of questions about the impact of treaty codification of customary norms and evolution of customary norms from treaties have given rise to a voluminous literature – with no clear answers to them.[135]

The relationship between customary law and general principles of law is also fraught with difficulties. It would appear, upon initial examination, that

132 *North Sea Continental Shelf Cases*, 41, para. 71 (emphasis in the original).

133 "Report of the International Law Commission," Sixty-Eighth Session, Draft Conclusion 11, para. 1(b).

134 Ibid., para. 1(c).

135 On the debates on some of these issues regarding the relationship between treaties and customary international law, see Lepard, *Customary International Law*, 30–32, 34, 191–207, 220–21.

the two bodies of law originated in different ways. Thus, customary norms were seen as arising from the behavior of states primarily in their interstate relations – including in their relations regarding trade, on the high seas, and on the battlefield, among others. They behaved a certain way toward one another, and came to believe that this behavior was legally required or permitted (or conversely, that certain actions from which they refrained were legally prohibited). By contrast, general principles of law developed from principles common to the national legal systems of the world, such as estoppel or *res judicata*. However, in practice, this apparent difference in provenance has collapsed, and the ICJ itself has recognized general principles of international law that are difficult to distinguish from norms of customary international law. To make matters even blurrier, the Court often refers simply to "general international law," without indicating whether it means customary law, general principles, or both.[136]

Moreover, some scholars have pointed out that the three "sources" mentioned in Article 38 of the ICJ Statute may no longer fully encapsulate the modern-day dynamic process of international lawmaking, and may need to be supplemented by other "sources" – including General Assembly resolutions and "soft law."[137] "Soft law" may encompass General Assembly resolutions as well as a wide variety of other nonbinding documents that still have a legal or quasi-legal character, such as resolutions of other important intergovernmental and nongovernmental bodies.

The precise role of General Assembly resolutions in relation to customary international law has generated a wide-ranging literature.[138] Some scholars view them as particularly potent and convincing evidence of *opinio juris*. These and other scholars may also believe that the voting behavior of states in relation to these resolutions itself constitutes a form of state practice. In these ways, General Assembly resolutions may provide strong evidence of new customary norms.

The ICJ arguably adopted just such an approach in the 1986 *Nicaragua Case*. In that case, the Court declared that "*opinio juris* may, though with all due caution, be deduced from, *inter alia*, the attitude of the Parties and the attitude of States towards certain General Assembly resolutions. … The effect of consent to the text of such resolutions … may be understood as an acceptance of the validity of the rule or set of rules declared by the resolution

136 On this issue, see generally ibid., 28–29, 162–68.

137 On soft law generally, see, e.g., Alan Boyle, "Soft Law in International Law-Making," in *International Law*, edited by Malcolm D. Evans 122 (Oxford: Oxford University Press, 3rd ed. 2010).

138 This literature is discussed in Lepard, *Customary International Law*, 33, 35, 208–17, 222–24.

by themselves. The principle of non-use of force, for example, may thus be regarded as a principle of customary international law."[139]

Nevertheless, the Court's holding in the *Nicaragua Case* was controversial. One reason is that under the UN Charter, General Assembly resolutions are mere recommendations, and are not legally binding on UN member states.[140] Accordingly, one view is that customary international law cannot be used as a "back door" to transform nonbinding resolutions into law. Another problem is that resolutions by themselves may reflect neither the practice of states (apart from the act of voting on the resolution) nor genuine acceptance of rules in resolutions as law (*opinio juris*).

For these and similar reasons, the 2016 draft conclusions of the ILC based on the work of Special Rapporteur Michael Wood adopt a cautious approach. They affirm, first, that "a resolution adopted by an international organization or at an intergovernmental conference cannot, of itself, create a rule of customary international law."[141] However, they go on to provide, somewhat vaguely, that such a resolution "*may* provide evidence for establishing the existence and content of a rule of customary international law, or contribute to its development."[142] They also state that a provision in such a resolution "may reflect a rule of customary international law if it is established that the provision corresponds to a general practice that is accepted as law (*opinio juris*)."[143] This statement again may be true on its face, but does not elaborate on the precise way in which provisions of resolutions intersect with customary law.[144] In short, the complex subject of the relationship between resolutions of international organizations and customary international law demands critical reexamination. A number of the contributors to this volume undertake just such a fresh inquiry.

Another problematic area concerns the relationship between customary international law and "soft law." Some commentators may be so frustrated with the apparent indeterminacy of customary law that they regard all of it as "soft law" – law that does not impose true binding legal obligations. However,

139 *Nicaragua Case*, 99–100, para. 188.
140 See UN Charter, art. 13 (providing that the General Assembly "shall initiate studies and make recommendations" for a variety of purposes).
141 "Report of the International Law Commission," Sixty-Eighth Session, Draft Conclusion 12, para. 1.
142 Ibid., para. 2 (emphasis added).
143 Ibid., para. 3.
144 For a more detailed and helpful discussion of the relationship between customary international law and resolutions adopted by international organizations, see Michael Wood, Special Rapporteur, "Third Report on Identification of Customary International Law," paras. 45–54.

the traditional doctrine maintains, as we have seen, that customary law is as binding as treaty law. In keeping with this doctrine, other scholars contrast soft law (such as aspirational norms in General Assembly resolutions) with "hard law" containing some element of state consent – including treaties and customary law. There is also disagreement among scholars about whether soft law merely encompasses norms with no legal authority or also includes norms with "persuasive" legal authority – meaning that states are at least legally obligated to give the norm great weight, similar to a legal presumption. It is possible that some customary law norms could create such persuasive obligations, and therefore be classified as "soft law" under this latter definition. In short, the precise relationship between customary law and soft law remains a subject rife with controversy.

There is another good reason to reexamine customary international law. The entrenched theory of customary international law described earlier in the chapter is monolithic in the sense that it is supposed to "work" equally well for identifying rules governing any kind of problem that states face.[145] For example, this theory and its accompanying doctrine is supposed to apply in the same way to rules of the law of the sea, international trade law, international humanitarian law, international human rights law, international aviation law, and international space law, among other areas. (Not coincidentally, these are some of the issue areas discussed by the contributors to this volume.) Nevertheless, experience demonstrates that courts in practice have adopted quite different approaches to finding customary law in different areas. Thus, for example, they have exhibited a tendency to focus on *opinio juris* rather than state practice in assessing the existence of customary human rights norms, or customary norms of international humanitarian law – a phenomenon that various contributors to this book discuss, and some critique. And normatively, it may be appropriate, in fact, to apply different approaches to different kinds of problems, including distinguishing those norms that mainly solve coordination problems,

[145] Special Rapporteur Michael Wood appears to adopt this view. For example, in his second report to the ILC, he stated: "The first report raised the question whether there might be different approaches to the identification of rules of customary international law in different fields. For example, there have been suggestions in the literature, occasionally echoed in practice, that in such fields as international human rights law, international humanitarian law and international criminal law, among others, one element may suffice in constituting customary international law, namely *opinio juris*. However, the better view is that this is not the case. There may, on the other hand, be a difference in application of the two-element approach in different fields (or, perhaps more precisely, with respect to different types of rules)." Michael Wood, Special Rapporteur, "Second Report on Identification of Customary International Law," para. 28 (citations omitted).

for example, from those that have direct and serious implications for the realization of ethical values.

In light of all of these unanswered questions concerning customary international law, theories about it abound. Each represents an attempt to solve some of the enigmas that characterize it. It would be impossible to summarize all of these theories here; suffice it to say that the literature on customary law is expansive, and growing – and that it has not yet found satisfactory answers to these questions.[146]

Prompted in part by the uncertainty enshrouding the concept of customary international law, the UN ILC launched an investigation of the subject in 2012. It appointed a Special Rapporteur – Sir Michael Wood, author of the Foreword of this volume – to undertake a study on the topic "Formation and evidence of customary international law." Mr. Wood prepared a preliminary note on the subject that year.[147] He submitted his first report in 2013.[148] The UN Secretariat also produced a memorandum that year that summarized the Commission's prior work of relevance to the topic.[149] The Special Rapporteur submitted his second report on the identification of customary international law in 2014.[150] This report focused on the nature and role of the two constituent elements of customary international law – state practice and *opinio juris* – and on how to ascertain their existence.[151] It proposed eleven draft conclusions. The ILC discussed this report in July 2014, and there was general support among its members for the two-element

[146] For representative book-length works, see, e.g., Michael Byers, *Custom, Power and the Power of Rules: International Relations and Customary International Law* (Cambridge: Cambridge University Press, 1999); *Custom's Future: International Law in a Changing World*, edited by Curtis A. Bradley (New York: Cambridge University Press, 2016); D'Amato, *The Concept of Custom in International Law*; Guzman, *How International Law Works*; Lepard, *Customary International Law*; Scharf, *Customary International Law in Times of Fundamental Change*; H.W.A. Thirlway, *International Customary Law and Codification: An Examination of the Continuing Role of Custom in the Present Period of Codification of International Law* (Leiden: A.W. Sijthoff, 1972); and Karol Wolfke, *Custom in Present International Law* (Dordrecht: Martinus Nijhoff Publishers, 2nd rev. ed. 1993).

[147] "Formation and Evidence of Customary International Law: Note by Michael Wood, Special Rapporteur," UN Doc. A/CN.4/653 (2012).

[148] Michael Wood, Special Rapporteur, "First Report on Formation and Evidence of Customary International Law," UN Doc. A/CN.4/663 (2013).

[149] "Formation and Evidence of Customary International Law: Elements in the Previous Work of the International Law Commission That Could be Particularly Relevant to the Topic: Memorandum by the Secretariat," UN Doc. A/CN.4/659 (2013).

[150] Michael Wood, Special Rapporteur, "Second Report on Identification of Customary International Law." The Commission changed the name of the topic to "identification of customary international law" in the preceding year.

[151] On the two-element approach, see ibid., paras. 21–31.

approach.[152] A Drafting Committee of the Commission then took up consideration of these eleven draft conclusions and provisionally adopted many of them.[153]

The Sixth Committee of the General Assembly in 2014 supported this work and in particular the preparation of a practical guide containing both conclusions and commentaries.[154] This guide would be of assistance to practitioners in identifying rules of customary international law.

The Special Rapporteur submitted his third report to the Commission in 2015.[155] This report contained final proposed draft conclusions relating to the relationship between state practice and *opinio juris*, the role of inaction as practice or evidence of *opinio juris*, the role of treaties and resolutions adopted by international organizations and conferences in the identification of customary law, the role of judicial decisions and writings, the relevance of practice of nonstate actors, the concept of "particular" or regional customary international law, and the persistent objector rule.[156]

In July 2015, the Drafting Committee provisionally adopted draft conclusions and issued their text.[157] The Sixth Committee of the General Assembly then discussed the draft conclusions and delegations expressed general support for them. A number of comments and suggestions were made by states and others.[158] The Special Rapporteur took these into account in issuing his fourth report in March 2016, which proposed minor modifications

152 See "Report of the International Law Commission," Sixty-Sixth Session (5 May–6 June and 7 July–8 August 2014), UN Doc. A/69/10 (2014), para. 149.

153 See "Identification of Customary International Law: Statement of the Chairman of the Drafting Committee, Mr. Gilberto Saboia, 7 August 2014," available at http://legal.un.org/docs/?path=../ilc/sessions/66/pdfs/english/dc_chairman_statement_identification_of_custom.pdf&lang=E.

154 See "Topical Summary of the Discussion Held in the Sixth Committee of the General Assembly During Its Sixty-Ninth Session, Prepared by the Secretariat," UN Doc. A/CN.4/678 (2014), paras. 52–59.

155 Michael Wood, Special Rapporteur, "Third Report on Identification of Customary International Law."

156 See generally ibid. On the concept of particular custom, the ILC's draft conclusions, based on those proposed by Michael Wood, recognize that there can be such a "rule of particular customary international law, whether, regional, local or other," that "applies only among a limited number of States." "Report of the International Law Commission," Sixty-Eighth Session, Draft Conclusion 16, para. 1. Consistent with the two-element definition of "general" customary law, the conclusions affirm that "to determine the existence and content of a rule of particular customary international law, it is necessary to ascertain whether there is a general practice among the States concerned that is accepted by them as law (*opinio juris*)." Ibid., para. 2.

157 See International Law Commission, "Identification of Customary International Law: Text of the Draft Conclusions Provisionally Adopted by the Drafting Committee," UN Doc. A/CN.4/L.869 (2015).

158 See generally UN Doc. A/C.6/70/SR.19-23 (2015).

to some of the draft conclusions provisionally adopted by the Drafting Committee.[159] At its sixty-eighth session held in 2016, the Commission asked the Drafting Committee to reconsider the draft conclusions. The Drafting Committee then adopted a revised set of conclusions.[160] The Commission as a whole discussed these and, on first reading, adopted a set of sixteen draft conclusions, with commentaries, based on the work of the Special Rapporteur and the Drafting Committee.[161]

Some of the draft conclusions adopted by the ILC in 2016 have been referred to in the preceding discussion of particular contentious issues involving customary law. Most importantly, as we have already seen, Draft Conclusion 2 reaffirmed the two-element definition of customary law, declaring: "To determine the existence and content of a rule of customary international law, it is necessary to ascertain whether there is a general practice that is accepted as law (*opinio juris*)."[162]

The work of the Special Rapporteur and the ILC shed light on many of the issues discussed in this book. Nevertheless, as the Special Rapporteur himself has acknowledged, the working out in practice of even agreed principles raises many complex problems. The scope of these problems is reflected in the broad range of academic and practical views expressed in the copious citations that appear in the Special Rapporteur's reports. Furthermore, while many of the contributors to this volume endorse some of the principles agreed to by the Commission (such as the requirement of the two elements of a general state practice and *opinio juris*), other contributors challenge them or call for further reflection. In short, the Commission's work, while important and very useful, is still an impetus to further inquiry.

1.4 OVERVIEW OF THE BOOK

The contributors to this volume would be superhuman if they were able to address, let alone resolve, all of the challenging questions concerning

159 See Michael Wood, Special Rapporteur, "Fourth Report on Identification of Customary International Law," UN Doc. A/CN.4/695 (2016). See also UN Doc. A/CN.4/695/Add.1 (2016) (containing a bibliography of writings on the identification of customary international law).

160 International Law Commission, "Identification of Customary International Law: Text of the Draft Conclusions Provisionally Adopted by the Drafting Committee," UN Doc. A/CN.4/L.872 (2016).

161 "Report of the International Law Commission," Sixty-Eighth Session, chapter V. The text of the draft conclusions adopted by the Commission appears in ibid., 76–79.

162 Ibid., Draft Conclusion 2.

customary international law identified throughout this chapter, including those questions left open in the work of the ILC. Nevertheless, they take on many of them in insightful ways as they reexamine this foundational legal source.

First, the contributors to Part I reexamine historical and theoretical perspectives on customary international law. J. Patrick Kelly engages in a penetrating review of the history of customary law ideas going back to the writings of the Catholic "scholastics," most notably Francisco de Vitoria and Francisco Suárez. He shows that the history of the theoretical doctrine of customary law is inextricably intertwined with great power politics, and in particular with efforts by powerful states to promulgate rules favoring their own economic interests at the expense of those of weaker states. He argues that they, and even the great theorists of customary international law, cloaked these economic interests under the mantle of "customary law." On the other hand, when certain allegedly customary rules were not to their liking, they profited from the creation and invocation of the persistent objector exception, which, Kelly argues, threatens to undermine the very legitimacy of customary law. Kelly therefore urges a fundamental reexamination of the premises and traditional doctrine of customary law, as well as reforms in its conceptualization, to make it apply more equitably.

Fernando Tesón addresses the history and theory of customary law from another angle: He is concerned that the original conceptual foundations of customary law, anchored in consistent state practice and *opinio juris*, are being eroded by diverse new conceptions of customary law promoting norms that masquerade as "customary law" but are, he says, "fake custom." He explores in some detail many of these conceptions that are based on "fallacies," including, for example, the belief that citing dozens of General Assembly resolutions endorsing a norm, "ad nauseam," in fact blesses it with the status of customary law. However, he also makes an appeal for recognition of some norms as international law – but not customary international law – based on their ethical character.

Niels Petersen reexamines the theory of customary international law by focusing on the role played by individual state consent. He explores this problem through new lenses, especially the one provided by game theory. Importantly, he argues that decision makers must distinguish among different categories of customary law norms using game theory, and apply different concepts of consent to each of these categories. Thus, he argues, some customary norms, such as those relating to simple coordination problems, may allow for exemption of particular states through persistent objection, while other customary norms, including those furthering important ethical values, should not permit such unilateral exemption.

The final contribution to Part I, by Thomas Kleinlein, probes the long-murky relationship between customary international law and general principles of law. He reviews prior attempts to clarify the conceptual distinctions between these two bodies of law, and shows how these attempts are inadequate. He then proposes a new way to demarcate the boundaries between customary law and general principles, drawing on the notion of "factual reciprocity." He also develops an approach to understanding the normativity of general principles that relies on the concepts of "changing identities" and "argumentative self-entrapment."

Having reexamined some of the historical and theoretical underpinnings of customary international law, the book turns to a closer analysis of the role of customary international law in particular issue areas, shining a light on both its strengths and weaknesses in regulating state behavior in these domains. Part II begins with an exploration of customary international humanitarian law, a body of law whose importance has grown exponentially in recent decades, as it has been repeatedly invoked by international criminal tribunals, the ICJ itself, and national courts.

A major contribution to the systematic identification of rules of customary humanitarian law was made by the ICRC in a groundbreaking and far-ranging study published in 2005 and supplemented by an online database that has been updated continually since then. One of the principal authors of this study, Jean-Marie Henckaerts, and his former colleague Els Debuf, who headed the ICRC's continuing project on customary international humanitarian law from 2011 to 2014, examine the relevance of this body of law today. They evaluate the impact of the ICRC's impressive study on the actual recognition and application of customary humanitarian law by courts and other relevant decision makers, explore various problematic issues of methodology that the ICRC had to confront, and use these issues as a springboard for undertaking a broader assessment of the theory and practice of customary international humanitarian law.

Noora Arajärvi then looks at the field of international criminal law, and how international criminal tribunals and other courts have used customary law in criminal prosecutions. She identifies various emerging trends in decisions of these tribunals and courts, including a de-emphasis of state practice and a focus on, and a broadening of, *opinio juris* to include moral concerns like the "demands of humanity." She views some aspects of these trends as positive, but others as problematic to the extent they effectively remove the state practice requirement for customary norms. She argues that doing so is injurious to legal certainty and the foundational principle of legality.

Part III turns attention to customary international human rights law, which is a close cousin of customary international humanitarian law. Customary law has played an increasingly prominent role in this field, too, as courts and other decision makers identify a wide variety of human rights norms, many originally expressed in declarations and treaties, as norms of customary law binding all states. However, this process has been controversial. The normative appeal of human rights norms is, at least from an ethical standpoint, indisputable; the problem is determining whether and how particular norms in fact satisfy appropriate criteria for customary law and therefore legally bind states.

My own chapter addresses some of the current challenges in identifying and applying customary international human rights law. I underscore that the traditional two-element definition of customary law does not work well for human rights norms, because there is, undoubtedly, a widespread state practice of violating many fundamental human rights, including the prohibition of torture, to take one example. I argue that these problems highlight a more systematic failing of the traditional definition. I then suggest a new interpretation of customary law along the lines intimated earlier in this chapter, and demonstrate how this new understanding can lead to better decision making about the customary law status of particular human rights norms, focusing as an example on the right to change one's religion or belief.

Anna Williams Shavers reexamines an especially contentious issue in the human rights field – women's rights – and their status in customary international law. Perhaps more so than in other areas of human rights law, the status of women's rights as customary law is precarious, because the legal disabilities that women suffer in many countries of the world are so entrenched and pervasive. For example, women are often denied the right to membership in a community such as a tribe on terms equal to men, are forbidden from owning or inheriting land, and are the victims of gender-motivated violence. Shavers argues that the new perspective on customary law developed in my chapter offers greater possibilities than the traditional doctrine for customary law to be effective in improving women's lives and upholding their rights, and can clarify the status of particular women's rights norms as customary law, *jus cogens*, and *erga omnes* norms.

Next, Part IV turns to two other issue areas in which customary international law is playing an increasingly prominent role: air and space law. These bodies of law have been governed largely by treaties, especially because they are of such recent vintage. Nevertheless, as treaty law in these domains has expanded over the last century, new norms of customary law consistent with the treaties have arguably emerged and can be useful to states as they attempt to regulate their activities, and those of private enterprises, in both airspace and outer space.

First, Sofia Michaelides-Mateou surveys the history of contemporary international air law, which dates back to the 1919 Paris Convention, and is today anchored in the 1944 Chicago Convention as well as manifold bilateral and multilateral air transport agreements. She demonstrates that a recurring theme in this history has been the battle among states between the competing norms of state sovereignty over the airspace above a state's territory and freedom of aircraft registered in one state to fly over the territory of another, referred to as "freedom of overflight." She critically evaluates the role of the treaty formulations of these norms in generating parallel customary international law norms, considering in particular a 2011 decision by the Court of Justice of the European Union that identifies relevant norms of customary air law. Her chapter provides an excellent case study of the complex interrelationship between treaty norms and customary law.

Second, Frans G. von der Dunk considers similar issues arising in the emerging law of outer space – also a relative newcomer in the international law domain. Again, this field offers a particularly appropriate case study for considering whether there can be "instant" customary international law, or at least rapidly forming customary law. Von der Dunk considers the impact on customary law of key space law treaties, as well as the complex tapestry of practice involving outer space – now including the spacefaring activities not only of states themselves but also of interstate space organizations. Von der Dunk trains close attention on the difficult problem of how customary law intertwines with treaty norms. He notes that in space law much of "state practice" actually consists of "paper practice" in the form of treaties and declarations, and discusses the special problems raised by paper practice. He helpfully explores a number of specific issues, including the customary law status of the norm requiring that space be used "exclusively for peaceful purposes," arrangements for international cooperation on space activities, and norms developed as part of the fight against space debris. He concludes that customary law has played a less prominent role in the field of space law than in other domains of international law.

Finally, Part V consists of my own concluding chapter. It offers my reflections on the many insights that can be gleaned from the contributions in the volume relating to the problem areas I identified earlier in this chapter. I highlight both the insights that appear to be shared among the authors as well as some of the areas in which the authors adopt differing approaches that in turn mirror many of the debates in the contemporary literature on customary international law. The book therefore does not pretend to resolve these complex problems and put an end to debate. Rather, it forms a humble part of a continuing quest by jurists and legal scholars to clarify the history and theory of customary international law as well as its practical role in fostering global cooperation to resolve many of the complex problems facing states and humankind as a whole today. In reexamining customary international law, it seeks to give new directions to this ongoing quest.

PART I

Reexamining Historical and Theoretical Perspectives on Customary International Law

2

Customary International Law in Historical Context

The Exercise of Power without General Acceptance

J. Patrick Kelly

2.1 INTRODUCTION

If one examines how international legal norms were formed and justified from a modern perspective, that history raises major concerns about the legitimacy of many putative norms of customary international law. A careful examination of that history suggests that to a large degree publicists and powerful nations ignored inconvenient state practice and generated customary international law norms based on prior assumed values or perceived self-interest irrespective of the general acceptance of a norm.

From a contemporary perspective, the elements of customary international law, state practice and *opinio juris*, are the means by which nations express their normative preferences in a decentralized system. State practice is the empirical element in customary international law formation providing evidence of customary norms. The states involved in an action or practice may justify their actions by reference to a norm or may disagree about the appropriate norm. Under customary international law theory the general acceptance of states or *opinio juris* determines whether a claimed norm embedded in state practice is legally binding.[1] Thus, it is the reaction of the states as a whole, not just that of the parties involved alone, that tells us how to interpret state

[1] See, e.g., *North Sea Continental Shelf Cases (Federal Republic of Germany v. Denmark; Federal Republic of Germany v. Netherlands)*, Judgment of 20 February 1969, 1969 ICJ Rep. 3, 43–44, para. 74 ("[A]n indispensable requirement would be that within the period in question, short though it might be, State practice, including that of States whose interests are specially affected, should have been both extensive and virtually uniform in the sense of the provision invoked; – and should moreover have occurred in such a way as to show a *general recognition* that a rule of law or legal obligation is involved") (emphasis added). At least since the late nineteenth century, with the rise of positivism and the secular state, customary rules arise from the common consent or consensus of states. See Lassa Oppenheim, *International Law*, Peace, Vol. 1 (London: Longmans, Green and Co., 2nd ed. 1912), §§ 11, 12 ("*Oppenheim's International Law* (2nd ed. 1912)").

practice.[2] The uniformity and generality of state practice may be an indication of *opinio juris*, that is, that a norm has been generally accepted as legally binding, but it is suggestive, not determinative.[3]

The general acceptance of states also performs the critical function of legitimizing a norm by the relevant political community, the international community of states. While legitimacy is an inherently subjective concept that can be evaluated from different perspectives, two important criteria of legitimacy resonate in modern international legal discourse: legal or formal legitimacy, and democratic legitimacy. Formal legitimacy or legality is the modern minimal criterion of legitimacy and the form of discourse in international affairs.[4] Formal legitimacy requires that legal norms and decisions be approved through prior defined legal processes accepted as valid.[5] In the domain of international law, the primary "right processes" are treaties formed by the express consent of participating states, such as the United Nations Charter, and customary international law as defined by both state practice and *opinio juris*, that is, the general acceptance of a norm as legally required.[6]

2 See *Delimitation of the Maritime Boundary in the Gulf of Maine Area (Canada v. United States of America)*, Judgment of 12 October 1984 Given by the Chamber Constituted by the Order Made by the Court on 20 January 1982, 1984 ICJ Rep. 246, 299, para. 111 ("*Gulf of Maine Case*"). See also Brian D. Lepard, *Customary International Law: A New Theory with Practical Applications* (New York: Cambridge University Press, 2010), 105–07. For a contrary view, see Anthony A. D'Amato, *The Concept of Custom in International Law* (Ithaca, NY: Cornell University Press, 1971).

3 See *Military and Paramilitary Activities in and against Nicaragua (Nicaragua v. United States of America)*, Merits, Judgment of 27 June 1986, 1986 ICJ Rep. 14, 97, para. 207 ("[A]s was observed in the *North Sea Continental Shelf* cases, for a new customary rule to be formed, not only must the acts concerned 'amount to a settled practice' but they must be accompanied by the *opinio juris sive necessitatis*. Either the States taking such action or other States in a position to react to it must have behaved so that their conduct is 'evidence of a belief that this practice is rendered obligatory by the existence of a rule of law requiring it. The need for such a belief, i.e. the existence of a subjective element, is implicit in the very notion of *opinio juris sive necessitatis*.'").

4 Max Weber developed the theory of formal legitimacy, asserting that legality or formal correctness would incline the citizenry toward compliance. See *Max Weber on Law in Economy and Society*, translated by Edward Shiles and Max Rheinstein (New York: Simon and Shuster, 1954), 8–9.

5 Legitimacy is the property of a rule or institution that exerts a compliance pull because the community believes that the rule or institution came into being or operates in accordance with generally accepted principles of "right process." See Thomas M. Franck, *The Power of Legitimacy Among Nations* (New York: Oxford University Press, 1990), 24.

6 Thomas Franck described customary international law and treaties as the secondary rules of right process in the international legal system using H.L.A. Hart's distinction between primary rules of substantive law and secondary rules of accepted processes to make law. Franck developed four criteria – determinacy, symbolic validation, coherence, and adherence – to determine the legitimacy of a process. See ibid., 206–07. For the view that customary international

By democratic legitimacy I mean the extent to which nations and societies are members of, participate in, and influence the political community determining norms. If a particular customary rule or standard is formed without the participation of a significant number of states or their interests and concerns are ignored or treated as irrelevant to norm formation, then a rule or standard may be seen not only as lacking general acceptance but also as lacking democratic legitimacy.

As the discussion that follows demonstrates, many international legal norms were not developed by the participation or acceptance of the overwhelming majority of states. If customary international law is an inductive, decentralized method of lawmaking formed by consistent state practice and the general acceptance of norms, then historically few customary international law norms met either of these requirements. Significantly, non-Western nations and societies as well as less powerful Western nations played little role in the formation of international legal norms. Their views were, by and large, ignored and considered irrelevant.[7] This tendency to ignore non-Western views about customary norms continued throughout the twentieth century, and is only gradually dissipating. Japan, Argentina, and China, for example, are quite aware of this history and have historically viewed themselves as recipients of international law rather than participants in the process.[8]

The claim here is that if one looks back at how norms were actually articulated and justified during the sixteenth century through much of the twentieth century, state practice and general acceptance played a minor, even inconsequential role in the formation of customary international law norms. Even many norms that were labeled as customary international law had their roots in an assumed universal natural law and remained deductive despite the label of "custom." Rather, customary international law development during this long gestation period might be characterized as dominated by the exercise of military and economic power and justified by Western legal maxims using a deductive methodology.[9] This disconnect between how norms were actually

law does not meet Franck's criteria of right process, see J. Patrick Kelly, "The Twilight of Customary International Law," 40 *Virginia Journal of International Law* 449 (2000), 457.

7 After nearly a century of ignoring Latin American views on state responsibility, Secretary of State Cordell Hull stated the view of the United States as follows: "The universal acceptance of this rule of the law of nations [prompt, adequate, and effective compensation], which, in truth, is merely a statement of common justice and fair-dealing, does not in the view of this government admit of any divergence of opinion." 19 *Department of State Press Releases* 139 (1938), 140.

8 See, e.g., Hanqin Xue, "Chinese Observations on International Law," 6 *China Journal of International Law* 83 (2007), 84–85.

9 For a revealing example of the use of deductive reasoning to justify norms deemed customary, see Clyde Eagleton, *The Responsibility of States in International Law* (New York: New York

determined and formal customary international law theory (requiring both state practice and *opinio juris*) raises significant questions about the legality and legitimacy of many purported customary international law norms. This tendency to treat extrinsic values such as the precautionary principle or the "demands of humanity" as customary norms rather than examine state practice and acceptance as law continues today.[10]

In order to understand the early formation of what are called customary international law norms, we must look beyond the formal requirement of state practice and general acceptance to the wider political and economic context.[11] From this wider lens, state practice and the general acceptance of states played only a limited role in norm development. Antony Anghie in his seminal work argued that much of modern international law and legal structures was forged from the European colonial encounter with non-European civilizations, with these cultures as the objects of reform.[12] James Gathii and Ileana Porras, among others, have modified this view by demonstrating that the competition and even violent encounters among European nations for trade and territory were similarly generative of international legal norms.[13] Other writers emphasize the positive aspects of the long, slow evolution of legal norms and institutions to limit and channel

University Press, 1928). There is a wide literature on colonialism and its aftermath as well as a modern conservative literature on international law as dominated by power and self-interest. For a discussion of how legal categories were used to justify conquest, see Robert A. Williams, Jr., *The American Indian in Western Legal Thought* (New York: Oxford University Press, 1992). For a critique of the legalistic approach to the use of force and an exposition of international law as power, see Michael J. Glennon, *Limits of War, Prerogatives of Power: Intervention After Kosovo* (New York: Palgrave, 2001).

10 On the precautionary principle, see Fernando R. Tesón, "Fake Custom," in this volume, and on the "demands of humanity" see Noora Arajärvi, "From the 'Demands of Humanity': The Formulation of *Opinio Juris* in Decisions of International Criminal Tribunals and the Need for a Renewed Emphasis on State Practice," in this volume.

11 For an argument that "bare" (uncodified) customary law often reflects the interests of the most powerful states, see Timothy Meyer, "Codifying Custom," 160 *University of Pennsylvania Law Review* 995 (2012), 1022 ("Powerful states play a disproportionate role in the formation of bare custom. The influence of the powerful may be due … to the application of political or economic pressure.… Powerful states are also generally more effective at publicizing their legal positions and, indeed, formulating claims as legal claims in a way likely to impact custom.").

12 Antony Anghie, *Imperialism, Sovereignty and the Making of International Law* (Cambridge: Cambridge University Press, 2007), 36–39.

13 For an insightful discussion of the role of commerce in colonial history, see James Thuo Gathii, *War, Commerce and International Law* (New York: Oxford University Press, 2010); Ileana Porras, "Constructing International Law in the East Indian Seas: Property, Sovereignty, Commerce and War in Hugo Grotius' De Jure Praedae – the Law of Prize and Booty, or 'On How to Distinguish Merchants from Pirates,'" 31 *Brooklyn Journal of International Law* 741 (2006).

state behavior.[14] As much as there is validity to this positive evolutionary perspective, particularly in the field of human rights, the development of international norms prior to the United Nations Charter primarily served to support the extension of power and facilitate its use rather than to limit power.[15]

This chapter begins with a brief analytical discussion of the history of international legal thought as articulated by the major publicists and chroniclers of each era.[16] This survey demonstrates the confluence of natural law ideas with the history of customary international law development in which idealized versions of European norms were universalized in order to justify the colonial enterprise and later treated as customary international law binding on all. Second, I examine the development of the law of state responsibility, with particular attention to the international minimum standard for compensation for expropriation. This body of law is an ongoing example of the use of power to impose norms, sometimes by force, contrary to the views of a significant group of states. Third, I examine the conflicted history of the customary international law of the territorial sea that culminated in a set of significantly different standards in a treaty regime. This example illustrates that in many areas treatises masked divergent claims, even among Western nations, about the content of norms. Finally, I examine the history of the persistent objector principle that threatens to undermine the claim of the legitimacy of customary international law as a form of norm creation. The persistent objector principle, if it is to be believed, creates a condition in which the majority of nations are bound to norms without their consent or participation, yet a state that persistently objects may exempt itself from an otherwise universal customary norm because international law is said to be essentially consensual.

2.2 HISTORICAL OVERVIEW

In order to evaluate the legality and legitimacy of putative customary international law norms, it is necessary to understand how the early writers of international legal thought developed and justified norms in their political and

14 For example, see Joel Trachtman, *The Future of International Law* (Cambridge: Cambridge University Press, 2013).

15 See Philip Trimble, "Globalization, International Institutions and the Erosion of National Sovereignty and Democracy," 95 *Michigan Law Review* 1944 (1995).

16 For more detailed discussions of this history, see Arthur Nussbaum, *A Concise History of the Law of Nations* (New York: Macmillan, rev. ed. 1954); W.G. Grewe, *The Epochs of International Law*, translated by Michael Byers (Berlin: de Gruyter, rev. ed. 2000); Martti Koskenniemi, *The Gentle Civilizer of Nations: The Rise and Fall of International Law 1870–1960* (Cambridge: Cambridge University Press, 2002).

economic context. The "Scholastics" – Francisco de Vitoria and Francisco Suárez – wrote to restore the intellectual rigor and the political standing of Catholicism during the challenge of the Protestant Reformation and to support the Spanish struggle for territories and markets in the newly discovered Americas.[17] Vitoria's two major lectures on international law are considered founding classics of international law.[18] While writing in the tradition of Aquinas, Vitoria distinguished himself by viewing *jus gentium* as natural law administered by a secular sovereign, not as divine law administered by the pope. Nevertheless this human law was discoverable by natural reasoning rather than built by state practice.[19] Indians, as non-Christians, were excluded from sovereignty, but their social organization and culture demonstrated that non-European people possessed reason and natural rights. Like Christians, they could not be deprived of their property or person without just cause. As rational beings Indians had access to and could understand the universal natural law of *jus gentium*.[20] This form of universalism was a projection of secular European humanism that minimized the identity of non-Christian people and excluded them from sovereignty.[21] With this construct of universal reason Vitoria had developed the means to bind non-European societies without their participation and against their will to assumed universal principles.[22]

While Vitoria recognized that Indians had jurisdiction over territory and a sense of property, they were nevertheless subject to universal *jus gentium* norms that, if violated, might justify punitive actions.[23] In *De Indis* he addressed the question of the legality of the Spanish conquest of native lands in the New World. Using his version of natural reason, Vitoria derived the right of states to hospitality within other states and of sociability in foreign countries. From these basic rights he further deduced a right to travel and a right to engage in trade.[24] For Vitoria it was a violation of *jus gentium* to treat foreigners inhospitably or hinder them from trading in the host country out of an overriding

[17] See Annabel Brett, "Francisco De Vitoria (1483–1546) and Francisco Suarez (1548–1617)," in *The Oxford Handbook of the History of International Law*, edited by Bardo Fassbender and Anne Peters 1086 (Oxford: Oxford University Press, 2012).

[18] The two lectures, *De Indis Noviter Inventis* [On the Indians Lately Discovered] and *De Jure Bellis Hispanorum in Barbaros* [On the Law of War Made by the Spaniards on the Barbarians], are collected in one volume. See Franciscus De Vitoria, *De Indis et De Ivre Belli Reflectiones*, edited by Ernest Nys and translated by John Paley Bate (1557), in *Classics of International Law*, edited by James Brown Scott 151 (William S. Hein & Co., 1995).

[19] Vitoria wrote: "What natural reason has established among nations is called *jus gentium*." Ibid., 151.

[20] Ibid., 127.

[21] See Koskenniemi, *The Gentle Civilizer of Nations*, 131–32; Anghie, *Imperialism*, 30.

[22] See Anghie, *Imperialism*, 20.

[23] See Brett, "Francisco De Vitoria (1483–1546) and Francisco Suarez (1548–1617)," 1086–87.

[24] Vitoria, *De Indis*, 152.

duty to treat others with love and fellowship.[25] A violation of such universal natural rights could provide cause to wage a "just war." According to Vitoria, the Spaniards could lawfully engage in trade among the native Indians as long as they did them no harm. Similarly, local princes had the right to trade with the Spaniards, but they could not hinder their subjects from carrying on trade with foreigners. If the indigenous people persisted in resisting Spanish incursion or attempted to expel them, then this hostility toward foreigners was just cause for war and would justify reparations, occupation, and even conquest to repair this injustice.[26]

In this view, once the Spanish were unjustly injured by indigenous people and in a state of war, it was permissible to take their property and kill all who took up arms against them.[27] His jurisprudence justified Spanish colonialism, including the taking of property as reparations and the exclusion of non-Christian states from sovereign rights.[28] The deductive rights to hospitality and sociability can be seen as the beginning of the law of state responsibility, with the corresponding right to remedy violations with self-help. Vitoria's universal *jus gentium* had resonance with secular rulers because it coincided with the interests of emerging colonial powers and justified the Spanish conquest of the Indies.

The Dutch jurist, theologian, and diplomat Hugo Grotius (1583–1645), often considered the father of modern international law, was a bridge between the natural law era and the rise of positivism. Like Vitoria, he derived his principles of international law from what he termed universal reason. His tract, *Mare Liberum*, argued for freedom of the seas in defense of Holland's interest as the preeminent sea power of the time. In his major work, *De Jure Belli Ac Pacis*,[29] he deduced universal international legal principles, including the fundamental principles of freedom of commerce and of navigation. In an important earlier work that became the basis of *Mare Liberum* and much of his later thinking, *De Jure Praedae* (The Law of Prize and Booty),[30] he emphasized and extended Vitoria's derivative right to trade by claiming that the doctrine of the Providential Function of Commerce was the source of the sacrosanct law of

25 Ibid., 151–53.
26 Ibid., 151–55.
27 Ibid., 181–83.
28 Anghie's view is that these encounters with non-Western societies helped define and expand the doctrine of sovereignty. Anghie, *Imperialism*, 29.
29 Hugo Grotius, *The Rights of War and Peace Including the Law of Nature and of Nations* (1625), translated by A.C. Campbell (New York: M. Walter Dunne, 1901). Available at http://oll.libertyfund.org/titles/553.
30 Hugo Grotius, *De Jure Praedae Commentarius* [Commentary on the Law of Prize and Booty] (1604), translated by Gwaldys L. Williams and Walter H. Zydel, in *The Classics of International Law*, edited by James Brown Scott (Oxford: Clarendon Press, 1950).

hospitality.[31] This placed the right to conduct commerce and to trade at the center of the privileges exercised by a sovereign.[32]

As with Vitoria, an offense against the natural rights of either commerce or hospitality entitled a sovereign to wage a just war on a local society for denying access to markets. Grotius, by elevating the right to conduct commerce as paramount, considered any interference with this right, even by a third party, such as Holland's European competitors, a potential justification for war against another European state.[33] In *De Praedae* Grotius extended this right to wage a just war even to private parties, such as privateers in service to the sovereign.[34] Grotius, for all his virtues in advancing international legal thinking,[35] wrote to justify aggressive Dutch commercial expansion and colonial adventures into what was known as the Indies.[36]

Both Vitoria in the sixteenth century and Grotius in the seventeenth century assumed natural principles, and then deduced further rights to justify the European conquest of new worlds. With these "universal" principles Grotius endorsed a rather extreme version of the right of states to make war, to punish violators of these principles, to take property, and to appropriate the unused or wasted land of indigenous peoples.[37]

The paradigm shift toward modern positivism, with the law theoretically based on the acts and practices of states, did not significantly alter the unequal legal relations. Vattel in his 1758 treatise redefined and subordinated natural law to a voluntary law of international relations based on the actual practice of states.[38] Natural law remained an important source of background norms that

[31] Ibid., 219.

[32] See Porras, *Constructing International Law*, 773. In discussing Vitoria's work, Grotius clarified his own priorities: "If in short, they (the Spaniards) should be disbarred from the practice of commerce – these causes might serve them as just grounds for war against the Indians; and indeed as grounds more plausible than others." Grotius, *De Jure Praedae Commentarius*, 219.

[33] See Porras, *Constructing International Law*, 773–74.

[34] In this way Grotius justified the capture of European vessels and their booty by Dutch privateers as prizes of war. See ibid., 774–80.

[35] For the view that Grotius was the "father" of the modern law of nations, creating the first formulation of a comprehensive legal order, see Michael P. Scharf, *Customary International Law in Times of Fundamental Change: Recognizing Grotian Moments* (New York: Cambridge University Press, 2013), 3–4.

[36] See Richard Tuck, *The Rights of War and Peace: Political Thought and the International Order from Grotius to Kant* (New York: Oxford University Press, 1999), 79–81.

[37] See ibid., 102–08.

[38] Emmerich de Vattel, *The Law of Nations; or, Principles of the Law of Nature Applied to the Conduct and the Affairs of Nations and Sovereigns*, translated by Joseph Chitty (London: Sweet, Stevens and Maxwell, 1834). For Vattel, the necessary, natural, or internal law of nations, while formally superior to voluntary law, binds only the conscience. The voluntary or external law of nations became the actual basis of practical action between nations. Ibid.,

justified state action, including colonial settlements where local inhabitants failed to honor their putative natural law obligation to cultivate the land for the good of mankind.[39] This paradigm shift had a powerful appeal to nation-states and their decision makers.[40] In the eighteenth and early nineteenth centuries, governments, particularly that of the United States, viewed Vattel's treatise as the primary authority on the law of nations.[41]

Vattel's positivism was particularized, voluntary, and not universal. In his view, customary international law was created by the tacit consent of states.[42] His natural law of *jus gentium* had been articulated as universal norms accessible to all by reason and at least theoretically bound sovereign states. In contrast to natural law, Vattel's customary international law was neither universal nor mandatory, binding only those states that chose to participate.[43] Important to the later discussion of the persistent objector principle, his *Law of Nations* recognized the right of states to choose to enter or exit customary law regimes voluntarily at any time.

Vattel's authority, however, had waned by the end of the nineteenth century.[44] His consent theory, as an explanation for the binding nature of customary international law, suffered from several defects. As a factual matter, few nations participated in the formation of custom or have ever expressed their will on a particular custom. Its contractual device, tacit consent, was an

Preliminaries, lxiv–lxvi. Wolff had developed a voluntary law of nations that was not part of the natural law, but derived from his conception of a *civitas maxima* an ideal republic to which nations should aspire. See Nicholas Greenwood Onuf, "Civitas Maxima: Wolf, Vattel, and the Fate of Republicanism," 88 *American Journal of International Law* 280 (1994), 295–99.

39 For a summary of the relevant passages of Vattel's works, see Tuck, *The Rights of War and Peace*, 194–96.

40 Vattel intimated that his version of voluntary law based on the sources of recognized practice would be more persuasive to nation-states than a theory based on nature as the one, unifying authority for all law. See Onuf, "Civitas Maxima," 299.

41 Charles G. Fenwick, "The Authority of Vattel," 7 *American Political Science Review* 395 (1913). His treatise was used as a textbook in universities in the United States and as the primary international law source cited by judges in their legal opinions and by lawyers in their briefs. See Arthur Nussbaum, *A Concise History of the Law of Nations* (New York: Macmillan, 1947), 161–62.

42 Tacit consent theory originated with the ancient Roman view that custom was a form of intentional lawmaking by the people. See Raphael M. Walden, "The Subjective Element in the Formation of Customary International Law," 12 *Israel Law Review* 344 (1977), 344–46 (discussing the Roman influences on classical writers).

43 He wrote: "Certain maxims and customs, consecrated by long use and observed by nations in their mutual intercourse with each other as a kind of law form the Customary Law of Nations, or the Custom of Nations. This law is founded on a tacit consent, or, if you please on a tacit convention of the nations that observe it towards each other. Whence it appears that it is not obligatory except on those nations who have adopted it, and that it is not universal, any more than the conventional law." Vattel, *The Law of Nations*, lxiv-lxvi.

44 See Nussbaum, *A Concise History of The Law of Nations* (1947), 163.

obvious fiction in an age of poor communications. It has little explanatory power and did not express actual practice.[45] Most importantly, the emerging social reality of new, non-Western nations, such as Turkey and Japan, participating in international affairs necessitated a universal theory of international law that bound non-European nations to European norms that had originally been based on natural law. A voluntary consent theory such as Vattel's would have created the uncomfortable possibility of opening norms to alternative views and to negotiation over content.

The later positivists in the late nineteenth and early twentieth centuries, such as W.E. Hall and Lassa Oppenheim, developed a universal social consensus theory, premised on the "common consent" of nations. "Common consent" expressed a communal theory of universal law based on the acceptance of the overwhelming majority of states.[46] It had the important practical effect of binding the states that emerged from the collapse of the Ottoman Empire to what up until that time had been known as European international law.[47] The common consent approach, which remains the reigning theory of customary international law today, bound new states without their consent or participation in a time of the expansion of the international community. It possessed a theoretical integrity because other, more traditional forms of customary law are based on the concept of social consensus.[48] This "common consent" approach was adopted by the Permanent Court of International

[45] See J.L. Brierly, *The Law of Nations: An Introduction to the International Law of Peace*, edited by Humphrey Waldock (New York: Oxford University Press, 6th ed. 1963), 49–56 (noting that implied consent is a fiction that is an inadequate explanation for the actual practice of states and for the binding nature of international law).

[46] Lassa Oppenheim's first edition (1905) through the eighth edition (1955) declare a community theory of customary international law based on the "common consent" of nations, not a consent theory based on will. In the second edition, Oppenheim wrote: "'Common consent' can therefore only mean the express or tacit consent of such an overwhelming majority of the members that those that dissent are of no importance whatever, and disappear totally from the view of one who looks for the will of the community as an entity in contradistinction to the wills of its single members." *Oppenheim's International Law* (2nd ed. 1912), 15–17.

[47] See, e.g., *Wheaton's Elements of International Law*, edited by Coleman Phillipson (London: Stevens and Sons, 5th ed. 1916), 14 ("The public law [of nations], with certain exceptions, has always been and still is limited to the civilized and Christian people of Europe or to those of European origin. This distinction between a European Law of Nations and that of other races of mankind has long been remarked by the publicists."). Oppenheim described a process of non-Western nations being received into the Family of Nations, which meant accepting the terms of the former "European Law of Nations." *Oppenheim's International Law* (2nd ed., 1912), § 28. He asserted that new states that are recognized and admitted into the family of nations thereby consent to existing custom. Ibid., § 12.

[48] Customary law in traditional societies is a socially determined, empirical law of a defined social group. It is not consensual or individually determined. See Ian Hamnett, *Chieftainship and Legitimacy* (London: Routledge & Kegan Paul, 1975), 11–13.

Justice ("PCIJ"),[49] the International Court of Justice ("ICJ"),[50] and the United States Supreme Court[51] in many opinions.

Armed with common consent theory, Western nations had the means to create and apply their version of universal customary international law norms to non-Western states even over the objections of these states. These norms were imposed by force, if necessary, under the remedy of self-help, even though other nations objected to the legality of many of these norms and viewed them as against their interests.[52] Attempts to codify these principles at international conferences over the objections of Latin American countries failed, with states nearly equally divided.[53] While these norms were articulated as based on the practice of states, state practice was scant and disputed. Norms were rationalized as based on "common consent," but were in fact drawn from principles of natural law or borrowed from domestic legal systems.[54] The international legal order had been transformed from one based on universal reason to one said to be constructed from customary practices of sovereigns based on common consent. Its legal principles, while developed in Europe and the United States, were nevertheless considered universal, applying to all states in the family of nations – European and non-European alike.

This system did not initially apply to the colonies of Asia and Africa. With the dawning of the positivist era in the nineteenth century, colonial powers excluded these societies and kingdoms from participation in international society by denying them the privilege of sovereignty and therefore the rights and protections of international law.[55] Oppenheim explained this strategy in simple syllogistic terms without irony.[56] He said that the "Law of Nations" is

49 See *Case of the S.S. "Lotus" (France v. Turkey)*, Judgment of 7 September 1927, PCIJ Series A, No. 10, 18.

50 See *Barcelona Traction, Light and Power Company, Limited (Belgium v. Spain)*, Preliminary Objections, Judgment of 24 July 1964, 1964 ICJ Rep. 6; Second Phase, Judgment of 5 February 1970, 1970 ICJ Rep. 3.

51 See, e.g., *The Scotia*, 81 U.S. 179 (1871), 187; *The Paquete Habana*, 175 U.S. 677 (1900), 708 ("This review of precedent and authorities on the subject appears to us to abundantly demonstrate at the present day, that by the *general consent* of the civilized nations of the world, and independently of any treaty or other public act, it is an established rule of international law ... that coast fishing vessels ... are exempt from capture as prizes of war.") (Emphasis added.)

52 See Charles Lipson, *Standing Guard: Protecting Foreign Capital in the Nineteenth and Twentieth Centuries* (Berkeley: University of California Press, 1985), 37–64 (describing the use of armed intervention and other strategies to impose the American and British view of an international minimum standard of compensation for expropriation).

53 See the discussion later in the chapter.

54 See discussion of Hall, Oppenheim, and Eagleton later in the chapter.

55 Anghie describes this process of excluding those nations considered "uncivilized" from the protections of international law in Anghie, *Imperialism*, 52–65.

56 See *Oppenheim's International Law* (2nd ed. 1912), §§ 26–29, 211.

the product of the "Christian Nations of Europe." In his view, membership in the Family of Nations and its laws is only available to "civilized" states. International law does not protect or give rights to states outside the circle of "civilized" states. Those states outside the circle and those in *terra nullus*, land not controlled by a state, may be subjected or occupied.[57] As "uncivilized" societies, the states and societies of Asia and Africa had no legal rights, and intervention in them was limited only by moral considerations. In the scramble for territory, resources, and prestige, morality seemed to be absent or of tertiary importance.[58] Sovereignty was used as a sword justifying conquest and the taking of property.[59]

Whether using universal natural law principles or universal customary international law based on "common consent" in a positivist era of state practice, international law constructs had the effect of justifying the use of power against the less powerful, including the use of violence and the taking of property and territory. The protections of international law only applied to the European states. Only by being accepted into the "family of nations" and impliedly accepting norms with which they may have disagreed did the invited states became sovereign and enjoy whatever protections might have existed under international law.[60]

The general point is that both the natural law publicists such as Vitoria and Grotius and the later positivists from Wheaton to Oppenheim developed analogous doctrines that performed similar functions. It mattered little whether these doctrines are characterized as having origins in natural law ideas utilizing a deductive methodology, or are characterized as "customary law" said to be based on state practice and common consent. Both natural law theorists

[57] For an extended discussion of the distinction between civilized and uncivilized states and its implications, see Anghie, *Imperialism*, 52–65.

[58] See Thomas Pekenham, *The Scramble for Africa: White Man's Conquest of the Dark Continent from 1876 to 1912* (New York: Avon Books, 1992).

[59] This utilitarian construction of sovereignty not only had broad implications justifying colonial expansion, but also provided the legal basis for unequal treatment within the continental United States. In *Johnson v. M'Intosh*, Justice John Marshall denied Native Americans sovereignty over their own land, and determined that Indians were incapable of owning land and could therefore not pass legal title. 21 U.S. 543 (1821), 591. In words reminiscent of Grotius's view of the "Providential Function of Commerce," Justice Marshall in *Worchester v. Georgia* justified war, conquest, and the taking of property as necessary because normal commercial relations were not possible with Indians. 31 U.S. 515 (1832), 558. As James Gathii explained, Justice Marshall developed two widely different legal regimes for commercial relations: a regime of liberal commerce for European sovereign states, and an illiberal one of subjugation in U.S.-Native American relations. Gathii, *War, Commerce and International Law*, 142–43.

[60] See *Oppenheim's International Law* (2nd ed. 1912), § 12 ("New States which came into existence and were … admitted into the Family of Nations thereby consented to the body of rules of international conduct in force at the time of their admittance.").

and positivist theorists declared norms to justify conquest and the expansion of trade and investment, not as an exchange among equals, but rather as the extension of state power through the forcible opening of markets and the protection of investment.[61] In these endeavors legal norms were neither neutral nor universal in their application. Rather, the concept of sovereignty was used as both a sword and a shield. As a sword, sovereignty conferred upon European states the right to wage a "just war" against nations not wishing to trade or allow annexation of their territory; as a shield, it protected these sovereign states from claims by allegedly non-sovereign and weaker societies.

2.3 STATE RESPONSIBILITY AND THE INTERNATIONAL MINIMUM STANDARD FOR EXPROPRIATION

With this history in mind, we turn to an examination of several areas where the methodology of customary international law was used by powerful states to develop norms in their self-interest despite widespread disagreement or protest. The first involved the development of the controversial international minimum standard of compensation for the expropriation of foreign property that is often articulated as requiring "prompt, adequate, and effective" compensation or "full compensation."[62] Much of the discussion in the literature over the last fifty years has concentrated on the challenge by the newly independent states created after the end of colonialism to the customary rules of investment law, including the minimum standard of compensation for expropriation.[63] These newly independent states used their majority at the United Nations General Assembly to pass resolutions declaring sovereignty over their natural resources and attempting to change the standard of compensation for expropriation to one of "national treatment."[64] Developed countries and many

61 For an extended discussion, see Gathii, *War, Commerce and International Law*, 145–90.

62 For a discussion of both full compensation and national treatment standards, see Ian Brownlie, *Principles of Public International Law* (Oxford: Oxford University Press, 6th ed. 2003), 508–12. For a clear statement of the formal international minimum standard in the Western literature during the late nineteenth and early twentieth centuries, see Charles G. Fenwick, *International Law* (New York: D. Appleton-Century Company, 2nd ed. 1934), 197–216.

63 See Rudolf Dolzer, "New Foundations of the Law of the Expropriation of Alien Property," 75 *American Journal of International Law* 553 (1981).

64 See GA Res. 1803 (XVII), 17 UN GAOR Supp. (No. 17) 15, UN Doc. A/5217 (1962); GA Res. 3201 (S-VI) (1974), Declaration on the Establishment of a New International Economic Order, S-6 UN GAOR Supp. (no. 1) 3. National treatment is a principle of equality requiring only the paying of the same compensation that a citizen of the expropriating country would receive, while the prompt, adequate, and effective compensation standard is articulated as an international standard superior to national law. See Brownlie, *Principles of Public International Law*, 508–12. In particular, legal scholar Ian Brownlie affirmed: "The rule supported by all leading 'Western' governments and a majority of jurists in Europe and North America is as follows: the

academics responded that "new states" are bound by customary international law that universally binds all states. Other academics suggested that when a majority of nations oppose an existing norm, general acceptance has been modified and customary international law must adjust.[65] Relatively few scholars have examined whether the international minimum standard has ever satisfied the requirements of customary international law in the first place.[66]

In retrospect, the natural rights of the Providential Function of Commerce for Grotius and of the right to hospitality and sociability in foreign lands of Vitoria can be seen as the normative source of the law of state responsibility toward aliens. These norms and their deductive progeny, such as the right to trade, provided a rationale even in a positivist era for commercial intervention, the exploitation of resources, and the protection of travelers, traders, and investors. In the nineteenth century there developed a practice by some governments of utilizing military interventions or demanding reparations for perceived mistreatment of their citizens and corporations abroad as a form of diplomatic protection. While alien investors fell under the territorial jurisdiction of the local state, treatises claimed, and some international arbitration practice supported the idea, that each state has the right to protect the person and property of its citizens abroad and receiving states have the corresponding duty to treat foreigners in their territory with a minimum standard of justice.[67] Legal scholar W.E. Hall, although an avowed positivist, developed the concept of a right of a state to protect its citizens abroad from the fundamental right of self-preservation.[68] According to Hall, the right of self-preservation not only applies to the situation where a state is under attack, but also extends to

expropriation of alien property is lawful if prompt, adequate, and effective compensation is provided for." Ibid., 509.

65 See, e.g., Burns H. Weston, "The Charter of Economic Rights and Duties of States and the Deprivation of Foreign-Owned Wealth," 75 *American Journal of International Law* 437 (1981).

66 Perhaps this gap in legal analysis is due to the early continuous and disparaging attack on the Calvo clause in state-investor contracts by the leading publicists of the time as incompatible with the international legal obligations of states. The Calvo clause required foreign investors to settle all disputes under the national law of the host state rather than the rules of international law or the investor's home state. See, for example, Eagleton, *The Responsibility of States*, 104–07 (citing consistent U.S. practice); ibid., 168–76 (discussing the "so-called" Calvo clause as superfluous to the concept of exhaustion of local remedies with no effect on international responsibility). See also Charles Cheney Hyde, *International Law: Chiefly as Interpreted and Applied by the United States* (Boston: Little, Brown and Co., 2nd ed. 1945), vol. 2, 994–98; *Oppenheim's International Law*, Peace, Vol. 1, edited by Hersch Lauterpacht (London: Longmans, Green, 8th ed. 1955), 345.

67 Oppenheim explains that aliens residing abroad, while subject to local rules, remain nevertheless under the protection of their home state. *Oppenheim's International Law* (2nd ed. 1912), §§ 319–20.

68 See W.E. Hall, *International Law* (Oxford: Oxford University Press, 3rd ed. 1890), §§ 83–87.

the protection of its subjects when an injury or injustice is committed abroad. Oppenheim, relying on Hall, justified this right of protection of citizens as a universally recognized customary rule of the law of nations.[69] While articulated as a customary law rule, the concept of aliens remaining under the protection of their home state was based on an asserted natural right. Instead of referring to state practice and demonstrating common consent or *opinio juris*, Oppenheim cited Hall and others who he said "deduce this indubitable right from the 'fundamental' right of self-preservation."[70] According to contemporary treatises, each state has the corresponding duty to provide foreigners with the minimum standards of treatment under international law.[71] Hall deduced further principles that permitted the use of force to vindicate these assumed natural rights. The only basis of these principles in state practice was a description of the actions and policies of Great Britain, which Hall assumed were authoritative.[72]

In the first significant treatise on the subject, written in 1915, Edwin Borchard formulated an extensive list of minimum rights owed to aliens, such as personal and religious liberty, the inviolability of domicile, and the right to equal protection of the laws, including access to the courts and the use of the executive branch to enforce these rights.[73] He described these rights as naturalistic principles, giving little attention to state practice or general acceptance. Clyde Eagleton, writing as late as 1928, did on occasion refer to examples of interventions and to arbitrations, but not in order to demonstrate general acceptance or analyze the variety of state practice. Rather, he assumed and asserted that responsibility in international law is based on "the same moral sense of obligation which influences mankind everywhere."[74] This underlying moral sense behind rules helps explain the little attention given to determining if there is, in fact, widespread consistent practice, or to ascertaining if there is general

69 See *Oppenheim's International Law* (2nd ed. 1912), § 319.

70 Ibid., § 319 at n.4.

71 Eagleton, *The Responsibility of States*, 82–85 (the international standard of justice limits how a state may treat aliens even if it results in discrimination in favor of aliens).

72 Hall, *International Law*, § 87.

73 Edwin M. Borchard, *The Diplomatic Protection of Citizens Abroad or the Law of International Claims* (New York: The Banks Law Publishing Co., 1919), 39–44. Borchard further includes the rights to sojourn and trade, borrowing these naturalistic concepts from earlier continental writers. See ibid., 42.

74 Eagleton, *The Responsibility of States*, § 2. He quotes Hall as follows: "The ultimate foundation of international law is an assumption that states possess rights and are subject to duties corresponding to the facts of their postulated nature. In virtue of this assumption … it is considered that their moral nature imposes upon them the duties of good faith, of concession of redress for wrongs, of regard for the personal dignity of their fellows, and to a certain extent of sociability." Ibid., 50.

acceptance or common consent. The common consent element was by and large assumed from membership in the family of nations and the moral sense common to all. This moral sense of the more powerful nations appeared to be highly selective, only applicable to their foreign property, while indigenous property was taken without compensation or even equal treatment.

In the realm of remedies, those states whose subjects were wronged may, according to Oppenheim and other international law publicists of his day, exercise reprisals, intervene, or even go to war against a state to force compliance with their demands.[75] The natural rights to travel and to engage in commerce were now justified in more positivist terms as being grounded in the right of diplomatic protection, which was expanded to protect businessmen and their property. While the right was termed "customary," it was in the early stages deduced from asserted fundamental principles or assumed as the natural order of international life.

These principles were supported on occasion by referring to the asserted legal rights and actions of the two most powerful nations of the time, Great Britain and the United States. In one sense it was supported by state practice: Powerful states perceived they had the right to intervene, did claim such a right, and did, in fact, intervene at their discretion. The United States, for example, had a policy of intervening in other states to vindicate its perceived international legal rights on the grounds of tortious injury to its nationals, the confiscation of their property, or the failure to provide them with a judicial remedy that in the sole judgment of the United States constituted a denial of justice.[76] Even in the face of this normative assault, the nations of Latin America, rather than accepting these policies as based on customary international law principles, protested and resisted them. These underlying facts undermine the notion that there was general acceptance of these principles even by the nation-states of the day. In the modern era the many new states that emerged from colonialism have similarly resisted such claims.

If we move from natural law methodologies and the formalism of treatises to the underlying economic and political context of those interventions, several European nations and the United States regularly intervened militarily as a matter of right or used the threat of intervention to settle expropriation disputes or to collect debts owed to their citizens as bondholders during the late nineteenth and early twentieth

[75] See *Oppenheim's International Law* (2nd ed. 1912), § 319. See also Hall, *International Law*, § 87.

[76] See the discussion of U.S. legal assertions and policy in Eagleton, *The Responsibility of States*, 160–68.

centuries.[77] Bond defaults in Latin America, for example, posed a policy dilemma for Great Britain. *Laissez faire* economic doctrine suggested that investors who had taken risks in the hope of high rewards should not be rescued from imprudent decisions. From a more long-term perspective, intervention would also undermine local social control and reduce stability important to the world financial system.[78] On the other hand, intervention promised immediate, short-term economic gains and the support of wealthy bondholders. The legal situation was similarly unclear. A default might be classified as a routine commercial contract not involving international responsibility or as confiscation or fraud that would incur international responsibility justifying intervention.[79] Great Britain decided, in general, to rely on its control of international financial markets with the implicit power to deny new capital to defaulting states rather than to intervene militarily in defaulting states.[80] The result was the slow settlement of government bond debt in Latin America in the late nineteenth century in a manner that did not undermine local authority and stability.[81]

The interplay between policy and asserted legal rights was more complicated with regard to British protection of direct foreign investment. Great Britain asserted the customary right to intervene in cases of the confiscation of the property of its nationals or of serious personal injuries to them, and did, in fact, intervene with some frequency.[82] Great Britain maintained that in cases of government fraud or robbery (including confiscation), it not only had the legal right to intervene but was morally obligated to intervene to correct an injustice.[83] This policy had a decidedly moral tone to it that might be seen as inconsistent with its utilitarian calculus with regard to government bond defaults.[84] It is not immediately clear why expropriation might not be seen

77 For a general description of state responsibility, including the right of a state to use war against or intervene in a state that fails to pay pubic debt owed to the aggrieved state's citizens, see *Oppenheim's International Law* (2nd ed. 1912), §§ 148–56.

78 See Lipson, *Standing Guard*, 44–46 (describing the use of armed intervention and other strategies to impose the American and British view of an international minimum standard of compensation for expropriated property regardless of national laws or contractual clauses).

79 Eagleton, *The Responsibility of States*, 170–71, 176–81.

80 See Lipson, *Standing Guard*, 46–48.

81 By 1890, defaults comprised only four percent of British-owned government securities in the region. See ibid., 47.

82 Lipson summarizes D.C.M. Platt as citing forty interventions, twenty-six of which were to enforce claims of British subjects for outrage or injuries, or to restore order and protect property. See ibid., 54 (referring to D.C.M. Platt, *Finance, Trade and Politics* (Oxford: Oxford University Press, 1968), 330.

83 See Lipson, *Standing Guard*, 55 (quoting Platt, *Finance, Trade and Politics*, 334–35).

84 The more utilitarian calculus for lost investment due to default or foreign competition is discussed in Lipson, *Standing Guard*, 44–50.

from a *laissez faire* perspective as a risk of highly profitable capital investments in relatively unstable foreign countries.

If we compare U.S. policy and interests, the United States was undergoing rapid internal economic growth and expanding its trade, military capability, and influence abroad. Rather than challenge European countries in their local markets with entrenched producers, it looked to Latin America for new markets, resources, and investment opportunities.[85] While this created a potential conflict with Great Britain, neither country wanted more territory or colonies, and importantly, their primary economic interests did not overlap significantly.[86] British and U.S. interests and policies thus converged with regard to each other's vital interests.

The dilemma for the United States was that it wanted regional hegemony over the Americas as defined in the Monroe Doctrine, but also believed that under customary international law Great Britain and Europe had the right to intervene to protect their investments.[87] The United States chose, with British support, to prevent European intervention by assuming ultimate responsibility to protect Great Britain and European investor rights in what was then known as the "Roosevelt corollary" to the Monroe Doctrine.[88] The result was regional hegemony, but it increased U.S. responsibility for local affairs in the Caribbean and led to more frequent interventions by the United States to quell local insecurity as well as protect investors under its broad version of the international minimum standard of protection.[89]

While the United States and Great Britain were asserting the right to intervene to protect investors, Latin American nations strongly resisted these claims, maintaining that foreign citizens and foreign corporations were owed only a standard of "national treatment," that is, equal treatment with domestic citizens.[90] These nations responded to U.S. interventions by articulating two interrelated doctrines – the Calvo doctrine and the Drago doctrine – to emphasize

[85] From 1897 to 1914, U.S. corporations invested nearly $1 billion in Latin America, which was equal to its private investment in the rest of the world. Ibid., 58.

[86] Great Britain had only 22 percent of its investment in those areas and was militarily and financially stretched by its many colonies in Africa and Asia, including the Boer War in South Africa. See ibid., 59–61.

[87] The United States asserted, and both treatise writers and claims tribunals supported, the right to protect its citizens abroad from injustice as an international delict of duty. See the discussion of U.S. legal claims and policy in Eagleton, *The Responsibility of States*, 157–68.

[88] See Dana Gardner Munro, *Intervention and Dollar Diplomacy in the Caribbean, 1900–1921* (Princeton: Princeton University Press, 1964), 65.

[89] Lipson discusses the role of international law in the policy dilemma. See Lipson, *Standing Guard*, 62–64.

[90] See generally Donald R. Shea, *The Calvo Clause: A Problem of Inter-American and International Law and Diplomacy* (Minneapolis: University of Minnesota Press, 1955).

their continuing disagreement with the international minimum standard of treatment and the use of military means to collect debt.[91] The Calvo doctrine, initiated by the Argentine jurist Carlos Calvo, required that foreign investors settle all disputes under the national law of the host state rather than the rules of international law or the investor's home state.[92] The Drago doctrine asserted that a public debt cannot justify armed intervention or occupation of the territory of debtor-states by creditor-states in order to collect the debt.[93] The Venezuelan Secretary of State Luis Drago protested that the collection of a loan by military means constituted an interference with the debtor-states' territorial sovereignty and the diminution of the sovereign equality of states.[94] By invoking the Drago doctrine Latin American nations were now using the sovereignty doctrine as a shield to protect themselves from intervention as a self-help remedy.

At the Second Hague Conference in 1906, just a few years later, states negotiated a convention disclaiming the use of armed force by one country on behalf of its citizens to recover public debt from another country.[95] The Convention did, however, specifically reserve the right to use force if a "debtor state refuses or neglects to accept an offer of arbitration … or, after the arbitration, fails to submit to the award."[96] Intervention was no longer a purely discretionary remedy.

The trajectory of the Calvo doctrine was somewhat similar. Latin American states added so-called Calvo clauses to their domestic statutes and constitutions and, to the extent possible, also inserted these clauses in concession and other state contracts. Calvo clauses required that foreign investors pursue remedies under the domestic law of the capital-importing country as the exclusive remedies on the basis of equal treatment with nationals.[97] These

91 See the discussion in Gathii, *War, Commerce, and International Law*, 145–58.

92 See Shea, *The Calvo Clause*, 16–21.

93 See Luis M. Drago, "State Loans in Their Relation to International Policy," 1 *American Journal of International Law* 692 (1907). The Drago doctrine emerged from a specific dispute after Venezuela refused to pay bondholders from Great Britain, Germany, and Italy. Venezuela proposed the formation of a commission to settle the claims. Great Britain and Germany launched a military blockade of Venezuela, and Venezuela soon capitulated, agreeing to arbitration. See Gathii, *War, Commerce and International Law*, 147–49.

94 Drago, "State Loans in their Relation to International Policy," 699. This position was deduced from a fundamental conception of sovereignty similar to Vattel's view that the concept of sovereign equality and its corollary principle of nonintervention are derived from the natural right of sovereignty inherent in a sovereign state. See Vattel, *The Law of Nations*, lxii and book II, chapter IV, 154–160.

95 Convention Respecting the Limitation on the Employment of Force for the Recovery of Contract Debts, Oct. 18, 1907, 36 Stat. 2241, art. 1.

96 Ibid.

97 See Shea, *The Calvo Clause*, 19 (explaining that under the Calvo doctrine, "aliens are not entitled to rights and privileges not accorded to nationals, and … therefore must seek redress for grievances only before local authorities").

clauses precluded the application of any international minimum standard of full compensation, or any resort to armed intervention to collect debt. The United States and European states viewed the Calvo clauses in contracts and in state constitutions prohibiting payment of full compensation not as legitimate "state practice" helping create a new customary international law norm, but rather as illegal attempts to avoid international legal obligations.[98]

If there was widespread acceptance of the full compensation standard and other norms of state responsibility, then one would expect overwhelming support. But at the Hague Conference for the Codification of International Law in 1930, for example, state delegates could not reach agreement or even consensus on the principles of state responsibility. They adjourned without adopting a convention. On the issue of the international minimum standard, states were nearly evenly split in their views.[99] Many Latin American nations did not bother to attend the conference. Far from evidencing common consent or general acceptance of the international minimum standard, these attempts at codification demonstrated widespread disagreement about norms and rancor over the gunboat diplomacy of the past. Rather, the language of customary international law and the uncritical acceptance of the policy positions of powerful nations by international scholars of the day were used to justify the domination by a few states over the protests of many states.

The other major source of authority for the international minimum standard, in addition to the naturalistic principles in treatises and the practices of intervention by the United States and European powers to defend it, was the extensive body of international claims arbitrations. These arbitrations, often viewed as a more acceptable alternative to intervention, were in many cases the product of threatened interventions, or emerged from diplomacy with an implied threat of intervention if arbitration was not successful.[100] Decisions

[98] Thus, the U.S. government affirmed: "This government [the U.S.] cannot admit that its citizens can, merely by making a contract with foreign powers ... destroy their dependence upon it or [its] obligation to protect [them] in case of a denial of justice." Moore, Digest VI (Feb. 15, 1888), 94. See the discussion in Eagleton, *The Responsibility of States*, 168–76.

[99] A motion to adopt the standard of national treatment for injury to aliens by private persons failed by 23 votes against and 17 votes in favor. An attempted compromise proposal in the Third Committee on a limited version of an international minimum standard received only a narrow majority of 21 to 17 votes. Green H. Hackworth, "Responsibility of States for Damages caused in their Territory to the Person or Property of Foreigners: The Hague Conference for the Codification of International Law," 24 *American Journal of International Law* 500 (1930), 513–16.

[100] Intervention was a fallback remedy even after the 1907 treaty limiting the use of force to collect debt. See *Oppenheim's International Law* (8th ed., 1955), 309, particularly n.3 (indicating that intervention is appropriate when a debtor-nation refuses an offer of arbitration or fails to pay an award).

issued by these arbitration panels referred to the natural law principles in treatises, and rarely undertook an examination of state practice and common consent except to the extent they referred to other arbitrations.[101] What emerged was an inconsistent and unsubstantiated set of rules.[102] Arbitration opinions, as subsidiary sources of international law, may be of some value to the extent that their reasoning is persuasive, but are not themselves authoritative or determinative of customary international law, which, as noted earlier, is determined by the practices and beliefs of states.[103]

As the nearly sole positivist source of legal material, arbitration decisions became more important than state practice or general acceptance in the evolution of the law of state responsibility. Calvo clauses in contracts and in state constitutions were viewed as ineffective in limiting international obligations and illegal.[104] The underlying narrative of an international minimum standard was contained in treatises and diplomatic correspondence, but only the pos ition of one side seemed to have relevance in the literature.[105] The Western

101 See Brownlie, *Principles of Public International Law* (Oxford: Oxford University Press, 3rd ed. 1979), 533–36. Brownlie states: "The justifications for the rule are based on the assumptions prevalent in liberal regimes of private property and in the principle that foreign owners are to be given the protection accorded to private right of nationals." Ibid., 533. Brownlie cites numerous international arbitration tribunals in discussing the adequate, effective, and prompt compensation standard. See ibid., 534–35.

102 In the context of state responsibility for acts of soldiers or other agents of the state that may be viewed as *ultra vires*, compare *U.S. v. Mexico*, 4 R.I.A.A. 110 (1926) (finding compensation for acts of Mexican troops acting outside their authority) with *U.S. v. Great Britain*, 6 R.I.A.A. 138 (1924) (involving a U.S. corporation in South Africa not receiving compensation for damages caused by acts of agent without permission of British government).

103 See Statute of the International Court of Justice ("ICJ Statute"), art. 38(1)(d) (describing judicial decisions and the teachings of the most highly qualified publicists, for example, treatise writers, as subsidiary means for determining rules of law). In this connection, the draft conclusions adopted by the International Law Commission on the identification of customary international law in 2016 provide, with reference to judicial and arbitration decisions: "Decisions of international courts and tribunals, in particular of the International Court of Justice, concerning the existence and content of rules of customary international law are a subsidiary means for the determination of such rules." "Report of the International Law Commission," Sixty-Eighth Session (2 May–10 June and 4 July–12 August 2016), UN Doc. A/71/10 (2016), 76–79, Draft Conclusion 13, para. 1. They also state, regarding the status of publicists: "Teachings of the most highly qualified publicists of the various nations may serve as a subsidiary means for the determination of rules of customary international law." Ibid., Draft Conclusion 14.

104 Both Eagleton and Hyde agree on this point. See Eagleton, *The Responsibility of States*, 168–76; Hyde, *International Law*, § 305, 994–95. Oppenheim summarizes the citations and concurs. See *Oppenheim's International Law* (8th ed. 1955), § 155a.

105 For example, note the dismissive tone of the discussion in Eagleton, *The Responsibility of States*, 168–76. Eagleton states: "The so-called 'Calvo Clause,' an application to contracts of the Calvo Doctrine already discussed, must be regarded as a superfluous statement of the rules upon which responsibility is founded.... The menace of the Calvo Clause lies in its

states controlled the literature and the debate, and had the military means to back up their asserted legal policy. As Tom Farer succinctly explained the situation,

> Latin American governments and scholars [have] consistently urged the view that international law require[s] nothing more than the equality of treatment for indigenous and foreign investors. Yet, although they [have] pulled all the right buttons on the international legal console and pedaled vigorously, they might as well have been silent for all the effect they have had on the views expounded in Western Universities and chancelleries or, for that matter, on the gunboats and marines dispatched to enforce the "law."[106]

The primary early judicial authority for the international minimum standard of full compensation for expropriation, the *Chorzow Factory* case of 1928, continues to resonate in modern judicial and arbitration decisions today.[107] In *Chorzow Factory*, the PCIJ held that Poland's expropriation of German-owned property in Upper Silesia violated a 1922 treaty. It did not rule that the expropriation violated customary international law. However, in dicta, the PCIJ discussed in naturalistic terms the principle that reparations must wipe out all the consequences of an illegal act.[108] It then supported this principle in rather weak terms, saying that the principle "seems to be established by international practice and in particular decisions of arbitral tribunals."[109] The opinion did not examine state practice beyond a general statement that the opinion was supported by arbitral decisions, nor did it discuss whether states had generally accepted the norm of full compensation for expropriation. While the PCIJ might have examined the many arbitration decisions involving European and Latin American states that would have given some support to its naturalistic approach to norms,[110] it apparently did not think that specific support was necessary.

purposeful effort of a state to decide unilaterally whether its local remedies are satisfactory, and ... to reduce its international obligations to impotence." Ibid., 168, 171.

106 Tom J. Farer, "The United States and the Third World: A Basis for Accommodation," 54 *Foreign Affairs* 79 (1975), 84.

107 *Factory at Chorzow (Germany v. Poland) (Indemnity)*, Judgment of 13 September 1928, PCIJ Series A, No. 17.

108 Ibid., 47 ("The essential principle contained in the actual notion of an illegal act – a principle which seems to be established by international practice and in particular by the decisions of arbitral tribunals – is that reparation must, as far as possible, wipe out all the consequences of the illegal act and reestablish the situation which would, in all probability, have existed if that act had not been committed. Restitution in kind, or, if this is not possible, payment of a sum corresponding to the value which a restitution in kind would bear.").

109 Ibid.

110 See Manley O. Hudson, *International Tribunals: Past and Future* (Washington: Carnegie Endowment for International Peace and Brookings Institution, 1944) (describing the history

The importance of the *Chorzow Factory* case cannot be overstated.[111] As a decision of the PCIJ, it became the primary historical source for many of the later judicial and arbitral decisions that apply its rule, announced in dicta, requiring full reparations for illegal expropriations and the just price of what was expropriated for legal expropriations.[112] Yet the source of the view of these decisions was a naturalistic principle originally based on deductive thinking, the repetition of this assumed principle in other treatises, and a series of earlier arbitration decisions, some of which were coerced.

This history of the recognition of these alleged customary international law norms illustrates that what is termed "state practice," if closely examined, may not reveal an underlying communal belief among states, but rather disagreement among them on the norm itself. The famous statement of Secretary of State Cordell Hull in 1938, in response to Mexico's expropriation of U.S.-owned agrarian properties, that a state owes an international duty of full compensation – defined as prompt, adequate, and effective compensation – is an instructive example.[113] A key, often-overlooked feature of the circumstances surrounding this statement is that the Mexican minister for foreign affairs did not acquiesce to this principle or change his position. He asserted that national treatment was the only duty owed to U.S. investors, as had many Latin American nations throughout the nineteenth and twentieth centuries. This national treatment view of Latin American nations is memorialized in the Montevideo Convention of 1933, which affirms: "The jurisdiction of states within the limits of national territory applies to all the inhabitants. Nationals and foreigners are under the same protection of the law and the national

of international tribunals and dividing it into four periods with, for example, about fifty arbitration cases involving Latin American states between 1872 and 1899). See also Patrick M. Norton, "Law of the Future or Law of the Past? Modern Tribunals and the International Law of Expropriation," 85 *American Journal of International Law* 474 (1991), 475.

111 Dolzer in his modern analysis of the state of the law of expropriation of alien property assumed that the Hull standard of prompt, adequate, and effective compensation was the reigning legal standard prior to World War II based on two arbitrations and the *Chorzow Factory* case. See Rudolf Dolzer, "New Foundations of the Law of Expropriation of Alien Property," 75 *American Journal of International Law* 553 (1981), 558–59.

112 See, e.g., *Amoco International Finance Corporation v. Iran (Iran-U.S. Claims Tribunal)*, 15 *Iran-U.S. T.R.* 189 (1987), paras. 113, 193 (describing the *Chorzow Factory Case* as the leading expression of the customary international law of expropriation). See also *Texas Overseas Petroleum Co. & California Asiatic Oil Co. v. Libyan Arab Republic*, 53 *Int'l. Law Rep.* 389 (1977), 17 *International Legal Materials* 1 (1978) (the arbitrator decided that the stabilization clause in the contract had "internationalized" the contract and applied the rules of customary international law, including the *Chorzow Factory* standard of restitution).

113 See the exchange of notes between U.S. Secretary of State Cordell Hull and the Mexican Minister of Foreign Affairs, 19 *Department of State Press Releases* (1938), 50–52, 135–37, 139–44.

authorities and the foreigners may not claim rights other or more extensive than those of nationals."[114] This 1938 U.S.-Mexico dispute, now framed by the prohibition on armed intervention in the Hague Convention of 1907,[115] was settled for an amount far below the standard of full compensation, providing no clear evidence of the appropriate norm accepted by the United States, Mexico, or other states. The full compensation view did not enjoy the support of Latin American nations in the nineteenth century, at the Hague Codification conference in 1930, or at the 1933 Montevideo conference. Since the end of colonialism, it has been actively opposed by the majority of nations.

To clarify the role that power rather than general acceptance played in the development of these norms, the primary defenders of the international minimum standard – the United States and Great Britain – generally opposed its application to themselves.[116] During the late nineteenth and early twentieth centuries, lynching and other mob violence were common forms of extralegal action in many southern states as well as in the north. Lynching was a form of illegal self-help, often with official sanction or support, visited upon not only African Americans but also upon many foreigners. Despite these attacks being an unassailable denial of justice under the presumed law of state responsibility, the United States specifically denied responsibility for these private acts of violence. When it did agree to provide compensation to victims, it asserted that doing so was a matter of grace, not legal responsibility.[117] After the New Orleans riots of 1851, in which the Spanish counsel was injured, Mr. Webster for the United States asserted that Spanish subjects were entitled to no more protection than U.S. citizens. In other words, he advocated a standard of national treatment. At the same time that the United States was denying that mob violence engendered state responsibility on its own part, it was vigorously asserting claims on behalf of Americans injured abroad by mob

[114] Montevideo Convention on the Rights and Duties of States, 49 Stat. 3097, T.S. No. 881 (signed Dec. 26, 1933, entered into force Dec. 26, 1934), art. 9. Importantly, Article 11 prohibits the use of force, threatened diplomatic representations, or any other coercive measures. Fifteen Latin American nations and the United States are parties to the Convention, but the United States made specific reservations to several of the articles.

[115] See notes 95 and 96 above and accompanying text.

[116] See Eagleton, *The Responsibility of States*, § 40 ("While the United States has perhaps been the chief offender in this respect, other states as well have sought to disclaim responsibility in principle for damages due to riotous disturbances within their own territories, while at the same time they have demanded reparations in behalf of their nationals similarly injured abroad.").

[117] See Amos S. Hershey, "The Calvo and Drago Doctrines," 1 *American Journal of International Law* 26 (1907), 32–35. He notes with evident embarrassment the inconsistency in U.S. policy in denying responsibility for acts of its agents and mob violence it could have prevented. See ibid., 34–36.

violence, declaring that states' refusal to provide compensation was a violation of the international minimum standard of justice.[118]

The historical development of the law of state responsibility to compensate for loss of property may be conceptualized as a colonial enterprise based on coercive use of power or as an attempt to extend Western property concepts to others based on universal principles, albeit through coercive means. No matter which narrative one chooses to accept, it is apparent that there was not, in fact, general acceptance of these principles by the overwhelming majority of nations in its period of formation or throughout the twentieth and twenty-first centuries.

Parts of this struggle seem antiquated. Developing countries now compete for foreign investment, including investment from newly emerging nations such as Brazil, South Africa, and South Korea, by signing bilateral investment treaties ("BITs") and passing domestic laws to satisfy investors.[119] Some level of protection for foreign investors is wise policy and has become standard public policy in nearly all nations that participate in the world economy because foreign investment plays a crucial role in economic development.[120] Foreign investment that contributes to export-driven trade has become a major force in reducing poverty.[121] Yet any attempt to codify, as international law, the standard of full compensation for expropriation or even of the wider body of the law of state responsibility remains a significant challenge.[122]

118 Eagleton discusses several such examples in Eagleton, *The Responsibility of States*, § 39.

119 See Zachary Elkins, Andrew T. Guzman, and Beth Simmons, "Competing for Capital: The Diffusion of Bilateral Investment Treaties, 1960–2000," 60 *International Organizations* 811 (2006), available in the Social Science Research Network Electronic Paper Collection, http://ssrn.com/abstract=1001169. The authors argue that the wide proliferation of bilateral investment treaties ("BITs") to protect foreign investors is driven by international economic competition among potential host countries, typically developing countries, for foreign direct investment.

120 For my views that are generally supportive of trade and foreign investment, see J. Patrick Kelly, "Trade, Globalization and Economic Policy," available at http://ssrn.com/abstract=2191073.

121 The recent globalization of the world economy has led to the largest increase in economic growth in human history and relief from poverty for more than one billion people. See Lawrence Chandy and Geoffrey Gertz, *Poverty in Numbers: The Changing State of Global Poverty from 2005 to 2015* (Washington, DC: Brookings, 2011).

122 The International Law Commission ("ILC") began its study in connection with the codification of the law of state responsibility in 1956. This project lasted through the lives of several special rapporteurs and produced at least thirty-two reports. In 2001, the ILC adopted the "Articles on State Responsibility." These articles have not been incorporated in a treaty, nor were they drafted or adopted by states. The delays and passage of time are a reflection of ongoing disputes among states about the appropriate legal norms, not a reflection of the quality of the Commission's work, which continues to be high and thoughtful. Many governments have objected that several articles do not reflect either state practice or *opinio juris*. See, e.g., "Symposium: The I.L.C.'s State Responsibility Articles," 96 *American Journal of International*

What does this history say about the role of state practice and *opinio juris* in customary international law formation? First, from the perspective of treatise writers and developed countries, the encounters between European powers or the United States and states of Latin America demonstrate that what we would term *opinio juris* or general acceptance appears to be neither present nor viewed by powerful states as either necessary or particularly relevant. If the *opinio juris* requirement for customary international law means that the views of all states potentially affected are relevant to a conclusion about the existence of a norm of customary international law, then discordant views and ambiguous practice on expropriation must lead to the conclusion that the full compensation norm does not meet the requirements of customary international law. The Permanent Court and arbitration panels were developing law independent of the requirements of customary international law and contrary to the express views and actions of a significant number of states.

Second, treatises, arbitration decisions, and judicial opinions relied on natural law principles and selected legal or moral maxims assumed to be accepted by all civilized people to justify their positions. This underlying moral sense helps explain why little attention was given to investigating state practice or to ascertaining if norms were actually generally accepted as law. The derivation and application of these moral maxims was highly selective and coincided with the self-interest of the most powerful states and rarely applied on behalf of weaker states. This is not to assert that there is no room in international law for moral sentiment, fundamental rights, and the concept of *jus cogens* to rescue humanity from its worse impulses. However, much of the law of state responsibility was based on the exercise of power to protect the position of the strong – not upon either an inquiry into general acceptance or an even-handed application of principles. Rather, this formalistic system of law was built on an idealized view of the behavior and sentiments of states rarely demonstrated in world history. It was not the experience of the nations and societies of Latin America, Asia, and Africa that were the subjects of interventions, endured the confiscation of their property, and suffered the death of those that resisted.

Third, these putative universal principles and norms were not articulated or applied in a neutral way. One's conclusion about legality in a natural law system depends on which principles or premises one chooses. Consider three possible formulations of the international standard for compensation

Law 773 (2002); "Symposium: Assessing the Work of the International Law Commission on State Responsibility," 13 *European Journal of International Law* 1053 (2002).

for expropriation. First, if one begins the analysis with the assumed principle of self-preservation as exemplified in an international minimum standard of justice under diplomatic protection, then expropriation without the payment of compensation is an illegal act for which reparations are due. Second, if one instead begins with the principles of the sovereign equality of states and exclusive territorial sovereignty, as did Carlos Calvo, then national treatment as nondiscrimination between foreign nationals and domestic citizens is a possible and appropriate norm. Third, if one starts with the principles of *laissez faire* economics, knowing the risks of moral hazard connected with rescuing investors from ill-considered, risky investments, one could accept national treatment or a policy of noninterference unless it put the world financial system at risk.

Finally, this history suggests that much of the law declared as customary international law in treatises – and particularly the presumed customary international law of state responsibility – may rest on quite weak legal foundations and be of questionable legitimacy without the general acceptance of these legal norms by the overwhelming majority of states. Treaties and other consensual arrangements may be necessary to provide greater clarity and legitimacy to norms. The legacy of this era is troubling, and creates significant problems for customary international law theory. Which of these early norms in treatises is generally accepted today? As described earlier in the chapter, the law of state responsibility arose not from state practice, but rather from courts and arbitration decisions citing publicists who had deduced norms from naturalistic maxims. Over time the treatises referred to these arbitration and court decisions to further bolster these maxims with a patina of state practice.[123] To what extent should the decisions of arbitrators and domestic courts be seen as authoritative with regard to a conclusion that a norm has been generally accepted or is based on consistent widespread state practice? Under Article 38(1)(d) of the Statute of the ICJ, judicial decisions and arbitrator opinions are treated not as authoritative, but as subsidiary means for ascertaining norms of customary international law to

[123] Compare *Oppenheim's International Law* (2nd ed. 1912), §§ 319–22 (basing a "universally recognized customary rule of the Law of Nations" of a right to protect one's citizens and their property abroad on a natural right of self-preservation) with *Oppenheim's International Law* (8th ed. 1955), §§ 319–22 (dropping the natural right language and citations, but bolstering this position by references to treatises, arbitrations, and the *Chorzow Factory Case*). With regard to the failure of a state fully to pay its debts to foreign nationals and asserted inadequate protection of their property, compare the summary discussion in *Oppenheim's International Law* (2nd ed. 1912), §§ 155–56 (based on no authority) with the lengthy and expanded discussion and voluminous citations in *Oppenheim's International Law* (8th ed. 1955), §§ 155, 155a, 155aa, 155b, 155c, 155d, 156.

the extent they are persuasive. Why should secondary and derivative sources be deemed more important than actual state practice and the normative attitude of states?

2.4 THE TERRITORIAL SEA

The history of the territorial sea is chronicled elsewhere,[124] and is of some importance in understanding the degree to which the rules of customary international law found in treatises and the rules of decisions by arbitrators are reliable indications of customary international law norms. Prior to the 1982 United Nations Convention on the Law of the Sea ("UNCLOS")[125] that resolved many conflicts, the governments of Great Britain and the United States not only claimed a territorial sea of three miles for themselves but also claimed that the three-mile limit was customary international law binding on all states.[126] Several of the major treatises of the day listed three miles as the customary international law limit of the territorial sea.[127] To what degree did this reflect customary law or rather was the policy of a few relatively powerful states?

By the beginning of the nineteenth century, there was a level of agreement on general concepts such as the freedom of the high seas and the existence of a residual band of coastal territory if control was effective and in continuous use.[128] There was, however, wide disagreement on the extent of this band. The Dutch jurist Bynkershoek in the eighteenth century had declared that a state's dominion extended as far as it could control its waters from shore – that is, to the extent of the reach of its cannons.[129] At the time this standard corresponded with a maritime league or about three nautical miles. This standard suffered from two significant problems: it was dependent on the limits of the

124 See, e.g., Jack L. Goldsmith and Eric A. Posner, *The Limits of International Law* (New York: Oxford University Press, 2005), 59–66; David J. Bederman, "The Sea," in *The Oxford Handbook of the History of International Law*, edited by Bardo Fassbender and Anne Peters 359 (Oxford: Oxford University Press, 2012).

125 The Convention was the culmination of a long process of negotiation that included three United Nations Conferences on the Law of the Sea (UNCLOS I of 1958, II of 1960, and III of 1973). UNCLOS III was necessary to address not only changes in technology, but also the rising political influence and interests of the many new states that had not participated in earlier conferences. See United Nations Convention on the Law of the Sea (1982), entered into force Nov. 16, 1994, 1833 UNTS 3.

126 See Brownlie, *Principles of Public International Law* (3rd ed. 1979), 192–93.

127 See, e.g., *Oppenheim's International Law* (2nd ed. 1912), 255–57.

128 See Kinji Akashi, "Cornelius Van Bynkershoek (1673–1743)," in *The Oxford Handbook of the History of International Law*, 1110.

129 See ibid., 1111.

then-current technology that had already begun to change, and several states made quite different claims.

Throughout the nineteenth century, Great Britain, as the paramount sea power, claimed a three-mile territorial sea as a fixed version of the cannon shot idea. In 1793, the United States, forced to declare its neutral waters during the war between France and Great Britain, announced that belligerents should respect its neutrality up to the "range of a cannon ball, usually stated at one sea league."[130] These policies do not create customary international law without an examination of other state practice and whether even these states accepted it as a binding legal obligation. There is much contrary evidence. Throughout much of the nineteenth century, the United States, when it was in its interest to do so, attempted to obtain recognition from Great Britain of a six-mile, and then later a five-mile, territorial sea.[131] During this same period Spain continued to claim jurisdiction of at least six miles as it had for more than a century.[132] Several Scandinavian countries claimed a four-mile territorial sea.[133] W.E. Hall in his 1890 edition doubted that the question had ever been settled. His personal view was that a state had a right to extend its territorial sea with the increased range of its guns, but a treaty agreement would be preferable.[134] Many British and American authorities continued to assert that there was worldwide customary international law rule of a three-mile territorial sea, as did the governments of the United States and Great Britain.[135] The Northern European maritime powers never accepted the cannon shot rule as a limitation on their jurisdiction.[136]

While the extent of the territorial sea might be seen as merely a housekeeping rule that requires only a bright-line standard, states have quite different interests concerning its breadth. The strength of a state's maritime forces, the relative level of its technology, and its access to capital to exploit resources in its coastal waters all affect whether it prefers a broad or narrow sea band. The great maritime powers, such as Great Britain and the United States, preferred broader freedom of the seas, relatively uninhibited by territorial waters,

130 John Bassett Moore, *Digest of International Law* (1906), vol. 1, 702–03, quoted in Lori F. Damrosch, Louis Henkin, Sean D. Murphy, and Hans Schmit, *International Law: Cases and Materials* (St. Paul: West Publishing, 5th ed. 2009), 1387.

131 See Hall, *International Law*, 152–53.

132 See ibid.

133 See ibid., 228; H.S.K. Kent, "The Historical Origins of the Three-Mile Limit," 48 *American Journal of International Law* 537 (1954), 550–52.

134 Hall, *International Law*, 152–55.

135 See ibid.; Kent, "The Historical Origins of the Three-Mile Limit."

136 See Wyndham L.Walker, "Territorial Waters: The Cannon Shot Rule," 22 *British Yearbook of International Law* 210 (1945), 231.

to pursue trade and to project power around the globe. On the other hand, coastal states, particularly less developed ones, wanted a wide territorial sea to exclusively exploit coastal resources and maintain security.

The positions of both the United States and Great Britain, which had been presented as unqualified and uncompromising with regard to their access to foreign waters, became flexible in order to exert broader jurisdiction in circumstances where it was in their interest to do so.[137] Great Britain exerted criminal jurisdiction beyond three miles for smuggling offshore. The United States similarly exercised customs jurisdiction up to twelve miles and enforced its ban on imported alcohol during prohibition to one-hour's sail from shore.[138] With the three-mile standard based on exerted power, and not general acceptance of the community, it is not surprising that Great Britain adopted inconsistent policies. It protected its fisheries at home from foreign exploitation with a limited territorial sea and asserted expansive trawling rights abroad.[139] The three-mile territorial sea might be seen as just the position of some states when convenient rather than a rule of law binding on all.[140]

Reminiscent of the deep disagreement about the minimum international standard of compensation, the attempt to codify maritime rules at the 1930 Hague Codification Conference failed. A significant consensus actually favored expansion of coastal state territorial waters, at least for some purposes.[141] Latin American states, among others, attempted to create a twelve-mile fisheries zone. After World War II, a number of developing nations directly challenged the supposed three-mile limit by extending their territorial sea in an effort to exclude foreign, more technologically advanced fishing fleets from their valuable resources. Developed states, on the other hand, favored greater access to fishing resources and the freer movement of their military fleets for national security purposes.[142] The zero-sum clash of wills and the lack of deliberative discussions that is characteristic of the customary law process had hardened positions. By the time of the 1958 negotiations on the Law of the Sea,

[137] Great Britain asserted jurisdiction beyond three miles for purposes of customs inspections and fishing rights. The United States similarly expanded jurisdiction in the Bering Strait after purchasing Alaska from Russia. See Goldsmith and Posner, *The Limits of International Law*, 63–66.

[138] Bederman, "The Sea," 376.

[139] See Goldsmith and Posner, *The Limits of International Law*, 65.

[140] See Kent, "The Historical Origins of the Three-Mile Limit," 537 (asserting that the three-mile limit emerged as a compromise between the cannon shot rule and the wider claims of Scandinavian countries).

[141] See Bederman, "The Sea," 372–77.

[142] See Peter Malanczuk, *Akehurst's A Modern Introduction to International Law* (London: Routledge, 7th ed. 1997), 178–79.

only a minority of the eighty-six nations attending the conference supported the asserted customary rule of a three-mile limit.[143]

The disputes from the 1930 Hague Conference, through the 1958 Law of the Sea Convention to their ultimate resolution in UNCLOS 1982, revealed that there had long been disagreement on the extent of the territorial sea and divergent views and interests concerning expanded jurisdiction for fisheries and other purposes.[144] The extended negotiations led to a series of compromises and creative alternatives that addressed the concerns of nearly all nations. Most significantly, the importance of the contentious territorial sea band was reduced by the successful negotiation of clear rules on transit passage and on an exclusive economic zone ("EEZ"). With these changes nations were willing to make trade-offs because their primary security and economic concerns had been addressed.[145] The territorial sea was extended to 12 miles, a new 200-mile EEZ protected fishing rights of developing countries, and the United States and other military powers obtained a special rule for international straits that protected access and confirmed the right of innocent passage.[146] A general consensus that had not been possible in the customary law era became possible once interests and positions were revealed and trade-offs were made. The result of the UNCLOS negotiations was that nations could agree on new common standards that each nation was willing to accept, even if these standards were the first preference of only a few nations.

The Law of the Sea treaty process provides insights into how treaty negotiations and their attention to diverse state concerns may resolve conflicting interests and positions that the customary international law process appears

143 See Donald R. Rothwell and Tim Stephens, *The International Law of the Sea* (Portland, OR: Hart Publishing, 2010), 61–66. The ILC-proposed draft articles for the territorial sea in 1956 set the stage for UNCLOS I in 1958, but did not recommend a specific standard for the breadth of the territorial sea because of the wide disagreement about that standard. See ibid., 62–64.

144 By 1955, *Oppenheim's International Law* treatise would assert that the three-mile limit was probably never generally accepted. See *Oppenheim's International Law* (8th ed. 1955), 490–92. Several European nations, including Spain, Portugal, and the Scandinavian states, claimed a larger limit. Ibid., 490 n.2. The 1930 Hague Codification Conference on Territorial Waters failed to resolve these differences. Ibid., 491–92. The United Kingdom and the United States continued to protest claims wider than three miles. See James Leslie Brierly, *The Law of Nations* (Oxford: Clarendon Press, 6th ed. 1963), 202–11 (describing the history of the territorial sea debate).

145 See Robert L. Friedheim, *Negotiating the New Ocean Regime* (Columbia: University of South Carolina Press, 1993), 78.

146 For a discussion of trade-offs that enabled a new consensus on various norms and standards in UNCLOS III, see ibid., 78–95. See also James K. Sebenius, *Negotiating the Law of the Sea* (Cambridge, MA: Harvard University Press, 1984) (analyzing the Law of the Sea Convention in terms of negotiations and complex bargaining).

to ignore or minimize. Just as we have seen concerning the law of state responsibility, Western treatises and even arbitration decisions masked disagreements about customary norms and resolved uncertainties in favor of the dominant powers of the era. Attempts to codify standards long thought to be mandatory in the Anglo-American literature revealed major disagreements about norms and different interests that required negotiation and compromise in order to reach agreement. The customary international law narrative favored the powerful maritime states, which could impose their will by boarding ships and repelling small boats of less powerful nations in their waters, had greater influence over the literature, and could select arbitrators and judges that reflected their positions. State practice of the less powerful nations was generally ignored. In contrast, UNCLOS and the multilateral treaty process, in general, provided the opportunity for wide-ranging negotiation, enabled the consideration of trade-offs to reconcile different normative perspectives by promoting compromises, and encouraged commitment to and compliance with the negotiated legal norms. In many respects we might see the UNCLOS process as a template for updating and legitimizing much of customary international law, including the law of state responsibility. Customary international law claims and isolated incidents based on dominant power may not adequately encourage and facilitate the development of international legal norms acceptable to nearly all states.

2.5 THE PERSISTENT OBJECTOR PRINCIPLE

Customary international law theory has had no persistent objector principle until recently. There is no mention of an opportunity to persistently object in the first eight editions of *Oppenheim's International Law*, nor in the *Chorzow Factory* case or the leading arbitrations of the day. Rather, Oppenheim assumed the existence of an international social community that creates rules binding on all members of the community.[147] The literature and the paramount states considered Latin American nations to be bound to follow customary international law norms in the late nineteenth century and throughout the twentieth century, including the disputed law of state responsibility, even though these nations continuously and strenuously objected during the purported period of formation of these norms. The persistent objector principle is inconsistent with the universal theory based on the "common consent" of the international

[147] *Oppenheim's International Law* (8th ed., 1955), 51 ("From this assumption there necessarily follows the acknowledgment of a body of rules of a fundamental character universally binding upon all members of that society.").

community that bound states such as Japan and Turkey at the turn of the nineteenth century into the twentieth century and new states that emerged from colonialism.

Similarly, the persistent objector principle is inconsistent with the concept of customary law found in domestic and traditional societies. Customary law is communally determined and independent of the idiosyncratic will of the individual.[148] Customary law, whether in traditional society, under the common law of England, or in international legal theory, is not based on individual consent.

During the second half of the twentieth century a remarkable change occurred in customary international law legal theory. Oppenheim's ninth edition for the first time included the persistent objector principle, a specific consent idea, while at the same time keeping the formulation of customary international law as expressing the "common consent" of nations.[149] This contractual idea would provide a potential means of exit from norms created by the emerging majority of developing nations that were exercising their new clout at the United Nations. If this principle is, in fact, part of the concept of customary international law, it created an anomaly. Newly independent states were bound by universal customary international law rules even though they played no role in their formation and did not have an opportunity to consent, but older, developed states could opt out of any new or modified customary international law rules with which they disagreed.

Supporters of the principle cite the ICJ's *Asylum Case* and the *Anglo-Norwegian Fisheries Case* as their lone evidence.[150] As D'Amato and others have persuasively demonstrated, the *Asylum Case* involved a special or regional custom, which is by its nature contractual, and not general

148 See Hamnett, *Chieftainship and Legitimacy*, 11–13.

149 *Oppenheim's International Law*, Peace, Vol. 1, edited by Sir Robert Jennings and Arthur Watts (Oxford: Oxford University Press, 9th ed. 2008), 29. Those supporting the persistent objector principle include Brownlie, Waldock, and the Akehurst treatise. See Brownlie, *Principles of Public International Law* (3rd ed., 1979), 10–11; Humphrey Waldock, "General Course on Public International Law," 106 *Recueil des cours* 1 (1962-II), 49–53; Malanczuk, *Akehurst's A Modern Introduction to International Law*, 39–48. Ted Stein authored the premiere study of the principle. See Ted L. Stein, "The Approach of the Different Drummer: The Principle of the Persistent Objector in International Law," 26 *Harvard International Law Journal* 457 (1985). The contrary view also has significant support. See Jonathan Charney, "The Persistent Objector Rule and the Development of Customary International Law," 56 *British Yearbook of International Law* 1 (1985); D'Amato, *The Concept of Custom in International Law*, 252–54; Jordan J. Paust, "Customary International Law: Its Nature, Sources and Status," 12 *Michigan Journal of International Law* 59 (1990), 64–67.

150 *Asylum Case (Colombia v. Peru)*, Judgment of 20 November 1950, 1950 ICJ Rep. 266; *Fisheries Case (United Kingdom v. Norway)*, Judgment of 18 December 1951, 1951 ICJ Rep. 116.

custom.[151] Nevertheless, the ICJ's opinion in the *Anglo-Norwegian Fisheries Case* does contain dicta that might be read to support the persistent objector principle.[152] Such an interpretation is unsupported by state practice and is consequently unpersuasive.[153] The more reasonable interpretation is that it is a discussion of a special or regional custom that is contractual, a deviation from general customary international law, or simply in error and should be ignored.[154] There are numerous contrary statements in other ICJ opinions both before and after the *Anglo-Norwegian Fisheries Case* clearly indicating that all nations are bound by customary norms.[155]

If the persistent objector principle is accepted, then customary law theory is inconsistent and incoherent. The majority of states have had no opportunity to consent or indeed participate in the formation of norms to which they are bound, while other states may opt out of changes to those norms. Paradoxically, Latin American nations would continue to be bound by rules to which they persistently objected. If the international order is premised on the express or implied consent of states, as the persistent objector principle suggests, then new states that have neither consented to, nor participated in, the formation of custom have the inherent right to opt out, as is the case with treaty law. If, as is frequently argued, this consent notion is premised on sovereignty,[156] then new states need not accept limitations on their sovereignty without their consent. If the international order is premised on

[151] See D'Amato, *The Concept of Custom in International Law*, 252–54; Malcolm N. Shaw, *International Law* (Cambridge: Cambridge University Press, 5th ed. 2003), 87. (In the *Asylum Case* Colombia claimed a special regional custom of Latin American states in granting asylum.)

[152] The Court held that the ten-mile bay closing line rule claimed by the United Kingdom had not become a general rule of customary international law and Norway could continue to use its system of straight baselines. In dicta it affirmed: "In any event the ten-mile rule would appear to be inapplicable as against Norway inasmuch as she has always opposed any attempt to apply it to the Norwegian coast." *Fisheries Case*, 131.

[153] Stein could find no examples of actual state practice. See Stein, "The Approach of the Different Drummer," 459 n.6.

[154] See the analysis in D'Amato, *The Concept of Custom in International Law*, 258–62.

[155] See, e.g., *North Sea Continental Shelf Cases*, 38–39 ("[G]eneral or customary law rules and obligations … by their very nature, must have equal force for all members of the international community, and cannot therefore be the subject of any right of unilateral exclusion exercisable at will by any one of them in its own favour."). Similarly, the Court in the *Gulf of Maine Case* explained that the customary principles of maritime law were "undoubtedly of general application, valid for all States and in relation to all kinds of maritime delimitation." *Gulf of Maine Case*, 292–93.

[156] See, e.g., Stein, "The Approach of the Different Drummer," 459, 464 (noting that the persistent objector rule is based on the idea that because the international legal order lacks a sovereign capable of imposing rules on a state, a rule that a state has continuously refused to accept cannot bind it).

consensus, then the idiosyncratic state is just as bound to universal law as are new states.

Upon closer examination, the emergence of the persistent objector principle appears to be the product of recent political and economic history, much like the saga of the international minimum standard, with little relationship to theory or practice. During the Cold War era, the Anglo-American literature regarded customary international law as universal, with the evident virtue that customary norms were binding on a recalcitrant Eastern Bloc. The original Restatement of the Foreign Relations Law of the United States, written during the height of the Cold War when it was thought important to bind the Soviet Union to the norms of customary international law, proclaimed a universal theory with no mention of a persistent objector principle.[157] If anything, the original Restatement appeared to reject consent as a basis for customary international law in asserting that the restrictive theory of sovereign immunity applied to all states, including the Soviet Union, despite its strenuous objection.[158]

However, in the 1960s and early 1970s, as the newly independent nations became a majority at the UN General Assembly, Western states began to lose control, or at least feared the loss of control, of the development of customary law regimes such as that of the territorial sea and the protection of foreign investment. Using democratic theory, the nonaligned nations challenged Western control of the international legal process.[159] The notion of the persistent objector can be seen as the Western counter-reformation to this attempted revolution. The persistent objector principle would allow the United States and other capital-exporting countries to exempt themselves from changes in foreign investment

157 See Restatement (Second) of the Foreign Relations Law of the United States, § 1, comment b (1965) ("Unless otherwise indicated, the rules described by the term 'international law' … are rules of general application applicable to any state."). The only option mentioned in the 1965 Restatement for a state disagreeing with a proposed norm was to protest and attempt to prevent its formation. The 1965 Restatement affirmed: "Because failure to object to practice may amount to recognition of it, the objection by a state to a practice of another is an important means of preventing or controlling in some degree the development of rules of international law." Ibid. There was no mention of the persistent objector principle or the idea that customary international law is based on consent.

158 For the Soviet position, see M.M. Boguslavsky, "Foreign Sovereign Immunity: Soviet Doctrine and Practice," 10 *Netherlands Yearbook of International Law* 167 (1979).

159 See Mohammed Bedjaoui, *Toward a New International Economic Order* (New York: Holmes and Meier, 1979), 138–44. Bedjaoui, former president of the ICJ, chronicled developing nations' challenges to traditional customary law principles and promoted UN resolutions as instruments of the progressive development of international law. See ibid., 133–44. He criticized as unjust the veto power of the permanent members of the Security Council and argued for the democratization of the United Nations and customary international law procedures. Ibid., 170–92.

law, including the standard of compensation for expropriation. The Reporters of the Restatement, after consulting with a State Department critical of the ICJ after the *Nicaragua Case*, adopted the persistent objector principle for the first time.[160]

As Ted Stein observed, the Reporters' conclusion that customary international law was part of federal common law presented the U.S. government with the rather horrifying prospect of hostile majorities at the UN making federal law through the adoption of resolutions or multilateral conventions.[161] Given the Reporters' view, the persistent objector principle provided the necessary escape device to preserve U.S. sovereignty. The Restatement position, like the dicta in the *Anglo-Norwegian Fisheries Case*, is based not on general state practice, but rather on unsubstantiated and incoherent assumptions about the international legal order.

In an attempt to justify the unjustifiable with history, the Restatement referred to Vattel as the source of the idea that the international legal system was consensual. But this confidence is misplaced. As discussed earlier, Vattel's customary international law bound only those states choosing to participate in it. Any nation could exercise its sovereign will to exit customary regimes both during and after formation. Such a theory would not have bound new states or the Soviet Union to customary law with which they disagreed. Indeed, it is a prescription for chaos.

If the persistent objector principle is customary international law, then the international system is an incoherent game that is consensual for some and a common consent theory for other, often less powerful states. Yet customary international law, if it is to have legal validity or legitimacy, must be a social consensus concept as it is in domestic and traditional societies. Powerful nations, utilizing the persistent objector concept, appear to assert that they will not accept normative principles based on general acceptance with which they disagree. This claim, if true, undermines the legitimacy and efficacy of customary international law as a coherent body of norms applicable to all. Given this history, the International Law Commission ("ILC"), in drafting conclusions on the identification of customary international law, should be quite

[160] See Restatement (Third) of the Foreign Relations Law of the United States, § 102, comment d. The Reporters' note borrowed from the classical consent theory of Vattel to assert that the principle of the dissenting state not being bound "is an accepted application of the traditional principle that international law essentially depends on the consent of states." Ibid., n.2. There were apparently significant clashes with the State Department on several issues. See "The Restatement of Foreign Relations Law of the United States, Revised: How Were the Controversies Resolved?" 81 *American Journal of International Law* 180 (1990).

[161] Stein, "The Approach of the Different Drummer," 472–73.

cautious in accepting the persistent objector principle as part of the structure of customary international law. If it does accept this principle, it would be recommending a major change in the way customary law has been articulated and applied through the centuries with little support in state practice.[162]

2.6 THE WAY FORWARD

To conclude, many international norms termed "customary" were a selected collection of assumed norms from European states reflecting their self-interest in a time of colonial expansion and later consolidation of their investments. The primary role of state responsibility law was to protect their foreign investment and businessmen with little respect for reciprocity on their part.[163] Treatise writers created a narrative of customary law based on little state practice or evidence of general acceptance of norms by the overwhelming majority of states. Rather, they placed great reliance on selected natural law principles, the diplomatic correspondence of the most powerful states, and arbitration decisions. It is striking that the writings of both publicists and arbitrators (who were typically selected from the dominant legal cultures), which are only subsidiary means for discovering rules of law, were treated as of greater importance than the practices and views of states.

If we return to our concern about the formal legality of customary international law and its democratic legitimacy, several of the norms of state responsibility do not appear to meet the customary international law criteria of consistent state practice and general acceptance. Fernando Tesón may well be right that in the modern view of custom state practice is of less importance if there is a broad, truly universal, and precise consensus.[164] But even in this view, Latin American nations, although weak militarily during this formative period, consistently objected to the putative international minimum standards and proposed an alternative, national treatment, that is standard practice in many developed states.

This history should serve as a caution to those authors who would utilize natural law principles to either inform customary international law, as would

162 In 2016 the Commission did adopt a draft conclusion endorsing the persistent objector principle. Draft Conclusion 15 declares: "Where a State has objected to a rule of customary international law while that rule was in the process of formation, the rule is not opposable to the State concerned for so long as it maintains its objection." "Report of the International Law Commission," Sixty-Eighth Session, Draft Conclusion 15, para. 1.

163 Beyond the incidents mentioned earlier in the chapter, the United States, for example, regularly adds reservations, understandings, and declarations to limit the application of international standards to its domestic legal standards.

164 See Fernando R. Tesón, "Fake Custom," in this volume.

Brian Lepard,[165] or as a separate source of international norms, as would Fernando Tesón.[166] Tesón writes persuasively that ideological advocates string nonbinding resolutions and declarations together to construct "fake custom" not moored in state practice or genuine general acceptance. But recharacterizing "fake custom" as ethical or morally binding principles does not solve the problems of genuine acceptance or inadequate specificity. In the human rights area there are some fundamental rights that are universal assumptions of civilization that are appropriately treated as custom and their legality has been confirmed in binding human rights treaties. However, to expand this small universe to environmental law or foreign investment law is to stretch what are general ethical concerns into the domain of policy decisions best left to more democratic processes.

Natural law systems can and have been manipulated depending on who decides what principles constitute "natural law" and which principles are selected and applied. The suggested binding ethical obligation to address climate change illustrates the problem. First, who decides the content of that obligation and the specific actions to be taken? Will it be the proclamation of a few powerful states with their own views and interests? Will it be judges or arbitrators not steeped in the complexities of economic incentives to discourage high carbon energy and encourage alternative energy sources? Second, general ethical obligations are inadequate to address complex decisions with competing interests, values, and perceptions. What are the most efficient, wise, or politically feasible means to achieve these goals? Which of the alternatives of a carbon tax, strict emission standards, a "cap and trade" system, or subsidies to alternative energy sources is best suited to address the problem, or are all of them required? Who will bear the costs and reap the benefits of each approach? Environmental issues are multipolar, legislative-type issues best addressed by multilateral negotiations among states that have the capacity and commitment to comply through their domestic political processes. Third, under what authority would judges make what are essentially regulatory decisions? This is a prescription for an impractical "juristocracy" removed from international and domestic political processes.[167]

There is a need for the protection of aliens and foreign investment in our globalized world, whether conceived of as an international minimum standard

[165] See Brian D. Lepard, "Toward a New Theory of Customary International Human Rights Law," in this volume.

[166] See Tesón, "Fake Custom," in this volume.

[167] For a nuanced, comparative law examination of the relative merits of transferring what are essentially political questions to judges, see Ran Hirschl, *Towards Juristocracy* (Cambridge, MA: Harvard University Press, 2004).

of state responsibility or as a matter of human rights. But what rights should be protected and what is the form of those rights? The taking of property by government may be seen as stealing in one context and appropriate land reform, resource-saving zoning, or environment-conserving regulation in others.

The international legal framework is changing rapidly, developing new forms of international institutions and processes to craft solutions to new problems. The evolving distribution of economic and political power and advances in telecommunication and transportation create the opportunity for more democratic and deliberative processes than are possible through the customary law process.[168] The way forward may be to develop more pluralist versions of international legal principles to move beyond the ethnocentric history of their development and imposition.[169] Some rules may need to be negotiated and reformulated to make them more representative of the interests and positions of a larger group of nations. This suggests that nations not represented in the original development of what might be called European International Law should now be heavily represented at the ILC and at treaty conferences to increase the legitimacy of the codification process of norm formation. The UN Law of the Sea negotiation illuminated a more flexible and effective process than is possible with customary law. The multilateral treaty process, particularly when informed by ILC draft recommendations, creates a legislative-like process that empowers all nations to participate, articulate their interests and concerns, make trade-offs, and ultimately agree on new common standards that each nation is willing to accept. In foreign investment law and other controversial areas the development of more legitimate and effective international lawmaking processes continues.

168 For an argument for increased reliance on treaty law and soft law, see Joel P. Trachtman, "The Growing Obsolescence of Customary International Law," in *Custom's Future: International Law in a Changing World*, edited by Curtis A. Bradley 172 (New York: Cambridge University Press, 2016); Kelly, "The Twilight of Customary Interantional Law," 530–35.

169 For an analysis of the role of Africa in international law development, both as a contributor and as a disempowered recipient, see James Thuo Gathii, "Africa and the History of International Law," in *The Oxford Handbook of the History of International Law*, 407.

3

Fake Custom

Fernando R. Tesón

3.1 INTRODUCTION

Customary law is the lifeblood of international law. It is also the most problematic concept in our discipline. One problem is the indeterminacy of the criteria by which lawyers identify customary rules. Following Hart, we can say that the rule of recognition of a legal system is the set of necessary and sufficient conditions to identify a norm as part of the system.[1] International law is problematic because its rule of recognition is seriously indeterminate.

I cannot here attempt to formulate a complete rule of recognition for the entire body of international law, so I will focus on a *partial* rule of recognition for custom. What are the necessary and sufficient conditions for the existence of a customary rule in international law? Traditional theory has identified state practice and *opinio juris* as the elements of custom. A rule is part of the system if (1) it can be gleaned from state practice and (2) that practice is accompanied by a belief on the part of state officials that the rule in question is required or permitted by law. I will not rehearse here the problems that even this basic rule of recognition has, so well discussed by many writers. These include questions such as: What is *opinio juris*? How dense or old should the practice be? What do we make of contradictory practice?[2]

I want to address instead a different phenomenon that has become increasingly common. This is the practice of claiming customary status for rules notwithstanding the fact that these rules cannot be traced back to any plausible rule of recognition. I call this practice "fake custom." The practice is

1 See H.L.A. Hart, *The Concept of Law* (Oxford: Oxford University Press, 2nd ed. 1990), 94–95.

2 See the classic study by Anthony D'Amato, Anthony A. D'Amato, *The Concept of Custom in International Law* (Ithaca, NY: Cornell University Press, 1971), 3–20, and the more recent book by Brian Lepard, Brian D. Lepard, *Customary International Law: A New Theory with Practical Applications* (New York: Cambridge University Press, 2010), 3–43.

widespread: International lawyers, norm entrepreneurs, and international courts perpetrate fake custom with alarming frequency. I distinguish fake custom from other practices. The assertion of fake custom differs from (a) the assertion that a certain customary law might be emerging, and (b) the assertion that a certain norm is desirable, just, or efficient. The speaker who says that a norm is emerging grounds his assertion in the observation of state practice; he does not claim that the norm is already customary law. The speaker who asserts that a norm is desirable, just, or efficient says nothing about whether the norm is custom. He may be a natural lawyer – that is, he might claim that international law includes norms that are desirable, just, or efficient. But the natural lawyer does not claim that the desired norm is custom; he claims that the norm is legally binding because it is morally binding.[3]

In contrast, the practitioner of fake custom tries to convince an audience who believes in custom as a source of international law that a rule is custom when in reality it is not. He really *wants* the rule to be law (he is a norm entrepreneur), and one of the ways to achieve that is to convince others that the rule *is* law. But fake customary rules are rules that are not law under any plausible theory of legitimate lawmaking. They are pieces of advocacy disguised as law. The speaker asserts them as law, but they are *putative* rules of law. That is, the speaker who asserts fake custom utters a false proposition of law. Now of course this exercise in advocacy is common in other areas of the law. But the phenomenon is more acute in international law because researching state practice is hard and time-consuming, so few people bother to check the truth of the assertion.

Fake custom is hard to unmask. The speaker hopes that if enough people repeat the proposition "X is custom," X will become custom in the eyes of most people, even if it is not. The lawyer who asserts fake custom, then, trades on the indeterminacy of the applicable rule of recognition and on the public's high informational costs of determining what states have done and not done in the past.

In domestic law, in contrast, it is easier to falsify a mistaken proposition of law, not only because most laws are written but also because courts continuously interpret and refine statutes, constitutions, and past decisions. The rule of recognition in domestic law is manageable because it is relatively determinate, so a speaker who tries to convince an audience that X is a rule of the system by merely repeating that it is will have a harder time. Propositions of domestic law are easier to test than propositions of international law.

3 See Fernando R. Tesón, "Natural Law as Part of International Law: The Case of the Armenian Genocide," 50 *University of San Diego Law Review* 813 (2013), and the discussion that follows.

The problem I identify also differs from the skeptical claims made by a number of authors about customary law. These authors are worried either about the incentives that states may have to comply with customary law[4] or about importing customary law into domestic law.[5] Their skeptical claims concern *genuine* customary law. They see problems with these norms even if they meet the classical definition (or something close to it). My worry is different, and prior, to theirs: I identify false claims about what custom is. Addressing this problem is a task that must be undertaken before we address the question of enforcement, or the question of the legal effect customary law has or should have in domestic law. I am concerned about weeding out false law.

In criticizing the abuse of custom, I remain agnostic about the substantive desirability of the positions defended with the techniques of fake custom I will soon describe. On the merits, I agree with some of those positions and disagree with others. My point is one of legal methodology, a conceptual point about soundness in legal argument, and a plea for transparency and intellectual honesty.

3.2 GENUINE CUSTOM

3.2.1 Classical Theory of Custom

In order to diagnose fake custom, I must first identify the real thing. I propose a rule of recognition for genuine custom. I distinguish between two concepts of custom which, I argue, are legitimate and supplement each other. Under the *classical* theory, a customary rule results from a relatively robust state practice over a relatively long period of time, practice that at some point in history has been internalized by the participants as legally required or permitted.

I think some of the problems with the traditional concept of *opinio juris* (such as how can we get into the heads of rulers to know what they believe and not believe?) can be solved by appealing to sociological elements of norm formation. A practice gets started more or less spontaneously and, at some point in the practice, its participants experience *normative pressure* to comply. This pressure is, as Hart explains, a disposition to strongly criticize violations and to respond to them, sometimes even with force.[6] Thus, there is no mystery about any "psychological" element in the classical definition of custom. Rather, a

4 See Jack Goldsmith and Eric Posner, *The Limits of International Law* (Oxford: Oxford University Press, 2006), 23–78.

5 See John O. McGinnis and Ilya Somin, "Should International Law Be Part of Our Law?" 59 *Stanford Law Review* 1175 (2007).

6 See Hart, *The Concept of Law*, 57.

customary norm is revealed when governments *with their actions* show that deviation from the norm is unacceptable. Analogous reasoning applies to *permissive* norms. When a practice develops that seems to depart from previous practice, then the *failure* by governments to criticize the new practice amounts to an endorsement of the permission enshrined in the new practice. A practice is robust when it is sufficiently dense and convergent.

The classical theory of custom is embodied in Article 38 of the Statute of the International Court of Justice ("ICJ"), and has been often reaffirmed in international and domestic jurisprudence. A good example is the customary rule discovered by the U.S. Supreme Court in the famous *Paquete Habana* case. There the Court researched diplomatic practice in order to establish that fishermen were exempted from the rule of capture prevalent at the time.[7] Another modern fine example of application of the classical theory of customary law is the study on international humanitarian law commissioned by the International Committee of the Red Cross.[8] In that study the authors researched a dense record of state practice – the practice of war – to extract conclusions about the laws of war supported by that practice.

The classical theory of custom is appealing because members of a community are supposed to honor the well-established usages of that community. Custom evokes the values of tradition, stability, fairness, and good faith, even in times of conflict. To appeal to custom is to reject the allure of opportunistic behavior: One should observe the well-established usages of one's community, even if by departing one could reap an opportunistic gain. This is particularly important in international law. When a new state joins the international community (as happened following the collapse of the Soviet Union and Yugoslavia), it should not do so on its own terms, but rather on the terms of that community. Those terms are defined, in great part, by long-standing practice reaffirmed as mandatory by the members of the community.

3.2.2 Modern Theory of Custom

It soon became evident to many observers that the classical theory of custom must be modernized, as it was increasingly difficult for states to interact in a mutually beneficial fashion with such a rigid method of creating norms. In the new world of speedy communication and instant interaction, the classical notion of custom proved inadequate to situations where the reality called for a

7 *The Paquete Habana*, 175 U.S. 677 (1900).

8 *Customary International Humanitarian Law*, edited by Jean-Marie Henckaerts and Louise Doswald-Beck, 2 vols., Vol. I: Rules, Vol. II: Practice (2 Parts) (Cambridge: Cambridge University Press and ICRC, 2005).

more flexible method of lawmaking. This *modern* view, then, accepted that a broad international *consensus* could create law, provided it was truly universal and reasonably precise. Under this modern notion of custom, a new rule can be created by a specific, strong international consensus, even if the norm is not sufficiently supported by prior state practice.

In the United States, the Supreme Court recognized this trend in the *Sosa v. Alvarez-Machain* case, decided in 2004. In laying down the standard for identifying customary norms for the purpose of jurisdiction under the Alien Tort Statute, the Court said that courts should not recognize a norm with no "less definite content and acceptance among civilized nations than the historical paradigms familiar when §1350 was enacted."[9]

While the Supreme Court applied this test in a specific statutory context, it can be generalized and exported to the *international* concept of customary law. We can then state the rule of recognition for international custom as follows.

Genuine customary law consists of (a) robust state practice (classical theory of custom) or (b) a *universal* and *sufficiently precise* international consensus (modern theory of custom). We could say, perhaps, that in the classical view state practice is central, while in the modern view *opinio juris* is decisive. The departure from the classical view is not as sharp as it seems, because custom in this modern sense requires *universal and specific international consensus*. A new customary rule cannot be established by a majority of states, either voting in a body like the United Nations General Assembly or in other international fora. For all intents and purposes, the modern theory of custom requires virtual unanimity for a rule to qualify. The salient characteristic of this modern lawmaking method is that universal, precise consensus is enough to create the rule; no prior or simultaneous practice is required. This is a reasonable and salutary addition to the theory of custom.

In his innovative book on customary law, Brian Lepard has suggested a theory of custom that at first blush endorses the modern theory. He writes that "a customary international norm arises when states generally believe that it is desirable now or in the near future to have an authoritative legal principle or rule prescribing, permitting, or prohibiting certain state conduct."[10] This belief need not be moored to preexisting or contemporary practice, so Lepard's theory superficially looks like the modern theory of custom that I have endorsed. On closer inspection, however, Lepard's definition is too broad because it fails to include the two crucial features of custom required

[9] *Sosa v. Alvarez-Machain*, 542 U.S. 692 (2004), 732, *reversing* 331 F.3d 604 (9th Cir. 2004).

[10] Lepard, *Customary International Law*, 8. See also ibid., 97–98.

by the modern theory: that the belief in the desirability of the norm should be *universal* and not proposed by a mere majority, and that the object of the agreement should be *specific and precise*, and not vague or aspirational.

On the issue of the requisite majority, Lepard offers a multilayered system under which the size of the majority of states necessary to create a new norm with their "beliefs" depends on the nature of the norm in question.[11] In spite of these distinctions, Lepard's use of the word "generally" and his endorsement of the international community as a sort of "global parliament" suggest a number well short of universal consent. And nowhere does Lepard include the important requirement of verbal precision and specificity.

Lepard's theory of custom, then, may lend itself to a form of fake custom. It will be sufficient for a norm entrepreneur to find that a significant number of states "generally" believe the norm he favors should be the law for him to peddle that norm as part of international law. The truth is that states "generally believe" objectionable or false things (see the example of criminalization of blasphemy later in the chapter). Moreover, the world is sharply divided over issues, and what a majority of states generally believe is fiercely opposed by the minority of states. For example, a great majority of states (encouraged by the Soviet Union) generally believed in the 1970s that governments should not pay full market compensation when nationalizing foreign property. Under Lepard's theory, such a belief would have already given rise to a customary law norm. Yet the customary process did not work that way. Western states were able to block this démarche (which, by the way, would have been harmful *to the very states that proposed it*, as it would have discouraged much-needed investment), and the law moved toward the liberal side again.

To be sure, and to his credit, Lepard would not validate customary norms, no matter how widely supported, that contravene ethical principles (a view I share, as described later). But there are still problems with his view. Suppose a majority of states generally believe that all states should cut carbon emissions by 50 percent in order to slow global warming. Suppose, however, that a minority of states oppose this. Some of them honestly doubt the soundness of the science on which such beliefs are based, others think that such a measure would be catastrophic to their economies, and still others think that the distribution of costs and benefits would be unfair. Now it is possible to argue that, if climate change is likely to cause the collapse of the Earth's biosphere or something similar in the long run, we have an ethical obligation to act.

[11] Ibid., 151–61.

What is the status of the proposed norm under Lepard's theory? Is the urgency to slow climate change enough to allow a majority to legislate in this way and ignore the opposition of a minority?[12] I do not think so. The international community has not reached the point (luckily, I would add) of naked majority rule, at least on any norm that is not peremptorily required by a clear ethical norm, such as the prohibition of official torture, in which case numbers do not count. If there is an obligation to act to slow global warming, it is an *imperfect* obligation – that is, an obligation that someone must discharge, but in accordance with all the circumstances surrounding the case, including the costs of compliance. Thus, for example, if the burdens of complying with the rule are unfairly distributed, then the obligation might be suspended.[13]

3.3 FAKE CUSTOM TECHNIQUES

How do fake custom arguments operate? Practitioners of fake custom resort to a number of techniques. Their arguments *appear* to be customary law arguments because they profusely cite documentary sources and other instances where the desired rule has been articulated. Here I offer a non-exhaustive list of fake custom techniques. These techniques are all fallacious in some respect, which is why I refer to them as "fallacies."

The *Ad Nauseam Fallacy*. The Ad Nauseam Fallacy technique consists of profusely citing nonbinding resolutions, speeches, memoranda, and the like that contain the rule in question; the more, the better. Nonbinding UN resolutions, for example, are favorite sources of fake custom, as are pronouncements by nongovernmental organizations and other advocacy groups. This imperceptible passage from wishful thinking into law is part and parcel of the fake custom technique.

Take as an example the precautionary principle, a norm favored by many environmentalists. According to that principle, "When an activity raises threats of harm to human health or the environment, precautionary measures should be taken even if some cause and effect relationships are not fully established scientifically. In this context the proponent of an activity, rather than the public, should bear the burden of proof."[14]

[12] If the carbon emission problem has the structure of a prisoners' dilemma, Lepard might require a higher level of support. See Lepard, *Customary International Law*, 159.

[13] I use the concept of imperfect obligation in the sense Immanuel Kant and John Stuart Mill used it, that is, as an obligation with latitude. A perfect obligation is one that leaves no latitude. See George Rainbolt, "Perfect and Imperfect Obligations," 98 *Philosophical Studies* 233 (2000).

[14] The formulation is from the Science and Environmental Health Network, available at www.sehn.org/precaution.html.

As noted above, I am not addressing here the merits of the principle. Rather, the issue is whether or not the principle is binding as a matter of customary law – that is, whether states that fail to prevent the potential dangerous activity are violating the law. A leading environmental treatise, in a chapter entitled "Customary International Law and Principles," lists the numerous times the principle appears in a number of nonbinding documents.[15] The implication is that this repetition (by anyone – speakers, nongovernmental organizations, resolutions of academic conferences) turns the principle into a norm of customary law.

The Ad Nauseam Fallacy method obviously begs the question. Citing a multitude of nonbinding documents does not turn a proposed norm into a binding customary norm because it neither is anchored in state practice (classic custom), nor is the object of a universal and specific consensus (modern theory of custom).[16] This is true especially with regard to states that have rejected the principle. If the precautionary principle were part of customary law, many states using technologies with uncertain consequences (do not *all* technologies have potential unforeseen bad consequences?) would be in continuous violation of international law. This is implausible. Again, the speaker hopes that repetition alone will create in her audience a sense of normativity that cannot be found in the practice or consensus of states.

The Treaty Fallacy. The Treaty Fallacy is the practice of saying that a customary norm is binding on state A by citing treaties to which A is not a party and even which A has expressly declined to join or has repudiated. The claim is that the rule is binding on nonparties as custom. It is a variation of the view that if many states adopt a rule, then it becomes binding on those who reject the rule. Lepard discusses an example of this rhetorical technique from international tax law. Some authors argue that the "arm's length" rule to determine taxable income of related corporations is customary international law based on the fact that it has been incorporated in many bilateral tax treaties.[17]

Lepard correctly rejects this conclusion. He notes that all states that have concluded bilateral tax treaties incorporating the rule have reserved the right to enter into such a treaty or not with other states, as they choose, even though all the treaties they have adopted in fact incorporate the rule. To recognize the arm's length standard as a binding customary rule on the basis

15 Alexandre Kiss and Dinah Shelton, *International Environmental Law* (Ardsley, NY: Transnational Publishers, 3rd ed. 2004), 206–12.

16 A resolution by the United Nations General Assembly adopted by consensus would not be enough, because governments know that these resolutions have no teeth and therefore cannot be deemed to be creating law.

17 See the discussion in Lepard, *Customary International Law*, 285–305.

of these treaties would have the effect of binding all states to observe the rule with respect to *all* their trading partners and therefore to bind at least some states to a rule in treaties that *others* have agreed upon. In this connection, Article 34 of the Vienna Convention on the Law of Treaties affirms that "a treaty does not create either obligations or rights for a third State without its consent."[18]

In the 1969 *North Sea Continental Shelf Cases*, the ICJ accepted that rules in treaties could sometimes create custom binding on nonparties, but the circumstances would have to be so extraordinary as to amount to virtually universal consent. Certainly a treaty does not create obligations for nonparties that have not independently acquiesced to the rules in the treaty.

The Legislative Fallacy. The Legislative Fallacy is the practice of asserting a customary norm binding on state A based on the fact that *other* states have adopted that norm in their own legislation. It is well established in international law that a state lacks jurisdiction to adopt legislation that is binding within the territory of other states. The contrary rule would mean, of course, that any number (such as a majority) of states would have the power to legislate for the entire world. I know of no plausible theory of legitimacy that would recognize this.

In the 2012 *Jurisdictional Immunities of the State Case*, the ICJ was faced with the question whether the immunity that sovereign states enjoy under customary law recognized a crimes-against-humanity exception.[19] The Court examined the laws of many states, including those of Europe and the United States, and found that they *failed* to recognize the exception. The legal position, then, was that the recognition by Italian courts of the exception was inconsistent with customary law, which mandated the recognition by domestic courts of absolute immunity for *all* acts *iuri imperii* committed by foreign armed forces in times of war.[20] This was not a case where a court found a customary rule to be binding on Italy by virtue of its having been enacted in other countries. On the contrary, it is a case where the Court *rejected* the existence of an exception to a binding rule of customary law, citing, among other sources of evidence, the fact that not even Italy's Western partners had recognized the exception domestically.

However, aside from the fact that states have no jurisdiction to bind other states by enacting domestic legislation, the Legislation Fallacy, if accepted, would have unsavory consequences, simply because often states enact

[18] Vienna Convention on the Law of Treaties, 1155 UNTS 331 (1969), art. 34.

[19] *Jurisdictional Immunities of the State (Germany v. Italy: Greece intervening)*, Judgment of 3 February 2012, 2012 ICJ Rep. 99.

[20] Ibid.

offensive legislation. Consider the criminalization of blasphemy. A coalition of fifty-six states, the Organization of the Islamic Conference, has recently sponsored, with some success, UN resolutions calling for the criminalization of blasphemy.[21] They have done this at the international level, but, as important, they have enacted this offense in their domestic legislation.[22] The problem is that the criminalization of blasphemy is in grave tension with the norm of freedom of expression recognized in human rights law.[23] If repeated domestic enactment of a norm creates customary law, then these states would have succeeded in introducing a permissive norm that authorizes governments to criminalize blasphemy, that is, to stomp out religious dissent. One reason why we have human rights law is not to authorize these exceptions. And at any rate, a government could not escape its constitutional obligation to protect free expression by arguing that international law permits its violation. The better position, I believe, is that these states are *violating* international law, not creating a new norm.

As an aside, any liberal government worth its salt must vigorously oppose such diplomatic moves. It matters little that proponents of this measure act peacefully and that they act out of a sincerely held conception of the good. By promoting the criminalization of blasphemy those governments incite repressive behavior and denial of important human rights. Liberal governments must confront diplomacy that promotes rights violations with the conviction that such a policy is not just a diverse conception of the good deserving of toleration and respect, but a morally objectionable policy, one that tries to rationalize repression at home and promote it outwardly.

[21] On March 27, 2008, the UN Human Rights Council adopted a resolution sponsored by the Organization of the Islamic Conference recommending the criminalization of "defamation of religions." See Human Rights Council Res. 7/19 (2008), "Combating Defamation of Religions," available at http://ap.ohchr.org/documents/E/HRC/resolutions/A_HRC_RES_7_19.pdf. Fortunately, this document has no legal force. Western observers have widely criticized the move. See Paula Schriefer, "The Wrong Way to Combat 'Islamophobia'," *New York Times*, Nov. 9, 2010, Op-ed section, available at www.nytimes.com/2010/11/10/opinion/10iht-edschriefer.html.

[22] For example, the Pakistani criminal code, Section 295-C, reads: "*Use of Derogatory Remarks in Respect of the Holy Prophet*: Whoever by words, either spoken or written, or by visible representation, or by any imputation, innuendo, or insinuation, directly or indirectly defiles the sacred name of the Holy Prophet Muhammed (peace be upon him) shall be punished with death, or imprisonment for life and shall also be liable to fine." Available at www.thepersecution.org/50years/paklaw.html.

[23] See Universal Declaration of Human Rights, GA Res. 217A (III) (1948), art. 19, and International Covenant on Civil and Political Rights, 999 UNTS 171 (1966), art. 19 ("ICCPR"). Almost all the members of the Organization of the Islamic Conference are parties to the Covenant. A list of states parties to the ICCPR is available at https://treaties.un.org/Pages/ViewDetails.aspx?src=TREATY&mtdsg_no=IV-4&chapter=4&clang=_en.

The *Selectivity Fallacy*. The Selectivity Fallacy is the practice of citing *only* the soft sources that support the desired norm, while omitting those that reject it. Examples abound. The precautionary principle, already cited, is only one of them; its defenders rarely cite dissenting voices. Another example is the opinion by the ICJ that declarations of independence do not violate international law.[24] The Court was asked to evaluate the conformity with international law of the declaration of independence by an assembly in the Serbian province of Kosovo. The Court concluded that the declaration was not in violation of international law. As the Court recognized, the parent states (those from which independence is sought) invariably and strenuously have objected to these declarations. Why doesn't their opposition count in assessing state practice? It is not hard for the Court to imagine that most states in the world would be hostile to declarations of independence by their own subjects and territories. Why then does it reach the conclusion that international law allows the declarations? (This opinion is silly on many counts, but here I address only the question of customary law.)[25]

The *Corrupt Pedigree Fallacy*. The Corrupt Pedigree Fallacy is an interesting phenomenon. It goes like this: A court (say, the ICJ) makes an assertion of law while deciding a case. For example, the ICJ says that "general practice" supports the rule that states do not have the right of collective self-defense against minor uses of force against them – a fallacious assertion made by the ICJ in the 1986 *Nicaragua Case*.[26] The Court failed to cite any practice, precedent, or consensus to support this assertion. Now this failure does not necessarily mean that the uttered proposition of law is false. Simply, the Court *itself* did not show it to be true; it cited no practice or consensus supporting the rule.

Now let us assume that the Court's assertion is indeed false; there is in fact no precedent, practice, or consensus supporting the rule. If this is so, further citations of this passage by lawyers will *consolidate and perpetuate* the legal error. A false proposition of law uttered by a court does not become true

[24] *Accordance with International Law of the Unilateral Declaration of Independence in Respect of Kosovo*, Advisory Opinion of 22 July 2010, 2010 ICJ Rep. 403.

[25] An anonymous reviewer has suggested that the Court only conceded that the parent states had objected to these declarations on the basis of *national* law, not international law. But it strains credulity to think that the parent states did not believe that under international law they had the right to keep their territory intact. One of the problems (not addressed in this chapter) in custom-type reasoning is the exaggeration of the *opinio juris* component of custom (also present in the *North Sea Continental Shelf Cases*). If parent states opposed these declarations of independence, then that opposition should count for purposes of customary analysis. It does not matter that these governments cited their own constitutions. (After all, why wouldn't they? The first and obvious violation of the rebel province is of the country's own constitution.)

[26] See *Military and Paramilitary Activities in and against Nicaragua (Nicaragua v. United States of America)*, Merits, Judgment of 27 June 1986, 1986 ICJ Rep. 14 ("*Nicaragua Case*").

by citing it over and over in subsequent litigation or academic writings. But then, something magical occurs: The repeated citations by the practitioners of fake custom become *themselves* "precedents" in support of the rule! Thus, a rule has been created out of thin air. In this way, a perpetuated judicial error replaces the stuff customary law is made of – practice and consensus.

The situation is even more serious when the Court makes a false assertion, not in a contentious proceeding, but in an advisory opinion. There, not only is the assertion false if it does not reflect practice or consensus, but it also has no legal force whatsoever. The assertion is just advisory. Yet practitioners of fake custom will treat it as an authoritative precedent regardless.

I believe the ICJ's view in the 2004 *Israeli Wall* advisory opinion that Israel lacked a right of self-defense against Palestinian attacks, and the view of the Court in the 2010 *Kosovo* advisory opinion that the principle of territorial integrity is applicable only among states and has no currency in domestic conflict, are mistaken assessments of the law.[27] Again, I may be wrong about this, but suppose I am right and these opinions wrongly stated the law. My point is that subsequently citing the errors as authoritative eventually will create the mirage of a new norm, one that, by definition, suffers from a congenital defect: It was never a customary law norm in the first place. Courts and commentators might perpetuate those judicial errors.

<u>The *False-Inferences-from-Vague-Generalities Fallacy*</u>. The False-Inferences-from-Vague-Generalities Fallacy is a common fake custom technique, and a variation of the Corrupt Pedigree Fallacy. A court says, without argument, that a broad corpus of law – say, the law of state responsibility or the law of self-determination – is now part of "general international law." Because of its breadth, this statement will almost always be true. Many of the rules in question are no longer mere treaty rules, but part of general international law. Still, it is virtually impossible to infer *specific* norms from this generality. For example, the ICJ has said in a nonbinding advisory opinion that "[t]he existence of the general obligation of States to ensure that activities within their

[27] The *Kosovo* opinion is cited above. The "*Israeli Wall*" opinion is *Legal Consequences of the Construction of a Wall in the Occupied Palestinian Territory*, Advisory Opinion of 9 July 2004, 2004 ICJ Rep. 136. For the Court's discussion of self-defense, see ibid., 194–95, paras. 138–42. Most of the commentary has been critical of the ICJ's treatment of self-defense in this opinion. See, e.g., Sean Murphy, "Self-Defense and the Israeli Wall Advisory Opinion: An Ipse Dixit from the ICJ?" 99 *American Journal of International Law* 62 (2005). So fake custom does not seem to have yet developed on this point. The question of territorial integrity as the right of a state to keep its territory together (and not, as the *Kosovo* Court said, a mere prohibition on outsiders breaking up the state's territory) is a much more open question, and it is hard to predict where the trend will go. Suffice it to say that I do not expect that states will accept an unrestrained right of secession. If so, the Court's bizarre suggestion may well fall into oblivion.

jurisdiction and control respect the environment of other States or of areas beyond national control is now part of the corpus of international law relating to the environment."[28]

Fair enough, but what can we infer from this statement in terms of precise norms? The answer is, virtually nothing, for two reasons. First, the opinion itself is not binding, so *the fact* that the Court said this cannot by itself create the norm. Second, the fact that the corpus of environmental law has generally become customary law does not mean that *specific* norms from that corpus are now customary law.

Suppose someone claims that this dictum means that all states have now a customary law obligation to reduce carbon emissions by 50 percent. This is of course absurd. The asserted specific environmental obligation must come from what states believe and do. This means that any responsible assertion of the law must examine the practice of states (classical theory) or the universal consensus of states (modern theory) to determine which environmental norms are binding and which are not.

A frequent ploy of fake custom practitioners is to avoid this step. In doing so, they perpetrate a double fallacy. First, they take the ICJ's nonbinding opinion as reflecting a true norm. Second, they purport to infer from the generality of the Court's statement any environmental rule they happen to favor, such as the obligation to curb carbon emissions.

So, either the Court expresses the rule in general, vague terms or in precise, definite terms. In the first case, no specific norm (such as "states have a duty to reduce carbon emissions by 50 percent") can be derived from the vague generality alone, even if the generality (such as "the laws regarding the protection of the environment are now part of customary law") is true. In the second case, when the Court states a precise norm, it has to be supported by either practice or universal agreement. In the example of carbon emissions, even if the Court had expressed the rule in sufficiently precise terms, it would not have met the test for customary law. In order for the Court's statement to be true, it must be true that states universally agree on that precise norm.

Often, then, practitioners of fake custom do not even bother to cite any documents; they simply assert, as in the example just given, that X is supported by "general practice." The audience, of course, does not have the means to refute this assertion. Contrast this with the assertion that X is supported by treaty. The audience can consult the treaty, a written document, and so (interpretation issues aside) can easily refute the assertion. A prominent feature

[28] *Legality of the Threat or Use of Nuclear Weapons*, Advisory Opinion of 8 July 1996, 1996 ICJ Rep. 226, 241–42, para. 29.

of fake custom is that its practitioners try to bamboozle their audience, who in order to check the truth of the statement (the assertion of the customary norm) would have to conduct complicated and time-consuming research on diplomatic history. Practitioners of fake custom trade on the audience's high informational costs.

3.4 FURTHER EXAMPLES OF JUDICIAL FAKE CUSTOM

Here I give some further examples of the use of fake custom in judicial opinions. These examples are from the ICJ. I hasten to say that not all international courts abuse custom in the same way. For example, the International Criminal Tribunal for the former Yugoslavia ("ICTY") has done a credible job of reviewing precedent to find customary rules with some respectable degree of robustness. And the ICJ itself has improved on this score, particularly in its decision in the 2012 *Jurisdictional Immunities of the State Case*.[29]

As already noted, in the 1986 *Nicaragua Case*, the Court reached the surprising conclusion that states did not have the right of collective self-defense against uses of force short of an armed attack. Until that decision, most scholars thought that states had the right of self-defense against any violation of Article 2(4) of the UN Charter, and that in those cases they had to abide, as always, by the rule of proportionality.[30] A minor armed attack, most people thought, authorized a minor defensive response, and this included the right to seek and receive the proportionate aid of allies. In reaching the opposite conclusion, the Court did not cite one single precedent. It only cited a non-binding General Assembly resolution and assumed that customary law could be deduced from that resolution.[31] Leaving aside the fact that the text of the resolution did not authorize the Court's conclusion on collective self-defense, sound legal method requires that the use of General Assembly resolutions

[29] See *Jurisdictional Immunities of the State (Germany v. Italy)*. I am referring to the Court's extensive review of national legislation and domestic judicial decisions in that case. This is a marked improvement over previous cases, where the Court contented itself with vague references to practice and lazy citations to UN General Assembly resolutions and similar documents.

[30] Article 2(4) of the UN Charter reads: "All Members shall refrain in their international relations from the threat or use of force against the territorial integrity or political independence of any state, or in any other manner inconsistent with the Purposes of the United Nations."

[31] The resolution in question is GA Res. 2625 (XXV) (1970). It can be found at www.un-documents.net/a25r2625.htm. In its 2005 ruling in the *Congo-Uganda Case*, the Court reiterated the view that certain paragraphs of Resolution 2625 were declaratory of customary law. Again, no precedents were cited in support of this statement. See *Armed Activities on the Territory of the Congo (Democratic Republic of the Congo v. Uganda)*, Judgment of 19 December 2005, 2005 ICJ Rep. 168, 226–27, para. 162 ("*Congo-Uganda Case*").

be supported by an examination of the practice of states.[32] But the Court did none of that.

In the *Nicaragua Case*, the most important case on use of force, the ICJ thus failed to cite any state practice in support of its conclusion. The Court's conclusion could have been defended, perhaps, on policy grounds. In particular, confining the exercise of the right of collective self-defense to situations involving full-fledged armed attacks arguably reduces the escalation of conflicts, since states will only be able to summon their allies in the worst cases (that is, assuming that international law puts effective constraints on state action in these kinds of cases). Had the Court ruled on policy grounds, instead of making up a rule from thin air, its conclusion would have been more credible.

In the 2005 *Armed Activities in the Territory of the Congo Case*, the Court resorted several times to customary international law. As in the *Nicaragua Case*, the Court concluded that the paragraphs in General Assembly Resolution 2625 concerning assistance to rebels were declaratory of customary law.[33] It cited no precedent in support of that conclusion. No one doubts that there is some default rule against such kind of intervention, but an examination of state practice would have been highly desirable here, if only to delineate the contours of that rule. For example, such an examination could have shed light on such questions as whether intervention in support of democratic rebels fighting a genocidal or otherwise illegitimate regime is also prohibited. Citing UN General Assembly resolutions is a lazy and inaccurate way to determine customary law. The Charter is crystal clear that UN General Assembly resolutions are not binding. Under some conditions they may provide some evidence of *opinio juris*, but in that case they need accompanying practice. And in the modern theory of custom, perhaps only a unanimous resolution equals universal agreement.

Elsewhere in this opinion, the Court again decided not to examine state practice in determining the nature of occupation in customary law. The Court turned only to the 1907 Hague Conventions. Now perhaps the Court got it right this time because it is likely that the 1907 Hague Conventions

[32] Resolution 2625 is a Cold War relic that should deserve little attention anyway. But even should one treat it, mistakenly, as reflecting customary law, it does not support the Court's reading. It does not even hint at the distinctions that the Court makes in the *Nicaragua Case*. It reads, in pertinent part: "Nothing in the foregoing paragraphs shall be construed as enlarging or diminishing in any way the scope of the provisions of the Charter concerning cases in which the use of force is lawful." Since the resolution nowhere discusses the contours of self-defense, it does not come close to suggesting that states that are the victim of military operations short of an armed attack do not have the right to ask assistance of third states.

[33] *Congo-Uganda Case*, 229–30, para. 172. See also ibid., 242, para. 214.

reflected customary law. Yet, again, that conclusion must be supported by an examination of actual state practice. My objection is not to the correctness of the holding itself, but to the soundness of the method used by the Court.

The failure of the ICJ to justify customary law's pedigree creates a corrupted chain of legal justification. The first time, the principle is said to be part of customary law, without any demonstration. The second time, since the Court had already said it is customary law, the Court will make it customary law by citing its own precedent.[34]

In its 2002 *Arrest Warrant* decision, the ICJ concluded that customary international law afforded foreign ministers absolute immunity from criminal jurisdiction.[35] However, one searches in vain for any citation of any international incident or precedent concerning this issue. Instead, the Court performed a purely functional analysis; it stated that foreign ministers enjoy absolute immunity because otherwise they could not fulfill their duties. This argument may be right or wrong, but my point here is that surely there are incidents in diplomatic history, bits of state practice, that the Court could have cited to support this view. And, distressingly, the Court took the controversial view that foreign ministers are immune for the acts perpetrated during their tenure even after they cease performing official functions.[36] This dictum, which was unnecessary for the resolution of the case, was totally unsupported. There was no citation of state practice or of any other authority, except the Court's rather feeble functional analysis.

In its conclusions, the Court told us that it "has carefully examined State practice, including national legislation and those few decisions of national higher courts, such as the House of Lords or the French Court of Cassation." Yet the Court declared itself "unable to deduce from this practice that there exists under customary international law any form of exception to the rule according immunity from criminal jurisdiction and inviolability to incumbent Ministers for Foreign Affairs, where they are suspected of having committed war crimes or crimes against humanity."[37] We are not told, however, what state practice the Court has examined, nor the reasoning by which the Court thinks this practice supports its view of the issue. This type of judicial technique is

34 Another example: In the *Oil Platforms Case*, the ICJ cites the *Nicaragua Case* for the dubious propositions that collective self-defense must be preceded by a formal request and that any use of force against the third-state victim must have been an "armed attack" and nothing short of that. *Oil Platforms Case (Islamic Republic of Iran v. United States of America)*, Judgment of 6 November 2003, 2003 ICJ Rep. 161, 186–87, para. 51.

35 *Arrest Warrant of 11 April 2000 (Democratic Republic of the Congo v. Belgium)*, Judgment of 14 February 2002, 2002 ICJ Rep. 3, 21–22, paras. 52–54.

36 Ibid., 25–26, para. 61.

37 Ibid., 24, para. 58.

regrettable and undermines the authority and persuasiveness of the Court's decisions.

Sometimes the ICJ refuses to infer normative consequences from practice without giving sufficient explanation of exactly why practice does not count. The Court does this by manipulating the concept of *opinio juris*. In its leading cases on custom, the 1969 *North Sea Continental Shelf Cases*, the Netherlands and Denmark offered in evidence several incidents in which states had used the method of equidistance to delimit their continental shelves. They argued that these incidents constituted enough practice to support a customary rule to that effect. The Court, however, refused to accept those incidents as evidence of custom. In doing so, the Court simply asserted that *opinio juris* was lacking, since the Netherlands and Denmark could not show that states used the equidistance rule out of a sense of legal duty.[38] But, of course, the proof that the Court required from Denmark and the Netherlands was impossible to produce. States do not proclaim that they are following international law when they agree to a delimitation or to anything else. Practice has to be *interpreted*. The outcome in that case, to my mind, rests solely on the fact that in the eyes of the Court the use of the equidistance method would have been unfair, not on a serious evaluation of precedent.

3.5 WHY FAKE CUSTOM SHOULD BE REJECTED

Genuine custom, both classical and modern, is an indispensable source of international law. But fake custom should be rejected. If international law is going to have relevance and gain the respect of the public and of our conventional colleagues, international lawyers should identify a workable, operational definition of customary law that can serve the ethical and functional goals that international law is supposed to serve. If we do not do so, customary law will become a pallid tool for advocacy and partisanship.

If international law lacks a reasonably robust account of the pedigree of customary law – an account of what counts as customary law – then it is hopelessly indeterminate. Anything goes. Almost any position we favor can be labeled "custom." This is exactly what is going on today in the world of international law. By the world of international law I mean not only international legal scholarship but also the decisions of some international courts and the stated views of governments.

[38] *North Sea Continental Shelf Cases (Federal Republic of Germany v. Denmark; Federal Republic of Germany v. Netherlands)*, Judgment of 20 February 1969, 1969 ICJ Rep. 3, 44, para. 77.

We are witnessing the phenomenon of custom inflation. Lawyers often label customary law any rule they favor. In doing so, they make no serious attempt to ground the favored rule in state practice or to justify it on policy or moral grounds, even less to find out whether the rule meets the rather strict requirements of *opinio juris*. Yet, as I said, the traditional appeal of customary law is that it reflects the aggregate sense of right and wrong in the community, one that either has been elaborated and has simmered over a relatively long period of time, or has been genuinely and universally agreed on by the international community. Genuine customary law reflects an equilibrium of some sort. The practice of fake custom misses all that. It misses what is most important about customary law – its ability to reflect institutional history and filter state expectations about what is lawful, mutually beneficial, ethical, or efficient and, for any of those reasons, expected.[39]

Because of the ubiquity and frequency of fake custom advocacy, in international legal practice customary law arguments have lost their robustness, and so the support that those positions may gain from being labeled "law" is just illusory. The problem with this trend is not so much that lawyers make value choices; everyone does. Rather, the problem is that they disguise a value choice as an objective norm, one that (they pretend) is not chosen by them as the best but is already enshrined in the law. This point requires elaboration.

3.6 CAN NATURAL LAW SAVE FAKE CUSTOM?

The practitioner of fake custom can perhaps retort in the following way: "The norms you derisively call fake custom are in reality norms that are highly desirable for reasons of morality, fairness, or efficiency. The concept of custom should not be understood in purely positivist terms. 'Custom' is a term of art. It includes not only diplomatic process – the practice and consensus of states – but also norms that are ethically required or desirable. If a reduction of carbon emissions is required for ethical reasons, then it is part of custom, understood in a non-positivist way. So custom includes norms that are required for positivist reasons (what you called classical and modern theories of custom) and norms that are required for ethical reasons. The obligation on the state not to torture, for example, does not depend on practice or consensus. It is an ethical

39 Thus I partly agree with Noora Arajärvi, "From the 'Demands of Humanity': The Formulation of *Opinio Juris* in Decisions of International Criminal Tribunals and the Need for a Renewed Emphasis on State Practice," in this volume. There she denounces, as do I, some forms of fake custom. However, unlike her, I would include ethical imperatives as part of international law. I just object to labeling those imperatives "custom."

obligation, and as such forms as much a part of international law as norms with a positivist pedigree."

This reply touches on the important jurisprudential question of the relationship between law and morality. Let us concede that the objector's jurisprudential position is correct and that morally binding rules are as much a part of international law as norms with a positivist pedigree (a position I myself accept, as explained later in the chapter). Morality may be binding on states, and in that sense some moral norms are part of international law.

The problem is that *this is not the argument that the practitioner of fake custom makes*. She does not claim that the obligation to reduce carbon emissions is legally binding because it is morally binding. She claims instead that such an obligation is grounded in *positivist* sources that her audience will recognize. She claims (falsely) that the obligation to reduce emissions is supported by practice (classical theory) or universal consensus (modern theory). She claims, that is, that people need not look beyond the positivist sources to find the obligation in question.

In truth, the practitioner of fake custom lacks the courage to say what she really thinks – that states *ought to* reduce carbon emissions *regardless* of practice or consensus, and that this non-positivistic obligation is part and parcel of international law. She conceals this because people are skeptical about natural law arguments. Most people have positivist intuitions. They believe that if a norm is supported only by moral reasons, then it is not law. That is why the norm entrepreneur wants the audience to believe that the obligation is hard law, as it were, and not just a moral stance. She will not succeed in mobilizing her audience if she confesses that the requirement to reduce emissions is a mere moral requirement. She has to fake positivist support for the norm.

The problem, in other words, is that lawyers often have a moral view on an issue. They are afraid of admitting this, so they dress that moral view in the garments of objective legal analysis. They present the value choice (or advocacy) as if it were the outcome of value-free legal reasoning. So I do not suggest that lawyers should avoid value choices. I suggest, instead, that lawyers and courts should acknowledge that often diplomatic history (in the form of state practice) is normatively indeterminate and that rules should be defended *on their merits*, and not by feigning positivist support for them.[40]

[40] Perhaps Ronald Dworkin's method of law-as-integrity comes close to this (whether or not he is right about his defense of specific rules). See Ronald Dworkin, "How Law is Like Literature," in Ronald Dworkin, A *Matter of Principle* 146 (Cambridge, MA: Harvard University Press, 1985). Dworkin thinks that propositions of law are the children of both history and philosophy. In international law, this means that an interpreter may not disregard practice or treaties, but must put them in their best possible light, which means making the best available *substantive* arguments for them.

3.7 CUSTOMARY LAW AS CLAIM-ORIENTED?

Can the technique of fake custom be nonetheless vindicated by a different respectable theory of law? Some writers have attempted to do so. One move is to say that custom is claim-oriented, and that in any international dispute the only issue is who has the better claim.[41] On this view, any claim that a party makes in an international dispute, no matter how unfounded, can potentially become custom. The very fact of articulating the claim turns it into a precedent – an embryonic rule, as it were – that can fail or succeed, depending on its comparative strength when measured against a rival claim. Suppose that a government argues in court that customary law allows sovereign states to renege from the voluntary acceptance of that court's jurisdiction for the settlement of disputes concerning their foreign debt.[42] Suppose this claim is unsupported by state practice or general consensus. Nonetheless, on the view we are discussing, the *very articulation* of this false claim enhances its normative status. If the Court allows the claim, it is thought, it has attained legal status; it has become, perhaps, a new rule of international law.[43]

There is a sense in which this claim is correct. A customary rule gets started at some point in time. If it is a classical norm, the practice has to get started. If it is a modern norm, there has to be a first statement, a proposal. In both cases, the first act encounters either acquiescence or resistance. If the first act encounters acquiescence (as the Truman Proclamation on the continental shelf did), then it ripens into a customary norm. If the first act encounters resistance (as has occurred with some statements regarding specific obligations to cut down on carbon emissions), then it will be an aborted norm. The startling feature of custom is that the *inaugural* act or articulation of the norm is fake custom, a false statement of the law. This has been known, of course, for a long time: in order to get a custom started, a state must violate existing law. If, notwithstanding the fact that the initial act was fake, other states accept the proposed norm, then it may mature into a genuine norm. A fake claim, *in this case*, may generate real custom.

However, this is a limited case that is confined to claims made by states in particularly solemn situations. Practitioners of fake custom are not entitled

41 See D'Amato, *The Concept of Custom in International Law*, 17–18. I am not sure how much practice D'Amato would require before concluding that a claim is plausible. He does write that what matters is the *relative* persuasiveness of the claim, and not any preconceived theory of custom. Ibid. I read this as suggesting that a claim may succeed if it defeats a weaker claim, regardless of whether the winning claim meets the more robust tests of custom that I have suggested.

42 Inspired by Argentina's default in 2014.

43 I say "perhaps," because the claim-oriented view must allow for a theory of judicial error.

to extend this feature of custom (that is, the fact that the inaugural act of custom is not law but a departure from law, and thus fake custom) to claims made by anyone, in any context, and then try to mimic the customary process by repeating the fake norm incessantly in the hope that sloppy international scholars will start treating it as customary law. Thus, the statements by activists, nongovernmental organizations, various sorts of international bureaucrats, interest groups, a majority of the UN General Assembly, and other norm entrepreneurs are congenitally unable to generate custom. The only kind of fake custom that has the power to generate law is the false legal statement or act by a government that is clearly followed by wide acquiescence in the international community.

If fake custom is not confined in this way, then anyone can claim anything they want, say it is law, and hope that their superior rhetoric will persuade the audience – in particular, a court. With such an approach, we do not need the classical or modern theories of custom; we do not need state practice or universal consent. Just about any claim will do. Nonetheless, the view as formulated should be rejected. In reality, the claim rests on the skeptical premise that there is no positive international law; all legal propositions are *ex aequo et bono*. Maybe that view is correct, and there is no international law; it is all a mirage. But if so, the theorist must recognize this fact, and not dress these claims in the garments of customary law.

3.8 ARE INTERNATIONAL HUMAN RIGHTS CUSTOMARY LAW?

No area of international law exemplifies fake custom better than the law of international human rights. I here defend two seemingly contradictory propositions: (1) most claims that human rights are custom are fake; and (2) most human rights are binding, not because they satisfy a positivist test, but because governments are morally required to respect human rights. I will only sketch my position here; a full defense and elaboration will have to await future research.

Suppose we try to determine if a human right listed in a declaration or a treaty is *also* part of customary law. To do so, we must see if the right in question meets the test of genuine custom. Under the first form of genuine custom, the classical theory of custom, the human right in question would result from a dense and robust practice by states that not only respect the right but feel normatively pressured to do so. The prohibition of genocide almost surely falls in that category. States refrain from genocide and feel strong pressure to continue refraining from genocide.

Under the second form of genuine custom, states must have reached a specific and universal consensus about the human right in question, even if that consensus is unsupported by state practice. Two examples that come to mind are the prohibition of official torture and the prohibition of indefinite arbitrary detention. There is no question that many governments violate these rights with alarming frequency. Hence, the classical theory of custom cannot support the view that these rights are part of customary law, because the practice is missing; in fact, there is significant *contrary* practice. But in these cases there is a specific, universal consensus about the existence of these rights. States (even the bad states!) publicly proclaim that they consider official torture and indefinite arbitrary detention as prohibited governmental activities, and that therefore citizens have a right not to suffer these affronts. If this is correct, then those two rights are customary law because they satisfy the second test for genuine custom. I do not regard this as a fake consensus; the states that overtly support the prohibition of torture yet continue to violate it are acting opportunistically. They will deny the facts, surely, or try to avoid condemnation in various ways. But their (hypocritical, one may say) admission that official torture is prohibited contributes to the consensus. They accept the rule; surely admitting that they are proud torturers has unacceptable reputational costs.[44]

But what is the customary status of other, very important human rights listed in treaties and declarations? To focus, let us consider a very specific human right – the right to criticize one's own government in print. The first task is to avoid the False-Inference-from-Vague-Generalities Fallacy. This would be to say that freedom of expression is "generally recognized" in documents and declarations, and *therefore* people have the customary human right to criticize their government in print. This is, as I explained, bad logic and fake custom. That *some* vague concept of free expression is "generally recognized" does not mean ipso facto that this *specific* right, the right to criticize one's government in print, is customary law. We must turn instead to our tests for genuine customary law.

I do not need to conduct extensive research to prove that this specific right is *not* supported by state practice. More than half the world represses dissent of any kind, and some governments, while more liberal in general with respect to speech, expressly prohibit criticism of the government.[45] Nor does this right, I'm afraid, meet the test for the second form of genuine custom.

44 At the other extreme, there are human rights in treaties that almost everyone agrees are not part of customary law – for example, the right to an annual paid vacation. See Lepard, *Customary International Law*, 326.

45 See Freedom House, *Freedom of the Press* (2014), 4, available at http://freedomhouse.org/sites/default/files/FOTP2014_Overview_Essay.pdf.

While governments certainly do not go around boasting of how much dissent they suppress, there is no consensus about the limits to free speech. For a few states, expression should be extremely robust; for others, expression admits of important legal restraints; and still others have expressly said that the right to free expression does *not* include the right to criticize the government.[46]

So it seems that even under a liberal theory of genuine custom we would have to conclude that the right to criticize one's own government in print is not part of customary law. An honest positivist lawyer (one who does not want to perpetrate fake custom) would have to say that the right in question may be protected by treaty (and even this is dubious, due to the generality of the term "freedom of expression" in human rights treaties) or that the right in question may be a moral right, but not a human right, under international law.

I have always found this view inadequate, but it is at least honest because it does not pretend that the right to criticize one's own government is customary law. The lawyer who says that this right is morally compelling but unfortunately not part of customary law is avoiding fake custom. Why then do I think the view is inadequate? Because *I do not believe that everything that is legally binding in international law must be traceable to treaty or custom.*[47] Specifically with respect to human rights, I think that *compelling human rights* are binding *in law* as much as if they had been enacted by treaty or custom. The right to criticize one's government in print is legally binding on governments because it is *morally* binding. Again, I cannot offer a full demonstration here, but I can safely assume that political speech is at the core of free expression, and that it would be essentially nullified if citizens could not criticize those who hold political power over them. So we do not need to straitjacket the right to criticize government into a contrived customary law claim where we make up norms out of nonexistent practice or imaginary consensus. Suppressing dissent is morally unacceptable, period, and international law does not deserve the label "law" if it does not uphold these basic ethical imperatives.

Now, I readily concede that determining which rights are morally binding in this way is not any easier than manufacturing a fake custom claim. But I am hopeful that a moral theory of human rights, by which I mean the rights we have against our governments, is less problematic than a full-fledged moral theory or a full-fledged theory of human nature. A properly enriched Lockean or Kantian approach would go a long way toward specifying which

[46] For examples, see Symposium, "Human Rights in Asia: China and the Bangkok Declaration," 2 *Buffalo Journal of International Law* 215 (1996), 220.

[47] For an application of this view, see my article, "Natural Law as Part of International Law: The Case of the Armenian Genocide."

rights are indispensable to free institutions.[48] The dilemma, to my mind, is this: Either international law does not recognize the right to criticize government or it does recognize this right. If the first, international law is a morally corrupt system that deserves neither our interest nor our allegiance. If the second, because the right to criticize government is not supported by positivist sources, then at least some moral requirements are part and parcel of international law. Legal language is a branch of moral language; it is not something inherently different. I accept, then, the second horn of the dilemma.

3.9 CONCLUSION

In summary, I propose distinguishing between *genuine* customary law and *fake* customary law. Genuine customary law in turn comprises two subcategories. First, genuine customary law includes classical international law as traditionally defined – a robust practice supported by strong pressure to conform (*opinio juris*). Second, genuine customary law includes a *specific, strong international consensus*, even if not supported by a robust practice.[49] My proposal is more liberal than the traditional version; it includes not only rules supported by state practice but also rules that have been widely agreed on by states, even if unsupported by practice. Genuine customary law thus defined reflects the aggregate sense of right and wrong in the community that has been elaborated and developed over a relatively long period of time or embodied in a strong consensus.

Fake custom, on the other hand, consists, as I explained, of those putative rules that are put forth by international lawyers and others but lack the pedigree of genuine custom. They are "rules" that international lawyers would *like* to be genuine rules of law, but in reality are not. A rule of fake custom is characterized, not by state practice or strong consensus, but by advocacy, partisan rhetoric, and unsupported assertion. The practice of fake custom has unfortunately degraded international law in the eyes of the general public, the courts, and the conventional legal community.

Rejecting fake custom does not mean adopting the positivist thesis of the separation between law and morality. On the contrary, an honest account of

[48] For a full defense of liberalism as the foundation of international law and justice, see Loren Lomasky and Fernando R. Tesón, *Justice at a Distance: Expanding Freedom Globally* (Cambridge: Cambridge University Press, 2015).

[49] To the examples discussed above I may add the execution of juveniles, declared unconstitutional (in part based on international consensus) by the U.S. Supreme Court. See *Roper v. Simmons*, 543 U.S. 551 (2005).

international obligation allows us to recognize norms that do not meet the test for custom but are nonetheless indispensable to a minimally justified international order and, for that reason, legally binding even in the absence of positivist support. But fake custom lacks the appeal of genuine law, is intellectually dishonest, and therefore has no place in international law.

4

The Role of Consent and Uncertainty in the Formation of Customary International Law

Niels Petersen

4.1 INTRODUCTION

The concept of customary law is a fascinating research topic.[1] There is no other source of international law that has been subject to an equally intensive scholarly debate. Yet many aspects of the formation of customary law still remain a mystery,[2] and one has the impression that there is little methodological guidance underlying the identification of customary norms. One of the areas of customary law doctrine in which this is particularly obvious is the question of how much state practice is needed for the formation of a customary norm. In this connection, there are two competing schools of thought that emphasize different characteristics of a customary norm.[3] Some scholars accent the practice requirement and see customary norms as "crystallization points" of patterns of state behavior,[4] while others focus on *opinio juris* and

1 See Michael Byers, *Custom, Power and the Power of Rules: International Relations and Customary International Law* (Cambridge: Cambridge University Press, 1999), xi.

2 See Martti Koskenniemi, "The Pull of the Mainstream," 88 *Michigan Law Review* 1946 (1990), 1947 (referring to customary law as a "theoretical minefield").

3 See Martti Koskenniemi, *From Apology to Utopia: The Structure of International Legal Argument* (Cambridge: Cambridge University Press, 2nd ed. 2005), 389–97.

4 See Maurice H. Mendelson, "The Formation of Customary International Law," 272 *Recueil des cours* 155 (1998); Christoph Engel, "The Emergence of a New Rule of Customary Law: An Experimental Contribution," 7 *Review of Law and Economics* 767 (2011).

perceive customary law as a type of tacit agreement,[5] which can only bind those states that have consented to it.[6]

In practice, however, we see a mixture of both positions, which creates certain tensions.[7] Customary norms can, on the one hand, be formed without the explicit consent of each individual state. The identification of a customary norm only requires the observation of a general and consistent pattern of state conduct.[8] States can thus also be bound if they were simply inactive during the phase of the formation of the customary rule or if they were not yet in existence as states.[9] On the other hand, every state has the opportunity to opt out of a specific customary norm if it explicitly objects to its formation and can thus be considered a "persistent objector,"[10] which can only be explained from a voluntarist standpoint focusing on consent.

5 Some authors even perceive state practice as a dispensable element of the definition of customary law. See, e.g., Bin Cheng, "United Nations Resolutions on Outer Space: 'Instant' International Customary Law?" 5 *Indian Journal of International Law* 23 (1965); Andrew T. Guzman, "Saving Customary International Law," 27 *Michigan Journal of International Law* 115 (2005); Curtis A. Bradley, "Customary International Law Adjudication as Common Law Adjudication," in *Custom's Future: International Law in a Changing World*, edited by Curtis A. Bradley 34 (Cambridge: Cambridge University Press, 2016). See also Brian D. Lepard, *Customary International Law: A New Theory with Practical Applications* (New York: Cambridge University Press, 2010), 98 (arguing that state practice is dispensable in most cases, while it is sometimes still necessary as critical evidence of *opinio juris*); Fernando R. Tesón, "Fake Custom," in this volume (arguing that a general consensus can sometimes lead to the emergence of a customary norm even if there is significant deviating state practice).

6 For such a voluntarist position, see, e.g., Godefridus J.H. van Hoof, *Rethinking the Sources of International Law* (Deventer: Kluwer Law and Taxation Publishers, 1983), 290; Prosper Weil, "Towards Relative Normativity in International Law?" 77 *American Journal of International Law* 413 (1983); Karol Wolfke, *Custom in Present International Law* (Dordrecht: Martinus Nijhoff Publishers, 2nd rev. ed. 1993), 87.

7 One expression of this mixture of both positions is the two-element approach, according to which the establishment of a norm of customary international law requires both state practice and *opinio juris*. On this approach, see Michael Wood, Special Rapporteur, "Third Report on Identification of Customary International Law," UN Doc. A/CN.4/682 (2015).

8 See Byers, *Custom, Power and the Power of Rules*, 130; Christian Tomuschat, "International Law: Ensuring the Survival of Mankind on the Eve of a New Century," 281 *Recueil des cours* 13 (1999), 326; Patrick Daillier, Mathias Forteau, Alain Pellet, and Nguyen Quoc Dinh, *Droit International Public* (Paris: LGDJ, 8th ed. 2009), 360.

9 On the debate on whether states are bound by customary rules that were formed before those states came into existence, see Georges Abi-Saab, *The Newly Independent States and International Law* (Geneva: Carnegie Endowment for International Peace, 1963), 8–10; Jonathan I. Charney, "The New States and International Legal Order," 118 *Recueil des cours* 1 (1966); Michael Schweitzer, *Das Völkergewohnheitsrecht und seine Geltung für neuentstehende Staaten* (Bad Homburg: Verlag Gehlen, 1969).

10 See *Fisheries Case (United Kingdom v. Norway)*, Judgment of 18 December 1951, 1951 ICJ Rep. 116, 131 (generally regarded as the main authority on the persistent objector principle). The term "persistent objector" was introduced into the discussion by Ian Brownlie in his treatise, Ian Brownlie, *Principles of Public International Law* (Oxford: Oxford University Press,

According to this interpretation of customary law, there is thus one decisive difference between legal obligations imposed by treaty and those stemming from custom: Treaty law is an opt-in system. A state is only part of the legal regime if it has explicitly consented to it. Customary law, in contrast, is an opt-out system. States are bound by customary rules unless they explicitly object to their formation. Despite this difference, there is one common denominator: In principle, a state cannot be bound by a customary norm against its will. The justification for this rule is the "*Lotus* principle," according to which states can only be bound by a legal norm if they have consented to it.[11] In *Lotus*, the Permanent Court of International Justice ("PCIJ") had to decide a dispute between France and Turkey following an accident between a French steamship and a Turkish steamer, which killed eight Turkish nationals. When Turkey tried the French officer on watch duty during the incident, France claimed that Turkey had no jurisdiction for such a criminal trial. The Court affirmed:

> The rules of law binding upon States therefore emanate from their own free will as expressed in conventions or by usages generally accepted as expressing principles of law and established in order to regulate the relations between these co-existing independent communities or with a view to the achievement of common aims. Restrictions upon the independence of States cannot therefore be presumed.[12]

Because international law did not contain an explicit limitation concerning Turkey's criminal jurisdiction in this case, the Court held that Turkey's

1966), 8. However, the principle has not remained without substantial critique. See, e.g., Jonathan I. Charney, "The Persistent Objector Rule and the Development of Customary International Law," 56 *British Yearbook of International Law* 1 (1985); Christian Tomuschat, "Obligations Arising for States without or against their Will," 241 *Recueil des cours* 195 (1993), 284–90; Patrick Dumberry, "Incoherent and Ineffective: The Concept of Persistent Objector Revisited," 59 *International Law & Comparative Law Quarterly* 779 (2010); J. Patrick Kelly, "Customary International Law in Historical Context: The Exercise of Power without General Acceptance," in this volume. For a defense of this principle and a more detailed discussion of it, see Ted L. Stein, "The Approach of the Different Drummer: The Principle of the Persistent Objector in International Law," 26 *Harvard International Law Journal* 457 (1985); Pierre-Marie Dupuy, "A propos de l'opposabilité de la coutume générale: enquête brève sur l'objecteur persistant," in *Le droit international au service de la paix, de la justice et du développement*, edited by Michel Virally 257 (Paris: Pedone, 1991); Prosper Weil, "Le droit international en quête de son identité," 237 *Recueil des cours* 9 (1992), 189–201; Wolfke, *Custom in Present International Law*, 66–67; Mendelson, "The Formation of Customary International Law," 227–44; Olufemi Elias, "Persistent Objector," in *Max Planck Encyclopedia of Public International Law*, vol. VIII, edited by Rüdiger Wolfrum 280 (Oxford: Oxford University Press, 2012).

11 *Case of the* S.S. *"Lotus" (France v. Turkey)*, Judgment of 7 September 1927, PCIJ Series A, No. 10, 18.

12 Ibid.

conduct did not violate international law.[13] The *Lotus* principle thus establishes a freedom of action for states.[14] States cannot be bound by legal norms unless they have explicitly consented to them. This principle is often thought to be a major obstacle to international law's ability to resolve collective action problems.[15]

This chapter analyzes the assumption that customary law norms cannot bind states against their will. Relying on game theory, it distinguishes between different types of situations and argues that the role of consent differs according to the structure of the social problem that a potential norm is supposed to address. I approach the topic in two steps. First, I provide a short review of the academic discussion on the issue of consent in the formation of customary law norms. Second, I propose a taxonomy of three different types of situations and suggest individual solutions for each of these categories.

4.2 THE DISCUSSION OF CONSENT IN INTERNATIONAL LAW SCHOLARSHIP

When we look at state practice, we might observe three different types of state conduct with respect to a specific customary rule. States may affirm the legal rule through their practice; they may abstain from any relevant action regarding the rule; or they may explicitly oppose the formation of the rule. There is consensus in international law scholarship that explicit opposition of some states does not hinder a rule of customary law from emerging. The question is, however, how much explicit consent we need. Where is the tipping point at which objections by states do not merely make them persistent objectors, but are an obstacle to the emergence of a norm itself?[16] For example, a positive practice of three states would in most cases not be sufficient to create a customary norm even if there is no contradictory state practice or protests by other states. Furthermore, there is disagreement whether persistent objectors can, at least in certain situations, be bound by a rule of customary law to which they have explicitly objected.[17]

13 Ibid., 19.

14 See Albert Bleckmann, "Das Souveränitätsprintip im Völkerrecht," 23 *Archiv des Völkerrechts* 450 (1985), 464–68.

15 See Andrew T. Guzman, "Against Consent," 52 *Virginia Journal of International Law* 747 (2012).

16 See Elias, "Persistent Objector," paras. 2–6.

17 See Lepard, *Customary International Law*, 152–53 (only allowing for persistent objection under very limited circumstances). See also the critics of the doctrine of persistent objection cited above, in note 10.

International law scholarship is almost mute on the question of how much consent is required for the formation of a customary norm.[18] The issue that has so far received the most attention is the question of whether the practice of all states should be considered equally. Many authors claim, in particular, that greater weight should be given to states that are specially affected by a rule.[19] This idea was also expressed in an obiter dictum in the *North Sea Continental Shelf Cases*, in which the International Court of Justice ("ICJ") argued that "State practice, *including that of States whose interests are specially affected*, should [be] both extensive and virtually uniform."[20]

The idea seems to be intuitive for certain cases. If we consider, for instance, a rule of the law of the sea, then it is plausible that the practice of land-locked countries has less of an influence on the formation of a customary rule. Certainly, even land-locked countries may have a "stake in the game" if they flag vessels or want to exploit maritime resources. However, in certain fields their interests are usually not as strong as those of coastal states. For example, land-locked countries do not usually have a significant fishing fleet, so they have little interest in rules distributing fishing rights. For this reason, their views and practices should, in principle, have less weight when identifying a customary rule. That means that the number of states necessary for the establishment of a state practice depends on the number of states that actually have an interest in this particular area. There are thus different standards for parts of the law of the sea or space law than for the law of diplomatic relations, for example.

In the jurisprudence of international courts or in international legal doctrine, we do not find any clear-cut rule on how much consent or how much consistent state practice is necessary for the formation of customary law. The reason for this vagueness is the structure of the problem. The more clear-cut rules are, the more likely it is that they are either over- or under-inclusive.[21] This is especially the case if the reality that the rules are meant to govern is

18 The notable exception is Lepard, *Customary International Law*, 158 (giving guidelines on the required level of consent and requiring different levels of consent depending on how much a customary norm restricts state autonomy).

19 Richard R. Baxter, "Treaties and Custom," 129 *Recueil des cours* 25 (1970), 66; Wolfke, *Custom in Present International Law*, 78; Anthony Clark Arend, *Legal Rules and International Society* (New York: Oxford University Press, 1999), 92–93. The idea is framed slightly differently by Anthony D'Amato. See Anthony A. D'Amato, *The Concept of Custom in International Law* (Ithaca, NY: Cornell University Press, 1971), 96–97. He attributes different weight to the degree of a state's "sophistication" in international law.

20 *North Sea Continental Shelf Cases (Federal Republic of Germany v. Denmark; Federal Republic of Germany v. Netherlands)*, Judgment of 20 February 1969, 1969 ICJ Rep. 3, 42, para. 74 (emphasis added).

21 On this point, see Koskenniemi, *From Apology to Utopia*, 591–92.

complex, as a complex reality cannot be grasped by simple rules. If we said that we always need at least the practice of *x* number of states for the formation of a customary norm, this rule would not take into account that there are areas, such as space law, in which only very few states are able to engage in relevant practice at all.[22] Furthermore, if we require a simple majority of states, we might not be able to take into account differences in the size and the political importance of a state. These illustrations show that the formation of customary law is a complex exercise that needs to leave some flexibility to the lawyer or judge interpreting instances of state practice and *opinio juris* and assigning legal significance to them.

Therefore, I will not be able to give any clear rules of interpretation in this chapter. I can only give some guidelines. In particular, I want to second-guess the consent requirement underlying the theory of customary international law – the dogma that states cannot be bound by a rule of customary international law against their will.[23] In his book on customary international law, Brian Lepard has advocated the introduction of a majority rule when it comes to the evaluation of contradictory state practice.[24] In this context, he distinguishes between different game-theoretical incentive structures.[25] According to Lepard, pure coordination problems require a lower level of consent than a prisoners' dilemma situation. In the following discussion I try to show that this approach of differentiating the degree of consensus or state practice required according to the structure of the problem is accurate. However, I propose some crucial modifications with regard to the treatment of different situations.

4.3 DIFFERENT STANDARDS DEPENDING ON THE STRUCTURE OF THE "GAME"

The rationale of the *Lotus* principle is the idea that every society should be the master of its own fate. It corresponds to the basic liberal principle articulated by Immanuel Kant that "[f]reedom (independence from being constrained by another's choice), insofar as it can coexist with the freedom of every other in accordance with a universal law, is the only original right belonging to every

22 On this point, see Frans von der Dunk, "Customary International Law and Outer Space," in this volume.

23 But see also Alain Pellet, "The Normative Dilemma: Will and Consent in International Law-Making," 12 *Australian Yearbook of International Law* 22 (1992), 37 (arguing that the principle only exists in theory because states often do not have the necessary information to protest in time against the formation of a customary norm).

24 See Lepard, *Customary International Law*, 152–53.

25 Ibid., 158–61.

man by virtue of his humanity."[26] There is one important restriction to Kant's dictum. Freedom is not unlimited, but can only be exercised as long as it does not come into conflict with the freedom of other actors of the legal order. There may be situations in which the exercise of one state's freedom restricts the freedom of another state or another legal subject. In such situations, the *Lotus* principle does not help us solve the problem in the abstract because we have conflicting claims based on freedom of action.[27]

In this connection, I believe that we have to differentiate between three different types of situations. The first concerns the preservation of common goods. In these situations, everyone contributing to the common good would be the socially optimal solution. However, everyone has an individual incentive not to contribute. Second, I consider norms of coordination. In game-theoretical terms, such situations have multiple equilibria. States thus have to settle on one particular equilibrium in order to achieve coordination. However, the choice of the concrete equilibrium does not make any difference from a social point of view. The third type of situation involves ethical values, which I define as rules or principles that do not protect the interests of a particular state, but of third entities, such as individual human beings.

4.3.1 *Common Goods and the Prisoners' Dilemma*

In the context of this essay, I define common goods as all goods whose provision or maintenance causes externalities.[28] The most important common good is a pure public good that is characterized by non-rivalry of consumption and non-excludability of benefits.[29] Non-rivalry of consumption means that the quality of the good is not affected by the number of persons using it. Goods are non-excludable if nobody can be physically excluded from using the good. The classic example of a pure public good is the provision of national defense. The military is not more or less effective if it has to protect more people. Furthermore, people cannot be excluded from the benefit of defense even if they do not want to share it. However, pure public goods do not occur often in practice. On the other hand, there are a number of impure public goods, which are characterized by partial non-rivalry

26 Immanuel Kant, *The Metaphysics of Morals*, edited and translated by Mary J. Gregor (Cambridge: Cambridge University Press, 1996), 393.

27 See Koskenniemi, *From Apology to Utopia*, 257.

28 For a corresponding definition, see Katharina Holzinger, "Common Goods, Matrix Games and Institutional Responses," 9 *European Journal of International Relations* 173 (2003), 175.

29 See Paul A. Samuelson, "The Pure Theory of Public Expenditure," 36 *Review of Economics & Statistics* 387 (1954).

and/or partial non-excludability.[30] The most important subcategory for our purposes is common pool resources, whose main characteristic is non-excludability. Examples of common pool resources in the international arena are the protection of the global climate or the preservation of fish stocks.

The problem with common goods is that the benefit of the use of these resources is private, while the costs are social.[31] If we consider clean air as a common good, driving a car yields private benefits for the driver of the car, while the costs – the pollution of the air – have to be borne by everyone and are thus socialized. The incentive structure of the provision or maintenance of common goods typically is that of an "n-dimensional" prisoners' dilemma.[32] Individuals have a private incentive to use the resources beyond the level that would be socially optimal.

Consider an imaginary international society with four states. Each state can decide either to make use of a certain contaminating industry or not to use it. The use of the industry would yield a private benefit of three units for that particular state, while yielding social costs of four units because of air pollution. These costs have to be equally borne by all four states. From a global perspective, the best decision would be not to use the industry because a benefit of three and costs of four add up to a negative number. If all states made use of their industry, they would each get a benefit of three units for the use of their industry. The total social benefit of using the industry would thus amount to twelve units. At the same time, the states would produce overall social costs of sixteen units (four units by each state).

Privately, however, every state has an incentive to use the contaminating industry, because it bears just one unit of its own total social costs since these are equally distributed among all states (see Table 4.1). Therefore, if a state is the only user of the contaminating industry, it has a private benefit of two units (a benefit of three less a cost of one, which is the social cost of four divided by four, the number of states sharing it). Similarly, if another state also uses the

[30] See Richard Cornes and Todd Sandler, *The Theory of Externalities, Public Goods, and Club Goods* (New York: Cambridge University Press, 2nd ed. 1996), 9.

[31] See the seminal work by Garrett Hardin, Garrett Hardin, "The Tragedy of the Commons," 162 *Science* 1243 (1968).

[32] See Russell Hardin, "Collective Action as an Agreeable N-Prisoners' Dilemma," 16 *Behavioral Science* 472 (1971). As there are many forms of impure public goods, the incentive structure is not necessarily that of an n-dimensional prisoners' dilemma. See Katharina Holzinger, *Transnational Common Goods: Strategic Constellations, Collective Action Problems, and Multi-Level Provisions* (New York: Palgrave Macmillan, 2008), 32. However, I will limit the analysis in this section to situations involving prisoners' dilemmas, as this is the most important constellation.

TABLE 4.1 *Payoffs for Each State in Games Dealing with Negative Externalities*

Number of other states polluting	0	1	2	3
Pollute	2	1	0	–1
Do not pollute	0	–1	–2	–3

contaminating industry, it has a private benefit of one unit (a benefit of three less a cost of two, which is the new social cost of eight divided among the four states). Each state is always worse off if it chooses not to use the contaminating industry, because it receives no private benefit but must still bear its one-fourth share of the total pollution costs.

Accordingly, the best of all worlds for one state would be the one where it is the only state to make use of its contaminating industry, while all the others refuse to do so in order to protect the environment (see the left-most column in Table 4.1 in the row labeled "Pollute"). But even if all other states make use of their contaminating industries, it is still individually rational for the fourth state to make use of its industry as well (see the right-most column in Table 4.1, indicating that the payoff to the fourth state is still higher if it pollutes [resulting in a payoff of –1] than if it does not pollute [resulting in an even worse payoff of –3]). Polluting thus provides a relatively bigger payoff (two units more) than not polluting does. The state has to bear its one-fourth share of the environmental costs caused by the other three states in any event. Therefore, it will also make use of its own industry and transfer part of the costs of its use to the other three states.

The most reasonable thing to do in such a situation from the standpoint of maximizing social welfare seems to be to strike an agreement through a treaty between all states concerned prohibiting the use of contaminating industries. As the game is played repeatedly in reality, there is a strong likelihood that states will honor the agreement if they want the other parties to the treaty to comply as well.[33] However, what do we do if there is no agreement? Let us assume that three states abstain from polluting the air with the expectation that the others act likewise, while a fourth state continues to use its contaminating industry. Is this practice sufficient to form a customary law norm protecting the clean air? Would this norm be binding for the fourth state, or could the latter be qualified as a persistent objector?

33 See George Norman and Joel P. Trachtman, "The Customary International Law Game," 99 *American Journal of International Law* 541 (2005), 553–62.

In the world of our model, it seems justified to recognize a customary norm and to extend its scope to the fourth state, even though it has not consented to the norm. We cannot invoke the sovereignty principle in favor of the fourth state because its behavior has negative external effects. The exercise of its freedom to pollute comes into conflict with the freedom of the other states and their inhabitants to enjoy clean air. If we privileged the active freedom of the fourth state against the passive freedom of the other three states, we would privilege freedom of action in general against the passive freedom not to be harmed. However, there seems to be no plausible argument to favor one type of freedom over the other.

As the potential customary norm supports socially optimal behavior and prevents external effects, normatively we should not require consensus for the formation of such a norm. Furthermore, the acceptance of persistent objectors in such situations would completely contradict the rationale behind the norm and defeat its purpose. While the persistent objector doctrine is supposed to protect the freedom of states, its invocation in this case would directly promote the violation of the freedom of the majority of states. The very purpose of the norm is to prevent defection, which is in the natural self-interest of each state.

In a second step, let us complicate our basic model. Up to now, we have assumed that payoffs are distributed equally across countries. However, this does not seem too realistic. There are some industrialized countries that benefit more from contaminating industries, while there are other countries that are affected more severely by certain environmental harms.[34] We might think, for example, of an island state whose existence is endangered by the rising sea level caused by global warming. Moreover, let us assume that for the industrialized state the benefit of the use of its contaminating industries outweighs the environmental costs affecting its territory even if all other states make use of their contaminating industry.[35]

[34] See Nico Krisch, "The Decay of Consent: International Law in an Age of Global Public Goods," 108 *American Journal of International Law* 1 (2014), 4 (calling public goods in situations with distributional implications "aggregate-effort goods").

[35] Some commentators argue, for example, that climate change might have net benefits for the United States. See Jason Scott Johnston, "Climate Change Confusion and the Supreme Court: The Misguided Regulation of Greenhouse Gas Emissions Under the Clean Air Act," 84 *Notre Dame Law Review* 1 (2008), 21; Robert Mendelsohn and James E. Neumann, "Synthesis and Conclusions," in *The Impact of Climate Change on the United States Economy*, edited by Robert Mendelsohn and James E. Neumann 315 (New York: Cambridge University Press, 2004), 321. For a criticism of this "Climate Change Winner Argument," see Jody Freeman and Andrew Guzman, "Climate Change and U.S. Interests," 109 *Columbia Law Review* 1531 (2009), 1536–44.

Now, the problem is not just one of finding a social optimum, as it was in the first step. There are also significant distributive implications. The industrialized state does not have any incentive to enter into an agreement protecting the environment, because even if every state pollutes, the industrialized state is still better off than if it were totally prevented from producing. In contrast, the prohibition of environmental harm is crucial for the survival of the island state. If we accept that each state has a "fundamental right to survival" as proclaimed by the ICJ in its advisory opinion on the use of nuclear weapons,[36] the arguments that have been presented earlier carry even more weight. The exercise by the industrialized state of its freedom to pollute severely impairs the freedom of the island state to survive, so that the industrialized state should be bound by an emerging customary norm even if it has not consented to it.

To complicate the matter further, let us assume in a third step that the private benefits of the industrialized state outweigh the total social costs that are caused by its industrial activity. For example, we could think of a conduct that produces a private benefit of five units and social costs of four units. From an economic point of view, it now seems to be more problematic to prohibit the contaminating behavior. We still observe the external effect of the behavior that impairs the freedom of other states to enjoy a pollution-free environment. However, the conduct is, in total, socially beneficial. The problem is only that the benefit is not distributed among those states that bear the costs. In a world with strict private property rights, the industrialized state would go ahead with its contaminating conduct and compensate the other states for their losses.[37] However, we lack such strict private property rights in the international arena with regard to environmental protection. Because of the complexity of the distribution problem, simple majority rules for establishing binding obligations, which provided clear benefits in the other situations, do not seem to be the right solution in this case. We either have to resort to solutions based on state consent or trust courts to find an equitable balance.

Furthermore, in this type of situation we would have a distribution problem of a different kind. Situations in which the benefit of industrial production outweighs the harm caused by industrial pollution require a certain level of technological development. Technologically more developed industries will either be less contaminating or more productive than industries of less developed countries. This brings us to a well-known dilemma of international

36 *Legality of the Threat or Use of Nuclear Weapons*, Advisory Opinion of 8 July 1996, 1996 ICJ Rep. 226, 263, para. 96.

37 This is the rationale of the Coase theorem. See Ronald H. Coase, "The Problem of Social Cost," 3 *Journal of Law & Economics* 1 (1960) (showing that externalities do not impair economic efficiency if property rights are well defined and transaction costs sufficiently low).

environmental law: If we impose the same standards on developing countries that we impose on developed countries, we might contribute to widening the developmental gap between developed and less developed countries, because the latter countries usually have less efficient technologies.[38] One of the rationales of well-designed emission trading systems is to deal with these kinds of distributive issues.[39] Again, legal obligations imposed by simple majority rules do not provide an adequate answer to the social dilemma.

Finally, we have an epistemological problem. In all of our model worlds, we have so far assumed that we have perfect information. We know the payoffs of the games and can thus calculate the socially optimal solution. However, this assumption is not realistic. Most often states not only have different interests with regard to certain social problems; they will also disagree with regard to the underlying facts, the costs, and the benefits of a certain measure. We often do not know what the socially optimal solution of a cooperation problem is.

Relying on the opinions of states and state practice is thus an epistemological tool. The more states support a certain rule, the more probable it is that this rule constitutes a socially optimal solution. However, it is not possible to establish a specific quota of support that has to be met for the formation of a customary norm. State support is only an indication of the rationality of a specific customary rule, but no guarantee of it. There are several reasons why even the majority opinion may not be rational. First, governments may take irrational decisions because of a lack of information or competence. Second, sometimes short-term interests may deviate from the long-term interests of a state. If the former trump the latter, states may make unsustainable decisions.[40] Finally, governments may have incentives to make policies that further certain particularistic interests to the detriment of the society as a whole.[41] The

[38] On the issue of differentiated responsibilities for developing countries in international environmental law, see Paul G. Harris, "Common But Differentiated Responsibility: The Kyoto Protocol and United States Policy," 7 *New York University Environmental Law Journal* 27 (1999); Duncan French, "Developing States and International Environmental Law: The Importance of Differentiated Responsibilities," 49 *International & Comparative Law Quarterly* 35 (2000); Graham Mayeda, "Where Should Johannesburg Take Us? Ethical and Legal Approaches to Sustainable Development in the Context of International Environmental Law," 15 *Colorado Journal of International Environmental Law & Policy* 29 (2004); Christopher D. Stone, "Common But Differentiated Responsibilities in International Law," 98 *American Journal of International Law* 276 (2004).

[39] This is the rationale behind the Clean Development Mechanism of the Kyoto Protocol to the United Nations Framework Convention on Climate Change, art. 12, March 16, 1998, reprinted in 37 *International Legal Materials* 22 (1998) (entered into force Feb. 16, 2005).

[40] See Fareed Zakaria, *The Future of Freedom: Illiberal Democracy at Home and Abroad* (New York: W.W. Norton & Company, 2003), 168–69.

[41] See Mancur Olson, *The Logic of Collective Action: Public Goods and the Theory of Groups* (Cambridge, MA: Harvard University Press, 1965), 127–28.

TABLE 4.2 *Simple Coordination Game*

	Left	Right
Left	1, 1	−1, −1
Right	−1, −1	1, 1

higher the support of a customary rule, the more likely it is that state conduct and *opinio juris* are not just the result of opportunistic behavior, but an expression of the willingness to find a solution to a collective action problem.

The same points are valid with regard to the question of whether we should allow persistent objectors to exempt themselves from a customary rule. The more widespread and diverse the support for an emerging customary rule, the more likely it is that the objection to an emerging customary rule will be based on the strategic interests of the objecting state. Because deviating conduct causes harm to the interests of the whole international community, persistent objection should not be permitted in cases of almost uniform support. The situation is different with regard to situations of high uncertainty and less widespread support. Here, we have to take into account that different societies may have different risk preferences that have to be respected. Therefore, persistent objection should, in principle, be possible if a specific state evaluates a certain social dilemma differently than does the majority of the international community.

4.3.2 *Norms of Coordination*

The second category in our taxonomy of norms is norms of coordination. In game-theoretical terms, coordination problems arise if a social problem has different equilibria on which states can focus. In such situations, states have to focus on one equilibrium to achieve optimal benefits and avoid the worst outcomes. The simplest coordination game, represented in Table 4.2,[42] is one that offers different options, and in which the states are indifferent with regard to which option to choose.

[42] The numbers in Table 4.2 represent the payoff for each of the two participants. Participant 1 can choose between the upper and the lower row, and participant 2 between the left and the right column. The payoffs of player 1 are shown on the left-hand side of each pair of numbers, while the payoffs of player 2 are shown on the right-hand side of each pair. For an introduction to game theory, see Stefan Magen, "Game Theory and Collective Goods," in *Economic Methods for Lawyers*, edited by Emanuel Towfigh and Niels Petersen 61 (Cheltenham, UK: Edward Elgar, 2015).

A prominent example of this type of situation is the problem of which side of the street to drive on. To an individual, it does not matter whether he drives on the left-hand side or the right-hand side of the street. What matters is that everybody drives on the same side of the street. Some rules of diplomatic communication may also have such a character. It is not so important how exactly communication is carried out, but it is important that there is some uniform way of communicating. The principal function of these coordination norms is thus the protection of expectations.[43] In most countries, I drive on the right-hand side of the street because I can expect all others to drive there, too.

Where customary norms govern these coordination situations, they are usually observed because states have an incentive to act in the same way in any event, even without the legal rule. If a state acts in a different way, this may be an indication that its perceived costs for the particular behavior are different than those for all other states. This might be, for example, because it has a certain, countervailing cultural tradition. If the state is willing to bear the costs of its deviating behavior and signals accordingly, then arguably international law should not prevent it from doing so to the extent that deviations do not impose overly significant costs on the other states. If a state clearly protests against the formation of a certain rule, other states know that the protester will react differently than they do. Consequently, if the principal aim of norms of coordination is the protection of expectations, there is no danger that these states will form false expectations about the conduct of the persistent objector.[44] Therefore, in simple coordination situations, there is no reason not to permit persistent objection.

However, coordination games can also be more complicated and involve some distributive issues. We can, for example, consider the "battle of the sexes" game, represented in Table 4.3.[45] In the classic version of a battle-of-the-sexes game, a couple discusses how to spend a Saturday night. While the man wants to see a play, the woman would much rather go to a baseball game. However, both prefer doing something together, rather than spending the evening apart.

[43] See Roger Guesnerie, "The Government and Market Expectations," 157 *Journal of Institutional & Theoretical Economics* 116 (2001), 124 (arguing that rules can be useful in shaping individual expectations even if they provide suboptimal solutions).

[44] The exception might be situations like the driving example where other participants do not have opportunities to react to deviant conduct even if they know that some other participants do not cooperate, because they do not know when and where they will meet the non-cooperators. However, such situations will be rare in international diplomacy.

[45] The numbers in the table represent the payoff for each of the two participants. The woman in our example can choose between the upper and the lower row, and her payoffs are represented on the left-hand side of each pair of numbers. The man can choose between the left and the right column, and his payoffs are represented on the right-hand side of each pair.

TABLE 4.3 *"Battle of the Sexes" Game*

	Baseball	Theater
Baseball	2, 1	0, 0
Theater	0, 0	1, 2

He is better off accompanying her to the baseball game than spending the evening alone in the theater.

In this game, all parties thus also have an incentive to arrive at a specific equilibrium to avoid their worst outcomes (0, 0, i.e., being alone). However, they do care which equilibrium is achieved, and they have competing interests in this respect. One example from international law of a battle-of-the-sexes game concerns the rules that govern delimitation of the continental shelf. Here states usually agree that it is necessary to have a clear delimitation in order to have legal certainty.[46] However, their interests may differ with regard to which kind of delimitation is preferable.

In the *North Sea Continental Shelf Cases*, decided by the ICJ in 1969, Denmark, Germany, and the Netherlands argued about the rule for the delimitation of their continental shelf.[47] Denmark and the Netherlands preferred the application of the equidistance principle, according to which all points of the continental shelf are attributed to the country to whose coast they are closest. However, the application of this principle is unfavorable for countries with a concave coastline, such as Germany. Consequently, Germany recognized the general utility of the equidistance principle, but claimed that states with a concave coastline should get a just and equitable share of the continental shelf, which takes into account the proportional length of their coastline. After negotiations failed, the three countries referred the case to the ICJ.

That the countries referred the case to a court already shows that the preferred option was to have legal certainty concerning the shape of the delimitation, regardless of what the actual line would look like. However, they had divergent preferences with regard to the exact shape of the line. In such a case, it is not prudent for courts to base their decisions only on rules to which all parties have consented. States prefer having a rule to not having any rule, and the courts do have to take a decision on what the rule should be, even though there is no consensus among the parties. Furthermore, simple majority rules

46 See Beth A. Simmons, "Capacity, Commitment, and Compliance," 46 *Journal of Conflict Resolution* 829 (2002), 832.

47 *North Sea Continental Shelf Cases.*

do not help in this kind of situation. This is because the interests of a specific state in the continental shelf depend on the natural environment of the state. If states with a concave coastline form only a minority of all coastal states and thus prefer a rule based on the length of the coastlines, then it is likely that their preferences will not be taken into account if the majority of coastal states do not have concave coastlines and thus prefer the equidistance principle. In this situation it seems inequitable to allow the majority of states to determine the rule. The position of the minority of states should not simply be disregarded, because it seems uniquely due to chance whether the majority of coastal states do or do not have concave coastlines and thus favor one rule or the other. The application of a rule favored by a majority thus only has limited epistemic value in such cases.[48]

In the *North Sea Continental Shelf Cases*, the ICJ found that although a majority of states seemed to prefer the equidistance rule, this rule could not be invoked against Germany as a binding rule of customary international law.[49] This raises the question how international courts like the ICJ should decide such cases if *non liquet* (an abstention from deciding) is not a viable option. In practice, courts tend to apply principles of bilateral equity in these situations.[50] Thus, in the *North Sea Continental Shelf Cases*, the ICJ refrained from imposing a concrete delimitation line on the parties. Instead, it gave the parties some principles that should guide their own negotiation of the delimitation line. It expressly referred to principles of equity in this context[51] and asked the parties to take all relevant geographic circumstances into account.[52] The Court ruled that if, after negotiations, there were still overlapping parts of the continental shelf on whose ownership the parties could not agree, these parts should be divided between the coastal states in equal portions.[53]

This determination of customary rules in the *North Sea Continental Shelf Cases* deviates from the classical focus on state practice and *opinio juris*. Instead, it refers to equity and justice. The applied standards of equity are, in the end, left to the deciding judge or judicial body. These judges may sometimes be able to refer to general, more abstract principles of international law,

48 On the general epistemic value of a rule adopted by a majority, see David Estlund, "Beyond Fairness and Deliberation: The Epistemic Dimension of Democratic Authority," in *Deliberative Democracy*, edited by James Bohman and William Rehg 173 (Cambridge, MA: MIT Press, 1997).

49 *North Sea Continental Shelf Cases*, 45–46, para. 82.

50 Koskenniemi, *From Apology to Utopia*, 461–73.

51 *North Sea Continental Shelf Cases*, 46–47, para. 85, 48–49, para. 88.

52 Ibid., 53, para. 101.

53 Ibid.

but even if such principles exist, the judges will still have a considerable margin of discretion.

However, there is probably no better way to deal with such situations, which are highly context-dependent. Already in the battle-of-the-sexes example, it does not seem to be desirable to have a constant rule that the couple either always attends baseball games or theater plays. What is needed instead is a procedural mechanism that determines which rule to prefer in the concrete case. The same is true for international law. There may be some instances where states only need an institution to resolve disputes, even if the dispute resolution is based on equity and not on rules to which states have previously consented.

4.3.3 *Norms Furthering Ethical Values*

States are the primary legislators in international law. They have the power to conclude treaties, and it is their practice and beliefs that determine the content of customary international law. However, not all norms of international law concern only the direct or indirect interests of states. There are also norms that concern the interests of other legal subjects.

The primary example is international human rights law, whose norms are supposed to protect citizens against mistreatment by their state. The problem with these types of norms is that citizens are not involved in the lawmaking process. States themselves decide about the limits of their power against their citizens. To a certain extent, they can thus conclude a treaty with other states to the benefit or the detriment of third persons, the individuals affected by their sovereign power. If a state does not ratify certain human rights treaties and objects to the formation of customary law norms that protect its citizens, these citizens cannot influence the international lawmaking process.

In a domestic democracy, where decisions are taken by a majority of citizens that might adversely impact the interests of a minority of individuals, these individuals are at least indirectly involved in the decision-making process. However, such a participation of individuals seems impractical in international law.[54] There are two possible solutions to the problem that have been proposed in the legal literature. On the one hand, scholars resort to natural

54 But see recent accounts in favor of a cosmopolitan democracy, including Jürgen Habermas, "Kommunikative Rationalität und grenzüberschreitende Politik: eine Replik," in *Anarchie der komunikativen Freiheit*, edited by Peter Niesen and Benjamin Herborth 406 (Frankfurt/Main: Suhrkamp, 2007); Daniele Archibugi, *The Global Commonwealth of Citizens: Toward Cosmopolitan Democracy* (Princeton: Princeton University Press, 2008).

law concepts.[55] They assume that it is possible to identify certain universal values that are valid for the whole of humankind and that bind every state of the international community by means of proper reasoning.

However, how do we determine these universal values? Different cultures and societies have different conceptions about what constitutes a good life. Some cultures champion individual rights, while others emphasize the value of the society and thus perceive obligations toward the society as a crucial element of social order. Even if it were possible, in theory, to determine certain universal values, we would need a person or a body that determines these universal values. As nobody acts behind a veil of ignorance, but has a certain social and cultural imprint that would influence his or her judgment, our judgment is in some way influenced by our social and cultural heritage, even if we think we know which values are universal. Therefore, it seems impossible to determine natural law–like universal values that form part of customary international law.[56]

On the other hand, we can think of a procedural way of involving the interests of individuals in the process of forming customary international law. One might think of considering only the practice of democratic states as relevant practice for the field of human rights law.[57] Then citizens would at least indirectly be involved in the process of lawmaking, as they could, to a certain extent, influence the conduct of their states through democratic processes. However, this approach has one significant conceptual problem as well: It has a predisposition toward democracy.[58] As only democracies participate in the game, it implies that democracy is the best government form for all states, all cultural environments, and all socioeconomic circumstances. However, the political science literature on democratization theory suggests that the effectiveness of democracy depends on several preconditions – such as a certain level of socioeconomic development, the dispersion of power resources, and social and cultural cohesion.[59]

55 See, e.g., Fernando R. Tesón, "The Kantian Theory of International Law," 92 *Columbia Law Review* 53 (1992); Antônio Augusto Cançado Trindade, "International Law for Humankind: Towards a New Jus Gentium," 316 *Recueil des cours* 9 (2005).

56 See Amartya Sen, *The Idea of Justice* (Cambridge, MA: Harvard University Press, 2009). Sen stresses the impossibility of identifying one global just institutional order.

57 In this connection, Brian Lepard proposes that greater weight should be given to the views of states that comply with fundamental ethical principles. See Lepard, *Customary International Law*, 155.

58 See Martti Koskenniemi, "'Intolerant Democracies': A Reaction," 37 *Harvard International Law Journal* 231 (1996), 232–33.

59 See Niels Petersen, "The Principle of Democratic Teleology in International Law," 34 *Brooklyn Journal of International Law* 33 (2008), 40–47 (with further references).

We thus have a tension between the preservation of the cultural autonomy of each individual state and the protection of its citizens against exploitation undertaken in the name of "cultural exceptionalism." The structure of the problem is a paradoxical one, so that there can be no clear-cut logical answer. However, I want to highlight two points that might help us deal with this problem in the context of customary international law.

First, conflicts about ethical values are often not so much about the general existence of these values, but more about the relationship between conflicting values. Nobody would deny that people have, in principle, a right to life or a right to respect for their privacy. However, there may be considerable disagreement about the extent to which these rights can be restricted for social purposes or to further competing values. Rights can thus rarely be perceived as absolute and unlimited.[60] Accordingly, we have to give states a margin of discretion in solving these conflicts. International courts can only control the limits of this margin of discretion.[61] In particular, they can assess whether there is a legitimate purpose for restricting an individual human right and whether there is a plausible relationship between the pursuance of the aim and the restriction of the right.[62]

But what about the recognition of the ethical values themselves? Do legal norms promoting certain ethical values only bind those states that have explicitly or implicitly accepted them, or can a customary law norm in this field also be binding on states that oppose the values underlying the norm? As a number of authors have argued, persistent objection should not be permitted in cases of a customary norm based on certain compelling ethical principles, such as fundamental human rights.[63] Allowing persistent objection with regard to fundamental rights would permit particular governments to oppose normative developments to the detriment of their population under the pretext of cultural exceptionalism. Accordingly, persistent objection to a fundamental human rights norm that is widely accepted in the international community should not be allowed. Cultural differences can, instead, be legitimately taken

60 See Yash Ghai, "Universalism and Relativism: Human Rights as a Framework for Negotiating Interethnic Claims," 21 *Cardozo Law Review* 1095 (2000), 1099.

61 Such a margin-of-appreciation doctrine for the field of human rights has been developed by the European Court of Human Rights. See *Handyside v. United Kingdom*, Judgment of 12 December 1976, (1976) 1 E.H.R.R. 737, paras. 48–50.

62 See Niels Petersen, "International Law, Cultural Diversity and Democratic Rule: Beyond the Divide between Universalism and Relativism," 1 *Asian Journal of International Law* 149 (2011), 154–56.

63 See Holning Lau, "Rethinking the Persistent Objector Doctrine in International Human Rights Law," 6 *Chinese Journal of International Law* 495 (2005), 503–05; Lepard, *Customary International Law*, 333–36. Both authors favor considerable exceptions for the application of the persistent objector doctrine in international human rights law.

into account by allowing states to exercise a margin of discretion with regard to the solution of conflicts between competing values. Therefore, states have to give reasons to justify their behavior if they want to restrict specific human rights.

4.4 CONCLUSION

The previous analysis demonstrates that we should rethink our approach to consent in the formation of customary international law. There are normative reasons not to stick to one uniform doctrinal approach, but rather to distinguish different types of social situations in determining such issues as the amount of state practice or *opinio juris* required for the emergence of a customary norm and whether persistent objection to a customary norm should be allowed.

In this chapter I have considered three such types of situations. First, there are customary rules regarding the protection of common goods. In these cases state consent is primarily an epistemological tool. States can, under certain circumstances, be considered bound by such a customary rule even if they object to the emergence of the rule. Second, there are customary norms concerning cooperation games. I have argued that in these cases states should, in principle, only be bound by the norm if they have not objected to it. However, there are often cases in which it may be necessary for courts to resort to considerations of bilateral equity in determining an applicable rule or in setting parameters for agreement among the states involved. Finally, I identified a category of customary rules that protect and further ethical values. I have argued that states should only have a margin of discretion in balancing competing ethical values. However, they should not be able to exempt themselves from such an ethical norm even by persistently objecting to its emergence.

The points I have highlighted in this chapter are certainly not exhaustive. There are still many issues that remain to be resolved. However, I hope that this chapter will help draw the attention of scholars to important issues that so far have been relatively neglected in the academic and professional debate on customary international law.

ACKNOWLEDGMENTS

Many thanks to Christoph Engel, Thomas Kleinlein, and Michael Kurschilgen for valuable comments on the earlier versions of this essay.

5

Customary International Law and General Principles

Rethinking Their Relationship

Thomas Kleinlein

5.1 INTRODUCTION

Rethinking the relationship between customary international law and general principles of law is like brooding over inequalities with two unknowns. Both customary international law and general principles are still "obscure" categories,[1] and, consequently, the "line of demarcation" between the two is also not very clear.[2] The vagueness of both concepts is also reflected in the fact that the assertion of either a customary rule or a general principle of law by the International Court of Justice ("ICJ") is only rarely accompanied by an adequate demonstration of its existence in international law.[3] According to the Committee on the Formation of Customary International Law of the American Branch of the International Law Association ("ABILA"), one "may posit distinctions between the two," but it is "difficult to reconcile these distinctions

1 Hilary Charlesworth, "Law-Making and Sources," in *The Cambridge Companion to International Law*, edited by James Crawford 187 (Cambridge: Cambridge University Press, 2012), 190.

2 Bin Cheng, *General Principles of Law as Applied by International Courts and Tribunals* (Cambridge: Grotius, 1987), 23. Symptomatically, Judge Sir Humphrey Waldock, in his 1962 General Course at The Hague, considered custom and general principles to be "two kinds" of unwritten law; for him, general principles "have tended to become absorbed into customary law and then to lose their identity as general principles of law." Humphrey Waldock, "General Course on Public International Law," 106 *Recueil des cours* 1 (1962), 39.

3 For an appraisal, see Rudolf H. Geiger, "Customary International Law in the Jurisprudence of the International Court of Justice: A Critical Appraisal," in Ulrich Fastenrath et al., *From Bilateralism to Community Interest: Essays in Honour of Bruno Simma* 673 (Oxford: Oxford University Press, 2011), with references; Giorgio Gaja, "General Principles of Law," in *Max Planck Encyclopedia of Public International Law*, vol. IV, edited by Rüdiger Wolfrum 370 (Oxford: Oxford University Press, 2012), 374, para. 20.

with any consistent usage."[4] Therefore, it comes as no surprise that Michael Wood – the International Law Commission's Special Rapporteur on the identification of customary international law – stated in his introductory "First Report on Formation and Evidence of Customary International Law" that "[t]he distinction between customary international law and 'general principles of law' is … important, but not always clear in the case law or the literature."[5]

Certainly, there is no point in trying to solve the inequalities of customary international law and general principles with mathematical precision. Nevertheless, I try to expose some landmarks that could help "demarcate" the line between customary international law and general principles. The chapter is divided into four parts. First, I analyze the different meanings of principles as a "source" of international law. Second, I consider different approaches to principles as a norm type in legal theory. Third, I discuss attempts in international legal doctrine to facilitate conceptual issues by either unifying general principles as a source with the source of customary international law or by equating general principles as a source and as a norm type. I argue, however, that both attempts avoid analyzing general principles as a source of international law.

Fourth and finally, I propose that the delimitation between customary international law and general principles of law as sources of international law should follow the distinction between situations dominated by factual reciprocity (which justify customary norms) and situations where such factual reciprocity is absent (which justify general principles). Customary international law is best understood as a relatively narrow category based on reciprocal state practice that is supported by *opinio juris*. With regard to general principles of international law, I develop an approach that is based on constructivist approaches in international relations theory. The jurisgenerative processes leading to the emergence of general principles of international law are processes of changing identities and argumentative self-entrapment, as I explore later in the chapter.

4 Committee on the Formation of Customary International Law, American Branch of the International Law Association, "The Role of State Practice in the Formation of Customary and Jus Cogens Norms of International Law," *Proceedings and Committee Reports of the American Branch of the International Law Association* 102 (1987–88), 111.

5 Michael Wood, Special Rapporteur, "First Report on Formation and Evidence of Customary International Law," UN Doc. A/CN.4/663 (2013), para. 36.

5.2 CONCEPTUALIZING THE RELATIONSHIP BETWEEN CUSTOMARY LAW AND GENERAL PRINCIPLES

The notion of general principles is indeed "ambivalent"[6] or "polysemic."[7] In particular, the concept of general principles refers to both a source of international law and a particular norm type in terms of legal theory. I discuss each of these in turn.

5.2.1 *General Principles of Law as a Source of International Law*

Sources of international law can be defined as the "*processes* by which international legal norms are created, modified, and annulled."[8] The doctrine of sources of international law determines the particular forms in which international law is created and can be ascertained.[9] Article 38(1) of the Statute of the ICJ ("Statute"),[10] which literally only identifies the legal norms that the Court "shall apply," is generally understood to codify the sources of international law.[11] Besides "international conventions," Article 38(1) of the Statute recognizes two sources of unwritten international law: "b. international custom, as evidence of a general practice accepted as law [and] c. the general principles of law recognized by civilized nations."[12]

6 See Emmanuelle Jouannet, "L'ambivalence des principes généraux face au caractère étrange et complexe de l'ordre juridique international," in *L'influence des sources sur l'unité et la fragmentation du droit international*, edited by Rosario Huesa Vinaixa and Karel Wellens 146 (Bruxelles: Bruylant, 2006) (referring to the ambivalent role of general principles with regard to the unity or fragmentation of international law).

7 See Samantha Besson, "General Principles in International Law – Whose Principles?" in *Les principes en droit européen/Principles in European Law*, edited by Samantha Besson and Pascal Pichonnaz 19 (Genève: Schulthess, 2011), 26 (explaining that the concept of principle can refer, for example, "to a legal source, a kind of legal norm, a degree of legal normativity or a quality of legal content"). See also James Crawford, *Brownlie's Principles of Public International Law* (Oxford: Oxford University Press, 8th ed. 2012), 37 ("The rubric 'general principles of international law' may alternately refer to rules of customary international law, to general principles of law as in Article 38(1)(c) [of the Statute of the ICJ], or to certain logical propositions underlying judicial reasoning on the basis of existing international law.").

8 Samantha Besson, "Theorizing the Sources of International Law," in *The Philosophy of International Law*, edited by Samantha Besson and John Tasioulas 163 (Oxford: Oxford University Press, 2010), 169–70 (emphasis in the original).

9 Thomas Skouteris, "The Force of a Doctrine: Art. 38 of the PCIJ Statute and the Sources of International Law," in *Events: The Force of International Law*, edited by Fleur Johns, Richard Joyce, and Sundhya Pahuja 70 (New York: Routledge, 2011).

10 Statute of the International Court of Justice ("ICJ Statute"), art. 38(1).

11 Skouteris, "The Force of a Doctrine," 71; Charlesworth, "Law-Making and Sources," 189.

12 ICJ Statute, art. 38(1)(b), (c).

The meaning of general principles of law "recognized by civilized nations" has been contentious since the deliberations of the Advisory Committee of Jurists for the Establishment of a Permanent Court of International Justice ("PCIJ") in 1921, which drafted the Statute of the PCIJ that in turn became the Statute of the ICJ in 1945.[13] Today, two views exist on how to interpret the phrase "general principles of law recognized by civilized nations" – one narrow and the other broader. The narrow view holds that such general principles must be recognized in municipal law.[14] In a postcolonial pluralistic world, the formulation of Article 38(1)(c) of the Statute referring to principles recognized "by civilized nations" should not limit the range of relevant municipal legal orders to the national law of specific states. Rather, under a modern interpretation, a majority of nations within each of the main families of laws must adhere to a principle, which shall be taken from domestic legal orders, in order for it to be recognized as a general principle of law under international law.[15]

An alternative broader understanding of general principles of international law distinguishes three categories of principles on the basis of their origin. According to this view, in addition to the aforementioned principles stemming from domestic law, Article 38(1)(c) of the Statute comprises, secondly, general principles originating in international relations and, thirdly, general principles applicable to all kinds of legal relations. Thus, general principles can either be transferred from national legal orders by qualified methods of comparative law (the first category), originate in international relations themselves (the second category), or be applicable to all legal relations (the third category).[16] The

[13] For an overview of representative positions, see Birgit Schlütter, *Developments in Customary International Law: Theory and the Practice of the International Court of Justice and the International ad hoc Criminal Tribunals for Rwanda and Yugoslavia* (Leiden: Martinus Nijhoff, 2010), 71–80.

[14] For examples of this view, see Michael Akehurst, "The Hierarchy of the Sources of International Law," 47 *British Yearbook of International Law* 273 (1974–75), 279; Michel Virally, "The Sources of International Law," in *Manual of Public International Law*, edited by Max Sørensen 144 (London: Kluwer, 1968); Schlütter, *Developments in Customary International Law*, 85; Besson, "General Principles in International Law," 35–37.

[15] Michael Bogdan, "General Principles of Law and the Problem of Lacunae in the Law of Nations," 46 *Nordic Journal of International Law* 37 (1977), 46 (submitting that "a legal principle can be deemed to be recognized by civilized nations if it is adhered to by the prevailing number of nations within each of the main families of laws, i.e. the romano-germanic family, the common-law family, the socialist family, the African family, the Moslem family and the family of the laws of the Far East"). For the debate concerning this wording, see Gaja, "General Principles of Law," para. 2, with further references.

[16] See Hermann Mosler, "Völkerrecht als Rechtsordnung," 36 *Zeitschrift für ausländisches öffentliches Recht und Völkerrecht* 6 (1976), 41–46 (also mentioning principles of legal logic); Blaine Sloan, "General Assembly Resolutions Revisited (Forty Years Later)," 58 *British Yearbook of International Law* 39 (1987), 79–80 (following Mosler); Hermann Mosler, "General Principles of International Law," in *Encyclopedia of Public International Law*, vol. II, edited by Rudolf

second category, consisting of principles originating in international relations, is understood to comprise principles inherent in the international legal community and principles generally recognized on the international level.[17]

For the German scholar and international judge Hermann Mosler, principles inherent in the international legal community "follow from the nature of the international community." He mentions principles concerning diplomatic and consular relations and the sovereign immunity of states as examples.[18] The freedom of maritime communication, by contrast, is a general principle not because it is inherent in the international community, but because it is generally accepted.[19] Despite their possible moral content, these principles are not derived from natural law. Rather, they essentially depend on the clear consent of states.[20] Mosler refers to the obligation to act in good faith and to the principle of proportionality as examples of the last, third category – that is, principles applicable to all kinds of legal relations.[21]

The broader view of the scope of general principles of law that includes principles originating in international relations themselves is more defensible. There is no need today to restrict Article 38(1)(c) of the Statute to principles recognized in domestic law.[22] Neither the wording of Article 38(1)(c) of the

Bernhardt 511 (Amsterdam: Elsevier/North Holland, 1995). The following scholars distinguish two categories of general principles – (1) principles derived from the law *in foro domestic*, and (2) principles generated on the international plane: Johan G. Lammers, "General Principles of Law Recognized by Civilized Nations," in *Essays on the Development of the International Legal Order in memory of Haro F. van Panhuys*, edited by Frits Kalshoven, Pieter Jan Kuyper, and Johan G. Lammers 59 (Alphen aan den Rijn: Springer, 1980); M. Cherif Bassiouni, "A Functional Approach to 'General Principles of International Law,'" 11 *Michigan Journal of International Law* 768 (1990), 772; Wolfgang Weiß, "Allgemeine Rechtsgrundsätze des Völkerrechts," 39 *Archiv des Völkerrechts* 394 (2001), 398 et seq.; and Niels Petersen, "Customary Law Without Custom? Rules, Principles, and the Role of State Practice in International Norm Creation," 56 *American University International Law Review* 275 (2007), 308.

17 See Mosler, "General Principles of International Law," 523; Alfred Verdross and Bruno Simma, *Universelles Völkerrecht: Theorie und Praxis* (Berlin: Duncker & Humblot, 3rd ed. 1984), paras. 606, 639; Bruno Simma and Philip Alston, "The Sources of Human Rights Law: Custom, Jus Cogens, and General Principles," 12 *Australian Yearbook of International Law* 82 (1988–89), 102.

18 Mosler, "General Principles of International Law," 522–23.

19 On this freedom, see *Corfu Channel (United Kingdom of Great Britain and Northern Ireland v. Albania)*, Judgment of 9 April 1949, 1949 ICJ Rep. 4, 22.

20 Besson regards it as a "theoretical benefit" of restricting general principles to those stemming from domestic laws that this recourse to municipal law "severs any direct connection between those principles and morality." Besson, "General Principles in International Law," 36. However, for an explicitly natural law approach to general principles of law, see *South West Africa (Ethiopia v. South Africa; Liberia v. South Africa)*, Judgment of 18 July 1966, Dissenting Opinion of Judge Tanaka, 1966 ICJ Rep. 6, 298.

21 Mosler, "Völkerrecht als Rechtsordnung," 44–45.

22 According to Bassiouni and Wolfrum, this is the majority view. See Bassiouni, "A Functional Approach," 772 and Rüdiger Wolfrum, "General International Law (Principles, Rules, and

Statute nor its legislative history[23] or object and purpose seem to point in such a direction.[24] Admittedly, individual members of the Advisory Committee of Jurists obviously had in mind principles "accepted by all nations *in foro domestico*."[25] Still, there are "no indications whatsoever to be found" in the Procès-Verbaux of the Proceedings of the Committee of Jurists that it was opposed to the idea that the Court would apply also general principles of *international* law.[26]

Furthermore, the argument can now also rely on Article 21(1)(b) and (c) of the Statute of the International Criminal Court,[27] which clearly distinguishes between general principles derived from international law and those derived from national law.[28] Any original limitation of general principles to those developed *in foro domestico* (i.e., within domestic legal orders) was due to the

Standards)," in *Max Planck Encyclopedia of Public International Law*, vol. IV, 344, 348, para. 28. See also Dionisio Anzilotti, *Cours de droit international, Premier Volume: Introduction – Théories générales* (Paris: Recueil Sirey, 1929), 117 ("Quant aux principes généraux de droit, dont parle le no. 3 de l'article 38, ce sont avant tout les principes généraux de l'ordre juridique international, et, en second lieu, les principes universellement admis dans les législations des peuples civilisés: une sorte, comme on l'a bien dit, de *novissimum ius gentium* au sens classique, *quasi quo iure omnes gentes utuntur* (§ 1er, *Inst.* I, 1)."); *Pulp Mills on the River Uruguay (Argentina v. Uruguay)*, Judgment of 20 April 2010, Separate Opinion of Judge Cançado Trindade, 2010 ICJ Rep. 135, 155–56, paras. 48–52. Cançado Trindade distinguishes between general principles of law proper to international law in general and principles of law proper to some domains of international law. For him, general principles of law emanate from "the universal juridical conscience," which he regards as "the ultimate material 'source' of all law." According to Cançado Trindade, the "gradual acknowledgment . . . of the principles proper to a domain like that of International Environmental Law" provides a "clear illustration." By contrast, Simma and Alston note that "the dominant view understands this concept in a narrow sense, as referring to legal principles developed *in foro domestico*." See Simma and Alston, "The Sources of Human Rights Law," 102. For a similar view, see Schlütter, *Developments in Customary International Law*, 75; Cheng, *General Principles of Law*, 390.

23 For the legislative history of Article 38 of the Statute, see Vladimir Duro Degan, *Sources of International Law* (The Hague: Martinus Nijhoff, 1997), 46–53; Ole Spiermann, "'Who Attempts Too Much Does Nothing Well': The 1920 Advisory Committee of Jurists and the Statute of the Permanent Court of International Justice," 73 *British Yearbook of International Law* 187 (2002), 212–18.

24 But see Besson, "General Principles in International Law," 35–36.

25 Spiermann, "'Who Attempts Too Much Does Nothing Well'," 217, with references. See also Maarten Bos, "The Recognized Manifestations of International Law: A New Theory of 'Sources,'" 20 *German Yearbook of International Law* 9 (1977), 33–42.

26 Lammers, "General Principles of Law," 66. See generally League of Nations, Advisory Committee of Jurists on the Establishment of a Permanent Court of International Justice, *Procès-Verbaux of the Proceedings of the Committee June 16th – July 24th 1920* (The Hague: Van Langenhuysen Brothers, 1920, repr. 2006).

27 Rome Statute of the International Criminal Court, 17 July 1998, 2187 UNTS 90, art. 21, para.1, (b) and (c).

28 See Wolfrum, "General International Law," para. 28.

fact that comparing domestic legal systems provided the only way to validate general principles in a reliable way at the time the Statute of the PCIJ was drafted.[29] The situation has changed as a result of the creation of countless international organizations and the expansion of international treaty law. Today, we can refer, for example, to the implicit consensus expressed in resolutions of the General Assembly of the United Nations (even if they are not directly binding themselves), to preambles of multilateral treaties, and to other expressions of consent in global transnational society.

There are at least three implications of the broader view. One is that it might need to be expanded even further. In particular, a fourth category of general principles could be added to the three categories mentioned above, which is closely related to the second category, that is, general principles originating in international relations. This category of "regime-specific principles" consists of principles set out in one particular treaty regime, such as the common heritage principle or the principle of sustainable development. Such principles could then be transferred from one particular treaty regime to other regimes or issue areas, thus acquiring an independent status.[30]

A second implication of the broader view is that general principles would gain greater practical importance in international law. General principles developed from municipal law – the exclusive focus of the narrow view – have not had much impact on the jurisprudence of international courts or tribunals.[31] In particular, the ICJ has referred to Article 38(1)(c) of the Statute only very rarely.[32]

The situation is different for principles derived from international relations or international treaties.[33] Generally, the ICJ has asserted the existence of principles in international law irrespective of their correspondence to principles in

29 See Simma and Alston, "The Sources of Human Rights Law," 102.

30 See Wolfrum, "General International Law," para. 29.

31 See ibid., para. 125. However, several influential scholars have regarded domestic law as an important means for developing international law. See, e.g., Hersch Lauterpacht, *Private Law Sources and Analogies of International Law (With Special Reference to International Arbitration)* (London: Longman, 1927); C. Wilfred Jenks, *The Common Law of Mankind* (New York: F.A. Praeger, 1958), 106; Wolfgang Gaston Friedmann, *The Changing Structure of International Law* (London: Stevens & Sons, 1964), 188–210.

32 On this point, see Gaja, "General Principles of Law," para. 32. Alain Pellet writes that he is aware of only four explicit references to Article 38(1)(c) in the entire case law of the Court since 1922. Remarkably, in each of these cases the Court ruled out the application of Article 38(1)(c). See Alain Pellet, "Article 38," in *The Statute of the International Court of Justice: A Commentary*, edited by Andreas Zimmermann 731 (Oxford: Oxford University Press, 2nd ed. 2012), 833, para. 253, with references.

33 See Wolfrum, "General International Law," para. 125. Pierre d'Argent has discussed recourse by the ICJ to principles of a customary nature. See Pierre d'Argent, "Les principes généraux à la Cour internationale de Justice," in *Les principes en droit européen/Principles in European Law*, edited by Samantha Besson and Pascal Pichonnaz 110 (Genève: Schulthess, 2011).

municipal laws,[34] or has referred to "general international law," encompassing both customary international law and general principles of law, as a generic category, without specifically referring to general principles of domestic law.[35] These general pronouncements imply that the ICJ itself has adopted a broader view of the scope of general principles. For this reason, too, a broader view would have more practical importance because it would be likely to be employed by the ICJ and other international courts.

A third, and most relevant, implication of a broader understanding of general principles is that it complicates the relationship between general principles and customary international law.[36] This relationship appears clear-cut on the basis of narrow conceptions of both customary international law and general principles. The traditional, narrow understanding of customary international law relies on international state practice accompanied by *opinio juris*,[37] and the narrow concept of general principles extracts them exclusively from municipal law. Understood in this way, both customary international law and general principles include "a requirement for concrete practice of sorts"[38] – either interstate practice in the case of customary law, or domestic practice in the case of general principles.[39] In both cases, the respective narrow view

34 See Gaja, "General Principles of Law," para. 32.

35 See, e.g., *North Sea Continental Shelf Cases (Federal Republic of Germany v. Denmark; Federal Republic of Germany v. Netherlands)*, Judgment of 20 February 1969, 1969 ICJ Rep. 3, 29, para. 37 (referring to delimitation on an equidistance-special circumstances basis); *Barcelona Traction, Light and Power Company, Limited (Belgium v. Spain)*, Second Phase, Judgment of 5 February 1970, 1970 ICJ Rep. 3, 32, para. 34 (listing the outlawing of acts of aggression and of genocide, and the principles and rules concerning the basic rights of the human person, including protection from slavery and racial discrimination, as examples of obligations *erga omnes* and clarifying that "[s]ome of the corresponding rights of protection have entered into the body of general international law . . .; others are conferred by international instruments of a universal or quasi-universal character"); ibid., 46, para. 87 ("the right of the State to have its nationals enjoy a certain treatment guaranteed by general international law"); *United States Diplomatic and Consular Staff in Tehran (United States of America v. Iran)*, Judgment of 24 May 1980, 1980 ICJ Rep. 3, 31, para. 62 (referring to the inviolability of the premises of a diplomatic mission and other obligations of the Iranian government).

36 On this point, see Committee on the Formation of Customary International Law, "The Role of State Practice," 111 ("It is difficult to distinguish 'general principles' from 'international custom' when both are viewed in their broader senses. . . . One may posit distinctions between the two, but it is difficult to reconcile these distinctions with any consistent usage.").

37 See Besson, "General Principles in International Law," 59 ("Custom requires state practice, and not necessarily state consent.").

38 Committee on the Formation of Customary International Law, "The Role of State Practice," 111.

39 On the requirement of practice, see, e.g., Restatement (Third) of the Foreign Relations Law of the United States, vol. 1 (1987), § 102, reporters' note, para. 7 ("references to 'general principles of international law' ordinarily mean principles accepted as customary international law whether or not they derive from principles common to national legal systems"); Committee

underlines that this practice must be "real." According to the narrow view of general principles, referring to domestic legislation – the law in the books – alone without considering actual enforcement deficits will therefore not suffice to establish a principle developed *in foro domestico*.[40]

On this theoretical basis, there might be an overlap of content between general principles and customary law, but conceptually, the normative origins of these two respective unwritten bodies of international law can be distinguished clearly. The drawback of this clear-cut distinction, however, is also evident: Such an understanding reduces the meaning and impact of both customary international law and general principles, limiting both the domains of international judicial institutions and the aspirations of international law scholars who build their arguments on unwritten international law.

By contrast, the broad view of general principles (as well as customary international law) raises the question of whether unwritten international legal norms that are not supported by solid and actual state practice can legitimately be considered either customary international law or general principles. If there is room for a distinct category of general principles of law that, like customary international law, originate in international relations themselves and are not adopted from domestic law, both international practice and scholarship are confronted with a considerable methodological uncertainty. There does not seem to exist any agreed-on method for establishing that a certain principle is "accepted" or even "inherent" in the international community.

5.2.2 *Principles as a Norm Type*

In legal theory, much effort has been devoted to defending principles as a distinct norm category. As we will see, some international law scholars have tried to make use of these categorizations. The debate in legal theory has referred to several aspects of legal principles.[41] Notably, principles are distinguished from rules. Scholars have proposed a number of criteria for purposes of making this distinction. For example, legal philosopher Joseph Raz argues that rules prescribe specific acts, whereas principles prescribe highly unspecific actions.

on the Formation of Customary International Law, "The Role of State Practice," 111–12 ("there must be some 'practice' with respect to these principles, at least to demonstrate that they are 'recognized'"); Theodor Meron, "International Law in the Age of Human Rights: General Course on Public International Law," 301 *Recueil des cours* 9 (2003), 393 (quoting the Committee on the Formation of Customary International Law).

40 See Meron, "International Law in the Age of Human Rights," 393, with further references in n.1486.

41 See generally Ralf Poscher, "Insights, Errors and Self-Misconceptions of the Theory of Principles," 22 *Ratio Juris* 425 (2009), 427–28.

According to Raz, the distinction between rules and principles is one of degree and many borderline cases exist.[42]

Dworkin, by contrast, logically distinguishes legal rules and legal principles. For Dworkin, rules are applicable in an "all-or-nothing" fashion. Principles, on the other hand, do not prescribe legal consequences that automatically follow when the conditions provided are met. Rather, principles state reasons that point in one direction but do not necessitate a particular decision. They have a dimension of weight or importance. Consequently, while a rule must be invalid if it conflicts with another rule, a conflict of principles can be resolved by taking into account the relative weight of each principle.[43] Other authors treat principles as reasons for the existence of certain rules,[44] or distinguish principles, which protect a common or individual good and are therefore value-related, from rules, which are in general conduct-related.[45] Some authors also point out that, unlike rules, principles have persuasive rather than binding authority.[46]

Robert Alexy begins with Dworkin's analysis but argues that the key to the distinction between rules and principles is that principles are optimization requirements. In other words, principles require that "something be realized to the greatest extent possible given the legal and factual possibilities." Rules, by contrast, are always either fulfilled or not. Alexy insists that the distinction is not one of degree, but of quality. In his words, a principle posits an "ideal-ought." Its weight in concrete cases is determined by its background justification as it applies to the given context. It is trumped whenever some competing principle has greater weight in the case at hand. Rules, by contrast, are not necessarily set aside just because their background justifications do not hold up in the context of a particular case.[47]

Due to this plenitude of diverse and even contrasting concepts of principles and rules, legal theory is, in the words of scholar Armin von Bogdandy,

[42] See, e.g., Joseph Raz, "Legal Principles and the Limits of Law," 81 *Yale Law Journal* 823 (1972), 838. See also George C. Christie, "The Model of Principles," 17 *Duke Law Journal* 649 (1968), 669; Graham Hughes, "Rules, Policy and Decision Making," 77 *Yale Law Journal* 411 (1968), 419.

[43] See Ronald Dworkin, *Taking Rights Seriously* (London: Duckworth, 1977), 24–28.

[44] See Neil MacCormick, "'Principles' of Law," 19 *Juridical Review* 217 (1974), 222.

[45] See Petersen, "Customary Law Without Custom?" 288. However, other authors regard principles as abstract but still conduct-related. See, e.g., Jouannet, "L'ambivalence des principes généraux," 5 ("on prend le principe général comme une norme qui indique un modèle abstrait de comportement").

[46] See, e.g., Brian D. Lepard, *Customary International Law: A New Theory with Practical Applications* (New York: Cambridge University Press, 2010), 167.

[47] Robert Alexy, *A Theory of Constitutional Rights*, translated by Julian Rivers (Oxford: Oxford University Press, 2002), 47–48, 58–59.

"not very helpful" in the search for a distinct concept of principles.[48] The baseline of the theoretical debate merely seems to be that principles are less specific than rules. Furthermore, adapting theoretical concepts developed for domestic law to international law obviously causes some difficulties. Apart from the question of whether or not a distinction between principles and rules has inherit merit,[49] a conceptually ambitious dichotomy of principles and rules was not apparently in the minds of the drafters of Article 38 of the ICJ Statute.[50] International judicial or arbitral decisions have not elaborated on such a dichotomy either. Rather, international courts and tribunals use the term "principles" in order to denote the general character and fundamental importance of the norm in question.[51]

Scholars of international law generally regard general principles of law as a vague and imprecise notion.[52] Michael Akehurst, for example, regards general principles of international law as broader principles of international law which are principles of customary law or derived from other sources.[53] According to Ian Brownlie's treatise *Principles of Public International Law*, a "rigid categorization of sources is inappropriate." Brownlie regards legal principles primarily as "abstractions."[54] In the view of the Committee on the Formation of Customary (General) International Law of the International Law Association, "principles operate at a higher level of generality than rules."[55] However, in light of the inevitable semantic indeterminacy of any legal norm, it remains

48 Armin von Bogdandy, "General Principles of International Public Authority: Sketching a Research Field," 9 *German Law Journal* 1909 (2008), 1910.

49 See András Jakab, "Re-Defining Principles as 'Important Rules': A Critique of Robert Alexy," in *On the Nature of Legal Principles*, edited by Martin Borowski 145 (Baden-Baden: Steiner, 2010), 145 (asserting that the concept of principles logically distinct from rules can be regarded as "simply superfluous"; according to Jakab, the designation as "principle" underscores importance, but it does not imply anything about logical structure).

50 See, e.g., Lord Phillimore, *Procès-Verbaux*, 335 (stating that by "general principles of law" he had intended to mean "maxims of law").

51 On this point, see Gaja, "General Principles of Law," para. 31.

52 See Virally, "Le rôle des 'principes' dans le développement du droit international," in *Recueil d'études de droit international: En hommage à Paul Guggenheim*, edited by Pierre Lalive and Jacques Freymond 531 (Genève: Tribune de Genève, 1968).

53 Akehurst, "The Hierarchy of the Sources of International Law," 279. Akehurst contrasts general principles of international law with general principles of law borrowed from municipal law as mentioned in Article 38 of the Statute. See also Virally, "The Sources of International Law," 144–45 (referring to "international constitutional law").

54 Crawford, *Brownlie's Principles of Public International Law*, 37.

55 International Law Association, London Conference (2000), Committee on the Formation of Customary (General) International Law, "Final Report of the Committee: Statement of Principles Applicable to the Formation of General Customary International Law," 69, § 2(i), Commentary.

doubtful whether a norm being "general" or "specific" is a sufficiently precise criterion for distinguishing legal principles from legal rules.[56]

In the field of international law, it seems more promising to analyze whether judicial arguments based on norm-type principles differ from other types of arguments. Turning away from an assumed ontological distinction between rules and principles therefore implies turning instead to "law in action" and to, in the words of legal scholar Ingo Venzke, the "continuous communicative processes of speaking and using the law."[57] From this point of view, principles can be distinguished on the bases of the distinct ways in which they are used in legal argumentation.

Writing in 1985, Martti Koskenniemi approached the topic of general principles by asking "what do lawyers mean?" when they have recourse to general principles. Koskenniemi distinguishes two views on legal principles in international law. According to the first view, principles bear a distinct normative function ("normative theory constructivism"). According to the second view, principles describe and organize the system of individual norms and are deprived of any independent normative content ("descriptive theory constructivism"). Koskenniemi adds, however, that considering these two views as fundamentally different would be an error: "Constructivist activity in both practice and theory consists in investing the law with evaluative and goal-rational meanings and thus carries normative consequences."[58]

Scholars who have analyzed international judicial practice more recently point to several particular functions of principles in international legal argument.[59] For example, they have noted that principles, in addition to filling in "gaps" in legal rules, guide the interpretation of other international norms. They rationalize, structure, and allocate burdens of justification

[56] Martti Koskenniemi, "General Principles: Reflections on Constructivist Thinking in International Law," 18 *Oikeustiede-Jurisprudentia* 121 (1985), 131.

[57] Ingo Venzke, "Contemporary Theories and International Law-Making," in *Research Handbook on the Theory and Practice of International Law-Making*, edited by Catharina Maria Brölmann and Yannik Radi 66 (Cheltenham, UK: Elgar, 2014, also available as ACIL Research Paper 2013–23), 69.

[58] Koskenniemi, "General Principles," 122, 128.

[59] For an overview, see Wolfrum, "General International Law," paras. 56–63 (principles may serve as a tool in the interpretation of positive legal norms; they are mechanisms for the progressive development of international law and serve as a substitute for necessary amendments; they may also serve as mechanisms to bridge different legal regimes and thus counterbalance the fragmentation of international law); Niels Petersen, "Rational Choice or Deliberation? Customary International Law between Coordination and Constitutionalization," 165 *Journal of Institutional and Theoretical Economics* 71 (2009), 79–82 (principles are supposed to rationalize and to structure the legal discourse, and they have an evolutionary function shaping international relations by guaranteeing progressive compliance).

in legal discourse.[60] In particular, principles guide the interpretation of other norms and make explicit certain value choices and interests. Recourse to principles also serves to cope with the fragmentation of international law by building bridges among different branches of international law.[61] The best example for this function still is the World Trade Organization Appellate Body's reference to the principle of sustainable development, which has opened the door to taking into consideration the full substance of what has been subsumed under the principle of sustainable development.[62] Furthermore, due to their abstractness, principles are open to new developments and can serve an evolutionary function and allow for the progressive development of international law.

5.2.3 *Simplification Strategies*

How then do the international legal source of "general principles of law recognized by civilized nations" and the philosophical norm type of "principles" interrelate? Theoretically, the intersection of principles as a source and as a norm type establishes three categories of general principles of law. The first category comprises those general principles of law that are not "principles" within the meaning of legal theory. This category seems to exist only on the basis of a strict norm-type concept of principles such as that of Alexy, who conceives principles as optimization requirements, ontologically different from rules. The aforementioned principles concerning diplomatic and consular relations provide a relevant example.

The second category comprises those general principles of law that are principles in a double sense, that is, that are a source of international law and at the same time a norm type. Arguably, unwritten international human rights norms provide an example of this category. International human rights qualify as optimization requirements just as domestic fundamental rights in Alexy's theory.[63]

The third category of general principles of law comprises those norm-type principles that cannot be related to the source of principles in Article 38(1)(c)

60 See Thomas Kleinlein, *Konstitutionalisierung im Völkerrecht: Konstruktion und Elemente einer idealistischen Völkerrechtslehre* (Berlin: Springer, 2012), 670–73.

61 With regard to the amelioration of fragmentation, see Thomas Kleinlein, "Judicial Lawmaking by Judicial Restraint? The Potential of Balancing in International Economic Law," 12 *German Law Journal* 1141 (2011).

62 World Trade Organization, "United States – Import Prohibition of Certain Shrimp and Shrimp Products," 12 October 1998, WT/DS58/AB/R, available at https://www.wto.org/english/tratop_e/dispu_e/58abr.pdf; see also Wolfrum, "General International Law," para. 63.

63 Kleinlein, *Konstitutionalisierung im Völkerrecht*, 667–68.

of the Statute, but can be based on state practice, in other words, that qualify as customary international legal norms within the meaning of Article 38(1)(b) of the Statute. This category, in turn, is particularly relevant if a narrow understanding of the source of general principles, which exclusively refers to principles developed *in foro domestico*, and a broad understanding of customary international law, is adopted. On this conceptual basis, unwritten international human rights norms would arguably fall into this category.

For reasons of conceptual clarity, international law scholarship has developed two "simplification strategies" to deal with the different meanings of "principle." The first strategy is simply to unite general principles of law and customary international law into one indistinguishable source of international law. The second strategy is to link the source of general principles to the norm type of principles. I discuss these strategies in the following two sections.

5.2.3.1 The Strategy of Uniting Customary International Law and General Principles of International Law

As indicated earlier in the chapter, distinguishing general principles from customary international law becomes particularly difficult under broad understandings of customary international law. The "modern" approaches derive custom by a deductive process beginning with general statements of rules rather than particular instances of practice, and abandon the state practice requirement.[64] In the end, this leads to "customary law without custom."[65] If the theory of customary international law emphasizes *opinio juris* over state practice, the barrier between customary international law and general principles originating in international relations themselves becomes "artificial" or even "illusory."[66] The normativity of both customary international law and general principles alike depends foremost on a "voluntary element"[67] called *opinio juris* or recognition. This coincident voluntary element is already reflected in the wording of Article 38(1) of the Statute, which demands that international custom be "accepted as law" and that general principles be "recognized by civilized nations."

Accordingly, many scholars cannot see additional value in distinguishing customary international law and general principles as two sources of

[64] See Anthea Elizabeth Roberts, "Traditional and Modern Approaches to Customary International Law: A Reconciliation," 95 *American Journal of International Law* 757 (2001), 758.

[65] Petersen, "Customary Law Without Custom?" 275 (claiming, on the basis of a distinction between legal rules and principles, that state practice is dispensable for establishing legal principles). See also Lepard, *Customary International Law*, 166 (suggesting an identity between many general principles of international law and customary international law).

[66] Lepard, *Customary International Law*, 163.

[67] Wolfrum, "General International Law," para. 54.

international law.[68] At the least, they regard it as difficult to draw a dividing line between the concepts.[69] Rather, they merge both sources into one category. On this basis, general principles are, in the words of Jan Klabbers, a "sort of 'custom lite'"; they are "rules which are perhaps a bit more 'necessary' … than other rules, and for which therefore there would apply less strict demands on state practice and *opinio juris*."[70] Framed like this, an understanding of general principles as a form of customary law resembles the so-called "sliding scale" approach to customary international law, which advocates a more flexible relationship between state practice and *opinio juris* and, in particular, allows for a strong *opinio juris* to compensate for lack of consistent state practice.[71] Even with regard to general principles developed in municipal law, the distinctiveness of the category has been questioned, because these domestic law principles may easily give rise to customary norms under a broad definition

68 For scholars adopting this view, see Cheng, *General Principles of Law*, 23–24, with references ("international custom or customary international law, understood in a broad sense, may include all that is unwritten in international law, *i.e.*, both custom and general principles of law"); Lord Phillimore, *Procès-Verbaux*, 311 (pointing out that "the rules of international law as recognized by the legal conscience of civilised nations" and "international jurisprudence as a means for the application and development of law" both deal with international custom); Restatement (Third), § 102, reporters' note, para. 7 ("references to 'general principles of international law' ordinarily mean principles accepted as customary international law whether or not they derive from principles common to national legal systems"); Lepard, *Customary International Law*, 166 ("It is, in fact, appropriate to treat a general principle of international law as also a norm of customary international law, so long as states generally believe that it is desirable now or in the near future to recognize the principle as an authoritative legal principle.").

69 See, e.g., Theodor C. van Boven, "Survey of the Positive International Law of Human Rights," in *The International Dimensions of Human Rights*, edited by Karel Vasak and Philip G. Alston, vol. 1 107 (Westport, Conn.: Greenwood Press, 1982) (relating to the relationship between customary law and general principles in international human rights law); Degan, *Sources of International Law*, 8; Rein Müllerson, "On the Nature and Scope of Customary International Law," 2 *Austrian Review of International and European Law* 341 (1997), 354–55.

70 Jan Klabbers, *International Law* (Cambridge: Cambridge University Press, 2013), 35.

71 See, e.g., Frederic L. Kirgis, Jr., "Custom on a Sliding Scale," 81 *American Journal of International Law* 146 (1987), 149 (explaining that on a "sliding scale, very frequent, consistent state practice establishes a customary rule without much (or any) affirmative showing of an *opinio juris*, so long as it is not negated by evidence of non-normative intent. As the frequency and consistency of the practice decline in any series of cases, a stronger showing of an *opinio juris* is required. At the other end of the scale, a clearly demonstrated *opinio juris* establishes a customary rule without much (or any) affirmative showing that governments are consistently behaving in accordance with the asserted rule."); John Tasioulas, "In Defence of Relative Normativity: Communitarian Values and the *Nicaragua* Case," 16 *Oxford Journal of Legal Studies* 85 (1996) (investigating two conceptions of customary international law, the first being of a positivistic variety and drawing on a statist conception of international society, and the second manifesting a natural law orientation and finding its rationale in a communitarian account of that society). Compare Müllerson, "On the Nature and Scope," 352–56; Roberts, "Traditional and Modern Approaches," 770–74.

of customary law that focuses on *opinio juris*, which may be evidenced by the appearance of these principles in domestic law.[72]

In my view, the merging of customary international law and general principles raises three problems. First, it is difficult to reconcile with Article 38 of the Statute. Article 38(1)(c) of the ICJ Statute would be rendered superfluous if it does not refer to a separate category of norms. Second, this unitary view of custom and principles often implies an understanding of customary international law that is inspired by the English common law. These Anglo-American roots of this approach might hamper its universal acceptance. It is probably not simple coincidence that it was Lord Phillimore, the United Kingdom member of the Advisory Committee of Jurists for the Establishment of a Permanent Court of International Justice, who argued that general principles came within the scope of customary law.[73] According to this Anglo-American understanding, customary international law is the product of legal or moral principles or judicial law making case-by-case rather than being created primarily through state practice and state belief.[74] Still, the affinity of the unitary view with the common law in itself is certainly not an insurmountable obstacle to adopting this view.[75]

However, third, a certain tension arises between the unitary view of custom and principles and actual international judicial practice. For example, the ICJ relatively frequently refers to "principles" or "general principles," without further clarification of their status.[76] One explanation for this judicial practice on the part of the ICJ is that it has adopted a narrow definition of customary

72 See, e.g., Lepard, *Customary International Law*, 165 ("if states believe that certain general principles of national law should create binding or persuasive obligations for all states, now or in the near future, then they may also give rise to customary norms").

73 *Procès-Verbaux*, 295, 311, and 316 (stating that "all the principles of common law are applicable to international affairs"). In this regard, Lepard explicitly refers to Lord Phillimore. See Lepard, *Customary International Law*, 163. See also Bos, "The Recognized Manifestations of International Law," 36. Further, see Waldock, "General Course on Public International Law," chapters 3 and 4, 39–69 (stating that international custom and general principles are "the 'common law' of the international community").

74 Compare Charlesworth, "Law-Making and Sources," 192 (noting that customary international law is sometimes presented as similar to the "common law"; according to Charlesworth, however, the analogy is imperfect, since customary international law is created primarily through evidence of state practice and state belief, rather than being an apparent product of any legal or moral principle or of judicial lawmaking case-by-case).

75 Consider, for example, the "continental" perspective of Baron Deschamps of Belgium, who, during the drafting of the Statute of the PCIJ, argued that customary law resulted "entirely from the constant expression of the legal convictions and the needs of the nations in their mutual intercourse," implying an emphasis on *opinio juris* and the flexible evolution of customary norms. See "Speech by Baron Deschamps on the Rules of Law to be Applied," *Procès-Verbaux*, 322.

76 For references, see Pellet, "Article 38," para. 248.

international law in Article 38(1)(b) of the Statute that requires both *opinio juris* and consistent state practice.[77] If it finds state practice in support of a norm to be insufficient, the ICJ seems to avoid characterizing the norm as customary international law and instead refers to it as a principle.[78] This move, however, presupposes a conceptual distinction between customary international law and general principles of law, suggesting that the Court is rejecting a merger of customary law and general principles.

5.2.3.2 The Strategy of Linking the Source to the Norm Type

Another approach, proposed by legal scholar Niels Petersen, links the source of general principles to the norm type of principles developed by Robert Alexy, as described above.[79] Petersen suggests treating these norm-type principles, which Alexy conceives as "optimization requirements," as general principles of law within the meaning of Article 38(1)(c) of the Statute.[80] Petersen regards rules, by contrast, as legal norms that relate to conduct. He considers legal rules to be part of customary international law and not general principles of law, and believes that they must be determined according to the traditional inductive approach of custom, requiring both *opinio juris* and state practice.[81]

The problem with this proposal is that it utilizes the very narrow concept of principles advocated by Robert Alexy. Aside from all the controversies surrounding Alexy's concept of principles as optimization requirements,[82] Petersen's proposal is of explanatory value only with regard to certain fields of international law, and in particular international human rights, an international right to democracy, and international environmental law. Indeed, certain constitutional principles in international law can be considered simultaneously as general principles in terms of the doctrine of sources and as principles in terms of legal

77 See Gaja, "General Principles of Law," para. 18.

78 Jan Wouters and Cedric Ryngaert, "Impact on the Process of the Formation of Customary International Law," in *The Impact of Human Rights Law on General International Law*, edited by Menno T. Kamminga and Martin Scheinin 111 (Oxford and New York: Oxford University Press, 2009).

79 Petersen, "Customary Law Without Custom?" 286 (referring to Alexy, *A Theory of Constitutional Rights*, 47–48). Petersen thereby modifies a proposal of Stefan Kadelbach and Thomas Kleinlein. Kadelbach and Kleinlein propose to conceive norms of international constitutional law both as general principles in terms of the doctrine of sources (Article 38(1)(c) of the Statute) and as principles in terms of legal theory. See Stefan Kadelbach and Thomas Kleinlein, "Überstaatliches Verfassungsrecht: Zur Konstitutionalisierung im Völkerrecht," 44 *Archiv des Völkerrechts* 235 (2006), 235, 255–65.

80 Petersen, "Customary Law Without Custom?" 306–07.

81 Ibid., 310.

82 See, e.g., Jakab, "Re-Defining Principles as 'Important Rules.'"

theory.[83] Still, it is obvious that not all principles covered by Article 38(1)(c) of the Statute are optimization requirements as narrowly understood by Alexy. They do not coincide necessarily. For example, the principle of good faith cannot be explained satisfactorily as an optimization requirement.[84] Good faith serves various functions in the interpretation of international treaties and beyond, which cannot be reduced to the structure of optimization requirements.[85]

The main deficit of both "simplification strategies," however, is that they cannot explain the specific jurisgenerative processes leading to the formation of general principles. This critique certainly implies a *petitio principii* with regard to the first "simplification strategy": Proponents of this approach beg the question by uniting customary international law and general principles precisely because they do not regard general principles as an independent source. By contrast, the fundamental proposition of the second "simplification strategy" is that the practice requirement is dispensable with regard to general principles. The reason provided for this dispensability of state practice is simply that principles are not conduct-related, but rather value-related. Depending on one's understanding of principles, this may be correct. However, such an argument avoids the question why – in the absence of state practice – principles can have any normative force at all, either binding or persuasive. It thus is unable to explain general principles as a "source" of international law. Analyzing general principles as a source, however, is important since their normativity and legitimacy – like the normativity and legitimacy of any norm of international law – depend on the processes by which they are created.[86]

5.2.4 *Developing a New Approach to the Normativity of General Principles: Changing Identities and Argumentative Self-Entrapment*

The problems with both strategies described above are consistent with the general weaknesses in the doctrine of sources. Legal scholar Hilary Charlesworth explains these weaknesses well in the following terms:

83 See Kadelbach and Kleinlein, "Überstaatliches Verfassungsrecht," 255–65; Stefan Kadelbach and Thomas Kleinlein, "International Law – a Constitution for Mankind?" 50 *German Yearbook of International Law* 303 (2007), 330–47; Kleinlein, *Konstitutionalisierung im Völkerrecht*, 617–81.

84 On the principle of good faith, see Robert Kolb, "Principles as Sources of International Law (With Special Reference to Good Faith)," 53 *Netherlands International Law Review* 1 (2006).

85 See Markus Kotzur, "Good Faith (Bona Fide)," in *Max Planck Encyclopedia of Public International Law*, vol. IV, 508, 513–14, paras. 19–24.

86 On this point, see Besson, "Theorizing the Sources of International Law," 164, 173–78. D'Argent describes the reluctance of the ICJ to rely on "principles" that are not customary international law. This reluctance may be due to the uncertainty about the processes by which unwritten norms of international law are created beyond customary international law. See d'Argent, "Les principes généraux à la Cour internationale de Justice," 118–19.

> Why does this list [in Article 38(1) of the Statute] exercise such sway? Part of the appeal of article 38(1) is that recourse to it allows international lawyers to sidestep complex debates about the function of international law and the relative legitimacies of state consent and claims of justice. It is a pithy mantra that offers a quasi-scientific formula for practitioners of international law, postponing (possibly indefinitely) discussion of the politics of the designated sources. The formal nature of article 38(1) obscures the fact that international law is generated by a multi-layered process of interactions, instruments, pressures and principles.[87]

In particular, any assertion of a general principle of law that is not derived from the law *in foro domestico*, but arises within the international legal order itself, is in danger of being a tautology. The assertion is tautological to the extent that international law as such cannot be conceived of as a source of international law unless it refers to one of the formally recognized processes of international lawmaking, such as treaty law or state practice accepted as law (in other words, customary international law).[88] Compared to the traditional doctrine of customary international law, general principles are the weaker limb in this regard.[89] Requiring both *opinio juris* and state practice, customary international law "at least benefits from some methodological objectivity and wide acceptance of the process."[90]

In reality, the jurisprudence of international courts and tribunals, resolutions of international organizations, and policy statements of international conferences all contribute to the recognition of a general principle. This is manifest, for example, in the field of environmental law, and in this context in principles like the principle of good neighborliness, the principle of sustainable development, and the preventive principle.[91] Accordingly, simply explaining the source of general principles as "judicial law" is an unsatisfactory way to avoid a tautology, which does not explain much. Clearly, a judge does more than merely identify a pre-existing principle, and thereby exercises a jurisgenerative function.[92]

To justify and legitimize this jurisgenerative function in relation to an asserted general principle of law, however, a judge will feel that it is not enough to deduce a general principle, but that she needs to refer to some sort of consent or recognition – a voluntary element – that backs the respective general principle. Therefore, it is crucial to pay close attention to the processes to which we refer when we identify a general principle. Arguably, these

87 Charlesworth, "Law-Making and Sources," 189.
88 See Besson, "General Principles in International Law," 41–42.
89 See Waldock, "General Course on Public International Law," 39–40.
90 Meron, "International Law in the Age of Human Rights," 393–94.
91 See Wolfrum, "General International Law," paras. 54–55.
92 Besson, "General Principles in International Law," 42.

jurisgenerative processes differ from the formation of customary international law. I now endeavor to develop an account of these processes, stressing the meaning of reciprocity in international law.

5.2.4.1 The Meaning of Reciprocity

According to the traditional, narrow understanding of customary international law, the requirement of state practice helps to ensure that customary international law is "workable." It is, in the words of the ABILA's Committee on the Formation of Customary International Law, a "guard against the impact of hypocrisy, as well as temporary posturing and other transitory phenomena,"[93] and therefore has a stabilizing function. This proposition, however, is only valid if state practice is based on reciprocity.

As Bruno Simma points out, expectations of reciprocity are the paramount rationale for the emergence of new customary rules. They motivate certain actions and omissions on the part of the actors involved, and may also moderate the claims put forward by a state that initiates a lawmaking process. In many fields, the anticipation of reciprocal concessions and reciprocal restraints may stimulate auto-limitation and thus account for the growth of general and concordant practice eventually accepted as law. States refrain from certain actions because they expect other states to behave accordingly in a similar situation in the future. Expectations of reciprocity also facilitate the acceptance of certain claims by those states that find themselves in a similar situation and are interested, sooner or later, in making the same demands.[94] Constant interactions, claims, and tolerances as to what sovereign states can do to and with each other should therefore be regarded as the "motor" leading to the formation of customary international law.

Thus, game theory[95] and rational choice institutionalism,[96] in which the rational self-interest of actors takes center stage, already explain a great

[93] Committee on the Formation of Customary International Law, "The Role of State Practice," 112–13.

[94] See Bruno Simma, "Reciprocity," in *Max Planck Encyclopedia of Public International Law*, vol. VIII, 651, 652, para. 3; see also Bruno Simma, *Das Reziprozitätselement in der Entstehung des Völkergewohnheitsrechts* (München and Salzburg: Fink, 1970).

[95] On game theory and customary international law, see, e.g., Jack L. Goldsmith and Eric A. Posner, "A Theory of Customary International Law," 66 *University of Chicago Law Review* 1113 (1999); Edward T. Swaine, "Rational Custom," 52 *Duke Law Journal* 559 (2002); George Norman and Joel P. Trachtman, "The Customary International Law Game," 99 *American Journal of International Law* 541 (2005); Andrew T. Guzman, "Saving Customary International Law," 27 *Michigan Journal of International Law* 115 (2005). For overviews, see Petersen, "Rational Choice or Deliberation?" 72–77; Lepard, *Customary International Law*, 59–73.

[96] See Robert O. Keohane, *After Hegemony: Cooperation and Discord in the World Political Economy* (Princeton: Princeton University Press, 1984) (asserting that, after the erosion of

deal about the emergence of norms on the basis of the cooperative strategic interaction of states. It is, however, important to take into account that norms of customary law are not created by reciprocal interaction alone. Their normative force can only be explained when the relevant actors also develop a corresponding *opinio juris*.[97]

In the absence of expectations of reciprocity, however, reliance on actual state practice will not be able to fulfill the described stabilizing function of customary norms.[98] There are some issue areas in which states normally lack expectations of reciprocal behavior by other states. For example, the performance of most substantive human rights obligations lacks the necessary element of reciprocity and cross-border state interaction. Human rights obligations do not "run between states," but operate on the domestic level.[99] For this reason, Simma and Alston proposed to use general principles as opposed to customary law to ground international human rights law in their intriguing article on "The Sources of Human Rights Law."[100] The absence of reciprocity also characterizes other issue areas governed by unwritten international law. For example, an international principle that demands state governments be democratically elected, often understood as customary international law, can barely be based on reciprocity. Like human rights, such a principle mainly operates on the domestic plane. Furthermore, structural reciprocity is lacking where an unwritten legal norm protects a community interest or a common good like international peace and security, or where it defines common values.[101] In these areas,

American hegemony, international regimes facilitate decentralized cooperation among egoistic actors); Robert Axelrod and Robert O. Keohane, "Achieving Cooperation Under Anarchy: Strategies and Institutions," in *Cooperation under Anarchy*, edited by Kenneth A. Oye 226 (Princeton: Princeton University Press, 1986) (arguing that a contextual approach to strategy helps to forge the links between game-theoretic arguments and theories about international regimes); Robert O. Keohane, "International Institutions: Two Approaches," in *International Institutions and State Power*, edited by Robert O. Keohane 158 (Boulder, Colo.: Westview Press, 1989) (contrasting "rationalistic" and "reflective" approaches to international institutions); Robert Axelrod, *The Complexity of Cooperation: Agent-Based Models of Competition and Collaboration* (Princeton: Princeton University Press, 1997) (applying complexity theory and computer modeling).

97 See Simma, *Das Reziprozitätselement*, 63–64.

98 See Petersen, "Customary Law Without Custom?" 301. See also Kleinlein, *Konstitutionalisierung im Völkerrecht*, 499–508.

99 See Simma and Alston, "The Sources of Human Rights Law," 99.

100 Ibid., 102–06.

101 For a typology of community interests protected by international law, see Isabel Feichtner, "Community Interest," in *Max Planck Encyclopedia of Public International Law*, vol. II, 477, 479–81, paras. 13–25. See also Niels Petersen, "The Role of Consent and Uncertainty in the Formation of Customary International Law," in this volume (distinguishing between common goods, coordination problems, and ethical values).

state practice does not seem to be a reliable requirement for the emergence of unwritten law since, by definition, the meaning of practice actually transcends the inter-state dimension. Furthermore, reciprocity is notoriously absent in the relations between international organizations and their member states. Therefore, a customary law of international organizations also seems to necessitate a specific theoretical underpinning.[102]

I argue that the conceptual differentiation between customary international law and general principles of law should follow the distinction between situations dominated by factual reciprocity (which justify customary norms) and situations where such factual reciprocity is absent (which justify general principles). On this account of the distinction between customary law and general principles, it is not important to distinguish "principles" from "rules," or norms *in foro domestico* from norms arising in international relations.

Admittedly, the opposition between issue areas characterized by reciprocal interaction and those characterized by non-reciprocal action does not create a very clear-cut "line of demarcation." For example, reciprocity is not entirely absent in the formation of unwritten international human rights law. As Simma and Alston have shown, a *droit de regard*, which entitles the United Nations to respond to gross violations of human rights, can be based on reciprocal state practice. For this argument, Simma and Alston refer to the reactions by target governments to the application of the Economic and Social Council Resolution 1503 procedure on handling complaints of human rights violations: By virtue of their regular participation, target governments also tacitly acknowledge that any alleged gross violations of human rights norms require some response.[103] The fact that reciprocity can be relatively, though not totally, absent in some cases, however, does not affect the merits of the conceptual distinction between customary international law and general principles. Rather, the content of customary law and general principles will overlap or be closely interwoven in such situations.

It is also somehow unconventional to draw the line between customary international law and general principles based on the criterion of reciprocity because it is easy to find examples of commonly recognized customary norms that are not based on reciprocity. For the limited purposes of this chapter, it is important to draw attention to the role of reciprocity in the formation of customary international law, and to the consequences of its absence.

102 See Cornelia Janik, *Die Bindung internationaler Organisationen an internationale Menschenrechtsstandards: Eine rechtsquellentheoretische Untersuchung am Beispiel der Vereinten Nationen, der Weltbank und des Internationalen Währungsfonds* (Tübingen: Mohr Siebeck, 2012), 431–88.

103 Simma and Alston, "The Sources of Human Rights Law," 98–99.

5.2.4.2 A Constructivist Approach to Principles in the Absence of Reciprocity

Bearing these caveats in mind, turning to general principles in the absence of reciprocal state interaction is appropriate. State practice is not only less likely to be consistent in the absence of reciprocity; it is also not a reliable criterion for establishing normative expectations based on unwritten law if not based on reciprocity. As the Committee on the Formation of Customary International Law of the ABILA has noted, "the concept of a 'recognized' general principle seems to conform more closely than the concept of 'custom' to the situation where a norm is widely accepted even though widely violated."[104]

Accordingly, I believe that the generation of general principles can be explained as a distinct process that occurs in the absence of reciprocal state interaction.[105] As already pointed out, it is of course a difficult task to determine in a methodologically sound manner whether a general principle is generally recognized at the international level or is "inherent" in the international legal community.[106] However, I argue that recognition of general principles should be based, above all, on a process of changing identities and of "argumentative self-entrapment"[107] in which states and other international actors are involved.

My approach to defining general principles and their relationship to customary law is based on "constructivist" approaches in international relations theory. Both sophisticated rational choice theory and moderate social constructivism theorize different modes of social interaction that are necessary to explain significant phenomena.[108] Correspondingly, it becomes possible to refer both to rationalism as the logic behind customary international law and to constructivism as the explanation for the emergence of general principles of law.

[104] Committee on the Formation of Customary International Law, "The Role of State Practice," 112 (giving prohibitions on the use of force as an example). By contrast, Meron suggests that general principles should also be supported by "practice." Meron, "International Law in the Age of Human Rights," 393. See also Paul Guggenheim, *Traité de Droit international public: Avec mention de la pratique international et suisse*, vol. 1 (Genève: Georg, 1953), 152 ("les principes généraux du droit reposent soit sur le droit conventionnel, soit sur le droit coutumier") ("the general principles of law are based either on conventional [treaty] law or on customary law").

[105] For a more elaborate version of the argument, see Kleinlein, *Konstitutionalisierung im Völkerrecht*, 636–61 (making special reference to constitutional principles).

[106] See, e.g., Anzilotti, *Cours de droit international*, 117–18 (noting that general principles are "acceptés tacitement dans l'ordre international" ("tacitly accepted in the international order"); with regard to principles that are exclusive to domestic legal orders and not recognized in the international legal order, Anzilotti perceives the international judge as a legislator).

[107] Thomas Risse uses this phrase. See Thomas Risse, "'Let's Argue!': Communicative Action in World Politics," 54 *International Organization* 1 (2000), 23.

[108] See ibid., 12.

Constructivism points to the constitutive role of ideas instead of pre-defined interests in international relations.[109] Constructivist scholars claim that interests are not simply "given" and then rationally pursued. Rather, a major factor in interest formation by actors, such as states, is the social construction of actors' identities. Through interaction and communication, actors generate shared knowledge and shared understandings and, accordingly, are socialized. Ends of social interaction are not predetermined, but can be discovered and learned. Socially shared ideas not only become the basis for subsequent interactions and thus regulate behavior, but also constitute the identity of actors. Collective norms and understandings constitute the social identities of actors and also define the basic "rules of the game" in which actors find themselves entrapped in their interactions.[110] For example, human rights norms increasingly define a "civilized state" in the modern world. Furthermore, it is difficult to find an international institution that would simply repudiate the demand for an embedding of its activity in the rule of law or in good governance.[111] Arguably, we can regard these phenomena as an acknowledgement by states and international organizations of general principles of law.

Social constructivists emphasize the role of a "logic of appropriateness," which encompasses two different modes of social action and interaction. On the one hand, actors regularly comply with norms that they have thoroughly internalized and thus take for granted. On the other hand, rule-guided behavior is a conscious process whereby actors figure out the situation in which they act, apply the appropriate norm, or choose among conflicting norms.[112] By these processes, international norms are formed and construed in interaction. These norms are continuously evolving.[113]

[109] See Nicholas G. Onuf, *World of Our Making: Rules and Rule in Social Theory and International Relations* (Columbia, SC: University of South Carolina Press, 1989) (Onuf actually coined the concept of "constructivism" in international relations); Friedrich V. Kratochwil, *Rules, Norms, and Decisions: On the Conditions of Practical and Legal Reasoning in International Relations and Domestic Affairs* (Cambridge: Cambridge University Press, 1989) (arguing that norms influence choices not by being causes for actions, but by providing reasons); Alexander Wendt, *Social Theory of International Politics* (Cambridge: Cambridge University Press, 1999) (developing a theory of the international system as a social construction).

[110] Risse, "'Let's Argue!'," 5.

[111] With regard to the rule of law and good governance, see von Bogdandy, "General Principles of International Public Authority," 1926.

[112] See James G. March and Johan P. Olsen, "The Institutional Dynamics of International Political Orders," 52 *International Organization* 943 (1998), 943; Risse, "'Let's Argue!'," 4–6.

[113] See Martha Finnemore, *National Interests in International Society* (Ithaca, NY: Cornell University Press, 1996), 5–7 (drawing on insights from sociological institutionalism to develop a systemic approach to the changing preferences and behavior of states by investigating an international structure not of power, but of meaning and social value).

Constructivist scholars also have described a norm "life cycle" that consists of a three-stage process. The characteristic mechanism of the first stage, "norm emergence," is persuasion by "norm entrepreneurs." Norm entrepreneurs – individuals, organizational platforms, or social movements – attempt to convince a critical mass of states to embrace new norms. The second stage, a "norm cascade," involves broad norm acceptance by states and international organizations, and the third stage involves norm internalization.

The second stage is characterized by a dynamic of imitation as those states that are the vanguard of new norms or "norm leaders" attempt to socialize other states to become "norm followers." Norm cascades are facilitated by a combination of pressure on states to conform to a new norm, a desire by states to enhance their international legitimacy, and a desire of state leaders to enhance their self-esteem. At the far end of the evolution of a norm cascade, norm internalization occurs; norms acquire a "taken for granted" quality and are no longer a matter of broad public debate.[114]

Admittedly, constructivists generally focus on norms as such and do not pay special attention to the distinction between legal and social norms. Nevertheless, I believe their insights help explain the evolution of general principles of law. In particular, I argue that in the absence of reciprocity as a reason for norm generation, the changing identities and argumentative self-entrapment of international actors are the driving forces behind the emergence of general principles.[115]

5.2.4.3 Changing Identities and Argumentative Self-Entrapment as the Driving Forces Behind the Emergence of General Principles of Law

I claim that constructivism can help international lawyers to understand what "recognition" of a general principle on the international plane means in the absence of reciprocity. These norms emerge in discourses that take place in international forums. They are not based on reciprocity, but on ideational factors. Identity changes seem particularly plausible in cases where reciprocity is relatively absent because the respective norms mostly operate on the domestic level. If unwritten international law is essentially not of an *inter*-state character, but refers to the *internal* situation within the state, it specifies the

[114] On the norm life cycle, see generally Martha Finnemore and Kathryn Sikkink, "International Norm Dynamics and Political Change," 52 *International Organization* 895 (1998).

[115] For a strong account of how international law enables and constrains international politics in different fields, based, *inter alia*, on constructivism, see Jutta Brunnée and Stephen J. Toope, *Legitimacy and Legality in International Law: An Interactional Account* (Cambridge and New York: Cambridge University Press, 2010).

design of the domestic legal order. Therefore, despite all necessary caveats, this internalization labeled "identity change" seems to be the most reliable basis for normative expectations.

International discourses among states in international forums which lead to the emergence of unwritten legal norms may be dominated by certain states. These discourses frame the image of a legitimate state government. Other states will not openly resist or openly express opposition in many situations because they might well have an interest in participating in these discourses to be perceived as legitimate actors, rather than staying outside or seeking to undermine the game. They might seek to minimize the impact of their commitments on their domestic orders, but will be careful in order to avoid reputational costs, and may even try to portray themselves as making normative "progress" in order to strengthen their legitimacy. Moreover, states may have an interest in the benefits of coordination and cooperation.

This change of "identity" is furthered and stabilized by nongovernmental organizations and actors of civil society that attach themselves to various international institutions and their policies and shape public debates and perceptions. A further factor is the participation of public officials in the various networks and regimes. If we assume that international discourse between states, at least in certain settings, requires a minimal degree of argumentative consistency, states will be entrapped by their own statements. In some cases, states might at first only create an "identity image" to enhance their reputation among other states. In the long run, however, their commitments can lead to a real change of identity. Therefore, even hypocrisy may develop a civilizing force.[116] As noted earlier, we might refer to this latter process as "argumentative self-entrapment."

The processes of identity change and argumentative self-entrapment explain how general principles of law are created. Identity change and argumentative self-entrapment may also explain how non-binding resolutions of international organizations gain normative force as articulating general principles of law. They can also explain how principles developed within a particular area of international law and the principles of a specific treaty regime "spread out" and turn into principles of a more general scope.[117]

Compared to solid and reciprocal interstate practice covered by *opinio juris*, these jurisgenerative processes are indeed rather weak. Furthermore, the normative force of argumentative entrapment might also be relevant with

116 See, e.g., Jon Elster, "Strategic Uses of Argument," in *Barriers to Conflict Resolution*, edited by Kenneth J. Arrow et al. 250 (New York: Norton, 1995).

117 On the development of general principles of this category, see Wolfrum, "General International Law," paras. 41–42.

regard to the other sources of international law. However, *self*-entrapment is particularly relevant in the absence of reciprocity. These caveats need not be a conceptual drawback of the proposed approach. It still serves to distinguish the normative origin and force of general principles of law from those of customary international law.

Admittedly, the conditions for the acceptance of general principles on the international plane are still vague and require specification. It will be crucial to analyze the institutional settings in which processes of self-entrapment take place in order to evaluate the legitimacy of the norms that emerge in these processes. Both customary international law and general principles are two-fold concepts that rest on two elements. These are state practice plus *opinio juris* in the case of customary international law, and identity change plus argumentative self-entrapment in the case of general principles. Parallels possibly also exist in the relationship between identity change elements. A lack of consistent state practice in a general setting in which state action is primarily guided by expectations of reciprocity may be compensated by a strong *opinio juris* on the basis of the sliding scale approaches to customary law I described above. Similarly, a lack of authentic identity change – in the case of hypocrites – may be compensated by the principled normative force of argumentative self-entrapment.

As pointed out above, scholarly attention should not focus on the processes that I aim to explain on the basis of constructivism in isolation. In addition, it is crucial to analyze what courts do and say. International judicial institutions refer to principles emerging in processes of identity change and argumentative self-entrapment and use them in order to guide their interpretations of other norms and solidify abstract principles in order to find solutions to concrete cases. They thus act as catalysts of these processes. In this regard, principles constitute a mechanism for progressive development of international law in both roles. This discussion of principles has revealed that generality and flexibility are accepted as the least common denominator of general principles. Due to this openness, general principles constitute the basis for new or at least modified international obligations.[118]

Constructivism therefore not only explains compliance with existing norms, but also explains the jurisgenerative processes by which legal norms emerge and evolve.[119] Application of the law and the emergence of new law are

[118] See ibid., para. 125.

[119] See Benjamin Herborth, "Verständigung verstehen: Anmerkungen zur ZIB-Debatte," in *Anarchie der kommunikativen Freiheit: Jürgen Habermas und die Theorie der internationalen Politik*, edited by Peter Niesen and Benjamin Herborth 166 (Frankfurt am Main: Suhrkamp, 2007); Tine Hanrieder, "The False Promise of the Better Argument," 3 *International Theory* 390 (2011), 403.

interdependent and intertwined processes. They are particularly interrelated in the case of general, unwritten norms. In this respect, it is plausible to closely link the norm construction process, the "source" of general principles, with the specific use of principles in legal argumentation. The genesis of these principles is accelerated by the fact that international actors need to justify their actions in different contexts in a fragmented international legal system, and by the open or silent interaction between international judicial institutions.

5.3 CONCLUSION

In order to analyze the relationship between customary international law and general principles of law, I have traced the different meanings of principles in international law as a source and as a norm type with particular functions in legal argumentation. Drawing a "demarcation line" between customary international law and general principles is not difficult on the basis of narrow concepts of both sources. Many scholars wish to attribute more ambitious functions to each of these sources in international law and therefore develop broader concepts of them. However, distinguishing the two sources then becomes more difficult.

I have sought to solve this problem by arguing that customary international law can be distinguished from general principles by looking at the role of reciprocal interactions between states. In particular, reciprocal state interaction justifies customary legal norms. Norms generated in issue areas where reciprocal state interaction is minimal or absent, on the other hand, are best regarded as general principles of law. The limited framework of this chapter has offered the opportunity to elaborate on the distinct processes leading to the emergence of general principles in the absence of reciprocity. Constructivist approaches to international law provide the theoretical basis of my explanation of these processes. However, much more research needs to be done in order to specify the threshold of normativity for norms that develop in these processes and to describe these processes in detail with regard to concrete principles.

ACKNOWLEDGMENTS

I am grateful to Anuscheh Farahat, Isabel Feichtner, Cornelia Janik, Stefan Kadelbach, Brian Lepard, Anna Katharina Mangold, and Niels Petersen for their very helpful comments on this chapter.

PART II

Reexamining Customary Humanitarian Law

6

The ICRC and the Clarification of Customary International Humanitarian Law

*Jean-Marie Henckaerts and Els Debuf**

6.1 INTRODUCTION: THE ICRC'S WORK ON CUSTOMARY INTERNATIONAL HUMANITARIAN LAW

In January 1995, the Intergovernmental Group of Experts for the Protection of War Victims proposed that the International Committee of the Red Cross ("ICRC") undertake a study on customary rules of international humanitarian law ("IHL") applicable in international and non-international armed conflicts.[1] This proposal was among a series of recommendations made by the Group aimed at enhancing respect for IHL. In December 1995, states endorsed this recommendation at the 26th International Conference of the Red Cross and Red Crescent and officially mandated the ICRC to prepare the study.[2]

After nearly ten years of extensive research and wide consultation involving more than 100 governmental and academic experts, the ICRC's study on customary IHL ("Study") was published in March 2005.[3] The Study comprises

* The views in this chapter are those of the authors alone. They do not necessarily reflect those of the ICRC.

1 Meeting of the Intergovernmental Group of Experts for the Protection of War Victims, Geneva, 23–27 January 1995, Recommendation II, 78 *International Review of the Red Cross* No. 310, 84 (1996), 84 (the recommendation proposed that "[t]he ICRC be invited to prepare, with the assistance of experts in IHL [international humanitarian law] representing various geographical regions and different legal systems, and in consultation with experts from governments and international organizations, a report on customary rules of IHL applicable in international and non-international armed conflicts, and to circulate the report to States and competent international bodies").

2 26th International Conference of the Red Cross and Red Crescent, Geneva, 3–7 December 1995, Resolution 1, para. 4, in "International Humanitarian Law: From Law to Action: Report on the Follow-Up to the International Conference for the Protection of War Victims," 78 *International Review of the Red Cross* No. 310, 58 (1996), 59.

3 *Customary International Humanitarian Law*, edited by Jean-Marie Henckaerts and Louise Doswald-Beck, 2 vols., Vol. I: Rules, Vol. II: Practice (2 Parts) (Cambridge: Cambridge University Press and ICRC, 2005). For more information, see www.icrc.org/eng/customary-law.

two volumes. The first volume, Volume I, sets out in a transparent manner the methodology followed and lists a total of 161 rules that were assessed to be of a customary law nature based on this methodology.[4] Volume II contains the practice on which the conclusions in Volume I are based. The practice in Volume II continues to be updated on the ICRC's freely accessible "online Customary IHL Database," launched in August 2010 and already containing about 80 percent more content than the original print version.[5]

The ICRC Study on customary IHL was not intended to be, and cannot be expected to be, exhaustive, both in terms of areas covered as well as in terms of the scope and extent of practice collected. The same holds true for the ICRC's Customary IHL Database. The Database does not purport to cover all practice worldwide, whether state practice or international practice. It aims to offer a collection of state and international practice that is sufficiently "dense" to allow for an assessment of any evolutions in the existence, scope, and meaning of the rules of customary international law identified by the ICRC in the Study.[6] For that reason, the ICRC strives to update continuously in the Database the practice of around 100 states, representing different regions and legal systems around the world. Efforts are also made to include in particular the practice of states that have a relatively comprehensive, clear, and public position and practice on a broad range of IHL topics.

Section 6.2 of this chapter illustrates the contemporary relevance of customary humanitarian law and gives examples of the use of custom in armed conflicts today. Section 6.3 highlights the impact the ICRC's work on customary IHL has had in this regard and provides examples of when and how the Study and Database are being used. Section 6.4 focuses on specific methodological issues with which a study on customary international law, such as the ICRC's, had to grapple. It tries to shed more light on how these theoretical issues play out in practice in a concrete assessment of customary law, based on an extensive collection of practice and assessment of *opinio juris*.

4 This volume has been translated into the official UN languages and several additional languages, namely: Arabic (Cairo: ICRC, 2007), Chinese (Beijing: China Law Press, 2007), Farsi (Tehran: Majd Publishers, 2008), French (Brussels: Editions Bruylant, 2006), Russian (Moscow: ICRC, 2006), Serbian (Belgrade: ICRC, 2005), Spanish (Buenos Aires: ICRC, 2007), and Turkish (Istanbul: Galatasary University, 2011). In addition, the rules have been translated into nearly fifty languages, available at: www.icrc.org/eng/resources/documents/misc/customary-law-translations.htm.

5 For more information, visit the Database at www.icrc.org/customary-ihl/eng/docs/home.

6 See also *Customary International Humanitarian Law*, Vol. I: Rules, xxxvi and xxxviii ("State practice has to be weighed to assess whether it is sufficiently 'dense' to create a rule of customary international law. [To do so,] State practice has to be virtually uniform, extensive and representative.... No precise number of States is required.... [T]he criterion is in a sense *qualitative* rather than quantitative.") (emphasis in the original).

6.2 THE RELEVANCE OF CUSTOMARY LAW IN INTERNATIONAL HUMANITARIAN LAW

While IHL is an extensively codified area of international law, customary law continues to play an important role, and perhaps increasingly so, in humanizing warfare and enhancing the protection of victims of armed conflicts. Customary law plays this key role for at least two reasons. First, customary IHL provides a common set of rules applicable to armed conflicts, binding all parties to these conflicts,[7] regardless of the differentiated levels of states' ratification of specific IHL treaties. Second, the formation of customary law has allowed IHL to adapt – perhaps in a more flexible manner than treaty law is able to do – to changes in the conduct of contemporary armed conflicts.

6.2.1 *The Unifying Function of Customary IHL*

The Geneva Conventions have today been universally ratified.[8] As a result, the Conventions are binding on all states as a matter of treaty law, regardless of whether the norms in them are also part of customary international law. However, the same cannot be said of other treaties of humanitarian law. For example, Additional Protocols I and II to the Geneva Conventions have been ratified by more than 170 and 160 states respectively.[9] This is an impressive ratification record by any measure. However, an important number of states still remain outside the framework of this treaty regime.[10] The same is true for other treaties, such as the 1954 Hague Convention on the Protection of Cultural Property in Time of Armed Conflicts and its Protocols, as well as the 1980 Convention on Certain Conventional Weapons and its Protocols.[11]

7 With the exception of states that have "persistently objected" to a rule according to the persistent objector rule, which is addressed later in this chapter.

8 South Sudan and Palestine were the most recent states to adhere to the Geneva Conventions, respectively on 13 January 2013 and on 2 April 2014.

9 For background on the Geneva Conventions, their Additional Protocols, and IHL more generally, see www.icrc.org/en/war-and-law and www.icrc.org/eng/war-and-law/treaties-customary-law/overview-treaties-and-customary-law.htm.

10 UN member states that are not yet party to Additional Protocol I are Andorra, Azerbaijan, Bhutan, Eritrea, India, Indonesia, Iran, Israel, Kiribati, Malaysia, Marshall Islands, Myanmar, Nepal, Pakistan, Papua New Guinea, Singapore, Somalia, Sri Lanka, Thailand, Turkey, Tuvalu, and the United States of America. UN member states that are not yet party to Additional Protocol II are Andorra, Angola, Azerbaijan, Bhutan, Democratic Republic of Korea, Eritrea, India, Indonesia, Iran, Iraq, Israel, Kiribati, Malaysia, Marshall Islands, Mexico, Myanmar, Nepal, Pakistan, Papua New Guinea, Singapore, Somalia, Sri Lanka, Syrian Arab Republic, Thailand, Turkey, Tuvalu, the United States of America, and Vietnam.

11 For a continuously updated list of states parties to the main IHL treaties, see www.icrc.org/ihl.

The non-universal ratification of important IHL treaties means that in different conflicts different treaty regimes apply. This situation is not satisfactory from the perspective of the legal protection of war victims.

Customary rules of IHL, by contrast, apply equally to all states and to all armed conflicts, regardless of the ratification record of the parties to the conflict.[12] For example, during the armed conflict between Ethiopia and Eritrea from May 1998 until June 2000, Eritrea was not yet a party to the Geneva Conventions and Additional Protocol I. Hence, these treaties were formally inapplicable to the conflict.[13] The Ethiopia-Eritrea Claims Commission had to grapple with this issue when it examined claims emerging from the conflict.[14] The Commission worked on the assumption that the Geneva Conventions, as well as Additional Protocol I, represented customary international law,[15] and relied heavily on customary international law to settle the claims before it.

The fact that different treaties have different levels of ratification also impacts coalition warfare when different coalition partners have not subscribed to the same treaties. In these cases, only customary humanitarian law provides a common set of rules that is applicable to all coalition partners. Therefore, even if a state is a party to a particular treaty, it may still be relevant to know to what extent (some of) its rules reflect customary law and are, as such, binding on coalition partners that have not ratified the treaty. This was the case, for example, during the First Gulf War in 1990–91, NATO's air operations over Kosovo in 1999, and more recently, coalition operations in Libya in 2011. Thus, concerning the Libya conflict, the International Commission of Inquiry stated in its June 2011 report:

[12] It should be noted that customary IHL distinguishes between armed conflicts of an international nature and non-international armed conflicts, just as IHL treaties do. While the customary rules applicable to both categories of armed conflict increasingly overlap, the two bodies of law are not fully identical in content.

[13] See common Article 2 of the 1949 Geneva Conventions and Article 3 of 1977 Additional Protocol I.

[14] The Commission was set up after the end of the armed conflict between Ethiopia and Eritrea in 2000 to "decide through binding arbitration all claims for loss, damage or injury by one Government against the other, and by nationals … result[ing] from violations of international humanitarian law." Agreement between the Governments of the State of Eritrea and the Federal Democratic Republic of Ethiopia, Algiers, 12 December 2000, art. 5(1).

[15] Either party to the arbitration proceedings could challenge this assumption, the challenging party having the burden of proof with respect to the Geneva Conventions and the Commission with respect to Additional Protocol I. See Eritrea-Ethiopia Claims Commission, Partial Award, *Prisoners of War, Eritrea's Claim* 17, 1 July 2003, § 41 and Partial Award, *Prisoners of War, Ethiopia's Claim* 4, § 32 (concerning the Geneva Conventions); Eritrea-Ethiopia Claims Commission, Partial Award, *Central Front, Eritrea's Claims* 2, 4, 6, 7, 8 *and* 22, 28 April 2004, § 23; and Partial Award, *Central Front, Ethiopia's Claim* 2, § 17 (concerning Additional Protocol I).

> In relation to the international armed conflict, the full provisions of the four Geneva Conventions, as well as customary international humanitarian norms relating to international armed conflict apply to engagements. Libya and most of the States involved in the military intervention [except Turkey and the U.S.] have also ratified Additional Protocol I to the Geneva Conventions Relating to the Protection of Victims of International Armed Conflict.[16]

The unifying role of customary IHL with respect to non-international armed conflicts is exemplified by the work of the International Commission of Inquiry on Darfur in 2004–05.[17] Because the Commission reviewed facts related to the conflict in Darfur (Sudan) at a time when Sudan was not yet a party to Additional Protocol II, customary IHL applicable in non-international armed conflicts was of particular relevance for the work of the Commission. The Commission deemed it sufficient to mention "only those customary rules on internal armed conflict which are relevant and applicable to the current armed conflict in Darfur," and listed twenty-four such rules.[18]

6.2.2 *The Adaptive Function of Customary IHL*

The adoption, ratification, and entry into force of treaties are regulated by strict formal procedures, which makes the treaty process at times lengthy and cumbersome, including the process for amending treaties. Treaties tend therefore to be more static than customary law, which is by nature based on a dynamic process. Thus, the formation of customary international law can be a more flexible process, and can at times adapt international law more easily to new realities on the ground. On the other hand, treaties can, at times, regulate new issues more quickly or provide a more detailed regulation beyond what the customary process can produce.[19]

16 "Report of the International Commission of Inquiry to Investigate All Alleged Violations of International Human Rights Law in the Libyan Arab Jamahiriya," UN Doc. A/HRC/17/44 (1 June 2011), para. 76.

17 See "Report of the International Commission of Inquiry on Darfur to the United Nations Secretary-General, pursuant to Security Council Resolution 1564 of 18 September 2004," 25 January 2005, available at www.un.org/news/dh/sudan/com_inq_darfur.pdf.

18 Ibid., para. 166. Some rules referred to by the Commission include: the obligation to distinguish between the combatants and civilians (Rule 1); the prohibition on deliberate attacks and indiscriminate attacks on civilians and civilian objects (Rules 1, 7, 11); the obligation to comply with the principle of proportionality (Rule 14) and take precautions in attack (Rules 15–21); the prohibition on the destruction of objects indispensable to the survival of the civilian population (Rule 54); the protection of cultural objects and places of worship (Rules 38–41); and the prohibition of pillage (Rule 52).

19 See, e.g., Convention on Cluster Munitions, Dublin, 30 May 2008 (development of a prohibition through treaty law long before any custom on the subject could develop) and Arms Trade

A particular weakness of international humanitarian treaty law is that it offers only a rudimentary framework for the regulation of non-international armed conflicts, in particular with respect to the conduct of hostilities. For example, common Article 3 of the Geneva Conventions, which regulates non-international armed conflicts, does not as such deal with the conduct of hostilities.[20]

Furthermore, Additional Protocol II similarly does not deal with the conduct of hostilities and a number of other issues in sufficient detail. For example, unlike Additional Protocol I, Additional Protocol II does not provide for the obligation to distinguish between military objectives and civilian objects. As a result, it does not contain any protection for civilian objects in general, nor does it define civilian objects and military objectives.[21] This is problematic in practice because, even in non-international armed conflicts, armed forces (both state armed forces and nonstate armed groups) are required to limit their military operations to military objectives. Additional Protocol II lacks other key provisions on the conduct of hostilities as well, such as provisions laying down the prohibition and definition of indiscriminate attacks and the obligation to take precautions in attack and against the effects of attack. While these shortcomings in treaty law have been rectified somewhat in subsequent treaties applicable to non-international armed conflicts,[22] it is through the parallel development of customary law that they have been rectified most effectively.

Treaty, New York, 2 April 2013 (development of a detailed regulatory framework far beyond a level of detail that can be achieved through the customary process).

20 Common Article 3 to the Geneva Conventions sets out the minimum rules applicable to non-international armed conflicts, including humane treatment of persons *hors de combat* without adverse distinction. In particular, violence to life and person, taking of hostages, outrages on personal dignity, and the passing of sentences and the carrying out of executions without a fair trial are prohibited. In addition, common Article 3 requires that the wounded and sick be collected and cared for, and permits parties to a non-international armed conflict to enter into special agreements that bring all or part of the other provisions of the Geneva Conventions into force. See common Article 3 to the Geneva Conventions of 12 August 1949 (adopted on 12 August 1949, entered into force on 21 October 1950).

21 Additional Protocol I, art. 52(1) provides: "Civilian objects shall not be the object of attack or of reprisals. Civilian objects are all objects which are not military objectives as defined in paragraph 2." Additional Protocol I, art. 52(2) provides: "Attacks shall be limited strictly to military objectives. In so far as objects are concerned, military objectives are limited to those objects which by their nature, location, purpose or use make an effective contribution to military action and whose total or partial destruction, capture or neutralization, in the circumstances ruling at the time, offers a definite military advantage."

22 See, e.g., Protocol on Prohibitions or Restrictions on the Use of Mines, Booby-Traps and Other Devices, as Amended, Geneva, 3 May 1996, arts. 2(6)-(7) and 3(7)-(11); Second Protocol to the Hague Convention of 1954 for the Protection of Cultural Property in the Event of Armed Conflict, The Hague, 26 March 1999, arts. 6–8.

The ICRC's study on customary international law indicates that the main rules on the conduct of hostilities, the use of means and methods of warfare, and the treatment of persons in the hands of a party to the conflict are part of customary law, not only in international but also in non-international armed conflicts. As a result, it can be said that the normative gap between the law on international and non-international armed conflicts has been significantly narrowed.

This is not to say that the customary law on international and non-international armed conflicts is now exactly the same. The ICRC Study shows that a difference continues to exist between the regulation of international and non-international armed conflicts.[23] Of the 161 rules the Study has identified, 12 apply to international armed conflicts only. These relate to what continues to be considered the "reserved domain" of international armed conflicts and include the definition of combatants and armed forces, conditions for prisoner of war status, the regulation of occupied territory, and the regulation of belligerent reprisals.[24]

On the other hand, the ICRC Study found that two rules apply to non-international armed conflicts only. These relate to the prohibition of belligerent reprisals and the granting of amnesty at the end of active hostilities.[25] With respect to the remaining 146 rules applicable in both international and non-international armed conflicts, three important nuances exist. First, the ICRC Study concluded that several rules were only "arguably" customary law in non-international armed conflicts, recognizing that practice was not that

23 The International Criminal Tribunal for the former Yugoslavia ("ICTY"), a tribunal that also relied significantly on customary IHL, found similarly that "only a number of rules and principles governing international armed conflicts have gradually been extended to apply to internal conflicts; and this extension has not taken place in the form of a full and mechanical transplant of those rules to internal conflicts; rather, the general essence of those rules, and not the detailed regulation they may contain, has become applicable to internal conflicts." ICTY, *Prosecutor v. Tadić*, Decision on the Defence Motion for Interlocutory Appeal on Jurisdiction, Appeals Chamber, 2 October 1995, Case No. IT-94-1-AR72, para. 126.

24 See *Customary International Humanitarian Law*, Vol. I: Rules, Rules 3 (definition of combatants), 4 (definition of armed forces), 41 (export and return of cultural property in occupied territory), 49 (war booty), 51 (public and private property in occupied territory), 106–08 (conditions for POW status, spies, mercenaries), 130 (transfer of own civilian population in occupied territory), and 145–47 (reprisals). For an analysis of whether even these areas could be merged, see Emily Crawford, "Blurring the Lines between International and Non-international Armed Conflicts: The Evolution of Customary International Law Applicable in Internal Armed Conflicts," 15 *Australian International Law Journal* 29 (2008); Emily Crawford, *The Treatment of Combatants and Insurgents under the Law of Armed Conflict* (Oxford: Oxford University Press, 2010); and Els Debuf, *Captured in War: Lawful Internment in Armed Conflict* (Paris/Oxford: Pédone/Hart, 2013), 110–11.

25 See *Customary International Humanitarian Law*, Vol. I: Rules, Rules 148 (reprisals in non-international armed conflicts) and 159 (amnesty).

dense in certain areas.[26] Second, the wording in the ICRC Study of some rules of customary humanitarian law is different for international and non-international armed conflicts based on the ICRC's assessment of differences in state practice.[27] Finally, some rules of customary IHL applicable in non-international armed conflict could only be identified as applicable to states but not to nonstate parties to armed conflict.[28] Hence, important differences in substance and scope of the rules applicable to international and non-international armed conflicts continue to exist.

6.3 THE IMPACT OF THE ICRC'S WORK ON CUSTOMARY IHL

Since its publication in 2005, the ICRC Study has been used by many as a legal reference to identify and interpret applicable rules of customary IHL, both in international and in non-international armed conflicts. Because of its origin – a mandate from the international community – the Study was intended as a working tool at the service of practitioners involved with humanitarian law, not a handbook of theoretical considerations. Given the time and resources needed to collect and assess practice and *opinio juris* for the purpose of identifying rules of customary IHL, the Study has proven to be very useful for practitioners, who would not have the time or resources to undertake this research themselves. This is also why the ICRC decided to make the Study available online and to continue updating the practice underlying it. The constant evolution of state and international practice affects the existence, scope, and meaning of the rules it underpins. The online Customary IHL Database allows both the ICRC and practitioners to monitor the evolution of practice and therefore of customary IHL.

Practitioners are using the Database with increased frequency and intensity.[29] Its users include a wide range of relevant actors,

[26] See ibid., Rules 21(target selection), 23–24 (specific precautions against the effects of attack), 44–45 (specific rules on the natural environment), 62–63 (improper use of flags, military or military emblems, insignia, or uniforms), and 82 (recording of the placement of landmines). For Rule 114 (return of the remains and personal effects of the dead), the study argues that the rule should apply equally in both international and non-international armed conflicts. See ibid., 412.

[27] See ibid., Rules 124 (ICRC access to persons deprived of their liberty), 126 (visits to persons deprived of their liberty), 128 (release and return of persons deprived of their liberty), and 129 (displacement).

[28] See ibid., Rules 141 (legal advisers for armed forces), 143 (dissemination among the civilian population), 144 (ensuring respect *erga omnes*), 149–50 (responsibility and reparation), 157–58 (jurisdiction over and prosecution of war crimes), and 161 (international cooperation in criminal proceedings).

[29] In 2013, the Database had 537,662 page views. That number has been increasing steadily since its publication online in August 2010. There were 113,446 views in 2010, 357,357 views in 2011, and 432,686 views in 2012.

including governments, armed forces, domestic and international courts taking important decisions on the applicability and interpretation of IHL, domestic and international commissions of inquiry, nongovernmental organizations and other institutions reporting on alleged violations of IHL, and, of course, the academic world.[30] Its most visited pages concern subjects that are at the center of current debates on IHL or that have raised concern in ongoing armed conflicts.[31] Many of its users come from countries affected by armed conflict or with a strong interest and involvement in the implementation, clarification, and development of IHL. Accordingly, the Database has become a useful and widely appreciated addition to the Study, and together they are considered important reference tools on customary IHL. The remainder of this section illustrates when, how, and by whom customary IHL and the ICRC's Study and Database have been used to identify, interpret, and apply customary IHL to reinforce the protection of victims of armed conflict.

With respect to international armed conflicts, the Study's rules have been relied on primarily, but not exclusively, in relation to states that are not parties to Additional Protocol I (including Israel and the United States of America). For example, the United Nations Fact-Finding Commission on the Gaza Conflict significantly relied in its 2009 report on rules of customary IHL regulating the conduct of hostilities because Israel had not ratified Additional Protocol I.[32] So did the United Nations Secretary-General's Panel of Inquiry on the 31 May 2010 flotilla incident off the coast of Israel.[33] Israeli courts and authorities themselves have also relied significantly on customary IHL and the ICRC Study in their findings and reports on issues related to the Israeli-Palestinian conflict.[34] In international armed conflicts where all states

30 For concrete examples, see the discussion later in the chapter.

31 In 2013, the top list of topics on which users consulted the Database included, in order of importance: (1) the principle of distinction, including specific rules and definitions of key concepts, (2) chemical weapons, (3) war crimes (definition, prosecution, responsibility), (4) proportionality in attack, (5) definition of military objectives, (6) torture, cruel and inhuman treatment, (7) rape and other forms of sexual violence, (8) attacks against persons *hors de combat*, (9) collective punishments, and (10) recruitment of child soldiers.

32 "Report of the United Nations Fact-Finding Mission on the Gaza Conflict," UN Doc. A/HRC/12/48 (25 September 2009), §§ 32 and 385 (Rules 7 and 9), § 431 (Rule 6), §§ 38, 489–492 and 528 (Rules 22–24), §§ 50 and 934 (Rule 54), § 1097 (Rule 97), § 1216 (Rule 145), § 1322 (Rule 44), § 1328 (Rule 103), and 1684 (Rule 2).

33 The Panel of Inquiry was established to investigate an incident that took place on the high seas off the shore of Gaza in May 2010. "Report of the Secretary-General's Panel of Inquiry on the 31 May 2010 Flotilla Incident," September 2011, Appendix I, § 33 (Rule 53), § 33 (Rule 53), § 35 (Rule 55), and § 47 (Rules 1, 5 and 6). Available at www.un.org/News/dh/infocus/middle_east/Gaza_Flotilla_Panel_Report.pdf.

34 See the discussion that follows.

involved are parties to Additional Protocol I, such as the 2008 conflict between Georgia and Russia, customary humanitarian law is of course less relevant.

In non-international armed conflicts, customary humanitarian law is relevant both for states that are not parties to Additional Protocol II and for states that are parties to Additional Protocol II. For conflicts within states that are not parties to Additional Protocol II, such as Afghanistan (prior to 2009), Somalia, Sri Lanka, Syria, or Sudan (prior to 2006), customary humanitarian law is or was the source of the majority of applicable humanitarian law rules, along with common Article 3 of the Geneva Conventions, which is or was the main humanitarian treaty provision in force. As a result, for example, in its report of 2011, the Secretary-General's Panel of Experts on Accountability in Sri Lanka relied extensively on rules of customary IHL, including several identified by the ICRC Study.[35] So did the International Commission of Inquiry on the Syrian Arab Republic in its reports on alleged violations of international human rights and humanitarian law in Syria (2012–13).[36]

In states that *are* parties to Additional Protocol II, such as Colombia or Libya, customary humanitarian law usefully complements the legal framework of that treaty.[37] For example, Colombia's operational law handbook refers

35 See "Report of the Secretary-General's Panel of Experts on Accountability in Sri Lanka," 31 March 2011, § 183 ("In order to determine the content and meaning of customary international law, the Panel relies upon various sources, including the ICRC's study, *Customary International Humanitarian Law* (2005), which comprehensively analyses state practice and attitudes."). For specific references to the study, see ibid., § 194 (Rule 1), § 196 (Rules 7 and 35), § 200 (Rule 2), § 201 (Rules 11–13), § 203 (Rule 14), § 204 (Rules 15–20), § 207 (Rules 25, 28, and 30–32), § 211 (Rules 53 and 55), § 215 (Rule 98), § 216 (Rule 118), § 217 (Rules 112–13 and 115–17), § 218 (Rule 115), § 237 (Rule 97), § 239 (Rules 23–24), § 240 (Rule 136), and § 241 (Rule 95).

36 In Annex II to its first report, on "Applicable Law," the Commission referred to the applicability of customary IHL and referred to the ICRC's Study as a "repository of the principles of customary IHL" (§ 11) and "an extensive study [in which] the ICRC identified 161 customary international humanitarian legal norms" (§ 20). The Commission also cited many of the Study's rules on specific topics. See "[First] Report of the Independent International Commission of Inquiry on the Syrian Arab Republic," UN Doc. A/HRC/21/50 (16 August 2012), 50 (Rule 158), 52 (Rule 14), 56 (Rules 99 and 123), 69 (Rules 6 and 14), and 75 (Rule 1). In later reports, the Commission continued to rely on customary IHL where necessary to complement or reinforce treaty provisions. See, e.g., "Report of the Independent International Commission of Inquiry on the Syrian Arab Republic," UN Doc. A/HRC/22/59 (5 February 2013), 15, 19, 23, 58, 66, 89–90, 110, 113, 116, 120, and 124; "Conference Room Paper: Assault on Medical Care in Syria," UN Doc. A/HRC/24/CRP.2 (13 September 2013), 2, 5; "[Seventh] Report of the Independent International Commission of Inquiry on the Syrian Arab Republic," UN Doc. A/HRC/25/65 (12 February 2014), 37, 55, and 58.

37 See *Customary International Humanitarian Law*, Vol. I: Rules. For example, see in particular Rules 7–24 on the conduct of hostilities; Rules 31–32 on humanitarian relief personnel and objects; Rule 34 on journalists; Rules 43–45 on the environment; Rules 115–16 on the dead; Rule 117 on the missing; and Rule 123 on persons deprived of their liberty, which are additional to the treaty rules found in Additional Protocol II.

to several rules of customary humanitarian law identified by the Study.[38] There is also significant case law from the Colombian constitutional court referring to customary humanitarian law and the ICRC's Study.[39] With respect to Libya, the International Commission of Inquiry established to investigate alleged violations of international human rights and humanitarian law in the Libyan Arab Jamahiriya (2011) relied on both treaty law binding upon Libya (including Additional Protocol II) and customary humanitarian law. When relying on the latter, the Commission systematically included references to the relevant rules identified in the ICRC Study.[40]

In addition to these references by international commissions relating to the conflicts in Sri Lanka, Syria, and Libya, several UN special rapporteurs have relied on customary humanitarian law and the ICRC's Study. One example is the report by several special rapporteurs of the UN Human Rights Council and the Representative of the Secretary-General on Internally Displaced Persons on their mission to Lebanon and Israel in the wake of the 2006 conflict.[41] Another example is the 2009 combined report of several mandate-holders

[38] See Colombia, *Manual de Derecho Operacional, Comando General de la Fuerzas Armadas*, Manual FF.MM 3–41 (Público, Primera Edición, 2009) (referring to Rules 1 and 21 (page 37), Rules 14 and 87 (page 38), Rule 140 (pages 38–39), Rule 9 (page 40), Rule 25 (pages 42–43 and 45), Rule 28 (page 43), Rule 27 (pages 44–45), Rule 31 (pages 45–46), Rule 34 (pages 46–47), Rules 15, 16, and 18 (page 52), Rules 19, 20, 21, 22, 129 b, and 70 (page 53), Rules 72, 73, 74, 77, 78, 79, 80, and 86 (page 54), Rules 46, 47, 48, 50, 52, 54, 65, and 53 (page 55) and Rule 8 (page 56)).

[39] See, e.g., Colombia, Constitutional Court, Sentencia C-291/07 (25 April 2007) (containing numerous references throughout the opinion to the ICRC Study).

[40] See "Report of the International Commission of Inquiry to Investigate Alleged Violations of International Human Rights Law in the Libyan Arab Jamahiriya," UN Doc. A/HRC/17/44 (1 June 2011), § 74 ("In relation to the non-international armed conflict which developed in Libya, of particular significance are the provisions of Additional Protocol II to the Geneva Conventions Relating to the Protection of Victims of Non-International Armed Conflict (AP II) together with the provisions of Common Article 3 of the Geneva Conventions ('Common Article 3'). The parties to the conflict are also bound by the provisions of customary international humanitarian law [with a reference to the ICRC's 2005 Study]."). For specific references to the Study, see ibid., § 103 (Rules 98, 99, 117, 123, 125, and 126), § 141 (Rule 34), § 156 (Rules 1, 11, and 14), § 157 (Rules 15–21), § 158 (Rules 31–32, 53, and 55), § 182 (Rule 70), § 183 (Rules 77 and 81), and § 186 (Rule 81).

[41] See "Report of the Special Rapporteur on Extrajudicial, Summary or Arbitrary executions, Philip Alston; the Special Rapporteur on the Right of Everyone to the Enjoyment of the Highest Attainable Standard of Physical and Mental Health, Paul Hunt; the Representative of the Secretary-General on Human Rights of Internally Displaced Persons, Walter Kälin; and the Special Rapporteur on Adequate Housing as a Component of the Right to an Adequate Standard of Living, Miloon Kothari, Mission to Lebanon and Israel (7–14 September 2006)," UN Doc. A/HRC/2/7 (2 October 2006), § 22 et seq. See also "Human Rights in Lebanon: Report of the Special Rapporteur on the Right to Food, Jean Ziegler, on His Mission to Lebanon," UN Doc. A/HRC/2/8 (29 September 2006), § 8 n.3.

of the UN Human Rights Council Special Procedures and the Special Representative of the Secretary-General for Children and Armed Conflict. This report referred to several rules in the Study as being part of customary humanitarian law.[42] A final example is the 2010 Joint Study on Global Practices in Relation to Secret Detention in the Context of Countering Terrorism, prepared by several special rapporteurs and working groups.[43] The Office of the High Commissioner for Human Rights has also relied on customary IHL and the ICRC's Study, for example when dealing with alleged violations of IHL in Colombia.[44]

Furthermore, in many states, customary international law can be invoked directly before national courts and tribunals. Such is the case in Israel, where the Supreme Court has on several occasions ruled on the customary nature of rules of humanitarian law.[45] In recent years, it has done so with reference to the ICRC Study. For example, in a judgment of December 2005 on the so-called "neighbour procedure" used by the Israeli Defence Forces ("IDF") to capture persons, the Israeli Supreme Court referred with approval to the

[42] "Human Rights Situation in Palestine and Other Occupied Arab Territories: Combined Report of the Special Rapporteur on the Right of Everyone to the Enjoyment of the Highest Attainable Standard of Physical and Mental Health, the Special Representative of the Secretary-General for Children and Armed Conflict, the Special Rapporteur on Violence Against Women, Its Causes and Consequences, the Representative of the Secretary-General on the Human Rights of Internally Displaced Persons, the Special Rapporteur on Adequate Housing as a Component of the Right to an Adequate Standard of Living, and on the Right to Non-Discrimination in This Context, the Special Rapporteur on the Right to Food, the Special Rapporteur on Extrajudicial, Arbitrary or Summary Executions, the Special Rapporteur on the Right to Education, and the Independent Expert on the Question of Human Rights and Extreme Poverty," UN Doc. A/HRC/10/22 (20 March 2009), § 11 (Rules 6–9, 11–13, 15–24, and 97), § 46 (Rule 54), § 66 (Rules 25 and 28–29), § 66 (Rule 38), and § 83 (Rules 24 and 129–131).

[43] "Joint Study on Global Practices in Relation to Secret Detention in the Context of Countering Terrorism, prepared by two Special Rapporteurs and Working Groups: Prepared by the Special Rapporteur on the Promotion and Protection of Human Rights and Fundamental Freedoms while Countering Terrorism, Martin Scheinin; the Special Rapporteur on Torture and Other Cruel, Inhuman or Degrading Treatment of Punishment, Manfred Nowak; the Working Group on Arbitrary Detention represented by its Vice-Chair, Shaheen Sardar; and the Working Group on Enforced or Involuntary Disappearances Represented by its Chair, Jeremy Sarkin," UN Doc. A/HRC/13/42 (19 February 2010), § 55 (referring to Rules 98–99, 123, and 125–26).

[44] See, e.g., Office of the High Commissioner for Human Rights, "Report on the Cemetery of Macarana, Department of Meta," 6 (citing Rules 112–17 as relevant norms of customary international humanitarian law regarding the issues of dead and missing persons).

[45] See, e.g., Israel, The Supreme Court sitting as the High Court of Justice, *Affo and Others v. Commander of the IDF in the West Bank* (10 December 1988), HCJ 785/87, HCJ 845/87, HCJ 27/88, reprinted in 29 *International Legal Materials* 139 (1990) (concerning the customary nature of Article 49 of the Fourth Geneva Convention).

Study's findings on the customary law nature of the requirements to give effective, advance warning (Rule 20) and to remove civilians from the vicinity of military objectives (Rule 24), as well as the prohibition of human shields (Rule 97).[46]

In its judgment of December 2006 on the policy of targeted killing, the Israeli Supreme Court referred with approval to the Study's conclusions concerning the principle of distinction between civilians and combatants and between civilian objects and military objectives (Rules 1 and 7), the principle that civilians are protected against attack, unless and for such time as they take a direct part in hostilities (Rule 6), the prohibition of indiscriminate attacks (Rule 11), and the prohibition against causing excessive incidental loss of civilian life, injury to civilians, damage to civilian objects, or a combination of these (Rule 14).[47] In a judgment of January 2008 concerning the reduction of fuel and electricity supply from Israel to Gaza, the Court also referred to customary IHL and the ICRC Study, stating that "each party to a conflict is obliged to refrain from disrupting the passage of basic humanitarian relief to populations needing it in areas under its control." However, it found that Israel had not violated this obligation.[48]

The U.S. Supreme Court cited the ICRC Study in its *Hamdan* decision relating to the U.S. military commissions, in which it stated that "one of the Red Cross' own treatises defines 'regularly constituted court' as used in Common Article 3 to mean 'established and organized in accordance with the laws and procedures in force in a country.'"[49] The War Crimes Section of the Court of Bosnia and Herzegovina relies significantly on customary IHL and has referred to the ICRC's Study (both the rules and the underlying practice) in its case law. In particular, it has done so to support its findings on issues such as the definition of specific war crimes, the nature of the obligation to prosecute war crimes, the applicability of the rules on command responsibility in non-international armed conflicts, the customary nature of the obligation to respect cultural property, and the prohibition of direct and indiscriminate

46 Israel, The Supreme Court sitting as the High Court of Justice, *Adalah and Others v. GOC Central Command, IDF and Others* (23 June 2005), HCJ 3799/02, §§ 20–21 and 24.

47 Israel, The Supreme Court sitting as the High Court of Justice, *The Public Committee against Torture in Israel and Others v. The Government of Israel and Others* (13 December 2006), HCJ 769/02, §§ 23, 29–30, and 41–42. See also references to the commentary of the Study in ibid., §§ 33–34, 40, 46.

48 See Israel, The Supreme Court sitting as the High Court of Justice, *Jaber Al-Bassiouni Ahmed and Others v. The Prime Minister and Minister of Defence* (30 January 2008), HCJ 9132/07, § 14 et seq.

49 United States of America, Supreme Court, *Hamdan v. Rumsfeld, Secretary of Defense, et al.*, 548 U.S. 557 (2006), 631.

attacks against civilians.[50] Courts dealing with war crimes cases in Germany[51] and the Netherlands[52] have also relied on and referred to the ICRC's Study.

At the international level, the International Criminal Tribunal for the former Yugoslavia ("ICTY") often operates on the basis of Article 3 of its Statute, which gives the Tribunal jurisdiction over "violations of the laws or customs of war."[53] The report of the UN Secretary-General submitted pursuant to the Security Council decision to establish the ICTY stated that "the application of the principle *nullum crimen sine lege* requires that the international tribunal [ICTY] should apply rules of IHL which are beyond any doubt part of customary law so that the problem of adherence of some but not all States to specific conventions does not arise."[54] As a result, in order to satisfy the principle of legality (*nullum crimen, nulla poena sine lege previa*), any conviction based on Article 3 of the Statute requires proof that the crime in question was part of customary international law at the time the alleged crime was committed.[55]

In practice, the ICTY has in fact required such proof, including a showing of adequate state practice and *opinio juris*. For example, in *Prosecutor v. Hadžihasanović and Kubura*, the Appeals Chamber of the Tribunal

[50] See, e.g., Court of Bosnia and Herzegovina, Section I for War Crimes, Case No. X-KR-06/290, Judgment of 28 November 2007, 21; Case No. X-KR-06/275, Judgment of 28 February 2008, 114; Case No. X-KR-08/488, Judgment of 10 July 2008, 11–12; Case No. X-KR-07/480, Judgment of 22 October 2008, 10; Case No. X-KR-08/502, Judgment of 28 November 2008, 19; Case No. X-KR-06/299, Judgment of 25 March 2009, 26; and Case No. X-KR-07/394, Judgment of 12 June 2009, 45.

[51] See Germany, Federal Prosecutor General at the Federal Court of Justice, "Investigation Proceedings Against Colonel Klein and Company Sergeant Major Wilhelm Because of Suspected Offences under the International Crimes Code and Other, Termination of Proceedings Pursuant to § 170, Para. 2, Sentence 1 of the Penal Procedure Code," 3 BJs 6/10–4 (16 April 2010), 58 (with regard to the definition of war crimes, relying on Rule 156) and 65–67 (with regard to the obligations of proportionality in attack and precautions against the effects on attack, relying on Rules 14 and 22).

[52] See Netherlands, Hague District Court, Criminal Law Section, *Mpambara Case*, Case No. 09/75009-06 and 09/750007-07, Landelijk Jurispr BK0520, Judgment of 23 March 2009, §§ 19 and 21–23. The court referred to the ICRC's Study in order to support the finding that both common Article 3 and, to a large extent, Additional Protocol II are part of customary international humanitarian law, and that gross violations of them are war crimes. The court stated in this connection: "The Court bases this assessment on the results of recent (2005) and extensive inquiries into the existence and contents of international customary law carried out by the International Red Cross, that presented the same conclusions." The court also referred to the ICRC Study to support its conclusion that several of the offences committed by the defendants constituted war crimes.

[53] Statute of the ICTY, art. 3.

[54] UN Secretary-General, "Report Submitted Pursuant to Paragraph 2 of Security Council Resolution 808 (1993)," UN Doc. S/25704 (3 May 1993), para. 34.

[55] See Theodor Meron, "The Revival of Customary Humanitarian Law," 99 *American Journal of International Law* 817 (2005).

concluded that the prohibitions of wanton destruction of cities, plunder of public or private property, attacks against cultural property, and, more broadly, attacks on civilian objects were customary norms whose violation, including in non-international armed conflicts, entails individual criminal responsibility under customary international law. In doing so, it cited practice recorded in Volume II of the ICRC Study rather than the black-letter rules in Volume I of the Study.[56] Earlier in the same case, the Appeals Chamber had to determine whether it could apply the principles of command responsibility to war crimes committed in a non-international conflict. Since Additional Protocol II is silent on the matter of command responsibility, the appeals chamber examined whether command responsibility applied in non-international armed conflict on the basis of customary international law and concluded that it did.[57] This conclusion confirms a similar finding in the ICRC Study.[58] More recent examples are the trial judgment in *Prosecutor v. Gotovina et al.*, in which the Trial Chamber cited the customary law nature of Rule 50 in the ICRC Study on seizure of property with approval, and the Trial Chamber judgment in *Prosecutor v. Dordjevic*. In the latter judgment the Chamber went even further than the Study with regard to the presumption of civilian status in cases of doubt by finding the rule to be applicable as a matter of customary law in non-international armed conflicts. It stated:

> The Chamber also recalls the principle of international humanitarian law that in case of doubt whether a person is a civilian, that person shall be presumed to be a civilian. … In international armed conflicts, the rule is codified in Additional Protocol I, Article 50(1). While Article 13 of Additional Protocol II does not contain the same text, the Chamber is of the view that the principle also applies in non-international armed conflicts. … While the ICRC's Customary International Humanitarian Law Study stopped short of finding the principle to be a customary rule of international humanitarian law given the lack of relevant state practice in regard to non-international armed conflicts, the Study noted that "the same balanced approach … with respect

[56] See ICTY, Appeals Chamber, *Prosecutor v. Hadžihasanović and Kubura*, Decision on Joint Defence Interlocutory Appeal of Trial Chamber Decision on Rule 98bis Motions for Acquittal, IT-01-47-AR73.3 (11 March 2005), §§ 29–30, 38, and 45–46.

[57] See ICTY, Appeals Chamber, *Prosecutor v. Hadžihasanović and Kubura*, Decision on Command Responsibility, IT-01-47-AR72 (16 July 2003), § 31.

[58] See *Customary International Humanitarian Law*, Vol. I: Rules, Rule 153: "Commanders and other superiors are criminally responsible for war crimes committed by their subordinates if they knew, or had reason to know, that the subordinates were about to commit or were committing such crimes and did not take all necessary and reasonable measures in their power to prevent their commission, or if such crimes had been committed, to punish the persons responsible."

to international armed conflicts seems justified in non-international armed conflicts."[59]

There are also examples where the conclusions of the Study have been confirmed by judicial or arbitral decisions. While the Study was not cited explicitly by the International Court of Justice ("ICJ") in the case of *Congo v. Uganda*, decided in 2005, the Court effectively confirmed a number of conclusions of the Study.[60] Another example is found in the work of the Ethiopia-Eritrea Claims Commission, mentioned earlier in the chapter. In a Partial Award of 19 December 2005 relating to issues on the conduct of hostilities, the Commission noted "with appreciation" the study of customary law by the ICRC and confirmed several of the findings of the Study.[61] In particular, the Commission confirmed the customary status of a number of provisions of Additional Protocol I.[62] Earlier, in a Partial Award of 28 April 2004, the Commission confirmed the prohibition of the rape of civilians by opposing or occupying forces as a matter of customary IHL.[63]

The practice collected for the Study and the Study itself have also been used as a reference by the Special Court for Sierra Leone, the Extraordinary Chambers in the Courts of Cambodia, and the International Criminal Court. Decisions of these tribunals have confirmed conclusions of the Study.[64]

An increasing number of state authorities have relied on or referred to the rules of customary IHL identified by the ICRC Study, without necessarily agreeing with all its conclusions. A recent example is the Israeli Ministry of Foreign Affairs report on the Israeli Defence Forces' military operation in

59 ICTY, Trial Chamber I, *Prosecutor v. Gotovina, Čermak and Markać*, Judgment, IT-06-90-T (15 April 2011), § 1779; Trial Chamber I, *Prosecutor v. Vlastimir Dordjevic*, Judgment, IT-05-87/1-T (23 February 2011), § 2066.

60 *Armed Activities on the Territory of the Congo (Democratic Republic of the Congo v. Uganda)*, Judgment of 19 December 2005, 2005 ICJ Rep. 168, 244, para. 219 (confirming the customary law status of Articles 25, 27, 28, 43, 46 and 47 of the Hague Regulations, which correspond to Rules 37, 38(A), 51(c), 52, 104, and 105 of the ICRC Study).

61 Eritrea-Ethiopia Claims Commission, Partial Award, *Western Front, Aerial Bombardment and Related Claims* (19 December 2005), § 330.

62 Ibid., § 95 (finding Articles 48, 51(2), 51(4)-(5), 52, 54(2), 57 and 58 of Additional Protocol I to be customary law).

63 See Eritrea-Ethiopia Claims Commission, Partial Award, *Central Front* (28 April 2004), §§ 37–38 (referencing Article 27 of the Fourth Geneva Convention and Article 76(1) of Additional Protocol I).

64 See, e.g., Special Court for Sierra Leone, Appeals Chamber, *Prosecutor v. Sam Hinga Norman*, Decision on Preliminary Motion based on Lack of Jurisdiction (Child Recruitment), Case No. SCSL-2004-14-AR72(E) (31 May 2004); Extraordinary Chambers in the Courts of Cambodia, *Kaing Case*, Judgment (26 July 2010); International Criminal Court, Trial Chamber I, *Prosecutor v. Thomas Lubanga Dyilo*, Judgment pursuant to Article 74 of the Statute (14 March 2012).

Gaza in December 2008 and January 2009. The report states that "Israel does not agree that all of the rules stated in the ICRC Customary International Law Study reflect customary international law, but it does agree that it accurately states the principle of distinction."[65] As another example, the Closing Submissions made by the UK Ministry of Defence in the Baha Mousa Public Inquiry in 2010 stated:

> The rules of [customary international law] most relevant to IHL are most conveniently set out and numbered by the ICRC in *Customary International Humanitarian Law, Vol. 1: Rules*. … The Government has concerns about this study, and in particular the methodology for deciding whether particular rules have entered the corpus of [customary international law]; however in relation to [rules 47, 87, 90, 91, 99, 118, 121, 122, 127, 128B, and 142 of the Study which are of most relevance to this inquiry] … the Government accepts that they reflect [customary international law].[66]

Since the Study's publication in 2005, the ICRC itself has also relied on it in many contexts. As stated in President Kellenberger's foreword to the Study, "the ICRC believes that the study does indeed present an accurate assessment of the current state of customary international humanitarian law. It will therefore duly take the outcome of this study into account in its daily work, while being aware that the formation of customary international law is an on-going process."[67] Examples of such reliance can be found in the 2009 and 2010 reports of the ICRC on its operations in Colombia.[68] The

65 Israel, Ministry of Foreign Affairs, "The Operation in Gaza (27 December 2008–18 January 2009) - Factual and Legal Aspects," 29 July 2009, available at www.mfa.gov.il/mfa/foreignpolicy/terrorism/pages/operation_in_gaza-factual_and_legal_aspects.aspx, § 96 n.70. In its discussion of the facts and its legal reading of them, the report continues to refer to specific parts of both Volume I (Rules) and Volume II (Practice) of the ICRC Study. See, e.g., ibid., §§ 96–115 (on the obligation not to target civilians) and §§ 120–38 (on the principle of proportionality and the obligation to weigh military objectives against incidental civilian harm and the obligation of attacking forces to take feasible precautions to minimize incidental civilian harm).

66 United Kingdom, Baha Mousa Public Inquiry, "Closing Submissions on Modules 1–3 on behalf of the Ministry of Defence," 25 June 2010, available at www.bahamousainquiry.org/linkedfiles/baha_mousa/hearings/oral_submission/sub000947.pdf, 28–33.

67 *Customary International Humanitarian Law*, Vol. I: Rules, xvii.

68 See ICRC, *Report 2009: Colombia*, Bogotá, April 2010, available in English at www.icrc.org/eng/assets/files/other/annual-report-2009-colombia-icrc.pdf, 13 (referring to Rule 55), 17 (Rule 1), 18 (Rules 98, 116–17), 21 (Rules 6–7), 22 (Rules 22–23), 23 (Rule 93), 24 (Rules 136–37), 26 (Rule 70), 27 (Rule 71), 29 (Rule 17), 36 (Rules 26 and 28), 38 (Rule 30), 40 (Rule 25), 46 (Rule 53), 47 (Rules 131–33), 53 (Rules 96 and 124B), 55 (Rule 119), 58 (Rule 118), 62 (Rules 139 and 141), and 63 (Rules 142–43). See also ICRC, *Informe 2010: Colombia [Report 2010 Colombia]*, Bogotá, March 2010, available in Spanish at www.icrc.org/spa/assets/files/other/icrc_003_t20102104.pdf, 25 (referring to Rule 117), 34 (Rule 22), 36 (Rules 70–71), 59 (Rules 135–37), 63 (Rules 87 and 96), 65 (Rules 118–19 and 124B), and 69 (Rule 100).

ICRC also increasingly relies on the rich collection of updated practice available in its online Database. It does so in its operational dialogue with parties to armed conflicts, relying on relevant national law and practice alongside treaty and customary rules of IHL. The collection of practice is also useful in the work of the ICRC in providing advice to states on the implementation of IHL in national legislation, and in its efforts to identify and monitor developing trends in state and international practice on particular IHL topics.

Finally, there are many examples of use of customary IHL, the ICRC's Study, and the ICRC's Database in reports by nongovernmental organizations. This is particularly the case in relation to countries that are not parties to the Additional Protocols.[69]

[69] See, e.g., Amnesty International, *The Conflict in Gaza: A Briefing on Applicable Law, Investigations, and Accountability* (London: Amnesty International, 2009), 15, 30 (references to Rule 156 on the definition of war crimes and to Rule 150 on reparation); Human Rights Watch, *War on the Displaced: Sri Lankan Army and LTTE Abuses against Civilians in the Vanni* (New York: Human Rights Watch, 2009), 21, 26 (references to Rule 158 on investigation and prosecution of war crimes, Rule 55 on access for humanitarian relief, and Rule 56 on freedom of movement of humanitarian relief personnel); Human Rights Watch, *Precisely Wrong: Gaza Civilians Killed by Israeli Drone-Launched Missiles* (New York: Human Rights Watch, 2009), 30–32 (reference to Rule 158 on investigation and prosecution of war crimes); Human Rights Watch, *Rain of Fire: Israel's Unlawful Use of White Phosphorus in Gaza* (New York: Human Rights Watch, 2009), 60–66 (references to Rule 85 on incendiary weapons and to Rule 156 on the definition of war crimes); Human Rights Watch, *The Human Cost: The Consequences of Insurgent Attacks in Afghanistan* (New York: Human Rights Watch, 2007), 83–89 (references to Rule 1 and 7 on distinction; Rule 2 on acts or threats of terror; Rule 4 on the definition of armed forces; Rule 8 on military objectives; Rule 12 on indiscriminate attacks; Rule 14 on proportionality; Rules 15–18 on precautions in attack; and Rule 65 on perfidy); Karen Human Rights Group, *Development by Decree: The Politics of Poverty and Control in Karen State* (April 2007), 118–19 (references to Rule 54 on attacking objects indispensable for civilian survival, Rule 55 on access for humanitarian relief, and Rule 131 on measures to be taken in case of displacement); National Lawyers Guild, *Onslaught: Israel's Attack on Gaza and the Rule of Law* (New York: National Lawyers Guild, 2009), 21–25 (references to Rule 71 on indiscriminate weapons, Rule 84 on incendiary weapons, and Rule 109 on wounded and sick); Human Rights Watch, *Razed to the Ground: Syria's Unlawful Neighbourhood Demolitions in 2012–2013* (January 2014), 39–41, 45–47 (apart from citing the Study as a general reference on customary IHL, the report refers to Rules 1, 7, 8, 10–17, and 24 on the conduct of hostilities, which were of particular relevance to its findings); Amnesty International, *Sudan: We Can't Endure Anymore: The Impact of Inter-Communal Violence on Civilians in Central Darfur* (March 2014), 19, 23, and 26 (references to, among others, Rules 54 (objects indispensable to the survival of the civilian population) and 55 (access to humanitarian relief for civilians in need)); Human Rights Watch, *Shaking the Foundations: The Human Rights Implications of Killer Robots* (May 2014), 14 (references to Rule 89 on violence to life and to Rules 1, 11 and 14, respectively, on the prohibition of direct attacks against civilians, the prohibition of indiscriminate attacks, and the principle of proportionality in attack).

6.4 METHODOLOGICAL ISSUES

The Study's methodology is explained in its introduction and has been summarized in an article that first appeared in the *International Review of the Red Cross*.[70] This part presents some of the salient issues that the Study had to deal with and that have been commented on since its publication.

Many of the issues discussed in the ICRC's Study on customary IHL have also been raised, and are the subject of debate, in the International Law Commission as part of its current work on the identification of customary international law.[71] The ICRC Study provides the Commission with a concrete example of how the theory of customary international law plays out in practice, in particular in the area of IHL. It is particularly noteworthy that the ICRC Study followed the two-element approach (requiring both practice and *opinio juris*), which the Commission has also deemed to be the most correct approach.[72] The ICRC's Study shows that this approach is workable.

More specifically, the following issues with which the ICRC had to deal in its Study are relevant for any assessment of customary international law, in any area of international law:

1. The relevance of physical and verbal acts of states
2. The distinction between the practice of contracting and of non-contracting states
3. The contribution of specially affected states
4. The required density of state practice
5. The assessment of *opinio juris*
6. The persistent objector rule

6.4.1 *The Relevance of Physical and Verbal Acts of States*

Most scholars and practitioners agree that both physical and verbal acts of states constitute practice that contributes to the creation of customary international

[70] Jean-Marie Henckaerts, "Study on Customary International Humanitarian Law: A Contribution to the Understanding and Respect for the Rule of Law in Armed Conflict," 87 *International Review of the Red Cross* No. 857, 175 (2005).

[71] For more information on the International Law Commission's work on this topic, see in particular the first, second, third, and fourth reports on the identification of customary international law by Michael Wood, Special Rapporteur, UN Doc. A/CN.4/663 (2013), UN Doc. A/CN.4/672 (2014), UN Doc. A/CN.4/682 (2015), and UN Doc. A/CN.4/695 (2016).

[72] See "Report of the International Law Commission," Sixty-Eighth Session (2 May–10 June and 4 July–12 August 2016), UN Doc. A/71/10 (2016), 76–79, Draft Conclusion 2, entitled "Two constituent elements," which states: "To determine the existence and content of a rule of customary international law, it is necessary to ascertain whether there is a general practice that is accepted as law (*opinio juris*)."

law.[73] Physical acts relevant to IHL include, for example, battlefield behavior, the use of certain weapons, and the treatment afforded to different categories of persons. Verbal acts include military manuals, national legislation, national case law, instructions to armed and security forces, military communiqués during war, diplomatic protests, executive decisions and regulations, pleadings before international tribunals, statements in international *fora*, and government positions on resolutions adopted by international organizations. This list shows that the practice of the executive, legislative, and judicial organs of a state can contribute to the formation of customary international law.

A study on customary international law, therefore, has to look at the combined effect of what states say (verbal acts) and what they do (physical acts). An examination of operational practice (physical acts) alone would not be enough. This is because, in order to ascertain the existence of customary international law, one has to look beyond a mere description of actual military operations (practice) and also examine the legal assessment of such operations by states (*opinio juris*).[74] This requires an analysis of official positions taken by the parties involved, as well as by other states. This is in line with the two-element approach also taken by the International Law Commission in its current work on the identification of customary international law. As noted earlier, the ICRC followed this approach in its study and found it to be practicable.

When a given operational practice – for example, the targeting of military installations – is generally accepted, this supports a potential rule underlying that practice, namely, in this example, the rule that military installations constitute lawful military targets. But when an operational practice is generally considered to be a violation of existing rules – for example, the targeting of civilian structures – that is all it is, a violation, not of a nature to modify

[73] See ibid., Draft Conclusion 6, entitled "Forms of practice," which provides: "1. Practice may take a wide range of forms. It includes both physical and verbal acts. It may, under certain circumstances, include inaction. 2. Forms of State practice include, but are not limited to: diplomatic acts and correspondence; conduct in connection with resolutions adopted by an international organization or at an intergovernmental conference; conduct in connection with treaties; executive conduct, including operational conduct 'on the ground'; legislative and administrative acts; and decisions of national courts. 3. There is no predetermined hierarchy among the various forms of practice." See also James Crawford, *Brownlie's Principles of Public International Law* (Oxford: Oxford University Press, 8th ed. 2012), 24. But see Anthony A. D'Amato, *The Concept of Custom in International Law* (Ithaca, NY: Cornell University Press, 1971), 88, 145 (contending that mere claims "cannot constitute the material component of custom," i.e., state practice, and that practice requires an act of a state rather than an argument of a state).

[74] See *Customary International Humanitarian Law*, Vol. I: Rules, xxxvii–xlviii; Henckaerts, "Study on Customary International Humanitarian Law," 178–82.

existing rules.[75] This explains why acts such as attacks against civilians, pillage, and sexual violence remain prohibited notwithstanding numerous reports of their commission. The conclusion that these acts are considered to be violations of existing rules can be derived only from the way they are viewed by states and relevant international bodies through verbal acts, such as military manuals, national legislation, national and international case law, resolutions of international organizations, and official statements. These verbal acts provide the lens through which to look at operational practice. They are evidence of both practice and *opinio juris* and as such of direct relevance to identifying customary rules of IHL.

As a result of the aforementioned considerations, the Study also had to take into account resolutions adopted by states in the framework of international organizations, in particular the United Nations and regional organizations.[76] However, the Study is premised on the recognition that, with a few exceptions, "resolutions are normally not binding in themselves and therefore the value accorded to any particular resolution depends on its content, its degree of acceptance and the consistency of state practice outside it."[77]

6.4.2 *The Distinction between the Practice of Contracting States and the Practice of Non-Contracting States*

The ICRC Study did not assume that a rule qualifies as customary law merely because it is contained in a widely ratified treaty. Widespread ratification was considered only an indication of the existence of a customary rule and was assessed in relation to other elements of practice and *opinio juris*, in particular the practice and *opinio juris* of states that are not parties to the treaty in question. Consistent practice and *opinio juris* of nonparty states was considered as important positive evidence. Contrary practice and *opinio juris* of nonparty states was considered as important negative evidence.

75 According to the ICJ, "If a State acts in a way prima facie incompatible with a recognized rule, but defends its conduct by appealing to exceptions or justifications contained within the rule itself, then whether or not the State's conduct is in fact justifiable on that basis, the significance of that attitude is to confirm rather than to weaken the rule." *Military and Paramilitary Activities in and against Nicaragua (Nicaragua v. United States of America)*, Merits, Judgment of 27 June 1986, 1986 ICJ Rep. 14, 98, para. 186.

76 *Customary International Humanitarian Law*, Vol. I: Rules, xli; Henckaerts, "Study on Customary International Humanitarian Law," 179.

77 *Customary International Humanitarian Law*, Vol. I: Rules, xxxv–xxxvi. See also "Report of the International Law Commission," Sixty-Eighth Session, Draft Conclusion 12, entitled "Resolutions of international organizations and intergovernmental conferences."

As a result, the distinction between contracting parties and non-contracting parties was taken into consideration in the assessment of each rule. In this connection, the Study used so-called "negative lists" – lists of countries that are not parties to relevant treaties – to identify the practice of nonparty states. It is interesting to note how these lists can differ considerably from one treaty regime to another. For example, the list of states parties to Additional Protocol I differs considerably from the list of states parties to the 1954 Hague Convention on the Protection of Cultural Property.[78]

This also means that to the extent that different treaties contain the same or similar rules, a state's ratification record with respect to all relevant treaties has to be taken into account. For example, although the United States is not a party to Additional Protocol I to the Geneva Conventions, it is a party to Protocol II and Amended Protocol II to the Convention on Certain Conventional Weapons ("CCW"), which contain a number of rules that are identical to those in Additional Protocol I. Thus, while the United States has not formally accepted the rules of distinction and proportionality and the prohibition of indiscriminate attacks through ratification of Additional Protocol I, it has formally accepted these rules, at least with respect to mines, booby traps, and other devices, through ratification of Amended Protocol II to the CCW, which applies in both international and non-international armed conflicts.[79]

As a result of the weight accorded to negative practice and *opinio juris* of non-contracting parties, the ICRC Study concluded that a number of provisions in Additional Protocol I were not customary law. These include the prohibition of reprisal attacks against civilians.[80]

The Study did not, however, limit itself to the practice of states that are not parties to the relevant treaties of IHL.[81] To limit the Study to a consideration

[78] Azerbaijan, Eritrea, India, Indonesia, Iran, Israel, Malaysia, Myanmar, Pakistan, Sri Lanka, Thailand, Turkey, and the United States are not parties to Additional Protocol I, but are parties to the 1954 Hague Convention on the Protection of Cultural Property (as of 28 August 2016). The same was true, until recently, for Iraq prior to its ratification of Additional Protocol I on 1 April 2010, and for Morocco, which ratified the Protocol on 3 June 2011.

[79] See Protocol on Prohibitions or Restrictions on the Use of Mines, Booby-Traps and Other Devices, as Amended, Geneva, 3 May 1996, arts. 2–3.

[80] This rule is set forth in Additional Protocol I, art. 51(6). For an assessment of the customary nature of this rule in light of negative practice and *opinio juris* of some states, see *Customary International Humanitarian Law*, Vol. I: Rules, 520–23.

[81] For example, Richard Baxter took the position that a court must look "exclusively to the conduct of non-parties in attempting to determine whether [a] treaty, in its law-creating aspect, was binding on all nations." See Richard R. Baxter, "Treaties and Custom," 129 *Recueil des cours* 25 (1970-I), 64 (referring to the ICJ's opinion in *North Sea Continental Shelf Cases*). But see Meron, "Revival of Customary Humanitarian Law," 833 and Brian D. Lepard, *Customary International Law: A New Theory with Practical Applications* (New York: Cambridge University Press, 2010), 197.

of the practice of only the 30-odd states that have not ratified the Additional Protocols, for example, would not comply with the requirement that customary international law be based on widespread and representative practice. Therefore, the assessment of the existence of customary law took into account the fact that, at the time of the publication of the ICRC Study, Additional Protocol I had been ratified by 162 states and Additional Protocol II by 158 states (as of 18 August 2016, 174 and 168, respectively). Similarly, the assessment of customary law took into account the fact that, at the time the ICRC Study was issued, the Geneva Conventions had been ratified by 192 states (now 196 states as of 18 August 2016). Although ratification does not *ipso facto* mean that a state party regards the ratified treaty rules as customary, such ratification does constitute an element to be taken into account in the overall assessment of practice.[82]

6.4.3 *The Contribution of Specially Affected States*

The Study duly noted the contribution of states that have had a greater extent and depth of experience in the field of the law of armed conflict and have typically contributed a significantly greater quantity and quality of practice than other states. A perusal of the Study and the updated practice on the online Database reveals the significant contribution to practice made by such states. For example, the United States, because of its experience with armed conflict, has contributed a significant amount of practice to the formation of customary humanitarian law. It also has taken positions on many points of interpretation of the law and these are often noted in the commentaries.

Hence, there are states that have contributed more practice than others because they have been involved more often in armed conflict and their position on the law is thus easy to identify.[83] Whether such practice counts more than the limited practice of other states in terms of satisfying the requirement of "widespread and representative" practice is a separate question. The statement of the ICJ in respect to the need for the practice of "specially affected" states to be included was made in the specific context of the law of the sea – and, in particular, in order to determine whether, after the passage of only

[82] On this point, see Lepard, *Customary International Law*, 193–94, 197.

[83] The selection of states whose practice is continuously updated on the ICRC's Customary IHL Database also continues to include, where feasible, states that engage in, or are likely to contribute, more practice than others because they are or have been involved more often in armed conflict or have a greater extent and depth of experience with and positions on IHL than others.

a short period of time, a rule in a treaty (that was not widely ratified) had become part of customary international law.[84]

Furthermore, the law of the sea governs situations that are based on inherent, geographic facts that objectively make certain states specially affected – for example, because they have a coastline, because they have a bay, because they are archipelagic, or because they are land-locked. It is questionable whether the same considerations can apply to humanitarian law, because humanitarian law governs situations of armed conflict that can potentially affect any state, since no state is inherently free from armed conflict. Therefore, all states have a legitimate interest in the development of humanitarian law and, as a result, it can be argued that there is no place for a rule on "specially affected" states in IHL.

6.4.4 *The Required Density of Practice*

While the ICJ has stated that practice has to be "extensive and virtually uniform" in order to establish a rule of customary international law,[85] there is no specific mathematical threshold for how extensive practice has to be. This is primarily so because the density of practice depends on the subject matter of the practice. Some issues arise more often than others and generate more practice. For example, the quantity of practice with regard to targeting is much greater than the quantity of practice with regard to the protection of the white flag of truce. Questions of targeting – such as the distinction between civilians and combatants and between civilian objects and military objectives – are discussed every day in connection with various armed conflicts, are addressed in nearly every military manual, and are often analyzed in international fora and judgments. Practice on the protection of the white flag of truce, on the other hand, is rather sparse. In general, the topic is rarely discussed, as there are relatively few concrete cases. Nevertheless, whatever practice there is on the protection of the white flag of truce is uniform and confirms the continued validity of the rule.

Such a differentiated approach is inevitable in any area of international law. Thus, in the S.S. *"Wimbledon" Case*, the Permanent Court of International Justice ("PCIJ") relied on two precedents only, those of the Panama and Suez

84 *North Sea Continental Shelf Cases (Federal Republic of Germany v. Denmark; Federal Republic of Germany v. Netherlands)*, Judgment of 20 February 1969, 1969 ICJ Rep. 3, 43, para. 74.

85 Ibid. See also "Report of the International Law Commission," Sixty-Eighth Session, Draft Conclusion 8, entitled "The practice must be general," which states in paragraph 1: "The relevant practice must be general, meaning that it must be sufficiently widespread and representative, as well as consistent."

canals, to find that the passage of contraband of war through international canals was not a violation of the neutrality of the riparian state.[86] Obviously, the Court could not cite more examples, as the number of international canals is limited. In this connection, Waldock observed that "on a question concerning international canals, of which there are very few in the world, the quantum of practice must necessarily be small."[87]

Furthermore, to quantify the density of practice correctly, it is necessary to determine the appropriate value of each element of practice. While some elements of practice may constitute single precedents, other elements may reflect numerous precedents. For example, this is particularly the case for military orders, instructions, and manuals. They reflect what armed forces are trained and instructed to do and what they end up doing most of the time. Hence, a single military manual may represent numerous precedents and thus a substantial quantum of practice.

Again, this may be compared to the facts in the S.S. "*Wimbledon*" *Case*, in which the PCIJ relied on two precedents only. But those two precedents represented a significant amount of practice, as many vessels, from all over the world, passed through the Panama and Suez canals. So a reference to just two precedents represented a wider body of practice than a first impression might suggest.

In addition, the nature of the rule has to be taken into account – whether it is prohibitive, obligatory, or permissive. For example, prohibitive rules, of which there are many in humanitarian law, are supported not only by statements recalling the prohibition in question but also by abstention from the prohibited act.[88] The prohibition against using certain weapons, such as biological weapons, is supported by the continued abstention from using such weapons. Such abstention alone is obviously not enough, however; evidence is required that states so abstain out of a sense of legal obligation, as discussed in the following subsection.[89]

6.4.5 *The Assessment of* Opinio Juris

As part of preparing the ICRC Study, after collecting and weighing the extent of the practice, a separate analysis had to be conducted in order to determine

86 See *Case of the S.S. "Wimbledon,"* Judgment of 17 August 1923, PCIJ Series A, No. 1, 1, 28.

87 C. H. M. Waldock, "General Course on Public International Law," 106 *Recueil des cours* 1 (1962), 44.

88 See "Report of the International Law Commission," Sixty-Eighth Session, Draft Conclusion 6, para. 1 ("Practice … may, under certain circumstances, include inaction.").

89 On this issue, see *Customary International Humanitarian Law*, Vol. I: Rules, xlvii–xlviii.

whether the practice attested to the existence of a rule of law because it was accompanied by *opinio juris* – a belief by states that legally they had to engage in the practice – or instead was inspired merely by nonlegal considerations of convenience, comity, or policy.[90] In the Study, the conclusion that practice reflects belief in the existence of a rule of law and not merely a policy was never based on any single instance or type of practice, but rather was the result of consideration of all the relevant practice. For example, it may be difficult to determine whether a state votes in favor of a resolution condemning attacks on cultural property in armed conflict because it believes this prohibition to reflect an existing or emerging rule of (customary) law, or whether it does so following a policy decision. Moreover, the vote could be based on both considerations at the same time. However, the totality of the practice and *opinio juris* on the subject of attacks on cultural property indicates that this prohibition is a rule of law, and not merely a matter of policy.

In the same vein, military manuals may put forward propositions that are based on law, but may also contain instructions based on policy or military considerations that go beyond the law. Of course, the instructions in these manuals should never require conduct that falls *below* (i.e., violates) the requirements of the law. During the drafting of the ICRC Study this distinction was always kept in mind when assessing the collected practice. Rules that appeared in military manuals were only recognized as legal rules if, taking into account the totality of practice and *opinio juris*, they were supported by other practice and *opinio juris* of such a nature as to show that states believed a rule of law to exist. It was recognized that some rules in military manuals were based merely on a policy consideration or a consideration of military or political expediency that can change from one conflict to the next.[91] For example, the fact that the United States decided, as a matter of policy rather than law, that it would apply the rules in its military manuals regardless of whether the conflict is characterized as international or non-international was recognized as a policy decision in the Study.[92] Hence, U.S. military manuals were never

[90] The distinction between states acting out of a sense of legal obligation and states acting for reasons of convenience, comity, or policy is clearly highlighted by the case law of the ICJ. See, for example, *North Sea Continental Shelf Cases*, 43, para. 77. See, also Michael Bothe, "Customary International Humanitarian Law: Some Reflections on the ICRC Study," 8 *Yearbook of International Humanitarian Law* 143 (2005), 161–62. See further Sean D. Murphy, *Principles of International Law* (St. Paul, MN: Thomas/West, 2006), 80–81.

[91] When a military manual quoted or referred to in the ICRC's Customary IHL Database includes a caveat as to its legal value, details of that caveat are included in the Database's source list.

[92] See U.S. Department of Defense, Directive 2311.01E, DoD Law of War Program, 9 May 2006, para. 4.1 ("It is DoD policy that: Members of the DoD Components comply with the law of war during all armed conflicts, however such conflicts are characterized, and in all other

cited as supporting evidence for rules applicable in non-international armed conflicts.

6.4.6 *The Persistent Objector Rule*

The Study may have caused some confusion by stating in the introduction that it took no view as to whether it is legally possible to be a "persistent objector" in relation to customary rules of IHL.[93] Although persistent objection may not be possible in the case of rules of *jus cogens*,[94] presumably not all rules of customary IHL are *jus cogens*, and therefore persistent objection to at least some of them would be possible.

The Study actually recognizes this fact. For example, with respect to Rule 45 on the prohibition of widespread, long-term, and severe damage to the natural environment, it noted that France, the United Kingdom, and the United States have persistently objected to the rule being applicable to nuclear weapons. Furthermore, the Study observed that the United States may be considered a persistent objector with respect to Rule 45 in general, including its application to conventional weapons. However, the persistent objector rule, as formulated by various authorities, requires that the state concerned must have objected to the emergence of a new norm during its formation and continue to object afterwards. Thus, it is not possible to be a "subsequent objector."[95] That there are no other examples of persistent objection in the Study should not come as a surprise. The 160 remaining rules in the Study reflect basic rules of IHL to which no state has felt the need to persistently object. These

military operations."). See also United States, *Operational Law Handbook*, International and Operational Law Department, The JAG Legal Center and School, U.S. Army, Charlottesville, Virginia (2012), 11; United States, *The Commander's Handbook on the Law of Naval Operations*, NWP 1-14M (July 2007), para. 5.2.

93 The persistent objector rule remains controversial. See e.g., Crawford, *Brownlie's Principles of Public International Law*, 28 (accepting that such a rule exists). For an overview of the main arguments set out in the literature, see Camilla G. Guldahl, "The Role of Persistent Objection in International Humanitarian Law," 77 *Nordic Journal of International Law* 51 (2008), 51–86. See also Maurice H. Mendelson, "The Formation of Customary International Law," 159 *Recueil des cours* 227 (1998).

94 See, e.g., Vaughn Lowe, *International Law* (Oxford: Oxford University Press, 2007), 58–60. See also Andrew Clapham, *Brierly's Law of the Nations* (Oxford: Oxford University Press, 7th ed. 2012), 62.

95 See Mendelson, "The Formation of Customary International Law," 244. See also "Report of the International Law Commission," Sixty-Eighth Session, Draft Conclusion 15, which affirms: "1. Where a State has objected to a rule of customary international law while that rule was in the process of formation, the rule is not opposable to the State concerned for so long as it maintains its objection. 2. The objection must be clearly expressed, made known to other States, and maintained persistently."

are rules that have been tried and tested in practice and make sense from a military and humanitarian point of view.

Furthermore, it is important to distinguish persistent objection, which only frees individual states from being bound by an existing customary rule, from situations in which the practice and *opinio juris* of many states is contrary to a potential rule. In the latter case the rule does not become part of customary international law at all. For this reason, the Study concluded that a number of rules were not customary law. For example, it concluded that the prohibition of reprisals against civilians in general, as contained in Additional Protocol I, was not customary law because there was sufficient contrary practice and *opinio juris*.

6.5 CONCLUSION

This chapter has sought to demonstrate that in today's international legal landscape, in which humanitarian law is extensively codified, customary law remains as relevant as ever. Section 6.2 gave several examples of the continued relevance of customary humanitarian law in armed conflicts in the Balkans, Afghanistan, Colombia, Israel, Libya, Somalia, Sri Lanka, and Syria. Section 6.3 illustrated the use made by states, domestic and international judicial and quasi-judicial bodies, international and nongovernmental organizations, and the ICRC itself of the ICRC's Study and Database in dealing with the legal aspects of such conflicts and alleged violations of IHL. These examples show that customary humanitarian law remains relevant in both international and non-international armed conflicts.

The assessment of customary international law is not an easy or quick task. It requires a long-term effort to collect practice from around the world. In the assessment of practice, numerous methodological issues can arise. In Section 6.4, this chapter sought to shed light on six such issues. These issues were particularly relevant to customary IHL. They were examined carefully as part of research for the ICRC Study. These issues have also emerged in the current work of the International Law Commission on the identification of customary international law. The chapter has tried to illustrate how the drafters of the ICRC Study addressed these methodological issues as they related concretely to the task of identifying rules of customary IHL.

Although the ICRC's Study has become to a large extent the starting point of any discussion of customary IHL, it should not be seen as the final word. This is because it cannot be exhaustive. Moreover, by definition, the formation of customary law is an ongoing process. The ICRC's Customary IHL Database aims to offer both the ICRC and other stakeholders the possibility of continuing to monitor the evolution of customary IHL.

7

From the "Demands of Humanity"

The Formulation of Opinio Juris *in Decisions of International Criminal Tribunals and the Need for a Renewed Emphasis on State Practice*

Noora Arajärvi

7.1 INTRODUCTION

> The requirement, as a constituent element of customary international law, of a general practice means that it is primarily the practice of States that contributes to the formation, or expression, of rules of customary international law.[1]

This chapter explores the role of *opinio juris* in the process of identifying rules of customary international law. In particular, it focuses on examples of case law in the field of international criminal law to illustrate the fluidity of approaches by international criminal tribunals ("ICTs") in identifying customary international law, as well as the indeterminacy of *opinio juris* within customary international law. It also argues that while some flexibility in the formulation of *opinio juris* is desirable, a rule of customary international law must be supported by actual state practice, as reaffirmed in the draft conclusions, quoted in the chapter-opening excerpt, of the International Law Commission ("ILC") on identification of customary international law.

The concept and identification of customary international law has been changing essentially through judicial interpretations.[2] Courts and tribunals have identified and applied rules of customary international law that have not been found through the elements of state practice and *opinio juris*, but rather

[1] "Report of the International Law Commission," Sixty-Eighth Session (2 May–10 June and 4 July–12 August 2016), UN Doc. A/71/10 (2016), 76–79, Draft Conclusion 4, para 1. Draft Conclusion 4 is entitled "Requirement of practice."

[2] Already more than four decades ago, a commentator noted that "the borderlines between interpretation of existing law and the making of new law are inevitably fluid." Wolfgang Friedmann, "The North Sea Continental Shelf Cases – A Critique," 64 *American Journal of International Law* 229 (1970), 235.

on the basis of other normative considerations, often embedded implicitly or explicitly within the notion of *opinio juris*. For example, the International Criminal Tribunal for the former Yugoslavia ("ICTY") has noted that a customary international law rule can materialize even if state practice is scarce or nonexistent, but "the demands of humanity or the dictates of public conscience" indicate the need for such a rule.[3] Legal scholar Ruti Teitel has described therefore a "paradigm shift" toward the "demands of humanity."[4]

I argue that this shift in the determination of customary international law rules in the domain of international criminal law is troublesome, for two reasons. First, criminal proceedings ought to respect the principle of legality, and recognizing customary international law norms that have not become well established through state practice and therefore known to criminal defendants may violate this principle. In short, the principle of legality sets the limits of criminal law and includes safeguards against abuse, such as "nothing is a crime except as provided by law, and no punishment may be imposed except as provided by law."[5] Second, the recognition of customary international law norms in general based on *opinio juris* alone is problematic because customary international law by definition should arise from, or at least contain, the element of practice.[6]

The aforementioned shift in the process of the formation of rules that are considered to fall under the umbrella of customary international law affects the legitimacy of the concept of customary international law as a whole, as well as the legitimacy of the resulting rules. Here I examine the identification and application of customary international law, with the main focus on ICTs. ICTs are at the forefront of determining the line – at times very thin – between legal rules and other normative frameworks. In the next sections I look at the methods and reasoning of international courts in identifying or "finding" customary international law where there is little or no evidence of practice. In

3 *Prosecutor v. Kupreškić*, 14 January 2000, IT-95-16-T, para 527, available at www.refworld.org/docid/40276c634.html.

4 This wording has been used by Ruti Teitel in her in-depth study of the concept of humanity in contemporary international law. See Ruti Teitel, *Humanity's Law* (New York: Oxford University Press, 2011).

5 For an extensive discussion of the principle of legality, see Lon Fuller, *The Morality of Law* (New Haven, CT: Yale University Press, 1964). See also Kenneth S. Gallant, *The Principle of Legality in International and Comparative Criminal Law* (Cambridge: Cambridge University Press, 2009); David Luban, "The Rule of Law and Human Dignity: Re-examining Fuller's Canons," 2 *The Hague Journal on the Rule of Law* 29 (2010).

6 As Suárez stated: "Custom is a kind of law [*ius*] introduced by usages and accepted as law." Francisco Suárez, *Selections from Three Works of Francisco Suárez, S.J.: De legibus, ac Deo legislatore*, translated by Gwladys L. Williams, Ammi Brown, and John Waldron, and edited by James Brown Scott (Oxford: Clarendon Press, 1944), 345–46, passage 6.7.1.1, quoted in David J. Bederman, *Custom as a Source of Law* (New York: Cambridge University Press, 2010), 139.

these instances, courts have often relied on *opinio juris*, or something that the courts count as *opinio juris*, while they are in fact incorporating social, political, and moral considerations into customary international law.

In this chapter, first, I discuss the conceptual differences between practice and *opinio juris*, invoking the resolutions of the UN General Assembly as an example of the ambiguity inherent in the process of identifying customary international law and of the uncertain relationship between these two traditional elements of customary international law. In the next section, I examine the applicability of human rights concepts – and concerns pertaining to humanity – in the determination of customary international law in international criminal proceedings. More precisely, I look at selected case law reflecting how ICTs have converted principles codified in human rights and humanitarian law treaties into customary international law applicable in these fora. Some of these principles stemming from human rights and humanitarian law are formulated as *opinio juris* in the decisions of the ICTs, reflecting the belief that they are legally binding – even when they may not have crystallized as customary international law applicable outside a specific treaty regime. The following section delves more deeply into the nature of customary international law. It sets out examples of the formulation of *opinio juris* in decisions of ICTs, and of how ICTs have used the "demands of humanity" to find *opinio juris* and dictate their identification of customary international law, even in the absence of significant state practice.

In the end, the chapter explores two key issues: the legitimacy of moral or "humanized" customary international law that focuses on *opinio juris* without regard to state practice; and the general lack of a unified approach among ICTs and other courts in determining the parameters of *opinio juris* in customary international law. I suggest that while there does not necessarily need to be a single definition of *opinio juris*, it is critical for ICTs to pay sufficient attention to state practice.

7.2 WHAT IS *OPINIO JURIS*?

I turn first to an exploration of the concept of *opinio juris*. According to the traditional doctrine of customary international law, both *opinio juris* and consistent state practice are required in order for the rule to pass into the domain of customary international law. Article 38(1)(b) of the Statute of the International Court of Justice ("ICJ") defines customary international law as "evidence of a general practice accepted as law."[7] Although the Statute sets

7 Statute of the International Court of Justice ("ICJ Statute"), art. 38(1)(b).

out the particular sources applicable in disputes heard by the ICJ, it also forms the basis of the formulation of customary international law in general. This definition translates into two elements required for customary international law to emerge: state practice and *opinio juris* – in other words, physical practice accompanied by a sense of legal obligation.[8]

The ICJ has articulated the elements of customary international law in the *North Sea Continental Shelf Cases* as follows: "Not only must the acts concerned amount to a settled practice, but they must also be such, or be carried out in such a way, as to be evidence of a belief that this practice is rendered obligatory by the existence of a rule of law requiring it."[9] The ICJ reaffirmed this two-element approach in the *Jurisdictional Immunities of the State Case*, stating, with a reference to its previous case law,[10] that "the existence of a rule of customary international law requires that there be 'a settled practice' together with *opinio juris*."[11] There is no exclusive method for determining where *opinio juris* arises from and how to define it in a coherent manner. However, it is the element of customary international law that transforms practice (of states, traditionally) into legally binding rules. The sense of legal obligation attached to practice is intended to reflect a general vision of states (and increasingly other actors on the international level) of what is or what ought to be governed by international law. In identifying *opinio juris*, the dilemma of distinguishing between *lex lata* and *lex ferenda* is highlighted. *Lex lata* refers to law as it is; *lex ferenda* refers to law as it ought to be.[12] The dilemma is this: How can a state have a genuine belief in the existence of a rule even before it has come to be accepted as such? While *lex lata* and *lex ferenda* have sometimes become intertwined in the interpretations of courts, it has been noted accurately, in relation to

[8] See Michael Wood, Special Rapporteur, "Second Report on Identification of Customary International Law," UN Doc. A/CN.4/672 (2014), paras. 21–31. See also "Report of the International Law Commission," Sixty-Eighth Session, Draft Conclusion 2, entitled "Two constituent elements," which provides: "To determine the existence and content of a rule of customary international law, it is necessary to ascertain whether there is a general practice that is accepted as law (*opinio juris*)."

[9] *North Sea Continental Shelf Cases (Federal Republic of Germany v. Denmark; Federal Republic of Germany v. Netherlands)*, Judgment of 20 February 1969, 1969 ICJ Rep. 3, 44, para. 77.

[10] See ibid.; *Continental Shelf Case (Libyan Arab Jamahiriya v. Malta)*, Judgment of 3 June 1985, 1985 ICJ Rep. 13.

[11] *Jurisdictional Immunities of the State (Germany v. Italy: Greece intervening)*, Judgment of 3 February 2012, 2012 ICJ Rep. 99, 122.

[12] See Ian Brownlie's presentation and the ensuing discussion in Ian Brownlie, "To What Extent are the Traditional Categories of *Lex Lata* and *Lex Ferenda* Still Viable?" in *Change and Stability in International Law-Making*, edited by Antonio Cassese and Joseph H. Weiler 66 (Berlin: Walter de Gruyter, 1988).

ICTs, that tribunals "cannot both apply the law strictly as it was and expand it" at the same time.[13]

Accordingly, *opinio juris* may reflect an ideal or wishful state of affairs – *lex ferenda* – as opposed to *lex lata*. The formation of what might be called "moral *opinio juris*," as a reflection of *lex ferenda*, may provide for a progressive method of developing international law in areas where treaties are scarce and practice is not yet widespread, but strong ethical grounds – which are reflected in the statements of states, and, perhaps, rational thought – all demand that such rules ought to exist. In his chapter, Brian Lepard explores the role of ethics in customary human rights law, and notes that "[u]sually ethics has found its way indirectly into the determination of customary law through the *opinio juris* requirement."[14] This approach has also been adopted in decisions of many ICTs, as I explore later in this chapter. Nonetheless, legitimate customary international law that is *lex lata* cannot crystallize in the absence of some evidence of practice regardless of any other persuasive factors. In the absence of practice, such norms may be a reflection of emerging customary international law, or fall within some other source of international law.[15] The "demarcation line" between customary international law and general principles is discussed in Thomas Kleinlein's chapter, where he highlights the clear distinction between the two as long as both are narrowly construed, while noting that broadening these categories risks overlap and conceptual confusion.[16] Although he approaches the subject from a different angle, his chapter also builds the notion of custom (as well as general principles) on a

[13] Darryl Robinson, "The Identity Crisis of International Criminal Law," 21 *Leiden Journal of International Law* 925 (2008), 946. See also Hugh Thirlway, "Reflections on *Lex Ferenda*," 32 *Netherlands Yearbook of International Law* 3 (2001); Major J. Jeremy Marsh, "*Lex Lata* or *Lex Ferenda*? Rule 45 of the ICRC Study on Customary International Humanitarian Law," 198 *Military Law Review* 116 (2008); Noora Arajärvi, "Between *Lex Lata* and *Lex Ferenda* – Customary International (Criminal) Law and the Principle of Legality," 15 *Tilburg Law Review* 163 (2010–2011).

[14] Brian D. Lepard, "Toward a New Theory of Customary International Human Rights Law," in this volume.

[15] For discussion, see Fabian O. Raimondo, *General Principles of Law in the Decisions of International Criminal Courts and Tribunals* (Leiden: Martinus Nijhoff Publishers, 2008); Ottavio Quirico, "A Formal Prescriptive Approach to General Principles of (International) Law," EUI LAW Working Papers, 2007/19 (2007); Hiram E. Chodosh, "Neither Treaty nor Custom: The Emergence of Declarative International Law," 26 *Texas International Law Journal* 87 (1991); and Hazel Fox, "Time History, and Sources of Law Peremptory Norms: Is There a Need for New Sources of International Law?" in *Time, History and International Law*, edited by Matthew Craven, Malgosia Fitzmaurice, and Maria Vogiatzi 119 (Leiden: Martinus Nijhoff Publishers, 2007).

[16] See Thomas Kleinlein, "Customary International Law and General Principles: Rethinking Their Relationship," in this volume.

form of practice – focusing on the reciprocal interactions between states, and not on the moral or ethical need for a rule.

ICTs have been criticized for adopting liberal methodologies in identifying customary rules and definitions.[17] Consequently, the question arises as to what extent inventive methods – "policy-directed choices" and "considerations of social and economic policy," among others – can be utilized in the discovery of *opinio juris*. Judge and legal scholar Antonio Cassese has asserted that the "international court must apply *lex lata*. … If it has instead recourse to policy considerations or moral principles, it acts *ultra vires*."[18] By its nature, however, the subjective element of customary international law – *opinio juris* – may entail some value-based and extralegal considerations as reflections of views of states on what is, or should be, accepted as law.[19]

The role of "soft law"[20] instruments in the formation of customary international law remains ambiguous, as recognized by Brian Lepard and Thomas Kleinlein in their respective chapters.[21] In particular, the resolutions of the UN General Assembly may be viewed as state practice, international practice, "paper practice," *opinio juris*, "implicit consensus," or simply reflections of existing or emerging customary international law, largely depending on the

[17] See Roozbeh (Rudy) B. Baker, "Customary International Law in the 21st Century: Old Challenges and New Debates," 21 *European Journal of International Law* 173 (2010) and Robert Cryer, "Of Custom, Treaties, Scholars and the Gavel: The Influence of the International Criminal Tribunals on the ICRC Customary Law Study," 11 *Journal of Conflict and Security Law* 239 (2006).

[18] Separate and Dissenting Opinion of Judge Cassese, *Prosecutor v. Erdemović*, IT-96-22-A, Appeals Chamber, 7 October 1997, para. 49.

[19] Amanda Perreau-Saussine has noted in relation to customary law in general that "for a sceptic … customary law is but a disguise for the furtherance of writers' or judges' motives, which are usually self-interested and sinister." Amanda Perreau-Saussine, "Three Ways of Writing a Treatise on Public International Law: Textbooks and the Nature of Customary International Law," in *The Nature of Customary Law: Legal, Historical and Philosophical Perspectives*, edited by Amanda Perreau-Saussine and James B. Murphy 228 (Cambridge: Cambridge University Press, 2007).

[20] For the purposes of distinguishing treaties from other international instruments, I use here the vocabulary of "hard" and "soft" law, although the practical usefulness of drawing such a distinction can be questioned. Dupuy notes in this connection: "'Soft' law is a paradoxical term for defining an ambiguous phenomenon." Pierre-Marie Dupuy, "Soft Law and the International Law of the Environment," 12 *Michigan Journal of International Law* 420 (1990), 420. See also Willem Van Genugten, Rob Van Gestel, Marc Groenhuijsen, and Rianne Letschert, "Loopholes, Risks and Ambivalences in International Lawmaking: The Case of a Framework Convention on Victims' Rights," 37 *The Netherlands Yearbook of International Law* 109 (2006), 123–26.

[21] See Lepard, "Toward a New Theory of Customary International Human Rights Law," in this volume; Kleinlein, "Customary International Law and General Principles," in this volume. For a list of further references, see Michael Wood, Special Rapporteur, "First Report on Formation and Evidence of Customary International Law," UN Doc. A/CN.4/663 (2013), para. 98.

standpoint of the observer.[22] On the one hand, the traditional view maintains that General Assembly resolutions are merely recommendations without contributing to practice or reflecting any views of states on their legally binding nature. This view is based on the plain language of Article 13 of the Charter of the United Nations, which affirms that the General Assembly shall "make *recommendations* for the purpose of … promoting international co-operation in the political field and encouraging the progressive development of international law and its codification."[23] Anthony D'Amato reiterates this point by noting that a clear separation of deeds and words is vital in ascertaining customary international law through acts and arguments of governments.[24]

On the other hand, General Assembly resolutions can be a rich source of evidence about the development of customary international law, as pointed out by legal scholar and ICJ judge Rosalyn Higgins.[25] She does, however, refrain from defining how and in what form the resolutions can be evidence of the development of customary international law or whether they merely reiterate preexisting customary international law. At the same time, she makes a nod toward accepting General Assembly resolutions as evidence of practice.[26]

An important factor in determining the effect of General Assembly resolutions on customary international law concerns their normative or nonnormative nature.[27] Legal scholar Maurice Mendelson articulates this issue as follows: "As a matter of principle, there is no reason why Assembly resolutions

22 According to D'Amato, "the articulation of a rule of international law – whether it be a new rule or departure from and modification of an existing rule – in advance of or concurrently with a positive act (or omission) of a state gives a state notice that its action or decision will have legal implications. In other words, given such notice, statesmen will be able freely to decide whether or not to pursue various policies, knowing that that their acts may create or modify international law." Anthony A. D'Amato, *The Concept of Custom in International Law* (Ithaca, NY: Cornell University Press, 1971), 75.

23 UN Charter, art. 13, para. 1 (emphasis added).

24 D'Amato states: "It is an extremely dubious proposition to rely upon the *arguments* of governments, expressed either through their attorneys or foreign offices, rather than their *acts*." D'Amato, *The Concept of Custom in International Law*, 134 (emphasis in the original).

25 See Rosalyn Higgins, *The Development of International Law Through the Political Organs of the United Nations* (Oxford: Oxford University Press, 1963), 2 ("With the development of international organizations, the votes and views of states have come to have legal significance as evidence of customary law. Moreover, the practice of states comprises their collective acts as well as the total of their individual acts.").

26 See ibid. (affirming that "international custom is to be deduced from the practice of states, which includes their international dealings as manifested by their diplomatic actions and public pronouncements").

27 These characteristics are also referred to using the adjectives, respectively, of "mandatory" and "nonmandatory." See Anthea Elizabeth Roberts, "Traditional and Modern Approaches to Customary International Law: A Reconciliation," 95 *American Journal of International Law* 757 (2001), 763.

should not in appropriate circumstances be treated as evidence of the *opinio juris* of states (or at least those voting in favor), bearing in mind there is no particular form prescribed by the law for the expression of such beliefs. But whether they do so depends very much on the terms of the resolution and the context."[28] Accordingly, resolutions that are merely recommendatory on their face do not possess the normative force from which *opinio juris* could be deduced. If the formulation of the text, however, is declaratory of preexisting legal rules and reinforces them, it can be taken as evidence of *opinio juris*.[29]

Legal expert Michael Scharf lists the problems arising from "instant custom" (which as such falls outside of the scope of this chapter) and General Assembly resolutions: the resolutions are not intended to have binding effect; they do not clearly differentiate between *lex lata* and *lex ferenda*; voting in favor of a resolution may be purely a political show-off; differentiating whether the resolutions provide for practice, *opinio juris*, or both, creates the problem of double counting; and finally, the self-contained nature of General Assembly resolutions, which is not related to real-world situations, undermines the rule of law.[30]

In their chapter, Jean-Marie Henckaerts and Els Debuf also recognize the ambiguity of deducing customary international law from a resolution, drawing an example from humanitarian law. They state: "For example, it may be difficult to determine whether a state votes in favor of a resolution condemning attacks on cultural property in armed conflict because it believes this prohibition to reflect an existing or emerging rule of (customary) law, or whether it does so following a policy decision. Moreover, the vote could be based on both considerations at the same time."[31] Interestingly, the ILC Special Rapporteur's second report on identification of customary international law includes

[28] Maurice Mendelson, "The International Court of Justice and the Sources of International Law," in *Fifty Years of the International Court of Justice: Essays in Honour of Sir Robert Jennings*, edited by Vaughan Lowe and Malgosia Fitzmaurice 63 (Cambridge: Cambridge University Press, 2008), 86.

[29] A similar condition in relation to treaty provisions was suggested by the ICJ in the *North Sea Continental Shelf Cases*. It there stated: "The provision concerned should, at all events potentially, be of a fundamentally norm-creating character such as could be regarded as forming the basis of a *general rule of law*." *North Sea Continental Shelf Cases*, 41–42, para. 72 (emphasis added). See also Mark E. Villiger, *Customary International Law and Treaties: A Manual on the Theory and Practice of the Interrelation of Sources* (The Hague: Kluwer Law International, 2nd ed. 1997), 186–91 ("The effects of resolutions upon the *underlying customary law* are *a priori* ambivalent. To the extent that the preparatory State practice adheres to, or invokes, the customary rule, this may confirm the rule.") (emphasis added.)

[30] See Michael P. Scharf, *Customary International Law in Times of Fundamental Change: Recognizing Grotian Moments* (New York: Cambridge University Press, 2013), 51–53.

[31] Jean-Marie Henckaerts and Els Debuf, "The ICRC and the Clarification of Customary International Humanitarian Law," in this volume.

General Assembly resolutions on the list of types of state practice as well as on the list of manifestations of "acceptance as law." The report notes that practice and *opinio juris* arise, or may be deduced from, voting in favor of or against a resolution and statements made in connection with the resolution.[32] It continues, however, to suggest that the final resolution itself may not be useful in identifying state practice, and states may have various motives – beyond the sense of legal obligation – when consenting to the text of a resolution.[33] The same issue has been highlighted in the ILC Special Rapporteur's third report, which states: "The General Assembly is a political organ in which it is often far from clear that [member states'] acts carry juridical significance."[34] The ILC's Draft Conclusion 12, adopted in 2016, reiterates that resolutions may carry evidentiary value for identifying custom, but cannot as such constitute it.[35]

Notably, the blurred understanding of the impact of General Assembly resolutions on customary international law has been reinforced by international courts. On many occasions they have referred to General Assembly resolutions as evidence of customary international law as a whole, or as evidence of either of the elements of customary international law (but more often of *opinio juris*).[36] The impact of international institutions and nonstate actors

32 Michael Wood, Special Rapporteur, "Second Report on Identification of Customary International Law," para. 41(i) (on resolutions as state practice), para. 76(g) (on resolutions as evidence of *opinio juris*).

33 See ibid.

34 Michael Wood, Special Rapporteur, "Third Report on Identification of Customary International Law," UN Doc. A/CN.4/682 (2015), para. 47.

35 See "Report of the International Law Commission," Sixty-Eighth Session, Draft Conclusion 12, para 1. Draft Conclusion 12 is entitled "Resolutions of international organizations and intergovernmental conferences."

36 See, e.g., *Legality of the Threat or Use of Nuclear Weapons*, Advisory Opinion of 8 July 1996, 1996 ICJ Rep. 226, 254–55, paras. 70–73. The Court stated there that General Assembly resolutions, in general, "may sometimes have normative value," and can contribute to the evidence of the existence of a rule or "the emergence of an *opinio juris*." It continued, however, by noting that "several of the resolutions under consideration in the present case have been adopted with substantial numbers of negative votes and abstentions; thus … they still fall short of establishing the existence of an *opinio juris* on the illegality of the use of such weapons." It so held despite the adoption of annual resolutions recalling GA Res. 1653 (XVI), adopted 24 November 1961. See also *Barcelona Traction, Light and Power Company, Limited (Belgium v. Spain)*, Judgment of 5 February 1970, 1970 ICJ Rep 3, Separate Opinion of Judge Ammoun, 302, para. 11. Judge Ammoun stated that "the positions taken up by the delegates of States … in the United Nations naturally form part of State practice." He further emphasized that General Assembly resolutions should be given more formal legal authority, affirming: "A marked trend in legal writing is becoming apparent, reflecting the new aspects of international life, which is in favour of attributing to the resolutions, and in particular to the declarations of the United Nations General Assembly, the status of at least a subsidiary source of international law, to be added to the classic sources in Article 38 of the Court's Statute."

on the formation of *opinio juris* is in fact important, and General Assembly resolutions can provide a well-articulated normative touchstone for the future evolution of state practice and *opinio juris*. On the one hand, General Assembly resolutions may reflect some of the existing or developing elements of customary international law, and reinforce them. On the other, General Assembly resolutions may act as a catalyst for a more formalized legal rule in the form of a treaty, or direct subsequent state practice, strengthening the basis for the development of customary international law on a given topic.

The advocates of modern, "revised," or "new" approaches to customary international law suggest that a customary rule can emerge even if practice is absent or scarce if *opinio juris* is strong, and if compelling – often moral and ethical – reasons call for such a rule.[37] The prime examples of such rules arising through this moralization of law – without the prerequisite of practice – are *jus cogens* norms, the peremptory norms of international law.[38] A conceptual

See also *Prosecutor v. Kupreškić et al.*, IT-95-16-T, Trial Chamber, 14 January 2000, para. 532 (finding that widespread *opinio juris* on the prohibition of reprisals against civilians was confirmed "by the adoption, by a vast majority, of a Resolution of the UN General Assembly in 1970," referring to GA Res. 2675 (XXV), adopted on 9 December 1970); *Prosecutor v. Blaškić*, IT-95-14-A, Appeals Chamber, 29 July 2004, para. 158 (holding that "evidence of the existence of *opinio juris* is demonstrated in the General Assembly Resolution 2444 (1968) … and in Resolution 2675 (1970)"). See also Brian D. Lepard, *Customary International Law: A New Theory with Practical Applications* (New York: Cambridge University Press, 2010), 279–81.

37 See, e.g., John Tasioulas, "In Defence of Relative Normativity: Communitarian Values and the Nicaragua Case," 16 *Oxford Journal of Legal Studies* 85 (1996); John Tasioulas, "Customary International Law and the Quest for Global Justice," in *The Nature of Customary Law: Philosophical, Historical and Legal Perspectives*, edited by Amanda Perreau-Saussine and James B. Murphy 307 (Cambridge: Cambridge University Press, 2007); Lepard, *Customary International Law*, 8, 98. See also Michael Wood, Special Rapporteur, "First Report on Formation and Evidence of Customary International Law," para. 98. The report notes, with references to a number of works, that modern approaches to customary international law seek "to reinterpret the constitutive elements of customary international law and, consequently, to reframe it as a source of international law." In short, this means replacing "the strictly additive (two-element) model of custom formation with a single-element theory, mostly by de-emphasizing one of the two standard requirements or by displacing them altogether." Ibid.

38 For discussion, see, for example, Michael Byers, "Conceptualising the Relationship between Jus Cogens and Erga Omnes Rules," 66 *Nordic Journal of International Law* 211 (1997), 221 ("*Opinio juris*, or something like *opinio juris*, appears to be at the root of the non-derogable character of *jus cogens* rules."); Ulf Linderfalk, "The Effect of Jus Cogens Norms: Whoever Opened Pandora's Box, Did You Ever Think about the Consequences?" 18 *European Journal of International Law* 853 (2008), 862 ("a norm of *jus cogens* may be said to presuppose the existence of two kinds of *opinio juris*," articulation of which can be found in Article 53 of the Vienna Convention on the Law of Treaties: first, being accepted and recognized by the international community of states, and second, as a norm from which no derogation is permitted); Lepard, *Customary International Law*, 243–60, esp. 246, 259 (noting that "a higher degree of consensus on *jus cogens* norms should be required than for 'ordinary' customary law norms"

understanding of customary international law that falls somewhere between the traditional and modern approaches would allow the inclusion of moral values in customary international law if treaties entered into and declarations made by a majority of states indicate that these substantive values are commonly accepted as legal norms, for example norms concerning the protection of basic human rights.[39]

Frederick Kirgis's "sliding scale" theory addresses the relative significance, or weight, of state practice and *opinio juris* in the formation of a customary international law norm.[40] The theory is based on the idea that "the more destabilizing or morally distasteful the activity ... the more readily international decision makers will substitute one element for the other, provided that the asserted restrictive rule seems reasonable."[41] This would imply that *opinio juris* may wholly, or at least mostly, be the foundation for a rule of customary international law. In other words, a customary international law rule may come into existence solely because of the existence of a very strong normative sense of legal obligation. Alternatively, it can arise out of an aspiration on the part of states that barely reaches the threshold of a sense of legal obligation so long as there is widespread state practice. Hence, according to this theory, *opinio juris* cannot be described in a unitary fashion, but can be anything between a bedrock of custom or just an afterthought following practice, if that.

A methodology similar to that set out by Kirgis has been occasionally utilized by ICTs in identifying customary international law, as I further examine in the next section. For example, in relation to international humanitarian law, the ICTY has held that some principles can be considered customary international law even if evidence of state practice is scarce or absent, as long as there is a strong ethical or moral basis for such a customary rule.[42] Hence,

and that in the formation and changing of *jus cogens* rules "consideration should be given to the impact of a change on the realization of fundamental ethical principles").

39 See, e.g., Frederick L. Kirgis, Jr., "Custom on a Sliding Scale," 81 *American Journal of International Law* 146 (1987); Roberts, "Traditional and Modern Approaches to Customary International Law," 757.

40 See Kirgis, "Custom on a Sliding Scale." See also Thomas Kleinlein's discussion of the "sliding scale" approach to customary international law and general principles. Kleinlein, "Customary International Law and General Principles," in this volume.

41 Kirgis, "Custom on a Sliding Scale," 149.

42 See, e.g., *Prosecutor v. Kupreškić*, Trial Chamber, para. 527 (holding, with regard to the prohibition of reprisals against civilians, that "*opinio necessitatis*, crystallising as a result of the imperatives of humanity or public conscience, may turn out to be the decisive element heralding the emergence of a general rule or principle of humanitarian law"). See also Jan Wouters and Cedric Ryngaert, "Impact on the Process of the Formation of Customary International Law," in *The Impact of Human Rights Law on General International Law*, edited by Menno T. Kamminga and Martin Scheinin 111 (Oxford: Oxford University Press, 2009), 112 ("The more important the common interests of the states or humanity are, the greater the weight that

opinio juris has become a normative tool used by ICTs to establish a desirable rule as law, which may or may not be supported by practice. More generally, the next section looks into the differences between international human rights law and international criminal law, their respective normative impact, and ICTs' approach to both areas of law in their identification of customary international law in criminal proceedings. It focuses in particular on how ICTs have used human rights norms and the "dictates of humanity" to ascertain customary international law.

7.3 THE DICTATES OF HUMANITY, HUMAN RIGHTS, AND INTERNATIONAL CRIMINAL LAW

International criminal law and human rights law address parallel issues, but with different motivations. Attempts to advance "humanity" are surely present in both, but human rights law – even though enforceable to an increasing extent – can be said to be more aspirational, encouraging states to direct their practices and policies in a more morally acceptable way. International criminal law, on the other hand, has a clear punitive element and places individual criminal responsibility at its center. As early as the years following the Nuremberg trials, the assimilation of these two areas of law was considered conceptually troublesome.[43] In relation to crimes against peace, the Nuremberg tribunal stated that any breach of the Paris Pact of 1928,[44] which created binding obligations on states, was illegal. It held, without exploring how a treaty binding on states could bind individuals, that such an illegal act constitutes a crime entailing individual responsibility.[45] Building on this precedent, the ICTY in its decisions has addressed the legitimacy of applying rules codified in human rights and humanitarian law treaties as the basis of establishing individual criminal responsibility. In doing so, it has imported human rights norms into international criminal law by framing them as customary international law.

The ICTY has discussed the applicability of human rights treaties as evidence of customary international law in criminal proceedings in a number

might be attached to *opinio juris* as opposed to state practice. If the stakes are high, inconsistent state practice may be glossed over, and a high premium may be put on states' statements and declarations, *inter alia* in multilateral fora, in identifying customary law combined with general principles of law.").

43 See, e.g., Georg Schwarzenberger, "The Judgment of Nuremberg," 21 *Tulane Law Review* 329 (1947).

44 General Treaty for the Renunciation of War as an Instrument of National Policy (also known as the Kellogg-Briand Pact), 27 August 1928, 94 LNTS 57.

45 For comments, see Schwarzenberger, "The Judgment of Nuremberg," 346–47.

of its earlier cases. For example, the Trial Chamber in the *Furundžija* case, decided in 1998, stated that the "general prohibition against torture has evolved in customary international law."[46] The Trial Chamber noted, however, that although torture is prohibited under general international law (and in particular, customary international law), customary international law does not necessarily provide a definition of torture as a war crime entailing individual criminal responsibility.[47] The definition of torture used in the 1984 UN Convention Against Torture ("Torture Convention")[48] had been applied by the International Criminal Tribunal for Rwanda ("ICTR") in the *Akayesu* case, also decided in 1998.[49] However, the ICTY there expressed the view that unless it could demonstrate that the same definition has crystallized in customary international law for the purposes of international criminal law – in other words, as a customary rule giving rise to individual criminal responsibility instead of state responsibility, which the Torture Convention imposes – it could not apply that definition directly.

The *Furundžija* Trial Chamber drew its reasoning from a previous decision of the ICTY, *Delalić*,[50] in which the Trial Chamber had derived the definition of torture as a war crime from a number of human rights instruments – both legally binding and nonbinding, and both international and regional. These included the 1948 Universal Declaration of Human Rights, the 1950 European Convention on Human Rights, the 1969 American Convention on Human Rights, the 1975 Declaration on Torture, the 1981 African Charter on Human and Peoples' Rights, and the 1985 Inter-American Convention to Prevent and Punish Torture.[51] In considering the treaty definition of torture, the *Delalić* Trial Chamber concluded that "the definition of torture contained in the Torture Convention includes the definitions contained in both the Declaration on Torture and the Inter-American Convention and thus reflects a consensus which the Trial Chamber considers to be representative of customary international law."[52] In *Furundžija*, the court confirmed the reasoning in *Delalić* by stating that "Trial Chamber II of the International Tribunal has rightly noted in *Delalić* that indeed the definition of torture contained in the

46 *Prosecutor v. Furundžija*, IT-95-17/1-T, Trial Chamber, 10 December 1998, para. 137.

47 Ibid., para. 159. See also Erika De Wet, "The Prohibition of Torture as an International Norm of *Jus Cogens* and Its Implications for National and Customary Law," 15 *European Journal of International Law* 97 (2004).

48 Convention against Torture and Other Cruel, Inhuman or Degrading Treatment or Punishment, UN Doc. A/39/51 (1984), 1465 UNTS 85.

49 *Prosecutor v. Akayesu*, ICTR-96-4-T, Trial Chamber, 2 September 1998.

50 *Prosecutor v. Delalić and Others*, IT-96-21-T, Trial Chamber, 16 November 1998.

51 Ibid., paras. 452–58.

52 Ibid., para. 459.

1984 Torture Convention is broader than, and includes, that laid down in the 1975 Declaration of the United Nations General Assembly and in the 1985 Inter-American Convention."[53]

The integration of human rights law relating to torture into international criminal law was further discussed in the *Kunarać* case decided by the ICTY's Trial Chamber in 2001, which adopted a more nuanced approach in determining the scope of a customary rule of international criminal law providing for the punishment of torture.[54] After reviewing many human rights instruments and case law from different legal systems, the *Kunarać* Trial Chamber concluded that "the definition of torture contained in the Torture Convention cannot be regarded as the definition of torture under customary international law which is binding regardless of the context in which it is applied. The definition of the Torture Convention was meant to apply at an inter-state level and was, for that reason, directed at the states' obligations. … The definition of torture contained in Article 1 of the Torture Convention can only serve, for present purposes, as an interpretational aid."[55] The main substantial difference in the reasoning of the court in *Kunarać* in comparison to *Delalić* was that it listed three elements of torture included in the Torture Convention that it did not consider as elements of torture from the specific viewpoint of international criminal law. The court in *Kunarać* found that it "must identify those elements of the definition of torture under human rights law which are extraneous to international criminal law as well as those which are present in the latter body of law but possibly absent from the human rights regime."[56]

This statement is commendable. It adopts an appropriate approach that requires the identification of customary international law in international criminal law independently from the norms of human rights law. Building on the reasoning in *Kunarać*, the Trial Chamber in the *Kupreškić* case discussed the status of persecution as a crime against humanity, and unequivocally concluded that "it would be contrary to the principle of legality to convict someone of persecution based on a definition found in international refugee law or human rights law."[57] The court underscored that human rights law imposes obligations on the state for the protection of individuals,[58] but importantly does not create individual criminal responsibility or define criminal conduct. Hence, it concluded that

[53] *Furundžija*, para. 160.
[54] *Prosecutor v. Kunarac*, IT-93-23-T & IT-96-23/1-T, Trial Chamber, 22 February 2001.
[55] Ibid., para. 482.
[56] Ibid., para. 488.
[57] *Prosecutor v. Kupreškić*, IT-95-16-T, Trial Chamber, para. 589.
[58] In this connection, legal scholar Louis Henkin has affirmed: "Human rights are moral-political claims by an individual against his or her society." Louis Henkin, "Human Rights and State 'Sovereignty,'" 25 *Georgia Journal of International and Comparative Law* 31 (1995), 40 n.34.

the dictates of humanity reflected in human rights law cannot automatically impose criminal responsibility under international criminal law. This position is in line with the need to separate legal rules from other normative moral systems, and complies with the principle of legality in criminal trials.

Judicial decision making ought to be an exercise in the application of legal rules to facts, in the spirit of *lex lata* – law as it is – as opposed to law as it ought to be, *lex ferenda*. This is also entailed in the principle of legality.[59] An articulation of the principle of legality is provided by legal philosopher Lon Fuller, who argues that it requires foreseeability and clarity of rules.[60] These attributes call for special attention when identifying and applying customary international law in criminal trials. Brian Lepard argues in his chapter that a norm could be considered customary law if states generally believe that "a norm *should* be law, rather . . . than that it is *already* law."[61] While this may be an applicable conceptualization in the areas of law that deal with interstate relations and the responsibility of states, such as human rights law, in international criminal law, where the courts are to determine the responsibility of individuals, the application of *lex ferenda* endangers the core notion of the rule of law and the principle of legality, including foreseeability and the *nullum crimen sine lege* (no crime without law) requirement.

All in all, importing noncriminal legal considerations (that may form *lex ferenda*) into the reasoning of ICTs will weaken the credibility and foreseeability of international criminal law, and may affect the normative eminence that separates it from other social norms, as noted by international relations scholar Hedley Bull. He argues: "If a distinction is not preserved between those rules of international conduct which have the status of law and those which do not, international law cannot survive as a distinct normative system at all."[62]

The distinction between norms of customary human rights law and customary criminal law has been elaborated in a dissenting opinion of Judge Hans-Peter Kaul of the International Criminal Court ("ICC") in the decision authorizing the ICC's investigation into the situation in Kenya in 2010.[63] This situation concerned the responsibility for alleged crimes against humanity committed during the 2007–08 post-election violence in Kenya. The ICC Prosecutor sought a formal authorization by the Pre-Trial Chamber to open

59 See note 5 above.
60 Fuller, *The Morality of Law*, 39.
61 Lepard, "Toward a New Theory of Customary International Human Rights Law," in this volume.
62 Hedley Bull, *The Anarchical Society: A Study of Order in World Politics* (New York: Columbia University Press, 1977), 159.
63 *Decision Pursuant to Article 15 of the Rome Statute on the Authorization of an Investigation into the Situation in the Republic of Kenya*, Dissenting Opinion of Judge Hans-Peter Kaul, ICC-01-09, Pre-Trial Chamber II, 31 March 2010.

an investigation into the situation. To grant such an authorization, the Pre-Trial Chamber must be satisfied that, among other requirements, there is a reasonable basis to believe that the acts in question qualify as crimes falling under the ICC's jurisdiction. The majority of judges, finding support from the case law of other ICTs on the definition of crimes against humanity, agreed that there was a reasonable basis for the Prosecutor to proceed with the investigation, because the attacks in question were directed against the civilian population, were widespread and systematic, and formed a part of state or organizational policy. However, Judge Kaul strongly dissented from this conclusion.

Judge Kaul noted that mere "cruelty or mass-victimization" does not make an act an international crime. Rather, he emphasized that the criminal nature of an act arises from "the constitutive contextual elements in which the act is embedded."[64] In deciding whether the situation in Kenya would fall under the jurisdiction of the court, and constitute crimes against humanity, Judge Kaul expressed the view that the approach of the majority of the Pre-Trial Chamber "expand[s] the concept of crimes against humanity to any infringement of human rights."[65] He then stated that "[a] distinction must be upheld between human rights violations on the one side and international crimes on the other side, the latter forming the nucleus of the most heinous violations of human rights representing the most serious crimes of concern to the international community as a whole."[66]

Judge Kaul, therefore, took a positivist stance and highlighted the special character of international crimes. Hence, he refused to allow norms of international human rights law – whether in treaty law or customary law – to be "imported" automatically into the sphere of international criminal law. Rather, he highlighted the importance of fidelity to the tribunal's constitutive document, the Rome Statute, and the definition of crimes appearing in it. This approach upholds the distinction between rules that criminalize the conduct of individuals and those of a more general nature, and consequently is in accordance with the principle of legality, holding that there can be no crime without law.

Likewise, in a dissenting opinion in the *Norman* case in the Special Court for Sierra Leone, Judge Geoffrey Robertson drew attention to the need to identify the process of the development of rules, here in the context of enlisting child soldiers. He affirmed: "[A]bhorrence alone does not make that conduct [enlisting child soldiers] a crime in international law. … So when did child enlistment … become a

64 Ibid., para. 52.

65 Ibid., para. 53.

66 Ibid., with a footnote referring to the fourth paragraph of the preamble of the Rome Statute.

war crime? That depends, as we shall see, on first identifying a stage – or at least a process – by which prohibition of child enlistment became a rule of law binding only on states. … Then, at the second stage, on further identifying a subsequent turning point at which that rule – a so-called norm of international law – metamorphosed into a *criminal law* for the breach of which individuals might be punished, if convicted by international courts."[67] Thus, Judge Robertson effectively maintained that customary rules of international criminal law cannot materialize just because the demands of humanity or morality call for them, but must instead be found in one of the traditional sources of international law, including customary law with its long-standing requirements of *opinio juris* and state practice. Admittedly, it may very well be appropriate to open the discussion on broadening the concept of sources of international law, but that is beyond the scope of this chapter.

While treaty-based or customary norms of international human rights law cannot automatically create customary norms of international criminal law, human rights law has provided many of the foundations for international criminal law. International criminal law has seen a proliferation in codification, adjudication, legal scholarship, and media attention in the past few decades. It has perhaps overshadowed attention to human rights, which has certainly led many journalists, and even scholars, to be confused about the separation of the two areas of law.[68] How are the aforementioned ethical, moral, political, and other nonlegal considerations then making their way into customary international law? The next section continues to examine the ways in which ICTs have validated findings of customary international law in the absence of state practice, relying only on *opinio juris*, and analyzes this trend through an examination of selected case law.

7.4 SOME EXAMPLES OF THE TREATMENT OF *OPINIO JURIS* IN INTERNATIONAL COURTS AND TRIBUNALS

7.4.1 *The Development of* Opinio Juris *in International Courts and Tribunals*

As noted earlier in the chapter, the ICJ in the *North Sea Continental Shelf Cases* held that for customary international law to crystallize, the acts in

67 Dissenting Opinion of Judge Geoffrey Robertson QC in *Prosecutor v. Norman*, SCSL-03-I, Decision on Preliminary Motion based on Lack of Jurisdiction, Trial Chamber, 31 May 2004. The substantive issue here – enlisting of child soldiers as an international crime – has been discussed in *Prosecutor v. Lubanga*, ICC-01/04-01/06, Trial Chamber I, 14 March 2012.

68 This confusion is illustrated in the discourse on victims' rights. For a critical account, see Dov Jacobs, "Puzzling over Amnesties: Defragmenting the Debate for International Criminal Tribunals," in *The Diversification and Fragmentation of International Criminal Law*, edited by Larissa van den Herik and Carsten Stahn 305 (Leiden: Martinus Nijhoff, 2012).

question must form a settled practice and also provide evidence of a belief that this practice is required by the existence of a rule of law requiring it.[69] This reflects the traditional understanding of customary international law, and the role of *opinio juris*: It is subsidiary to, and complements, the actual practice, which is the bedrock in the formation of customary international law.

In the *Nicaragua Case*, decided in 1986, the ICJ began to shift this focus.[70] Instead of concentrating on state practice, it emphasized the importance of *opinio juris* in the formation of customary international law, which is then, in turn, confirmed by practice.[71] In other words, the Court gave priority to the words of states over their deeds, providing an initial stepping stone for the widening of the concept of customary international law to encompass norms arising largely from *opinio juris*.[72] In analyzing the principle of nonintervention under customary international law, the Court stated that examples of "*opinio juris* regarding the existence of the principle of non-intervention in customary international law are numerous and not difficult to find," and that this *opinio juris* "is backed by established and substantial practice." The ICJ failed, however, to show evidence of such existing practice beyond the two states involved in the proceedings.[73] It aspired to stress the underlying goals of international peace and security on practical and moral grounds, and noted that the rejection of a customary rule prohibiting the use of force and intervention in the affairs of sovereign states would not only reduce the significance of international law but also adversely affect confidence in the Court.[74]

The *Nicaragua Case* and ICT decisions that emphasize *opinio juris* at the expense of conforming state practice raise the fundamental issue of how political, social, and moral considerations – and especially the demands of humanity broadly understood – can metamorphose into a belief in, or conviction about,

69 *North Sea Continental Shelf Cases*, 44, para. 77.

70 See *Military and Paramilitary Activities in and against Nicaragua (Nicaragua v. United States of America)*, Merits, Judgment of 27 June 1986, 1986 ICJ Rep. 14 ("*Nicaragua Case*"). On this point, see also Lepard, *Customary International Law*, 132.

71 To some extent the shift began in the *Continental Shelf Case (Libyan Arab Jamahiriya v. Malta)*, Judgment of 3 June 1985, 1985 ICJ Rep 13.

72 On this point, see, for example, Roberts, "Traditional and Modern Approaches to Customary International Law," 757; Anja Seibert-Fohr, "Modern Concepts of Customary International Law as a Manifestation of a Value-Based International Order," in *Unity and Diversity in International Law: Proceedings of an International Symposium of the Kiel Walther Schücking Institute of International Law, 4–7 November 2004*, edited by Andreas Zimmermann and Rainer Hofmann 257 (Berlin: Duncker & Humblot, 2006).

73 See *Nicaragua Case*, 106–10, paras. 202–09. For discussion, see Hilary C.M. Charlesworth, "Customary International Law and the Nicaragua Case," 11 *Australian Yearbook of International Law* 1 (1984–87).

74 Charlesworth, "Customary International Law and the Nicaragua Case," 27–29.

the legal necessity of practice. Legal scholar Karol Wolfke notes that *opinio juris* brings a "naturalistic tinge" to the identification of customary international law, because practice may arise on the basis of some preexisting, higher belief, duty, or right.[75] The struggle to find the right balance between this "naturalistic tinge" and reliance on practice is reflected in the discussion in the case law on the general problem of how customary international law should be identified.

A review of decisions by ICTs, with a particular focus on the ICTY, reveals that the methods used to identify customary international law and *opinio juris* can roughly be divided into four categories, although these often overlap. First, they may find customary international law by employing the traditional method of state practice supported by *opinio juris*. Second, they may rely on *opinio juris* over practice – understood to include a broad spectrum of different considerations. Third, they may deduce customary rules from treaties, national legislation, and other (binding or nonbinding) documents. And fourth, they may refer to previous case law as a confirmation of the customary status of a norm. In the following analysis, I focus on the last three categories, in which the relative importance of *opinio juris* has outshined that of the actual practice, or the ICT directly infers customary international law from existing case law, strongly emphasizing moral and ethical concerns.[76]

The next subsection focuses on the identification of elements of crimes under customary international law, exemplifying the aforementioned methods of identification. I then touch on the lack of unity among ICTs in interpreting the notion and role of *opinio juris* in customary international law by looking at some examples of modes of liability under customary international law.

7.4.2 Opinio Juris *in Defining the Elements of Crimes*

Former president of the ICTY Theodor Meron has stated that "international criminal tribunals have taken an essentially conservative and traditional approach to the identification and application of customary international law

[75] Karol Wolfke, *Custom in Present International Law* (Dordrecht: Martinus Nijhoff, 2nd ed. 1993), 46. Wolfke also accurately points out that "some authors use the term *opinio juris sive necessitatis* also in a more general meaning – namely, that practice should be accompanied by a conviction of acting according to a general sense of law, social needs, morality, etc." Ibid.

[76] These developments have also been noted in the first report of the Special Rapporteur of the International Law Commission on customary international law. See Michael Wood, Special Rapporteur, "First Report on Formation and Evidence of Customary International Law," para. 70.

principles."[77] This indeed is evidenced in some decisions of the ICTs, but does not reflect the plethora of case law and approaches adopted by all of them.[78] As already noted, the ICTY has found customary international law to exist without substantive state practice in a number of cases – particularly those where it has inferred the existence of a customary rule of international criminal law from treaty-based or customary human rights norms. In some cases the existence of strong *opinio juris* has been sufficient for the court to conclude that a norm has become part of customary international law. I discuss some of these in further detail here.

One of the most striking deliberations highlighting *opinio juris* and undercutting the element of practice was the ICTY Trial Chamber judgment in the *Kupreskić* case, discussing the prohibition of reprisal attacks against civilians. In that case, six individuals were accused of attacking a village in Central Bosnia, killing 116 inhabitants and destroying houses and mosques. The Trial Chamber affirmed:

> Admittedly, there does not seem to have emerged recently a body of State practice consistently supporting the proposition that one of the elements of custom, namely *usus* or *diuturnitas* has taken shape. This is however an area where *opinio iuris sive necessitatis* may play a much greater role than *usus*, as a result of the aforementioned Martens Clause. In the light of the way States and courts have implemented it, this Clause shows that principles of international humanitarian law may emerge through a customary process under the pressure of the demands of humanity or the dictates of public conscience, even where State practice is scant or inconsistent. The other element, in the form of *opinio necessitatis*, crystallising as a result of the imperatives of humanity or public conscience, may turn out to be the decisive element heralding the emergence of a general rule or principle of humanitarian law.[79]

The Trial Chamber stated that the Martens Clause had become part of customary international law.[80] By way of background, the Martens Clause is a basic principle of humanitarian law, dating back to the preamble of the 1899 Hague Convention with Respect to the Laws and Customs of War on Land. It states, in short, that in cases not covered by the law in force, all persons

77 Theodor Meron, "Editorial Comment: Revival of Customary Humanitarian Law," 99 *American Journal of International Law* 817 (2005), 821.

78 In this connection, Roozbeh Baker states: "While the majority of ICTY and ICTR jurisprudence follows generally accepted international law, certain case-law does not, and in fact conflicts with long held international norms." Baker, "Customary International Law in the 21st Century," 184.

79 *Prosecutor v. Kupreškić*, Trial Chamber, para 527.

80 Ibid., para. 525.

remain under the protection of the principles of humanity and the dictates of public conscience.[81] While the clause does not provide any substantive rules of international law, it offers a minimum standard for the clarification of the rules of international humanitarian law. The Martens Clause, however, is best classified not as a rule of customary international law, but as a general principle of international law, providing interpretative assistance in determining the substantive rule arising from treaties or customary international law. This is an important distinction not only conceptually, as "principles are less specific than rules,"[82] but for the outcome: ICTs cannot apply principles that are vague and nonspecific, but are bound to apply specific (prohibitive) legal rules in order to adhere to the principle of legality. On the distinction between rules of customary international law and general principles, Thomas Kleinlein notes in his chapter that international courts in general have not been helpful in elaborating this dichotomy, but rather "use the term 'principles' in order to denote the general character and fundamental importance of the norm in question."[83]

In *Kupreskić*, the court considered that *opinio juris* had greater importance than practice in determining if a customary rule existed. Hence, the opinion reflects an emphasis on *opinio juris* over practice.[84] This broad understanding of customary international law accepts that various considerations feed into the element of *opinio juris*, and can contribute to the formation of principles of international criminal law through the customary process. The court stated that these considerations were paramount in the notion of *opinio juris*, and consequently ruled that *opinio juris* provided sufficient justification for the conclusion that a customary international rule governing reprisals against civilians had crystallized.[85]

Conceptually, the court first broadened the internal nature of *opinio juris* and the limits of that concept by looking for evidence of *opinio juris* beyond the sense of *legal* obligation in the concepts of "the demands of humanity" and "the dictates of public conscience." Second, it afforded *opinio juris* greater influence than practice on the formation of customary international law. In addition to referring to the "requirements of humanity and the dictates of public conscience," the court in *Kupreškić* conducted an inquiry into

81 See Rupert Ticehurst, "The Martens Clause and the Laws of Armed Conflict," 79 *International Review of the Red Cross* No. 317, 125 (1997); Antonio Cassese, "The Martens Clause: Half a Loaf or Simply Pie in the Sky?" 11 *European Journal of International Law* 187 (2000).

82 Kleinlein, "Customary International Law and General Principles," in this volume.

83 Ibid.

84 For a sliding-scale approach that might allow such an emphasis, see Kirgis, "Custom on a Sliding Scale."

85 *Prosecutor v. Kupreškić*, para. 531.

the nature of a customary rule prohibiting reprisals against civilians before the drafting of the First Protocol to the Geneva Conventions in 1977 ("First Protocol"), which relates to the protection of victims of international armed conflicts and modern international warfare.[86] The court looked into national declarations and military manuals, establishing that only the United States Military Manual of 1956 and the Dutch Soldiers Handbook of 1974 explicitly took a stance against such reprisals. However, in response to the prohibition of reprisals against civilians as incorporated in the First Protocol, in 1978 the U.S. government adopted a more reserved position out of a concern about limiting its options in case another state were to use such reprisals as a means of warfare. The court found that it was impossible to establish constant and widespread state practice relating to a prohibition of reprisals against civilians, and instead emphasized the existence of a strong sense of such a legal obligation. Nonetheless, the ICRC study on customary international humanitarian law has found preexisting practice in the form of various instruments, national legislation, military manuals, and documents adopted by the United Nations – and by reference to *Tadić* and the subsequent *Kupreskić* decisions themselves.[87]

In *Prosecutor v. Krstić*, another ICTY case, General Krstić was prosecuted for acts that took place in Srebrenica in 1995.[88] More precisely, Krstić was charged with murders under Articles 3 and 5 of the ICTY Statute – war crimes and crimes against humanity – and with persecution and extermination. Alternative counts of genocide and complicity to commit genocide were also included in the indictment. Among other acts, he was accused of crimes against humanity committed in the form of deportation or forcible transfer of women, children, and elderly persons.[89]

The Trial Chamber, in accordance with the ICTY Statute, had to apply the existing definition of genocide under customary international law. Article 4(2) of the Statute of the ICTY defines genocide, replicating the definition set out in Article 2 of the 1948 Convention on the Prevention and Punishment of the Crime of Genocide ("Genocide Convention"),[90] which has crystallized as

86 Ibid., para. 532.

87 See *Customary International Humanitarian Law*, edited by Jean-Marie Henckaerts and Louise Doswald-Beck, Vol. II: Practice, Part 2 (Cambridge: Cambridge University Press and ICRC, 2005), 3405–27.

88 *Prosecutor v. Krstić*, IT-98-33-T, Trial Chamber, 2 August 2001.

89 Ibid., para. 479.

90 Article 2 of the 1948 Genocide Convention, and Article 4(2) of the ICTY Statute, define genocide as follows: "Genocide means any of the following acts committed with intent to destroy, in whole or in part, a national, ethnical, racial or religious group, as such: (a) killing members of the group; (b) causing serious bodily or mental harm to members of the group; (c) deliberately

customary international law through state practice and universal *opinio juris*.[91] The ICTY correctly noted that it must interpret the definition of genocide in light of the status of customary international law at the time the alleged offences took place – in July 1995, when the Srebrenica massacre occurred. To determine the definition of genocide in 1995, the court looked at the text as well as the object and purpose of Article 2 of the 1948 Genocide Convention. In addition, the court scrutinized relevant case law, especially that of the ICTR, and the Report of the ILC on the Draft Code of Crimes against Peace and Security of Mankind. The court also took into account the definition of genocide appearing in the Rome Statute of the ICC, which was adopted in 1998. The chamber observed that even though the Rome Statute and the draft text of the Statute elaborated by the Preparatory Commission for the ICC were drafted only after the crimes took place (in 1995), they "proved helpful in assessing the state of customary international law which the Chamber itself derived from other sources."[92] The starting point of the court's analysis was not the actual practice of states, but rather the possible crystallization of customary international law through treaties and other documents. This serves as an example of deducing customary rules from treaties, national legislation, and other (binding or nonbinding) documents as opposed to practice supported by *opinio juris*.

The *Krstić* court took the opportunity to discuss the formation of customary international law and its elements drawn from treaty law in more detail. It expressed the view that the draft text of the Rome Statute prepared by the Preparatory Commission for the ICC was evidence of *opinio juris*, because all the states attending the Rome Conference, whether or not they signed the Rome Statute, had had the opportunity to raise their opinions at the meeting of the Preparatory Commission. Instead of further analyzing the nature of the *opinio juris* and its differentiation from state practice, the court straightforwardly pointed to tangible evidence of (international) *opinio juris* – the documents and cases. The court could have articulated state practice in support of the definition of the *mens rea* element of genocide – an intent to destroy all or part of the group – as it is codified in the Genocide Convention (and

inflicting on the group conditions of life calculated to bring about its physical destruction in whole or in part; (d) imposing measures intended to prevent births within the group; (e) forcibly transferring children of the group to another group."

91 While the customary international law nature of the prohibition of genocide is not challenged, it is interesting to note that in 1951 the ICJ stated that such a prohibition exists, for it is part of "the most elementary principles of morality," even in the absence of any conventional obligation. *Reservations to the Convention on the Prevention and Punishment of the Crime of Genocide*, Advisory Opinion of 28 May 1951, 1951 ICJ Rep. 15, 23.

92 *Prosecutor v. Krstić*, para. 541.

possibly other sources), at least by showing that no contrary state practice existed. Here, by contrary state practice I mean any practice that would define the requisite *mens rea* for genocide in a manner other than that set out in the Genocide Convention.

The court's reasoning – and the doctrine of customary international law in general – would also have profited from a more profound analysis by the court of the notion of *opinio juris*. In particular, it could have better explained how the act of participating in the Rome Conference evidences a sense of legal obligation pertaining to substantive rules of customary international law.

As the *Krstić* decision shows, the ICTY has found support in treaties, national legislation, and previous decisions for practice, *opinio juris*, and even customary international law as such, without specific analysis of the elements of customary international law. The court has simultaneously cited codified law and previous decisions of ICTs, including its own, especially in cases where it has not looked at the physical practice of states or of the international community. In short, it has relied on "paper practice," meaning that instead of looking at the actual (physical) practice of states, it finds "practice" in individual or collective statements of states expressing support for (or condemning) certain acts.[93]

Another example of a method deducing customary international law from existing instruments and documents is the ICTY Appeals Chamber judgment in *Blaškić*, decided in 2004.[94] In this judgment the Appeals Chamber considered different crimes of persecution in order to determine whether they were prohibited under customary international law at the time of their commission. The Chamber justified characterizing these crimes as persecution by analogy to other crimes identified in the ICTY Statute, stating that the crimes

[93] On paper practice, see Bruno Simma and Philip Alston, "The Sources of Human Rights Law: Custom, Jus Cogens, and General Principles," 12 *Australian Yearbook of International Law* 82 (1988–89), 89 ("[Practice] has changed from something happening out there in the real world, after the diplomats and the delegates have had their say, into paper practice: the words, texts, votes and excuses themselves. The process of customary law-making is thus turned into a self-contained exercise in rhetoric."); Kristin N. Wuerffel, "Discriminating Among Rights? A Nation's Legislating Hierarchy of Human Rights in the Context of International Human Rights Customary Law," 33 *Valparaiso University Law Review* 369 (1998), 409 ("By means of this paper practice, customary human rights norms have emerged more deliberately than traditional customary norms. For instead of relying on the consistent but arbitrary practice of a norm, states have explicitly stated their adherence to human rights norms in such instruments."); Niels Petersen, "Customary Law Without Custom? Rules, Principles, and the Role of State Practice in International Norm Creation," 23 *American University International Law Review* 275 (2007), 278 ("Not only explicit conduct, but also paper practice – such as the conduct and pronouncements of international organizations – is recognized as practice by a majority of legal scholars.").

[94] *Prosecutor v. Blaškić*, Appeals Chamber.

"must constitute a crime of persecution of gravity equal to the crimes listed in Article 5 of the Statute,"[95] which defines "crimes against humanity." Article 5 provides: "The International Tribunal shall have the power to prosecute persons responsible for the following crimes when committed in armed conflict, whether international or internal in character, and directed against any civilian population: (a) murder; (b) extermination; (c) enslavement; (d) deportation; (e) imprisonment; (f) torture; (g) rape; (h) persecutions on political, racial and religious grounds; (i) other inhumane acts."[96] Instead of looking at state practice defining whether the crimes in question would qualify as crimes against humanity, the court stated that it had to determine whether the acts "constitute a denial of or infringement upon a fundamental right laid down in international customary law."[97]

In looking at the specific charges of persecution, the court attempted to analyze the customary international law status of each of them. First, according to the Chamber, killing and causing serious injury can be characterized as persecution, because the "inherent right to life and to be free from cruel, inhuman or degrading treatment or punishment is recognized in customary international law and is embodied in Articles 6 and 7 of the ICCPR, and Articles 2 and 3 of the ECHR."[98] It also made a reference to the above-discussed *Kupreškić* Trial Chamber judgment. Hence, the Chamber deduced that killing and causing serious injury could be crimes of persecution under customary international law from human rights instruments that impose obligations on states rather than individuals, and found support for the conclusion in its previous case law.

Second, the Trial Chamber determined whether destruction and plunder of property were a form of persecution under customary international law by making reference to various treaties. In particular, it referred to Geneva Convention IV, on the protection of civilians in international armed conflict, as an "expression of customary international law," to the First Additional Protocol, setting forth additional rules applicable in international armed conflicts, and to the judgment of the Trial Chamber in *Kupreškić*.[99] In reference to the norm prohibiting pillage, the court stated that it is considered to be part of customary international law because pillage is expressly prohibited in Geneva

95 Ibid., para. 135.

96 Statute of the ICTY, art. 5.

97 *Prosecutor v. Blackic*, para. 139.

98 Ibid., para. 143.

99 Ibid., paras. 145–46 (quoting the *Kupreškić* Trial Chamber judgment, stating the act "may constitute a gross or blatant denial of fundamental human rights, and, if committed on discriminatory grounds, it may constitute persecution").

Convention IV, Additional Protocol II, the Hague Regulations of 1907, the Nuremberg Charter, and Control Council Law No. 10, and because it was the subject of proceedings at the Nuremberg trials and other post–World War II trials, with a mention of three such cases. Again, the court made no explicit mention of the constituent elements of customary international law, practice and *opinio juris*. The court followed the same methodology of citing international instruments, some post–World War II cases, and its earlier judgment in the *Krnojelac* case in also concluding that deportation, forcible transfer, and forcible displacement could amount to persecution as a crime against humanity.[100]

Third, whereas the Trial Chamber in *Blaškić* had not elaborated on whether the attacks on cities, towns, and villages were acts of persecution, the Appeals Chamber undertook an analysis of the customary prohibition of those acts. The Chamber again made recourse to the First and Second Additional Protocols of the Geneva Conventions in concluding that a norm protecting civilians from indiscriminate attacks is part of customary international law. Moreover, the Appeals Chamber supported this conclusion by effectively finding the existence of *opinio juris* in General Assembly Resolutions 2444 (1968) and 2675 (1970), which affirm that military action cannot be launched against civilians, and that civilians cannot be the object of military operations, and further in the *travaux préparatoires* of the Additional Protocols to the Geneva Conventions.[101]

Thus, the Appeals Chamber found the elements of persecution as a crime against humanity under customary international law by reference to international legal documents, without any explicit mention of state practice. The main sources for its conclusions were international human rights and humanitarian treaties, supported by international case law – largely the decisions of the ICTY itself. The methodology of the court seems very linear and does not do justice to customary international law as a complex source of international law based on practice supported by a sense of legal obligation, which cannot be straightforwardly deduced from international documents, or even existing case law.

Similarly, in some cases, as Jean-Marie Henckaerts and Els Debuf note in their chapter, the ICTY has cited the ICRC Study on Customary Humanitarian Law as proof of the status of a customary norm.[102] They also highlight some

100 Ibid., paras. 150–53.

101 See ibid., para. 158 ("Evidence of the existence of *opinio juris* is demonstrated in the General Assembly Resolution 2444 (1968) … and in Resolution 2675 (1970). … The travaux préparatoires of the Additional Protocols also provide further confirmation of the customary status of this prohibition.").

102 See Jean-Marie Henckaerts and Els Debuf, "The ICRC and the Clarification of Customary International Humanitarian Law," in this volume.

"examples where the conclusions of the Study have been confirmed by judicial or arbitral decisions."[103]

However, there are some problems with the ICTY relying on the ICRC Study to determine the content of customary humanitarian law. First, this can become a circular exercise because of the Study's references to the decisions of the ICTY – and other tribunals – as proof of custom, which then are viewed as being confirmed when re-cited by a court or tribunal. In practice, perhaps, this is unproblematic, but on the conceptual level this methodology circumvents – or at least moves to the back-burner – the requirement of state practice in the formation of customary international law. Second, while the ICRC Study provides a thorough scrutiny of the substantive issues of humanitarian law and provides a vast amount of evidence in favor of rules of customary international humanitarian law, it is a "snapshot"[104] of what was interpreted by the ICRC to be customary at a certain point in time. As Judge Koroma pointed out in his foreword to the ICRC Study, customary international law is "notoriously imprecise."[105]

Returning to the *Kupreškić* case, the court, in discussing the definition of "civilian" for the purposes of crimes against humanity,[106] again resorted to an inventive method of identifying customary international law. The court noted that "the Security Council, in establishing the International Tribunal, may have defined the crime in Article 5 more narrowly than is necessary under customary international law," but that a wide definition of "civilian" and "population" was intended, and that the limitation in Article 5 of the Statute of the ICTY was in fact a departure from customary international law.[107] Because of the supposedly wider concept of "crimes against humanity" under customary international law than under the ICTY Statute, the court concluded that the definition of a civilian should also be correspondingly broader in this context. The court found support for this conclusion in the 1985 *Barbie* decision of the French Court of Cassation, even though the court

103 Ibid.

104 Jean-Marie Henckaerts, "Customary International Humanitarian Law: A Response to U.S. Comments," 89 *International Review of the Red Cross* No. 866, 473 (2007), 487.

105 Foreword by Dr. Abdul G. Koroma, in *Customary International Humanitarian Law*, xviii. For further discussion, see Noora Arajärvi, *The Changing Nature of Customary International Law: Methods of Interpreting the Concept of Custom in International Criminal Tribunals* (London: Routledge, 2014), esp. chapter 3.

106 Under humanitarian law, "civilians" are afforded broader protection than combatants, and no attacks can be directed against them. Therefore, the distinction between civilians and combatants is important in an armed conflict, and hence in determining accountability for violations against civilians.

107 *Prosecutor v. Kupreškić*, Trial Chamber, paras. 545–47.

acknowledged that this decision was based on general principles rather than on customary international law, and in the ICTY's *Vukovar* Rule 61 Decision of 3 April 1996.[108] The court could have strengthened its argument by analyzing some national legislation and case law as evidence of practice contributing to the customary international law character of this broader definition. On the other hand, such an analysis might have led the court to conclude that the definition has not crystallized under customary international law. The latter outcome, however, may not have been a desired or just one from an ethical standpoint. Nonetheless, as this chapter aims to highlight, courts – especially international courts – should exercise the utmost caution, in particular in criminal proceedings, in looking for or providing novel definitions for crimes. This is because they must respect the principle of legality by applying law as it is, *lex lata*.

7.4.3 *The Fragmentation of Judicial Approaches in ICTs – Modes of Liability*

As exemplified by the case law discussed earlier, while there has been a trend in international courts and tribunals to generally refer to their own case law as well as the interpretations of customary international law in the decisions of other courts and tribunals (at least within a specific field of public international law), some courts have adopted a different approach, resulting in a "fragmentation" of judicial approaches to finding customary international law. Here, I briefly discuss two examples of different approaches where ICTs have determined modes of liability based on customary international law.

One such example involves the concept of "joint criminal enterprise" ("JCE"). JCE imposes individual criminal responsibility on each member of an organized group (for example, a government) for crimes committed by the group within their common plan or purpose. This "common purpose" liability stems from post–World War II war crimes trials,[109] but was formulated in its modern form in the ICTY Appeals Decision in *Tadić*.[110] There are potentially three types of "JCE," which differ with respect to the requisite *mens rea*: "JCE I," in which all members of the JCE act together pursuant to a common

[108] Ibid., paras. 548–49 ("Thus the presence of those actively involved in the conflict should not prevent the characterization of a population as civilian and those actively involved in a resistance movement can qualify as victims of crimes against humanity.").

[109] For an overview, see Jens David Ohlin, "Three Conceptual Problems with the Doctrine of Joint Criminal Enterprise," 5 *Journal of International Criminal Justice* 69 (2007).

[110] See *Prosecutor v. Tadić*, IT-94-1-A, Appeals Chamber, 15 July 1999.

design and share the same *mens rea*[111]; "JCE II," addressing the "concentration camp" cases, where the accused participates, with knowledge of the systematic ill-treatment, in an institutional framework inflicting such ill-treatment[112]; and "JCE III," in which the accused is held liable for criminal acts committed by other members of the group even though they fall outside the common plan, so long as these acts are reasonably foreseeable and the accused still willingly participates in the common plan.[113]

Courts and scholars have generally recognized that JCE I and JCE II have crystallized under customary international law, but the third type, JCE III, has been far more controversial.[114] Even though JCE III has been recognized and accepted by the ICTY as a part of customary international law in *Tadić* and subsequent cases, many commentators have taken the view that the ICTY constructed JCE III without any proper basis in international law, and in the absence of state practice and *opinio juris*.[115] While the ICTY, the ICTR, the Special Court for Sierra Leone ("SCSL"), and the Extraordinary Chambers in the Courts of Cambodia ("ECCC") have all considered the applicability of JCE III, it still remains an ambiguous and controversial form of criminal responsibility.[116]

Michael Scharf points out that JCE was never specifically mentioned in the Nuremberg Charter or the judgment, but that they did lay the foundations for the modern application of JCE in the form of common plan liability.[117] Scharf concludes that JCE (without specifying the form of JCE) became a part of customary international law in 1946 and that domestic and hybrid courts can

111 Ibid., para. 196.

112 Ibid., para. 202. The Appeals Chamber in *Vasiljević* added that the accused must also possess the intention of *furthering* the system of ill-treatment. See *Prosecutor v. Vasiljević*, IT-98-32-A, Appeals Chamber, 25 February 2004, para. 101.

113 *Prosecutor v. Tadić*, para. 204. See also Michael P. Scharf, "Seizing the 'Grotian Moment': Accelerated Formation of Customary International Law in Times of Fundamental Change," 43 *Cornell International Law Journal* 439 (2010).

114 See, e.g., Darryl Robinson, "The Two Liberalisms of International Criminal Law," in *Future Perspectives on International Criminal Justice*, edited by Carsten Stahn and Larissa van den Herik 115 (The Hague: T.M.C. Asser Press, 2010), 119–24.

115 See, e.g., Verena Haan, "The Development of the Concept of Joint Criminal Enterprise at the International Criminal Tribunal for the Former Yugoslavia," 5 *International Criminal Law Review* 167 (2005); Mohamed Elewa Badar, "'Just Convict Everyone!': Joint Perpetration from *Tadić* to *Stakić* and Back Again," 6 *International Criminal Law Review* 293 (2006); Antonio Cassese, "The Proper Limits of Individual Responsibility under the Doctrine of Joint Criminal Enterprise," 5 *Journal of International Criminal Justice* 109 (2007).

116 See, e.g., Nolwenn Guibert and Tilman Blumenstock, "The First Judgement of the Special Court for Sierra Leone: A Missed Opportunity?" 6 *Law and Practice of International Courts and Tribunals* 367 (2007); Dov Jacobs and Noora Arajärvi, "International Criminal Court," 7 *The Law and Practice of International Courts and Tribunals* 115 (2008).

117 Scharf, *Customary International Law in Times of Fundamental Change*, 69, 74–76.

therefore try crimes based on JCE liability. However, he also takes note of the arguments against the customary nature of JCE by the Khmer Rouge defendants in the ECCC. The defendants protested that the cases evidencing JCE as part of customary international law were "unpublished cases," and therefore they could not have had knowledge of such developments in law. In this context, Scharf also notes that "international judicial decisions, like domestic court cases, can evidence state practice and *opinio juris*, establishing customary international law."[118] The ECCC held in 2010 – and confirmed in 2011 – that JCE III was not a sufficiently clear and unambiguous form of liability, did not exist under customary international law in 1975–79, and consequently was not applicable in the proceedings of that court.[119]

In *Prosecutor v. Brdanin*, decided in 2004, the ICTY itself attempted to reverse its position on JCE III (considering both JCE I and JCE III simultaneously), narrowing its scope.[120] The decision was, however, subsequently overturned on appeal. In that case, Brdanin was accused of a number of crimes under JCE based on a permanent forcible removal of Bosnian Muslims and Bosnian Croats from the territory of the Autonomous Region of Krajina. The Trial Chamber considered and dismissed the applicability of any of the three categories of JCE, holding that JCE was not an appropriate form of responsibility when the accused was "structurally remote" from the actual acts.[121] Brdanin was convicted of aiding and abetting the commission of the crimes.[122] Both the Defense and the Prosecutor appealed, the latter claiming, among other alleged errors, that the interpretations of JCE I and JCE III by

[118] Ibid., 80–81, 85.

[119] See *Prosecutor v. Ieng, Ieng and Khieu*, 002/19-09-2007-ECCC/OCIJ (PTC 35, 37, 38, and 39), Pre-Trial Chamber Decision on the Appeals against the Co-Investigative Judges' Order on Joint Criminal Enterprise, 20 May 2010; Trial Chamber Decision on the Applicability of Joint Criminal Enterprise, 12 September 2011. See also Robert Charles Clarke, "Return to Borkum Island: Extended Joint Criminal Enterprise Responsibility in the Wake of World War II," 9 *Journal of International Criminal Justice* 839 (2011).

[120] *Prosecutor v. Brdanin*, IT-99-36-T, Trial Chamber Judgment of 1 September 2004, paras. 340–56. For a historical review of JCE and a critical opinion on its interpretation by the Trial Chamber, see Allen O'Rourke, "Joint Criminal Enterprise and Brđanin: Misguided Overcorrection," 47 *Harvard International Law Journal* 307 (2006).

[121] *Prosecutor v. Brdanin*, para. 351. See also Antonio Cassese, "The Proper Limits of Individual Responsibility under the Doctrine of Joint Criminal Enterprise," 5 *Journal of International Criminal Justice* 109 (2007), 126 ("To extend criminal liability to instances where there was no agreement or common plan between the perpetrators and those who participated in the common plan would seem to excessively broaden the notion, which is always premised on the sharing of a criminal intent by all those who take part in the common enterprise.").

[122] For analysis of the Trial Chamber decision, see Katrina Gustafson, "The Requirement of an 'Express Agreement' for Joint Criminal Enterprise Liability: A Critique of *Brdanin*," 5 *Journal of International Criminal Justice* 134 (2007).

the Trial Chamber were too narrow. The Appeals Chamber agreed with the Prosecutor.

The Appeals Chamber ruled that JCE did not have to include the persons committing the physical acts, and that there did not have to be an agreement between the accused and the actual perpetrator for JCE responsibility to apply.[123] While the discussion largely centered on the requisite *actus reus* of JCE, the Appeals Chamber reflected on the previous jurisprudence on JCE in general – mainly its own – and, at the end of the opinion, noted that there was no reason to depart from *Tadić*.[124] It did not, however, delve more deeply into the notion of JCE as part of customary international law, nor did it directly refer to any "state practice" or "*opinio juris*."

As noted earlier, in the case of *Prosecutor v. Ieng, Ieng and Khieu*, the ECCC in 2010 limited JCE III by declaring that it did not form part of customary international law between 1975 and 1979, when the crimes in that case took place.[125] This ruling evidently was opposed to the analysis and outcome in the ICTY's ruling in *Tadić*. The ECCC essentially maintained that the ICTY had stretched the limits of customary international law to reach the conclusion that JCE III had crystallized.[126] It noted that neither the legal instruments nor the case law relied on in *Tadić* provided sufficient evidence of the customary international law status of JCE III.[127]

In analyzing the concept of JCE III, the ECCC first noted that it must consider "not only whether JCE existed under customary international law at the relevant time, thus being punishable under international criminal law, but also whether it was sufficiently foreseeable and accessible to the Charged Persons."[128] It then examined the findings in *Tadić*, other ICTY cases, and case law dealing with the crimes committed in World War II. It concluded that JCE I and JCE II "are forms of responsibility that were recognised in customary international law since the Post-World War II

[123] *Prosecutor v. Brdanin*, IT-99-36-A, Appeals Chamber Judgment of 3 April 2007, paras. 410–32. Judge Shahabuddeen disagreed with the majority by holding that the required link between the accused and the crime can only be established if the physical perpetrator was a member of the JCE. See Partly Dissenting Opinion of Judge Shahabuddeen, paras. 18–19.

[124] *Prosecutor v. Brdanin*, Appeals Chamber Judgment, para. 390.

[125] *Prosecutor v. Ieng, Ieng and Khieu*, Pre-Trial Chamber Decision. This was confirmed in 2011 by the Trial Chamber. See Trial Chamber Decision on the Applicability of Joint Criminal Enterprise, 12 September 2011.

[126] The appeals to the Pre-Trial Chamber argued that "the *Tadić* Appeals Chamber wrongly determined that JCE liability existed under customary international law as it relied on too few cases. … JCE liability has never been a form of liability in general and consistent State use." *Prosecutor v. Ieng, Ieng and Khieu*, para. 51.

[127] Ibid., paras. 79–81.

[128] Ibid., para. 45.

international instruments and international military case law."[129] On the other hand, in relation to JCE III, the court found that "[h]aving reviewed the authorities relied upon by *Tadić* in relation to the extended form of JCE (JCE III), the Pre-Trial Chamber is of the view that they do not provide sufficient evidence of consistent state practice or *opinio juris* at the time relevant to Case 002."[130] Hence, unlike some other decisions of ICTs, discussed earlier in the chapter, the ECCC noted the need for both state practice and *opinio juris* in formulating customary international law. While the ECCC perhaps could have tweaked its reasoning to place greater emphasis on one element of customary international law over the other in order to establish JCE III, its choice not to do so may be more connected to the type of customary international law rule at hand than conscious fidelity to proper legal method and the principle of legality. In particular, here the ECCC was determining a mode of liability, and not the legal status of a morally and ethically appalling act.

As these cases demonstrate, the status of JCE III under customary international law remains unclear. It is yet to be seen whether recognition of JCE III was simply a short-lived expansion of individual criminal responsibility, invented by the ICTY, or whether it will continue to be recognized and applied by the ICTY and other ICTs.[131] Given the wide-spanning critiques of the doctrine, coupled with diverging interpretations of existing practice and the exclusion of JCE III from the scope of the Rome Statute of the ICC, it may be safest to lay JCE III to rest and look to the other forms of liability, JCE I and II, which have a stronger basis in customary international law and

[129] Ibid., para. 72.

[130] Ibid., para. 77. For further analysis of the decision, see Michael G. Karnavas, "Joint Criminal Enterprise at the ECCC: A Critical Analysis of the Pre-Trial Chamber's Decision against the Application of JCE III and Two Divergent Commentaries on the Same," 21 *Criminal Law Forum* 445 (2010).

[131] Both the Trial Chamber and the Appeals Chamber of the Special Court for Sierra Leone embraced the ICTY's interpretation of the concept of JCE by reducing the required link between the action or inaction of a member of the JCE and the commission of the crime. See *Prosecutor v. Sesay, Kallon and Gbao*, SCLS-04-15-T-1234, Trial Chamber, 2 March 2009 and SCLS-04-15-A, Appeals Chamber, 26 October 2009, para. 394 ("The Trial Chamber held that to establish the liability of JCE members, the principal perpetrator of the crime need not be a member of the JCE, but may be used as a tool by one of the JCE members"), and ibid., para. 401 ("the Appeals Chamber is satisfied that the holdings reflect customary international law at the time the crimes in the present case were committed"). The court did not refer to state practice or *opinio juris*, but cited a number of ICTY cases in support of the customary international law concept of JCE. For a critical analysis, see Wayne Jordash and Scott Martin, "Due Process and Fair Trial Rights at the Special Court: How the Desire for Accountability Outweighed the Demands of Justice at the Special Court for Sierra Leone," 23 *Leiden Journal of International Law* 585 (2010), esp. 598–607.

in treaty law.[132] On a more general level, the interpretations of JCE III under customary international law also illustrate that there is quite some diversity in the ways customary international law is identified even within the same field of public international law.

Another example of a recent departure from the emphasis on *opinio juris* in the jurisprudence of ICTs at the expense of state practice is the decision of the Appeals Chamber of the Special Court for Sierra Leone in *Prosecutor v. Charles Taylor*, announced in 2013. Among other issues, the Appeals Chamber discussed the customary law elements of *mens rea* for aiding and abetting as a form of criminal responsibility. In other words, it addressed whether an accused can be held criminally liable if he willingly performed the requisite *actus reus*, knowing the impact of his conduct on the commission of the crime.[133]

In the appeal proceedings, the Defense stated that "knowledge of the consequences" is not a sufficient standard for aiding and abetting liability, and is not supported by customary international law.[134] It argued that the Trial Chamber had erroneously relied on, for example, Article 25(3) of the Rome Statute of the ICC, the Draft Articles of the International Law Commission on Internationally Wrongful Acts, and the ICTY judgment in *Furundžija*, as setting forth the "purpose" standard, as these do not provide evidence of state practice or *opinio juris*.[135] The Defense argued in particular that the *Furundžija* Trial Chamber failed to analyze and show the existence of both practice and *opinio juris*, and contended that its discussion of these elements of customary international law was "manifestly incorrect, incomplete and insufficient."[136] In conclusion, the Defense stated that the "*opinio juris* of States has not coalesced around a knowledge standard of *mens rea* for aiding and abetting."[137] The Prosecution disagreed with these statements, siding with the interpretation of the standard of *mens rea* for aiding and abetting adopted by the ICTY and ICTR.

In resolving this dispute, the SCSL Appeals Chamber examined the development of customary international law, engaging in a broad analysis

132 See Rome Statute of International Criminal Court, 17 July 1998, 2187 UNTS 90, art. 25(3). For discussion, see Defence Observations on Article 25(3)(d), Situation in the Democratic Republic of Congo in the Case of the *Prosecutor v. Germain Katanga*, ICC-01/04-01/07, 15 April 2013; Gerhard Werle, "Individual Criminal Responsibility in Article 25 ICC Statute," 5 *Journal of International Criminal Justice* 953 (2007); Jens David Ohlin, "Joint Intentions to Commit International Crimes," 11 *Chicago Journal of International Law* 693 (2011).

133 *Prosecutor v. Charles Taylor*, SCSL-03-01-A, Appeals Chamber, 26 September 2013.

134 Ibid., para. 407.

135 Ibid., para. 408.

136 Ibid.

137 Ibid.

of post–World War II case law,[138] the Draft Code of the International Law Commission,[139] some (inconsistent) domestic case law,[140] and case law of ICTs. It did not agree with the Defense's criticism of the identification of customary international law in *Furundžija*. Furthermore, it noted that some later ICTY cases[141] have followed the analysis of the *Tadić* Trial Chamber, which drew from the Nuremberg trials in holding that knowledge alone can be sufficient to establish culpable intent. Notably, the Appeals Chamber did not dissect the elements of customary international law in its analysis, but rather relied on existing case law in identifying customary law. In its discussion of Taylor's personal culpability, however, the Chamber noted that "existing customary international law can be modified if the combination of *opinio juris* and state practice show a continuing and consistent adherence to the new custom by the international community."[142]

Finally, the Appeals Chamber entered into a discussion of the requirement of "specific direction" as a necessary part of the *actus reus* for aiding and abetting liability under customary international law (recognizing that the Statute of the SCSL is silent on the issue).[143] It noted that it should take into account decisions of the ICTY and ICTR Appeals Chamber, as well as decisions of the ECCC and STL, but must make the final assessment of the law itself.[144] On the basis of the reviewed post–World War II case law and subsequent state practice, it held that such a requirement of specific direction for aiding and abetting liability under customary international law did not exist.[145]

By contrast, the ICTY Appeals Chamber held in *Perisić*,[146] decided in February 2013 – that is, seven months prior to the *Taylor* Appeals judgment – that specific direction *is* a necessary part of the *actus reus* for aiding and abetting liability. However, the court there did not make any explicit reference to customary international law, and did not elaborate on any state practice or *opinio juris* that may contribute to such a rule. This example illustrates the very different ways in which ICTs – the SCSL and the ICTY Appeals Chambers – have interpreted the customary status of the same rule, and both within a time frame of less than a year.

138 Ibid., paras. 417–27.
139 Ibid., para. 428.
140 Ibid., paras. 429–30.
141 The court referred to *Prosecutor v. Delalic*, IT-96-21-T, Trial Chamber, 20 February 2001, and *Prosecutor v. Aleksovski*, IT-95-14/1-T, Trial Chamber, 24 March 2000.
142 *Prosecutor v. Charles Taylor*, para. 457.
143 Ibid., paras. 471–73.
144 Ibid., para. 472.
145 Ibid., para. 474.
146 *Prosecutor v. Perišić*, IT-04-81-A, Appeals Chamber, 28 February 2013.

The SCSL Appeals Chamber in *Taylor* distinguished its approach from that of the ICTY Appeals Chamber in *Perisić* as follows:

> In the absence of any discussion of customary international law, it is presumed that the ICTY Appeals Chamber in *Perisić* was only identifying and applying internally binding precedent. ... [T]he ICTY Appeals Chamber's jurisprudence does not contain a clear, detailed analysis of the authorities supporting the conclusion that specific direction is an element of the *actus reus* of aiding and abetting liability under customary international law.[147]

In effect, the SCSL Appeals Chamber stated that the ICTY in no way showed that the specific direction element is part of customary international law, but applied it nonetheless. The ICTY did so regardless of its mandate, which requires it to apply legal rules that are "beyond any doubt part of customary law so that the problem of adherence of some but not all States to specific conventions does not arise."[148]

The critique by the SCSL in *Taylor* of the ICTY's reasoning in *Perisić* is well founded. It properly implies that direct reliance on previous case law does not constitute a sufficient analysis of whether a rule has crystallized as customary international law, and may pave the way for faulty outcomes that are not founded on existing and consistent practice supported by *opinio juris*.[149] Accordingly, courts, including the ICTY, should engage in a critical qualitative reexamination of their analyses and the evidence they looked at in reaching their conclusions in previous cases, rather than blindly duplicating the interpretations they adopted in these cases.

The ICTY has not continued to follow this "internally binding precedent" of the "specific direction" requirement. The ICTY Appeals Chamber – with mostly different judges on the bench than in *Perisić* – held in *Šainović*, decided in January 2014, that "specific direction" is in fact not a requirement for responsibility to arise under aiding and abetting liability.[150] The court, like the SCSL in the *Taylor* case, reexamined the customary international law definition of the elements of aiding and abetting liability by reference to existing case law, including post–World War II cases, and

147 *Prosecutor v. Charles Taylor*, paras. 476–77.

148 UN Secretary-General, "Report Submitted Pursuant to Paragraph 2 of Security Council Resolution 808 (1993)," UN Doc. S/25704 (3 May 1993), para. 34. See also *Prosecutor v. Blaškić*, Appeals Chamber, para. 141 ("while the Statute of the International Tribunal lists offences over which the International Tribunal has jurisdiction, the Tribunal may enter convictions only where it is satisfied that the offence is proscribed under customary international law at the time of its commission").

149 This is an example of the "corrupt pedigree fallacy" described by Fernando Tesón in his chapter. See Fernando R. Tesón, "Fake Custom," in this volume.

150 *Prosecutor v. Šainović et al.*, IT-05-87-A, Appeals Chamber, 23 January 2014.

its own jurisprudence, which it reviewed to show how the definition has developed.[151] The court noted that when the case law is conflicting, it must determine its approach according to "cogent reasons in the interest of justice … mindful of its duty to act in the interests of legal certainty and predictability while ensuring that justice is done in all cases."[152] Eventually, the court also looked at national legislation and case law on aiding and abetting liability, while recognizing that there is no uniformly adopted definition. It did not explicitly articulate these as evidence of customary international law, but stated that they may be relied upon as a source of international principles.[153] It concluded that there is "not a general, uniform practice in national jurisdictions."[154] Furthermore, the court analyzed the definition provided in the 1996 Draft Code of Crimes against the Peace and Security of Mankind adopted by the International Law Commission and the Rome Statute of the ICC.[155] Finally, the court stated, in no uncertain terms, that it "unequivocally rejects the approach adopted in the *Perisić* Appeal Judgment as it is in direct and material conflict with the prevailing jurisprudence on the *actus reus* of aiding and abetting liability and with customary international law in this regard."[156] This approach was confirmed by the Appeals Chamber in *Popović et al.* in January 2015.[157]

In May 2013 – between the *Perisić* and *Šainović* Appeals judgments, and prior to the *Taylor* judgment of the SCSL – the Trial Chamber delivered its judgment in *Stanišić and Simatović*, which followed *Perišić* in holding that specific direction is an element of the *actus reus* of aiding and abetting, leading to the acquittal of the defendants.[158] The Trial Chamber did not discuss the customary status of this requirement of specific direction, but proceeded with simply referencing the previous case law of the court.

In December 2015, the Appeals Chamber quashed the Trial Chamber's decision, upholding the *Sainović* Appeals Chamber's denunciation of the specific direction requirement, and ordered a re-trial.[159] The Appeals Chamber's reasoning was two-fold: The Trial Chamber had committed an error of law in its interpretation of the *actus reus* requirement of aiding and abetting liability, and its reasoning of *mens rea* in JCE was flawed. With two judges dissenting, it

[151] Ibid., paras. 1649–51.
[152] Ibid., para. 1622.
[153] Ibid., paras. 1643–46.
[154] Ibid., para. 1646.
[155] Ibid., paras. 1647–48.
[156] Ibid., para. 1650.
[157] *Prosecutor v. Popović et al.*, I T-05-88-A, Appeals Chamber, 30 January 2015.
[158] *Prosecutor v. Stanišić and Simatović*, IT-03-69-T, Trial Chamber, 30 May 2013.
[159] *Prosecutor v. Stanišić and Simatović*, IT-03-69-A, Appeals Chamber, 9 December 2015.

confirmed that "it has been established that specific direction has never been part of the elements of aiding and abetting liability under customary international law, which the Tribunal has to apply."[160]

Similarly to the divergent interpretations of JCE explored earlier in the chapter, the jurisprudence of ICTs identifying the status of customary international law in relation to the requirement of "specific direction" has been only gradually elaborated by the ICTY.[161] The *Šainović* Appeals Chamber attempted to mend the flawed interpretation of customary international law adopted by the *Perisić* court. However, it could have gone a step further in properly articulating the elements (or lack thereof) of state practice and *opinio juris*. On the other hand, it did bring the practice of states – even if somewhat opaquely formulated – back into the discourse. On the basis of the analysis provided in the judgments on "specific direction," it appears that the *Perišić* holding was a mistake, "a distinct outlier," and will not be followed in the future by other ICTs.[162]

In short, we have seen in this section that many ICTs, but especially the ICTY, have adopted a variety of judicial methodologies that minimize the importance of state practice. These include focusing on *opinio juris* without regard to practice; identifying customary international law rules based on international documents and "paper practice" without regard to actual practice; and identifying customary international law rules based on prior decisions of other ICTs or the ICT making the decision itself. I have demonstrated that ICTs have at times employed all of these strategies. Moreover, some ICTs, like the ECCC, have called these non-traditional methodologies into question.

On the other hand, even if a "customary international law" norm is initially identified using a dubious methodology, such as reliance on *opinio juris* in the absence of practice, if that norm is subsequently applied by courts – for instance, as "internally binding precedent" – it may be argued that this constant judicial usage contributes to the crystallization of the rule in question as part of legitimate international law. It may be viewed as a self-generating crystallization of a rule. In other words, even if the rule was not customary law in reality at its inception, the subsequent judicial practice and acceptance

160 Ibid., para 128.

161 See Marko Milanović, "The Self-Fragmentation of the ICTY Appeals Chamber," 23 January 2013, available at www.ejiltalk.org/the-self-fragmentation-of-the-icty-appeals-chamber.

162 See Marko Milanović, "ICTY Appeals Chamber Reverses Stanisic and Simatovic Acquittal, Orders Retrial, Kills Off Specific Direction (Again!)," 15 December 2015, available at www.ejiltalk.org/icty-appeals-chamber-reverses-stanisic-and-simatovic-acquittal-orders-retrial-kills-off-specific-direction-again.

eradicates the "mishap" of the initially faulty interpretation. The courts are then, in retrospect, creating a self-fulfilling prophecy, intentionally or not.[163]

It would be conceptually flawed, however, to characterize the resulting rule as customary international law. The rule would have a "corrupt pedigree" as described by Fernando Tesón.[164] As this chapter has underlined, customary international law by definition requires the element of practice. Although practice can be broadly conceived, reliance exclusively on the "practice" of ICTs in identifying customary international law is not sufficient for custom to crystallize. This view is supported also by the ILC's Special Rapporteur in his third report on the identification of customary international law, which notes that "while the decisions of international courts and tribunals as to the existence of rules of customary international law and their content are not 'practice,' they do serve an important role as 'subsidiary means for the determination of rules of law.'"[165]

The various methodologies discussed here that ICTs have used to broaden the scope of customary international law – for instance, the greater emphasis on *opinio juris* over practice, and the deduction of customary international law directly from treaty law – find some support among practitioners and scholars.[166] Nevertheless, these methodologies should be used only with caution. Focusing on *opinio juris* rather than actual practice can create uncertainty and unpredictability in criminal trials, especially when a fluid, morally charged analysis of *opinio juris* is embraced. As noted throughout this chapter,

[163] Patrick Norton quotes Junius in his paper: "One precedent creates another. They soon accumulate and constitute law. What yesterday was fact, today is doctrine." Patrick M. Norton, "A Law of the Future or a Law of the Past? Modern Tribunals and the International Law of Expropriation," 85 *American Journal of International Law* 474 (1991), 474. Anthony D'Amato has also noted that "customary law is formed in much the same way that common law is formed. In a common-law jurisdiction, we start with a dispute between two parties, a conflict as to which rule of law (whether it is an old rule or one that is advanced as the best rule for the occasion) is applicable to their dispute, and a resolution of the dispute by the court. The court's 'holding' is the rule that governs the dispute (sometimes the court does not make the holding explicit)." Anthony D'Amato, "Customary International Law: A Reformulation," 4 *International Legal Theory* 1 (1998), 5.

[164] See Fernando R. Tesón, "Fake Custom," in this volume.

[165] Michael Wood, Special Rapporteur, "Third Report on Identification of Customary International Law," UN Doc. A/CN.4/682 (2015), para. 59.

[166] For discussion, see, for example, Birgit Schlütter, "Constitutionalisation at its Best or at its Worst? Lessons from the Development of Customary International Criminal Law," paper presented at Biennial Conference of the European Society of International Law, 18–20 May 2006, on "International Law: Do We Need It?" available at www.esil-sedi.eu/sites/default/files/Schleutter.PDF, esp. 6–7; Mia Swart, "Judicial Lawmaking at the Ad Hoc Tribunals: The Creative Use of the Sources of International Law and 'Adventurous Interpretation,'" 70 *Zeitschrift für ausländisches öffentliches Recht und Völkerrecht* 459 (2010).

criminal trials must be conducted with respect for the principle of legality, and ICTs must refrain from resorting to *lex ferenda* in the identification of customary international law rules. As with certain forms of criminal modes of liability that I have discussed, it is not for the courts to invent such categories (as the *Tadić* court was criticized for doing in relation to JCE III). Rather, it is their responsibility to apply the existing law that arises from established practice supported by *opinio juris*.

Of course, in human rights law and international criminal law – areas closely touching on fundamental moral issues – the undertones of normative considerations, eventually imported into *opinio juris*, may enhance the crystallization of norms into customary international law, with the support of various instruments, statements, and decisions. In determining the elements of crimes or a mode of liability, ICTs should act according to the existing, crystallized legal rules and not pass moral judgment, regardless of the gravity of the acts or the ethical grounds for condemning them. More specifically, in identifying applicable customary international law rules, they must examine state practice supported by *opinio juris*. By contrast, we have seen that in determining the status of JCE III in international criminal law, ICTs have used a piecemeal approach, often looking exclusively at existing case law of ICTs, with only occasional attempts to ascertain whether practice exists and is unified – as exemplified by the ICTY Appeals Chamber decision in *Brdanin*. While international criminal justice has faced significant critiques from all directions, it should serve – in both theory and practice – as a global project in bringing perpetrators to account for violations of international criminal law. To achieve this end, it must allow for pluralistic approaches without compromising the core principles of human dignity and accountability for violations of that dignity, which constitute a kind of "moral minimum."[167]

7.5 CONCLUSIONS

We have seen in this chapter that in a number of cases ICTs have used the vocabulary of state practice and *opinio juris* without referring to actual evidence of either. In other cases, ICTs have omitted the traditional language of

[167] In this connection, Larry May asserts: "What is most appealing about moral minimalism is that it explains the nearly universal recognition of such norms as self-preservation and self-defence. … [O]nly those human rights that protect the security of the individual can, when abused, trigger justified international intervention." Larry May, *Crimes against Humanity: A Normative Account* (Cambridge: Cambridge University Press, 2005), 34. See also the response to May by David Luban in David Luban, "Beyond Moral Minimalism," 20 *Ethics and International Affairs* 353 (2006).

customary international law altogether and founded customary international law on "paper practice" and previous case law.[168] The main discussion has focused on three often overlapping methods of identifying customary international law that ICTs have utilized, namely identifying customary international law based on evidence of *opinio juris* where evidence of practice is scarce or nonexistent; deducing customary international law directly from treaties, national legislation, and other documents (either as evidence of "paper practice" or *opinio juris*, or both); and citing earlier case law as a confirmation of the customary status of a norm. This illustrates, in brief, how the interpretation of the content and limits of *opinio juris* vary within one field of international law, and even within the jurisprudence of the same tribunal (such as the ICTY). As a consequence, the foreseeability of applicable legal rules is undermined. Accordingly, there is a need for a re-emphasis on the importance of state practice in the identification of rules of customary international law. This would not only lead to greater consistency in the determination of customary international law by ICTs, but also result in more uniformity in the treatment of sources of international law in general.

The analysis in this chapter has also focused on the role of *opinio juris* in the judgments of ICTs. According to legal scholar Larry May, *opinio juris* relating to a norm consists of a motivation "to follow the norm out of a sense of legal or *moral* obligation."[169] Even though this looks like an expansion of the definition – with the inclusion of a sense not only of legal but also of moral obligation – it is a reflection of an already existing broader understanding of *opinio juris*, at least on the part of criminal tribunals.

Some practice, however, must be present in the identification of customary international law. The ILC's Special Rapporteur, Michael Wood, thus correctly affirms: "As the International Court has consistently made clear, it is 'State practice from which customary law is derived.'"[170] Practice is necessary, first, for the norm to be recognized as "true" customary international law that reflects, not the desired state of law (*lex ferenda*), but the factual legal rules in existence (*lex lata*). Second, it is critical because it retains fidelity to the principle of legality in criminal proceedings that ensures the foreseeability and clarity of rules, which are inherently linked to the application of *lex lata*. Applying *lex lata* – law as it stands – carries the expectation that the law is

[168] For further analysis, see Arajärvi, *The Changing Nature of Customary International Law*, chapters 2 and 3.

[169] May, *Crimes against Humanity*, 50 (emphasis added).

[170] Michael Wood, Special Rapporteur, "Second Report on Identification of Customary International Law," para. 33 (quoting the ICJ's opinion in *Jurisdictional Immunities of the State (Germany v. Italy)*).

known to the individuals accused of international crimes and does not impose unforeseeable responsibility.

The SCSL stated in its 2013 *Taylor* judgment that "existing customary international law can be modified if the combination of *opinio juris* and state practice show a continuing and consistent adherence to the new custom by the international community."[171] This statement illustrates that while "the demands of humanity" may call for better, wider-encompassing legal rules, legal certainty in the formulation of the sources of law cannot be overlooked. Within the domain of customary international law, this can best be preserved through reliance on practice as the foundation of customary international law.

Of course, *opinio juris* is a fluid element of customary international law by its nature, influenced but not directly determined by the development of societal and moral norms. Therefore, it is impossible to determine it in a unitary manner applicable any time, any place, and in all fields of international law. Moral and societal norms have an impact on the formation and composition of *opinio juris*, which in turn affects the formation and substance of customary international law – especially when judicial bodies adopt active interpretations. This may, then, have a self-generating impact on subsequent practice and on the developing sense of legal obligation. In this way courts may legitimately contribute to the formation of customary international law.

To conclude, this review of the decisions of international courts and tribunals has shown that *opinio juris* is not a unitary phenomenon, and practice is not always elaborated in identifying customary international law. Case law of ICTs illustrates that the relative weight and content of these two elements of customary international law are given varying interpretations based on the type of court, the subject matter under discussion, and the extralegal normative considerations, including the demands of humanity, which may be central in a case where grave violations of the world's ethical code have been committed.

Courts should retain practice, even if broadly defined, as the bedrock of customary international law for the reasons elaborated above. Practice provides concrete evidence of the state of law reflected in the widespread and consistent conduct of states and other relevant actors, and hence corresponds to the principle of legality, which is a key to fair legal proceedings.

What is needed, therefore, is an approach that accepts a broadened notion of "moral" *opinio juris*, but that is also ultimately grounded in practice. This could result in the desired balance of respect for positive law and the principle of legality on the one hand while addressing the demands of humanity on the other.

[171] *Prosecutor v. Charles Taylor*, para. 457.

PART III

Reexamining Customary Human Rights Law

8

Toward a New Theory of Customary International Human Rights Law

Brian D. Lepard

8.1 INTRODUCTION

The status of particular human rights as customary international law has provoked heated controversy. This controversy has become all the more important because international tribunals as well as domestic courts have been called upon to determine the human rights content of customary law, and are doing so with increasing frequency. In large part this is due to the veritable explosion of international human rights law since 1945, the year of the adoption of the United Nations Charter.[1]

International and national courts and tribunals have adopted divergent approaches to the identification and application of customary human rights law – even though it is now playing an increasingly prominent role in their decisions. What accounts for this legal cloudiness and confusion? In large part the pervasive enigmas characterizing the entire field of customary law, which I reviewed in Chapter 1, are responsible. But there are also problems unique to human rights norms that make the traditional approach to customary international law, requiring the two elements of consistent practice and *opinio juris*,[2] difficult to apply to them – not the least of which is their widespread violation. In this chapter I attempt to formulate a new approach both to the formation of customary international law generally and to the determination of the customary law status of human rights norms in particular.

[1] On international human rights law, see generally, e.g., Philip Alston and Ryan Goodman, *International Human Rights: Text and Materials* (Oxford: Oxford University Press, 2013).

[2] As noted in Chapter 1, the International Law Commission and its Special Rapporteur on the identification of customary international law, Michael Wood, have reaffirmed the traditional "two element" definition of customary international law. See, e.g., "Report of the International Law Commission," Sixty-Eighth Session (2 May–10 June and 4 July–12 August 2016), UN Doc. A/71/10 (2016), 76–79, Draft Conclusion 2.

I first review the evolution of international human rights law, including its foundational documents and institutions. I then examine some threshold questions about the impact of treaties and UN General Assembly resolutions on customary human rights law in light of this history. Next, I give examples of the ways in which both international and national courts have grappled with the problem of determining whether particular norms have attained the status of customary law. I show that they are not consistent in their methodologies. With these problems in mind, I explore in greater detail why we need a new theory of customary human rights law. I then sketch a new theory that can resolve some of the problems I have described and that is based on the concept of "fundamental ethical principles" in international law. I identify some of these key principles, most importantly that of "unity in diversity." I explain how this new approach can be applied to clarify the customary law status of particular human rights norms in contemporary treaties, declarations, and state practice. I provide an example of this approach, focusing on the right to change one's religion or belief. Finally, I review some advantages of the proposed theory, identify some possible critiques of it, and offer my responses to these critiques.

8.2 THE EVOLUTION OF INTERNATIONAL HUMAN RIGHTS LAW

The UN Charter laid the foundation for the far-ranging international human rights system by proclaiming that one of the organization's fundamental purposes was to "reaffirm faith in fundamental human rights, in the dignity and worth of the human person, [and] in the equal rights of men and women."[3] To fulfil this purpose, Article 55 of the Charter requires the United Nations as an organization to "promote ... universal respect for, and observance of, human rights and fundamental freedoms for all without distinction as to race, sex, language, or religion."[4] And under Article 56, UN member states "pledge themselves to take joint and separate action in co-operation with the Organization for the achievement" of the organization's purpose of promoting respect for fundamental human rights.[5] On the other hand, these human rights provisions were not uncontroversial in 1945; states worried that they might undercut state sovereignty. Accordingly, the framers of the Charter also included Article 2(7), which affirms that nothing in the Charter "shall authorize the United Nations

[3] UN Charter, preamble.
[4] Ibid., art. 55.
[5] Ibid., art. 56.

to intervene in matters which are essentially within the domestic jurisdiction of any state." The drafters were careful to affirm that this principle of non-intervention would not prejudice peace enforcement measures that the UN Security Council had the authority to mandate pursuant to Chapter VII of the Charter.[6]

Three years after agreement on the UN Charter, the UN General Assembly followed up on the human rights promise in the Charter by adopting the Universal Declaration of Human Rights as a "common standard of achievement for all peoples and all nations," thereby serving, at a minimum, as a moral yardstick for the measurement of progress in the enjoyment of human rights.[7] The Universal Declaration identifies many civil and political rights, as well as economic, social, and cultural rights, to which everyone is entitled.

For example, among other civil and political rights, the Universal Declaration recognizes freedom from discrimination on the grounds of race, color, sex, language, religion, political opinion, nationality, property, birth, or other status; the rights to life, liberty, and security of person; freedom from slavery or servitude; freedom from torture and other cruel, inhuman, or degrading treatment or punishment; the right to recognition before and equal protection of the law; the right to an effective remedy for human rights violations; freedom from arbitrary arrest, detention, or exile; the right to a fair and public hearing by an independent and impartial tribunal; the right to be presumed innocent until proven guilty; the right to privacy; freedom of movement and residence; the right to seek and enjoy asylum from persecution; the right to a nationality; the right to marry; the right to own property; freedom of thought, conscience, and religion; freedom of opinion and expression; freedom of peaceful assembly and association; and the right to take part in government, directly or through elected representatives.[8]

The Universal Declaration also upholds a more limited array of economic, social, and cultural rights. These include the right to social security; the right to work and to just and favorable conditions of work and to protection against unemployment; the right to rest and leisure; the right to a standard of living adequate for one's health and well-being and that of one's family, including food, clothing, housing, medical care, and necessary social services; the right to education; and the right to participate in the cultural life of one's community.[9]

The Universal Declaration was a groundbreaking document, and one that now undergirds the entire international human rights system and human

6 Ibid., art. 2, para. 7.
7 Universal Declaration of Human Rights, GA Res. 217A (III) (1948), preamble.
8 See ibid., arts. 2–21.
9 See ibid., arts. 22–27.

rights discourse. It inspired the adoption of numerous binding multilateral treaties on human rights. A day before the General Assembly voted to approve the Universal Declaration, it adopted the text of the 1948 Convention on the Prevention and Punishment of the Crime of Genocide ("Genocide Convention").[10] Eighteen years later, after nearly two decades of painstaking negotiations, the General Assembly adopted two prominent treaties that, together with the Universal Declaration, constitute the "International Bill of Rights." These are the International Covenant on Civil and Political Rights ("ICCPR")[11] and the International Covenant on Economic, Social and Cultural Rights ("ICESCR").[12] These treaties had 168 and 164 states parties, respectively, as of August 2016.[13]

Meanwhile, regional organizations had gotten on the "human rights bandwagon." During the arduous drafting of the ICCPR and ICESCR at the global level, the Council of Europe pressed forward with the creation of its own regional human rights treaty and enforcement regime. It adopted the European Convention on Human Rights in 1950.[14] Similarly, the Organization of American States, after promulgating the American Declaration on the Rights and Duties of Man[15] the same year that the General Assembly approved the Universal Declaration, adopted the 1969 American Convention on Human Rights.[16]

The UN, in turn, continued active treaty-making. It drafted and adopted treaties on the elimination of racial discrimination in 1965,[17] on the elimination of discrimination against women in 1979,[18] on the right not to be tortured in 1984,[19] and on the rights of the child in 1989.[20] Other treaties on the rights of

[10] Convention on the Prevention and Punishment of the Crime of Genocide, 78 UNTS 277 (1948).

[11] International Covenant on Civil and Political Rights, 999 UNTS 171 (1966) ("ICCPR").

[12] International Covenant on Economic, Social and Cultural Rights, 993 UNTS 3 (1966) ("ICESCR").

[13] See http://treaties.un.org (last accessed 26 August 2016).

[14] Convention for the Protection of Human Rights and Fundamental Freedoms, 213 UNTS 222 (1950).

[15] American Declaration on the Rights and Duties of Man (1948), adopted by the Ninth International Conference of American States, Bogotá, Colombia, 1948, available at http://cidh.oas.org/Basicos/English/Basic2.American%20Declaration.htm.

[16] American Convention on Human Rights, 1144 UNTS 123 (1969).

[17] International Convention on the Elimination of All Forms of Racial Discrimination, 660 UNTS 195 (1966).

[18] Convention on the Elimination of All Forms of Discrimination against Women, 1249 UNTS 13 (1979).

[19] Convention against Torture and Other Forms of Cruel, Inhuman or Degrading Treatment or Punishment, 1465 UNTS 85 (1984).

[20] Convention on the Rights of the Child, 1577 UNTS 3 (1989).

specific populations followed, including a treaty on the rights of persons with disabilities, approved in 2006.[21]

The UN General Assembly has also adopted many declarations on particular rights. These include the 1981 Declaration on the Elimination of All Forms of Intolerance and of Discrimination Based on Religion or Belief,[22] and the 2007 Declaration on the Rights of Indigenous Peoples.[23]

The UN has furthermore established a variety of institutions for addressing human rights problems and hearing complaints of human rights violations. In 2006, the General Assembly created the intergovernmental Human Rights Council to succeed the Commission on Human Rights that was established pursuant to the UN Charter, and that originally drafted the Universal Declaration.[24] Since 1993, a High Commissioner for Human Rights has been charged with overseeing the UN system's human rights activities and serving as a human rights advocate.[25] With the exception of the Genocide Convention, a body of experts has been established for each of the aforementioned human rights treaties, and that body is charged with supervising the treaty's implementation and hearing complaints of violations of it. These bodies include, for example, the Human Rights Committee established under the ICCPR.[26]

Paralleling this development of international human rights treaties at the global level was the elaboration of a historically distinct body of law dealing with armed conflict – international humanitarian law. Although its roots were separate from those of human rights law, growing out of a concern for protecting combatants and noncombatants in armed conflict rather than a philosophy of universal human rights, this legal domain has now expanded dramatically and intersected with international human rights law. International humanitarian law today, as explained by Jean-Marie Henckaerts and Els Debuf in their chapter,[27] is founded on the Genocide Convention as well as the four Geneva Conventions of 1949. Moreover, a subset of international humanitarian law, international criminal law, was given new impetus with the adoption in 1998 of the Rome Statute of the International Criminal Court.[28] Earlier, in 1993

21 See Convention on the Rights of Persons with Disabilities, 2515 UNTS 3 (2006).

22 GA Res. 36/55 (1981).

23 GA Res. 61/295 (2007).

24 For the General Assembly resolution creating the Council, see GA Res. 60/251 (2006).

25 For the General Assembly resolution creating the post, see GA Res. 48/141 (1993).

26 The provisions of the ICCPR dealing with the Human Rights Committee's responsibilities and procedures are found in ICCPR, arts. 28–45. On the work of the Human Rights Committee, see generally Yogesh Tyagi, *The UN Human Rights Committee: Practice and Procedure* (Cambridge: Cambridge University Press, 2011).

27 Jean-Marie Henckaerts and Els Debuf, "The ICRC and the Clarification of Customary International Humanitarian Law," in this volume.

28 See Rome Statute of the International Criminal Court, 17 July 1998, 2187 UNTS 90.

and 1994, respectively, the UN Security Council established the International Criminal Tribunal for the former Yugoslavia ("ICTY") and the International Criminal Tribunal for Rwanda ("ICTR"). As discussed in the preceding chapters, other special-purpose criminal tribunals followed suit, such as the Special Court for Sierra Leone and the Extraordinary Chambers in the Courts of Cambodia.

This accelerating development of international human rights law and humanitarian law globally had a dramatic impact on national laws and institutions. Many countries adopted constitutions that drew inspiration from the Universal Declaration.[29] Likewise, national legislatures have adopted statutes that codify many of the rights proclaimed in international human rights declarations or guaranteed in treaties that their states have ratified.[30] National courts have increasingly referred to international human rights and criminal law in interpreting their constitutions or national legislation relating to human rights.[31] Some courts have heard cases under national universal jurisdiction statutes that directly invoked international criminal law.[32] Accordingly, national courts have themselves become major "players" in applying and interpreting international human rights and criminal law. Although human rights and humanitarian law are today closely intertwined, here I focus on international human rights law, especially because international humanitarian law is

[29] See, e.g., Hurst Hannum, "The Status of the Universal Declaration of Human Rights in National and International Law," 25 *Georgia Journal of International and Comparative Law* 287 (1995–1996), 313–15, 355–76.

[30] See, e.g., the 1998 Human Rights Act adopted by the UK Parliament, which implements the United Kingdom's obligations under the European Convention on Human Rights, to which the United Kingdom is a party. For the text of the Act, see www.legislation.gov.uk/ukpga/1998/42/contents/enacted

[31] See, e.g., *Suresh v. Canada*, decided in 2002, in which the Supreme Court of Canada stated that "in seeking the meaning of the Canadian Constitution, the courts may be informed by international law." *Suresh v. Canada (Minister of Citizenship and Immigration)*, [2002] 1 S.C.R. 3 (2002), para. 60. In construing a constitutional provision on fundamental justice in the context of evaluating the lawfulness of a deportation proceeding that could lead to a detainee being tortured abroad, the Court determined that there were "compelling indicia" that the prohibition of torture had achieved the status of a *jus cogens* norm, most importantly, "the great number of multilateral instruments that explicitly prohibit torture," the fact that "no state has ever legalized torture or admitted to its deliberate practice," and endorsement of this status by many tribunals and scholars. See ibid., paras. 61–64.

[32] For example, Belgium adopted a universal jurisdiction statute in 1993. See Law of 16 June 1993 "concerning the Punishment of Grave Breaches of the International Geneva Conventions of 12 August 1949 and of Protocols I and II of 8 June 1977 Additional Thereto," as amended by the Law of 19 February 1999 "concerning the Punishment of Serious Violations of International Humanitarian Law." However, under pressure, Belgium modified the law in 2003 to reduce its scope. See Human Rights Watch, "Belgium: Universal Jurisdiction Law Repealed," August 2, 2003, available at www.hrw.org/news/2003/08/01/belgium-universal-jurisdiction-law-repealed.

addressed directly in the contributions by Noora Arajärvi as well as Jean-Marie Henckaerts and Els Debuf.

8.3 INITIAL QUESTIONS ABOUT THE IMPACT OF TREATIES AND UN GENERAL ASSEMBLY RESOLUTIONS ON CUSTOMARY HUMAN RIGHTS LAW

The elaboration of the network of treaties, declarations, and human rights–related institutions at the global, regional, and national levels described in the preceding section is certainly an impressive achievement. But what is the role of customary international law in the human rights domain and in this ever-expanding process of human rights norm creation, interpretation, and application? The customary law status of the rights recognized in the Universal Declaration and other instruments is now very much contested despite the existence of this large corpus of human rights norms.

As noted in Chapter 1, Article 38 of the Statute of the International Court of Justice ("ICJ") sets out the widely accepted "sources" of international law, including treaties, customary law, and general principles of law.[33] The status of treaties is evident enough. They clearly bind those states that have ratified them. But can they also bind nonparties? The formal answer is "no." Thus, Article 34 of the Vienna Convention on the Law of Treaties provides that "a treaty does not create either obligations or rights for a third State without its consent."[34] Many states that commit serious human rights violations are not parties to one or more human rights treaties, and are accordingly not bound by them.

On the other hand, as the ICJ itself has acknowledged, a human rights norm in a treaty may at some point in time be recognized as customary law (either before or after conclusion of the treaty) and therefore be binding, as customary law, on states not party to the treaty. Article 38 of the Vienna Convention explicitly recognizes this possibility, affirming that "nothing in articles 34 to 37 precludes a rule set forth in a treaty from becoming binding upon a third State as a customary rule of international law, recognized as such."[35] The problem, of course, as highlighted in Chapter 1, is determining just when and how a human rights treaty norm attains this status. This raises additional questions like the following: When does a treaty norm merely codify a pre-existing customary human rights obligation? When can a treaty norm create

33 Statute of the International Court of Justice ("ICJ Statute"), art. 38(1)(a)-(c).

34 Vienna Convention on the Law of Treaties, 1155 UNTS 331 (1969), art. 34.

35 Ibid., art. 38.

"new" customary law, and how? Can the treaty itself constitute a form of state practice? Can it provide evidence of *opinio juris*? Again, when and how?

Another legal problem is that the many UN General Assembly declarations and resolutions on human rights discussed earlier, including the iconic Universal Declaration itself, are not formally "law." Under Article 13 of the UN Charter, they constitute mere "recommendations" to member states.[36] Moreover, Article 38 of the ICJ Statute makes no reference to UN General Assembly declarations or resolutions as a source of international law that can be considered by the Court. Nevertheless, the wide acceptance of these resolutions, and their recognition in a variety of national constitutions, laws, and judicial opinions, raises the questions of whether and how they might contribute to the recognition of customary human rights norms – as evidence of either state practice, *opinio juris*, or both.

A final legal problem that I address in more detail in the following sections is that despite the web of human rights treaties, declarations, national laws, and judicial opinions that has been woven in the post–World War II era, human rights violations are rampant. It would be quite appropriate to say that there is, indeed, a "widespread" and "consistent" "practice" by states of trampling on human rights that exists alongside a practice of sometimes honoring them. So the argument can legitimately be made that an honest application of the two-element test for customary law must result in a conclusion that human rights norms *cannot* satisfy the test because there is simply insufficient consistent state practice in favor of human rights. Treaties and declarations, the argument goes, might evidence *opinio juris*, but they cannot compensate for a blatant absence of confirming state practice upholding their lofty norms.

8.4 EFFORTS BY INTERNATIONAL AND NATIONAL COURTS TO IDENTIFY CUSTOMARY HUMAN RIGHTS NORMS

The troubling questions mentioned in the preceding section have not impeded courts from engaging in the sometimes tortuous process of figuring out whether a putative human rights norm (often, but not necessarily, expressed in a treaty or declaration) is in fact a norm of customary law. International and domestic courts have been called upon to do so in a plethora of contexts.

At the apex of the international judicial system, the ICJ has characterized a number of human rights norms as customary law, and some of them as *jus cogens* and *erga omnes* norms. As noted in Chapter 1, it has affirmed, for example, that genocide is prohibited by customary international law, most recently

36 See UN Charter, art. 13, para. 1.

in the 2015 judgment in the *Genocide Convention Case (Croatia v. Serbia)*.[37] In several judgments it has also declared the prohibition of genocide to be a *jus cogens* peremptory norm,[38] and has concluded that the Genocide Convention (and presumably the customary norms paralleling it) set forth *erga omnes* obligations.[39]

In the 1970 *Barcelona Traction Case*, the ICJ stated, rather laconically, that "the basic rights of the human person, including protection from slavery and racial discrimination," have risen to the level of customary international law.[40] The ICJ also affirmed in its 2012 judgment in the case between Belgium and Senegal on the obligation to prosecute or extradite under the Torture Convention (the *Obligation to Prosecute or Extradite Case*) that "in the Court's opinion, the prohibition of torture is part of customary international law and it has become a peremptory norm (*jus cogens*)."[41]

As just noted, the ICJ's reasoning about why particular human rights deserve customary law status is often opaque. It has frequently declared that certain human rights norms are customary law without undertaking a rigorous analysis of whether these norms satisfy the traditional requirements of consistent state practice and *opinio juris*, even where it has mentioned these requirements.

For example, in declaring genocide to be prohibited by customary law, the ICJ has relied on the Genocide Convention, and also invoked moral principles. Thus, in its 2015 judgment in the *Genocide Convention Case (Croatia v. Serbia)*, the ICJ affirmed that "the Court has also repeatedly stated that the Convention embodies principles that are part of customary international law."[42] It referred to its own statement in the 1951 *Genocide Convention Advisory Opinion* that "the origins of the Convention show that it was the

37 See *Application of the Convention on the Prevention and Punishment of the Crime of Genocide (Croatia v. Serbia)*, ICJ Judgment of 3 February 2015, para. 87 ("*Genocide Convention Case (Croatia v. Serbia)*"). See also, e.g., *Armed Activities on the Territory of the Congo (New Application: 2002) (Democratic Republic of the Congo v. Rwanda)*, Jurisdiction and Admissibility, Judgment of 3 February 2006, 2006 ICJ Rep. 6, 31–32, para. 64 ("2006 *Armed Activities Case (Congo v. Rwanda)*"); *Application of the Convention on the Prevention and Punishment of the Crime of Genocide (Bosnia and Herzegovina v. Serbia and Montenegro)*, Judgment of 26 February 2007, 2007 ICJ Rep. 43, 110–11, para. 161.

38 See, e.g., 2006 *Armed Activities Case (Congo v. Rwanda)*, 31–32, para. 64 (affirming that it is "assuredly the case" that the prohibition of genocide is a norm of *jus cogens*).

39 See, e.g., *Barcelona Traction, Light and Power Company, Limited (Belgium v. Spain)*, Second Phase, Judgment of 5 February 1970, 1970 ICJ Rep. 3, 32, paras. 33–34.

40 Ibid., para. 34.

41 *Questions Relating to the Obligation to Prosecute or Extradite (Belgium v. Senegal)*, Judgment of 20 July 2012, 2012 ICJ Rep. 422, 457, para. 99 ("*Obligation to Prosecute or Extradite Case*").

42 *Genocide Convention Case (Croatia v. Serbia)*, para. 87.

intention of the United Nations to condemn and punish genocide as 'a crime under international law' involving a denial of the right of existence of entire human groups, a denial which shocks the conscience of mankind and results in great losses to humanity, and *which is contrary to moral law* and to the spirit and aims of the United Nations."[43] This statement thus referred to moral law. The ICJ in that opinion went on to affirm that because of this purpose, "the principles underlying the Convention are principles which are recognized by civilized nations as binding on States, even without any conventional obligation" (presumably, and as confirmed by the 2015 judgment, as customary law). The 1951 advisory opinion also affirmed that the "Convention was manifestly adopted for a purely humanitarian and civilizing purpose. It is indeed difficult to imagine a convention that might have this dual character to a greater degree, since its object on the one hand is to safeguard the very existence of certain human groups and on the other *to confirm and endorse the most elementary principles of morality*."[44] What is notable about this opinion and the ICJ's quotations of it in its 2015 judgment is the extent to which the ICJ does not engage in any explicit inquiry into *opinio juris* or state practice as such, but rather invokes principles of ethics and morality to support the customary law status of the norm.

In its 2012 judgment in the *Obligation to Prosecute or Extradite Case*, the ICJ stated that torture is prohibited by customary law, and declared that the prohibition of torture "is grounded in a widespread international practice and on the *opinio juris* of States."[45] In this way, it invoked the two-element definition of customary law. On the other hand, in support of this proposition, the Court referred exclusively to treaties, declarations, national laws, and denunciations of torture by states, rather than to actual practices relating to torture. Thus, it said that the prohibition

> appears in numerous international instruments of universal application (in particular the Universal Declaration of Human Rights of 1948; the 1949 Geneva Conventions for the protection of war victims; the International Covenant on Civil and Political Rights of 1966; General Assembly resolution 3452/30 of 9 December 1975 on the Protection of All Persons from Being Subjected to Torture and Other Cruel, Inhuman or Degrading Treatment or Punishment), and it has been introduced into the domestic law of almost

[43] *Reservations to the Convention on the Prevention and Punishment of the Crime of Genocide*, Advisory Opinion of 28 May 1951, 1951 ICJ Rep. 15, 23 ("*Genocide Convention Advisory Opinion*") (emphasis added).

[44] Ibid. (emphasis added).

[45] *Obligation to Prosecute or Extradite Case*, 457, para. 99.

> all States; finally, acts of torture are regularly denounced within national and international fora.[46]

This was the extent of the Court's analysis of both state practice and *opinio juris*. While national laws, treaties, and declarations are sometimes regarded as state practice, as discussed in other chapters, the sources referred to by the Court are most often viewed as evidence of *opinio juris*. Notably, the Court did not discuss actual practices of states in torturing or not torturing detainees (or subjecting them to other forms of cruel, inhuman, or degrading treatment or punishment falling short of torture).

While not expressly called upon to do so by their mandates, some of the expert bodies established under human rights treaties have expressed the view that particular rights in the treaties are now part of customary law. For example, the Human Rights Committee created by the ICCPR issued a general comment in 1994 on the permissibility of reservations to the ICCPR. It stated that a number of rights had achieved the status of customary law and, indeed, *jus cogens*. It maintained that under customary international law,

> a State may not reserve the right to engage in slavery, to torture, to subject persons to cruel, inhuman or degrading treatment or punishment, to arbitrarily deprive persons of their lives, to arbitrarily arrest and detain persons, to deny freedom of thought, conscience and religion, to presume a person guilty unless he proves his innocence, to execute pregnant women or children, to permit the advocacy of national, racial or religious hatred, to deny to persons of marriageable age the right to marry, or to deny to minorities the right to enjoy their own culture, profess their own religion, or use their own language.[47]

In making this assertion, the Committee did not refer to either state practice or *opinio juris*.

Regional human rights commissions and courts have also identified and applied customary human rights law. For example, the Inter-American Commission on Human Rights has recognized a number of rights as having the status of customary law, and indeed, of *jus cogens*. Thus, in the case of *Domingues v. United States*, decided in 2002, the Commission stated that the prohibition of execution of individuals who were juveniles at the time of commission of a crime had become a norm of customary law as well as a *jus cogens* norm that bound the United States, and from which it could not

46 Ibid.

47 Human Rights Committee, General Comment No. 24, UN Doc. CCPR/C/21/Rev.1/Add.6 (1994), para. 8.

exempt itself even through persistent objection.[48] The Commission did so after a fairly exhaustive review of state practice concerning juvenile executions as well as expressions of *opinio juris* in the form of treaties and declarations prohibiting the juvenile death penalty. Furthermore, in an advisory opinion issued in 2003 and requested by Mexico, the Inter-American Court of Human Rights declared that the norms of equality and nondiscrimination had "entered the realm of *jus cogens*" (and therefore customary law as well) at least in part because the right to equal protection of the law "derives 'directly from *the oneness of the human family* and is linked to the essential dignity of the individual.'"[49]

The European Court of Human Rights ("ECHR") has at times identified and applied customary international law rules on issues not explicitly addressed by the European Convention on Human Rights. For example, it has referred to and applied the customary law of state succession[50] as well as the customary law of state responsibility.[51] The ECHR has expressed the view that the prohibition of genocide is a norm of *jus cogens*.[52] And similarly, it has stated that the prohibition of torture is a peremptory norm.[53] Both these conclusions imply that it recognizes these norms also as ones of customary international law. By contrast, it has stated in a 2015 judgment that there is no obligation of a state under customary international law to criminalize genocide denial, because of a lack of consistent state practice.[54] And it has also found, in another judgment

48 *Domingues v. United States*, Inter-American Commission on Human Rights, Report No. 62/02, Case 12.285 (22 October 2002), para. 85.

49 Inter-American Court of Human Rights, Advisory Opinion OC-18/03 of 17 September 2003 Requested by the United Mexican States, "Juridical Condition and Rights of the Undocumented Migrants," paras. 100–101 (quoting Inter-American Court of Human Rights, Advisory Opinion OC-4/84 of 19 January 1984 Requested by the Government of Costa Rica, "Proposed Amendments to the Naturalization Provision of the Constitution of Costa Rica," para. 55) (emphasis added).

50 See, e.g., *Case of Ališić and Others v. Bosnia and Herzegovina, Croatia, Serbia, Slovenia and the Former Yugoslav Republic of Macedonia*, Application No. 60642/08, Judgment of 6 November 2012, referral to the Grand Chamber on 18 March 2013, para. 40.

51 See, e.g., *Case of Bureš v. the Czech Republic*, Application No. 37679/08, Judgment of 18 October 2012, final on 18 January 2013, para. 54.

52 See *Case of Jorgic v. Germany*, Application No. 74613/01, Judgment of 12 July 2007, final on 12 October 2007, para. 68.

53 See, e.g., *Case of Al-Adsani v. the United Kingdom*, Application No. 35763/97, Judgment of 21 November 2001, para. 61 (affirming that "the Court accepts, on the basis of [other judicial] authorities, that the prohibition of torture has achieved the status of a peremptory norm in international law"); *Case of Demir and Baykara v. Turkey*, Application No. 34503/97, Judgment of 12 November 2008, para. 73 (reiterating this conclusion).

54 See *Case of Perinçek v. Switzerland*, Application No. 27510/08, Judgment of 15 October 2015, para. 266 (affirming that "nor does it appear that there existed a customary international law rule requiring Switzerland to criminalise genocide denial. State practice, as can be seen from paragraphs 87–97 above, is far from generalised and consistent").

issued in 2015, that the definition of the crime of genocide under customary international law did not, at least as of 1953, include "political groups" among those groups protected. In so ruling, it relied primarily on the definition of genocide contained in Article 2 of the 1948 Genocide Convention.[55]

Moreover, in delineating the content of certain rights under the Convention, the ECHR has at least alluded to views of experts that particular rights are now protected by customary international law. For example, in its 2008 judgment in the *Case of Bevacqua and S. v. Bulgaria*, it cited (apparently with approval) the views of the UN Commission on Human Rights' Special Rapporteur on Violence Against Women that "there is a rule of customary international law that 'obliges States to prevent and respond to acts of violence against women with due diligence.'"[56] In the same judgment, it noted that the Special Rapporteur's "conclusion was based mainly on analysis of developments in the case-law of several international bodies," including the ECHR itself, the Inter-American Court of Human Rights, the Inter-American Commission on Human Rights, and the expert committee monitoring implementation of the UN Convention on the Elimination of All Forms of Discrimination against Women.[57] The Court went on to find that Bulgaria had violated Article 8 of the Convention, protecting family life, by failing to take sufficient measures in response to violent behavior by the husband of one of the applicants, thus amounting to "a failure to assist the applicants contrary to the [State's] positive obligations under Article 8 of the Convention to secure respect for their private and family life."[58] While the Court did not refer to customary law in the operative part of its decision, it may have indirectly used customary law to confirm an interpretation of the Convention.[59] Importantly, it relied on indirect evidence of customary law and did not engage in an extensive review of state practice and *opinio juris*.

At the national level, many courts have now opined on the content of customary human rights law, in a wide variety of contexts. One unusual context involves U.S. courts hearing cases brought under the Alien Tort Claims Act ("ACTA") (also known as the "Alien Tort Statute," or "ATS"), which first appeared in U.S. federal law in 1789. That Act grants original jurisdiction to U.S. federal district courts over "any civil action by an alien for a tort only,

55 See *Case of Vasiliauskas v. Lithuania*, Application No. 35343/05, Judgment of 20 October 2015, paras. 171–78.

56 *Case of Bevacqua and S. v. Bulgaria*, Application No. 71127/01, Judgment of 12 June 2008, final on 12 September 2008, para. 53.

57 Ibid.

58 Ibid., para. 84.

59 For reflections on the role of customary law in decisions of the Court, see Ineta Ziemele, "Customary International Law in the Case Law of the European Court of Human Rights – The Method," 12 *The Law and Practice of International Courts and Tribunals* 243 (2013).

committed in violation of the law of nations or a treaty of the United States."[60] The phrase "law of nations" in this statute has been interpreted to mean customary international law.

Since 1980, many cases have been decided under this provision that have allowed non-U.S. citizens to pursue civil claims against various persons, both individuals and corporations, for alleged violations of particular asserted norms of customary international human rights law. The seminal case permitting this litigation was that of *Filartiga v. Pena-Irala*, decided by the U.S. Second Circuit Court of Appeals in 1980. In that case, the court determined that the norm prohibiting torture had become part of customary international law, "as evidenced and defined by the Universal Declaration of Human Rights."[61]

Filartiga gave a "green light" to litigation of claims of violations of customary international human rights law, and opened the floodgates in U.S. courts. Plaintiffs brought many claims alleging successfully that, in addition to the prohibition of torture, the prohibitions of genocide and other human rights violations had passed into customary international law and therefore were actionable under the ATCA. In each case, courts examined whether the human right concerned could legitimately be considered protected by customary international law, often by determining whether there was sufficient state practice and *opinio juris*. In some cases courts decided there was not sufficient state practice or *opinio juris*, such as in the case of the right not to be subjected to "cruel, inhuman or degrading treatment or punishment" – a lesser offense than torture.[62] However, other courts have disagreed with this view.[63] Many of these judicial opinions focus on treaties, declarations, and

[60] See Alien Tort Claims Act, 28 U.S.C. § 1350.

[61] *Filartiga v. Pena-Irala*, 630 F.2d 876 (2nd Cir. 1980), 882.

[62] See, e.g., *In re Chiquita Brands Int'l, Inc.*, 792 F. Supp.2d 1301 (S.D. Fla. 2011), 1323 (affirming that such a claim is not "sufficiently established or universally recognized under international law to satisfy *Sosa*'s requirements for recognizing new ATS claims"); *Aldana v. Del Monte Fresh Produce, N.A., Inc.*, 416 F.3d 1242 (11th Cir. 2005), 1247, *cert. denied*, 549 U.S. 1032 (2006) (stating rather cryptically that "we see no basis in law to recognize Plaintiffs' claim for cruel, inhuman, [or] degrading treatment or punishment," and emphasizing that a finding that such a claim was actionable under the ATCA could not be based solely on a treaty like the ICCPR).

[63] See, e.g., *Al-Quraishi v. Nakhla*, 728 F. Supp.2d 702 (D. Md. 2010), 756–60, *rev'd on other grounds*, *Al-Quraishi v. L-3 Services, Inc.*, 657 F.3d 201 (4th Cir. 2011) (holding the prohibition of cruel, inhuman, or degrading treatment or punishment to be a norm of customary international law and actionable under the ATCA after a comprehensive review of authorities); *Sarei v. Rio Tinto Plc*, 650 F. Supp.2d 1004 (C.D. Ca. 2009), 1028 (noting a recent trend toward federal courts recognizing a universal prohibition against cruel, inhuman, or degrading treatment or punishment); *Bowoto v. Chevron Corp.*, 557 F. Supp.2d 1080 (N.D. Cal. 2008), 1092 (stating that "the prohibition of cruel, inhuman and degrading treatment has been widely recognized in numerous sources of international law").

government statements rather than state practice regarding detainee treatment as such.[64]

The U.S. Supreme Court has in two opinions limited the scope of cases that can be brought under the ATCA. First, in *Sosa v. Alvarez-Machain*, decided in 2004, the Court essentially endorsed the holding in *Filartiga*.[65] The Court concluded that the ATCA was primarily jurisdictional, but that in enacting it Congress also intended to provide a cause of action for certain serious crimes recognized under customary international law in 1789, such as violations of "safe conducts," infringement of the rights of ambassadors, and piracy. Accordingly, drawing on these precedents, the Court concluded that the ATCA could provide jurisdiction and a cause of action for a narrow range of violations of customary international human rights law, namely for violations of norms with no "less definite content and acceptance among civilized nations than the historical paradigms familiar when §1350 was enacted."[66] It went on to say that "whether a norm is sufficiently definite to support a cause of action should (and, indeed, inevitably must) involve an element of judgment about the practical consequences of making that cause available to litigants in the federal courts."[67] The Court found that under the facts in *Sosa*, which involved the abduction of a Mexican national by U.S. Drug Enforcement Agent officers in Mexico and his detention in a facility in Texas without appropriate legal authorization, there was no customary norm prohibiting "arbitrary" detention that was sufficiently definite to provide jurisdiction or a cause of action under the ATCA.[68]

The second Supreme Court case dealing with the scope of the ATCA was *Kiobel v. Royal Dutch Petroleum Co.*, decided in 2013.[69] It involved allegations that Royal Dutch Petroleum and other corporations that were engaged in oil exploration and production in Nigeria aided and abetted the Nigerian government in violating the human rights of the plaintiffs, who were residents of Nigeria who now lived in the United States. The Second Circuit Court of Appeals ruled that the case could not be brought under the ATCA because under customary international law there was no cause of action against corporations for human rights violations, only against individual perpetrators.[70] On appeal, the U.S. Supreme Court ruled in April 2013 that the ATCA has no

64 See, e.g., *Bowoto v. Chevron Corp.*, 557 F. Supp.2d at 1092.

65 *Sosa v. Alvarez-Machain*, 542 U.S. 692 (2004).

66 Ibid., 732.

67 Ibid., 732–33 (citations omitted).

68 See ibid., 733–38.

69 569 U.S. ___, 133 S.Ct. 1659 (2013).

70 See *Kiobel v. Royal Dutch Petroleum Co.*, 621 F.3d 111 (2nd Cir. 2010).

extraterritorial application, and thus should not grant jurisdiction for lawsuits involving torts committed outside the United States that did not "touch and concern" U.S. territory.[71] Judges hearing cases since the issuance of the *Kiobel* opinion have thus had to determine whether there is a sufficient connection with the United States to allow the case to be heard.

Other national courts have considered the content of customary human rights law in the context of evaluating the constitutionality of national laws, including in states whose constitution itself makes direct or indirect reference to customary law. They have thus expressed an opinion on the customary law status of various rights. National courts have been particularly apt to consider that subset of customary human rights norms that have reached the status of *jus cogens*. For example, a number of national courts have ruled that torture violates a norm of customary law as well as a peremptory norm. Thus, in *Suresh v. Canada*, the Supreme Court of Canada found "compelling indicia" that the prohibition of torture had achieved *jus cogens* status, including the many treaties and national laws prohibiting it and the failure of states to admit to it.[72] The former UK House of Lords has declared that "there is no doubt that the prohibition on torture" is a *jus cogens* norm.[73] Furthermore, the Supreme Court of Tonga has affirmed that "it is now accepted by most international jurists that the prohibition against torture is part of customary international law, and, furthermore it is a *jus cogens* rule from which States cannot derogate – whether they are a party to the various treaties which prohibit it or not."[74] Many of these statements are based largely on international treaties and declarations and national laws, coupled with references to the decisions of various international tribunals, rather than on surveys of actual state practices involving treatment of detainees.

The preceding review of international and national judicial decisions involving customary international human rights law demonstrates that courts have not uniformly applied the two-element test. Judicial practice in this regard varies widely. Indeed, many decisions tend to focus on evidence of *opinio juris*

71 See 133 S.Ct. at 1669.

72 *Suresh v. Canada (Minister of Citizenship and Immigration)*, paras. 61–64.

73 *Jones v. Ministry of Interior Al-Mamlaka Al-Arabiya AS Saudiya (the Kingdom of Saudi Arabia)*, [2006] UKHL 26 (14 June 2006), para. 43 (opinion of Lord Hoffmann, citing *R. v Bow Street Metropolitan Stipendiary Magistrate, Ex p Pinochet Ugarte (No. 3)*, [2000] 1 AC 147). See also *A (FC) v. Secretary of State for the Home Department*, [2005] UKHL 71 (8 December 2005), para. 33 (opinion of Lord Bingham of Cornhill). The UK Supreme Court, the successor to the House of Lords, has referred approvingly to the statement of Lord Bingham in *A (FC)* concerning the *jus cogens* status of the prohibition of torture. See *Youssef (Appellant) v. Secretary of State for Foreign and Commonwealth Affairs (Respondent)*, [2016] UKSC 3 (27 January 2016), paras. 17–18 (opinion of Lord Carnwath).

74 *Tavake v. Kingdom of Tonga*, [2008] TOSC 14 (19 December 2008), para. 52.

and give state practice (other than "paper practice" in the form of treaties, declarations, national laws, and government statements[75]) little or no attention.

8.5 WHY WE NEED A NEW THEORY OF CUSTOMARY HUMAN RIGHTS LAW

This survey of court decisions involving the identification of customary human rights norms discloses some problems with the traditional definition and theory of customary law that I explored in Chapter 1. There are at least two major problems, one of which I have already touched upon.

First, the reality is that very often there appears to be a consistent state practice of *violating* many rights, not respecting them. Some jurists have creatively confronted this problem by regarding treaties, declarations, rhetorical statements by states defending human rights, and national laws prohibiting human rights violations as the relevant state practice.[76] We have seen this emphasis on "paper practice" in a number of the decisions above, including the ICJ's judgment in the 2012 *Obligation to Prosecute or Extradite Case*. However, this juridical turn is not very satisfactory, as emphasized by such scholars as Bruno Simma and Philip Alston.[77] They have argued that it is simply intellectually dishonest to maintain that there is a widespread state practice of *not* torturing, for example, which would clearly be required by the traditional definition of customary law. Indeed, Simma and Alston have proposed that human rights advocates would do better to argue that human rights norms are general principles of law, as defined in Article 38(1)(c) of the ICJ Statute.[78]

Second, the omnipresence of human rights violations also casts doubt on the existence of *opinio juris* as traditionally defined. States often seem to believe

75 On "paper practice," see, e.g., Noora Arajärvi, "From the 'Demands of Humanity': The Formulation of *Opinio Juris* in Decisions of International Criminal Tribunals and the Need for a Renewed Emphasis on State Practice," in this volume; Frans von der Dunk, "Customary International Law and Outer Space," in this volume.

76 The draft conclusions adopted by the International Law Commission in 2016 appear to validate such an approach. In particular, Draft Conclusion 6 affirms that "forms of State practice include, but are not limited to: diplomatic acts and correspondence; conduct in connection with resolutions adopted by an international organization or at an intergovernmental conference; conduct in connection with treaties; executive conduct, including operational conduct 'on the ground'; legislative and administrative acts; and decisions of national courts." "Report of the International Law Commission," Sixty-Eighth Session, Draft Conclusion 6, para. 2.

77 See Bruno Simma and Philip Alston, "The Sources of Human Rights Law: Custom, Jus Cogens, and General Principles," 12 *Australian Yearbook of International Law* 82 (1988–89).

78 See ICJ Statute, art. 38(1)(c).

not that they are already bound to observe certain human rights norms, but that the norms are still in the process of formation and that they may therefore comply with them, or fail to do so, at their pleasure, and depending on whether or not they perceive their vital security interests to be threatened. This was certainly the attitude of many Western states regarding their practices of "enhanced interrogation" in connection with the "war on terrorism." While they gave lip service to the prohibition on torture, their attitude toward the norm was that "torture" was hazily defined under customary international law, and therefore they could narrow the concept to suit their interests. Statements and documents along these lines might well weaken other apparent evidence in favor of *opinio juris* prohibiting torture.

These two problems are reflected in the above judicial opinions. On the one hand, many opinions make little reference to state practice on human rights other than paper practice. One reason may be that violations are so pervasive and courts are naturally drawn, therefore, to emphasize *opinio juris*. On the other hand, the judicial opinions have tended to cite treaties and declarations as both state practice and *opinio juris* (if they even identify these separate elements of customary law explicitly). These sources are most naturally viewed as evidence of what states believe the law *ought to* require of all states. Courts have not rigorously investigated whether states observe human rights norms (when states do so) *because* they believe they are already legally obligated to do so – the traditional definition of *opinio juris*.

Scholars have dealt with these problems in various ways, and accordingly adopted different views of the legal status of the rights articulated in the Universal Declaration. At one extreme, some scholars maintain that all of the substantive rights listed in the Universal Declaration have, by virtue of the widespread acceptance of the Declaration over a more than sixty-year period since its adoption, entered the realm of customary law, despite widespread human rights violations. For example, John Humphrey, who served as Director of the UN Human Rights Division during the drafting of the Universal Declaration, affirmed in 1979 that "the justiciable provisions of the Declaration, including certainly, those enunciated in articles two to twenty-one inclusive, have now acquired the force of law as part of the customary law of nations."[79]

At the other end of the spectrum, some scholars maintain that the listing of rights in the Universal Declaration has no bearing whatsoever on their status

[79] Prof. John P. Humphrey, "The Universal Declaration of Human Rights: Its History, Impact and Juridical Character," in *Human Rights: Thirty Years after the Universal Declaration: Commemorative Volume on the Occasion of the Thirtieth Anniversary of the Universal Declaration of Human Rights*, edited by Dr. B.G. Ramcharan 21 (The Hague: Martinus Nijhoff Publishers, 1979), 29.

as customary law.[80] They view it as a merely hortatory instrument that, at best, may be evidence of *opinio juris* (though they doubt even that) and provides absolutely no evidence of the *sine qua non* for a customary norm – consistent state practice. They believe that the record of state practice tends to suggest that states do *not* consistently honor human rights. This view is supported by the fact, pointed out earlier in the chapter, that under Article 13 of the UN Charter, all General Assembly resolutions are only recommendations to UN member states.

Most scholars take a position somewhere between these extremes: They believe that the customary law status of particular rights must be evaluated through a careful consideration of state practice and *opinio juris* relating to each right.[81] Under this approach, some rights appearing in the Universal Declaration will qualify as customary law, and others will not. This approach is consistent with that adopted by such scholars as Anthony D'Amato, who emphasizes that consistent state practice in accordance with a norm is the essence of customary law and that courts and scholars violate its essential foundations when minimizing the significance of state practice.[82]

These debates on the relative importance of state practice and the proper view of *opinio juris* in relation to customary human rights law highlight some characteristics of human rights norms that distinguish them from other kinds of norms forming part of customary law, and that relate to the two key problems with the traditional definition I identified earlier in the chapter. First, human rights norms are based on ethical principles, not merely the self-interest of states. Moreover, it will often be in states' perceived short-term interest to violate these ethics-based norms, for example, in order to extract information from suspected terrorists. This means there is a permanent tension between states' self-interest and the demands of human rights norms – a tension that is less salient than in the case of more "practical" norms fostering interstate cooperation. And this tension can lead to widespread human rights abuses in practice. However, does this mean that a customary human rights norm can never emerge?

80 See, e.g., J. Patrick Kelly, "The Twilight of Customary International Law," 40 *Virginia Journal of International Law* 449 (2000), 486–91.

81 Bruno Simma and Philip Alston adopt this view. See Simma and Alston, "The Sources of Human Rights Law," 100.

82 See Anthony A. D'Amato, *The Concept of Custom in International Law* (Ithaca, NY: Cornell University Press, 1971), 87–88 (affirming that without the quantitative element of state acts, "one could not tell which of the numerous and often contradictory articulated norms were actually embodied in customary law.... The state's act is visible, real, and significant; it crystallizes policy and demonstrates which of the many possible rules of law the acting state has decided to manifest.").

Furthermore, if states have a "natural" incentive to violate human rights to achieve short-term goals, then they may also be unlikely to engage in behavior favoring human rights with the belief that they are doing so out of compliance with international human rights norms. They are more likely to believe, and claim, that behaving in this way is required by their own national law or is simply their policy choice. "*Opinio juris*" will be very difficult to find in the traditional sense. Again, does this mean that a customary human rights norm can never emerge?

The clear answer is "no," at least if the opinions of the aforementioned courts are to be accepted, and if states' rhetorical assertions of their acceptance of the legally binding character of human rights norms are to be believed. Accordingly, some new understanding of customary law is necessary that takes account of, and remedies, these deficiencies in applying the traditional approach to human rights norms.

8.6 A NEW THEORY OF CUSTOMARY INTERNATIONAL LAW

To help resolve these types of problems and debates, I propose a new theory of customary international human rights law grounded in the more comprehensive theory of customary law outlined in my book, *Customary International Law: A New Theory with Practical Applications*.[83] In particular, I argue that a careful study of the evolution of customary international law coupled with ethical insights gleaned from contemporary international law (including the Universal Declaration itself) point to a new understanding of customary international law as an informal process of lawmaking by the global community of states that complements the more formal and institutionalized process of treaty-making. In my view, this conception actually best comports with the use that states and courts have made of customary law.

According to this new understanding, a rule or principle ought to be considered customary law if states generally believe that it is desirable, now or in the near future, to make the rule or principle legally authoritative for all members of the global community of states and irrespective of any treaties that states may or may not ratify. Moreover, in assessing state beliefs, it is necessary to evaluate the degree to which a norm is consistent with certain fundamental ethical principles in contemporary international law anchored in a preeminent principle of "unity in diversity." State practice is important *evidence* of this belief that a norm should be universally binding. However, it is not by itself an essential

[83] See Brian D. Lepard, *Customary International Law: A New Theory with Practical Applications* (New York: Cambridge University Press, 2010).

independent requirement for recognition of a norm as customary law.[84] This is particularly true for norms, such as human rights standards, that have a potent ethical content.

The theory emphasizes *opinio juris* as opposed to state practice, but also redefines *opinio juris* as a belief by states that a norm *should* be law, rather than a belief by states that it is *already* law. (This definition applies directly in the case of new norms. In the case of existing norms, *opinio juris* should be viewed as a belief by states that a norm *should continue to be law*.) The theory furthermore introduces an analysis of the impact of a norm on the realization of fundamental ethical principles, which can assist in making inferences about what states believe if their views are not clear. The theory thereby solves some of the serious problems with recognizing many human rights standards as customary law under the conventional doctrine. At the same time, the theory insists on a rigorous inquiry into the views of states using many sources of evidence of those views, including but not limited to state practice and the many human rights declarations and treaties reviewed in the preceding sections.

It is natural that customary law came to be identified with consistent state practice, because state practice is very often the best kind of evidence that states have a belief that a norm should be law. But that is just what state practice is – evidence of this belief. The key requirement is this lawmaking intent by states. One finds in many of the judicial opinions mentioned earlier in the chapter a focus on this lawmaking intent, rather than on actual state practices concerning human rights, as well as references to state practice as evidence of *opinio juris*. The ICJ suggested this relationship between state practice and *opinio juris* in its statement in the 1969 *North Sea Continental Shelf Cases* that "not only must the acts concerned [constituting state practice] amount to a settled practice, but they must also be such, or be carried out in such a way, as to be *evidence of a belief that this practice is rendered obligatory by the existence of a rule of law requiring it.*"[85]

The proposed theory also explicitly addresses the role of ethical analysis. By contrast, the traditional doctrine fails explicitly to articulate a role for ethics, even though from the beginning customary law has, indeed, been affected

84 As indicated in Chapter 1, a number of other scholars have advocated viewing state practice not as an independent requirement, but as evidence of *opinio juris*. See, e.g., Andrew T. Guzman, *How International Law Works: A Rational Choice Theory* (Oxford: Oxford University Press, 2008), 200.

85 *North Sea Continental Shelf Cases (Federal Republic of Germany v. Denmark; Federal Republic of Germany v. Netherlands)*, Judgment of 20 February 1969, 1969 ICJ Rep. 3, 44, para. 77 (emphasis added).

by ethics. Usually ethics has found its way indirectly into the determination of customary law through the *opinio juris* requirement.[86] That is, a court or other decision maker is more likely to find that states believe that they are already bound to follow a particular norm as a legal norm if it advances ethical principles. For example, in the well-known case of *The Paquete Habana*, the U.S. Supreme Court, in concluding that a customary norm had developed that exempted civilian fishing vessels from capture in wartime, emphasized "considerations of humanity" and that the norm promoted the ethical goal of protecting innocent vessels and fishermen.[87] Perhaps most significantly for human rights norms, ethics obviously has supported a finding that the *opinio juris* requirement is met in the case of many human rights standards, such as the prohibition of genocide. As noted above, in the 1951 *Genocide Convention Advisory Opinion* the ICJ said that this prohibition confirms "the most elementary principles of morality." And in the 2015 *Genocide Convention Case (Croatia v. Serbia)*, the ICJ explicitly quoted this language while specifically identifying the genocide prohibition as customary international law.

Nevertheless, it is critical to explain how and why ethics should play such a role in the formation of customary international law. I have proposed a role for a particular body of ethical principles, which I refer to as "fundamental ethical principles." I suggest that these principles form a "background" value system that can inform our interpretation and assessment of the beliefs of states about whether a norm ought to be a legal norm (i.e., *opinio juris*). Fundamental ethical principles are principles that states have already directly or indirectly endorsed in international legal texts, including the UN Charter and the Universal Declaration, and that are logically related to a paramount ethical principle, which I refer to as "unity in diversity."

Unity in diversity asserts that morally all states and peoples should be united, respectively, as members of a community of states and a community of individuals. It is thus grounded in a concept, quite familiar to the great natural law theorists, such as Hugo Grotius, of the "unity of the human family." For example, in his influential work "On the Law of War and Peace," Grotius described "the mutual tie of kinship among men."[88] At the same time, the principle of unity in diversity insists on respect for national and other affiliations, as well as individual freedom and diversity of thought, conscience, belief, religion, and expression. This is why I refer to it as "unity in diversity."

86 This point is made by Noora Arajärvi in her chapter. See Arajärvi, "From the 'Demands of Humanity,'" in this volume.

87 See *The Paquete Habana*, 175 U.S. 677 (1900), 708.

88 Hugo Grotius, *De Jure Belli ac Pacis Libri Tres*, translated by Francis W. Kelsey (New York: Oceana; London: Wildy and Sons, 1964), book 2, chap. 25, ¶ 6, 582.

8.7 RELEVANT FUNDAMENTAL ETHICAL PRINCIPLES IN INTERNATIONAL LAW

There are many examples of acceptance of the principle of unity in diversity by states in international legal documents. For example, the UN Charter clearly envisions a community of states that seek to collaborate to achieve peace and human rights, while respecting national sovereignty. It affirms that "we the peoples of the United Nations" adopted the Charter to "practice tolerance and *live together in peace with one another as good neighbours*."[89] Furthermore, the Universal Declaration of Human Rights announces in Article 1 that "all human beings are born free and equal in dignity and rights. They are endowed with reason and conscience and should act towards one another in a spirit of brotherhood."[90] At the same time, it recognizes the value of freedom of thought, conscience, and religion, as well as of freedom of opinion and expression, in Articles 18 and 19, respectively.[91]

Many other principles are related to this preeminent principle logically, and have also been endorsed by states, as I have explored elsewhere. These include the equal dignity of all human beings; universal human rights and universal human duties to respect human rights; a trust theory of government and limited state sovereignty; the right to life, physical security, and subsistence; the right to freedom of moral choice, including freedom of thought, conscience, opinion, religion, and expression; open-minded consultation as a means of finding solutions to problems; individual moral responsibility for criminal behavior; the interdependence between peace and human rights; and the observance of humanitarian rules in military action.[92]

In addition, it is possible generally to rank principles and rights based on the proximity of their connection with the paramount principle of unity in diversity as "fundamental," "compelling," and "essential." Fundamental human rights are those rights recognized in international law, including the Universal Declaration, that morally are deserving of significant weight because of their logical relationship to the principle of unity in diversity, and that morally merit a significant degree of preemptive effect. It appears that all the rights recognized in the Universal Declaration have this minimal status. Compelling human rights are those fundamental human rights that

89 UN Charter, preamble (emphasis added).

90 Universal Declaration, art. 1.

91 See ibid., arts. 18, 19.

92 See Brian D. Lepard, *Rethinking Humanitarian Intervention: A Fresh Legal Approach Based on Fundamental Ethical Principles in International Law and World Religions* (University Park: Pennsylvania State University Press, 2002), 39–98.

morally are deserving of especially high weight because of their direct and immediate logical relationship to unity in diversity, and that morally merit a high degree of preemptive effect. Finally, essential human rights are those compelling human rights that are among the most minimal requirements for the enjoyment of equal human dignity. They deserve the highest weight morally because they are so closely related to the preeminent principle of unity in diversity. In addition, because of their moral importance, they should preempt any possible reasons for not respecting them in all, or virtually all, cases.[93]

8.8 EVALUATING THE CUSTOMARY LAW STATUS OF PARTICULAR HUMAN RIGHTS

What implications does this theory have for evaluating the customary law status of particular human rights? First, the test for a customary norm I have set out – that states generally believe that a particular norm ought to be law, now or very soon – by its nature requires a norm-by-norm analysis. Accordingly, it is not appropriate to conclude that every single substantive right listed in the Universal Declaration is *ipso facto* customary law unless there is evidence that states have this belief with respect to all those rights. I argue that the evidence strongly indicates that states did not in 1948, nor do they now, believe that the listing of a right in the Universal Declaration automatically confers on it the status of binding law. The Universal Declaration is a General Assembly resolution, which is formally only a recommendation to UN member states, and its drafters, including Eleanor Roosevelt, took great pains to insist that it was not a legally binding document.[94] There is little evidence that states have changed their views on this score.

On the other hand, I have argued that there is indeed quite compelling evidence that states generally believe that all of the human rights proclaimed in the Universal Declaration have at least persuasive legal authority, even if not binding legal authority.[95] This means that states are legally obligated under customary law to give these rights great weight in their decision making. I elaborate on the concept of persuasive obligations in my book on customary international law.[96] This conclusion follows not only from the *travaux préparatoires* of the Universal

93 See ibid., 57–58; 58 Fig. 2.

94 For example, Roosevelt, who chaired the UN Commission on Human Rights during the drafting of the Universal Declaration, said that "it is not and does not purport to be a statement of law or of legal obligation." 19 *Bulletin of State Department* (1948), 751, quoted in H. Lauterpacht, *International Law and Human Rights* (N.p.: Archon Books, 1968), 399.

95 See Lepard, *Customary International Law*, 318–27.

96 See ibid., 54–57.

Declaration, but also from its status as a solemn resolution of the General Assembly that was furthermore christened with the title of "declaration" – a status indicating that member states of the UN are not simply free to disregard its norms at will.[97] Indeed, the ICJ has implied in some of its judgments that the Universal Declaration establishes norms that states must conscientiously consider and not wholly ignore, even if they are not *ipso facto* obligated to respect them.[98]

Beyond this minimal obligation that all states have under customary law to give great weight to the norms in the Universal Declaration, particular rights have achieved the necessary *opinio juris* to become fully binding customary law. State practice is not wholly irrelevant to this analysis, as it can be a good indicator of states' beliefs, but it also is not determinative with regard to ascertaining the status of norms such as those in the Declaration that are so laden with ethical content.

Let me give just one example here, involving the right to change one's religion or belief. Article 18 of the Universal Declaration protects this right. It provides: "Everyone has the right to freedom of thought, conscience and religion; this right includes freedom to change his religion or belief, and freedom, either alone or in community with others and in public or private, to manifest his religion or belief in teaching, practice, worship and observance."[99] The 1966 ICCPR does not explicitly mention a right to "change" one's belief – a term opposed by various Islamic states[100] – but does protect a right to "have or adopt" a religion or belief of one's choice.[101] The drafters universally understood this right to encompass a right to "change" one's religion or belief.[102] Nevertheless, a number of scholars have argued that this right simply is not part of customary international law because so many states violate it – and in particular, Islamic states.[103] These states often

97 See ibid., 216, 319.

98 See, e.g., *United States Diplomatic and Consular Staff in Tehran (United States of America v. Iran)*, Judgment of 24 May 1980, 1980 ICJ Rep. 3, 42, para. 91 (affirming that "wrongfully to deprive human beings of their freedom and to subject them to physical constraint in conditions of hardship is in itself manifestly incompatible with the principles of the Charter of the United Nations, *as well as with the fundamental principles enunciated in the Universal Declaration of Human Rights*") (emphasis added).

99 Universal Declaration, art. 18.

100 On this point, see Lepard, *Customary International Law*, 349–52.

101 See ICCPR, art. 18, para. 1 (providing in part that the right to freedom of thought, conscience, and religion "shall include freedom to have or to adopt a religion or belief of his choice").

102 See Lepard, *Customary International Law*, 351–52.

103 See, e.g., Richard B. Lillich, "Civil Rights," in *Human Rights in International Law: Legal and Policy Issues*, vol. 1, edited by Theodor Meron 115 (Oxford: Clarendon Press, 1984), 158 n.242 (doubting that even a general right to freedom of religion is part of customary international law because of the absence of confirming state practice); International Law Association, Buenos Aires Conference (1994), Committee on the Enforcement of Human Rights Law, "Final Report on

have laws preventing Muslims from renouncing their faith, treating religious conversion as a severe crime of apostasy that is in some cases punishable by death.[104]

Using the new definition of customary international law I have proposed, however, I argue that this right should indeed be considered protected by customary international law. A thorough analysis of all relevant evidence of states' beliefs indicates that a majority of them believe this norm should be legally recognized as binding on all states. This is evidenced by the Universal Declaration, the ICCPR, national laws, and numerous government statements.[105] Even Islamic states, while opposing the word "change," conceded during the drafting of the ICCPR that an individual should be free to renounce an existing religion or belief and adopt a new one.[106] While many states violate the norm in practice, Islamic states among them, these violations do not indicate a general belief among all states that the norm should not be universally binding. Moreover, to the extent there is any doubt about state beliefs, we should make reference to fundamental ethical principles to resolve this doubt. I suggest that freedom to change one's religion or belief, which is necessary for diversity of opinion, belief, and expression, is an essential human right because it lies at the heart of the preeminent principle of unity in diversity. This elevated moral status means that any doubt about state beliefs should be resolved in favor of recognizing the norm as customary law.[107]

Which human rights norms recognized as customary international law under the proposed approach also deserve to be treated as norms of *jus cogens*? I have suggested that, in general, a *jus cogens* norm is a norm that (1) states generally believe should be strongly peremptory in character because of the importance of the values it promotes; (2) states generally believe furthers such important values that it should bind all states, even states that have persistently objected to it; (3) states generally believe in particular furthers such important values that it should preempt any contrary provision of an agreement between states and indeed should render such an agreement entirely void, including rendering void provisions in the agreement that do not contravene the norm; and (4) states generally and reasonably believe either further compelling or essential ethical principles or are at least consistent with fundamental

the Status of the Universal Declaration of Human Rights in National and International Law," in *Report of the Conference* 525 (London: W. Clowes and Sons, 1994), 548 (similar, and referring to the contrary practice of Muslim states regarding the freedom to change one's religion).

104 See generally Lepard, *Customary International Law*, 346.

105 See generally ibid., 346–67.

106 See ibid., 351–52.

107 For a fuller discussion, see ibid., 359–60, 364–67.

ethical principles.[108] I should note that "compelling" and "essential" ethical principles are defined in a manner similar to "compelling" and "essential" human rights.[109] I have also suggested that a higher degree of consensus should be required to recognize *jus cogens* norms than for "ordinary" customary law norms.[110]

Similarly, I have proposed that an *erga omnes* norm (creating an *erga omnes* obligation) should be defined as a norm otherwise meeting the above criteria for customary law to the extent it is clear that (1) states generally believe that the norm creates an obligation actually owed to all other states based on the content of the norm; (2) states generally believe that every other state therefore has a legal interest in the norm's observance and a right to bring a claim for its violation in a forum with jurisdiction; and (3) states generally and reasonably believe that the norm furthers fundamental ethical principles or is at least consistent with them.[111]

To return to the above example, what should be the *jus cogens* and *erga omnes* status of the right to change one's religion or belief using these standards? I have argued that it indeed meets the above tests for *jus cogens* status, for which there is compelling evidence, including the fact that states believe that no exemption for persistent objection to it should be allowed. For example, it is included in the list of nonderogable rights under Article 4(2) of the ICCPR. I have argued that it also meets the three criteria for an *erga omnes* norm.[112]

8.9 ADVANTAGES OF THE PROPOSED THEORY

As illustrated in part by this example, the new theory of customary human rights law I have proposed offers a number of advantages in comparison with the traditional definition of customary law. First, the theory solves the problem identified by Simma and Alston, among others, that consistent state practice in favor of human rights often does not exist. It does so by viewing state practice as evidence, among many other sources, of *opinio juris*. In short, under the proposed approach, state practice does not *have* to be consistent to find the existence of a customary human rights norm.

Second, there are good reasons for this new understanding. There is evidence that it is in fact applied by the ICJ and other courts, as suggested above,

[108] See ibid., 243–44. On *jus cogens* norms, see generally ibid., 243–60.
[109] See ibid., 81–82, 83 Fig. 5.1.
[110] See ibid., 246–47.
[111] Ibid., 262. On *erga omnes* norms, see generally ibid., 261–69.
[112] See ibid., 364–67.

including in the ICJ's 2012 *Obligation to Prosecute or Extradite* judgment. It allows customary human rights norms to be recognized as law despite the persistent temptation of states to flout these norms to pursue their own interests.

Third, the proposed approach is more intellectually honest and rigorous than the traditional definition. When applying this definition, jurists often conflate "actual" practice with "paper" practice in determining whether the state practice requirement is fulfilled. Somehow all this "practice" gets mixed together and some kind of overall practice emerges. Not surprisingly, however, jurists often seem to give greater weight to the paper practice, and rarely mention the actual practice (of torturing, for example). The better, more candid, view is that what is called paper "practice" is really evidence of *opinio juris*.[113]

Fourth, the approach reinterprets *opinio juris* in a way that is more consistent with the actual jurisprudence of courts hearing human rights cases. It asks whether states believe there *ought to be* a legal rule binding on all states, now or in the near future – not whether they believe they are already bound by a rule. Such an understanding of *opinio juris* allows human rights law to evolve more easily. And, importantly, it avoids the "paradox" of *opinio juris* regarding new norms that I described at some length in Chapter 1.

Finally, the theory incorporates an explicit ethical component into the determination of customary international law. It is obvious from the above review of international and national court judgments that courts have recognized that human rights norms have an intrinsic ethical purpose and have referred to ethical principles supporting the norms. However, they have done so haphazardly and not systematically, often obfuscating their reasoning. Some academic approaches to customary law have also admirably introduced ethical reasoning into the evaluation of *opinio juris*, but again in a very broad and general way.[114]

By contrast, the proposed theory explicitly identifies relevant fundamental ethical principles, all of which have been endorsed by states themselves, and explains their background role in the identification of customary law. It introduces rigor into the ethical component of customary law analysis regarding human rights norms. Moreover, according to the theory, these principles can serve as a "check" on the recognition of unethical customary norms that

[113] A number of other scholars have adopted a similar view of the evidentiary role of state practice in determining *opinio juris*. See, e.g., Anna Williams Shavers, "Using Customary International Law to Improve Women's Lives," in this volume.

[114] See, e.g., John Tasioulas, "Customary International Law and the Quest for Global Justice," in *The Nature of Customary Law: Legal, Historical and Philosophical Perspectives*, edited by Amanda Perreau-Saussine and James Bernard Murphy 307 (Cambridge: Cambridge University Press, 2007), 310 (referring to "the ethical appeal of a candidate norm" as one of the criteria for determining whether a norm should attain the status of customary international law).

directly contravene fundamental human rights. Thus, for example, resolutions adopted by the UN Human Rights Council endorsing criminal laws prohibiting and punishing the "defamation of religion" should be discounted as evidence of *opinio juris* because they would violate the essential human right to freedom of expression.[115]

In brief, the proposed theory of customary human rights law sharpens the inquiry into the customary law status of particular norms, rather than engaging in "fuzzy" analyses that mix together both actual and paper practice. It abandons the futile attempt to squeeze human rights norms into old customary law pigeonholes. And, I argue, it better explains what both international and national courts are actually holding with respect to the customary law status of particular human rights.

8.10 POTENTIAL CRITIQUES OF THE PROPOSED THEORY AND SOME RESPONSES

Nevertheless, the proposed approach might be critiqued on a number of scores. Let me identify possible critiques and offer some responses to them.

First, it could be argued that the proposed theory is attractive on some level, but is not a theory of "customary" international law, which requires some form of consistent and widespread state practice.[116] While it is true that the theory broadens the concept of customary law, it does not dispense with the state practice element. Rather, it reconceptualizes the traditional state practice "requirement" as a requirement that state practice be considered as evidence of *opinio juris*. As such evidence, it will almost always be the case that *some* kind of conforming state practice will be required to find a customary human rights norm. For example, to sustain a finding that torture is prohibited by customary law, it will be important to establish that at least *some* states actually exercise restraint in the treatment of detainees and refrain from torturing them. Of course, other sources of evidence of *opinio juris* are relevant as well, including national laws and regulations prohibiting torture, as well as international treaties and declarations that do likewise. In short, the proposed theory does not delete the state practice requirement; rather, it instructs jurists

115 On the defamation of religion resolutions, see Brian D. Lepard, "Parochial Restraints on Religious Liberty," in *Parochialism, Cosmopolitanism, and the Foundations of International Law*, edited by M.N.S. Sellers 225 (New York: Cambridge University Press, 2012), 231–32, 245–46.

116 A number of the contributors to this volume have emphasized the importance of establishing the existence of consistent state practice in support of a customary norm. See, e.g., Arajärvi, "From the 'Demands of Humanity,'" in this volume.

on how best to view state practice in the larger analysis of the existence of a customary norm – as one source of evidence, among others, of *opinio juris*.[117]

In addition, the theory's redefinition of *opinio juris* as forward-looking and based on the beliefs of states "generally" about what the law should be, or should continue to be, could be viewed as a way of allowing simple majorities of states to legislate for all states – and not always in favor of norms that promote human rights. This is a critique of my theory made very articulately by Fernando Tesón in his stimulating chapter.[118]

In response to this critique, it is important to underscore, first, that the traditional definition of customary law allows for some kind of majority lawmaking. That is, barring the case of a persistent objector, a "widespread" practice and *opinio juris* among at least a majority of states can generate a rule binding on all states. Universal consensus on a customary norm has never been required under the traditional definition. So the legitimacy issues raised by majority lawmaking exist even under current understandings of customary international law.

However, the definition of *opinio juris* that I propose contains a number of safeguards. First, not all states' views deserve the same weight in assessing whether "majority" support exists. I have argued that states' views should be weighted differently on the basis of multiple factors, depending on the nature of the problem the putative rule is trying to solve. One key factor relevant to human rights is the degree to which a particular state takes into account the views of its citizens as part of its policy-making process.[119] For example, the views of states that form their policies (and therefore views on the desirability of a legal norm) through democratic procedures ought to be given more weight than the views of autocratic states that ignore the wishes of their populations. Such weighting is justified by the fundamental ethical principle, described at greater length in my book on customary international law, of open-minded consultation and by the fundamental human right to democracy.[120] It would

[117] I should note in this connection that the role of state practice as evidence of *opinio juris* will depend on the nature of the norms in question. For example, in the case of international criminal law, the ethical and legal principle of legality means that in interpreting state beliefs about the desirability of imposing individual criminal liability for certain acts, we should be cautious in assessing these beliefs and presume that states do not wish to impose such liability unless defendants were reasonably on notice of the criminal nature of their acts – and actual conforming state practice would be a principal way of giving such notice. I agree with Noora Arajärvi, then, that in the field of international criminal law conforming state practice is normally important to establish. See ibid. However, under my theory this is because it deserves more weight as evidence of *opinio juris*, rather than because it is an independent requirement for customary international criminal law in its own right.

[118] See Fernando R. Tesón, "Fake Custom," in this volume.

[119] See Lepard, *Customary International Law*, 155–56.

[120] See ibid., 90–91, 156.

prevent, to take an example offered by Fernando Tesón, a simple majority of UN member states that are autocratic states and that favor a norm requiring the criminalization of blasphemy to create such a customary rule.[121] While this kind of weighting process is imprecise, it is essential in making judgments about which norms should be recognized as universally binding customary law to ensure some form of democratic accountability for these judgments.[122]

Second, I have argued that some kinds of rules require a form of "supermajority" in support of them – including rules that solve prisoners' dilemmas. Rules of *jus cogens* also require a higher level of support, as noted above. So not all rules can be established by the views of a simple majority of states.

Third, the proposed test for *opinio juris* requires that states generally believe that a rule would be desirable to implement "now or in the near future" – not far into the future as part of an aspirational agenda. States must be willing to recognize, and abide by, the legal norm now or soon. This requirement puts a check on the transformation of clearly aspirational norms into binding law, and thus helps to demarcate *lex ferenda* from *lex lata*, a common and legitimate concern of several of the contributors to this volume, including Noora Arajärvi.[123] In this way the theory prevents creation of the kind of "fake custom" described by Tesón that results from recognition as law of norms that are merely the "wish lists" of their promoters.

Fourth, the proposed new understanding of *opinio juris* requires that states believe it is desirable to implement an "authoritative" legal rule or principle. This means that they must favor a rule that limits their discretion. It must impose either a binding obligation on them, which would completely preempt their own decision making, or a persuasive obligation on them, which would require that they give the rule great weight in their decision making. It is not sufficient that states believe that a particular *action* would be "desirable." Thus, for example, the mere belief by most (or all) states that it would be desirable for states to adopt laws prohibiting the "defamation" of religion does not establish *opinio juris* in favor of an international rule *requiring* states to adopt such laws. This feature of the proposed test would significantly restrict the creation of new customary laws because this is a high barrier to clear.

121 See Tesón, "Fake Custom," in this volume.

122 I should note that the weighting factors I propose apply to all states, whether developed or developing, and whether of the West or East, North or South. In this way the approach is globally inclusive, and helps to address concerns that many recognized norms of customary law are those favored by Western states rather than by non-Western states. For example, the views of democratic non-Western states should be given a similar weight to those of democratic Western states. On these types of concerns, see J. Patrick Kelly, "Customary International Law in Historical Context: The Exercise of Power without General Acceptance," in this volume.

123 See Arajärvi, "From the 'Demands of Humanity,'" in this volume.

Fifth, under the proposed definition of *opinio juris*, states must believe that it is desirable to recognize an authoritative *legal* rule. It is not sufficient for them to believe in the desirability of an authoritative moral, political, or social rule. They must believe, in other words, that some legal remedy must be available for states or individuals whose rights are infringed by violations of the rule. Again, this limitation restricts the rampant and free-wheeling recognition of otherwise desirable norms as customary law. It may well be the case that states believe that it would be desirable to recognize a universal *moral* rule, but not a legal one – such as a moral rule calling on individuals to exercise restraint in their speech about people with a different religion or belief system.

All of these limitations incorporated in the theory, including the need, normally, for some state practice as evidence of *opinio juris*, mean that the theory does not simply allow a majority of states to impose on others as customary law whatever they believe to be desirable. However, Tesón makes another important point, which is that many apparent expressions of *opinio juris* involve very vague and abstract "rules."[124] He argues that verbal precision and specificity are essential. I accept this argument. I believe that a requirement of precision is implicit in the concept of an "authoritative legal rule or principle," but in any event agree with this point.

Another potential critique of the proposed theory is that by minimizing the role of state practice, and reconceptualizing *opinio juris* as a belief by states about what the law should be, it opens the door to judges "finding" customary law based on their personal preferences. One answer to this critique is that the proposed definition of *opinio juris* focuses on the beliefs of *states*, rather than the views of judges, nongovernmental organizations, or scholars. It respects the autonomy and perspectives of states in this way. And, of course, it does not render state practice irrelevant, but merely seeks to explain its proper role in the analysis of customary law.

It might be argued, too, that the proposed theory fails to differentiate between customary law and general principles of law. It is true that the theory moves customary law closer to general principles by recognizing the evidentiary function of state practice. On the other hand, it continues to maintain a distinction between these two bodies of law, principally on the basis of the degree of generality of the rule in question and whether it establishes binding or persuasive obligations.[125]

[124] See Tesón, "Fake Custom," in this volume.

[125] For a fuller discussion of the relationship between customary international law and general principles of law, see Lepard, *Customary International Law*, 162–68. In this respect my theory's explanation of the dividing line between customary law and general principles differs from that proposed by Thomas Kleinlein, who believes that customary norms are best distinguished from

The insertion of ethical reasoning into the identification of customary law may also be critiqued. Indeed, in his chapter Niels Petersen challenges the idea that truly "universal" values exist; he says that "it seems impossible to determine natural law-like universal values that form part of customary international law."[126] However, at least at a broad level of generality, we have seen that states themselves *have* agreed on certain values as universal in documents like the Universal Declaration of Human Rights. There may be contentious arguments about just how competing values are to be reconciled, or what practical implications these values have for particular human rights, but the values themselves have indeed been universally endorsed and the theory is grounded in them. The theory is also careful not to conflate customary law with ethical principles. Rather, it very deliberately refers to ethical principles only as a background value system. States themselves still decide on which norms would be desirable to implement as authoritative legal norms within the framework of this value system.

8.11 CONCLUSION

I have sketched here the outlines of a new theory of customary international human rights law. It seeks to provide more practical guidance to international and national tribunals, and other decision makers, on finding and applying customary human rights law. Moreover, it does a better job than the traditional definition of explaining how tribunals are already identifying customary human rights norms. Consistent with the theory, these tribunals have tended to focus on evidence of *opinio juris*, have adopted a forward-looking definition of *opinio juris*, and have discounted the importance of consistent state practice (other than "paper practice") relating to human rights. My hope is that the theory opens promising new avenues not only for ascertaining the content of customary human rights law, but also for promoting certain fundamental ethical principles underlying that law.

general principles because they are based on reciprocity. See Thomas Kleinlein, "Customary International Law and General Principles: Rethinking Their Relationship," in this volume.

126 Niels Petersen, "The Role of Consent and Uncertainty in the Formation of Customary International Law," in this volume.

9

Using Customary International Law to Improve Women's Lives

*Anna Williams Shavers**

9.1 INTRODUCTION

As we have seen throughout this volume, it is generally accepted that in order to establish a rule of customary international law, attention must be directed to the practice and *opinio juris* of states.[1] In his book, *Customary International Law: A New Theory with Practical Applications*,[2] legal scholar Brian Lepard seeks to develop a legal principle that customary international law can be established even if the existence of consistent state practice is absent. As he explains in Chapter 8 of this volume, he advocates a new definition of customary international law, asserting: "A customary international law norm arises when states generally believe that it is desirable now or in the near future to have an authoritative legal principle or rule prescribing, permitting, or prohibiting certain conduct."[3]

* This chapter grew out of my presentation at the "Reexamining Customary International Law" symposium held in Washington, DC, in November 2010, sponsored by the International Legal Theory Interest Group of the American Society of International Law. I participated in the conference and presented a paper there shortly after I first read Professor Brian Lepard's book, *Customary International Law: A New Theory with Practical Applications*. This chapter incorporates further clarifications of my thoughts on Professor Lepard's theory and women's rights.

1 See, e.g., *Military and Paramilitary Activities in and against Nicaragua (Nicaragua v. United States of America)*, Merits, Judgment of 27 June 1986, 1986 ICJ Rep. 14, 97, para. 183. The ICJ ruled that the basic rules contained in the Geneva Conventions have passed into the corpus of general customary law. See ibid., 114. See also "Report of the International Law Commission," Sixty-Eighth Session (2 May–10 June and 4 July–12 August 2016), UN Doc. A/71/10 (2016), 76–79, Draft Conclusion 2, entitled "Two constituent elements" (stating that "to determine the existence and content of a rule of customary international law, it is necessary to ascertain whether there is a general practice that is accepted as law (*opinio juris*)").

2 Brian D. Lepard, *Customary International Law: A New Theory with Practical Applications* (New York: Cambridge University Press, 2010).

3 Ibid., 8. For further explanation of Lepard's theory, see Brian D. Lepard, "Toward a New Theory of Customary International Human Rights Law," in this volume.

As described by one commentator, Lepard's new theory addresses "the level of evidence required to demonstrate the existence of *opinio juris* in circumstances where states have not made their own views clear."[4] Lepard joins others who have challenged the traditional sources of customary international law.[5] Under his theory, a norm of customary international law can be established even if consistent state practice does not exist. State practice becomes evidence of the belief required under Lepard's definition. One essential element in the development of his theory is the identification and inclusion of "fundamental ethical principles," which are defined as "all of those ethical principles apparent in contemporary international law that are logically related to a preeminent ethical principle of 'unity in diversity.'"[6] Lepard asserts that this principle of unity in diversity "maintains that all human beings should seek to be unified as members of one human family while respecting one another's right to diversity of language, religion, and culture and individual freedom of thought, conscience, belief, and expression."[7] He categorizes these fundamental ethical principles in descending order of importance as "essential," "compelling," and "fundamental."[8]

To make his case, Lepard first examines the enigmatic nature of customary international law, as he has done here in Chapter 1, devoting particular attention to the customary law status of human rights, and applies game theory to explain the positions that states might take regarding customary international law norms. He focuses on some of the enigmas of traditional customary international law doctrine, including determining the existence of *opinio juris*, the necessity of a state practice requirement, the definition of *jus cogens* and *erga omnes* customary norms, the persistent objector doctrine,[9] and the role of ethics in the formation of customary international law.[10] He then proceeds to

4 Aurel Sari, "Book Reviews: *Customary International Law: A New Theory with Practical Applications*," 24 *Leiden Journal of International Law* 531 (2011), available at www.aurelsari.co.uk/2011/01/customary-international-law-a-new-theory-with-practical-applications/.

5 See, e.g., Roozbeh (Rudy) B. Baker, "Customary International Law in the 21st Century: Old Challenges and New Debates," 21 *European Journal of International Law* 173 (2010), 180–83; Anthea Elizabeth Roberts, "Traditional and Modern Approaches to Customary International Law: A Reconciliation," 95 *American Journal of International Law* 757 (2001), 758; Hilary C.M. Charlesworth, "Customary International Law and the Nicaragua Case," 1984–87 *Australian Yearbook of International Law* 1.

6 Brian D. Lepard, "How Should the ICC Prosecutor Exercise His or Her Discretion? The Role of Fundamental Ethical Principles," 43 *John Marshall Law Review* 553 (2010), 553.

7 Ibid. (citing Lepard, *Customary International Law*, 78–81).

8 Lepard, *Customary International Law*, 81–82. See also ibid., 83, Fig. 5.1.

9 See, e.g., ibid., 229–42; Restatement (Third) of the Foreign Relations Law of the United States, § 102, comment b ("A principle of customary law is not binding on a state that declares its dissent from the principle during its development.").

10 See generally Lepard, *Customary International Law*, 1–13.

develop his new theory of customary international law as explained here in Chapter 8, where he discusses the application of the theory to international human rights law and certain norms in particular.[11]

In this chapter, I apply Lepard's theory to the human rights of women and argue that the theory is helpful and appropriate to apply in analyzing the customary law status of these rights. I first explore the suppression of women's rights based on state and local law and how this suppression has been addressed by international law. I then attempt to create a solution that could lead to the recognition of women's humans rights as customary international law based on a modern aspirational view of customary international law,[12] and in particular on Lepard's definition of it.

9.2 CUSTOMARY INTERNATIONAL LAW AND HUMAN RIGHTS

Lepard adds to the growing number of scholars who recognize the potential of customary international law in protecting human rights. As Lepard notes in Chapter 1, the International Court of Justice ("ICJ") has increasingly considered and relied on customary international law to resolve disputes, including those involving human rights.[13]

Many scholars have argued, and courts have recognized, that particular norms protecting human rights are now a part of customary international law.[14] However, there is continuing debate about which rights so qualify and whether all human rights have attained the status of customary law. In the preceding chapter in this volume Lepard recognizes the lack of universal agreement about the customary law status of the norms in the three human rights instruments commonly referred to as the "International Bill of Human Rights": The Universal Declaration of Human Rights ("UDHR"),[15] the International Covenant on Civil and Political Rights ("ICCPR"),[16] and the International Covenant on Economic, Social and Cultural Rights

11 See Lepard, "Toward a New Theory of Customary International Human Rights Law," in this volume.

12 On modern views of customary international law, see generally Roberts, "Traditional and Modern Approaches to Customary International Law."

13 See Lepard, *Customary International Law*, 3–6.

14 See e.g., Tom Dannenbaum, "Translating the Standard of Effective Control into a System of Effective Accountability," 51 *Harvard International Law Journal* 113 (2010), 135–36; Anthony D'Amato, "Human Rights as Part of Customary International Law: A Plea for Change of Paradigms," 25 *Georgia Journal of International & Comparative Law* 47 (1995–96); Louis B. Sohn, "The New International Law: Protection of the Rights of Individuals Rather Than States," 32 *American University Law Review* 1 (1982), 12–13.

15 Universal Declaration of Human Rights, GA Res. 217A (III) (1948) ("UDHR").

16 International Covenant on Civil and Political Rights, 999 UNTS 171 (1966) ("ICCPR").

("ICESCR").[17] One scholar has described these instruments as providing the "shared moral consciousness"[18] that results in a legal obligation with respect to certain human rights. Other commentators have suggested that customary human rights law has been established based on either the UDHR in its entirety[19] or some select provisions of it.[20] Nevertheless, debates persist about just which human rights are now part of customary law.

Lepard suggests that the guidelines he has proposed for determining the existence of customary international law can resolve these debates. As noted earlier, under his theory we focus not on universal or widespread practice, but on evidence that "states generally believe that it is desirable now or in the near future to have an authoritative legal principle or rule prescribing, permitting, or prohibiting certain conduct."[21] The question for analysis he suggests is: "Do states generally believe it is desirable, now or in the near future, to recognize some or all of the human rights proclaimed in the Universal Declaration as binding or persuasive legal obligations for all states?"[22] In response to this question, he demonstrates, by examining the language of the relevant instruments[23] and UN resolutions and records of discussions, that there is evidence that states intended to create some legal human rights obligations binding on all states apart from treaties.[24]

In addition, some national courts have adopted the view that treaties and declarations can be evidence of customary human rights law. For example, U.S. courts have looked to Section 702 of the Restatement (Third) of the Foreign Relations Law of the United States[25] and other sections of the Restatement to define violations of customary international law.[26] The former

[17] International Covenant on Economic, Social and Cultural Rights, 993 UNTS 3 (1966) ("ICESCR").

[18] Joan F. Hartman, "'Unusual' Punishment: The Domestic Effects of International Norms Restricting the Application of the Death Penalty," 52 *University of Cincinnati Law Review* 655 (1983), 676.

[19] See generally Karen Parker and Lyn Beth Neylon, "Jus Cogens: Compelling the Law of Human Rights," 12 *Hastings International & Comparative Law Review* 411 (1989), 442; Richard B. Lillich, "Invoking International Human Rights Law in Domestic Courts," 54 *University of Cincinnati Law Review* 367 (1985), 394–96; Kate Parlett, *The Individual in the International Legal System* (Cambridge and New York: Cambridge University Press, 2011), 301–07, 312–21, 322–23; Lepard, *Customary International Law*, 318–19 (describing this view).

[20] See Beth Stevens and Michael Ratner, *International Human Rights Litigation in U.S. Courts* (Irvington-on-Hudson, NY: Transnational Publishers, 1996), 66–69.

[21] Lepard, *Customary International Law*, 112.

[22] Ibid., 319.

[23] See ibid., 312–30.

[24] See ibid.

[25] Restatement (Third), § 702.

[26] See, e.g., *Kadic v. Karadzic*, 70 F.3d 232 (2nd Cir. 1995), 241; *Chubb & Son, Inc. v. Asiana Airlines*, 214 F.3d 301 (2nd Cir. 2000), 307–08 ("Customary international law results from a

section identifies a number of human rights that it maintains have risen to the level of customary law.[27]

Lepard suggests that by including in the analysis of *opinio juris* a consideration of fundamental ethical principles, human rights treaties may be evidence that states believe that the human rights norms in them should have at least persuasive authority apart from the treaties, meaning that they should guide states in their decision making.[28] Fundamental ethical principles require respect for human rights, and in some instances limitations on state sovereignty. As Dinah Shelton has noted, due in part to increasing globalization, the "international protection of human rights" reflects "universal values about human dignity that limit the power of the state and reduce the sphere of sovereignty."[29] Two of the fundamental ethical principles identified by Lepard that are reflected in international law and that are particularly relevant to human rights are the equal dignity of all human beings and the universal human duty to respect human rights.[30]

Lepard goes through a similar analysis with the UN Charter and the ICCPR. He discusses, but rejects, the argument by some scholars that the lack of "any enforcement mechanism or system of reparations" in these treaties is evidence against the conclusion that they help create customary international law.[31] Lepard concludes that some of these instruments provide evidence of the requisite *opinio juris* for a persuasive obligation that is now part of customary international law, as well as the requisite *opinio juris* to establish that certain rights listed are now "fully binding" under customary international law.[32]

In this connection, section 702 of the Restatement (Third)[33] provides that a state violates international law if, as a matter of state policy, it practices,

general and consistent practice of states followed by them from a sense of legal obligation," quoting Restatement (Third), § 102(2)).

27 See Restatement (Third), § 702.

28 See Lepard, *Customary International Law*, 328–30.

29 Shelton, "Protecting Human Rights in a Globalized World," 277–78.

30 See Lepard, *Customary International Law*, 82–86. For evidence of states' recognition of these principles, see, e.g., UDHR, art. 1 (providing that "all human beings are born free and equal in dignity and rights. They are endowed with reason and conscience and should act towards one another in a spirit of brotherhood.")

31 See Lepard, *Customary International Law*, 327 (citing Arthur M. Weisburd, "Customary International Law: The Problem of Treaties," 21 *Vanderbilt Journal of Transnational Law* 1 (1988), 25–29).

32 Lepard, *Customary International Law*, 327–28. Lepard cites Richard B. Lillich, "Civil Rights," in *Human Rights in International Law: Legal and Policy Issues*, vol. 1, edited by Theodor Meron 115 (Oxford: Clarendon Press, 1984), 118 (stating with respect to provisions of the ICCPR that they "now can be said to have helped create norms of customary international law – including ones having *jus cogens* status – binding even states which have yet to ratify it").

33 Restatement (Third), § 702.

encourages, or condones certain conduct that violates "fundamental rights," including genocide and slavery.[34] The Restatement list has been suggested by some commentators, including Lepard, as identifying rights that are now fully binding under customary international law.[35] Lepard, however, urges that this should not be an exclusive list.[36] There is support for this position in the comments to the section, which state that "the list is not necessarily complete, and is not closed."[37] Lepard suggests that a determination of the human rights that are "fully binding" and are now customary international law can benefit from a classification of rights according to the same nomenclature for fundamental ethical principles, namely a ranking of human rights as "essential," "compelling," or "fundamental."[38] He defines "essential" human rights as those that are "very closely related to 'unity in diversity' and should, because of their moral importance, preempt any possible reasons for not respecting them in all, or virtually all, cases."[39] He suggests that some limitations may be permissible for compelling and fundamental rights, but not essential rights.[40]

In some areas of law, it appears to be essential to prove the existence of both consistent state practice and *opinio juris* to establish the existence of a customary international law norm. These are, of course, the two elements emphasized by the International Law Commission in the draft conclusions it adopted in 2016.[41]

However, there is a strong case for demanding less extensive evidence of consistent state practice in the case of human rights norms – a position consistent with Lepard's approach. Lepard finds support for an approach that deemphasizes concrete evidence of state practice regarding human rights norms in Theodor Meron's observation that the ICJ has also placed less emphasis on state practice, "especially … inconsistent or contrary practice,"[42] in evaluating the customary law status of human rights.[43] This approach also seems warranted because, as Rebecca J. Cook has observed, state practice may be slow to conform to human rights treaties because these treaties are often viewed

34 Ibid., § 702, reporters' note 11 (identifying prohibitions against genocide, slavery, murder or disappearance, torture or other cruel, inhuman or degrading treatment, prolonged arbitrary detention, and systematic racial discrimination as norms of customary international law).

35 Lepard, *Customary International Law*, 331.

36 Ibid. (noting his discussion of freedom of religion or belief in chapter 24).

37 Restatement (Third), § 702, comment a.

38 Lepard, *Customary International Law*, 82–86. See also ibid., 85, Fig. 5.2.

39 Ibid., 84.

40 Ibid., 84–85.

41 See "Report of the International Law Commission," Sixty-Eighth Session, Draft Conclusion 2.

42 Theodor Meron, *Human Rights and Humanitarian Norms as Customary Law* (Oxford: Clarendon Press, 1989), 113–14.

43 Lepard, *Customary International Law*, 332.

by states as "likely to jeopardize the sovereignty of state parties without, at the same time, offering them a commercial advantage that may render a compromise of sovereignty worthwhile."[44] Human rights treaties have as their purpose the protection of individual rights. Therefore, the impact of human rights treaties is considered "less certain than that of commercial treaties."[45]

The question remains as to whether it is all or only certain human rights norms that qualify as *jus cogens* norms. I use the four-part test suggested by Lepard[46] to make the case that women's human rights are *jus cogens* norms. Customary international human rights norms that rise to the level of *jus cogens* may also impose obligations *erga omnes*. In support of his position that "[h]uman rights norms provide a strong case for *erga omnes* status," Eric Posner argues that human rights violations by one state may cause harm in foreign states because of the destabilization in the offending state that results in effects across the border in those foreign states.[47]

Arguably, the issues of reservations, derogations, and persistent objector status may be more troublesome with respect to the development of customary international law in the human rights context. States may seek to derogate from human rights commitments. The derogations available for human rights treaties, however, may serve as only weak evidence that certain rights are not *jus cogens*, because, as Christopher Michaelsen has noted, "only a very limited number of states have officially made use of those derogation clauses."[48]

44 Rebecca J. Cook, "Reservations to the Convention on the Elimination of all Forms of Discrimination against Women," 30 *Virginia Journal of International Law* 643 (1990), 650 (citing Pierre-Henri Imbert, "Reservations and Human Rights Conventions," 6 *Human Rights Review* 28 (1981), 30).

45 Ibid. But see *Barcelona Traction, Light and Power Company, Limited (Belgium v. Spain), Second Phase*, Judgment of 5 February 1970, Dissenting Opinion of Judge Riphagen, 1970 ICJ Rep. 3, 337–38, para. 6 (suggesting that even in international commerce state practice is not the determining factor for customary international law, stating that "as in the protection of international commerce, the different methods adopted by the municipal law of different countries are irrelevant to the attainment of the objectives of the rules of customary international law").

46 Lepard, *Customary International Law*, 243–44.

47 Eric A. Posner, "Erga Omnes Norms, Institutionalization, and Constitutionalism in International Law," 165 *Journal of Institutional and Theoretical Economics* 2 (2009), 13, available at http://ssrn.com/abstract=1211424. See also Donna E. Arzt, "Three Degrees of Separation: The Evolving Convergence of Human Rights Law, Humanitarian Law, and Refugee Law," in *War in the Twentieth Century: Reflections at Century's End*, edited by Michael A. Hennessy and B. J. C. Mckercher 167 (Westport, CT: Praeger, 2003), 169.

48 Christopher Michaelsen, "Permanent Legal Emergencies and the Derogation Clause in International Human Rights Treaties: A Contradiction?" in *Post 9/11 and the State of Permanent Legal Emergency: Security and Human Rights in Countering Terrorism*, edited by Aniceto Masferrer 287 (Dordrecht: Springer, 2012), 289 (noting that a "prominent exception to this trend was the United Kingdom which, in late 2001, derogated from obligations under

At the same time, as Lepard explains, it is possible to conclude that there may be reasons to prohibit limitations or derogations regarding some rights other than their *jus cogens* character. Thus, the existence of such prohibitions on derogations of certain rights does not necessarily mean that the rights are *jus cogens*. Their status as *jus cogens* norms must first be established under his four-part test.[49]

9.3 WOMEN'S RIGHTS AS HUMAN RIGHTS

If there are enigmas present in defining and applying customary international law generally, these enigmas become even more pronounced when trying to define women's human rights under customary international law. Some feminists attribute this to the fact that the development of the law on human rights, including the concept of *jus cogens*, has been from a male perspective,[50] with little input from women,[51] and based on the view that sex discrimination is not as damaging as discrimination based on other characteristics, such as race.[52]

An analysis generally of the benefit of customary international law, and more specifically Lepard's theory of customary international law, to women as a means of improving their lives requires first an analysis of how domestic and international law have failed to help women. This can be accomplished by using a form of analysis referred to by feminists as "asking the woman question." As Katherine Bartlett describes it, "[i]n law, asking the woman question means examining how the law fails to take into account the experiences and values that seem more typical of women than of men, for whatever reason, or how existing legal standards and concepts might disadvantage women."[53]

Asking the woman question in consideration of whether particular rights are now part of customary international law raises complex issues. This is because customary international law regarding the rights of particularly vulnerable groups is new and evolving. Women have been recognized as such

both the European Convention on Human Rights (ECHR) and the International Covenant on Civil and Political Rights (ICCPR)").

49 See Lepard, *Customary International Law*, 339.

50 See, e.g., Hilary Charlesworth and Christine Chinkin, *The Boundaries of International Law: A Feminist Analysis* (Executive Park, NY: Juris Pub.; Manchester, UK: Manchester University Press, 2000), 1, 195.

51 See Berta Esperanza Hernandez-Truyol, "Women's Rights as Human Rights – Rules, Realities and the Role of Culture: A Formula for Reform," 21 *Brooklyn Journal of International Law* 605 (1996), 608; Jo Lynn Southard, "Protection of Women's Human Rights under the Convention on the Elimination of All Forms of Discrimination against Women," 8 *Pace International Law Review* 1 (1996), 87.

52 See Charlesworth and Chinkin, *The Boundaries of International Law*, 137.

53 Katharine T. Bartlett, "Feminist Legal Methods," 103 *Harvard Law Review* 829 (1990), 837.

a vulnerable group from the inception of the journey started by nations to define human rights. Indeed, the UN Charter and the UDHR both prohibit discrimination regarding the enjoyment of human rights on the basis of sex.[54]

As J. Patrick Kelly notes in Chapter 2, the identification of a need to protect certain rights (as in the case of rights of aliens) requires further inquiry into the specific rights that must be protected – and whether a common consensus exists with respect to those specific rights.[55] In the case of a norm of nondiscrimination based on gender, there is increasing recognition of such a norm in treaties and declarations following the UN Charter and the Universal Declaration, and a number of authorities now recognize the norm as a norm of customary international law. To give a few examples, in 1993, the UN World Conference on Human Rights in Vienna confirmed that women's rights are human rights.[56] The Convention on the Elimination of All Forms of Discrimination against Women ("CEDAW"),[57] the Declaration on the Elimination of Violence against Women ("DEVAW"),[58] and the Inter-American Convention on the Prevention, Punishment and Eradication of Violence against Women ("IACPW")[59] are some of the human rights instruments that have focused on women's human rights. Regarding the customary law status of women's rights – a subject I analyze in more detail later in the chapter – the comments to the "Human Rights" section of the Restatement (Third) of the Foreign Relations Law of the United States noted that at the time the American Law Institute ("ALI") adopted the Restatement in 1987, "freedom from gender discrimination,"

[54] See UN Charter, art. 1, para. 3; UDHR, art. 2.

[55] See J. Patrick Kelly, "Customary International Law in Historical Context: The Exercise of Power without General Acceptance," in this volume.

[56] Vienna Declaration and Programme of Action, adopted by the World Conference on Human Rights in Vienna on 25 June 1993, UN Doc. A/CONF.157/23, 12 July 1993, para. 18, available at www.ohchr.org/en/professionalinterest/pages/vienna.aspx ("The human rights of women should form an integral part of the United Nations human rights activities, including the promotion of all human rights instruments relating to women.").

[57] Convention on the Elimination of All Forms of Discrimination against Women, Dec. 18, 1979, 1249 UNTS 13 ("CEDAW"), GA Res. 34/180, 34 UN GAOR Supp. (No. 46) at 193, UN Doc. A/34/46, entered into force Sept. 3, 1981. CEDAW also has an Optional Protocol that permits individuals or groups to lodge complaints against states that have ratified the Protocol. See Optional Protocol to the Convention on the Elimination of All Forms of Discrimination Against Women, GA Res. 54/4, annex, 54 UN GAOR Supp. (No. 49) at 5, UN Doc. A/54/49 (Vol. I) (2000), entered into force Dec. 22, 2000. The CEDAW Committee has also issued general recommendations on particular issues affecting women. See, e.g., General Recommendation No. 19, UN Doc. No. A/47/38 (1992) (addressing gender-based violence).

[58] GA Res. 48/104, 48 UN GAOR Supp. (No. 49) at 217, UN Doc. A/48/49 (1993).

[59] Reprinted in 33 *International Legal Materials* 1534 (1994), entered into force March 5, 1995.

even though not universally practiced, "may already be a principle of customary international law."[60]

Because of the discrimination that continued to exist against women, despite the nondiscrimination provisions of the UDHR, the ICCPR, and the ICESCR, the UN General Assembly adopted CEDAW in 1979.[61] As of August 2016, 189 countries had ratified CEDAW.[62] As Rebecca J. Cook has explained, "[CEDAW] is the definitive international legal instrument requiring respect for and observance of the human rights of women; it is universal in reach, comprehensive in scope and legally binding in character."[63] CEDAW contains a broad definition of discrimination against women in Article 1, affirming:

> For the purposes of the present Convention, the term "discrimination against women" shall mean any distinction, exclusion or restriction made on the basis of sex which has the effect or purpose of impairing or nullifying the recognition, enjoyment or exercise by women, irrespective of their marital status, on a basis of equality of men and women, of human rights and fundamental freedoms in the political, economic, social, cultural, civil or any other field.[64]

In part because of the inclusion of a number of specific measures that states are required to implement, CEDAW has been described as "essentially an international bill of rights for women and a framework for women's participation in the development process,"[65] and as being instrumental in bringing about changes in women's lives. For example, Amnesty International reports that CEDAW "has encouraged the development of citizenship rights in

60 Restatement (Third), § 702, comment l. See also Geoffrey A. Hoffman, "In Search of an International Human Right to Receive Information," 25 *Loyola of Los Angeles International & Comparative Law Review* 165 (2003), 186.

61 See CEDAW, preamble ("Concerned, however, that despite these various instruments extensive discrimination against women continues to exist").

62 A listing of all parties to CEDAW and the Optional Protocol is available at https://treaties.un.org/Pages/ViewDetails.aspx?src=TREATY&mtdsg_no=IV-8&chapter=4&lang=en (last accessed 29 August 2016).

63 Cook, "Reservations to the Convention on the Elimination of All Forms of Discrimination against Women," 643. See also Hilary Charlesworth, Christine Chinkin, and Shelley Wright, "Feminist Approaches to International Law," 85 *American Journal of International Law* 613 (1991), 624 (noting that despite the absence of women on international treaty bodies, CEDAW is the only one that has been criticized by the Economic and Social Council for its gender imbalance). See generally Nienke Grossman, "Sex on the Bench: Do Women Judges Matter to the Legitimacy of International Courts?" 12 *Chicago Journal of International Law* 647 (2012).

64 CEDAW, art. 1.

65 International Women's Rights Action Watch, *The Convention on the Elimination of All Forms of Discrimination against Women* (Minneapolis, MN: Humphrey Institute of Public Affairs, 1988), 1.

Botswana and Japan, inheritance rights in the United Republic of Tanzania, [and] property rights and political participation in Costa Rica, [and] has fostered development of domestic violence laws in Turkey, Nepal, South Africa, and the Republic of Korea."[66]

The 1995 United Nations Fourth World Conference on Women in Beijing[67] included in its adopted Platform for Action on human rights for women the acknowledgment that the achievement of women's freedom from discrimination "is undermined by the discrepancies between some national legislation and international law and international instruments on human rights."[68] It also focused on the need to have all states become party to CEDAW and other human rights instruments and to eliminate reservations that are incompatible with the object and purpose of CEDAW.[69]

Although the UDHR, ICCPR, and ICESCR are commonly described together as the International Bill of Human Rights, complaints about violations of human rights often rely on the UDHR and ICCPR, without reference to the ICESCR. This is in part because there is less universal agreement on the rights guaranteed by the ICESCR. Nevertheless, it is viewed by many scholars as the primary instrument within the International Bill of Human Rights that provides protections against particular actions that have special consequences for women.[70] For example, Article 7 of the ICESCR provides women with a right to "equal remuneration" and "guaranteed conditions of work not inferior to those enjoyed by men."[71]

In addition, CEDAW and subsequent instruments that address the denial of rights of women have been subjected to numerous reservations by states

[66] Amnesty International USA, "A Fact Sheet on CEDAW: Treaty for the Rights of Women," August 25, 2005, available at www.amnestyusa.org/sites/default/files/pdfs/cedaw_fact_sheet .pdf.

[67] See "Report of the Fourth World Conference on Women, Beijing Declaration, Annex 1," UN Doc. A/CONF.177/20 (1995), para. 32, available at www.un.org/womenwatch/daw/beijing/ fwcwn.html.

[68] *Beijing Declaration and Platform for Action*, in "Report of the Fourth World Conference on Women, Beijing, 4–15 September, 1995," vol. 1, UN Doc. A/CONF.177/20/Rev.1, UN Sales No. 96.IV.13 (1996), para. 219, available at www.un.org/womenwatch/daw/beijing/platform/ human.htm.

[69] See generally Belinda Clark, "The Vienna Convention Reservations Regime and the Convention on Discrimination against Women," 85 *American Journal of International Law* 281 (1991), 306.

[70] See Christine M. Chinkin, "Resolving Conflicting Human Rights Standards in International Law," 85 *American Society of International Law Proceedings* 336 (1991), 351. See also Brad R. Roth, "The CEDAW as a Collective Approach to Women's Rights," 24 *Michigan Journal of International Law* 187 (2002), 190 (discussing bifurcation of human rights between the ICCPR and ICESCR).

[71] ICESCR, art. 7(a)(i).

parties.[72] The justifications asserted by states for reservations that relate to the granting of rights to women are often based on the provisions of state constitutions or other state laws, as well as assertions that the state making the reservation is a party to other international human rights treaties that protect rights conflicting with the granting of rights to women, such as treaties guaranteeing religious rights. States may also invoke respect for the rights of indigenous peoples to implement their own customs, and customary domestic law more generally, as grounds for limiting the rights of women under CEDAW. In any event, these reservations raise the question of whether they are sufficiently widespread to impede the formation of a customary law rule – or at least help qualify the reserving states as persistent objectors to any such rule.

Taking into account this historical context relating to the recognition of women's rights in international human rights law, in the following sections I first look at the role of international law to date in combating three particular forms of discrimination against women. I then apply Lepard's theory of customary law to determine the customary law status of women's rights as well as their status as norms of *jus cogens* and as *erga omnes* norms.

9.4 THE ROLE OF INTERNATIONAL LAW IN ADDRESSING CONFLICTS BETWEEN WOMEN'S HUMAN RIGHTS AND DOMESTIC STATUTORY AND CUSTOMARY LAWS

An examination of cases in three areas of the law – (1) nationality and membership in a citizenship group, (2) land tenure rights, and (3) violence against women – helps demonstrate that the application of international law has helped improve women's lives. However, it also shows that discriminatory domestic statutory and customary laws in these fields continue to present significant challenges to the achievement of gender equality.[73]

First, the rights and privileges of nationality and citizenship have historically been denied to women in various situations. Even when women

[72] Regarding reservations to CEDAW, see generally "The United Nations Human Rights Treaties, Reservations, Declarations, Objections and Derogations – CEDAW," available at www.bayefsky.com/docs.php/area/reservations/node/2/treaty/cedaw/opt/0.

[73] This section discusses only a small sample of situations where discriminatory laws have disadvantaged women. See generally Jessica Neuwirth, "Inequality before the Law: Holding States Accountable for Sex Discriminatory Laws under the Convention on the Elimination of All Forms of Discrimination against Women and through the Beijing Platform for Action," 18 *Harvard Human Rights Journal* 19 (2005), 19 (noting that "[w]ife obedience is mandated by law in Mali, wife beating is permitted by law in Northern Nigeria, women do not have the right to vote in Kuwait, [and] in Pakistan, the attestation of a woman regarding financial obligations is worth half the attestation of a man").

are viewed as full citizens, they may lose this status upon a decision to "marry out" of the defined citizenship group.[74] Defining nationality and tribal membership based on patrilineal lines has led to the exclusion of women from political rights and other benefits of community membership, including the transmission of their nationality to their children. In this area, a comparison of two cases, *Santa Clara Pueblo v. Martinez* (a decision of the U.S. Supreme Court)[75] and *Sandra Lovelace v. Canada* (an opinion of the UN Human Rights Committee),[76] reveals how international law has been used to end discriminatory practices in pursuit of freedom from sex inequality.

In *Martinez*, a full-blooded member of the Santa Clara Pueblo tribe and her daughter brought an action in U.S. federal court on behalf of similarly situated women and children. Their lawsuit was based on a federal law that provided that "[n]o Indian tribe in exercising powers of self-government shall … deny to any person within its jurisdiction the equal protection of its laws."[77] They brought the lawsuit[78] to challenge a membership ordinance of the Santa Clara Pueblo Council. The ordinance provided that children became members of the Santa Clara Pueblo if they were born to Santa Clara Pueblo men who married women who were not Santa Clara Pueblo, but children born to Santa Clara Pueblo women who married men who were not Santa Clara Pueblo did not become members of the tribe.[79] In addition, naturalization was prohibited. The U.S. Court of Appeals for the Tenth Circuit ruled that the federal courts had jurisdiction to hear the tribal matter, and that, in enacting the relevant federal law, Congress intended to make important civil rights in the Constitution applicable to tribal members.[80] As the Court of Appeals noted, if it was a valid concern of the tribe that the inclusion of children of mixed marriages in the tribe would "swell the population … and diminish the individual shares of … property,"

74 See generally Robyn Emerton, *Women's Human Rights: Leading International and National Cases* (London and Portland, OR: Cavendish, 2005), xxxviii–xl (noting that some of these laws are based on the disfavoring of dual citizenship); Lucy Williams, "Agency and Citizenship in Cross-Border Marriages," in *Contours of Citizenship: Women, Diversity and Practices of Citizenship*, edited by Margaret Abraham et al. 193 (Farnham, UK and Burlington, VT: Ashgate, 2010).

75 436 U.S. 49 (1978).

76 UN Human Rights Committee, Communication No. R.6/24, UN Doc. Supp. No. 40 (A/36/40) (1981), 166 ("*Lovelace*").

77 Title I of the Indian Civil Rights Act of 1968, 25 U.S.C. § 1302(8).

78 *Martinez v. Santa Clara Pueblo*, 402 F. Supp. 5 (D. N. Mex. 1975).

79 Ibid., 6.

80 *Martinez v. Santa Clara Pueblo*, 540 F.2d 1039 (10th Cir. 1976).

then the children of all mixed marriages could have been excluded from membership, rather than only the mixed marriages where the tribal member was a woman.[81]

However, the U.S. Supreme Court reversed this holding.[82] Once the Supreme Court ruled and overturned this Court of Appeals decision, no further review of the case was available. Rather, it was up to Congress to act to address these tribal membership issues. Unfortunately, Congress took no action to change the result.

The Canadian case of *Sandra Lovelace v. Canada* resulted from a petition to the UN Human Rights Committee ("HRC"), and demonstrates how legal action can have a beneficial result for women when international law is invoked. *Lovelace* also involved the denial of rights of tribal membership to women based on marriage. This included the loss of the right to live on the tribal reserve. The Canadian Indian Act recognized indigenous customary law, and provided in section 12(1)(b) that an Indian man who marries a non-Indian woman does not lose his Indian status, while an Indian woman who marries a non-Indian man does. The petitioner filed a communication with the HRC, which is established under Article 28 of the ICCPR,[83] and pursuant to the First Optional Protocol of the ICCPR,[84] which Canada had ratified. She alleged that the Indian Act was discriminatory and contrary to Articles 2(1), 3, 23(1) and (4), 26, and 27 of the ICCPR.[85]

The HRC concluded that the enforcement of the Indian Act to deny Sandra Lovelace membership in her tribe was a "breach by Canada of article 27 of the Covenant."[86] Article 27 reads as follows: "In those States in which ethnic, religious or linguistic minorities exist, persons belonging to such minorities shall not be denied the right, in community with the other members of their group, to enjoy their own culture, to profess and practise their own religion, or to use their own language."[87]

81 Ibid., 1047.

82 *Santa Clara Pueblo v. Martinez*, 436 U.S. 49 (1978).

83 ICCPR, art. 28.

84 Optional Protocol to the ICCPR, adopted and opened for signature, ratification and accession by GA Res. 2200A (XXI) of 16 December 1966.

85 See *Lovelace*, para. 1. Lovelace also contended that she was not required to exhaust local remedies as generally required by Article 5(2)(b) of the First Optional Protocol, since the Supreme Court of Canada, in *The Attorney-General of Canada v. Jeanette Lavell, Richard Isaac et al. v. Yvonne Bédard*, [1974] S.C.R. 1349, held that section 12(1)(b) was fully operative, irrespective of its inconsistency with the Canadian Bill of Rights on account of discrimination based on sex. See ibid.

86 *Lovelace*, para. 19.

87 ICCPR, art. 27.

The HRC concluded that Article 27 should be construed along with other articles of the ICCPR,[88] including Article 26. Article 26 prohibits discrimination on a number of grounds, including sex, and provides:

> All persons are equal before the law and are entitled without any discrimination to the equal protection of the law. In this respect, the law shall prohibit any discrimination and guarantee to all persons equal and effective protection against discrimination on any ground such as race, colour, sex, language, religion, political or other opinion, national or social origin, property, birth or other status.[89]

As a result of the HRC opinion and accompanying pressure from women, the Indian Act was amended.[90] The amendments provided for the reinstatement of status to women whose status had been revoked upon marriage to a non-Indian man.

Other cases that involve the use of international law to achieve favorable results for women in the area of membership rights include (1) *Shirin Aumeeruddy-Cziffra and 19 Other Mauritian Women v. Mauritius* (an opinion of the UN HRC),[91] in which the HRC determined that a Mauritian immigration law discriminated against women on the ground of sex and that Mauritius was in breach of ICCPR Article 2(1), Article 3, and Article 26 in relation to Articles 17(1) and 23(1); and (2) *Attorney-General v. Dow*,[92] decided by the Botswana Court of Appeal in 1992.

Attorney-General v. Dow involved the Botswana domestic Citizenship Act, which, among other provisions, stated that a child born in Botswana would be considered a citizen of Botswana by birth and descent if his father was a citizen of Botswana (without regard to the mother's citizenship, if she was married to the father).[93] The Botswana Court of Appeal rejected arguments that these discriminatory laws were necessary "to preserve the male orientation of Botswana society,"[94] pointing out that "tradition and custom have never been static."[95] The Court

88 See *Lovelace*, para. 7.4, 11 (noting that Articles 12, 17, and 23, and Articles 2 and 3, may also be applicable to the claims of discrimination).

89 ICCPR, art. 26.

90 See An Act to Amend the Indian Act, S.C. 1985, c. 27, Bill C-31.

91 UN Human Rights Committee, Communication No. 35/1978 (9 April 1981), UN Doc. CCPR/C/OP/1 (1984), 67.

92 *Attorney-General v. Dow*, 1992 B.L.R. 119; 103 I.L.R. 128 (Bots. Ct. App. 1992), available at www.law.georgetown.edu/rossrights/docs/cases/Dow.html, reprinted in *The Citizenship Case: The Attorney-General of The Republic of Botswana v. Unity Dow Court Documents, Judgements, Cases and Materials*, edited by Unity Dow 123 (Gaborone, Botswana: Lentswe La Lesedi (Pty) Ltd., 1995).

93 See ibid.

94 Ibid. (opinion of Judge President Amissah).

95 Ibid.

declared that sex discrimination is generally prohibited by the Botswana Constitution and also applied international law to reach its conclusion, affirming: "Botswana is a member of the community of civilised states which has undertaken to abide by certain standards of conduct, and, unless it is impossible to do otherwise, it would be wrong for its Courts to interpret its legislation in a manner which conflicts with the international obligations Botswana has undertaken."[96]

Regional intergovernmental organizations in Europe, Africa, and the Americas have also referred to international law as a source of protection for a woman's right to membership in a community and to nationality. One example is found in the application of the American Convention on Human Rights ("American Convention" or "Convention"),[97] adopted by the Organization of American States ("OAS"), to proposed amendments in the 1980s to Costa Rica's naturalization laws.[98] The proposed naturalization law amendments permitted husbands to sponsor their wives for citizenship, but prohibited wives from sponsoring their husbands. Article 20 of the American Convention, entitled "Right to Nationality," provides that every person "has the right to a nationality" and "has the right to the nationality of the state in whose territory he was born if he does not have the right to any other nationality." It also asserts that "[n]o one shall be arbitrarily deprived of his nationality or of the right to change it."[99] Article 24 furthermore states: "All persons are equal before the law. Consequently, they are entitled, without discrimination, to equal protection of the law."[100] In concluding that the proposed amendments contained discriminatory provisions, the Inter-American Court of Human Rights stated that issues of membership and nationality are "linked

[96] Ibid. The Court took into consideration the African Charter on Human and Peoples' Rights, CEDAW, and the Convention on the Rights of the Child.

[97] American Convention on Human Rights, 1144 UNTS 123 (1969) ("American Convention").

[98] See Advisory Opinion OC-4/84, "Proposed Amendments to the Naturalization Provisions of the Constitution of Costa Rica," Inter-Am. Ct. H.R. (ser. A) (Jan. 19, 1984), reprinted in 5 *Human Rights Law Journal* 161 (1984), 168, available at www1.umn.edu/humanrts/iachr/b_11_4d.htm. The Inter-American Commission on Human Rights ("IACHR") and the Inter-American Court of Human Rights are primarily responsible for monitoring the implementation by states parties of the human rights obligations contained in the Charter of the OAS and the American Convention. The IACHR is the principal body of the inter-American system charged with human rights protection. The Commission investigates petitions alleging violations of human rights by the member states. The Inter-American Court issues advisory opinions and decides the merits of contentious cases. See generally Thomas Buergenthal, "The Advisory Practice of the Inter-American Human Rights Court," 79 *American Journal of International Law* 1 (1985), 25.

[99] American Convention, art. 20.

[100] Ibid., art. 24.

to the demands imposed by the international system for the protection of human rights."[101]

The ownership of land and other property can improve women's economic opportunities and well-being. Unfortunately, however, women have often been denied ownership rights. According to one nongovernmental organization, the exclusion of women from property ownership "contributes to women's low social status and their vulnerability to poverty."[102] To give one example, customary inheritance laws have been used to deny women's property rights even when a state's constitution or other domestic law includes equal protection provisions.[103]

Two cases from Africa relating to property rights demonstrate the importance of international law to women's lives. In 1999, the Zimbabwe Supreme Court decided the case of *Magaya v. Magaya*.[104] In this much criticized opinion,[105] the Court upheld an estates law that preferred males to females as heir to the deceased's estate, thereby rejecting the claim that the law constituted *prima facie* discrimination against females and was consequently a breach of the Constitution of Zimbabwe.[106] The Court stated that the grant of the heirship to the son was consistent with "the nature of African society."[107] It also ruled that the grant was consistent with an exception to the equal protection provision of the Constitution, Section 23, which favored African customary law.[108]

[101] Advisory Opinion OC-4/84, para. 38. The legislation that gave effect to the Court's opinion, the Citizenship Act 1998, became effective on 24 April 1998.

[102] International Center for Research on Women, *Property Ownership for Women Enriches, Empowers and Protects: Toward Achieving the Third Millennium Development Goal to Promote Gender Equality and Empower Women* (Washington, DC: International Center for Research on Women, 2005), 2 ("*Property Ownership*"), available at www.icrw.org/docs/2005_brief_mdg-property.pdf.

[103] See generally Shelly Kreiczer Levy and Meital Pinto, "Property and Belongingness: Rethinking Gender-Biased Disinheritance," 21 *Texas Journal of Women & Law* 119 (2011), 119 (arguing that "the law also should not protect gender-biased bequests").

[104] 3 L.R.C 35; 1999 (1) ZLR 100(S) (Zimbabwe Supreme Court).

[105] See, e.g., Uche Ewelukwa Ofodile, "The Universal Declaration of Human Rights and the African Child Today: Progress or Problems?" 25 *American University International Law Review* 37 (2010), 54–56. See also Valerie Knobelsdorf, "Zimbabwe's Magaya Decision Revisited: Women's Rights and Land Succession in the International Context," 15 *Columbia Journal of Gender & Law* 749 (2006), 760–61.

[106] Section 23 of the Constitution at the time read in part: "(1) Subject to the provisions of this section – (a) no law shall make any provision that is discriminatory either of itself or in its effect; and (b) no person shall be treated in a discriminatory manner by any person acting by virtue of any written law or in the performance of the functions of any public office or any public authority."

[107] *Magaya*, 3 L.R.C 35, 43. The Court noted that the Constitution did not specifically prohibit discrimination based on sex.

[108] In this connection, the Court pointed out that section 23(3) "expressly exempted matters involving the devolution of property on death and customary law involving Africans from the discrimination provisions." Ibid., 41; 1999 (1) ZLR 100, 105.

In three consolidated cases decided in 2004, the *Bhe* cases,[109] the South African Supreme Court reached a different result. The cases involved constitutional challenges to the rule of male primogeniture as it applied in the African customary law of succession. The Court held that statutory provisions and regulations that prevented the inheritance of property by females were unconstitutional. In reaching its decision, the South African Supreme Court, unlike the Zimbabwean court, relied on international law, as required by the South African Constitution. Section 39(1) of the Constitution in relevant part provides that "when interpreting the Bill of Rights, a court, tribunal or forum ... (b) must consider international law."[110] In particular, the Court held that the principle of male primogeniture discriminates unfairly against women, and noted that South Africa is a party to a number of international instruments that "underscore the need to protect the rights of women, and to abolish all laws that discriminate against them."[111] The use of international law made a difference in how property inheritance affected women's lives.

Gender-based violence is another problem facing women that can be addressed by international law. The Inter-American Commission on Human Rights ("IACHR") has declared: "Gender-based violence is one of the most extreme and pervasive forms of discrimination, severely impairing and nullifying the enforcement of women's rights, [and there is a] strong connection between the problems of discrimination and violence against women."[112] A particularly pervasive and complex issue is the domestic violence committed against women by their partners and the appropriate action of the state in response to such domestic violence.

The benefits of applying international law to domestic violence situations can be demonstrated by one case, the U.S. case involving Jessica Gonzales, which was heard by two separate bodies, the U.S. Supreme Court and a regional body, the IACHR.[113] In the 2005 case of *Town of Castle*

[109] *Bhe and Others v. The Magistrate, Khayelitsha and Others Case CCT 49/03; Shibi v. Sithole and others Case CCT 69/03; South African Human Rights Commission and another v. President of the Republic of South Africa and another Case CCT 50/03*, October 2004, 2005 (1) BCLR 1 (CC) (South Africa) (collectively, the "*Bhe* cases").

[110] South African Constitution, § 39, available at www.constitutionalcourt.org.za/site/theconstitution/thetext.htm.

[111] *Bhe and Others*, 2005 (1) BCLR 1 (CC), para. 51.

[112] *Jessica Lenahan (Gonzalez) et al. v. United States*, Case 12.626, Report No. 80/11, Inter-Am. Comm.H.R., para. 110 (July 21, 2011) (released publicly on August 17, 2011) ("Lenahan Final Report").

[113] As noted earlier, the IACHR investigates petitions of alleged violations of human rights by the member states of the OAS. The United States is one of the thirty-five members of the OAS. Human rights obligations of OAS member states are contained in the OAS Charter, the 1948 American Declaration of the Rights and Duties of Man, and the 1969 American Convention

Rock v. Gonzales,[114] the U.S. Supreme Court ruled that Jessica Gonzales's constitutional rights to due process had not been violated when the government failed to protect her and her children when a restraining order issued against her husband was not enforced.[115] The Supreme Court decided that there was no basis in law to uphold her claims against either the individual police officers involved or the town because the restraining order had not created an enforceable property interest.

In December 2005, after her case was dismissed by the U.S. Supreme Court, Gonzales submitted her petition to the IACHR.[116] She asserted that the U.S. Supreme Court and the Castle Rock Police Department violated her human rights as provided in the American Declaration on the Rights and Duties of Man (hereinafter "the American Declaration").[117] In its final report on the case, the IACHR found that the United States violated Gonzales's human rights.[118] The IACHR concluded that the United States had incurred international responsibility under several articles of the American Declaration, including its articles on the right to equality before the law and the obligation not to discriminate (Article II), the right to life (Article I), and the right to special protection (Article VII).[119] The Commission noted that both international and regional human rights systems recognize a "strong link between discrimination, violence and due diligence."[120] The IACHR listed several international instruments and cited opinions issued by human rights bodies[121] in support of

on Human Rights. The United States signed the American Convention on Human Rights in 1977, but has not yet ratified it.

114 545 U.S. 748 (2005).

115 Jessica Gonzales filed a lawsuit under a federal statute, Rev. Stat. § 1979, 42 U.S.C. § 1983, which provides a remedy for deprivation of rights secured by the Constitution of the United States when that deprivation takes place "under color of any statute, ordinance, regulation, custom, or usage, of any State or Territory." She claimed that her procedural due process rights under the Due Process Clause of the Fourteenth Amendment were violated when the police failed to provide protection pursuant to a validly obtained protective order. *Town of Castle Rock*, 545 U.S. at 754.

116 See *Jessica Gonzales v. United States*, Petition No. 1490-05, IACHR Report No. 52/07, OEA/Ser.L./V/II.128, Doc. 19, para. 1 (July 24, 2007), available at http://cidh.org/annualrep/2007eng/USA1490.05eng.htm ("Gonzales, Admissibility Report").

117 Ibid., paras. 22, 23. The American Declaration on the Rights and Duties of Man ("American Declaration") was adopted by the Ninth International Conference of American States held in Bogota, Colombia in 1948.

118 *Jessica Lenahan (Gonzalez) et al. v. United States*, Case 12.626, Report No. 80/11.

119 Ibid., paras. 102–04.

120 Ibid., para. 111.

121 Ibid., para. 124 (referring to "General Assembly resolutions adopted by consensus, broadly-approved declarations and platforms, treaties, views from treaty bodies, custom, jurisprudence from the universal and regional systems, and other sources of international law") (citations omitted). See also ibid., paras. 132–33.

an international consensus that violence against women is a human rights problem that requires state action.[122]

9.5 A NEW THEORY OF WOMEN'S RIGHTS UNDER CUSTOMARY INTERNATIONAL LAW

As the previous section demonstrates, because of the general devaluing of women,[123] they are denied rights of membership and property ownership and are subjected to violence. We have seen that national court decisions have often upheld discriminatory practices against women under state or local law, including customary law, many without referring to international law standards on women's rights at all. Moreover, as discussed earlier, many states continue to make reservations and derogate from treaties designed to protect and provide equality for women. In short, despite the increasing reliance of some courts and bodies on international law to achieve equality for women and hold those who inflict violence on women accountable, progress in implementing women's rights has been neither as fast nor as expansive as many women would hope.

This is where customary international law can play an important role in strengthening the ability of international law to improve women's lives and combat these and other forms of discrimination against them. Lepard's theory of customary international law is promising as a basis for pursuing the goals of equality and protections for women's lives more effectively.

Other scholars and advocates have similarly recognized the value of establishing the right to gender equality as customary international law.[124] A more expansive view of the establishment of customary international human rights norms can aid in this effort. In this connection, some of the other contributors to this volume appear to endorse the recognition of customary law norms based in part on their moral underpinnings and objectives. For example, Jean-Marie Henckaerts and Els Debuf argue in Chapter 6 that with respect to international humanitarian law there should be a focus on individual victims

[122] Ibid., paras. 123–24. See generally Catharine A. MacKinnon, "Creating International Law: Gender as Leading Edge," 36 *Harvard Journal of Law & Gender* 105 (2013).

[123] See, e.g., David S. Mitchell, "The Prohibition of Rape in International Humanitarian Law as a Norm of Jus Cogens: Clarifying the Doctrine," 15 *Duke Journal of Comparative & International Law* 219 (2005), 226 (discussing how women's lives remain undervalued).

[124] See, e.g., Hilary Charlesworth and Christine Chinkin, "The Gender of Jus Cogens," 15 *Human Rights Quarterly* 63 (1993), 63–65; Ladan Askari, "Girls' Rights Under International Law: An Argument for Establishing Gender Equality as a Jus Cogens," 8 *Southern California Review of Law and Women's Studies* 3 (1998); Charlotte Bunch, "Women's Rights as Human Rights: Toward a Re-Vision of Human Rights," 12 *Human Rights Quarterly* 486 (1990), 486–87.

and therefore less emphasis on the explicit consent of states before they can be bound by certain norms as customary law. They thus stress that a merit of customary rules of IHL is that they "apply equally to all states and to all armed conflicts, regardless of the [treaty] ratification record of the parties to the conflict" – a situation that is more "satisfactory" "from the perspective of the legal protection of war victims."[125]

I argue that women's lives and the abuses they suffer must be considered in establishing norms of customary international law. As previously noted, the UDHR may provide evidence of both the *opinio juris* and state practice necessary to establish the status of the rights it proclaims as customary law.[126] Development of a customary international law norm for specific denials of rights to women, however, is preferred rather than a general norm under customary international law prohibiting conduct that applies to women as equally as it does to men. For example, the UDHR and ICCPR have led to the establishment of a customary international law norm that prohibits slavery. Slavery is likely to be viewed in traditional terms under this general norm. This norm may not address modern-day slavery, which includes sex trafficking affecting primarily girls and women.[127]

To assess the effect of Lepard's theory in this effort, once again it is necessary to "ask the woman question." Here, to paraphrase his inquiry, we must ask: "Do states generally believe it is desirable, now or in the near future, to recognize some or all of the human rights of women proclaimed in human rights instruments as binding or persuasive legal obligations for all states?"[128]

In this connection, Charlotte Bunch has stated that, in linking women's rights to human rights, it is necessary to consider the human rights concept from a feminist perspective to take greater account of women's lives.[129] This requires that the "human rights vision" not be a male-oriented vision, but instead a vision that "incorporate[s] gender perspectives."[130] The application of

[125] Jean-Marie Henckaerts and Els Debuf, "The ICRC and the Clarification of Customary International Humanitarian Law," in this volume.

[126] See the discussion earlier in the chapter. See also Roshni Patel, "The Trafficking of Women in India: A Four-Dimensional Analysis," 14 *Georgetown Journal of Gender & Law* 159 (2013), 170 (noting that the UDHR "is considered to be customary international law, and India is expected to adhere to it").

[127] See United Nations Convention against Transnational Organized Crime; Protocol to Prevent, Suppress and Punish Trafficking in Persons, Especially Women and Children; Protocol Against the Smuggling of Migrants by Land, Sea and Air, Nov. 15, 2000, UN Doc. A/55/383 (2000), reprinted in 40 *International Legal Materials* 335 (2001).

[128] Lepard, *Customary International Law*, 319.

[129] See Bunch, "Women's Rights as Human Rights," 493–95.

[130] Ibid., 497.

Lepard's theory to the achievement of women's human rights accommodates this approach.

Lepard illustrates the application of his theory to human rights by analyzing one aspect of religious freedom, "the right to change one's religion or belief."[131] He poses five questions that can be answered to evaluate whether a norm has become customary international law and its status as a *jus cogens* norm or as an *erga omnes* obligation: "1) whether all states in the world today are legally obligated to ensure freedom to change one's religion or belief as a right guaranteed by customary international law; 2) the specific content of this right and any limitations on it; 3) whether states may exempt themselves from the right by persistently objecting to it or entering into contrary treaties; 4) whether the right is a norm of *jus cogens*; and 5) whether the right creates obligations *erga omnes*."[132]

A variation of these five questions can serve as the basis for establishing the existence of customary international law relating to women's human rights and evaluating the legal status of such customary norms. Of course, in answering each of these questions, it is important to look at clear evidence of states' views, as well as their practices. This is critical to avoid the recognition of "fake custom," as rightly emphasized by Fernando R. Tesón in Chapter 3.[133] Women's rights should not be recognized as customary law simply because an advocate (like me) desires to champion women's rights.

9.5.1 *Are Women's Rights Protected by Customary International Law?*

The initial problem to resolve is determining whether, and which, women's rights are today protected by customary international law. Lepard's first two questions above relate to this determination. In relation to women's rights, the first two questions posed by Lepard should read:

1. *Whether all states in the world today are legally obligated to ensure women's freedom from sex inequality as a right guaranteed by customary international law and*
2. *The specific content of this right and any limitations on it.*

The starting point here is Lepard's classification of human rights. Using Lepard's taxonomy, the initial question is whether women's human rights are fundamental, compelling, or essential rights from an ethical perspective.[134]

131 Lepard, *Customary International Law*, 346–67.
132 Ibid., 347.
133 See Fernando R. Tesón, "Fake Custom," in this volume.
134 See Lepard, *Customary International Law*, 359. On the definition of essential rights, see ibid., 86, Fig. 5.3; ibid., 341–42.

In this connection we should consider the list of essential human rights suggested by Lepard, and then subject it to a critique based on whether these rights include discrimination against women specifically. This analysis may lead to the addition or clarification of other essential rights that have been ignored because of the traditional male-oriented vision of essential rights. As Lepard notes, it is likely that some rights deserve to be classified as *jus cogens* norms "whose status as *jus cogens* rights is less generally accepted, and yet are strong candidates for closer analysis."[135] As he suggests, morally essential rights are strong candidates for *jus cogens* status,[136] and such essential rights should include the requirement of "nondiscrimination in the enjoyment of all these rights, including on the grounds of sex."[137]

The denial of rights to women on the basis of their sex is condemned in general international human rights documents as well as those specifically focusing on the rights of women. This stems from the moral belief that oppression of women is unacceptable because there is no salient moral difference between the treatment of men and women. This belief, expressed in a wide variety of international human rights instruments, provides support for the principle that conflicting cultural values should be suppressed in favor of sex equality.

While Lepard's analysis of the specific freedom to change one's religion or belief lends itself to a separate analysis of questions (1) and (2), the broad nature of women's human rights lends itself more to a joint consideration of these questions. For example, violence against women, the denial of membership or nationality and accompanying rights, and the lack of recognition of women's property rights trigger a number of different human rights and interests.

To recall, Lepard states his theory as follows: "A customary international law norm arises when states generally believe that it is desirable now or in the near future to have an authoritative legal principle or rule prescribing, permitting, or prohibiting *certain conduct*."[138] If we interpret the term "certain conduct" to require separate consideration of each type of gender discrimination, this suggests that an appropriate approach is to focus on the establishment of customary international law regarding specific practices and the treatment

[135] Ibid., 342.

[136] Based on the tests Lepard describes earlier, he lists as morally essential rights the "rights to subsistence, including adequate food, clothing, shelter and medical care; [and] to freedom of moral choice, including freedom of thought, conscience, and religion and freedom of opinion and expression." Ibid.

[137] Ibid.

[138] Ibid., 8 (emphasis added).

of women, rather than applying a broad principle that women should be treated in a nondiscriminatory manner. However, a practice-specific approach may be more problematic than an approach based on the broad issue of sex inequality. It is not advisable to establish a customary international law norm for each type of discrimination suffered by women. Otherwise, this could lead to the fragmentation of international law on women's human rights and the establishment of a hierarchy of those rights. Instead, the focus should be on whether a broad principle of nondiscrimination against women has attained the status of customary law.

Because of the diverse issues involved in women's human rights, there has been doubt expressed about whether they have reached the level of customary international law, primarily because of a lack of consistent state practice in favor of them.[139] The cases discussed in the previous section may be cited as evidence that customary international law does not exist on these issues. These cases may be evidence that consistent state practice in the treatment of, and granting of human rights to, women is absent. However, the better view, as Lepard suggests, is that a customary international law norm can be established if there is sufficient *opinio juris*, despite the lack of consistent state practice in the treatment of and protection provided to women. As Lepard points out, "even unenforced laws may be evidence of *opinio juris*."[140] More generally, such laws and other evidence of the belief of states that rules in declarations and treaties regarding women's human rights do and should establish "persuasive or binding obligations"[141] for all states can create customary law even though many of the obligations are not enforced or are violated.

If it is agreed that rights included in general human rights instruments have become customary international law because there is extensive evidence of sufficient *opinio juris*, even if not perfectly consistent state practice, then women must be equally treated. Because sex-based discrimination is prohibited by these and other international agreements, many scholars have concluded that a norm of nondiscrimination based on gender has already passed into customary international law. And the Restatement (Third) recognizes that even though gender-based discrimination is still practiced in many states

139 See, e.g., Hurst Hannum, "The Status of the Universal Declaration of Human Rights in National and International Law," 25 *Georgia Journal of International and Comparative Law* 287 (1995–96), 342–43 (noting that while there is widespread acceptance of a right to equal treatment under the law, in keeping with Articles 1, 2, 6, and 7 of the UDHR, suggesting its potential customary law character, "state practice does not support a conclusion that there is full compliance with the principle of equality," giving as an example the fact that "women are prevented from exercising their human rights on an equal footing with men in many states").

140 Lepard, *Customary International Law*, 176.

141 Ibid., 207.

in varying degrees, freedom from gender discrimination as state policy may already be a principle of customary international law.[142]

To review, many instruments now prohibit sex-based discrimination and can support such a conclusion if we treat them as evidence of *opinio juris* and focus on such *opinio juris* as opposed to state practice. (Of course, under some approaches, including that endorsed by the International Law Commission, the adoption of these instruments itself may constitute part of state practice.[143]) I have already noted that the UN Charter (in Article 1(3)) and the UDHR (in Article 2) prohibit discrimination in respect of human rights on various grounds, including sex. We also saw that the ICCPR and the ICESCR contain general provisions prohibiting nondiscrimination on the basis of gender in relation to the rights they protect. Furthermore, the World Conference on Human Rights, held in Vienna in 1993, confirmed women's human rights as universal norms. In particular, the Vienna Declaration and Programme of Action of the World Conference on Human Rights was adopted by 171 states and emphasizes that the rights of women and girls are "an inalienable, integral and indivisible part of human rights."[144] Also as indicated above, states have adopted many international instruments that specifically address the human rights of women, such as CEDAW, DEVAW, the Convention on the Nationality of Married Women,[145] and the Inter-American Convention on the Prevention, Punishment and Eradication of Violence against Women.

Some observers might cite the adoption of these specialized instruments as support for an argument that because the UDHR, ICCPR, and ICESCR do not address women's human rights specifically, they cannot be used as evidence of the formation of customary norms on women's rights, even if they are valid evidence that some human rights have achieved the status of customary international law. These skeptical observers might also emphasize the lack of enforcement mechanisms in these general human rights instruments, and in gender-specific instruments in particular, as a reason not to treat them as evidencing *opinio juris* in favor of binding customary law norms.[146]

On the other hand, a growing number of scholars and advocates have concluded that the combination of gender-specific instruments like CEDAW

[142] Restatement (Third), § 702.

[143] See, e.g., "Report of the International Law Commission," Sixty-Eighth Session, Draft Conclusion 6, para. 2.

[144] Vienna Declaration and Programme of Action, para. 20.

[145] Convention on the Nationality of Married Women, GA Res. 1040, UN GAOR, 11th Sess., Supp. No. 17, at 18 (1957), 309 UNTS 65, entered into force 11 August 1958.

[146] On this point, see Lepard, *Customary International Law*, 327 (citing Weisburd, "Customary International Law," 25–29). See also Donna E. Young, "Culture Confronts the International," 60 *Albany Law Review* 907 (1997), 912.

and other general documents such as the UN Charter, UDHR, and ICCPR demonstrate that customary international law now includes women's human rights norms and prohibits discrimination on the basis of sex.[147] For example, Major David J. Western has argued that CEDAW is reaching the status of customary international law because of the legal obligations it imposes,[148] while Chantalle Forgues has affirmed that "CEDAW articulates the basic customary international law against gender discrimination in general."[149]

Regional agreements also provide additional evidence of *opinio juris* in favor of freedom from sex inequality and therefore help establish that it is a right under customary international law.[150] And regional human rights bodies have suggested that certain norms in these instruments may now be general principles of law or customary international law and that national law must therefore comply with these norms. For example, with respect to the application of the American Convention on Human Rights to naturalization laws proposed in Costa Rica discussed in an earlier section, the IACHR required that the domestic law on nationality rights be reconciled with the "demands imposed by the international system for the protection of human rights."[151] To take another example, the judge in the Tanzanian case of *Ephraim* v. *Pastory*[152] found that a Tanzanian customary law on inheritance rights was discriminatory not only because of specific prohibitions against discrimination in the Tanzanian Constitution but also because the country had made the UDHR a part of the constitution and had ratified the ICCPR, CEDAW, the African Charter on Human and Peoples' Rights, and its Protocol on the Rights of

147 See, e.g., *Bringing Equality Home: Implementing the Convention on the Elimination of All Forms of Discrimination Against Women, CEDAW*, edited by Ilana Landsburg-Lewis (New York: United Nations Development Fund for Women, 1998); Henry J. Steiner and Philip Alston, *International Human Rights in Context: Law, Politics, Morals* (Oxford: Oxford University Press, 2nd ed. 2000), 69, 72. But see Arthur M. Weisburd, "The Effect of Treaties and Other Formal International Acts on the Customary Law of Human Rights," 25 *Georgia Journal of International & Comparative Law* 99 (1996), 118.

148 Major David J. Western, "Islamic 'Purse Strings': The Key to the Amelioration of Women's Legal Rights in the Middle East," 61 *Air Force Law Review* 79 (2008), 125.

149 Chantalle Forgues, "A Global Hurdle: The Implementation of an International Nondiscrimination Norm Protecting Women from Gender Discrimination in International Sports," 18 *Brigham Young University International Law Journal* 247 (2000), 262.

150 See generally OHCHR and IBA, *Human Rights in the Administration of Justice: A Manual on Human Rights for Judges, Prosecutors and Lawyers*, chapter 3 (New York and Geneva: United Nations, 2003) (discussing African Charter on Human and Peoples' Rights); Convention for the Protection of Human Rights and Fundamental Freedoms ("European Convention"), adopted November 1950, entered into force on September 3, 1953, available at www.ohchr.org/Documents/Publications/training9chapter3en.pdf.

151 Advisory Opinion OC-4/84, Inter-Am. Ct. H.R. (Ser. A) No. 4 (1984), para. 38.

152 *Ephrahim v. Pastory and Kaizilege* (Tanzania High Court), [1990] LRC (Const) 757; (2001) AHRLR 236 (TzHC 1990).

Women.[153] He stated: "The principles enunciated in the above-named documents are a standard below which any civilized nation will be ashamed to fall."[154] This opinion suggests that these principles may well now be part of customary international law.

Consistent with Lepard's theory, these many instruments on women's rights have contributed to the formation of customary international law because they are evidence of *opinio juris*, the central ingredient of customary law. As indicated by the IACHR in the *Gonzales* case discussed earlier,[155] in addition to judicial opinions,[156] evidence of *opinio juris* can be provided by advisory opinions of human rights bodies and human rights instruments. The IACHR there referred to "General Assembly resolutions adopted by consensus, broadly-approved declarations and platforms, treaties, views from treaty bodies, custom, jurisprudence from the universal and regional systems, and other sources of international law"[157] as evidence of a broad international consensus on the principle that states must exercise due diligence in protecting women from domestic violence. This consensus may also reflect *opinio juris*. Indeed, the IACHR emphasized that the "United Nations Special Rapporteur on Violence against Women [has] established that the duty of due diligence has attained the status of a norm of customary international law, which obligates States to prevent and respond with due diligence to acts of violence against women."[158]

Evidence of *opinio juris* regarding women's rights can be found not only in instruments relating to human rights but also in treaties and other instruments relating to international humanitarian law and international refugee law. For example, Donna E. Arzt has suggested that the law of war or humanitarian law[159] and refugee law[160] along with human rights law have increasingly

[153] For the Protocol, see African Union, Protocol to the African Charter on Human and People's Rights on the Rights of Women in Africa, 11 July 2003, available at www.refworld.org/docid/3f4b139d4.html.

[154] *Ephrahim v. Pastory and Kaizilege*, para. 10.

[155] Lenahan Final Report.

[156] See, e.g., *Filartiga v. Pena-Irala*, 577 F. Supp. 860 (E.D.N.Y. 1984) (emphasizing judicial opinions, conventions, and declarations instead of state practice in determining the content of customary human rights law on torture).

[157] Lenahan Final Report, para. 124.

[158] Ibid., n.208.

[159] See the discussion of international humanitarian law in Jean-Marie Henckaerts and Els Debuf, "The ICRC and the Clarification of Customary International Humanitarian Law," in this volume. Humanitarian law comprises international rules, such as those in the Geneva Conventions and the Hague Conventions, that limit the conduct of armed conflict for humanitarian reasons. See generally Theodor Meron, "The Humanization of Humanitarian Law," 94 *American Journal of International Law* 239 (2000), 243.

[160] The 1951 Convention Relating to the Status of Refugees ("1951 Convention") and its subsequent 1967 Protocol govern refugee status and are the principal United Nations instruments

recognized that there is overlap among the three areas of law,[161] which have undergone a "gender awakening" to the fact that sexual assault and rape against women are human rights abuses.[162]

Although it is generally recognized that "[t]ime is another important element in the process of creation of customary international law,"[163] and many gender-specific human rights instruments are fairly recent in origin, it can be argued that the basis for many women's rights relates back to the UDHR and ICCPR, which have been in existence for many decades, and which include sex as a prohibited ground of discrimination in their antidiscrimination provisions.[164] The earlier view that customary international law must be based on the practice of states continued over an extended period of time is becoming less widespread.[165] New, more widely accepted theories of customary international law accept that today a practice can achieve customary international law status in a short period of time.[166] Lepard's decreased emphasis on state practice is consistent with these theories and facilitates this goal.

establishing the legal rights of refugees. See 1951 Convention Relating to the Status of Refugees, art. 33, July 28, 1951, 19 UST 6276, 189 UNTS 137 and 1967 Protocol, available at www.unhcr.org/protect/PROTECTION/3b73b0d63.pdf.

161 See Arzt, "Three Degrees of Separation," 167. See also *Application of the Convention on the Prevention and Punishment of the Crime of Genocide (Bosnia and Herzegovina v. Yugoslavia)*, Preliminary Objections, Judgment of 11 July 1996, 1996 ICJ Rep. 595, 648 ("The human rights and humanitarian principles contained in the Genocide Convention are principles of customary international law.").

162 Arzt, "Three Degrees of Separation," 191 n.23 (noting that violence against women is recognized in humanitarian law because women "are indeed the targeted victims of war and human rights atrocities" such as sexual assault and rape; in human rights law, which has focused on issues such as domestic violence "which involve abusive acts by private, non-state actors"; and in refugee law, which recognizes that victims of female genital mutilation ("FGM") may qualify for a grant of asylum under the 1951 Refugee Convention category of "membership in a social group" even though sex is not listed as one of the grounds used to define a refugee). A similar case can be made for forced marriages, which have been recognized as human rights violations suffered by women during war, violations of equality of marriage in human rights instruments, and in some cases persecution that qualifies for a grant of asylum. See generally CEDAW, art. 16(1)(b) (freedom to choose a spouse and marry); Kim Thuy Seelinger, "Forced Marriage and Asylum: Perceiving the Invisible Harm," 42 *Columbia Human Rights Law Review* 55 (2010).

163 *Dispute Regarding Navigational and Related Rights (Costa Rica v. Nicaragua)*, Separate Opinion of Judge Sepúlveda-Amor, 2009 ICJ Rep. 214, 279, para 25. See also Michael P. Scharf, *Customary International Law in Times of Fundamental Change: Recognizing Grotian Moments* (New York: Cambridge University Press, 2013), 1, 5 (discussing extraordinary situations that lead to the "unusual rapidity and acceptance" of some new rules of customary international law).

164 See UDHR, art. 2; ICCPR, art. 2(1).

165 See, e.g., Baker, "Customary International Law in the 21st Century," 179.

166 See Paul C. Szasz, "General Law-Making Processes," in *The United Nations and International Law*, edited by Chris C. Joyner 27 (Washington, DC: American Society of International Law; Cambridge: Cambridge University Press, 1997), 31 (in part because of "the general

In brief, a strong argument can be made that freedom from discrimination on the basis of sex is an essential human right from a moral perspective. Moreover, there is strong evidence that states not only recognize the essential moral status of this right but generally believe that it should be enjoyed by all women as a legal right. International instruments and decisions of courts and regional and international human rights bodies evidence that states generally believe that women should have the legal right to be free from discrimination on the basis of sex with respect to human rights and that states should have the obligation to protect human rights without discrimination on the basis of sex. As Lepard asserts, to the extent there is any doubt about state beliefs, we should err on the side of presuming such a belief based on the essential character of the right concerned. And this belief, in turn, establishes *opinio juris* and justifies recognizing a general norm of nondiscrimination based on gender as a rule of customary international law.

There is also a plethora of state practice of recognizing a norm prohibiting gender discrimination – thus satisfying the traditional requirement of consistent state practice for establishing customary law according to the two-element definition recently reaffirmed by the International Law Commission. To the extent that there are many examples of states continuing to discriminate against women either *de jure* or *de facto*, as described earlier, these evidences should be discounted in light of the clear *opinio juris* in favor of the norm. This *opinio juris*, coupled with state practice of asserting a nondiscrimination norm, should help respond to the concerns of those scholars, such as Noora Arajärvi, who understandably resist a de-emphasis on state practice as an essential component of customary law in order to ensure the predictability of the law and observance of the principle of legality.[167]

What is the impact on this conclusion of the many reservations to CEDAW and other treaty provisions on women's rights that I described earlier? On the one hand, if the international community permits these reservations, they might constitute state practice contrary to the rights of women and thus prevent these rights from being recognized as customary international law. On the other hand, if customary international law is thought of in more progressive terms and we reject the need for evidence that there is universal or near-universal state practice, then these reservations may not prevent formation of a customary rule. Moreover, in evaluating state practice, it may be possible to

acceleration of international interactions … the speed by which customary international law is created is also increasing").

[167] See Noora Arajärvi, "From the 'Demands of Humanity': The Formulation of *Opinio Juris* in Decisions of International Criminal Tribunals and the Need for a Renewed Emphasis on State Practice," in this volume.

discount certain customary state law as well as derogations and reservations that fail to protect women's rights because they are invalid and unlawful under rules of treaty law.[168] In other words, they would be treated as violations of existing customary norms protecting women's rights rather than as contrary practice preventing the formation of a customary rule. A perspective, like Lepard's, that emphasizes *opinio juris* over state practice in the human rights area may allow for formation of customary norms protecting women's rights, notwithstanding the presence of contrary state laws or treaty reservations – and this is a key benefit of such a perspective.

Furthermore, there is ample evidence that each of the specific rights discussed in the preceding sections are essential rights that should be recognized as customary law and enjoyed by all women free from sex inequality. More specifically, the denial of membership and full citizenship to women interferes with their essential rights of nationality and full participation in society, the denial of property and inheritance rights to women can interfere with their essential right to subsistence, and violence against women interferes with essential rights to life and physical security. Again, the morally essential character of these rights should help tip the balance in favor of recognizing them as customary law even if state practice is not perfectly consistent with them. Let me elaborate on each of these rights and evidence of *opinio juris* in favor of them.

First, regarding the right of membership and citizenship, as Ruth Lister has noted, while many would consider citizenship a gender-neutral concept, it is often "deeply gendered."[169] She asserts that if "[c]itizenship is a *status* bestowed on those who are full members of a community,"[170] then one of the key elements is equality.[171] Rebecca J. Cook has emphasized the importance of certain rights associated with citizenship that should be enjoyed by women, such as the "capacity to possess citizenship and nationality separate from their husband," and "their ability legally to transmit [that nationality] on to [their] children."[172] Article 9 of CEDAW articulates the equality principle with specific reference to citizenship, providing that "States Parties shall grant women equal rights with men to acquire, change or retain their nationality."[173]

168 See generally Ryan Goodman, "Human Rights Treaties, Invalid Reservations, and State Consent," 96 *American Journal of International Law* 531 (2002).

169 See Ruth Lister, *Citizenship: Feminist Perspectives* (Basingstoke, UK: Macmillan, 1997), 1.

170 Ibid., 14 (quoting T.H. Marshall, *Citizenship And Social Class* (Cambridge: Cambridge University Press, 1st ed. 1950), 28) (emphasis in the original).

171 Ibid., 14, 91–116 (discussing a gender-neutral vs. a gender-differentiated approach under which there is equality with men but recognizing "particular concerns and contributions").

172 Cook, "Reservations to the Convention on the Elimination of All Forms of Discrimination against Women," 693.

173 CEDAW, art. 9, para. 1.

It furthermore affirms that "States Parties shall grant women equal rights with men with respect to the nationality of their children."[174] These provisions are strong evidence not only of the essential character of citizenship rights but also of *opinio juris* relating to the desirability of granting women such rights universally.

Property rights and inheritance rights are closely related to rights of citizenship. Article 15 of CEDAW requires that states parties "accord to women equality with men before the law" and "accord to women, in civil matters, a legal capacity identical to that of men and the same opportunities to exercise that capacity. In particular, they shall give women equal rights to conclude contracts and to administer property."[175] In addition, CEDAW provides that women should have the same rights as men "in respect of the ownership, acquisition, management, administration, enjoyment and disposition of property."[176] The CEDAW Committee's General Recommendation No. 29, on "Economic Consequences of Marriage, Family Relations and their Dissolution," and relating to Article 16 of CEDAW, was adopted in 2013.[177] It addresses the need to protect women's equal rights to property upon divorce or the death of their spouses.

Furthermore, the Millennium Development Goals adopted by the UN General Assembly in 2000[178] emphasize the elimination of obstacles to the ownership of property by women as a means to help achieve the third millennium development goal to promote gender equality and empower women.[179] These obstacles include domestic statutory and customary state laws, as we saw in earlier discussions.[180] Several commentators have discussed how these laws are inconsistent with CEDAW as well as other international human rights norms.[181] Susan Deller Ross has pointed out, however, that judges like Tanzanian Judge Mwalusanya in *Ephrahim v. Pastory* "are pioneers in

174 Ibid., para. 2.

175 Ibid., art. 15, paras. 1, 2.

176 Ibid., art. 16, para 1(h). Article 16 of CEDAW generally obligates states parties to establish equal property rights for women in relation to marriage, divorce, and death. See also ibid., art. 14, para. 2(g).

177 UN Doc. CEDAW/C/GC/29 (2013), available at http://tbinternet.ohchr.org/_layouts/treatybodyexternal/Download.aspx?symbolno=CEDAW/C/GC/29.

178 The Millennium Project was commissioned by the UN Secretary-General. See Report to the Secretary-General, *Investing in Development: A Practical Plan to Achieve the Millennium Development Goals* (London and Sterling, VA: Earthscan, 2005).

179 See International Center for Research on Women, *Property Ownership*.

180 Ibid., 5.

181 See, e.g., Sara Hossain, "Women's Rights and Personal Laws in South Asia," in *Human Rights of Women: National and International Perspectives*, edited by Rebecca J. Cook 465 (Philadelphia: University of Pennsylvania Press, 1994), 467–73.

safeguarding women's human rights while reminding the government that it is a signatory to international human rights instruments guaranteeing equality and freedom from discrimination on the basis of sex."[182] The UN Population Fund ("UNFPA") reports that measures "to protect women's personal security and their rights in marriage, property, [and] inheritance … are being expanded and increasingly enforced."[183] Even those who may not believe that a customary international law norm already exists regarding sex equality in inheritance rights may agree that the evidence supports a conclusion that such a norm is developing.[184] In short, there is also emerging *opinio juris* sufficient to recognize equal rights to property and inheritance as a norm of customary international law.

Violence against women takes many forms, and, as noted earlier, many scholars have recognized that states are required to "to prevent and respond to acts of violence against women with due diligence" as a rule of customary international law.[185] The UN Special Rapporteur on Violence against Women, Yakin Ertürk, arrived at this conclusion "on the basis of the practice and the *opinio juris*" of states.[186] The adoption of instruments and laws focusing on violence against women, as well as increased attention to this issue in the courts and human rights bodies, have led some scholars to conclude that this "evidences a universal trend toward *jus cogens* status for gender based abuses, particularly violence."[187] Specific acts of violence have also been addressed. For example, as Lepard notes,[188] the UN General Assembly adopted a resolution in 2004 affirming with respect to honor crimes that it is "the obligation of all States to promote and protect human rights and fundamental freedoms, including the right to life, liberty and security of person, as stated in the Universal Declaration of Human

[182] Susan Deller Ross, *Women's Human Rights: The International and Comparative Law Casebook* (Philadelphia: University of Pennsylvania Press, 2008), 190.

[183] United Nations Population Fund ("UNPF"), *The State of World Population Report 2000: Lives Together, Worlds Apart: Men and Women in a Time of Change* (New York: UNFPA, 2000), 1, available at www.unfpa.org/swp/2000/english/index.html.

[184] See, e.g., Sarah J. Conroy, "Women's Inheritance and Conditionality in the Fight Against AIDS," 28 *Wisconsin International Law Journal* 705 (2011), 719 n.55.

[185] See, e.g., UN Commission on Human Rights, "Integration of the Human Rights of Women and the Gender Perspective: Violence Against Women: The Due Diligence Standard as a Tool for the Elimination of Violence Against Women: Report of the Special Rapporteur on Violence against Women, Its Causes and Consequences, Yakin Ertürk," UN Doc. E/CN.4/2006/61 (2006), para. 29, available at www.unhcr.org/refworld/docid/45377afb0.html.

[186] Ibid. See also ibid., paras. 19–29.

[187] Mitchell, "The Prohibition of Rape," 225 n.19 (quoting Dawn Askin Kelly, *War Crimes against Women: Prosecutions in International War Crimes Tribunals* (The Hague and Cambridge, MA: Martinus Nijhoff Publishers, 1997), 242).

[188] See Lepard, *Customary International Law*, 322.

Rights."[189] Once again, these statements evidence a strong *opinio juris* in favor of a customary norm prohibiting violence against women and requiring states to prevent and respond to acts of violence against women with due diligence.

9.5.2 *Can States Exempt Themselves from Customary Norms Regarding Women's Rights?*

The next question to address is whether states can exempt themselves from the aforementioned customary norms regarding women's rights. This relates to Lepard's third question, which is "whether states may exempt themselves from the right by persistently objecting to it or entering into contrary treaties."

According to Lepard's theory, some customary norms, including *jus cogens* norms, do not allow any exemptions based on persistent objection to them, or by reason of entering into contrary treaties. Whether or not such exemptions from a norm are allowed depends, again, on the views of states about the permissibility of such exemptions. These views may be manifest in treaty provisions on derogations from comparable treaty norms, among other sources.

Applying this question to customary norms relating to women's rights, it is first of all relevant to note that CEDAW does not contain a derogation clause. Even if it is argued that some rights are derogable because of Article 4 of the ICCPR, which allows states parties to derogate from enumerated rights in a time of national emergency,[190] the text of Article 4 itself states that no lawful derogation may involve discrimination solely on the ground of sex, among other characteristics.[191] In short, the better view is that neither CEDAW nor the ICCPR allows derogations from the treaty norm of nondiscrimination based on sex. This is evidence that states believe that no exemptions should be allowed with respect to the comparable customary norm of nondiscrimination based on gender.

On the other hand, as emphasized earlier, many states have entered reservations to treaty articles they deem incompatible with their customary or religious

[189] "Working Towards the Elimination of Crimes Against Women and Girls Committed in the Name of Honour," GA Res. 59/165 (2004).

[190] Article 4(1) of the ICCPR provides that "in time of public emergency which threatens the life of the nation and the existence of which is officially proclaimed, the States Parties to the present Covenant may take measures derogating from their obligations under the present Covenant to the extent strictly required by the exigencies of the situation, provided that such measures are not inconsistent with their other obligations under international law and do not involve discrimination solely on the ground of race, colour, sex, language, religion or social origin." ICCPR, art. 4, para. 1.

[191] See ibid. See also Arzt, "Three Degrees of Separation," 4 n.5; Human Rights Committee, General Comment 29, "States of Emergency (Article 4)," UN Doc. CCPR/C/21/Rev.1/Add.11 (2001), paras. 11–13.

law relating to women's rights. Many of the 189 states parties to CEDAW have made reservations to Articles 15 and 16 relating to women's rights to property, inheritance, and land on the ground that their national law, tradition, religion, or culture is not consistent with these provisions of CEDAW.[192] These reservations reflect discriminatory attitudes in some cultures toward women based on religion or other beliefs, and could be asserted as evidence that states believe that persistent objection should be allowed to comparable customary norms.

More generally, the concept of cultural relativism is used by some states to justify making reservations to CEDAW and other treaties that allow them to avoid human rights obligations toward women.[193] In particular, several Middle Eastern nations have entered reservations to CEDAW as a condition of their ratification, refusing to accept articles they deem incompatible with Islamic Sharia law.[194] Other states parties to CEDAW have filed official objections against these reservations, alleging that they are invalid because, according to the Vienna Convention on the Law of Treaties, reservations may not circumvent the main object and purpose of a treaty.[195] The objections are based on Articles 2(f) and 5(a) of CEDAW, which require all states parties to modify customary and cultural practices that discriminate against women and constitute obligations that relate to the main purpose of the treaty.[196]

In evaluating the legal effect of these treaty reservations, three of Lepard's fundamental ethical principles are particularly relevant here, and must be balanced: the fundamental ethical principles of unity in diversity,[197] open-minded consultation,[198] and state autonomy.[199] As Lepard states in relation to

192 For a survey of the wide practice of making reservations to CEDAW, see Hilary Charlesworth et al., "Feminist Approaches to International Law," 632; Cook, "Reservations to the Convention on the Elimination of All Forms of Discrimination against Women."

193 See, e.g., Dinusha Panditaratne, "Towards Gender Equality in a Developing Asia: Reforming Personal Laws Within a Pluralist Framework," 32 *New York University Review of Law & Social Change* 83 (2007), 108 (discussing reservations made by Asian countries).

194 See generally Western, "Islamic 'Purse Strings,'" 121–23.

195 See ibid. See also Southard, "Protection of Women's Human Rights," 21; Belinda Clark, "The Vienna Convention Reservations Regime and the Convention on Discrimination against Women," 85 *American Journal of International Law* 281 (1991).

196 See CEDAW, art. 2(f) (requiring states parties to "take all appropriate measures, including legislation, to modify or abolish existing laws, regulations, customs and practices that constitute discrimination against women"); ibid., art. 5(a) (requiring states parties "to modify the social and cultural patterns of conduct of men and women, with a view to achieving the elimination of prejudices and customary and all other practices which are based on the idea of the inferiority or the superiority of either of the sexes or on stereotyped roles for men and women").

197 Lepard, *Customary International Law*, 78–81.

198 Ibid., 90–91.

199 Ibid., 87–88.

the persistent objector doctrine, "An interest in respecting state autonomy as an ethical value, coupled with the fundamental ethical principle of unity in diversity . . . initially lend support to respecting a state's wishes not to be bound [by a customary law norm] – but only under limited conditions."[200] In particular, one condition is that a state not reserve the right to violate fundamental human rights. Similar principles and a similar condition should apply to the making of valid treaty reservations.

Thus, while a determination of compliance with the treaty obligations may need to take into account some aspects of a state's culture,[201] blatant discriminatory conduct permitted by some of the existing reservations to CEDAW should not be allowed, as doing so would defeat the object and purpose of the treaty.[202] These reservations are in conflict with CEDAW Article 5, which calls for the modification of social and cultural patterns, sex roles, and stereotyping that are based on the idea of the inferiority or the superiority of either sex.[203] Therefore, such reservations are not valid under treaty law. Moreover, because they are not valid, and because they purport to permit violations of fundamental human rights, they should not be treated as satisfying the requirements for persistent objector status. Furthermore, we should be wary of finding these requirements to be easily satisfied because, as J. Patrick Kelly discusses in Chapter 2, recognition of persistent objector status can undermine the effectiveness of customary international law norms.[204]

In short, there are strong reasons for finding that, in Lepard's words, "states generally believe [that the customary norm of nondiscrimination based on sex furthers] such important values that [it] should bind all states, even states that have persistently objected [to it]."[205] In other words, states do not believe that persistent objection should be allowed to the general norm of nondiscrimination based on sex because it promotes the fundamental and important value of equality. Moreover, even if there is doubt about state beliefs on this score because of the record of reservations to CEDAW and other treaties dealing with women's rights, these doubts should be resolved against allowing persistent objection because states have viewed gender nondiscrimination as an essential right, as underlined earlier in the chapter. According to Lepard's theory, "where states reasonably believe that a norm directly advances

[200] Ibid., 230.

[201] See, e.g., International Center for Research on Women, *Property Ownership*, 2 ("no single global blueprint can address the complex landscape of property and inheritance practices – practices that are country and culture-specific").

[202] See Restatement (Third), § 312(3).

[203] CEDAW, art. 5.

[204] See Kelly, "Customary International Law in Historical Context," in this volume.

[205] Lepard, *Customary International Law*, 230.

fundamental ethical principles, and particularly compelling or essential ones, we should presume that they disfavor allowing persistent objection."[206] This presumption should definitely apply here.

Even though persistent objector status should not be recognized with respect to freedom from sex inequality, there may be some room for states to make certain distinctions between men and women, particularly where their purpose is actually to enhance the enjoyment of women's rights. In this connection, Lepard's theory does allow some limited permissible exceptions when they are consistent with the purpose of a norm.[207] He even allows some exceptions with respect to *jus cogens* norms. Thus, he suggests that some *jus cogens* norms may be "strongly peremptory" rather than completely peremptory. He provides an example involving race. He points out, on the one hand, that the definition of "genocide" under the Genocide Convention in Article II includes an intention to "destroy, in whole or in part, a … racial … group."[208] He notes that this is a "completely peremptory" norm that permits no exceptions. On the other hand, he observes that the generally accepted *jus cogens* norm prohibiting racial discrimination may be more appropriately referred to as a "strongly peremptory norm." This is because some exceptions may be permitted to allow a state to take "special measures" favoring a particular racial group to help advance the group if it has suffered from past discrimination.[209]

Similarly, with respect to women's rights, the general rule, as we have seen, is a prohibition against sex inequality, but some limited exceptions may be permissible based on the state or culture. For example, the European Group of National Human Rights Institutions[210] issued a white paper[211] in which it concluded that since gender equality is a "proactive principle," implementation of nondiscrimination may require "positive or affirmative action" in favor of women. The report emphasized that these measures were not to be viewed as derogations from equality, but rather as consistent with Article 4(1) of CEDAW, which provides that it is acceptable to use temporary measures to elevate the status of women who have suffered discrimination.[212]

[206] Ibid., 365.

[207] See ibid., 248.

[208] See Genocide Convention, art. II.

[209] Lepard, *Customary International Law*, 248.

[210] The European Group is a representative group of thirty-six National Human Rights Institutions ("NHRIs") within the Council of Europe. See http://bit.ly/1nRsSc4.

[211] European Group of National Human Rights Institutions, *Written Contribution by the European Group of National Human Rights Institutions to General Discussion of the Committee on the Elimination of Discrimination against Women on Access to Justice* (18th February 2013), available at http://bit.ly/1nRsSc4.

[212] Ibid., 2.

The extent to which these exceptions may be permitted is controversial.[213] Reference to Lepard's reliance on fundamental ethical principles, however, should provide some guidance. In particular, the "preeminent ethical principle" of "unity in diversity"[214] would seem to allow limited situations where modest exceptions to the fundamental ethical principles of equality, nondiscrimination, and human dignity are accommodated.[215] Invoking the fundamental principle of open-minded consultation can be the basis for developing a process to engage in the necessary investigations and dialogue to reach the appropriate balance.[216] At the same time, it is clear, as emphasized earlier, that states generally believe that no state can exempt itself from the basic norm of nondiscrimination based on gender through persistent objection, through treaty reservations, or through the adoption of discriminatory national laws. This is true even if the norm is not *jus cogens*. I next turn to the question of whether it is indeed a *jus cogens* norm.

9.5.3 *Is the Norm of Nondiscrimination Based on Gender a* Jus Cogens *Norm?*

Yet another question to address under Lepard's typology is whether a particular right (in this case a right to nondiscrimination based on gender) is a *jus cogens* norm. If women's human rights norms are determined to be *jus cogens*, then these norms will definitely prevail over other inconsistent treaty rules and not allow exemptions based on persistent objection to them.[217] Dinah Shelton has also stated, "Although the idea of *jus cogens* originated solely as a limitation on

[213] See, e.g., Directorate General for Internal Policies, "Policy Department C: Citizens' Rights and Constitutional Affairs, Gender Equality: How Could the Convention on the Elimination of All Forms of Discrimination against Women (CEDAW) be Implemented in the EU Legal Framework?" Note, PE453.193 (2011), 16 ("While differential treatment of women and men is permitted under the EU law in the form of provisions allowing Member States to take positive action measures or specific measures to ensure full equality of women and men in practice, the law does not impose positive obligation to introduce such measures. Furthermore, the permissibility of such measures is the subject of continuing consideration by the CJEU.") (referring to C. McCrudden and S. Prechal, *The Concepts of Equality and Non-Discrimination in Europe: A Practical Approach* (Brussels: European Commission, 2009), 38), available at www.europarl.europa.eu/RegData/etudes/etudes/join/2014/493040/IPOL-FEMM_ET(2014)493040_EN.pdf.

[214] See Lepard, *Customary International Law*, 83.

[215] See ibid., 82–86, 230, 257.

[216] See ibid., 90–91.

[217] See Michael Ewing-Chow, "First Do No Harm: Myanmar Trade Sanctions and Human Rights," 5 *Northwestern University Journal of International Human Rights* 153 (2007), 169 (noting that a treaty in conflict with a *jus cogens* norm is void, citing Vienna Convention on the Law of Treaties, art. 53).

the treaty-making power of states, today an assertion that a norm is *jus cogens* seems more often intended to override the will of persistent objectors to the emergence of the norm as customary international law."[218] All states are bound by these norms regardless of state practice. Any objection to or disavowal of the norm is invalid.

In the case of women's rights, the right of women to be free from gender-based violence and other forms of sex inequality is so vital that morally it must be considered impossible for individual states to contract out of these obligations. Moreover, there is evidence, reviewed earlier in the chapter, that states recognize these rights as norms that admit no derogation. Therefore, these rights should be considered preemptory rules and *jus cogens* norms. The right to freedom from gender discrimination should be treated as one of those rights, like racial nondiscrimination,[219] that is so morally essential as to constitute *jus cogens*.

Applying the four criteria that Lepard has proposed for identifying *jus cogens* norms[220] also supports this conclusion. First, the evidence presented in the preceding sections establishes that states generally believe that freedom from sex inequality should be strongly preemptory in character because of the importance of the values this freedom furthers. Second, states also generally believe that the norm should bind all states, even states that have made reservations to applicable treaties like CEDAW or have otherwise persistently objected to it. Third, states generally believe that the norm of freedom from sex inequality should preempt any contrary provision of an agreement between states and indeed should render such an agreement entirely void. States' belief that freedom from sex inequality should preempt contrary agreements is evidenced by CEDAW's lack of a provision permitting derogations and the fact that many states parties to CEDAW have objected to the assertion of reservations by other parties to some CEDAW provisions. Finally, states generally and reasonably believe that the norm of freedom from sex inequality furthers compelling or essential ethical principles. As discussed earlier in the chapter, there is growing evidence that states regard freedom from sex inequality as an essential human right that is linked directly to the "preeminent ethical principle of unity in diversity"[221] and justifiably limits state sovereignty.

218 Dinah Shelton, "Normative Hierarchy in International Law," 100 *American Journal of International Law* 291 (2006), 304.

219 See Ian Brownlie, *Principles of Public International Law* (Oxford: Oxford University Press, 6th ed. 2003), 515.

220 See Lepard, *Customary International Law*, 365–66 (application of criteria to right to change religion or belief).

221 See ibid., 78–81.

For all these reasons, even though it may be possible in some limited situations to justify exceptions to specific norms regarding sex inequality, the general norm of freedom from sex inequality should still be considered *jus cogens*.

In keeping with this analysis, a number of scholars have concluded that freedom from discrimination based on sex is not only a customary law norm but also a *jus cogens* norm that must trump competing norms, including those based on religion or culture. Thus, for example, Jordan Paust declares that the protection of women's human rights requires "the primacy of fundamental universal and peremptory *jus cogens* rights of women over contradictory claims in the name of the limited right to practice one's religion."[222]

Furthermore, several commentators have discussed how violations of women's human rights contained in CEDAW and other instruments are being increasingly recognized as violations of norms of *jus cogens*.[223] As noted earlier, Charlesworth and Chinkin have taken the position that women's rights should be considered *jus cogens* norms.[224] Paust has stated that there is "the need to protect fundamental universal rights of women to dignity and equality and their absolute, non-derogable, and peremptory *jus cogens* rights to freedom from torture and cruel, inhuman, and degrading treatment."[225] Rhonda Copelon has argued for the classification of the norm prohibiting gender-based violence as *jus cogens*.[226] Other scholars have specifically taken the position that rape in wartime is a violation of a *jus cogens* norm.[227]

9.5.4 *Does the Norm of Nondiscrimination Based on Gender Create* Erga Omnes *Obligations?*

The final question Lepard suggests we ask concerning a right established by a customary law norm is whether the right creates obligations *erga omnes*. Here, the question is whether women's human right to be free from sex inequality entails an obligation owed by the state not only to a particular other state but to the entire international community.

222 Jordan J. Paust, "International Law, Dignity, Democracy, and the Arab Spring," 46 *Cornell International Law Journal* 1 (2013), 14.

223 See, e.g., Mitchell, "The Prohibition of Rape," 226 (discussing sexual violence and rape in conflict and *jus cogens*).

224 See Hilary Charlesworth and Christine Chinkin, "The Gender of Jus Cogens."

225 Paust, "International Law, Dignity, Democracy, and the Arab Spring," 14.

226 Rhonda Copelon, "Recognizing the Egregious in the Everyday: Domestic Violence as Torture," 25 *Columbia Human Rights Law Review* 291 (1994), 365–66.

227 See Kelly D. Askin, "Prosecuting Wartime Rape and Other Gender-Related Crimes under International Law: Extraordinary Advances, Enduring Obstacles," 21 *Berkeley Journal of International Law* 288 (2003).

Arguably, once a human right is established as a *jus cogens* norm, it creates obligations *erga omnes*.[228] Eric Posner has noted that there are only a few international law rules that have been identified as *erga omnes* norms.[229] He lists aggression, genocide, slavery, and racial discrimination as four clear examples, but notes that others, including sex discrimination, are plausible.[230] We must therefore ask: If a state violates its obligation to ensure freedom from sex inequality, do other states than have a right to complain and seek a legal remedy?

Lepard's theory requires that we apply three tests to answer this question.[231] The first, whether states generally believe that the obligation to protect freedom from sex inequality is actually owed to all other states, must be answered "yes" if freedom from sex inequality is a universal customary norm, as I have argued here. It is also true that the evidence presented here demonstrates that states generally and reasonably believe that this norm furthers fundamental ethical principles, which is the second test.

The third test is the most problematic here, as with most norms involving a state's failure to honor its citizens' human rights. Can we demonstrate that states generally believe that there should be a right of other states to bring a claim in a forum with jurisdiction? Lepard's theory suggests that, as with the freedom to change religion or belief, if freedom from sex inequality is a morally essential right, then this test is satisfied. As he notes, in the *Barcelona Traction* case, the ICJ held that the "basic rights of the human person" created *erga omnes* obligations.[232] Eric Posner concludes that human rights "provide a strong case for *erga omnes* status" because of the injuries that other states may suffer as a result of the offending state's actions.[233] These conclusions should extend specifically to women's human rights.

At one level, injuries to other states from violations of women's rights may be only "moral," as in the case of human rights norms generally. On the other hand, some injuries to other states may be direct. For example, states may be required to give asylum to women who flee their home states because of violations of their human rights. Or states may experience the negative effects of human trafficking, such as increased violence, because another

[228] See, e.g., Posner, "Erga Omnes Norms," 14 (noting lack of clarity as to whether there is a meaningful difference between *jus cogens* norms and *erga omnes* norms).
[229] Ibid., 2. See also Maurizio Ragazzi, *The Concept of International Obligations Erga Omnes* (Oxford: Oxford University Press, 1997).
[230] Posner, "Erga Omnes Norms," 2.
[231] See Lepard, *Customary International Law*, 366–68.
[232] See *Barcelona Traction Case*, 32.
[233] Posner, "Erga Omnes Norms," 13.

state has failed to protect vulnerable girls and women from being subjected to trafficking.[234]

Therefore, it is reasonable to conclude that Lepard's third test for *erga omnes* status is fulfilled, because states generally believe that all states may be affected by violations of women's rights, morally and directly, and consequently should be able to bring a legal claim based on these violations in a forum with appropriate jurisdiction. For all these reasons, a compelling case can be made that women's rights should be treated as *erga omnes* obligations.

9.6 CONCLUSION

Lepard's theory can help establish that women's human rights are customary international law norms. Significant evidence shows that even in the absence of widespread or universal practice, states believe that freedom from sex inequality is a desirable norm to implement now or in the near future, and is thus a customary norm. Moreover, I have shown that it is a norm admitting no exceptions for persistent objectors, is a *jus cogens* norm, and establishes *erga omnes* obligations.

By recognizing freedom from sex discrimination and other women's rights as customary law, greater progress will be made in achieving freedom from sex inequality and improving women's lives. Further efforts must be made to determine how to implement and enforce these rights. The necessary focus on the individual requires that individual women be given the right to make complaints that their rights under customary international law and relevant treaties are being violated. Often women's human rights are violated by nonstate actors. In these situations the state must be required to ensure the protection of women from these acts. The preferred method is to have states incorporate these rights into their domestic law, accompanied by appropriate enforcement measures. A realistic approach would also accommodate the filing of individual complaints, as well as complaints by other states, with international bodies when states have failed to provide adequate domestic relief to women residing in them. More study and thought must be devoted to the enforcement of women's human rights when states fail to act to protect them.

[234] See generally Karen Parker and Jennifer F. Chew, "Compensation for Japan's World War II War-Rape Victims," 17 *Hastings International & Comparative Law Review* 497 (1994), 519 n.126, 521 (discussing protection from slavery, including modern-day slavery, as an obligation *erga omnes* arising out of international human rights law).

PART IV

Reexamining Customary Air and Space Law

10

Customary International Law in Aviation

A Hundred Years of Travel through the Competing Norms of Sovereignty and Freedom of Overflight

Sofia Michaelides-Mateou

10.1 INTRODUCTION: THE EVOLUTION OF INTERNATIONAL AVIATION LAW

Flight technology goes back to 1783, when the first manned flight was made in a hot air balloon.[1] The first national legislation relating to air law was passed the following year, in 1784, when the French enacted a law requiring balloons to fly with a special licence.[2] With technological developments, the legal framework regulating air law rapidly transcended national boundaries and spanned international horizons. Today, the framework of law and policy within which international air transportation operates is a complex system of multinational treaties and bilateral agreements, national laws, regulations, policies, and informal arrangements – but also, as I explore in this chapter, customary international law.

The multilayered system of aviation law I have just described has developed at the international level amid a persisting tension between two competing norms. Since the earliest years of aviation, some states advocated for a principle of complete state sovereignty over their airspace, while other states preferred to recognize a principle of "freedom of the air." Regarding the former principle, many centuries ago a state's complete and exclusive sovereignty over its territory was recognized in accordance with the maxim that first appeared in the writings of the thirteenth-century Accursius of Bologna, "*Cuius est solum, eius est usque ad caelum et ad inferos*." According to this maxim, a landowner's

[1] On November 21, 1783, Jean-François Pilâtre de Rozier and François d'Arlandes made the first flight in a hot air balloon created by the Montgolfier brothers in France. See Sofia Michaelides-Mateou, *Air Law: A Practical Perspective* (Greece: Ant. N. Sakkoulas Publishers, 2010), 54 (published in English and Greek in the European Studies in Law series).

[2] See Ronald I.C. Bartsch, *International Aviation Law: A Practical Guide* (Surrey, UK: Ashgate Publishing, 2012), 2.

rights extended up to the heavens and down to the depths of the earth.[3] The right of states to limit flights over their airspace, stemming from the norm holding that a state has complete and exclusive authority over its territory and airspace, was embodied in the first air law treaty, the 1919 Convention Relating to the Regulation of Aerial Navigation ("Paris Convention").[4] It was also featured in the Convention on International Civil Aviation of 1944 ("Chicago Convention").[5]

In keeping with this principle, there is no accepted right under customary international law for one state to fly its planes in the airspace over another state – often referred to as "freedom of overflight" – despite advocacy of this principle by many states. The situation is starkly different in maritime law, under which freedom of innocent passage at sea, including the freedom to fly over the high seas, is a well-established principle of customary international law recognized in international treaties like the UN Convention on the Law of the Sea ("UNCLOS").[6]

The tension between the norms of sovereignty and freedom of overflight is the cornerstone of international air law. It has been the focal point of disputes and discussions among states since the beginning of aviation in the early eighteenth century, when the first German air balloons flew over French airspace and the two states met at Paris, eventually culminating in the Paris Convention, in an attempt to find ways to address the tension.[7]

Another difference between air law and maritime law involves the relative importance of customary international law in relation to treaty law. Because air travel is a relatively recent phenomenon, it has been regulated primarily by treaties, such as the Paris Convention and the Chicago Convention. Customary international law has played a less important role. By comparison, the law of the sea originally developed as customary law, and only in modern decades has been codified in international treaties like UNCLOS.

Despite these apparent differences between air law and maritime law, the two may be slowly converging. Thus, the content of customary international

[3] See I.H.Ph. Diederiks-Verschoor, *An Introduction to Air Law* (The Hague: Kluwer Law International, 7th ed. 2001), 4.

[4] See Convention Relating to the Regulation of Aerial Navigation, signed at Paris, 13 October 1919, with Additional Protocol, signed at Paris, 1 May 1920, [1922] League of Nations Treaty Series 99; 11 LNTS 173 ("Paris Convention").

[5] ICAO Doc. 7300/9 (9th ed. 2009), available at www.icao.int/publications/Documents/7300_cons.pdf.

[6] See United Nations Convention of the Law of the Sea ("UNCLOS"), Montego Bay, 10 December 1982, reprinted in 21 *International Legal Materials* 1261 (1982). Available at https://treaties.un.org/Pages/ViewDetailsIII.aspx?src=TREATY&mtdsg_no=XXI-6&chapter=21&Temp=mtdsg3&clang=_en.

[7] See Diederiks-Verschoor, *An Introduction to Air Law*, 2.

law in relation to the competing principles of state sovereignty and freedom of overflight is gradually evolving, thanks in part to the adoption of numerous air transport and "open skies" agreements by which states grant certain rights, including rights of overflight, to other states. As a result of these treaties, there may well be a limited customary norm allowing certain kinds of overflights. The existence of these treaties alongside the long-standing Chicago Convention and other treaties reiterating the state sovereignty norm provides an intriguing case study of the interrelationship between treaty law and customary international law.

The chapter first provides an overview of customary international air law. Next, it looks at the role of treaties and their relationship with customary international law generally. It then reviews key treaties on international air law, including the Paris Convention and the Chicago Convention. In light of this analysis of important treaties, it engages in a closer examination of which norms of air law have attained the status of customary international law. As part of this analysis, it explores the relationship between customary international air law and the customary international law of the sea, including differences and similarities between the two bodies of customary law.

The chapter then focuses on the conflicting norms of state sovereignty and freedom of overflight. It considers to what extent these norms have passed into customary law and whether some freedoms of overflight are now part of customary law.

Next, the chapter devotes significant attention to the implications for these issues of the 2011 judgment of the Court of Justice of the European Union ("CJEU") on the EU Emission Trading Scheme ("ETS"), which directly addressed the customary law status of a number of norms of air law. That judgment resulted from a challenge by three air carriers and the Air Transport Association of America to the lawfulness under customary international air law of the extension of the ETS – essentially a "cap and trade" scheme – to greenhouse gas emissions from air travel in an EU directive issued in 2008.[8] In particular, the directive restricted the total amount of emissions allowed for all "flights which depart from or arrive in an aerodrome situated in the territory of a Member State." Under this language, the directive's restrictions extended to flights to or from a non-EU state, and parts of which may take place over the high seas.[9]

[8] See Directive 2008/101/EC of the European Parliament and of the Council of 19 November 2008, amending Directive 2003/87/EC so as to include aviation activities in the scheme for greenhouse gas emission allowance trading within the Community, OJ L 8/3, 13.1.2009. Available at http://eur-lex.europa.eu/LexUriServ/ LexUriServ.do?uri=OJ:L:2009:008:0003:0021:EN:PDF.

[9] Ibid., Annex 1(c), "Aviation."

The plaintiffs argued that this attempt by the EU to regulate emissions from flights originating in a non-EU state, or with a non-EU state as a final destination, and to flights over the high seas violated various asserted customary air law norms, including norms of sovereignty over the airspace above a country and freedom to fly over the high seas. The CJEU held that while the EU must comply with customary international law, and while most of the asserted norms were indeed norms of customary international law, the EU directive did not infringe on them, and the claimants could not successfully challenge the EU directive. The Court reasoned that every flight subject to the directive had a physical presence – whether at its origin or destination – within an EU member state.[10]

The chapter critiques important aspects of this judgment on the basis of its analysis of the content of customary international air law. Most importantly, the judgment is at odds with the clear import of the customary norm of exclusive sovereignty over territorial airspace and the customary norm of freedom to fly over the high seas. The EU directive is an unacceptable and unlawful encroachment on these norms.

Finally, the chapter concludes that while customary international law has had a greater influence on maritime law than on air law, its role in air law is being strengthened. As the CJEU decision emphasizes, customary international law is an important part of international air law. It contains many of the foundational norms of air law. At the same time, these norms are evolving as both state practice (including through treaties) and *opinio juris* change and adapt to new conditions.

10.2 CUSTOMARY LAW AS A SOURCE OF INTERNATIONAL AIR LAW

International air law today forms an important part of international law as a result of the frequency of cross-border air travel. International air law consists mainly of written law. Written sources of international air law are multilateral conventions, the primary source of air law, and bilateral agreements between states relating to air flight. Furthermore, air law encompasses a variety of written sources other than treaties, including national law, agreements between states

[10] See *Air Transport Association of America and Others v. Secretary of State for Energy and Climate Change*, C-366/10, Judgment of the Court (Grand Chamber), 21 December 2011 (hereinafter "*Air Transport Association of America and Others*"), paras. 124–30. In InfoCuria – Case-law of the Court of Justice. Available at http://curia.europa.eu/juris/document/document.jsf?docid=117193&mode=req&pageIndex=1&dir=&occ=first&part=1&text=emissions%2Btrading%2Bscheme&doclang=EN&cid=15541#ctx1.

and airline companies (as in the case where the state is the sole or major shareholder of an airline), and private contracts between airline companies, such as code sharing and interlining agreements. However, international air law also includes unwritten sources of law, as recognized in Article 38 of the Statute of the International Court of Justice ("ICJ"), namely customary international law and general principles of law.[11] I focus here on customary international air law.

As Brian Lepard explains in Chapter 1, customary international law is the oldest source of international law, for it dates back to the first norms regulating conduct between countries based on their practices and their belief that legal norms had evolved regulating those practices. Thus, according to international law scholar Ian Brownlie, "Custom is not a special department or area of public international law: it *is* international law."[12]

We have also seen that under traditional doctrine, customary international law arises when two conditions have been satisfied. First, there must exist an established, widespread, and consistent practice by states. Second, there must exist a psychological belief by states that the practice is legally required or necessary (referred to as *opinio juris sive necessitatis*, or more simply as *opinio juris*).[13] These two elements were referred to by the ICJ in the 1985 *Continental Shelf Case (Libyan Arab Jamahiriya v. Malta)*[14] as well as the 1969 *North Sea Continental Shelf Cases*.[15] They have also been reaffirmed by the International Law Commission in its study of customary international law. In particular, Draft Conclusion 2 of the ILC, adopted in 2016, states: "To determine the existence and content of a rule of customary international law, it is necessary to ascertain whether there is a general practice that is accepted as law (*opinio juris*)."[16] Draft Conclusion 3 reaffirms that both elements must be separately proved. Thus, paragraph 2 of that conclusion asserts: "Each of the two constituent elements is to be separately ascertained. This requires an assessment of evidence for each element."[17]

11 See generally Diederiks-Verschoor, *An Introduction to Air Law*, 1.

12 Ian Brownlie, *The Rule of Law in International Affairs: International Law at the Fiftieth Anniversary of the United Nations* (The Hague/London/Boston: Martinus Nijhoff, 1998), 18 (emphasis in the original).

13 See, e.g., Hugh Thirlway, "The Sources of International Law," in *International Law*, edited by Malcolm D. Evans 95 (Oxford: Oxford University Press, 3rd ed. 2010), 102.

14 *Continental Shelf Case (Libyan Arab Jamahiriya v. Malta)*, Judgment of 3 June 1985, 1985 ICJ Rep. 13, 29–30, para. 27.

15 *North Sea Continental Shelf Cases (Federal Republic of Germany v. Denmark; Federal Republic of Germany v. Netherlands)*, Judgment of 20 February 1969, 1969 ICJ Rep. 3, 44, para. 77.

16 "Report of the International Law Commission," Sixty-Eighth Session (2 May–10 June and 4 July–12 August 2016), UN Doc. A/71/10 (2016), 76–79, Draft Conclusion 2.

17 Ibid., Draft Conclusion 3, para. 2.

This long-standing two-element definition of customary international law that has been endorsed by both scholars and the International Law Commission is valid and should govern the determination of customary international air law – notwithstanding some critiques that have been made of it, including by Brian Lepard in this volume.[18] The question in the domain of air law is therefore whether there is a general practice among states relating to a particular asserted norm of air law and whether states accept the norm that is the subject of the practice as binding law.

Since all states undertake flights or have domestic air carriers, they all can participate in the formation of a "general practice." However, the practices of various states may differ. For example, some may have entered into bilateral "open skies" agreements (discussed later in the chapter), while others may not have done so. Furthermore, it might be argued that the practices of particular states that have far more extensive air operations than others ought to "count" more than the practices of states with limited air activity, and that the views of these states should similarly be given greater weight in the ascertainment of *opinio juris*.

In this connection, the ICJ has stated that to establish a rule of customary international law, state practice must be both virtually uniform, in the sense that different states must not have engaged in substantially different conduct, and extensive and representative, meaning that the practice must be general but also "include that of States whose interests are specially affected."[19] This appears to require that at least a large majority of states undertake consistent practices relevant to air law. At the same time, it could leave open the argument that states with more extensive air operations are "specially affected" and therefore that their practices and views about the status of air norms as law should be given proportionately greater consideration. However, the better perspective is that in the context of air law, all states conducting air operations are "specially affected," irrespective of their size, the scope of their own air operations, and the number and size of their domestic and international carriers. Accordingly, in assessing general practice and *opinio juris* the behavior and attitudes of all states should be given equal consideration. Furthermore, a significant majority of states must engage in a similar or uniform practice for a related norm to be recognized as customary law.

Although there is general agreement on the aforementioned doctrines of customary international law, and in particular the two-element definition, the

[18] See Brian D. Lepard, "Toward a New Theory of Customary International Human Rights Law," in this volume.

[19] *North Sea Continental Shelf Cases*, 43, para. 74.

actual process by which rules of customary international rules develop as well as the identification of such rules are still largely unsettled, as illustrated by many of the other chapters in this volume. One area of particular difficulty involves the question of the relationship between treaties and customary international law. For example, when, if ever, can rules in bilateral or multilateral treaties evolve into customary law norms binding all states? This problem is especially acute in international air law in relation to the impact of air treaties on customary law, as I examine in the following sections.

10.3 THE ROLE OF TREATIES AND THEIR RELATIONSHIP WITH CUSTOMARY INTERNATIONAL LAW

A treaty, which may also be referred to as a "convention" or an "agreement," is an official, express written agreement that is legally binding on the states that ratify it.[20] The obligation to observe treaties is itself based on a rule of customary international law, namely "*pacta sunt servanda*," which means "agreements must be kept." In this connection, Article 26 of the Vienna Convention on the Law of Treaties, which codifies this customary rule,[21] provides: "Every treaty in force is binding upon the parties to it and must be performed by them in good faith."[22] This customary international law principle creates the obligation for states that are parties to a treaty to honor their obligations under the treaty.[23] In general, treaties are only binding on these states parties. In this connection, the great international law scholar Vattel wrote: "As it is evident that a treaty binds none but the contracting parties, the conventional law of nations is not a universal but a particular law."[24] This general principle is codified in Article 34 of the Vienna Convention on the Law of Treaties, which states that "a treaty does not create either obligations or rights for a third State without its consent."[25]

[20] See Malcolm N. Shaw, *International Law* (Cambridge: Cambridge University Press, 2003), 88–92, esp. 88.

[21] The Vienna Convention on the Law of Treaties, 1155 UNTS 331 (1969), codified many preexisting customary rules on treaties between states, but also established new treaty rules for states parties. It was adopted on 22 May 1969 and opened for signature on 23 May 1969. Available at https://treaties.un.org/doc/publication/unts/volume%201155/volume-1155-i-18232-english.pdf.

[22] Ibid., art. 26.

[23] On *pacta sunt servanda*, see generally Christopher Greenwood, "Sources of International Law: An Introduction," available at http://legal.un.org/avl/pdf/ls/Greenwood_outline.pdf.

[24] Emer de Vattel, *The Law of Nations, or, Principles of the Law of Nature, Applied to the Conduct and Affairs of Nations and Sovereigns, with Three Early Essays on the Origin and Nature of Natural Law and on Luxury*, edited and with an Introduction by Béla Kapossy and Richard Whitmore (Indianapolis: Liberty Fund, 2008), 43. Available at http://oll.libertyfund.org/titles/vattel-the-law-of-nations-lf-ed.

[25] Vienna Convention on the Law of Treaties, art. 34.

Importantly, however, the Vienna Convention clarifies that a norm of customary international law expressed in a treaty binds all states independently of the treaty.[26] In particular, Article 38 affirms: "Nothing in articles 34 to 37 precludes a rule set forth in a treaty from becoming binding upon a third State as a customary rule of international law, recognized as such."[27] In other words, a rule in a treaty that initially binds only the parties can evolve into a rule of customary international law binding all states. Of course, treaties may also codify preexisting customary international law, which already binds all states apart from the treaty.

The ICJ has recognized these dual roles of treaties in relation to customary international law – either giving rise to new customary norms or codifying preexisting ones.[28] For example, in the 1985 *Continental Shelf Case (Libyan Arab Jamahiriya v. Malta)*, it stated that "multilateral conventions may have an important role to play in recording and defining rules deriving from custom, or indeed in developing them."[29] In the 1986 *Nicaragua Case*,[30] the United States argued that the Court should not apply the rules of customary international law because they had been "subsumed" and "supervened" by those of international treaty law, particularly the rules in the UN Charter.[31] The ICJ rejected this argument, concluding that customary international rules on the use of force continued to exist alongside treaty law. It found, furthermore, that the areas governed by the two sources of law do not overlap exactly and the rules therefore do not have the same content.[32]

In the *Nicaragua Case*, the ICJ referred to its earlier observation in the 1969 *North Sea Continental Shelf Cases*[33] that the degree of ratification of a treaty was important with regard to the assessment of whether its rules had evolved into customary international law. The Court stated in the *North Sea Continental Shelf Cases*:

> With respect to the other elements usually regarded as necessary before a conventional rule can be considered to have become a general rule of international law, it might be that, even without the passage of any considerable

[26] See generally Thirlway, "The Sources of International Law," 97.

[27] Vienna Convention on the Law of Treaties, art. 38.

[28] On this point, see generally Jean-Marie Henckaerts, "Study on Customary International Humanitarian Law: A Contribution to the Understanding and Respect for the Rule of Law in Armed Conflict," 87 *International Review of the Red Cross* No. 857, 175 (2005), 183.

[29] *Continental Shelf Case (Libyan Arab Jamahiriya v. Malta)*, 29–30, para 27.

[30] *Military and Paramilitary Activities in and against Nicaragua (Nicaragua v. United States of America)*, Merits, Judgment of 27 June 1986, 1986 ICJ Rep. 14 ("*Nicaragua Case*").

[31] Ibid., 93, para. 174.

[32] See ibid., 94, para. 176.

[33] *North Sea Continental Shelf Cases*, 42, para. 73.

> period of time, *a very widespread and representative participation in the convention* might suffice of itself, provided it included that of States whose interests were specially affected.[34]

The Court went on to say that in that case, even if allowance was made for the existence of a number of states to whom participation in the 1958 Geneva Convention on the Continental Shelf was not open, the number of ratifications and accessions secured – thirty-nine at that time – was insufficient.[35] By contrast, in the *Nicaragua Case*, the Court placed a great deal of weight on the fact that the UN Charter was almost universally ratified in assessing the customary law status of the rule in Article 2(4) of the Charter prohibiting the use force by one state against another.[36] In the 1985 *Continental Shelf Case (Libyan Arab Jamahiriya v. Malta)*, the ICJ effectively concluded that a treaty may reflect customary law even if it has not yet entered into force, so long as there is sufficiently similar practice, including practice by affected states, so that there would be very little possibility of any opposition to the rule.[37]

The ICJ has also addressed in various cases the time period required for the formation of a customary rule, including one that originated in a treaty. In the 1969 *North Sea Continental Shelf Cases*, the Court said that the passage of only a short period of time would not necessarily preclude the formation of a customary rule during that time frame.[38] It stated, however, that it would be an "indispensable requirement" that within even that short time, "State practice, including that of States whose interests are specially affected, should have been both extensive and virtually uniform in the sense of the provision invoked; – and should moreover have occurred in such a way as to show a general recognition that a rule of law or legal obligation is involved."[39]

The ICJ, other courts, and various experts believe that some of the norms in particular treaties have passed into customary law, as we saw in the earlier example of the *Nicaragua Case*. To give another relevant example, the ICJ has recognized and applied many provisions of the Vienna Convention on the Law of Treaties on the ground that these provisions state rules that are

34 Ibid. (emphasis added).

35 Ibid. On the number of ratifications, see ibid., 25, para. 26.

36 See *Nicaragua Case*, 99–100, para. 188.

37 *Continental Shelf Case (Libyan Arab Jamahiriya v. Malta)*, 29–33, paras. 27–34. In that case the Court determined that the concept of an exclusive economic zone ("EEZ") had become part of customary international law, even though the UN Convention on the Law of the Sea had not yet entered into force. It noted that the number of claims to an EEZ had risen to fifty-six, which included several specially affected states. For a discussion of the case, see Henckaerts, "Study on Customary International Humanitarian Law," 183.

38 *North Sea Continental Shelf Cases*, 42, para. 74.

39 Ibid.

applicable as customary law to all states, including states that are not party to the Convention.[40] Even though only 114 states have ratified the Vienna Convention as of August 2016,[41] many other courts have agreed with the ICJ that the main provisions of the Convention codify customary law and are therefore applicable to all states, irrespective of whether they are a party to the Convention.[42]

Rules of multilateral treaties that did not codify preexisting customary law but were "new" rules may nevertheless, over time, pass into customary law binding on all states. This is most likely to occur when the drafters of the treaties intended them to be universally ratified. Of course, it is also critical that states generally, including nonparties, come to accept the treaty rules as binding upon them under customary law and apart from the treaty.[43]

When treaty provisions become binding upon nonparties as a result of a customary process, the norms are only customary law for them, whereas parties to the treaty are bound by both the treaty norms and the parallel customary international law norms. Soviet legal scholar Grigory Tunkin argued that the latter norms should be referred to as "mixed norms" or "treaty-customary" norms.[44] One must, however, take into account a number of important differences between treaty norms and customary norms. For example, international treaties may generally be amended or terminated by states parties, whereas customary norms may be changed only by state practice accepted as law. Treaty norms may also be more rigid than customary norms, which may be more flexible. However, it is now more common for treaty provisions to be changed by subsequent practice, especially in the case of bilateral treaties.[45] Finally, treaty norms are often more specific than customary norms. I discuss the application of these concepts to multilateral air law treaties in the following sections.

The application of customary norms to particular states can also be modified by treaty commitments undertaken by those states, so long as the norms are not peremptory norms.[46] If the treaty norms are widely accepted, this could

40 See generally Thirlway, "The Sources of International Law," 100.

41 See https://treaties.un.org/Pages/ViewDetailsIII.aspx?src=TREATY&mtdsg_no=XXIII-1&chapter=23&Temp=mtdsg3&clang=_en (last accessed 29 August 2016).

42 See Greenwood, "Sources of International Law."

43 On this point, see Brian D. Lepard, *Customary International Law: A New Theory with Practical Applications* (New York: Cambridge University Press, 2010), 191–204.

44 See Grigory Tunkin, "Is General International Law Customary Law Only?" 4 *European Journal of International Law* 534 (1993), 539.

45 See ibid., 539–40.

46 See Vienna Convention on the Law of Treaties, art. 53 (providing in part that "a treaty is void if, at the time of its conclusion, it conflicts with a peremptory norm of general international law").

also result in a modification of the underlying customary norm that applies to nonparties.

10.4 KEY TREATIES ON INTERNATIONAL AIR LAW AND THEIR RELATIONSHIP TO CUSTOMARY INTERNATIONAL LAW

In light of the discussion in the preceding section on the relationship between treaties and customary international law, I now examine some key provisions of important air law treaties. In the following sections I evaluate the extent to which they codified existing customary law and whether or not they have now generated new norms of customary law.

International treaties on air law originated in the early 1900s, when the French jurist Fauchille suggested that a code of international air navigation be drafted. The first intensive attempt at codification was in 1910, when German balloons flew above French territory. This attempt led to the holding of the Paris Conference in October 1919.[47] The Paris Conference was convened as a forum for states to exchange views regarding sovereignty over airspace. The Conference resulted in the adoption of the first international public air law treaty – the 1919 Paris Convention. The Paris Convention regulated flights of aircraft between different states. The preamble affirmed that the drafting states recognized "the necessity of an early agreement upon certain principles and rules calculated to prevent controversy."[48]

Most importantly, the Paris Convention addressed the fundamental, contentious question of whether states had sovereignty over their airspace or whether there should be freedom of overflight. The drafters of the Convention opted unequivocally in favor of absolute state sovereignty over the airspace above a country. This principle was affirmed in Article 1, which provided: "The High Contracting Parties recognize that every Power has complete and exclusive sovereignty over the air space above its territory. For the purpose of the present Convention, the territory of a State shall be understood as including the national territory, both that of the mother country and of the colonies, and the territorial waters adjacent thereto."[49] At the same time, the Convention recognized a limited right of innocent passage (overflight) through a state's airspace. Thus, Article 2 declared: "Each contracting State undertakes in time of peace to accord freedom of innocent passage above its territory to the aircraft of the other contracting States, provided that the conditions laid down in the present

47 Diederiks-Verschoor, *An Introduction to Air Law*, 2.

48 Paris Convention, preamble.

49 Ibid., art. 1.

Convention are observed. Regulations made by a contracting State as to the admission over its territory of the aircraft of the other contracting States shall be applied without distinction of nationality."[50] Under Article 6, aircraft "possess the nationality of the State on the register of which they are entered,"[51] and under Article 8, they must be registered to one state only.[52] Eventually, thirty-two states ratified the Paris Convention.

In 1944, states adopted the Chicago Convention to elaborate on the norms in the 1919 Paris Convention and replace it. The fifty-four states that met in Chicago to draft the Convention recognized the need to provide an operational framework for aviation, establish order in the skies, deal with traffic rights, and promote the safe and orderly development of international civil aviation. The Chicago Convention aimed at regulating civil aviation internationally on a worldwide scale, and established the International Civil Aviation Organization ("ICAO") to develop the principles and techniques of international air transportation and to foster the planning and development of international air transport.

Once again, the drafting states had to address conflicting views among them about whether there should be a right of overflight over a state's airspace. And once again, they chose to reaffirm the principle of absolute state sovereignty over airspace codified in Article 1 of the Paris Convention. Thus, Article 1 of the Chicago Convention provides, repeating Article 1 of the Paris Convention almost verbatim: "The contracting States recognize that every State has complete and exclusive sovereignty over the airspace above its territory."[53] At the time of the drafting of the Chicago Convention, the allocation of traffic rights among states was a critical and contentious issue. Again, the Convention generally protected the sovereignty of states. Article 6 of the Convention goes on to state in this connection: "No scheduled international air service may be operated over or into the territory of a contracting State, except with the special permission or other authorization of that State and in accordance with the terms of such permission or authorization."[54]

Although they agreed on this rule, the states drafting the Chicago Convention could not reach consensus on the scope of the freedoms of the air. I return to this subject in a later discussion. Furthermore, the Chicago Convention addressed the regulation of aircraft flying over the high seas. The Convention stipulates that "over the high seas, the rules in force shall be

50 Ibid., art. 2.
51 Ibid., art. 6.
52 Ibid., art. 8 (providing that "an aircraft cannot be validly registered in more than one State").
53 Chicago Convention, art. 1.
54 Ibid., art. 6.

those established under this Convention."[55] In turn, under the Convention, an aircraft is considered to be a national of the state in which it is registered pursuant to Article 17, which parallels Article 6 of the Paris Convention. Accordingly, the state of registration of an aircraft flying over the high seas generally has jurisdiction over the aircraft while it flies over the high seas.[56]

Today, the Chicago Convention is the cornerstone of the international legal regime governing civil aviation. As of August 2016, it had been ratified by 191 states, representing nearly all members of the United Nations, with just a few exceptions.[57]

In addition to the Paris and Chicago Conventions, there are two other important, broad multilateral treaties dealing with civil aviation. The first is the Warsaw Convention, adopted ten years after the Paris Conference, in 1929.[58] The Warsaw Convention regulated the international transportation of passengers and goods. It determined liability of the owner or operator of the carrier for any injury, death, or property damage. The second is the 1999 Montreal Convention, which replaced the Warsaw Convention.[59] It protects airline customers and prescribes the conditions and amounts of air carrier liability. It provides a two-tier system of liability in the event of death or bodily injury of a passenger. As of August 2016, there were 120 parties to the convention.[60] In this chapter I focus on the customary law status of certain norms in the Paris and Chicago Conventions, rather than on the status of the norms in the Warsaw and Montreal Conventions.

10.5 CUSTOMARY INTERNATIONAL AIR LAW AND ITS RELATIONSHIP TO AIR LAW TREATIES

Having explored some key air law treaties, I turn now to a closer examination of which norms in these treaties have attained the status of customary international law. I focus on the long-standing tension between the norms of state sovereignty and freedom of overflight.

55 Ibid., art. 12.

56 See generally Michael Milde, *International Air Law and ICAO* (Utrecht: Eleven International Publishing, 2008), vol. 4 of *Essential Air and Space Law*, edited by Marietta Benkö, 46.

57 See the list of states parties available at http://www.icao.int/secretariat/legal/List%20of%20Parties/Chicago_EN.pdf. The Chicago Convention came into force in April 1947 after twenty-six states ratified it.

58 The Convention for Unification of Certain Rules Relating to International Carriage by Air was signed in Warsaw on 12 October 1929 ("Warsaw Convention").

59 Convention for the Unification of Certain Rules for International Carriage by Air – Montreal, 28 May 1999, entered into force on 4 November 2003 ("Montreal Convention").

60 For a list of states parties as of August 2016, see www.icao.int/secretariat/legal/List%20of%20Parties/Mtl99_EN.pdf.

First of all, states have repeatedly rejected a broad norm of freedom of overflight. They did so in 1919, during the drafting of the Paris Convention, and again in 1944, when the Chicago Convention was elaborated. Accordingly, it cannot be maintained that such a far-reaching norm is part of customary international law.

On the contrary, the Paris and Chicago Conventions provide strong evidence that a norm of relatively absolute sovereignty over the air space above a state has now become part of customary international law. Both treaties evidence a belief by the parties that such a norm is desirable. It has survived many challenges over the last 100 years. The number of states that have ratified the Chicago Convention and thus endorsed the norm constitutes a substantial portion of the 196-odd independent sovereign states in the world – 191, or about 97 percent. This is similar to the near-universal ratification of the UN Charter referred to by the ICJ in the *Nicaragua Case* in finding the UN Charter norm prohibiting the unilateral use of force by one state against another to be part of customary international law. On the other hand, it is far higher than the relatively low percentage of ratification of the Geneva Convention on the Continental Shelf referred to by the ICJ in the *North Sea Continental Shelf Cases*.

However, the norm of a state's absolute and complete sovereignty over the airspace above its territory has not remained static. A number of bilateral and regional treaties have sought to restrict this sovereignty. For example, under its foundational treaties, the EU has over the last decades developed a single internal market in which nationals of one EU member state can invest in, establish, and control airlines licensed in any other EU member state. The fact that airlines in the EU are set up and licensed under a common set of rules and can operate any route within the EU has led to recognition of the notion of an "EU carrier." One of the obligations of an EU member state, then, is not to discriminate among such EU carriers in the regulation of flights within its airspace.

Indeed, the CJEU has identified and upheld just such an obligation. In November 2002, the Court held, in the case of *Commission of the European Communities v. United Kingdom of Great Britain and Northern Ireland*,[61] that if a bilateral air services agreement between an EU member state and a third country permits only the designation of airlines that are owned and controlled by nationals of that EU member state, the designation is discriminatory and

[61] *Commission of the European Communities v. United Kingdom of Great Britain and Northern Ireland*, Case C-466/98, 31 January 2002, available at http://eur-lex.europa.eu/legal-content/EN/TXT/?uri=CELEX%3A61998CJ0466.

consequently violates EU law. As a result of this decision, every EU member state must grant equal market access for routes to destinations outside the EU to any EU carrier with an establishment in its territory. The Court held, in effect, that some issues covered in bilateral air services agreements are within exclusive EU competences and consequently should not be negotiated by EU member states on an autonomous basis.[62] Moreover, under the decision, the air service agreements between EU member states and third countries are required to be amended in order to conform to this legal requirement.[63]

This shows that the system of EU treaties, and their norm of nondiscrimination, can override the foundational customary norm of absolute and complete sovereignty over airspace (which includes the right to exercise that sovereignty through bilateral agreements like air service agreements). A more interesting question is whether the EU treaties may, along with other treaties and practices, have led to universal limitations on the customary norm of absolute sovereignty, and effectively modified that norm. In a later discussion I return to a fuller consideration of the extent to which the customary norm of sovereignty over airspace has been modified by various treaties and state practice relating to various "freedoms of the air." Before undertaking that investigation, however, to better understand the content of customary international air law, it is instructive to compare its evolution to that of maritime law and norms regarding the law of the sea – the subject to which I now turn.

10.6 THE RELATIONSHIP BETWEEN CUSTOMARY INTERNATIONAL AIR LAW AND THE CUSTOMARY INTERNATIONAL LAW OF THE SEA

It is helpful to compare the development of air law with maritime law because both bodies of law deal with human activity within specific geographic and physical areas having certain characteristics, and contain treaties that regulate such activities.[64] Moreover, the drafters of the Paris Convention of 1919 and the 1944 Chicago Convention were aware of the customary law of the sea, and kept this in mind while choosing to adopt, or not adopt, certain principles that were already part of that law. Accordingly, these air law treaties incorporate

62 See ibid., para. 96.

63 See European Commission Mobility and Transport, "Air – External Aviation Policy – Horizontal Agreements," available at http://ec.europa.eu/transport/modes/air/international_aviation/external_aviation_policy/horizontal_ agreements_en.htm.

64 See John Cobb Cooper, *Explorations in Aerospace Law: Selected Essays*, edited by Ivan A. Vlasic (Montreal: McGill University Press, 1968), 3, cited in Jae Woon Lee, "Revisiting Freedom of Overflight in International Air Law: Minimum Multilateralism in International Air Transport," 38 *Air & Space Law* 351 (2013), 354 n.13.

certain general principles of law that were originally developed in the context of the law of the sea. As a result, a review of the development of the international law of the sea can facilitate an understanding of legal instruments relating to air law, as well as an analysis of which norms in or outside these legal instruments may now be part of customary international air law.[65]

A key difference between the two fields is that the law of the sea developed over the course of many centuries, while air law has been created much more recently. The first legislation dealing specifically with conflicts arising out of the use of the sea was adopted in Venice and Genoa as well as other port cities along the Adriatic Sea in medieval times. Many other national laws were adopted, and seafaring states entered into treaties relating to the sea. All of this legislation and treaty law gave rise to a veritable and rich customary law of the sea. Much later, at the end of the twentieth century, significant efforts were made to codify the law of the sea, in particular as part of the UN Conference on the Law of the Sea. States gathered there to refine and articulate in a global treaty the norms that had developed on the law of the sea since the beginning of civilization, and in particular from the fifteenth century. That grand treaty was UNCLOS. It was signed in 1982 and entered into force in 1994. As of August 2016 it had been ratified by 168 states and is now the most important treaty defining the rights and obligations of states with respect to their use of the sea.[66]

Some of the norms in UNCLOS reflect preexisting customary law, while others changed preexisting customary law. Article 2 declares that the sovereignty of a coastal state extends beyond its land territory and internal waters to an adjacent belt of sea known as the "territorial sea," the breadth of which is set to a limit not exceeding 12 nautical miles, measured from baselines determined in accordance with Article 3 of the Convention.[67] However, importantly, UNCLOS limits that sovereignty. It provides in particular that ships of one state may exercise a right of "innocent passage" through the territorial sea of another state. This originated as a customary law norm. Article 17 of UNCLOS affirms in this connection that "ships of all States, whether coastal or land-locked, enjoy the right of innocent passage through the territorial sea."[68]

65 On this point, see Barbara Kwiatkowska, *International Organisations and the Law of the Sea: Documentary Yearbook*, vol. 1 (Dordrecht: Martinus Nijhoff, 1985), 244.

66 See generally Lesther Antonio Ortega Lemus, *Brief Outline of the History and Development of the Law of the Sea*, 1–9, available at www.academia.edu/1193093/Brief_Outline_of_the_History_and_Development_of_the_ Law_of_the_Sea. On the number of states parties, see https://treaties.un.org/Pages/ViewDetailsIII.aspx?src=TREATY&mtdsg_no=XXI-6&chapter=21&Temp=mtdsg3&clang=_en (last accessed 29 August 2016).

67 UNCLOS, art. 2. See also ibid., art. 3.

68 Ibid., art. 17, para. 3.

UNCLOS also creates the concept of an exclusive economic zone ("EEZ"). Article 55, dealing with the specific legal regime of the EEZ, states: "The exclusive economic zone is an area beyond and adjacent to the territorial sea, subject to the specific legal regime established in this Part, under which the rights and jurisdiction of the coastal State and the rights and freedoms of other States are governed by the relevant provisions of this Convention."[69]

Furthermore, UNCLOS codifies a long-standing customary norm protecting the freedom of all states to navigate on and use the high seas. The principle of freedom of passage on the high seas was paramount in the development of international maritime law. Hugo Grotius emphasized this principle in his influential book *Mare Liberum*. He wrote that the sea was free to all and that no state had the right to deny others access to it.[70] This principle has now become widely accepted in customary international law.[71] It is reflected in many international conventions, and in particular UNCLOS.

Thus, Article 87 of UNCLOS, entitled "Freedom of the high seas," affirms that "the high seas are open to all States, whether coastal or land-locked. Freedom of the high seas is exercised under the conditions laid down by this Convention and by other rules of international law."[72] For purposes of this rule, the term "high seas" is defined to refer to all parts of the sea that are not included in the EEZ, the territorial sea, the internal waters of a state, or the archipelagic waters of an archipelagic state.[73]

Importantly, a number of UNCLOS's provisions relate directly to regulation of the airspace above the sea. For example, Article 2, mentioned earlier, goes on to affirm that the sovereignty of the coastal state extends to the air space over the territorial sea, in addition to the bed and subsoil of the territorial sea.[74] Furthermore, paragraph 1 of Article 87, on freedom of the high seas, addresses certain air rights of states. It provides in relevant part that freedom of the high seas "comprises, inter alia, both for coastal and land-locked States:

a. *freedom of navigation*;
b. *freedom of overflight*;

[69] Ibid., art. 55.

[70] See generally Hugo Grotius, *Mare liberum, 1609–2009*, edited by Robert Feenstra (online publication: Brill, 2009), cited in Lee, "Revisiting Freedom of Overflight in International Air Law," 355 n.14.

[71] See, e.g., Shaw, *International Law*, 507, and Brownlie, *Principles of Public International Law*, 186.

[72] UNCLOS, art. 87, para. 1.

[73] Ibid., art. 86.

[74] Ibid.

c. freedom to lay submarine cables and pipelines, subject to Part VI;
d. freedom to construct artificial islands and other installations permitted under international law, subject to Part VI;
e. freedom of fishing, subject to the conditions laid down in section 2;
f. freedom of scientific research, subject to Parts VI and XIII."[75]

This article specifically asserts that freedom of the high seas includes freedom of overflight and navigation. This means that the high seas and the air space above them cannot be subject to the sovereignty of any state.

Unlike the law of the sea, international air law is only a century old. The drafters of the Paris Convention of 1919 and the Chicago Convention of 1944 chose to adopt and reinforce the concept of territorial sovereignty by applying it to the airspace above a state's land territory as well as the airspace above the territorial sea. As noted earlier, Article 1 of the Chicago Convention affirms that "the contracting States recognize that every State has complete and exclusive sovereignty over the airspace above its territory."[76] Article 2 goes on to clarify that for purposes of the Convention, "the territory of a State shall be deemed to be the land areas *and territorial waters adjacent thereto* under the sovereignty, suzerainty, protection or mandate of such State."[77] This rule parallels the customary right to exercise sovereignty over the territorial sea reiterated in Article 2 of UNCLOS.

However, the drafters of both the Paris Convention and the Chicago Convention rejected the adoption of a doctrine parallel to that of "freedom of innocent passage" through a state's territorial sea that had become part of customary maritime law and was later codified in Article 17 of UNCLOS. The Chicago Convention recognizes no such right of innocent passage (overflight) of a state's aircraft through the airspace above the land territory or territorial sea of another state.

At the same time, the drafters of the Paris Convention and the Chicago Convention sought to integrate those treaty norms with customary maritime law where air law and maritime law intersect. The Chicago Convention, for example, implicitly respects freedom of the high seas, including the impermissibility of any one state exercising jurisdiction over the airspace above them, by providing that "over the high seas, the rules in force shall be those established under this Convention."[78]

[75] Ibid., art. 87, para. 1 (emphasis added).
[76] Chicago Convention, art. 1.
[77] Ibid., art. 2 (emphasis added).
[78] Ibid., art. 12.

10.7 THE CONFLICTING NORMS OF STATE SOVEREIGNTY AND FREEDOM OF OVERFLIGHT IN CUSTOMARY INTERNATIONAL AIR LAW

We have seen that the law of the sea, including as expressed in UNCLOS, attempts to strike a balance between the norms of sovereignty and freedom of navigation and passage, which otherwise are in conflict. A similar tension exists in international air law. I will now explore in more detail the evolution of respective norms of sovereignty and freedom of overflight, and evaluate how customary international law may be evolving to reconcile these norms.

State sovereignty is a fundamental norm of customary international law generally. Indeed, some scholars view it as a norm of *jus cogens*.[79] Under customary international law, a sovereign state is one that has a permanent population, defined territorial boundaries, a government, and the capacity to enter into relations with other states. These customary requirements for statehood were codified in Article 1 of the 1933 Montevideo Convention.[80]

We have seen that a broad norm of state sovereignty is also a fundamental principle of international air law. It is recognized in the very first article of both the Paris and Chicago Conventions, and states have, through these treaties and their practices, clearly accepted it as a norm of customary international law. It is, in fact, the cornerstone of international aviation law. As evidenced by Articles 1 and 2 of the Chicago Convention, as well as Article 2 of UNCLOS, under customary international law state sovereignty extends to the airspace above the state's territory and its territorial waters. As codified by Article 6 of the Chicago Convention, the customary norm of sovereignty over airspace also includes the rule that no aircraft can enter the air space of another state without the permission of that state.[81] Given the rapid evolution of air flight technology and the corresponding rapid development and reaffirmation of these treaty norms, this is one of those cases, as recognized by the ICJ in the *North Sea Continental Shelf Cases* discussed earlier in the chapter, where a customary norm developed very quickly.

79 See, e.g., Ian Brownlie, *Principles of Public International Law* (Oxford: Oxford University Press, 7th ed. 2008), 510–11.

80 See Montevideo Convention on the Rights and Duties of States, signed at Montevideo, Uruguay on 26 December 1933, during the Seventh International Conference of American States, art. 1. Available at https://www.ilsa.org/jessup/jessup15/Montevideo%20Convention.pdf. Article 1 states: "The state as a person of international law should possess the following qualifications: a permanent population; a defined territory; capacity to enter into relations with the other states."

81 See generally Peter P.C. Haanappel, *The Law and Policy of Air Space and Outer Space: A Comparative Approach* (The Hague: Kluwer Law International, 2003), 3.

On the other hand, as emphasized in the preceding section, there is no generally recognized right of passage under customary international law of the aircraft registered in one state through the airspace above another state, which I have referred to as "freedom of overflight."[82] Neither the Paris Convention nor the Chicago Convention recognizes such a general freedom. And there is no other broad, quasi-universal international treaty protecting freedom of overflight.[83] While certain regional treaties, like those of the EU, permit overflight among their parties, these regional agreements do not evidence acceptance by those or other states of a universal norm permitting overflight (except, as discussed later in this section, under very limited conditions).

The history of the drafting of the Paris Convention and Chicago Convention is instructive on this point. Prior to World War I, and later at the 1919 Paris Conference, states generally agreed that the airspace above the high seas was free and open for use by every state. However, different views among states prevailed regarding freedom of flight in the airspace over a state's territory and territorial waters. There were two main competing theories. France argued that because freedom of the high seas was established in maritime law, the same principle should apply to the space above a state's territory. France took the position, therefore, that the airspace over a state's territory should be completely free and that there should be complete freedom of the air. The United Kingdom believed, by contrast, that because states exercised absolute sovereignty over and beneath the surface of their territories, they were entitled to exercise similarly exclusive jurisdiction in the airspace above their territories. It thus argued that the airspace above a state was part of its sovereign territory.[84]

With the inauguration of the first scheduled air service between Paris and London, there was a greater focus among states on security issues, and states perceived a need for existing regulations to be embodied in a treaty. A choice had to be made between the principle of a free airspace, similar to the principle of freedom of the high seas in maritime law, and the principle that each state had sovereignty over its airspace. As a result of World War I and the need for states to defend their security interests, states ultimately preferred the latter view.[85]

Thus, as we have seen, Article 1 of the 1919 Paris Convention proclaimed this principle of absolute sovereignty over the airspace above the territory and territorial waters of a state. To recall, Article 1 states: "The High Contracting

[82] See Shaw, *International Law*, 464.
[83] See Lee, "Revisiting Freedom of Overflight in International Air Law," 351.
[84] On this debate, see Shaw, *International Law*, 463.
[85] See Diederiks-Verschoor, *An Introduction to Air Law*, 2.

Parties recognize that every Power has complete and exclusive sovereignty over the air space above its territory."[86] Only twenty-five years later, states reaffirmed this principle in Article 1 of the 1944 Chicago Convention. As I have suggested, these nearly universal affirmations of the principle have led to its widespread recognition as a norm of customary international law. Indeed, the ICJ itself has identified the norm of sovereignty over airspace as a norm of customary international law based on Article 1 of the Chicago Convention and other treaties. In the 1986 *Nicaragua Case*, the Court declared:

> The basic legal concept of State sovereignty in customary international law, expressed in, *inter alia*, Article 2, paragraph 1, of the United Nations Charter, extends to the internal waters and territorial sea of every State and to the air space above its territory. As to superjacent air space, the 1944 Chicago Convention on International Civil Aviation (Art. 1) reproduces the established principle of the complete and exclusive sovereignty of a State over the air space above its territory. That convention, in conjunction with the 1958 Geneva Convention on the Territorial Sea, further specifies that the sovereignty of the coastal State extends to the territorial sea and to the air space above it, as does the United Nations Convention on the Law of the Sea adopted on 10 December 1982. *The Court has no doubt that these prescriptions of treaty-law merely respond to firmly established and longstanding tenets of customary international law.*[87]

In that case, the Court also stated that "the principle of respect for territorial sovereignty is … directly infringed by the unauthorized overflight of a State's territory by aircraft belonging to or under the control of the government of another State."[88]

However, despite the broad language of Article 1 of the Paris and Chicago Conventions affirming absolute sovereignty over airspace, the Chicago Convention does recognize some "freedoms of the air" that regulate and limit this sovereignty. I have already referred in this connection to the rule in Article 12 on regulation of flights over the high seas. During the drafting of the Chicago Convention, the states involved could not reach consensus on the scope of the freedoms of the air. Some countries, such as the United States, favored maximum freedom of the air, while others, such as the United Kingdom, preferred a regulated air space.[89] These debates echoed those between France and the United Kingdom during the drafting of the Paris Convention in 1919. In the

86 Paris Convention, art. 1.
87 *Nicaragua Case*, 111, para. 212 (emphasis added).
88 Ibid., 128, para. 251.
89 See Lee, "Revisiting Freedom of Overflight in International Air Law," 360.

end, the states that negotiated the Chicago Convention failed to reach an agreement with regard to traffic rights that was satisfactory to all of them and therefore could be included in the Convention itself.

Instead, the result of these contentious negotiations was a compromise. Certain freedoms of the air were recognized in two separate agreements annexed to the Chicago Convention. These agreements could be ratified by those states that were willing to accept the rights granted in them. These agreements identified five freedoms of the air. The International Air Services Transit Agreement ("IASTA") of 1944 (known as the "Two Freedoms Agreement" or "Transit Agreement") and the International Air Transport Agreement ("IATA") of 1944 (known as the "Five Freedoms Agreement" or "Transport Agreement") stipulate the extent to which states grant each other particular freedoms of the air.

Both agreements grant a limited freedom of overflight to the aircraft of states parties in identical language in Article 1, which affirms: "Each contracting State grants to the other contracting States the following freedoms of the air in respect of scheduled international air services: 1. The privilege to fly across its territory without landing; 2. The privilege to land for non-traffic purposes."[90]

In accordance with this article, the Transit Agreement grants a state party the right to overfly the territory of another state party without landing. It also grants a state the freedom to land in a foreign country for non-traffic purposes, in other words for technical reasons, such as an emergency (often referred to as a "technical landing"). The Transit Agreement had 130 parties as of August 2016.[91]

The Transport Agreement also grants these two freedoms in its Article 1, but furthermore provides for an additional three freedoms in that same article. The third freedom grants the right to fly passengers, mail, and cargo from the registration state of the air carrier to a foreign contracting state. The fourth freedom grants the right to fly passengers, mail, and cargo from another contracting state to the state of registration of the air carrier. And the fifth freedom grants the right to fly passengers, mail, and cargo from the state of registration to a second country and then from that second country to a third country other than the state of registration of the air carrier. In all cases, the scheduled origin or the final destination

90 See International Air Services Transit Agreement 1944, signed at Chicago on 7 December 1944 ("Transit Agreement"), art. 1, sec. 1, available at www.mcgill.ca/iasl/files/iasl/chicago1944b.pdf; International Air Transport Agreement 1944, signed at Chicago on 7 December 1944 ("Transport Agreement"), art. 1, sec. 1, available at www.mcgill.ca/iasl/files/iasl/chicago1944c.pdf.

91 See the list of parties available at www.icao.int/secretariat/legal/List%20of%20Parties/Transit_EN.pdf (last accessed 29 August 2016).

of the chain of transportation must be in the registration state of the air carrier.[92] The Transport Agreement had a mere eleven parties as of August 2016.[93]

Why has the Transit Agreement been much more widely ratified than the Transport Agreement? One reason for the wider acceptance of the Transit Agreement is that it does not grant commercial rights, but only deals with the freedoms of overflight and technical landing.[94] In addition, states may prefer to enter into bilateral treaties rather than a multilateral air service treaty like the Transport Agreement because they have more control over the choice of other treaty partners as well as the advantage of reciprocity.[95]

Today, in addition to the Transit and Transport Agreements appended to the Chicago Convention, numerous multilateral and bilateral agreements afford states the contractual right to fly aircraft and operate air service that depart from the customary international air law principle that a state has complete and exclusive sovereignty over its airspace.[96] Under these agreements a state grants aircraft registered in another state the right to fly within its sovereign airspace. These agreements effectively recognize additional "freedoms of the air." Of course, the words "freedom" and "right" are perhaps somewhat misleading, as a country's airline only has the right to operate international air services and fly and land in another country in accordance with the permission granted by that country, as reflected in these agreements.

Some of these agreements are multilateral and others are bilateral. An example of a multilateral agreement is the 2000 agreement between the United States, Brunei Darussalam, Chile, New Zealand, and Singapore.[97] Bilateral agreements also provide for additional freedoms. An example of such an agreement is the 2007 agreement between India and Malaysia.[98]

Indeed, after the failure of the states at the Chicago Conference to agree on universal rules on traffic rights and freedoms of the air, many states turned to the use of such bilateral agreements. Bilateral agreements can generally

92 See Transport Agreement, art. 1, sec. 1.

93 See the list of parties available at www.icao.int/secretariat/legal/List%20of%20Parties/Transport_EN.pdf (last accessed 29 August 2016).

94 On this point, see R.A. Doganis, "Transport: A Case Study in International Regulation," 7 *Journal of Transport Economics and Policy* 109 (1973).

95 See Divya Mohan, "Role of Chicago Convention and ICAO in the Development of International Air Law: A Critical Approach" (paper on file with the author).

96 Haanappel, *The Law and Policy of Air Space and Outer Space*, 104–05.

97 Multilateral Agreement on the Liberalization of International Air Transport, available at http://www.state.gov/documents/organization/114408.pdf.

98 See Memorandum of Understanding, available at www.dgca.nic.in/bilateral/bilateral_idx.htm. For the text of bilateral air service agreements between India and other countries, see www.dgca.nic.in/bilateral/bilateral_idx.htm.

take one of two forms.[99] The first form is an agreement that specifies the operational routes of the airline. Such an agreement also often stipulates the capacity that should be provided on each route and requires that the capacity be equal for the designated carriers of the two states. Other agreements, such as the air service agreements between the United Kingdom and France, may even require that routes be operated in a pool by the specified airlines.

The second form of bilateral agreement is an agreement, referred to as the "Bermuda type," after an agreement signed in 1946 between the United Kingdom and the United States relating to air services between their territories. This agreement is commonly referred to as the "Bermuda 1 Agreement." The agreement was important because it was largely a compromise between the extreme positions taken during the negotiation of the Chicago Convention. It set a precedent for future bilateral agreements. It was replaced in 1977 with what became known as the "Bermuda 2 Agreement."

The Chicago Convention of 1944, the Transport Agreement, the Transit Agreement, and the network of multilateral and bilateral air services agreements just described constitute the foundation of the international regulatory framework for international air transportation. Originally, this framework was relatively rigid; routes were fixed and assigned to particular airlines – often government-owned airlines – and competition among airlines was intentionally limited. However, in the mid-1970s, the practice of airline deregulation and liberalization in the United States spread to many countries.[100] This process of liberalization resulted in a vast expansion in commercial air travel, along with many technological developments. It also led to a multiplication of air services agreements and the inclusion of more liberal and less restrictive terms in them, as originally exemplified by Bermuda-type agreements.

Indeed, since the early 1990s there has been a trend toward liberalization of air services agreements. The first liberalized bilateral air services agreement, known as an "open skies" agreement, was between the United States and the Netherlands, and was concluded in 1992.[101] Open-skies agreements expand international passenger and cargo flights by removing state interference regarding routes, capacity, and pricing. They thus allow carriers to provide more affordable, convenient, and efficient air travel and foster increasing economic growth.[102]

[99] See generally Doganis, "Transport," 110.

[100] See Peter Haanappel, "The Transformation of Sovereignty in the Air," 20 *Air & Space Law* 311 (1995), 313. Available at www.kluwerlawonline.com/document.php?id=AILA1995042.

[101] See Lee, "Revisiting Freedom of Overflight in International Air Law," 363.

[102] See U.S. Department of State, "Open Skies Partnerships: Expanding the Benefits of Freer Commercial Aviation," Fact Sheet – Bureau of Public Affairs, 29 March 2011. Available at www.state.gov/r/pa/pl/159347.htm.

More than 400 open-skies agreements were concluded from 1992 to October 2012, involving 145 states, representing 76 percent of ICAO's membership.[103] Liberalization of air traffic has also been established through regional agreements such as those within the EU and among EU member states, the 2007 EU-U.S. Air Transport Agreement (hereafter referred to as the "EU-U.S. Open Skies Agreement"),[104] the 2002 bilateral air service agreement between Australia and New Zealand,[105] and the agreement between the EU and Israel, which was signed in Luxembourg on 4 November 2013.[106] Additionally, in November 2013, Singapore offered to negotiate an open-skies agreement with Turkey.[107] Even though the open-skies agreements concern commercial flights and focus mainly on the third and fourth freedoms of the air mentioned earlier, a clear shift from "protective skies" to "open skies" is evident.

As the above review demonstrates, the framework of air law and policy within which international carriage by air operates has developed from its foundational years to its current intricate system made up of a number of multilateral treaties, a corpus of bilateral agreements and informal agreements, and laws, regulations and policies on an international, regional, and domestic level.[108] But what is the role of customary international law in this system today? And have all of these modern air transport agreements, including

[103] ICAO Working Paper, *Expanding Market Access for International Air Transport (Presented by the Secretariat)*, ATConf/6-WP/13 (2012), para. 2.1. Available at www.icao.int/Meetings/atconf6/Documents/WorkingPapers/ATConf6-wp013_en.pdf.

[104] Decision 2007/339/EC of the Council and the Representatives of the Governments of the Member States of the European Union meeting within the Council, of 25 April 2007, on the signature and provisional application of the Air Transport Agreement between the European Community and its Member States, on the one hand, and the United States of America, on the other hand, approved the "Open Skies" Agreement concluded with the United States of America. The agreement provides for all transatlantic routes to be opened up to European and American companies. The EU-U.S. Open Skies Agreement is available at http://eur-lex.europa.eu/legal-content/EN/TXT/?uri=URISERV%3Al24483.

[105] Agreement between the Government of Australia and the Government of New Zealand relating to Air Services, done at Auckland on 8 August 2002. Available at www.aph.gov.au/binaries/house/committee/jsct/augustandseptember2002/treaties/nzopenskies_nia.pdf. See generally Mohan, "Role of Chicago Convention and ICAO," 7.

[106] European Commission Press Release, *Aviation: EU and Israel Sign Agreement*, IP/13/519, Brussels, 10 June 2013. Available at http://ec.europa.eu/transport/modes/air/international_aviation/country_index/doc/ip-13-519_-_en.pdf.

[107] See Serkan Demirtaş, "Singapore Offers Open Skies Deal with Turkey," *Singapore – Hürriyet Daily News*, Nov. 2, 2013. Available at www.hurriyetdailynews.com/singapore-offers-open-skies-deal-with-turkey.aspx?pageID=238&nID=57223&NewsCatID=345.

[108] See generally Ismael Saka Ismael, "A Critical Analysis of 'Freedom of the Air,'" 1 *UDUS Law Journal* 66 (1999). Available at http://unilorin.edu.ng/publications/ismaelsi/A%20CRITICAL%20ANALYSIS%20OF.pdf.

open skies agreements, changed the long-standing customary norm of state sovereignty over the airspace above a state's territory?

The preceding analysis suggests that even though the "Chicago Convention system" has to some extent been modified and even "watered down" as a result of the many multilateral and bilateral agreements enacted since 1944,[109] the principle of a state's sovereignty over its airspace contained in Article 1 remains the cornerstone of customary international air law today and has not been significantly changed. A number of pieces of evidence from the above historical review point to this conclusion.

First, although the Transit Agreement and Transport Agreement appended to the Chicago Convention allow for five freedoms of the skies, it is significant that the drafters of the Convention failed to agree on including these five freedoms in the Convention itself. Under the Convention, airlines do not have the automatic right to operate scheduled international flights. Rather, special permission must be negotiated between states and agreed on in bilateral or multilateral agreements or granted by unilateral state action. This tends to show that the drafters did not believe that freedoms of the air must be observed by states apart from their treaty obligations – that is, as norms of customary international law. Instead, they gave to states parties of the Convention the freedom to decide whether or not to grant these rights by ratifying the separate appended agreements or entering into other agreements.

Second, the prevalence of regional and bilateral air transport agreements tends to indicate that states wish to reserve the right to restrict their airspace and only allow freedoms to airlines of particular other states, and only on terms to which they explicitly consent. It is true that some scholars of international law maintain that a far-ranging network of bilateral treaties with similar terms – such as bilateral investment treaties, or tax treaties – can be both evidence of a consistent state practice and evidence of *opinio juris*, thus tending to show that the terms may well have passed into customary international law.[110] However, the better view, as argued by such scholars as Brian Lepard, is that the choice of states to adopt bilateral treaties rather than

[109] See Shaw, *International Law*, 467 n.24.

[110] For example, the American Law Institute's Restatement (Third) of the Foreign Relations Law of the United States asserts that a "wide network of similar bilateral arrangements on a subject may constitute practice and ... result in customary law." Restatement (Third) of the Foreign Relations Law of the United States, § 102, comment i. The draft conclusions adopted by the ILC in 2016 express a more cautious view about the prevalence of a common provision in treaties generally, providing: "The fact that a rule is set forth in a number of treaties *may, but does not necessarily*, indicate that the treaty rule reflects a rule of customary international law." "Report of the International Law Commission," Sixty-Eighth Session, Draft Conclusion 11, para. 2 (emphasis added).

a quasi-universal multilateral treaty suggests that they believe that they are not constrained, and should not be constrained, by any norms in these treaties to which they did not explicitly consent.[111] It thus demonstrates that the requisite *opinio juris* is lacking. In short, in their treaties and in their practice, states have insisted that there is no general freedom of overflight or other freedoms of the air apart from rights granted to aircraft of a different state pursuant to a treaty or other explicit permission of the state concerned. Accordingly, the conclusion is warranted that there is no such broad freedom in contemporary customary international law.

Other scholars have agreed that the fundamental customary norm of state sovereignty remains intact even in the face of a plethora of air services agreements. Thus, according to Peter Haanappel, these agreements do not "fundamentally change the notion of sovereignty; rather, they modify [it], they liberalise its exercise."[112] They do not by themselves detract from the notion of sovereignty provided for by Articles 1 and 6 of the Chicago Convention.[113] As Haanappel underscores, there has been no real transformation of the principle of sovereignty in the air embedded in Article 1 of the Chicago Convention, which is a provision that declares preexisting customary international law. Rather, there has been an "evolution in the exercise of national sovereignty."[114]

Does this mean that the network of multilateral and bilateral agreements providing for various freedoms of the air has had no impact on the original customary norm of state sovereignty? Not necessarily. The principle of state sovereignty in air law that was recognized by customary law and codified in the Paris and Chicago Conventions has now been "modernized" by recent rules related to transit agreements and freedoms of the air.[115] It could be persuasively argued that, alongside the customary norm of state sovereignty over air space, there has developed a limited customary norm allowing freedom of air flight under certain conditions.

In particular, many of the norms in UNCLOS relating to air travel have now arguably passed into customary international law, especially because UNCLOS is a broad, multilateral treaty, with an intended universal membership, and as noted earlier has been ratified by 168 states, representing more than 85 percent of the number of member states of the United Nations. It may be recalled that paragraph 1 of Article 87 refers to a number of rules relating to the high seas, and that this provision in particular guarantees freedom of overflight

[111] See Lepard, *Customary International Law*, 200–04.
[112] Haanappel, "The Transformation of Sovereignty in the Air," 314.
[113] Ibid.
[114] Ibid.
[115] See Martin Dixon, *International Law* (Oxford: Oxford University Press, 7th ed. 2013), 178.

of the high seas to all nations.[116] This freedom was also earlier codified in Article 2 of the 1958 Geneva Convention on the High Seas,[117] which as of August 2016 had been ratified by sixty-three states.[118] The preamble to the Geneva Convention specifically states that the treaty was intended to "codify the rules of international law relating to the high seas" – in other words, to codify customary international law.[119] Accordingly, there is strong evidence, including these widely endorsed treaty provisions, that this particular freedom of overflight is now a norm of customary international law. The CJEU in fact reached such a conclusion in its 2011 decision in *Air Transport Association of America and Others v. Secretary of State for Energy and Climate Change*, which I discuss in more detail in the following section.[120]

Moreover, the first two freedoms of the air codified in Article 1 of the 1944 Transit Agreement and 1944 Transport Agreement are possible candidates for recognition as customary norms that restrict the absolute state sovereignty otherwise upheld by Article 1 of the Chicago Convention itself. This is because these two freedoms have been accepted by 130 states as parties to the Transit Agreement, and these norms have been endorsed in the treaties for seventy years.

However, on closer inspection, the evidence suggests that the first freedom – the privilege of aircraft registered to a state party and conducting scheduled international air services to fly across the territory of another state party without landing, or "freedom of overflight" – is still not a norm of customary law, apart from freedom of overflight over the high seas. That is because it appears that the parties to the Transit Agreement only intended to grant such a privilege in relation to other states parties – not to states generally. States continue to reserve the right to deny overflight rights to aircraft of other states in the absence of a treaty. Thus, there is still insufficient state practice, and insufficient *opinio juris*, to support recognition of freedom of overflight as a norm of customary law.

On the other hand, there may be more compelling reasons to recognize at least a part of the second freedom of the air, as provided in Article 1 of the Transit and Transport Agreements, as a norm of customary international law.

[116] See UNCLOS, art. 87, para. 1.

[117] See Convention on the High Seas, done at Geneva on 29 April 1958, 450 UNTS 11, art 2 (providing that freedom of the high seas includes, for both coastal and non-coastal states, "freedom to fly over the high seas").

[118] See https://treaties.un.org/Pages/ViewDetails.aspx?src=TREATY&mtdsg_no=XXI-2&chapter=21&clang=_en (last accessed 29 August 2016).

[119] Geneva Convention on the High Seas, preamble.

[120] See *Air Transport Association of America and Others*, paras. 103–04.

That allows a privilege of aircraft of another state party to make unscheduled "technical landings" in the territory of a state party, such as in the case of an emergency. Certainly, at least in the narrower case of emergencies, there has generally been a consistent practice of allowing such landings. Very few cases exist where a state denied aircraft of another state the right to make an emergency landing. And there is stronger evidence that states believe that such a legal right may already exist and should exist, including the text of Article 1 of the Transport and Transit Agreements. A right to make emergency landings would not significantly detract from the general sovereignty that states retain over their airspace. Of course, a more comprehensive survey of state practice would be necessary to establish more definitively the existence of such a new norm of customary law.

10.8 THE 2011 JUDGMENT OF THE CJEU ON THE EU EMISSION TRADING SCHEME AND ITS IMPLICATIONS FOR CUSTOMARY INTERNATIONAL AIR LAW

Many of the aforementioned issues regarding the content of customary international air law – and in particular the competing norms of sovereignty and freedom of overflight – were addressed in 2011 by the CJEU in the case of *Air Transport Association of America and Others*, to which I have just referred. That case involved the Emission Trading Scheme ("ETS") adopted by the EU and its relationship to customary international law. Here I give some information on how the case arose.

Efforts to address the drastic effects of global climate change by the international community resulted in the United Nations Framework Convention on Climate Change ("UNFCCC")[121] and the Kyoto Protocol.[122] However, neither agreement regulates greenhouse gas emissions from international aviation. The EU has signed and ratified both the UNFCCC and the Kyoto Protocol, and is therefore subject to obligations to reduce emissions. In 2003, the EU issued Directive 2003/87/EC, which established a regional EU Emissions Trading Scheme ("EU ETS") beginning in 2005 for the exchange of greenhouse gas emission allowances.[123] It is a "cap and trade" scheme. Initially,

[121] United Nations Framework Convention on Climate Change (entered into force 21 March 1994), 31 *International Legal Materials* 849 (1994) ("UNFCCC"). Available at https://cil.nus.edu.sg/1992/1992-united-nations-framework-convention-on-climate-change/.

[122] Kyoto Protocol to the United Nations Framework Convention on Climate Change, UN Doc. FCC/CP/1997/L.7/Add.1 (1997) (entered into force 16 February 2005) ("Kyoto Protocol"). Available at http://unfccc.int/resource/docs/convkp/kpeng.pdf.

[123] See Directive 2003/87/EC of the European Parliament and of the Council of 13 October 2003, establishing a scheme for greenhouse gas emission allowance trading within the Community

the EU ETS did not include greenhouse gas emissions from air transport. However, in 2008, the EU issued Directive 2008/101/EC,[124] which included aviation in the EU ETS.

Importantly, and of direct relevance to the case, the 2008 Directive limited the total amount of emissions permitted for all "flights which depart from or arrive in an aerodrome situated in the territory of a Member State," including flights to a non-EU destination or with a non-EU origin.[125] As a result of the Directive, from 2012 on, all flights departing from and arriving in the EU were to be included in the EU ETS. This means that air carriers have to acquire and surrender emission allowances for their flights. Noncomplying carriers face a stiff penalty for each missing allowance. The Directive therefore impacted not only EU carriers but also aircraft that were registered in non-EU member states and aircraft flying over the high seas, despite the absence of mutual consensus between the EU and the affected states.[126]

The Directive was criticized by many countries. A number of them, including China, India, and the United States, enacted legislation designed to prevent their airline operators from complying with the Directive.[127] A Joint Declaration by representatives of twenty-one states, including China, India, Japan, the United States, and the United Arab Emirates, was adopted on 30 September 2011.[128] It opposed the inclusion of non-EU carriers in the ETS. It stated that doing so was inconsistent with applicable international law, and it urged the EU and its member states to refrain from including flights by non-EU carriers to and from the EU in its ETS.[129]

Three U.S. airline operators (American, Continental, and United) and the Air Transport Association of America legally challenged the measures in the

and amending Council Directive 96/61/EC, OJ L 275/32, 25.10.2003. Available at http://eur-lex.europa.eu/legal-content/EN/TXT/PDF/?uri=CELEX:32003L0087&from=EN.

124 Directive 2008/101/EC.

125 Ibid., Annex 1(c), "Aviation."

126 See Theodore Konstadinides, "When in Europe: Customary International Law and EU Competence in the Sphere of External Action," 13 *German Law Journal* 1177 (2012), 1191. Available at http://static1.squarespace.com/static/56330ad3e4b0733dcc0c8495/t/576099243c44d8a0f9a59785/1465948456114/GLJ_Vol_13_No_11.pdf.

127 See Henrik Horn, "The ECJ Judgment on the Extensions of the ETS to Aviation: An Economist's Discontent," IFN Working Paper No. 980, Research Institute of Industrial Economics, 26 September 2013. Available at www.ifn.se/wfiles/wp/wp980.pdf.

128 Joint Declaration by Argentina, Brazil, Chile, China, Colombia, Cuba, Egypt, India, Japan, Republic of Korea, Malaysia, Mexico, Nigeria, Paraguay, Qatar, Russian Federation, Saudi Arabia, Singapore, South Africa, the United States of America, and the United Arab Emirates, 30 September 2011, C-WP/13790, Appendix. Available at www.greenaironline.com/photos/ICAO_C.194.WP.13790.EN.pdf.

129 See ibid., paras. 5–8.

United Kingdom before the High Court on the basis that the EU Directive was unlawful under international treaty law and customary international law.[130] First, the claimants argued that the EU breached international treaty obligations, and specifically Article 2(2) of the Kyoto Protocol, which provides that ICAO has the exclusive responsibility for reducing greenhouse gas emissions for the aviation industry. They contended that the EU, as a signatory of the Kyoto Protocol, should work through ICAO. The claimants further pointed out that, in accordance with the EU-U.S. Open Skies Agreement, it was agreed that matters related to emissions trading would be handled within the context of ICAO and not unilaterally.

Second, the claimants argued that the EU breached Article 15 of the Chicago Convention, which prohibits the imposition of a charge other than for the use of airports and air navigation facilities. They argued accordingly that the EU scheme imposed an illegal charge or tax on aircraft operators.

Third, the claimants contended that the EU breached customary international law norms, and in particular the norm of state sovereignty, reflected in various treaties, such as the Chicago Convention, the EU-U.S. Open Skies Agreement, and other bilateral agreements. It did so, they alleged, because it applied the ETS to parts of flights that take place outside the airspace of EU member states and imposed extraterritorial obligations on foreign airlines, thereby contravening the fundamental customary international law principle of state sovereignty.

The High Court of Justice of England and Wales, Queen's Bench Division (Administrative Court), stayed the proceedings and referred the matter to the CJEU for a preliminary ruling regarding two issues. The first issue involved the conditions under which international treaties and customary law principles could be relied on when determining the validity of EU law. The second issue involved the legal validity of Directive 2008/101/EC.

The CJEU thus had to consider, among other questions, whether the Directive infringed on the following four principles of customary international law relied on by the claimants: (1) the principle that each state has complete and exclusive sovereignty over its airspace; (2) the principle that no state may validly purport to subject any part of the high seas to its sovereignty; (3) the principle of freedom to fly over the high seas; and (4) the principle that aircraft overflying the high seas are subject to the exclusive jurisdiction of the country in which they are registered. The claimants thus argued that including in the Directive flights from non-EU member states, outside EU airspace, created, in the words of one scholar, an "extraterritorial rule that

[130] See *Air Transport Association of America and Others*.

contravenes both the sovereign rights of third countries and the freedom of the high seas."[131]

In its judgment issued in December 2011, the Court confronted the initial question of the relationship of customary international law to EU law. The Court referred to Article 3(5) of the Treaty on European Union ("TEU"), which provides that "the EU shall uphold and promote … the strict observance and the development of international law."[132] The Court relied on this provision to confirm that the EU is bound to adhere to international law in its entirety, including customary international law.[133] The Court then stated: "Thus, it should be examined first whether the principles to which the referring court makes reference are recognised as forming part of customary international law. If they are, it should, secondly, then be determined whether and to what extent they may be relied upon by individuals to call into question the validity of an act of the European Union, such as Directive 2008/101, in a situation such as that in the main proceedings."[134]

The CJEU proceeded to identify the relevant norms of customary international law in the case. It acknowledged the existence of the first three principles of customary international law that the claimants relied on, namely the principle that each state has complete and exclusive sovereignty over its airspace, the principle that no state may validly purport to subject any part of the high seas to its sovereignty, and the principle that the aircraft of any state have the freedom to fly over the high seas.

The Court declared that these three principles embody the current state of customary international maritime and air law. It observed that they have been codified in various treaties, including the Chicago Convention, the Geneva Convention on the High Seas, and UNCLOS. It also noted that decisions of the Permanent Court of International Justice and ICJ had recognized these principles.[135]

By contrast, with regard to the fourth asserted principle of customary international law, that aircraft overflying the high seas are subject to the exclusive jurisdiction of the state of registration, the Court found that such a principle did not yet exist in customary law. It stated that there is insufficient evidence to establish that the principle of customary international law, recognized as such, that a vessel on the high seas is in principle governed only by the law of its flag would apply by analogy to aircraft overflying the high seas.[136]

[131] Konstadinides, "When in Europe," 1191.

[132] Consolidated Version of the Treaty on European Union, art. 3, para. 5. Available at http://eur-lex.europa.eu/resource.html?uri=cellar:2bf140bf-a3f8-4ab2-b506-fd71826e6da6.0023.02/DOC_1&format=PDF.

[133] *Air Transport Association of America and Others*, para. 101.

[134] Ibid., para. 102.

[135] Ibid., para. 104.

[136] Ibid., para. 106.

The Court next examined whether and under what circumstances the three customary international principles it recognized could be relied on by the claimants. The CJEU stressed that these principles may be relied on by individuals for the purposes of examining the validity of an act of the EU where those principles put into question the competence of the EU to adopt that act and where that act may affect rights or create obligations under EU law.[137] It is possible, the Court stated, that where the Directive creates obligations under EU law regarding the claimants, as in this case, those claimants may rely on customary international law principles, and therefore the Court could examine the validity of the Directive in light of them.[138]

In this connection, legal scholar Theodore Konstadinides has argued that the Court effectively created a new test that hinges on two conditions under which an individual may rely on customary international law to challenge the validity of an EU act. First, the customary norm must be capable of calling into question the competence of the EU to adopt that act. Second, for an individual to raise the matter in a national court, the EU act must affect the individual's rights derived from EU law or create obligations under EU law.[139]

The Court went on to determine how it would apply principles of customary international law in the case. It clarified that "as a principle of customary international law does not have the same degree of precision as a provision of an international agreement, judicial review must necessarily be limited to the question whether, in adopting the act in question, the institutions of the European Union *made manifest errors of assessment concerning the conditions for applying those principles.*"[140]

The CJEU determined that the only principles of customary international law that could be relied on for purposes of assessing the validity of the Directive were, "within the limits of review as to a manifest error of assessment attributable to the European Union regarding its competence, in the light of those principles, to adopt that directive": (1) "the principle that each State has complete and exclusive sovereignty over its airspace"; (2) "the principle that no State may validly purport to subject any part of the high seas to its sovereignty"; and (3) "the principle which guarantees freedom to fly over the high seas."[141]

The Court concluded that under the above principles of customary international law, "European Union law and, in particular, Directive 2008/101 cannot render Directive 2003/87 applicable as such to aircraft registered in third

[137] Ibid., para. 107.
[138] Ibid., para. 109.
[139] On this part of the Court's opinion, see Konstadinides, "When in Europe," 1195.
[140] *Air Transport Association of America and Others*, para. 110 (emphasis added).
[141] Ibid., para. 111.

States that are flying over third States or the high seas."[142] It said that the EU "must respect international law in the exercise of its powers, and therefore Directive 2008/101 must be interpreted, and its scope delimited, in the light of the relevant rules of the international law of the sea and international law of the air."[143]

At the same time, the Court affirmed that "European Union legislation may be applied to an aircraft operator when its aircraft is in the territory of one of the Member States and, more specifically, on an aerodrome situated in such territory, since, in such a case, that aircraft is subject to the unlimited jurisdiction of that Member State and the European Union."[144] Critically, the Court concluded that the Directive did not infringe on the sovereignty that non-EU states enjoy over the airspace above their territory, because non-EU aircraft are physically in the territory of an EU member state at the time of their arrival or departure and are therefore subject to the unlimited jurisdiction of the EU.[145]

In addition, the Court held that the customary law principle of freedom to fly over the high seas was not affected by the Directive because aircraft flying exclusively over the high seas are not subject to it. The Court underscored that only airline operators that have chosen to operate a commercial air route arriving at or departing from an aerodrome within an EU member state are subject to the allowance trading scheme imposed by the Directive.[146] Moreover, it found that the EU could properly require the operator of an aircraft to surrender emission allowances "calculated in the light of the whole of the international flight that its aircraft has performed or is going to perform" from or to an airport within the EU even though part of the flight occurred outside the territory of the EU. In other words, customary international law did not require any apportionment of the allowances based on the percentage of the flight that took place over EU territory.[147]

The Court concluded that the EU "did have competence, in the light of the principles of customary international law capable of being relied upon in the context of the main proceedings, to adopt Directive 2008/101, in so far as the latter extends the allowance trading scheme laid down by Directive 2003/87 to all flights which arrive at or depart from an aerodrome situated in the territory of a Member State."[148]

[142] Ibid., para. 122.
[143] Ibid., para. 123.
[144] Ibid., para. 124.
[145] Ibid., para. 125.
[146] Ibid., paras. 126–27.
[147] Ibid., paras. 128–29.
[148] Ibid., para. 130.

The CJEU's decision is significant because it directly addresses both the role of customary international air law in EU law and some aspects of the content of customary international air law. Regarding the former, the decision helpfully emphasizes that the EU is obligated to respect customary international air law. This is an important statement because it allows EU secondary law to be subject to an external check based on customary law. In this way, customary international law may in the future influence EU policy in relation to external action in the aviation and maritime industries in respect of its extraterritorial jurisdiction.[149]

On the other hand, the decision sets a high bar to any claimant successfully challenging an EU act as violating customary international law. Because of the Court's view that judicial review must be limited to the question of whether the EU committed a *manifest* error of assessment when adopting the act in question – a very high standard – it appears that future claimants may not have great success in relying on customary international air law norms unless they can show such a serious error on the part of the EU. This requirement, therefore, may impede litigation challenging EU acts on the basis of customary law. As Konstadinides has affirmed, "[I]t can be argued that the obligation springing from EU law to respect customary international law in the exercise of its powers is not vigorous enough to curtail EU competence in the sphere of external action."[150]

The CJEU's decision furthermore sheds light on the CJEU's interpretation of the content of customary international air law.[151] The Court correctly emphasized that a number of rules form part of current customary international maritime and air law and that they have been codified in various provisions of the Chicago Convention, the 1958 Geneva Convention on the High Seas, and the 1982 UNCLOS. In particular, it affirmed the customary law status of the exclusive sovereignty of each state over its airspace, the prohibition on states exercising jurisdiction over the high seas, and the freedom to fly over the high seas.

All of these conclusions about the customary law status of these norms appear warranted in light of the analysis earlier in the chapter. However, the Court's application of these principles to the EU Directive can be criticized. Thus, the principle that a state has exclusive jurisdiction over its territory, including its airspace, is widely accepted as part of customary international law. Contrary to the Court's judgment, there is no exception in customary international law that would justify the extraterritorial application of EU law

149 See Konstadinides, "When in Europe," 1197.

150 Ibid.

151 See ibid., 1190.

to non-EU carriers. Consequently, because the Directive imposes a legal obligation on non-EU member states, and inflicts financial costs and imposes a penalty for operators that do not comply, it clearly contravenes the principle of sovereignty by intervening in the jurisdiction of another state.[152]

It is also well established in customary international law that no state may subject any part of the high seas to its jurisdiction and that all states must respect freedom to fly over the high seas. This rule is supported both by long-standing state practice and *opinio juris*. The provisions of UNCLOS are clear evidence in support of both this practice and belief by states. Applying EU law to flights over the high seas – including flights that are not exclusively over the high seas – would therefore be contrary to customary international law. The principle of freedom of the seas applies to enforcement acts, such as policing over the high seas, as well as to legislation that is intended to apply to parts of the high seas. The Court correctly stated these rules, but it is doubtful whether the Directive could lawfully impose a tax or penalty based on the portions of flights that occurred over the high seas, even if the flights originated in or terminated in an EU member state. At a minimum, the Court should have exempted that portion of such flights that took place over the high seas from the EU emission allowance scheme.

Furthermore, the Court found insufficient evidence in favor of a rule that an aircraft flying over the high seas is under the exclusive jurisdiction of the state of registration. However, there is indeed compelling evidence of such a customary rule. As we saw in an earlier discussion, this rule has been codified in Articles 12 and 17 of the Chicago Convention and has long been accepted. Moreover, significant state practice supports it.

10.9 CONCLUSION: THE INCREASING ROLE OF CUSTOMARY INTERNATIONAL AIR LAW

I have argued in this chapter that customary international law is playing an increasingly vital role in the rapidly expanding commercial aviation industry. That industry is striving to meet passenger and market demands and safely fly millions of passengers across continents in what is still the safest means of transportation. International carriage by air is interwoven with many complex legal and business-related issues, which greatly impact states, governments, the aviation industry, and the general public.

We have seen that customary international air law is not as extensive as customary international maritime law, given the more recent development of

[152] See ibid., 1192.

flight technology. Nevertheless, although international air law is only a century old, a strong case can be made that certain foundational norms codified in key treaties like the 1919 Paris Convention and the 1944 Chicago Convention have passed into the realm of customary international law because there is sufficient evidence of both *opinio juris* and state practice – with these and other treaties providing evidence of both. These customary law principles include the norms of a state's sovereignty over its airspace, the absence of any state's sovereignty over the high seas, freedom to fly over the high seas, and the exclusive jurisdiction of the state of registration of an aircraft over that aircraft when it is flying over the high seas. The CJEU in its 2011 decision in *Air Transport Association of America and Others* concurred that the first three norms are customary norms, but disagreed with the customary law status of the fourth.

On the other hand, a careful examination of the complex network of treaties and bilateral air transport agreements reveals that although many agreements allow for freedom of overflight, there is no generally accepted norm allowing such overflight – unlike the norm of freedom of innocent passage that has become part of customary international maritime law. However, I have suggested that there may well now be a customary norm at least allowing emergency landings in a state.

These conclusions, we have seen, require a thoughtful analysis of whether a particular treaty or series of treaties evidence a general *opinio juris*. I have argued that broad multilateral treaties like the Chicago Convention and UNCLOS provide much better evidence of *opinio juris* than do bilateral treaties such as open skies agreements, even though the terms of the latter may be very similar. Nevertheless, the vast and growing network of bilateral agreements may be giving rise to new norms of customary law. We can thus expect that the role of customary law in air law will increase. Certainly the 2011 decision of the CJEU gave support to such increased influence by asserting that EU acts must comply with customary international air law, even though it also set a high procedural bar to claims invoking customary international law. In short, customary international air law's role is likely to "ascend" in the coming years as it regulates in new ways the competing norms of sovereignty and freedom of overflight.

11

Customary International Law and Outer Space

Frans G. von der Dunk

11.1 INTRODUCTION: THE LAW OF OUTER SPACE

Following land, sea, and airspace, outer space has often been hailed as the "fourth domain" for humankind to venture into – and hence require law, notably international law, to help establish or maintain some form of equilibrium between individual interests of relevant states and other internationally relevant categories of stakeholders. Clearly, it is the youngest human-occupied domain among them. Whereas land masses and seas have been populated or traversed ever since (and even before) states came into existence, which then developed international law norms, and humankind took to the air more than a century ago with the first treaties soon to follow,[1] the first man-made artifact –Sputnik-1 – entered what is commonly known as outer space in 1957, with the first human entering space four years later.

Almost immediately, international law relating to the realm of outer space developed. One year after Sputnik-1, the General Assembly of the United Nations created an *ad hoc* Committee on the Peaceful Uses of Outer Space ("COPUOS") to discuss the legal issues relevant to space activities.[2] Within another year that Committee was made permanent. Its member states included the Soviet Union and the United States, the then-two superpowers, which also dominated the use of outer space.[3]

1 See Sofia Michaelides-Mateou, "Customary International Law in Aviation: A Hundred Years of Travel through the Competing Norms of Sovereignty and Freedom of Overflight," in this volume.

2 See "Question of the Peaceful Use of Outer Space," UN GA Res. 1348 (XIII), of 13 December 1958, *Resolutions adopted on the Reports of the First Committee*, General Assembly – Thirteenth Session, 5.

3 See "International Co-operation in the Peaceful Uses of Outer Space," UN GA Res. 1472 (XIV) A, of 12 December 1959, *Resolutions adopted on the Reports of the First Committee*, General Assembly – Fourteenth Session, 5.

A General Assembly declaration setting out fundamental legal principles applicable to activities in outer space followed in 1963.[4] Only four years later, most of those principles found their way into the Outer Space Treaty,[5] the first international treaty exclusively and comprehensively dealing with outer space and space activities. As of January 2016, the Treaty enjoyed the support as parties of 104 states, including all major spacefaring nations in the world, plus the participation of another 25 states that had signed the treaty but not ratified it.[6] These signatory states are bound not to defeat the object and purpose of the Treaty, even though they are not formally parties to it.[7]

As more and more states became involved in space activities and an increasing number of practical applications of space technology engaged intergovernmental organizations and private actors, the law relevant to outer space grew and also became more diverse. Four more treaties were developed by COPUOS, and the General Assembly adopted a number of additional resolutions. Outside of the United Nations, various other intergovernmental organizations started to assert certain regulatory competences in the context of space activities, such as the International Telecommunication Union ("ITU")[8]

4 "Declaration of Legal Principles Governing the Activities of States in the Exploration and Use of Outer Space," UN GA Res. 1962 (XVIII), of 13 December 1963, UN Doc. A/AC.105/572/Rev.1 (1963), 37.

5 Treaty on Principles Governing the Activities of States in the Exploration and Use of Outer Space, including the Moon and Other Celestial Bodies (hereafter "Outer Space Treaty"), London/Moscow/Washington, done 27 January 1967, entered into force 10 October 1967, 610 UNTS 205, TIAS 6347, 18 UST 2410, UKTS 1968 No. 10, Cmnd. 3198, ATS 1967 No. 24, 6 *International Legal Materials* 386 (1967).

6 Status as of 1 January 2016. See UN Doc. A/AC.105/C.2/2016/CRP.3 (2016), 10.

7 See Vienna Convention on the Law of Treaties, 1155 UNTS 331 (1969), art. 18(a) (providing in part that "a State is obliged to refrain from acts which would defeat the object and purpose of a treaty when ... it has signed the treaty").

8 The ITU was first established under the International Telegraph Convention, Paris, done 17 May 1865, entered into force 1 January 1866, 130 CTS 198, 56 BFSP 295. However, its current legal foundation is the ITU Constitution (Constitution of the International Telecommunication Union, Geneva, done 22 December 1992, entered into force 1 July 1994, 1825 UNTS 1, UKTS 1996 No. 24, Cm. 2539, ATS 1994 No. 28, Final Acts of the Additional Plenipotentiary Conference, Geneva, 1992 (1993), 1) and the ITU Convention (Convention of the International Telecommunication Union, Geneva, done 22 December 1992, entered into force 1 July 1994, 1825 UNTS 1, UKTS 1996 No. 24, Cm. 2539, ATS 1994 No. 28, Final Acts of the Additional Plenipotentiary Conference, Geneva, 1992 (1993), 71), both amended a few times since 1992. In 1959, at a World Administrative Radio Conference ("WARC") in Geneva, Switzerland, the participating states agreed that space communications as well as traditional telecommunications would henceforth be handled by the ITU. See, e.g., Francis Lyall, *International Communications – The International Telecommunication Union and Universal Postal Union* (Farnham, UK and Burlington, VT: Ashgate, 2011), 110; Milton L. Smith, *International Regulation of Satellite Communication* (Dordrecht: Martinus Nijhoff, 1990), 23–28; Francis Lyall, *Law and Space Telecommunications* (London: Dartmouth, 1989), 324.

and the World Trade Organization ("WTO").[9] A host of regional and bilateral treaties were concluded on specific space projects or cooperative ventures. And even national laws implementing the international responsibilities and liabilities of states on a domestic level became a common feature of space law.[10]

Apart from the few UN resolutions referred to earlier, these legal instruments relating to outer space all take the form of so-called black-letter law – treaties on the international level and national laws on the domestic level. So where does customary international law come in? What role does it play in outer space, either along the same lines as elsewhere in public international law or differently from it?

These are the questions I seek to explore in this chapter. I argue, first, that customary law in general is a source of international law that is fundamentally different from treaty law in a number of respects. Whereas the latter is in essence binary in character as to its formal applicability, customary international law represents a process of moving along a sliding scale from a clear and undisputed lack of international binding force to a (hopefully) clear and undisputed legal rule.

Second, I apply this conception of customary law to the specific realm of space law. I focus in particular on the Outer Space Treaty and its "attitude" toward customary international law, as well as the specifics of space activities. This means that much "state practice" actually consists of "paper practice," as opposed to actual activities in outer space.

9 The WTO was established by the Agreement Establishing the World Trade Organization, Marrakesh, done 15 April 1994, entered into force 1 January 1995, 1867 UNTS 154, UKTS 1996 No. 57, ATS 1995 No. 8, 33 *International Legal Materials* 1125, 1144 (1994).The principles of the GATS (General Agreement on Trade in Services) by way of the Fourth Protocol to the General Agreement on Trade and Services of 15 April 1994, Geneva, done 15 April 1997, entered into force 5 February 1998, WTO Doc. S/L/20 of 30 April 1996 (96–1750), 2061 UNTS 209, ATS 1998 No. 9, 33 *International Legal Materials* 1167 (1994), 36 *International Legal Materials* 354 (1997) rapidly became applied to the telecommunications sectors, notably including satellite communications. See Peter Malanczuk, "The Relevance of International Economic Law and the World Trade Organization (WTO) for Commercial Outer Space Activities," in *International Organisations and Space Law*, edited by Ray Harris 305 (Noordwijk: ESA Publications Division, 1999); Ian Walden, "International Telecommunications Law," in *Telecommunications Law and Regulation*, edited by Ian Walden 747 (Oxford: Oxford University Press, 3rd ed. 2009); Raj Bhala and Kevin Kennedy, *World Trade Law: The GATT-WTO System, Regional Arrangements, and U.S. Law* (Charlottesville, VA: Lexis Law Pub., 1998), 1289 et seq. See generally GATS, Marrakesh, done 15 April 1994, entered into force 1 January 1995, 1869 UNTS 183, UKTS 1996 No. 58, Cm. 3276, ATS 1995 No. 8.

10 See, e.g., *National Regulation of Space Activities*, edited by Ram S. Jakhu (Dordrecht; Heidelberg; London; New York: Springer, 2010); *Nationales Weltraumrecht/National Space Law*, edited by Christian Brünner and Edith Walter (Vienna; Cologne; Graz: Böhlau, 2008); *National Space Legislation in Europe*, edited by Frans G. von der Dunk (Leiden: Martinus Nijhoff, 2011).

Third, I argue that the special character of space activities as being almost inherently of a dual-use character also results in a special, somewhat limited role of customary international law in outer space. This argument is investigated in somewhat further detail in the context of the treaty phrase "exclusively for peaceful purposes."

Fourth, a second dimension particular to space activities, that of international cooperation, is investigated since it is also referred to as a "quasi-legal" obligation in many relevant documents. I further analyze this dimension with reference to the financial structure of various institutional mechanisms for international cooperation.

I then scrutinize another example, or "showcase" – that of fighting space debris – along the same lines. I turn next to a final example that brings two lines of arguments together: how certain international mechanisms of cooperation have addressed the issue of "peaceful purposes."

Finally, I summarize why and how customary international law has become a source for lawmaking in the domain of space activities to a different, and usually also lesser, extent, as compared to other major domains of international law.

11.2 WHAT, EXACTLY, *IS* CUSTOMARY INTERNATIONAL LAW ANYWAY?

To understand the role of customary international law in space law, it is first important to clarify the meaning of customary international law. Traditionally, reference is made in defining customary international law to the famous clause of the Statute of the International Court of Justice ("ICJ"), which states that the two primary sources of public international law are "a. international conventions, whether general or particular, establishing rules expressly recognized by the contesting states; [and] b. international custom, as evidence of a general practice accepted as law."[11] In short, the Statute refers to treaties and customary international law.

In the abstract, these two sources could hardly be more different from each other. Treaties can literally be seen, even touched; they have a physical form, manifesting themselves in paper documents well-kept in some state's archives. They comprise a very precisely determined set of words, where supposedly every comma has been, if not negotiated, at least considered; there is a precise date on which, or a precisely defined set of conditions under which, they enter into force; and the complete text is solemnly sealed by the signatures of

[11] Statute of the International Court of Justice ("ICJ Statute"), art. 38(1)(b).

high-level representatives of the state's parties. To the extent doubt may arise regarding certain aspects of a treaty, there is even a "meta-treaty," the aforementioned Vienna Convention on the Law of Treaties, that provides authoritative rules on how to interpret and apply treaties. As a consequence, treaties are considered a relatively precise means to determine the status of certain perceived rights and obligations of states vis-à-vis each other, the community of states as a whole, or occasionally specific other subjects or objects of public international law.

Customary international law is very different. As we have seen in preceding chapters, the definition in the ICJ Statute has been generally perceived by experts and state advocates alike (as well as the ICJ itself[12]) as comprising two distinct elements: (1) the *usus*, or "general practice" element, and (2) the *opinio juris sive necessitatis*, or "accepted-as-law" element. For example, legal scholar Hugh Thirlway has affirmed that "State practice, to be significant, must be accompanied by a conviction of adhering to an *existing* rule of law."[13] The International Law Commission, too, has endorsed this two-element definition.[14] Thus, customary international law arises if two questions are answered in the positive: "(a) is there a general practice; [and] (b) is it accepted as international law?"[15] In the words of legal scholar Malcolm N. Shaw, the one concerns "overt action," the other "subjective conviction."[16]

Almost by definition, therefore, customary international law is *not* represented in one authoritative version. It *cannot* be seen or touched – and consequently also remains imprecise and subject to doubt. Even the distinction between the two constitutive elements of customary international law has been a constant issue for debate.[17] There is also an inherent paradox looming here. As Brian Lepard explains, "States must act in a certain way … because they believe they are legally obligated to do so [without a treaty formally and clearly providing evidence thereof]. However,

[12] See, e.g., *North Sea Continental Shelf Cases (Federal Republic of Germany v. Denmark; Federal Republic of Germany v. Netherlands)*, Judgment of 20 February 1969, 1969 ICJ Rep. 3, 44, para. 77.

[13] Hugh Thirlway, "The Sources of International Law," in *International Law*, edited by Malcolm D. Evans 117 (Oxford: Oxford University Press, 2003), 125 (emphasis in the original).

[14] See "Report of the International Law Commission," Sixty-Eighth Session (2 May–10 June and 4 July–12 August 2016), UN Doc. A/71/10 (2016), 76–79, Draft Conclusion 2.

[15] James Crawford, *Brownlie's Principles of Public International Law* (Oxford: Oxford University Press, 8th ed. 2012), 23.

[16] Malcom N. Shaw, *International Law* (Cambridge: Cambridge University Press, 4th ed. 1997), 59.

[17] See, e.g., Thirlway, "The Sources of International Law," 125–26; Shaw, *International Law*, esp. 59. See also Crawford, *Brownlie's Principles of Public International Law*, 23.

before a legal norm comes into existence already, such a belief would be mistaken."[18]

Furthermore, while the practice of states and their belief in the legally binding character of that practice is supposed to give rise to customary international law, no practice or belief is normally labeled as such in any formal sense by these states. It is *interpretation in hindsight* of that practice-plus-belief – by academic experts or (in specific dispute contexts) state advocates, arbitrators, or judges, including those of the ICJ – that leads to recognition of a rule as rising to the level of customary international law.[19]

Of course, treaties also give rise, time and again, to disputes regarding their proper application, interpretation, and implementation; in that sense, they, too, are often not able to erase all doubt as to what the law is. The major difference with customary law, however, is that such uncertainties all play out within the context, and even the text, of the treaty itself. With few exceptions, the words and their proper application or meaning are disputed instead of the very existence of the treaty.[20]

With customary international law, by contrast, the more fundamental *a priori* question has to be answered whether it actually *exists* in the context where it is disputed. *Then* it has to be determined what it means (even if these two questions are generally discussed side-by-side without the judge or analyst necessarily realizing the distinction between them). In both cases, these questions are answered as part of *ex post facto* interpretations, usually offered by relative "outsiders" (as opposed to the states affected themselves), which unavoidably bring in a broader measure of subjectivity.

Moreover, those persons attempting to identify a rule of customary law must answer a myriad of more specific questions, such as the following: How "consistent" must "state practice" be for it to constitute customary international

[18] Brian D. Lepard, "The Legal Status of the 1996 Declaration on Space Benefits: Are Its Norms Now Part of Customary International Law?" in *Soft Law in Outer Space*, edited by Irmgard Marboe 289 (Vienna: Böhlau, 2012), 292. See also Lepard's more detailed argument in Brian D. Lepard, *Customary International Law: A New Theory with Practical Applications* (New York: Cambridge University Press, 2010), esp. 22–23, and the points he makes in Chapter 1 of this volume. This issue also relates to the general reticence of many scholars to accept something as "law" which is not necessarily "hard" in all respects. See, for example, the (rather theoretical and abstract) analysis in George C. Shaffer and Mark A. Pollack, "Hard vs. Soft Law: Alternatives, Complements, and Antagonists, in International Governance," 94 *Minnesota Law Review* 706 (2010), esp. 713–16.

[19] See also Crawford, *Brownlie's Principles of Public International Law*, 23 (referring to "the conclusion drawn by someone (a legal adviser, a court, a government, a commentator)"); Shaffer and Pollack, "Hard vs. Soft Law," 750.

[20] For the "standard" means of interpretation of treaty clauses and treaties, see, e.g., Vienna Convention on the Law of Treaties, arts. 31, 32. See also the general discussion on "precision of rules" as a constitutive part of "hard (treaty) law" in Shaffer and Pollack, "Hard vs. Soft Law," 714–15.

law?[21] How long must this practice have persisted?[22] How many states must have followed such a "state practice"? How many of them have to be "specially affected" in that particular area of international interaction?[23] What behavior would qualify a state as a "persistent objector," allowing it to escape being bound by a customary rule that is otherwise of presumably global application?[24] What behavior, by contrast, would amount to "acquiescence" by a state to a presumed rule of customary international law in the absence of a positive reaction by that state to the rule?[25] What would constitute a "region" for the purpose of determining regional or local customary law?[26]

The final major distinction that arises between treaty law and customary international law concerns the time frame of the existence or absence of relevant obligations. In the case of treaty law, there is in principle at least a black-and-white moment when a treaty enters into force, both in general and for a particular state – even if prior to that moment general obligations not to defeat the object and purpose of the treaty exist for all states that have signed it, whether or not they have ratified it.[27] Likewise, at the other end of the "obligation timeline," most treaties contain rules on their own termination as a whole and on the effect of withdrawal of an individual state party. These rules also consequently pinpoint a particular day of the calendar as the day on which treaty obligations end for a particular state party or for all of them.[28]

[21] See, e.g., Tullio Treves, "Customary International Law," in *The Max Planck Encyclopedia of Public International Law*, vol. II, edited by Rüdiger Wolfrum 945 (Oxford: Oxford University Press, 2012); Crawford, *Brownlie's Principles of Public International Law*, 25.

[22] See, e.g., Shaw, *International Law*, 59–62; Thirlway, "The Sources of International Law," 126–27; Crawford, *Brownlie's Principles of Public International Law*, 24–25; Treves, "Customary International Law," 943.

[23] See, e.g., Shaw, *International Law*, 62–63; Crawford, *Brownlie's Principles of Public International Law*, 24.

[24] On the concept of the "persistent objector," see, e.g., Olufemi Elias, "Persistent Objector," in *The Max Planck Encyclopedia of Public International Law*, vol. VIII, 280 (referring, *inter alia*, to a number of ICJ judgments at 282–84); Crawford, *Brownlie's Principles of Public International Law*, 28; Thirlway, "The Sources of International Law," 129–30. For reaffirmation of the persistent objector doctrine by the International Law Commission, see "Report of the International Law Commission," Sixty-Eighth Session, Draft Conclusion 15, para. 1.

[25] On "acquiescence," see, e.g., Nuno S.M. Antunes, "Acquiescence," in *The Max Planck Encyclopedia of Public International Law*, vol. I, 53 (referring, *inter alia*, to a number of ICJ judgments at 54). See also Shaw, *International Law*, 70–71.

[26] See, e.g., Thirlway, "The Sources of International Law," 128–29; Crawford, *Brownlie's Principles of Public International Law*, 29–30; Shaw, *International Law*, 72–73.

[27] See Vienna Convention on the Law of Treaties, art. 18(a).

[28] See also ibid., arts. 54–64 (providing for applicable law even where a particular treaty happens *not* to have (appropriately) provided for such rules itself). These articles determine, among

Customary law, by contrast, has been appropriately likened by one scholar

> to the gradual formation of a road across vacant land. After an initial uncertainty as to direction, the majority of users begin to follow the same line which becomes a single path. Not long elapses before that path is transformed into a road accepted as the only regular way, even though it is not possible to state at which precise moment this latter change occurs.[29]

In short, as opposed to the essentially binary character of treaty law as to its formal applicability (it either applies or it does not), customary international law represents a process of moving along a sliding scale from a clear and undisputed *absence* of any state practice and *opinio juris* to an (almost) undisputed full-fledged *presence* of relevant state practice and *opinio juris*.[30]

11.3 THE ROLE OF CUSTOMARY INTERNATIONAL LAW IN OUTER SPACE: GENERAL REMARKS

With this general analysis of the respective natures of treaty law and customary law in mind, I now turn to a broad analysis of the role of customary international law regarding outer space. Importantly, the "baseline" for assessing the role of customary international law in outer space and vis-à-vis outer space activities is the most fundamental treaty of space law: the Outer Space Treaty. That foundational treaty provides that "States Parties to the Treaty shall carry on activities in the exploration and use of outer space, including the Moon and other celestial bodies, in accordance with international law."[31] While the clause goes on to single out specifically the UN Charter[32] as well as major principles regarding the maintenance of international peace and security and the promotion of international cooperation and understanding, the general reference to "international law" certainly includes customary international law.

This clause has been generally perceived to mean, following the principle of *lex specialis derogat legi generali*,[33] that where space law itself is absent,

other issues, under what circumstances and conditions a treaty and the obligations arising under it can be terminated, denounced, or suspended.

29 Charles de Visscher, *Theory and Reality in Public International Law* (Princeton: Princeton University Press, 3rd ed. 1960), 149 (as quoted in Shaw, *International Law*, 62).

30 On this argument, see further Frans G. von der Dunk, "*Contradictio in terminis* or *Realpolitik*?" in *Soft Law in Outer Space*, 31, 52–53. Interestingly, Shaffer and Pollack make the argument that the distinction between hard law and soft law is also not a binary one. See Schaffer and Pollack, "Hard vs. Soft Law," 709, 712 ff.

31 Outer Space Treaty, art. III.

32 See ibid. (referring to "international law, including the Charter of the United Nations").

33 According to this principle, specific rules trump general rules with which they otherwise conflict. On this principle, see, e.g., Nele Matz-Lück, "Treaties, Conflicts between," in *The*

moot, or fundamentally open to conflicting interpretations (and therefore there is no specific and precise rule), states and courts may resort to general international law to find legal answers to legal problems involving outer space. General international law in turn incorporates general customary international law. This makes customary international law directly relevant to outer space.[34]

However, with respect to activities in outer space, as on earth, customary international law is typically considered a far less helpful legal source for assessing and addressing a certain situation than treaty law. It is often (even though only implicitly) resorted to as a stop-gap subsidiary source when there is no applicable treaty to use for the purpose.

This becomes clear by revisiting the twofold approach to customary international law described earlier in the chapter. This bifurcated approach has often been criticized,[35] and in particular the *usus* element of the two elements has been controversial.

Regarding the specifics of the application of the *usus* concept in the context of outer space, one should note that "state practice" would in the context of general international law normally be supposed to refer to what states *do*, as opposed to what they *say* or, more often, *write*. For example, if a coastal state's navy regularly intercepts foreign vessels in a particular maritime area, that physical practice of interception constitutes "classical" state practice. If it is backed up by the proper pronouncements by the coastal state (for example, that the state's navy is entitled to do so because of the legal character of the area being that of territorial waters), this practice may come to be accepted as giving rise to a rule of customary international law, namely that that area should be considered territorial waters of the coastal state.

The problem, however, is that many states also "act" by creating – in writing or through oral statements of state officials – policies, laws, and regulations. That is, after all, what states typically do – and states are the only entities

Max Planck Encyclopedia of Public International Law, vol. IX, 1098; Thirlway, "The Sources of International Law," 136–37.

34 See further, e.g., Olivier Ribbelink, "Article III," in *Cologne Commentary on Space Law*, edited by Stephan Hobe, Bernhard Schmidt-Tedd, and Kai-Uwe Schrogl, vol. I 67 (Cologne: Carl Heymanns Verlag, 2009), 67–69; Francis Lyall and Paul B. Larsen, *Space Law – A Treatise* (Farnham, UK and Burlington, VT: Ashgate, 2009), 42–43; Bin Cheng, *Studies in International Space Law* (Oxford: Oxford University Press, 1997), 228–29.

35 See, e.g., Lepard, "The Legal Status of the 1996 Declaration," 293–94; Brian D. Lepard, "Toward a New Theory of Customary International Human Rights Law," in this volume.

generally entitled under international law to make laws and regulations. Thus, what states *say* and *write* also constitutes state practice, even if at the same time the mere fact of writing a rule into a law or regulation may very well reflect the *opinio juris* of that state relating to the rule, *opinio juris* being the other necessary element of customary international law. In these cases, *usus* and *opinio juris* may refer to, and be evidenced by, the very same documents; the borderline between the two elements is not nearly as precise as is often assumed.

This analysis becomes particularly relevant with regard to outer space and space activities. The rather expensive and risky nature of space activities, certainly in the early stages of the space era, means that by definition they remained limited in quantity and extent as far as actually *doing* anything out in space. Moreover, because such activities largely take place in areas that are difficult for humans to access and that are even difficult to monitor in a reliable manner by remote means, it would be fairly challenging to determine whether the "state practice" in outer space demonstrates the uniformity and consistency that supposedly must exist in order for a rule of customary law to be established.

If state practice were to refer exclusively to practice consisting of actually doing something in outer space as opposed to "state practice on paper," for many years it would not have been necessary to look beyond the practices of the United States and the Soviet Union to determine what rules of customary international law existed with regard to outer space. Even today, for the vast majority of states, a "space activity" means an activity involving a partnership with one or more of the leading spacefaring nations, or alternatively limited operations in a few niche areas where these states can afford to be active.

The traditional focus on "physical" rather than "paper" state practice thus raises important questions regarding the qualification of "paper practice" as "state practice" for the purpose of establishing customary international law.[36] For example, should the customary international law status of the moon be exclusively left to U.S. practice, since the United States is responsible for the only "practice" of alighting citizens there to scurry around? (Significantly, there were no more than twelve American astronauts doing so in any event.) Could the scope of state practice be possibly extended beyond that of the United States to include the Russian, Chinese,

[36] On the issue of paper practice, see also Noora Arajärvi, "From the 'Demands of Humanity': The Formulation of *Opinio Juris* in Decisions of International Criminal Tribunals and the Need for a Renewed Emphasis on State Practice," in this volume; Lepard, "Toward a New Theory of Customary International Human Rights Law," in this volume.

Japanese, Indian, and European[37] "state practice" of unmanned landings on the moon?[38]

Alongside this physical practice concerning the moon, there was a distinct effort during the 1970s to address the legal status of the moon by way of a treaty, especially because of states' concerns about the apparently impending commercial exploitation of its natural resources. The so-called Moon Agreement was adopted in 1979 and came into force in 1984.[39] The negotiations on the Moon Agreement notably included the United States and the Soviet Union, even though in the end both, as well as many other states following their lead, failed to ratify the treaty. Apparently, the participation of the superpowers in these treaty negotiations indicated that neither of them considered any customary international law that might have existed on the subject to be very helpful, or at least that they desired to create clarity on legal rules relating to the moon.

As a consequence, my conclusion regarding the legal status of the moon and rules on its usage – for example, for commercial exploitation – is twofold. First, there is no widely applicable treaty regime, as the Moon Agreement was only ratified by a limited number of non-major spacefaring nations. Second, at the same time, it is also effectively impossible to distinguish any particular customary rule on the subject. If one looks at those states that landed humans on the moon, it would be a rule dictated by U.S. state practice only.

[37] Of course, it should be noted that "Europe" as such is not a state. Rather, I use the term "Europe" as shorthand for the European Space Agency ("ESA"), an intergovernmental organization established under the ESA Convention and currently comprising twenty-two European member states. See Convention for the Establishment of a European Space Agency ("ESA Convention"), Paris, done 30 May 1975, entered into force 30 October 1980, UKTS 1981 No. 30, Cmnd. 8200, 14 *International Legal Materials* 864 (1975), reprinted in *Space Law – Basic Legal Documents*, C.I.1. See generally http://en.wikipedia.org/wiki/European_Space_Agency (last accessed 16 August 2016). See also the discussion later in the chapter on the role of intergovernmental organizations in space law.

[38] See, e.g., http://en.wikipedia.org/wiki/Moon_landing (last accessed 16 August 2016), which lists the major efforts at unmanned landings on the moon by those nations.

[39] See Agreement Governing the Activities of States on the Moon and Other Celestial Bodies, New York, done 18 December 1979, entered into force 11 July 1984, 1363 UNTS 3, ATS 1986 No. 14, 18 *International Legal Materials* 1434 (1979), which currently counts 16 states parties, none of them, however, major spacefaring nations (status as of 1 January 2016). See UN Doc. A/AC.105/C.2/2016/CRP.3 (2016), 10. See further Stephan Hobe et al., "The 1979 Agreement Governing the Activities of States on the Moon and Other Celestial Bodies," in *Cologne Commentary on Space Law*, edited by Stephan Hobe, Bernhard Schmidt-Tedd, and Kai-Uwe Schrogl, vol. II 325 (Cologne: Carl Heymanns Verlag, 2013); Cheng, *Studies in International Space Law*, 357–80; Carl Q. Christol, *The Modern International Law of Outer Space* (Elmsford, NY: Pergamon Press, 1982), 246–363; Lotta Viikari, *From Manganese Nodules to Lunar Regolith* (Rovaniemi, Finland: University of Lapland, 2002), esp. 90–124; Fabio Tronchetti, *The Exploitation of Natural Resources of the Moon and Other Celestial Bodies* (Leiden: Martinus Nijhoff, 2010), 38–61.

This is politically unacceptable, and thus in conflict with broad customary international law principles of international cooperation. The rule would also be dependent on only six events (moon landings) – none of which went beyond some preliminary scientific exploration. If one looks at those states that landed human artifacts on the moon, one ignores the relevance of human action *in situ* in the context of establishing state practice – and still only has as practice activities limited to preliminary scientific exploration. If, by contrast, one includes "paper practice," one enters into the politics-driven debate on whether the moon should be a global commons open to anyone interested in investing in it or whether the moon should become an international area subject to internationalized control – and gone is any hope of discovering the uniformity of state practice required to give rise to customary international law.

Furthermore, the concept of customary international law itself, as I have already briefly touched upon, *does* recognize a distinction between states specially affected by a particular legal realm, area, or subject matter and those not so specially affected, and gives greater weight to the practices and views of the former group of states. However, the traditional definition of customary law does *not* do so to the extent of denying all other states any say on what the customary international rules should look like.[40] The example here would be the noteworthy case of Antarctica. This case is especially relevant for outer space since the area is considered, with a few exceptions, a global commons comparable to outer space.[41] Here, a special legal regime was developed, with only a limited number of states being active in Antarctica. Nevertheless, states' activities resulted in the quick adoption of a treaty, later backed up with further treaties, not in a customary law regime. Furthermore, there was general acceptance of that treaty, after considerable discussions, by most other states that later became interested in Antarctica as well.[42]

It is hard to imagine that the formal character, the visibility, and the "touchability" of the Antarctic Treaty were not instrumental in confronting those initially nonparticipating states with the fait accompli of the Antarctic Treaty's regime, and thus convincing them to try to join rather than fight the club of states

40 Compare, for example, Treves, "Customary International Law," 945; Crawford, *Brownlie's Principles of Public International Law*, 24; Shaw, *International Law*, 62–63.

41 Thus, Article 4 of the Antarctic Treaty virtually froze the territorial claims of a few states parties to that Treaty from the beginning. See Antarctic Treaty, art. 4, Washington, done 1 December 1959, entered into force 23 June 1961, 402 UNTS 71, TIAS 4780, 12 UST 794, UKTS 1961 No. 97, Cmnd. 913, ATS 1961 No. 12. The later treaties and agreements also restricted the individual discretion of these states parties to act vis-à-vis Antarctica so substantially that for all practical purposes Antarctica may now indeed be deemed a global commons.

42 See Silja Vöneky and Sange Addison-Agyei, "Antarctica," in *The Max Planck Encyclopedia of Public International Law*, vol. I, 420.

parties. If, by contrast, international law on Antarctica would have developed as customary international law, quite possibly various states would have taken the opportunity to become persistent objectors, or at least would have created their own interpretation of presumed rules of customary international law, taking advantage of the inherent imprecision of these customary rules.

Transplanted to the realm of outer space, this example supports the conclusion that the use of customary international law as a source for international obligations is relatively complicated, and by and large agreement through treaty-like arrangements should be preferred.[43] At the same time, the problems of arriving at the necessary consensus for achieving treaties with broad, hopefully even worldwide, application would mean that customary international law could still play a major role in bridging the gap between full-fledged absence of law and any hoped-for treaty in a particular area. The inherent sliding scale along which customary law comes into existence allows individual states various moments at which to reflect on whether the direction such a legal development is taking is to their liking or even merely helpful and sensible from a broader perspective. This can in the end pave the way for either a space treaty or a full-fledged rule of customary international space law.

11.4 THE SPECIAL CHARACTER OF SPACE LAW: THE SECURITY AND DUAL-USE DIMENSION

When it comes to substantive space law, the first area where space law is special in relation to the role of customary international law concerns the innate "dual-use" character of most, if not all, space assets and activities. That is, space assets can simultaneously be used for peaceful and military purposes.[44] The launch vehicles that put satellites into orbit are technically almost indistinguishable from rockets capable of carrying nuclear warheads[45]; remote

[43] This aspect of my argument echoes some of the same points made by J. Patrick Kelly, who argues that treaties have the ability to balance competing interests better than customary international law, whose ambiguity can too easily be exploited by great powers to pursue their own preferences. See J. Patrick Kelly, "Customary International Law in Historical Context: The Exercise of Power without General Acceptance," in this volume.

[44] See, e.g., Fabio Tronchetti, *Fundamentals of Space Law and Policy* (New York; Heidelberg; Dordrecht; London: Springer, 2013), 61 et seq. See also N.L. Remuss, "Space and Security," in *Outer Space in Society, Politics and Law*, edited by Christian Brünner and Alexander Soucek 519 (Vienna and New York: Springer, 2011); Henry R. Hertzfeld and Raymond L. Jones, "International Aspects of Technology Controls," in *Outer Space in Society, Politics and Law*, 638.

[45] Note, for example, that in the context of disarmament treaties between the United States and the Soviet Union/Russia the conversion of these "swords" into "ploughshares" is subjected to severe constraints in order to preclude the possibility of easy re-conversion. See also 51 U.S.C. §

sensing satellites can be used for spying[46]; and the GPS satellite navigation system is owned, operated, and controlled by the U.S. military, even as many civil and commercial applications now start to depend on its availability.[47]

This means that space activities across the board tend to have a possible impact on national security. National security relates, in the final analysis, to the sheer survival of the state as a relevant entity and thus in legal terms is closely linked to questions of state sovereignty. With such issues of survival ultimately at stake, states are generally less willing to subject themselves to the imprecision that tends to characterize customary international law. On the one hand, they wish to maximize their own options to protect their existence and limit their own obligations under international law. On the other hand, they try to minimize the options of some other states and maximize the applicability of international law to those other states – in a context almost by definition ruled by distrust and suspicion. This is not to say that international security law is a zero-sum game. Concerns about increasing predictability, maximizing a law-abiding profile (in particular in a democratic rule-of-law environment), and respecting the rights and interests of third-party, neutral states also affect states' decision-making processes when they are developing or accepting international obligations on the international level. None of this, however, negates the obvious preference for black-letter treaties over customary law in the security domain. This inherently makes treaty law, being relatively clear, that much more preferable than customary international law in the eyes of states as an instrument for protecting their national security interests.

Moreover, the general atmosphere of distrust and suspicion makes monitoring other parties' behavior relatively more important than in less security-relevant realms. The rights, obligations, and procedures for monitoring, inspecting, and (if acceptable to the parties) sanctioning other states' space activities by definition are not easily arranged by way of customary law; they require precise arrangements and agreements.[48] Even in Europe, despite its

50134, 3 Jan. 2012; Pub. L. 111–314, § 3, Dec. 18, 2010, 124 Stat. 3400 (providing for the United States' implementation of these treaty requirements).

46 For example, regarding the United States, see the Kyl-Bingaman Amendment of 1996 (§ 1064, 1997 Defense Authorization Act, P.L. No. 104–201) of the Land Remote Sensing Policy Act (Public Law 102–555, 102nd Congress, H.R. 6133, 28 October 1992, 15 U.S.C. 5601, 106 Stat. 4163), which was adopted to ensure that very high resolution data on Israel generated by U.S.-licensed remote sensing satellite operators would not be disseminated.

47 See 51 U.S.C. § 50112, 3 Jan. 2012; Pub. L. 111–314, § 3, Dec. 18, 2010, 124 Stat. 3397 (seeking to ensure that interests in civil and commercial applications are taken into consideration as much as possible within the context of a military satellite system).

48 Thus, major international treaties addressing security and arms control all include key provisions on such monitoring and inspection clauses, from the broad obligation not to interfere with "national technical means of verification" (including satellites) of Article V of the SALT

post–World War II record of regional integration, including some cooperation on military and security issues and the conduct of joint military exercises, often within the European Union ("EU") context,[49] states still prefer, as in other parts of the world, to rely on themselves for national security.[50]

As noted earlier in the chapter, this general analysis is of particular relevance in the context of space activities and space law, resulting in states being very careful not to act in a manner that could be interpreted as state practice sanctified by *opinio juris*, which could possibly result in a rule of customary international law that could be used against them. As a consequence, relatively little customary international law can be discerned in this particular legal domain.

Furthermore, while the various space treaties, in particular the Outer Space Treaty, may have given rise to at least some customary norms that would be applicable outside the group of states bound by them as treaty norms, this development would occur only to a limited extent. In particular, it would occur only to the extent that such a norm can be viewed as an "extension" of a similar rule of "general" customary international law that is also already generally recognized outside the domain of outer space and space activities. This conclusion follows from Article III of the Outer Space Treaty, as discussed earlier, which requires states parties to carry on their outer space activities "in accordance with international law." With the exception of a few "showcases" addressed later, there are precious few customary rules derived from the space treaties that do not directly follow from such broader international law – and that consequently are unique to space law.

I Interim Agreement to the establishment of a full-fledged Comprehensive Nuclear Test-Ban Treaty Organization to monitor compliance with the Comprehensive Test Ban Treaty and the obligations not to test any nuclear weapons (including in outer space) (see Articles II-VI), covering a full sixty-seven pages. For the SALT I Interim Agreement, see Interim Agreement on Certain Measures with Respect to the Limitation of Strategic Arms, Moscow, done 26 May 1972, entered into force 3 October 1972, TIAS 7504, 23 UST 3462. For the Comprehensive Test Ban Treaty, see Comprehensive Test Ban Treaty, New York, done 24 September 1996, not yet entered into force, Cm. 3665, 35 *International Legal Materials* 1439 (1996), S. Treaty Doc. No. 105–28 (1997).

49 See Treaty on European Union as amended by the Treaty of Lisbon amending the Treaty on European Union and the Treaty establishing the European Community, Lisbon, arts. 21–46, done 13 December 2007, entered into force 1 December 2009, OJ C 115/1 (2009). See also Treaty establishing the European Community as amended by the Treaty of Lisbon amending the Treaty on European Union and the Treaty establishing the European Community (hereafter "Treaty on the Functioning of the European Union"), arts. 326–34, Lisbon, done 13 December 2007, entered into force 1 December 2009, OJ C 115/47 (2009).

50 For further discussion, see Frans G. von der Dunk, "Europe and Security Issues in Space: The Institutional Setting," 4 *Space and Defense* 71 (2010). See also Shaffer and Pollack, "Hard vs. Soft Law," 730.

11.5 THE FIRST SHOWCASE: "PEACEFUL PURPOSES"

The general situation sketched in the preceding section to a major extent confines the impact of customary international law on the legal framework applicable in the space arena to an almost secondary role of interpreting treaty clauses that have not been duly defined. In the particular area of security-related treaty clauses, the most important one concerns the proper interpretation of Article IV of the Outer Space Treaty, which provides in its second paragraph: "The Moon and other celestial bodies shall be used by all States Parties to the Treaty *exclusively for peaceful purposes*."[51] The meaning of "exclusively for peaceful purposes" is not further spelled out, except to the extent that the same article provides:

> The establishment of military bases, installations and fortifications, the testing of any type of weapons and the conduct of military manoeuvres on celestial bodies shall be forbidden. The use of military personnel for scientific research or for any other peaceful purposes shall not be prohibited. The use of any equipment or facility necessary for peaceful exploration of the Moon and other celestial bodies shall also not be prohibited.[52]

Originally, the intentional vagueness of the clause allowed both the United States and the Soviet Union to uphold their respective interpretations, and hence to ratify the Treaty in the first place. The United States had argued that military use, as long as it is defensive in nature, is serving peaceful purposes, and hence allowed. By contrast, the Soviet Union had taken the position that any military use is by definition not peaceful, and therefore forbidden, with the exception of the few specific cases mentioned in the clause itself. For that very reason, any effort – either in black-letter law or by way of customary acquiescence – at further specification of the statement in the final treaty would have been doomed to fail.[53]

As time wore on, however, it became clear that the legal attitude to permissible military use of outer space was shifting. In spite of the Soviet Union's

[51] Outer Space Treaty, art. IV, para. 2 (emphasis added).

[52] Ibid.

[53] It may be noted that a similar clause ("for exclusively peaceful purposes") was inserted in Article II of the ESA Convention principally in order to exclude any potential involvement of ESA in security-related space activities. One could of course argue that the lack of "precision of rules" mentioned earlier detracts from the "hardness" of the treaty, or even presents a "soft law" element within it. See, e.g., Shaffer and Pollack, "Hard vs. Soft Law," 714–15, 719. Yet this does not detract from the formally binding character of the provisions. With the developments described later in the chapter, moreover, the range of acceptable interpretations increasingly narrowed, allowing as of now much less dispute about what the term could be held to mean. See ibid., 749.

apparent assertion to the contrary, it did use space infrastructure for military purposes, such as reconnaissance and satellite navigation. In 1996, its successor state, Russia, offered open access to certain positioning, timing, and navigation signals of its GLONASS satellite navigation system, much like the United States did with respect to its GPS system owned, operated, and controlled by the military.[54] While this means the systems and their signals were increasingly opened up for nonmilitary purposes, it did not change the fact that both systems also continued to be used by the countries' respective militaries. Notably, both systems distinguished between lower-precision signals to which nonmilitary users had access and high-precision signals that remained encrypted and accessible only by the respective military forces.

In addition, the general international legal attitude to the use of force was changing. The UN Charter had explicitly recognized only two categories of cases where the use of armed force was allowed: that of self-defense (including, if applicable, collective self-defense),[55] and the mandated use of force against states as authorized by the UN Security Council invoking its Chapter VII enforcement powers to respond to a threat to the peace, breach of the peace, or act of aggression.[56] Outside of the UN Charter, a broader customary right of self-defense or a more general right to use force as a proportional reprisal had often been claimed – but equally often been disputed, or at least been eyed suspiciously as giving rise too easily to abuse.

In view of the reference in Article III of the Outer Space Treaty to general international law and the UN Charter in particular, the result is that any changing interpretation of the exceptions to the prohibition of the use of force in the international community also gives rise to a concomitant change of the interpretation of the treaty phrase "peaceful purposes." Thus, any use of force currently in conformity with the accepted interpretation of the laws on the use of force would *ipso facto* be permissible as compliant with the "peaceful purposes" provision. I come back to this issue in the next section in the specific context of international organizations.

11.6 THE SPECIAL CHARACTER OF SPACE LAW: THE DIMENSION OF INTERNATIONAL COOPERATION

A second major area where space activities are unique, giving rise to a special role for customary law, is that of international cooperation. Even today, space

[54] See, e.g., Lyall and Larsen, *Space Law – A Treatise*, 389 et seq. See also Norbert Frischauf, "Satellite Navigation," in *Outer Space in Society, Politics and Law*, 124.

[55] See UN Charter, art. 51.

[56] See ibid., arts. 42 et seq.

activities are high-risk and require a high level of investment. Accordingly, except for a few major spacefaring nations, all countries need to cooperate internationally to partake of the full range of benefits that space activities and space applications may bring.

This principle of international cooperation is enshrined in the Outer Space Treaty. The Treaty declares: "States Parties to the Treaty shall carry on activities in the exploration and use of outer space … in the interest of … promoting international cooperation and understanding."[57]

More importantly, this treaty-based obligation of international cooperation gave rise to an unprecedented role of intergovernmental organizations in outer space. These organizations have not just played a regulatory or political role but have also had a major operational role, pooling huge amounts of national technical and material resources for the greater common good of the totality of the member states. Regarding the distinction discussed earlier between "physical" and "paper" practice, this also means that in this particular area of space activity a considerable amount of physical practice *is* present.

Even as they have recently been privatized,[58] the International Telecommunications Satellite Organization ("INTELSAT"),[59] the International Maritime Satellite Organization ("INMARSAT"),[60] and,

57 See Outer Space Treaty, art. III. See also ibid., art. VI (referring to responsibility for "activities … carried on in outer space … by an international organization") and art. XIII (referring to "activities … carried on within the framework of international intergovernmental organizations").

58 See, e.g., *The Transformation of Intergovernmental Satellite Organisations*, edited by Patricia K. McCormick and Maury J. Mechanick (Leiden: Martinus Nijhoff, 2013).

59 INTELSAT was originally established by the Agreement Relating to the International Telecommunications Satellite Organization ("INTELSAT") (hereafter "INTELSAT Agreement"), Washington, done 20 August 1971, entered into force 12 February 1973, 1220 UNTS 21, TIAS 7532, 23 UST 3813, UKTS 1973 No. 80, Cmnd. 4799, ATS 1973 No. 6, 10 *International Legal Materials* 909 (1971) and the Operating Agreement Relating to the International Telecommunications Satellite Organization ("INTELSAT") (hereafter "INTELSAT Operating Agreement"), Washington, done 20 August 1971, entered into force 12 February 1973, 1220 UNTS 149, TIAS 7532, 23 UST 4091, UKTS 1973 No. 80, Cmnd. 4799, ATS 1973 No. 6, 10 *International Legal Materials* 946 (1971). After its establishment it was privatized under the Agreement Relating to the International Telecommunications Satellite Organization ("ITSO"), Washington, done 20 August 1971, entered into force 12 February 1973, as amended 13 November 2000, amended version entered into force 30 November 2004, Cm. 5092, reprinted in *Space Law – Basic Legal Documents*, C.V.1.

60 INMARSAT was originally established by the Convention on the International Maritime Satellite Organization ("INMARSAT") (hereafter "INMARSAT Convention"), London, done 3 September 1976, entered into force 16 July 1979, 1143 UNTS 105, TIAS 9605, 31 UST 1, UKTS 1979 No. 94, Cmnd. 6822, ATS 1979 No. 10, 15 *International Legal Materials* 1052 (1976) and the Operating Agreement on the International Maritime Satellite Organization ("INMARSAT") (hereafter "INMARSAT Operating Agreement"), London, done 3 September 1976, entered into force 16 July 1979, 1143 UNTS 213, TIAS 9605, 31 UST 1, UKTS 1979 No. 94, Cmnd. 6822,

for Europe, the European Telecommunications Satellite Organization ("EUTELSAT")[61] for many years dominated international satellite communications as intergovernmental organizations operating a telecommunication satellite infrastructure for the benefit of their respective sets of member states.[62] The INTERSPUTNIK International System and Organization of Space Communications[63] and the Arab Corporation for Space Communications ("ARABSAT")[64] still continue to do so.

In Europe, moreover, following the success of EUTELSAT, another intergovernmental organization was established to operate a satellite weather forecasting system, EUMETSAT,[65] which as of August 2016 counted thirty member states.[66] Finally, since 1975 the European Space Agency ("ESA")[67]

ATS 1979 No. 10, 15 *International Legal Materials* 233 (1976). After its establishment it was privatized under the Convention on the International Mobile Satellite Organization (hereafter "IMSO Convention"), London, done 3 September 1976, entered into force 16 July 1979, as amended 1998, amended version entered into force 31 July 2001, ATS 2001 No. 11.

61 EUTELSAT was originally established by the Convention Establishing the European Telecommunications Satellite Organization ("EUTELSAT") (hereafter "EUTELSAT Convention"), Paris, done 15 July 1982, entered into force 1 September 1985, UKTS 1990 No. 15, Cm. 956, Cmnd. 9069, reprinted in, *Space Law – Basic Legal Documents*, C.II.1, and the Operating Agreement Relating to the European Telecommunications Satellite Organization ("EUTELSAT") (hereafter "EUTELSAT Operating Agreement"), Paris, done 15 July 1982, entered into force 1 September 1985, UKTS 1990 No. 15, Cm. 956, Cmnd. 9154, reprinted in *Space Law – Basic Legal Documents*, C.II.2. After its establishment it was privatized under the Convention Establishing the European Telecommunications Satellite Organization ("EUTELSAT") (hereafter "EUTELSAT Convention" as amended), Paris, done 15 July 1982, entered into force 1 September 1985, as amended 20 May 1999, amended version entered into force 28 November 2002, Cm. 4572, reprinted in *Space Law – Basic Legal Documents*, C.II.1.

62 As of 2000, the year privatization became more or less irreversible for all three organizations, INTELSAT counted 143 member states, INMARSAT 87 member states, and EUTELSAT 47 member states, generally testifying to their great success.

63 INTERSPUTNIK was established by the Agreement on the Establishment of the "INTERSPUTNIK" International System and Organization of Space Communications (hereafter "INTERSPUTNIK Agreement"), Moscow, done 15 November 1971, entered into force 12 July 1972, 862 UNTS 3, TIAS 859 (1973) No, 12343, reprinted in *Space Law – Basic Legal Documents*, C.VIII.1.

64 ARABSAT was established by the Agreement of the Arab Corporation for Space Communications ("ARABSAT"), Cairo, done 14 April 1976, entered into force 15 July 1976, reprinted in *Space Law – Basic Legal Documents*, C.VII.1, 44 *Telecommunications Journal* 422 (1977).

65 EUMETSAT was established by the Convention for the Establishment of a European Organization for the Exploitation of Meteorological Satellites ("EUMETSAT") (hereafter "EUMETSAT Convention"), Geneva, done 24 May 1983, entered into force 19 June 1986, as amended 14 July 1994, entered into force 27 July 1994, UKTS 1999 No. 32, Cm. 1067, Cmnd. 9483, 44 ZLW 68 (1995).

66 See the list of member states at www.eumetsat.int/website/home/AboutUs/WhoWeAre/MemberStates/index.html (last accessed 16 August 2016).

67 ESA was established by the ESA Convention.

has combined the know-how and financial resources of twenty-two member states (as of August 2016) to undertake the full range of space activities imaginable, from scientific deep space research to launch services and space station operations.[68]

11.7 THE SECOND SHOWCASE: FINANCING JOINT SPACE ACTIVITIES THROUGH ORGANIZATIONS

The starting point to note here is that – as is the case with intergovernmental organizations in general as well – these organizations are ultimately still controlled by their member state constituencies. In the respective constitutive documents of these organizations the role and competences of their major organs are defined in a way that maintains rather absolute deference to the sovereign member states. This, then, raises the question of the role of the organizations' "practice" in helping create customary international law. It should be reiterated that, as compared to "general" customary international law, in this particular context, a considerable amount of "physical practice" can be discerned.

For example, the Council of the ESA is the highest organ of that organization. It is comprised of all ESA member states, and tasked, *inter alia*, with responsibility for approving programs, activities, budgets, and policies by a simple majority vote, unless otherwise provided.[69] Does this mean that all decisions of the Council and the activities following from them could be regarded as "joint" state practice and expressions of a "joint" *opinio juris* of the member states? Or would only those decisions where unanimity of the Council members was required count as joint state practice and *opinio juris*?[70]

While arguments could be made both ways, the detailed nature of the ESA Council's decisions and activities makes it unlikely that they could be seen as true potential candidates for a rule of customary law. They would normally be much too idiosyncratic, dealing with specific and unique circumstances in each and every case, to give rise to any consistent "state practice" along with a commensurate consistent belief by member states that the practice is required *ipso facto* by law.

In particular, the intricate system of ESA combines mandatory and optional programs – the core of ESA's "physical practice" – within one international intergovernmental institution. The mandatory programs are focused on science

68 On the number of member states, see www.esa.int/About_Us/Welcome_to_ESA/New_Member_States (last accessed 16 August 2016).

69 See ESA Convention, arts. XI(5), (6) (esp. *sub* (d)).

70 On this issue, see, e.g., Treves, "Customary International Law," 946–48.

and require all member states to contribute according to a preset scale. The optional programs are focused on more operational and application-oriented space activities, allowing for an à la carte approach for member states, both in terms of their participation per se and their level of financial contribution once they decide to participate.[71]

The result is a uniquely flexible framework that balances the sovereign discretion of member states to spend resources on space programs with the fundamental need to cooperate on those programs. The ESA framework thus accommodates the interests of individual states while maintaining a coherent and efficient manageable program. It has worked well over the almost four decades of existence of the Agency, is not currently subject to any legal controversy whatsoever, and has meanwhile been so successful that it has been emulated by EUMETSAT.[72] The flexibility of ESA's structure is very likely *the* trait of the Agency that prospective international space cooperation organizations in other parts of the world would most like to adopt and copy.

This, however, still would not mean that this dual system of mandatory and optional activities can be deemed to be part of customary international law. The member states of ESA comply with it because of the ESA Convention (the treaty that established ESA), the mechanisms provided by that treaty, and the competences of ESA organs to develop programs as spelled out by the treaty. They have not complied because of some inherent belief that every scientific activity in outer space should be conducted by or through ESA, and should be financed by all ESA member states according to a predetermined scale of contributions. If international operational space organizations should indeed be created in the future in Africa, Latin America, or Southeast Asia, nothing would keep them from deciding on a rather different system of organizing their activities, no matter how much states in these regions may currently admire ESA's example.

The same holds true for the financial contribution systems applicable to INTELSAT, INMARSAT, and EUTELSAT in their pre-privatized stages, which were generally identical to one another. Under these systems, the financial contributions by the respective member states toward the costs of building, maintaining, and operating a satellite infrastructure through their public telecommunication operators were adjusted in light of their actual proportion

[71] See ESA Convention, arts. V(1)(a) and (b), XI(5)(a), (b), and (c), and XIII.

[72] See, e.g., Kevin Madders, *A New Force at a New Frontier* (Cambridge: Cambridge University Press, 2000), 189–95; Gabriel Lafferranderie, *European Space Agency* (The Hague: Kluwer Law International, 2005), 74–89. On EUMETSAT, see further, e.g., F.G. von der Dunk, "European Satellite Earth Observation: Law, Regulations, Policies, Projects, and Programmes," 42 *Creighton Law Review* 397 (2009), 403–06.

of use of the infrastructure.[73] This approach was considered hugely successful in many respects. INMARSAT followed it because of INTELSAT's success, and then EUTELSAT adopted the same approach in turn. This same general approach was later adopted by INTERSPUTNIK after the downfall of communism in the Soviet Union, the leading country in that organization.[74] And ARABSAT adopted it as well.[75] However, this financial approach, while universally implemented during these organizations' pre-privatization phases, was ultimately discarded as part of the privatization processes for INTELSAT, INMARSAT, and EUTELSAT.

The question then again arises as to whether this system of matching *a priori* investment with *a posteriori* actual usage is a possible candidate for a rule of customary international law. The better view is that it is not such a rule; rather, it was simply a matter of common (business) sense. Again, legally speaking, nothing would keep, for example, a future African international satellite organization from adopting another financial approach – and indeed, the three original major proponents of such a financial system have now replaced it with straightforward commercial and private operation of their respective systems.

Finally, in the context of ESA yet another, even more complicated, financial approach was developed: that of geographical distribution or "fair return." In general, under this approach member states were supposed to see their contributions to specific ESA programs "returned" to their domestic space industry in the form of ESA contracts.[76] For some time this system was legally under challenge, in particular from the perspective of the EU, from which it could be viewed as anti-competitive and therefore possibly in violation of the EU's competition regime.[77] Nevertheless, for political reasons ESA's regime

73 See INTELSAT Agreement, art. V; INTELSAT Operating Agreement, arts. 3(c), 4, 6–8; INMARSAT Convention, arts. 5(1)-(2), 19; INMARSAT Operating Agreement, arts. III, V, VI(1); Annex to the INMARSAT Operating Agreement; EUTELSAT Convention, art. V; EUTELSAT Operating Agreement, arts. 4, 6, 7.

74 See INTERSPUTNIK Agreement, art. 15(1).

75 See ARABSAT Agreement, art. 6(2).

76 In general, see, e.g., *A Coherent European Procurement Law and Policy for the Space Sector*, edited by Stephan Hobe, Mahulena Hofmannová, and Jan Wouters (Berlin; Münster; Vienna; Zürich; London: LIT Verlag, 2011), 70–78; Bernhard Schmidt-Tedd, "The Geographical Return Principle and its Future within the European Space Policy," in *Contracting for Space*, edited by L. Jane Smith and Ingo Baumann 85 (Farnham, UK and Burlington, VT: Ashgate, 2011), 87; Lafferranderie, *European Space Agency*, 108–15; Madders, *A New Force at a New Frontier*, 384–88.

77 It would principally fall within the scope of the EU prohibition on state aid. See Treaty on the Functioning of the European Union, art. 107(1). Further, see, e.g., Frans G. von der Dunk, "ESA and EC: Two Captains on One Spaceship?" in *Proceedings of the Thirty-Second Colloquium on the Law of Outer Space* (Reston, VA: AIAA, 1990), 427–29; Frans G. von der Dunk, "Perspectives for a Harmonised Industrial Policy of ESA and the European Union,"

on this issue has never been formally attacked, and it persists today as a major element of the ESA structure.

Ultimately, therefore, whatever the extent to which the general practice of an intergovernmental organization could be considered a "joint state practice" of its member states, these financing issues, problems, and approaches are too idiosyncratic and need to be far too detailed in order to be acceptable and workable to even come near to a consistent (joint) state practice and attendant *opinio juris*. In essence, despite the adoption of these quite uniform and popular financing systems, states do not exhibit the requisite *opinio juris* because they want to retain the right to agree on some other financing scheme in the future, or in other space organizations. They do not really believe that these systems should be legally binding in the absence of treaty commitments. Neither the "investment-equals-usage-level" approach of the international satellite organizations nor the "investment-equals-contract-volume" approach of ESA can in any way be deemed to obligate even the respective member states beyond the very specific and detailed rules of the constitutive documents of these organizations and other internal regulations. Moreover, they cannot have any customary international legal effect outside of these respective member state constituencies.

11.8 THE THIRD SHOWCASE: FIGHTING SPACE DEBRIS

The main exception to the limited role of major international cooperation in a customary law context lies in the area of combating the ever-increasing problem of space debris.[78] Not surprisingly, customary law is more relevant here because this is a problem that is affecting *all* states of the world involved or interested in space activities, regardless of the international space organizations to which they belong.

The process of tackling this vexing problem started with major space agencies cooperating through the Inter-Agency Space Debris Coordination Committee ("IADC"). Through the IADC, these agencies agreed in 2002 on a policy and practical level to start conducting their respective space operations in a manner less conducive to the generation of harmful

in *"Project 2001 Plus" – Global and European Challenges for Air and Space Law at the Edge of the 21st Century*, edited by Stephan Hobe, Bernhard Schmidt-Tedd, and Kai-Uwe Schrogl 181 (Cologne; Berlin; Munich: Carl Heymanns Verlag, 2006). However, it is important to note that in reality EU law itself also allowed for exceptions to application of the competition regime, as long as they were agreed to at the EU level itself. See especially Treaty on the Functioning of the European Union, art. 107(3).

[78] However, for another potential candidate for customary international law status evolving from an international cooperational/organizational context, see von der Dunk, "*Contradictio in*

space debris.[79] As a next step, the United Nations, acting in effect as the representative of the international community of states, officially recognized the validity and value of the IADC document in a General Assembly resolution adopted in 2007.[80] It thereby elevated these practical guidelines to what should probably be called "soft law" – law that is highly authoritative from a political perspective but is not yet enforceable hard law in the normal sense of the word.[81]

Meanwhile, the process has reached a third phase, in which the major states involved have chosen to start applying relevant aspects of those guidelines as license requirements for private space operators.[82] They have done so only on a domestic level so far – without question, however, imposing legally binding obligations on licensees. If, somewhere down the road, these processes will have indeed spread to all spacefaring nations in a more or less consistent fashion – for example, by these nations faithfully following the IADC Guidelines and the UN resolution – then clearly a state practice with attendant *opinio juris* amounting to a rule of customary international law would have emerged. That rule might be written as follows: "Thou shalt not leave thy junk in outer space, and either safely de-orbit, re-orbit, or boost it into deep space, as well as minimize intentional break-up, and take other preventive measures as listed."[83] This may well turn out to be the first major substantive rule of outer

terminis or *Realpolitik*?" 55 (discussing the Charter on Space and Major Disasters and the extent to which states requested to provide support under it might be legally bound to do so).

79 This ultimately resulted in the IADC Space Debris Mitigation Guidelines, IADC-02-01, Revision 1, September 2007.

80 See Space Debris Mitigation Guidelines of the United Nations Committee on the Peaceful Uses of Outer Space of 2010, endorsed by GA Res. 62/217 of 21 December 2007, A/RES/62/217 (2007). These Guidelines almost literally repeat the IADC Guidelines, so that the main effect is the elevation in the political and proto-legal status of them.

81 See, e.g., Steven Freeland, "The Role of 'Soft Law' in Public International Law and its Relevance to the International Legal Regulation of Outer Space," in *Soft Law in Outer Space*, 9, 19–23.

82 Notably, France, Italy, Japan, the United Kingdom, and the United States have done so. See, e.g., Lotta Viikari, *The Environmental Element in Space Law* (Leiden: Martinus Nijhoff, 2008), 96. Kosuge and Takeuchi also discuss from this perspective Russia, China, and India, as well as the European Space Agency as far as their own (inter)governmental launches are concerned. See Toshio Kosuge and Yu Takeuchi, "From Guideline to International Treaty for Rule of Law Concerning Mitigation of Space Debris?" in *Proceedings of the International Institute of Space Law 2010* 291 (Reston, VA: AIAA, 2011). For further discussion, see, e.g., Kelly Gable, "Rules Regarding Space Debris: Preventing a Tragedy of the Commons," in *Proceedings of the Fiftieth Colloquium on the Law of Outer Space* 262 (Reston, VA: AIAA, 2008).

83 Compare IADC Space Debris Mitigation Guidelines, §§ 3.4, 4, 5 (providing for key elements of debris mitigation policies and laws, including the limitation of debris released during normal operations, the minimization of the potential for on-orbit breakups, and the minimization of the potential for post mission breakups).

space law principally developed on a customary international law basis, as opposed to being developed as a rule of treaty law.

The main difference between this supposed prospective rule of customary international law and the financial schemes discussed in the preceding section, which I have argued have not attained customary law status, lies in the implicit involvement of third parties also making use of the same global commons of outer space. The financial schemes discussed earlier involve a completely internal arrangement between certain partners in a joint venture regarding its financing. If the venture fails, or has major flaws, the states harmed thereby would only be those that are party to the joint venture or organization. By contrast, a rule of customary international law on space debris would address the actual use of those global commons. A spacefaring state's negligence of the risk of space debris also puts the legal interests and rights of third states at risk, and hence threatens the very international sustainability and status of outer space.

11.9 THE FOURTH SHOWCASE: INMARSAT, INMARSAT, AND "PEACEFUL PURPOSES" REVISITED

Both specific traits of space activities – the security dimension and the dimension of international cooperation through operational organizations – came together perhaps most visibly and uniquely in the INMARSAT and Inmarsat context and their role in various war-related activities. The former organization gained worldwide exposure during the Persian Gulf War in early 1991, when war correspondents were able to give live reports from Baghdad and other areas in the Persian Gulf of missiles flying overhead or bombs going off around them using INMARSAT satellites and terminals. At the time INMARSAT was still operating as a public international consortium of member states.

Yet another issue that drew global attention to INMARSAT was the appearance of photos in the press showing U.S. forces using INMARSAT terminals during operations related to the Persian Gulf War in 1991. INMARSAT's Director General raised concerns with the U.S. government regarding this usage, and called attention to the opinion by the organization's legal adviser that had been released four years earlier.

That opinion had been drafted in response to concerns that were privately raised by some members of the organization in response to extensive use of INMARSAT shipboard terminals by the United Kingdom during the Falklands War of 1982. The opinion addressed Article 3 of the INMARSAT Convention, which describes the organization's purpose, and provides as follows:

> (1) The purpose of the Organization is to make provision for the space segment necessary for improving maritime communications and, as practicable, aeronautical communications, thereby assisting in improving communications for distress and safety of life, communications for air traffic services, the efficiency and management of ships and aircraft, maritime and aeronautical public correspondence services and radio determination capabilities; ...
> (3) The Organization *shall act exclusively for peaceful purposes.*[84]

Interpreting the clause in a strict sense, the opinion of the Legal Adviser was that the use of INMARSAT shipboard terminals on ships engaged in armed conflict, even in situations in which they would be acting in self-defense, would not be considered a use for peaceful purposes. Accordingly, it concluded that such use was in violation of the INMARSAT Convention.

INMARSAT was then privatized, following market and regulatory pressures in the EU and the United States. It was transformed into a private satellite infrastructure operator, known as "Inmarsat," and a rudimentary intergovernmental oversight organization known as "IMSO."[85] Substantively, Article 3 of the INMARSAT Convention was not changed and became Article 3 of the new IMSO Convention. However, after this restructuring, it was now up to IMSO to ensure that the company Inmarsat would be "acting exclusively for peaceful purposes."[86]

Inmarsat, the private operator, then became involved in a discussion on the proper meaning and effect of this phrase. Although the question of the legality of the use of Inmarsat's capabilities was again raised during the U.S. military operations in Afghanistan and Iraq beginning in 2003, the question seems to have troubled Inmarsat's management less than it did in previous years. For example, Inmarsat openly announced: "Global security events in recent years have had a positive effect on the group's revenues, particularly in the land sector. In 2003, despite decreased demand for our services from Afghanistan and neighboring countries, revenues were higher than in the previous year because of demand fed by the conflict in Iraq."[87]

84 INMARSAT Convention, art. 3 (emphasis added).

85 See, e.g., Patricia K. McCormick, "Neo-Liberalism: A Contextual Framework for Assessing the Privatisation of Intergovernmental Satellite Organisations," in *The Transformation of Intergovernmental Satellite Organisations*, edited by Patricia K. McCormick and Maury J. Mechanick 1 (Leiden: Martinus Nijhoff, 2013). On INMARSAT specifically, see, e.g., David Sagar and Patricia K. McCormick, "Inmarsat: In the Forefront of Mobile Satellite Communications," in *The Transformation of Intergovernmental Satellite Organisations*, 41.

86 See IMSO Convention, art. 3, which states: "The purpose of the Organization is to ensure that the basic principles set forth in this Article shall be observed by the Company, namely: ... (c) acting exclusively for peaceful purposes."

87 Inmarsat Group Limited, Annual Review 2003, 17, available at www.inmarsat.com/wp-content/uploads/2013/10/Inmarsat_Annual_Review_2003.pdf (last accessed 29 August 2016).

Moreover, Inmarsat made this statement at the same time that it announced plans to construct a Ka-band broadband system that will be substantially faster than its Broadband Global Area Network service. It did so primarily in response to the requests of the U.S. government to meet military needs, such as unmanned aerial vehicle downloads.[88] All this took place without any corrective action on the part of IMSO officials. Clearly, "the times they are a-changing" when it comes to the interpretation of "peaceful purposes" that is considered appropriate and correct. In other words, the interpretation of this particular clause of the Outer Space Treaty is changing as a consequence, not of a formal "restatement" or "redefinition" of the term by another document like a treaty or protocol, but because of changing "collective state practice" in the context of this particular organization, as the most prominent forum in which the issue had to be legally addressed.

11.10 CONCLUSIONS

In sum, customary international law plays a more marginal role in space law than it does in general international law due to the inherent security dimension of space activities and space law and due to customary law's general lack of precision in scope and content. By and large, the role of customary international law in space activities remains limited to further clarifying general concepts of law found in treaties, of which the term "peaceful purposes" represents the main successful example.[89]

Even in the area in which space law has made significant novel contributions to general international law – in particular, the establishment of a number of key intergovernmental organizations actually undertaking space activities on behalf of the respective member state constituencies, thus giving rise to "physical practice" potentially qualifying as "joint state practice" – it is rather difficult to discern any consistent state practice-*cum-opinio juris*. This is because of the fundamental requirement of detailed and specific regulations

88 See *Defense Systems*, 20 August 2010, available at www.defensesystems.com/Articles/2010/08/20/ Inmarsat-addresses-growing-military-broadband-needs.aspx (last accessed 29 August 2016).

89 By contrast, for example, when it comes to the term "national activities in outer space" of Article VI of the Outer Space Treaty, which requires authorization and continuing supervision, no consistency in the state practice of the fifteen or so states currently having established national space laws can be discerned. On this point, see, e.g., Frans G. von der Dunk, "Towards 'Flags of Convenience' in Space?" in *Proceedings of the International Institute of Space Law 2012* 822 (The Hague: Eleven International Publishing, 2013). As a consequence of this lack of consistency, what precisely is to be considered "*national* activities"? Activities conducted by nationals? Activities conducted from national territory? Both? This issue remains unclear, as individual states have implicitly adopted various interpretations, including the ones indicated earlier in the chapter, but also more complicated ones.

and arrangements for usually unique situations, contexts, or events. The main exception here might be the one concerning space debris, helped no doubt by the fact that every state is in the same boat here. Another possible exception is the question of how to interpret "peaceful purposes" in the constitutive treaties of INMARSAT and Inmarsat, where through a largely customary law process more military-related activities are being treated as "peaceful." Only with the ongoing "normalization" and privatization of at least some major areas of space activity will the importance of security issues as opposed to intergovernmental cooperation wane sufficiently for this situation fundamentally to change.

Thus, while customary international law certainly has a role to play in the context of space activities, it would be mainly within the context of treaty law, as either leading the way to formalized treaty arrangements or further developing the details of legal rights and obligations within existing treaty law. This is not to say, however, that customary international law does not and should not play a paramount role in the future formation of space law; on the contrary, its inherent flexibility as opposed to the relative inflexibility of treaty law is indispensable in the context of an area where so much is changing all the time.

PART V

Insights from Reexamining Customary International Law

12

Concluding Reflections

Brian D. Lepard

12.1 INSIGHTS FROM REEXAMINING CUSTOMARY INTERNATIONAL LAW

The essays in this volume provide new perspectives on many of the problems and mysteries enshrouding customary international law identified in the first chapter of the book. In this concluding chapter I offer my own reflections on some of the insights that can be gleaned from the contributors.

First of all, a number of the contributors have referred to the importance of critically examining the history of customary international law and not regarding it as "ahistorical." As J. Patrick Kelly illuminates in his chapter, the modern doctrine of customary international law was developed by powerful states with colonial interests. Even if its essential foundations – state practice, coupled with *opinio juris* – have parallels in many domestic legal systems, including those of developing countries, and appear to be "neutral," they have often been interpreted so as to vindicate the views and interests of powerful states. Kelly offers several compelling examples of this interpretive trend, including the standard of "prompt, adequate, and effective" compensation for expropriation of property of foreign investors, which clearly favored the developed states. At a minimum, then, those decision makers charged with "finding" or "interpreting" customary international law should be aware of these kinds of biases that may have crept into judicial decisions in particular issue areas.

More broadly, Kelly's critique suggests certain reforms in the way we think about state practice and *opinio juris* – the constituent elements of customary law that have recently been reaffirmed by the International Law Commission and its Special Rapporteur, Michael Wood.[1] For example, it would tend to

[1] See, e.g., "Report of the International Law Commission," Sixty-Eighth Session (2 May–10 June and 4 July–12 August 2016), UN Doc. A/71/10 (2016), 76–79, Draft Conclusion 2; "Foreword by Michael Wood," in this volume.

support the "legislative model" rather than the consent model. The legislative model would give a more equitable voice to less powerful states. And Kelly's analysis suggests that in assessing state practice and *opinio juris*, fair consideration should be given to the practices of less influential states, as well as to their views about the existence or desirability of a legal norm pertaining to those practices. It implies, too, that decision makers should give due regard (however much that is) to resolutions of inclusive bodies like the UN General Assembly as well as, under limited conditions, views expressed through broad multilateral treaties as possible evidence of *opinio juris*. These juridical practices might help counterbalance implicit biases that have permeated the record of interpretation of customary international law based on great power interests.

On the other hand, as Fernando Tesón underscores, it is critical that these reforms not mask a hidden agenda on the part of decision makers of "wishing" into existence norms favored by less powerful states that do not enjoy the consensus of opinion and the concordance of widespread state practice necessary to justify recognition of a customary law norm. Tesón would presumably argue that the practices and views of powerful states continue to be relevant and cannot be dismissed as illegitimate if recognized customary law norms are to enjoy wide support and be effective in regulating actual state behavior. The support of at least some powerful states is, as a practical matter, typically required to achieve such effective regulation. For this reason Tesón argues for a requirement of unanimous agreement on norms not supported by widespread state practice for them to achieve customary law status.

Thus, both Kelly and Tesón would seem to argue that in these different ways politics cannot be divorced from customary law. For Kelly, we must be suspicious that customary law is just another political tool used by the powerful; for Tesón, we must be mindful that claims about the customary law status of norms that run counter to the views of politically powerful states may result in "fake" customary law that has no real impact, and may even do damage to the reputation, and implementation, of "real" customary law. Moreover, the game theory analysis so aptly described by Niels Petersen views customary law as a way for states to achieve political goals in their own short-term or long-term self-interest. He argues that we can make better judgments about how to recognize customary law, the legitimacy of demanding individual state consent to a customary norm, and the respective roles of state practice and *opinio juris* if we candidly identify and assess the political "games" that states play and the way states use customary norms to solve the underlying problems depicted by these games.

On the other hand, the traditional doctrine of *opinio juris* rightly demands that we identify what states believe the law is, or should be (according to some theories) – not what it is in their political interest to do. Views of states that are purely a matter of politics, or even policy, should be distinguished from views about legality. This is a point made by Jean-Marie Henckaerts and Els Debuf in their discussion of the evidentiary role of military manuals, where they recognize that some rules in these manuals were based on political expediency and did not reflect views about the current or desirable status of the law. Noora Arajärvi raises a related concern, namely that court decisions that elevate *opinio juris* over state practice and find customary law based only, or primarily, on the former may be illegitimately injecting political considerations into the determination of customary law. And Frans G. von der Dunk underscores, similarly, that "soft law" is the product of a political process, but is not enforceable hard law.

Thus, these authors would seem to agree that while customary law can serve political ends, it cannot degenerate into merely a political process if it is to serve the functions of law, one of which is to regulate political behavior. On the other hand, the reality is that the lawmaking process has inevitable political elements. If decision makers can be conscious of these, they may actually be better able to identify and interpret customary law in a politically unbiased way that also advances both states' political interests and the interests of their residents, including respect for human rights.

A number of the contributions, including my own, explore the relationship between ethics and customary law. We have seen that the traditional doctrine purports to be ethically neutral, but these contributions generally challenge that notion. For example, Kelly points out that the Western powers, and Western treatise writers, often invoked supposedly universal moral maxims to justify purported norms of customary law without any real showing of consensus on the norms (*opinio juris*) or state practice supporting them. Moreover, he argues that their policies of intervention in less developed countries were not in fact "moral."

It seems fair to say that all of the contributors believe that moral considerations can support *opinio juris* and ultimately the recognition of customary international law norms, so long as sufficient state practice also exists. For example, Tesón acknowledges that some customary rules may be grounded in morality – but must also be supported by state practice. Without state practice, they are "fake custom." Provocatively, he endorses the recognition of compelling human rights, and moral rules, as international law even without state practice – but says they should be recognized as a separate category of international law, not customary international law. His view has certain affinities with those of Bruno Simma and Philip Alston, who similarly have argued that human rights, because based on morality rather than practice, are more legitimately protected by general principles of law than customary law.[2] However, Tesón appears to suggest that compelling human rights form part of a "new" source of international law not explicitly specified in Article 38 of the Statute of the International Court of Justice ("ICJ"), a novel proposition that merits further exploration.

The chapters on humanitarian law and human rights law also suggest that customary law can play a useful role – and even an essential one – in promoting ethical values such as the humane treatment of civilians and the realization of human rights. Henckaerts, Debuf, and Arajärvi all argue, normatively, for the importance of customary humanitarian law, but make a plea for a kind of "quality control" and a cautiousness in recognizing ethical norms without sufficient supporting state practice. To this extent, their views resonate with Tesón's own admonition to be on guard against "fake custom," and with points made by Michael Wood in his Foreword.

Henckaerts and Debuf maintain that a rigorous study of state practice and expressions of *opinio juris*, like that undertaken by the ICRC, can provide a necessary "check" on overambitious ethical lawmaking. So, too, Arajärvi critiques a judicial trend toward finding "moral *opinio juris*" and argues in favor of a kind of "moral minimalism" in international criminal law. This would allow some consideration of morality in the determination of *opinio juris*, but also insist on sufficient state practice in order to satisfy the principle of legality. This principle, she maintains, holds more sway in international criminal law, which binds individuals, as opposed to international human rights law, which binds states. Petersen would seem to agree that even customary rules that further ethical values, rather than state interests, should be supported by some kind of general practice. However, he believes that states should not be allowed to "opt out" of being bound by such ethically portentous norms even through persistent objection to them.

On the other hand, some contributors suggest that ethical values themselves may legitimately "tip the scale" in favor of recognition of particular ethics-based norms as legally binding customary law. I argue that fundamental ethical principles are not themselves customary law, and that in general some kind of state practice will be required to show that states have the requisite belief in the desirability of instituting a legal rule, which is how I define *opinio juris*. Nevertheless, if state views are ambiguous, recourse may be had to

[2] See Bruno Simma and Philip Alston, "The Sources of Human Rights Law: Custom, Jus Cogens, and General Principles," 12 *Australian Yearbook of International Law* 82 (1988–89).

these background principles, themselves accepted by states, to determine if the critical line between non-law and customary law has been crossed. Anna Williams Shavers echoes this view. She notes that a kind of "shared moral consciousness" can help establish *opinio juris*. She proposes that an analysis that explicitly incorporates a role for ethics be applied to women's rights, concluding that it results in recognition of a general norm of gender equality as well as other rights of women in customary international law.

Can these different perspectives on the proper relationship between ethics and customary law be reconciled? It seems fair to conclude that no contributor endorses the view that ethical values are ever, by themselves, customary law. All make reference to the traditional two-element definition of customary law, but argue either for applying it rigorously or for refining it in some way to take account of moral values. And all maintain that any such process of incorporating moral values into the identification of customary law must be done in a systematic way, not based on the whim or personal moral predilections of a judge or other decision maker.

Some of the contributors touch on the important problem of identifying *jus cogens* "super norms." Kelly acknowledges the legitimacy of these norms, as well as ordinary human rights norms grounded in morality, but argues that we must be skeptical about whether or not asserted *jus cogens* norms are merely the preferences of powerful states. Henckaerts and Debuf accept that some, but not all, norms of international humanitarian law fall into this privileged category and thus bind all states, even persistent objectors. This general doctrinal point is reiterated by Shavers in her chapter. I argue that fundamental ethical principles, and especially "essential ethical principles," can play a role in identifying *jus cogens* norms, and Shavers draws extensively on the tests I propose to conclude that the norm prohibiting discrimination on the basis of gender, as well as other rights protecting women, should be treated as having this high-level status.

A couple of the authors also shed light on the problem of defining *erga omnes* norms. I suggest a definition in my chapter in relation to human rights norms. Again, Shavers delves into this question in some detail. Adopting the definition that I propose, she concludes that a norm of gender nondiscrimination creates *erga omnes* obligations of states, and that any state can bring legal action against a fellow state for its violation. Both of our chapters, while recognizing that many *jus cogens* norms will qualify as *erga omnes* norms (and vice versa), nevertheless endorse the view that they are distinct categories of norms and that a rigorous analysis is required regarding the *erga omnes* status of particular customary law norms, whether or not they rise to the level of *jus cogens*.

Why is customary law law? Is it because of consent, because customary law is a form of global legislation, or for some other reason? A number of the contributions shed light on these questions. Some debunk the view that customary international law is, at bottom, based on the consent of an individual state subject to it. Kelly observes that Vattel's "specific consent" theory was replaced by the now-dominant theory of "common consent," allowing, in effect, a majority of states to make law binding on a minority of states without the latter's consent. The problem is that powerful nations used the fiction of "common consent" to foist purported norms of customary international law on less well-endowed states, and therefore without the genuine consensus of opinion required for customary law. At the same time, Kelly argues, the persistent objector doctrine, expansively interpreted, opens the door to creating a consent-based opt-out system, but largely for powerful states. Newly emerged states, he says, are held to be bound to observe all existing customary law rules without their explicit consent. He ultimately argues against this doctrine, and a consent-based notion of customary international law, because in his view such a notion would undermine the very concept of law. He appears, therefore, to have some sympathy with the legislative model, which he believes should be expansively interpreted to ensure fair representation of the views, and practices, of less influential states, thus resulting in "democratic legitimacy" in customary lawmaking.

Tesón, on the other hand, explicitly criticizes the legislative model, at least insofar as it could be interpreted to allow the will of a simple majority of states to create a customary norm (via the operation of *opinio juris*) without genuinely widespread state practice. But he does not appear to advocate an explicit consent theory, either. Rather, in his view, the consistent state practice requirement in tandem with a robust requirement for a broad-based *opinio juris* serve as "brakes" on expansive lawmaking by simple majority. His lack of support for consent as a foundational basis for international law is underscored boldly by his advocacy of treating certain morally compelling human rights as international law, *ipso facto*, without regard to state consent.

Petersen undertakes a finely reasoned analysis of just when and how consent is required for the formation of customary norms, and draws careful distinctions among types of customary norms in this regard. Thus, he suggests that specific consent should not be required for norms solving common goods problems, but is a legitimate factor in determining whether a state is bound by a norm solving a coordination problem. In the case of customary norms furthering ethical values, he maintains that while states should be given some leeway in deciding how to reconcile competing ethical values, they should not be allowed to exempt themselves wholly from ethics-based customary norms even by persistently objecting to them.

Most of the contributors thus tend to align themselves with the legislative model that does not insist on specific consent as a condition for the formation of every customary law norm. They adopt some version of a "majoritarian" principle regarding both state practice and *opinio juris*, with various qualifications. For example, Petersen cautions that the solution favored by a majority of states to certain coordination problems may not, in fact, be an optimal solution. Tesón undertakes a sharper critique of the legislative model, maintaining that if a "modern" theory of customary law is invoked, not requiring "robust state practice," then a "universal and sufficiently precise" international consensus must exist to establish what he calls "genuine" customary law; majority support is, in his view, not enough.

Regarding the persistent objector doctrine, some contributors believe that the doctrine still plays a useful role as a "safety valve," allowing states to exempt themselves from some customary norms that do not rise to the level of *jus cogens*. As just noted, Petersen engages in a nuanced analysis of different types of norms and argues that persistent objection should be allowed for some but not for others. In particular, he maintains that persistent objection should not be permitted if a norm protects a common good and enjoys almost universal support, or if it promotes ethical values. Henckaerts and Debuf reaffirm that persistent objection cannot relieve a state from the obligation to observe norms of *jus cogens*. However, they note that the ICRC study on customary international humanitarian law now confirms that persistent objection *is* permissible with respect to norms not reaching this rarified status, and give a number of examples of these norms. Shavers argues that reservations to CEDAW, the UN treaty on women's rights, that contravene the object and purpose of the treaty, which includes the elimination of prejudicial attitudes toward women, should not be treated as meeting the requirements for persistent objector status to a norm prohibiting gender-based discrimination. She goes on to conclude that states generally believe that no persistent objector exception should be allowed for this norm in any event, and that for this and other reasons it qualifies as a norm of *jus cogens*.

Kelly seems to go even further and favors burying the persistent objector doctrine entirely. He engages in a penetrating critique of the doctrine, affirming that it is not an essential component of the theory of customary law, having been introduced relatively recently. As noted earlier in the chapter, he argues that it undermines the character of customary law as law, and, moreover, has been used exclusively to benefit the great powers.

Some of the authors seek to explain rules of customary international law, and make normative judgments about the relative importance of state practice or *opinio juris* with respect to a particular rule, by drawing upon insights from game theory. Petersen makes an important contribution in this regard. This kind of analysis opens the door to a recognition that not every rule of customary law ought to be evaluated in the same way, because different rules serve different purposes. Such an approach also permits judges and decision makers to engage in more rigorous, and legitimate, reasoning about the customary status of various norms. These kinds of distinctions may still be legitimate and not introduce wholly different analyses for norms governing different subject areas – an approach that Michael Wood finds problematic and a reason for reaffirming a unified approach to the determination of customary international law.[3]

Thomas Kleinlein, too, helpfully employs the concept of reciprocity in interactions among states to distinguish customary law, which is justified by factual reciprocity, from general principles of law, which govern situations in which factual reciprocity is lacking. Whether or not they refer to concepts derived from game theory, all the authors appear to recognize that a variety of goals can justify the status of customary law as law, including the goals of providing common goods for states and their peoples, promoting cooperation among them to achieve their own interests, and facilitating the realization of certain broader ethical values.

What insights can be gleaned from the contributions concerning the role of the state practice requirement? First, all the contributors emphasize that state practice cannot be dispensed with altogether as a normal requirement for customary international law. Indeed, many emphasize its critical importance if customary law is not merely to represent *lex ferenda* or wishful thinking. Perhaps my own theory departs the most from the mainstream in this respect by regarding state practice as evidence of *opinio juris*. (Notably, Anna Shavers also endorses this perspective.) Nevertheless, in judicial "practice," normally some kind of general state practice consistent with a norm will be required to demonstrate that states actually have the requisite *opinio juris*. My theory simply clarifies the role of state practice in the ultimate analysis, and does not justify the wholesale disregard of such practice.

A number of the contributors have illuminated the problem of what can count as "practice." In general, they support the traditional view, endorsed by Michael Wood and the International Law Commission, that many types of state acts can do so. In particular, Henckaerts and Debuf emphasize that

3 See "Foreword by Michael Wood," in this volume.

the ICRC study on customary international humanitarian law adopts a broad perspective, and they do so as well, counting many different types of "verbal" and "physical" acts of states. Of course, such a perspective is consistent with a view of practice as evidence of *opinio juris*, as I have advocated, because it is desirable to locate as much evidence of *opinio juris* as possible. Moreover, a view of state practice as evidence of *opinio juris* definitely legitimizes the relevance of "verbal" acts in determining customary law because they clearly bear on *opinio juris*.

In evaluating relevant state practice, a contentious issue, as discussed in Chapter 1, is how to determine a state's "practice" when a state is composed of multifarious agencies and institutions. Henckaerts and Debuf note that the approach of the ICRC study is, in fact, to consider the acts and practices of many different government departments and organs, including national legislatures, courts, executives, and militaries. On the other hand, the authors of the study were also careful to attempt to distinguish expressions of "policy" by these various agencies from legal opinions, and therefore *opinio juris* – a sometimes difficult task. Tesón suggests that national laws, by themselves, cannot give rise to sufficient state practice or *opinio juris*. He certainly believes that recourse alone to such laws in determining *opinio juris* – what he calls the "legislative fallacy" – could lead to recognition of customary rules of international law that are not only not truly accepted as international law by states, but are objectively immoral, such as excessive limits on freedom of expression. Yet Tesón still recognizes the relevance of national legislation in the determination of *opinio juris* in a broader context. Thus, he notes that in the 2012 *Jurisdictional Immunities of the State Case* the ICJ properly referred to national laws that fail to recognize a "crimes against humanity" exception to state sovereign immunity as evidence of an *opinio juris* that such an exception does not currently exist in customary international law. In other words, national legislation can be important evidence of *opinio juris* when considered along with other evidence of *opinio juris*. This view is adopted, too, by other contributors. For example, Arajärvi points out the relevance of national legislation in assessing *opinio juris* relating to international criminal law. And of course, as Kleinlein emphasizes, similar national laws can contribute directly to the establishment and recognition of general principles of law.

Some commentators address the role of protest as practice and evidence of *opinio juris*. Kelly implies that protests – and certainly protests by less powerful states – should be given appropriate weight in assessing whether there is sufficient *opinio juris* in favor of a norm. He argues, as we have seen, that the protests of these states against Western-imposed norms on the minimum standard of compensation for expropriated property were ignored. Protest may also be relevant not only to the question of whether or not there is adequate *opinio juris* to recognize a norm in the first place but also to the question of whether a particular state qualifies as a "persistent objector" to a norm that otherwise is recognized as customary law. Similarly, "nonactions" or "abstentions" may be relevant state practice, as well as evidence of *opinio juris*. As Henckaerts and Debuf emphasize, abstentions from various acts in war, like the use of biological weapons, count as state practice in favor of the prohibition of those acts under customary law. And Petersen likewise implies that abstentions must be considered in evaluating both state practice and *opinio juris*.

Some of the authors address the question of how widespread a practice must be to generate a customary law norm. They seem to agree that a number larger than just a few states is normally required to create a general norm of customary law binding on all states. Petersen thus suggests that practice by three states, for example, is not sufficient. As already noted, many of the contributors discuss at some length the problem of how large a "majority" of states engaging in a practice is required.

On the other hand, as Henckaerts and Debuf point out, some norms involve such rare behavior – like the waving of a white flag of truce – that there will naturally be only a few instances of state practice, by a few states, and yet this behavior can evidence customary law. Furthermore, where only a limited number of states are "specially affected" by a norm – like seafaring states, or spacefaring states – the contributors generally concur with the ICJ's implication in the *North Sea Continental Shelf Cases* that it is appropriate to give special weight to the practices (and views) of these states. However, the authors tend to limit this concept to such cases where objectively only certain states are affected by a rule. Thus, Petersen accepts the idea as "intuitive" only with respect to norms like those just mentioned concerning the law of the sea or outer space. Frans von der Dunk implies that there may be some special role for the views of spacefaring nations in creating customary international space law norms, but that the customary international law process demands that all states should have at least some voice in developing these norms. He points out that treaties have been the lawmaking method of choice for space law precisely because spacefaring nations can quickly adopt them and in effect induce non-spacefaring states to go along with the new treaty regime.

Where all states have some interest in the rule, the contributors doubt that the practices or views of some states are entitled to more weight than others. Thus, for example, Henckaerts and Debuf argue that while some states, such as the United States, have generated more "practice" in the field of international humanitarian law because of their frequent involvement in armed conflict, no states should be considered to have a greater "say" in the development of international humanitarian law than others because of being "specially affected." This is because all states may be involved in armed conflict at some time and therefore have an equal interest in international humanitarian law. Along the same lines, Sofia Michaelides-Mateou takes the position that because all states conduct air operations, all are "affected" and therefore should have an equal voice in the establishment of customary air law norms, regardless of their own size or that of their airline industry or air force.

The authors' contributions also shed light on the problem of whether the practices of powerful states are entitled to special weight in determining the content of customary law. Kelly would obviously argue that they are not; indeed, he suggests that the entire recent history of customary law is one of unfair domination by the practices of powerful states, which have manipulated even the doctrine of customary law to legitimate their own self-interested behavior. He thus invites us to give special attention to the practices and views of less powerful states that have too often been the victims of Western intervention and subjugation. Other contributors similarly advocate a more egalitarian conception of customary law formation. However, some admit that powerful states may necessarily generate more state practice (as Henckaerts and Debuf point out with respect to the United States and international humanitarian law), or may lead the way in forging new norms, whether via treaty or customary law (as in the case of the United States and the Soviet Union, as space pioneers, with respect to norms of space law). Furthermore, as already noted, the contributors give some credence to the idea that the views and practices of "specially affected" states, which may also be more powerful ones in relation to a given issue area, might be entitled to extra consideration – but only if, objectively, they are affected more directly than other states, and not just because of their military or economic might.

Some of the authors also address the question of whether the practices of democratic states should be given some kind of special weight in the ascertainment of customary law. The traditional rule holds, of course, that they should not in light of the principle of the sovereign equality of states. Kelly, among others, seems to endorse such equality in advocating that greater attention be paid to the views of less powerful states – presumably whether or not they are democratic in character. He thus pleads for greater "democracy" *among* states in customary lawmaking. Petersen also appears to discount the relevance of internal democracy in evaluating a state's contribution to customary law formation because of the broad diversity of values among cultures.

On the other hand, I have argued, as discussed in Chapter 8, that a fundamental ethical principle of open-minded consultation, accepted by states themselves, in tandem with the accepted human rights norm of democratic government, imply that customary international law ought to favor the views of states that also take into account their own citizens' views. Without such a weighting, the traditional customary law doctrine can reach morally troubling results. For example, according to the traditional doctrine, we might legitimately conclude, as Tesón points out, that the views and practices of states suppressing freedom of expression ought to "count" just as much as those favoring freedom of expression in determining the customary law status of the norm of liberty of speech.

All the authors are in apparent agreement that a practice need not persist for some predetermined length of time in order to generate a new customary rule. They thus reject the once-common doctrine, articulated by such treatise writers as Blackstone, that a custom must have existed from "time immemorial" – or at least a very long time indeed – to attain the privileged status of law. A number of the contributions recognize that new customary norms developed quite quickly and echo the general idea put forward by Michael Scharf, among others, that there can be "Grotian Moments" of speedy norm formation. For example, Michaelides-Mateou observes that a customary norm of state sovereignty over airspace above state territory developed very rapidly with the advent of air flight. On the other hand, all of the contributors are doubtful that a General Assembly resolution standing alone can generate customary law in an "instant" without, at a minimum, a more rigorous inquiry into whether it actually establishes *opinio juris*, and in the view of most authors, without some evidence of state practice apart from the resolution.

Indeed, many of the chapters touch on the concept of *opinio juris* and explore its definition and role in the identification of customary international law. The authors are in agreement that there can be many sources of evidence of *opinio juris*, just as there can be many sources of evidence of state practice. So long as appropriate caution is exercised, they believe that treaties, their drafting history, advisory opinions of various bodies, international judicial opinions, national laws, administrative regulations, and statements by governments may be evidence of *opinio juris*. However, they also agree that it is essential to focus on the precise assertions made by states, including whether they believe that there is or ought to be a legal rule binding on all states apart from treaties.

In Chapter 1 I raised the problem of the "naturalistic fallacy" that may infect the traditional doctrine of *opinio juris* – namely that what "is" (i.e., what states believe the law currently to be) may not be a good indicator of what "ought to be" (i.e., what states believe the law *should* be). The contributors do not address this question directly. However, a number of them agree that moral considerations – which include views of states about what "ought" to be – have a proper, though not exclusive, place in the evaluation of *opinio juris*. Indeed, *opinio juris* should allow for this kind of dynamism in the evolution of customary law, while being focused on the views of states about what the law should be now or in the near future, not in some distant utopic era.

In this connection, some of the contributors, particularly Anna Shavers, appear to endorse the suggestion that I and others have put forward that the *opinio juris* test should be reinterpreted to focus on what legal rules states believe are desirable to recognize now or in the immediate future. As I noted in Chapter 1, this interpretation also avoids the chronological paradox of *opinio juris*. And it allows customary law to change more easily, for it dispenses with the pretense that states must erroneously believe that a new or modified rule is already law for it to become law. In this way, it may also help counteract any existing biases of customary law in favor of powerful states, which are described so well by Kelly.

However, Tesón engages in a cogent critique of certain aspects of this definition. In particular, he says that this definition is "too broad because it fails to include the two crucial features of custom required by the modern theory: that the belief in the desirability of the norm should be *universal* and not proposed by a mere majority, and that the object of the agreement should be *specific and precise*, and not vague or aspirational." I responded to these points in Chapter 8, emphasizing that the traditional theory of customary law does not require either unanimous practice or *opinio juris*. Furthermore, state practice is still normally important evidence of *opinio juris*. And finally, the required belief of states in the desirability of a legally authoritative *rule or principle* also implies an appropriate degree of specificity and precision, which I agree are necessary.

Many of the authors have reexamined the problem of the degree of consensus among states on *opinio juris* that is required for a customary law to form. Their discussion echoes that of how widespread state practice must be. It is noteworthy that many of them blend their discussion of the required universality of practice and *opinio juris*, again suggesting that these concepts are closely related and that what may ultimately matter the most are the views of states about what the law is or should be.

The contributors do not focus on the question of whether the views of nonstate actors can "count" in the determination of *opinio juris*. However, Noora Arajärvi observes that the impact of nonstate actors on the development of *opinio juris* is important today. My own view is that for customary international law to retain its character as international law, we must focus on the views and practices of states – acknowledging, however, that these can be shaped by the programs and opinions of nongovernmental organizations and nonstate actors. Indeed, we should be open to considering whether states may have changed their beliefs about desirable legal rules in light of these broader opinion trends within their countries and globally.

As pointed out in Chapter 1, the ICJ, while stating the requirement of the two elements of state practice and *opinio juris* in a few cases, has also seemed to ignore one or the other element in many of its decisions. This was true, for example, in the *Nicaragua Case*, and a number of the contributors underscore the Court's relegation of state practice to a subsidiary role in this decision. Similarly, Arajärvi points out that the ICTY Trial Chamber in *Prosecutor v. Kupreškić* explicitly found customary law where state practice was lacking. However, she and other contributors express concern that these kinds of decisions undermine the legitimacy of customary law – and at a minimum are problematic in the context of criminal law by violating the principle of legality.

At the same time, a common theme among the contributions is that widespread state practice alone is not sufficient to generate customary law. Rather, all find *opinio juris* to be essential, whether it focuses on state beliefs about the status of norms as existing law or takes account of the normative and moral views of states. Some of the authors are also troubled by the tendency of certain treatise writers, arbitration panels, and courts to declare some norms to be customary law *tout court*, apparently based only on alleged state practice and without any serious inquiry into the existence of *opinio juris*. This is certainly a point strongly emphasized by Kelly.

A number of the contributors reaffirm that treaties may codify preexisting customary law norms, which continue to coexist alongside the treaties. For example, Henckaerts and Debuf as well as Arajärvi note that many international humanitarian law treaties were intended to codify preexisting customary rules. Likewise, Michaelides-Mateou recalls that UNCLOS codified preexisting customary norms of the law of the sea. Nevertheless, difficult questions persist about how a customary norm paralleling a treaty relates to the treaty norm and about how a state might be bound by each respective norm.

Some of the authors note, conversely, that treaties may help give rise to new customary law. Under "paper practice" approaches they may serve as a form of state practice. And they may simultaneously evidence *opinio juris* if it is clear from their drafting history and the text, among other sources of evidence, that states believe the norms in the treaties ought to be binding on all states even outside the treaty framework. This is a position I elaborated in my own chapter, and Anna Shavers concurs that treaties on women's rights provide evidence of *opinio juris* because they are intended to be universally ratified and articulate universal norms. Similarly, Michaelides-Mateou argues that certain provisions of a treaty, like the Chicago Convention, that was intended to be universally ratified, and that is indeed very widely ratified, may be good evidence of *opinio juris*. She argues in particular that the treaty norm of state sovereignty over territorial airspace is for this reason now part of customary law.

Nevertheless, some of the contributors are concerned that tribunals may make unwarranted "leaps" from treaty texts or drafts to conclusions about *opinio juris*. Thus, Henckaerts and Debuf emphasize the importance of focusing on the practice and views of nonparties to a treaty in helping establish that its norms have passed into customary law. Arajärvi critiques the ICTY's decision in *Krstić* for viewing the draft text of the Rome Statute of the International Criminal Court as evidence of *opinio juris* merely because all states participating in the Rome Conference had an opportunity to express their opinions on the draft. And Michaelides-Mateou contends that bilateral air law treaties must be regarded with some suspicion in the determination of *opinio juris*. She points out that the widespread use by states of bilateral treaties, rather than multilateral treaties, to regulate a particular area tends to show that they do not believe that the norms in those treaties should be universally binding outside the treaties, and therefore is evidence *against opinio juris*. Furthermore, von der Dunk doubts that all norms in space law treaties can or should readily pass into customary law, especially when the treaties seek to regulate complex matters and create institutional mechanisms for the resolution of particular problems relating to activities in outer space – and when customary law opens up the possibility of gaining persistent objector status.

Kleinlein's chapter helpfully reexamines the controversial relationship between customary law and general principles of law. He argues that customary norms are characterized by "factual reciprocity," while general principles are not. He maintains, therefore, that the distinction between customary rules and general principles does not lie in the difference between "rules" and "principles," or between international norms and domestic ones. This is certainly a persuasive argument. However, as other authors such as Petersen have pointed out, there may indeed be customary norms, such as those relating to human rights, that are not characterized by factual reciprocity and have an ethical foundation. Thus, while such reciprocity is a feature of a broad range of customary norms (and in particular those designed to solve common goods problems or coordination problems), it may not be central to other customary norms. Again, for example, there are good reasons to consider many international human rights norms as customary norms as well as general principles, especially because they may be supported by a wide range of state practice as well as *opinio juris*.

A number of contributors address the role of General Assembly resolutions as state practice or as evidence of *opinio juris*. For example, Tesón says that General Assembly resolutions may provide some evidence of *opinio juris*, under some conditions, but must be accompanied by practice to generate customary law. Arajärvi engages in a thoughtful examination of the role of these resolutions in relation to customary law. She argues that General Assembly resolutions that by their plain text are merely recommendatory cannot generate *opinio juris*. She also points out that states will be reluctant to approve resolutions if they fear that the resolutions will later be considered to contain legal obligations. However, she believes that where the text of a resolution clearly declares the existence of preexisting rules, then it may be evidence of *opinio juris*. And she goes on to note that General Assembly resolutions can lay the groundwork for recognition of a more formal rule of customary law in the future. Shavers concurs that under certain circumstances General Assembly resolutions can be strong evidence of *opinio juris*.

In my own chapter I suggest that General Assembly resolutions may be evidence of *opinio juris* – which I argue is the essence of customary law – depending on a wide variety of factors, necessitating a careful analysis of the text of and circumstances surrounding particular resolutions. I argue that the Universal Declaration of Human Rights, a very special resolution, is important evidence that today we should recognize a minimal persuasive obligation under customary law of all states to give great weight in their policies to respecting the rights proclaimed in the Declaration. However, the norms in other General Assembly resolutions may not merit this status.

Taken as a whole, the contributions to this volume certainly suggest that the traditional "one size fits all" doctrine of customary international law may not work with equal effectiveness for all issue areas, and that it is appropriate at least to refine the doctrine, or apply it differently, given particular problem contexts. For example, Tesón argues that customary law can encompass both the traditional model, relying on state practice, as well as a "modern" theory that relies solely on *opinio juris* – so long as *opinio juris* is universally shared among states. Moreover, in the case of ethical norms, he argues for independent recognition of these norms as international law, even though they may not meet either the traditional or modern definition of customary law. Petersen draws his own helpful distinctions between customary norms solving common goods problems, solving coordination problems, and promoting ethical values, arguing that the required degree of "consent" (including *opinio juris* and state practice) should differ for each of them.

Arajärvi suggests that the traditional definition of *opinio juris* may need to be modestly extended to include moral considerations in the case of international criminal law, but without sacrificing the state practice requirement. My own chapter argues that human rights norms may need special consideration both in terms of the importance of state practice and the degree of consensus required. The chapters by Michaelides-Mateou and von der Dunk on air and space law demonstrate not only that special considerations may exist in determining customary international law in certain areas, such as space law, in which few actors are directly involved, but also that the relative importance of customary international law in relation to treaties can differ markedly depending on the issue context.

Finally, some of the contributions to this volume have shed light on the concept of "soft law." For example, I have argued that some customary law human rights norms impose only "persuasive" obligations and therefore might be classified as soft law under some definitions of it. Arajärvi affirms that General Assembly resolutions, while "soft law" by themselves, can be evidence of *opinio juris* and therefore help generate customary law – so long as there is also adequate state practice supporting that law. And von der Dunk has referred to the importance of soft law norms in outer space law that eventually might evolve into true customary law.

12.2 THE FUTURE OF CUSTOMARY INTERNATIONAL LAW

All of the contributions to this volume demonstrate the imperative of reexamining customary international law. Furthermore, they highlight that the purpose of this reexamination should not be to undermine customary international law, or discredit it, but rather to help it better fulfill the goals that states themselves have laid out for it: to help them solve common problems, promote their own interests, and achieve a better life for their residents.

Customary international law is a social process, and jurists should not believe themselves to be bound to traditional doctrine merely because it is old. After all, there was a time when this doctrine itself was a new interpretation of customary law. It is desirable that the field of international law be in a constant state of self-examination and dynamic change. To give a couple of examples, most jurists are quite happy that long-standing notions of absolute state sovereignty that allowed a state to mistreat its own residents without justified critique from other states, as well as the doctrine of lawful acquisition of territory by conquest, are now relics of less enlightened times.

Moreover, as some of the contributors have underscored, much of what we perceive as "traditional" doctrine is in fact not very old and was always quite contested – like the persistent objector exception. This is another reason to feel free, as have the authors here, to reevaluate customary law doctrine.

Such a reevaluation may, of course, result in a confirmation of some aspects of existing doctrine – as we have seen it has, among these contributors, and also in the work of Special Rapporteur Michael Wood and the International Law Commission. However, it may also disclose issues that deserve further examination and clarification.

Indeed, the contributors to this volume have identified many such issues and proposed resolutions to them. A hopeful sign is that there is much they agree on; where apparent disagreement exists, it tends not to concern the importance or foundations of customary law, but issues that may, eventually, find a resolution. Furthermore, that very discord suggests that the issues involved are complex and deserve more attention from scholars and jurists.

What is most evident from the investigations undertaken in this volume is that customary international law is not vanishing, or becoming irrelevant. Its importance is growing in nearly every field of international relations. Customary international law has a bright future – a future that can only become brighter through continued reexamination of its history, doctrine, and current role in building a more ordered, and just, global community of states and people.

Index

www.ingramcontent.com/pod-product-compliance
Lightning Source LLC
LaVergne TN
LVHW011531200926
848484LV00001B/230

* 9 7 8 1 1 0 7 1 4 6 9 1 4 *